JAMES BALDWIN

JAMES BALDWIN

COLLECTED ESSAYS

Notes of a Native Son
Nobody Knows My Name
The Fire Next Time
No Name in the Street
The Devil Finds Work
Other Essays

Toni Morrison, *editor*

THE LIBRARY OF AMERICA

Contents

NOTES OF A NATIVE SON
    Autobiographical Notes 5
    Everybody's Protest Novel 11
    Many Thousands Gone 19
    Carmen Jones: The Dark Is Light Enough 35
    The Harlem Ghetto 42
    Journey to Atlanta 54
    Notes of a Native Son. 63
    Encounter on the Seine: Black Meets Brown 85
    A Question of Identity 91
    Equal in Paris 101
    Stranger in the Village 117

NOBODY KNOWS MY NAME
    The Discovery of What It Means To Be an
       American 137
    Princes and Powers. 143
    Fifth Avenue, Uptown: A Letter from Harlem 170
    East River, Downtown: Postscript to a Letter from
       Harlem. 180
    A Fly in Buttermilk 187
    Nobody Knows My Name: A Letter from the
       South 197
    Faulkner and Desegregation 209
    In Search of a Majority 215
    Notes for a Hypothetical Novel. 222
    The Male Prison 231
    The Northern Protestant 236
    Alas, Poor Richard 247
    The Black Boy Looks at the White Boy 269

THE FIRE NEXT TIME
    My Dungeon Shook: Letter to My Nephew. 291
    Down at the Cross. 296

NO NAME IN THE STREET 349

THE DEVIL FINDS WORK 477

OTHER ESSAYS

Smaller Than Life 577
History as Nightmare 579
The Image of the Negro 582
Lockridge: 'The American Myth' 588
Preservation of Innocence 594
The Negro at Home and Abroad 601
The Crusade of Indignation 606
Sermons and Blues 614
On Catfish Row 616
They Can't Turn Back 622
The Dangerous Road Before Martin Luther King . . . 638
The New Lost Generation 659
The Creative Process 669
Color 673
A Talk to Teachers 678
"This Nettle, Danger . . ." 687
Nothing Personal 692
Words of a Native Son 707
The American Dream and the American Negro . . . 714
On the Painter Beauford Delaney 720
The White Man's Guilt 722
A Report from Occupied Territory 728
Negroes Are Anti-Semitic Because They're Anti-White . . 739
White Racism or World Community? 749
Sweet Lorraine 757
How One Black Man Came To Be an American . . . 762
An Open Letter to Mr. Carter 766
Last of the Great Masters 770
Every Good-bye Ain't Gone 773
If Black English Isn't a Language, Then Tell Me,
   What Is? 780
Open Letter to the Born Again 784
Dark Days 788
Notes on the House of Bondage 799
Introduction to Notes of a Native Son, 1984 808
Freaks and the American Ideal of Manhood 814
The Price of the Ticket 830

Chronology 845
Note on the Texts 856
Notes 860

NOTES OF A NATIVE SON

FOR
PAULA MARIA

Contents

Autobiographical Notes 5

I

Everybody's Protest Novel 11
Many Thousands Gone. 19
Carmen Jones: The Dark Is Light Enough 35

II

The Harlem Ghetto 42
Journey to Atlanta 54
Notes of a Native Son 63

III

Encounter on the Seine: Black Meets Brown 85
A Question of Identity 91
Equal in Paris 101
Stranger in the Village 117

Autobiographical Notes

I WAS BORN in Harlem thirty-one years ago. I began plotting novels at about the time I learned to read. The story of my childhood is the usual bleak fantasy, and we can dismiss it with the restrained observation that I certainly would not consider living it again. In those days my mother was given to the exasperating and mysterious habit of having babies. As they were born, I took them over with one hand and held a book with the other. The children probably suffered, though they have since been kind enough to deny it, and in this way I read *Uncle Tom's Cabin* and *A Tale of Two Cities* over and over and over again; in this way, in fact, I read just about everything I could get my hands on—except the Bible, probably because it was the only book I was encouraged to read. I must also confess that I wrote—a great deal—and my first professional triumph, in any case, the first effort of mine to be seen in print, occurred at the age of twelve or thereabouts, when a short story I had written about the Spanish revolution won some sort of prize in an extremely short-lived church newspaper. I remember the story was censored by the lady editor, though I don't remember why, and I was outraged.

Also wrote plays, and songs, for one of which I received a letter of congratulations from Mayor La Guardia, and poetry, about which the less said, the better. My mother was delighted by all these goings-on, but my father wasn't; he wanted me to be a preacher. When I was fourteen I became a preacher, and when I was seventeen I stopped. Very shortly thereafter I left home. For God knows how long I struggled with the world of commerce and industry—I guess they would say they struggled with *me*—and when I was about twenty-one I had enough done of a novel to get a Saxton Fellowship. When I was twenty-two the fellowship was over, the novel turned out to be unsalable, and I started waiting on tables in a Village restaurant and writing book reviews—mostly, as it turned out, about the Negro problem, concerning which the color of my skin made me automatically an expert. Did another book, in company with photographer Theodore

Pelatowski, about the store-front churches in Harlem. This book met exactly the same fate as my first—fellowship, but no sale. (It was a Rosenwald Fellowship.) By the time I was twenty-four I had decided to stop reviewing books about the Negro problem—which, by this time, was only slightly less horrible in print than it was in life—and I packed my bags and went to France, where I finished, God knows how, *Go Tell It on the Mountain*.

Any writer, I suppose, feels that the world into which he was born is nothing less than a conspiracy against the cultivation of his talent—which attitude certainly has a great deal to support it. On the other hand, it is only because the world looks on his talent with such a frightening indifference that the artist is compelled to make his talent important. So that any writer, looking back over even so short a span of time as I am here forced to assess, finds that the things which hurt him and the things which helped him cannot be divorced from each other; he could be helped in a certain way only because he was hurt in a certain way; and his help is simply to be enabled to move from one conundrum to the next—one is tempted to say that he moves from one disaster to the next. When one begins looking for influences one finds them by the score. I haven't thought much about my own, not enough anyway; I hazard that the King James Bible, the rhetoric of the store-front church, something ironic and violent and perpetually understated in Negro speech—and something of Dickens' love for bravura—have something to do with me today; but I wouldn't stake my life on it. Likewise, innumerable people have helped me in many ways; but finally, I suppose, the most difficult (and most rewarding) thing in my life has been the fact that I was born a Negro and was forced, therefore, to effect some kind of truce with this reality. (Truce, by the way, is the best one can hope for.)

One of the difficulties about being a Negro writer (and this is not special pleading, since I don't mean to suggest that he has it worse than anybody else) is that the Negro problem is written about so widely. The bookshelves groan under the weight of information, and everyone therefore considers himself informed. And this information, furthermore, operates usually (generally, popularly) to reinforce traditional attitudes.

Of traditional attitudes there are only two—For or Against—and I, personally, find it difficult to say which attitude has caused me the most pain. I am speaking as a writer; from a social point of view I am perfectly aware that the change from ill-will to good-will, however motivated, however imperfect, however expressed, is better than no change at all.

But it is part of the business of the writer—as I see it—to examine attitudes, to go beneath the surface, to tap the source. From this point of view the Negro problem is nearly inaccessible. It is not only written about so widely; it is written about so badly. It is quite possible to say that the price a Negro pays for becoming articulate is to find himself, at length, with nothing to be articulate about. ("You taught me language," says Caliban to Prospero, "and my profit on't is I know how to curse.") Consider: the tremendous social activity that this problem generates imposes on whites and Negroes alike the necessity of looking forward, of working to bring about a better day. This is fine, it keeps the waters troubled; it is all, indeed, that has made possible the Negro's progress. Nevertheless, social affairs are not generally speaking the writer's prime concern, whether they ought to be or not; it is absolutely necessary that he establish between himself and these affairs a distance which will allow, at least, for clarity, so that before he can look forward in any meaningful sense, he must first be allowed to take a long look back. In the context of the Negro problem neither whites nor blacks, for excellent reasons of their own, have the faintest desire to look back; but I think that the past is all that makes the present coherent, and further, that the past will remain horrible for exactly as long as we refuse to assess it honestly.

I know, in any case, that the most crucial time in my own development came when I was forced to recognize that I was a kind of bastard of the West; when I followed the line of my past I did not find myself in Europe but in Africa. And this meant that in some subtle way, in a really profound way, I brought to Shakespeare, Bach, Rembrandt, to the stones of Paris, to the cathedral at Chartres, and to the Empire State Building, a special attitude. These were not really my creations, they did not contain my history; I might search in them in vain forever for any reflection of myself. I was an interloper;

this was not my heritage. At the same time I had no other heritage which I could possibly hope to use—I had certainly been unfitted for the jungle or the tribe. I would have to appropriate these white centuries, I would have to make them mine—I would have to accept my special attitude, my special place in this scheme—otherwise I would have no place in *any* scheme. What was the most difficult was the fact that I was forced to admit something I had always hidden from myself, which the American Negro has had to hide from himself as the price of his public progress; that I hated and feared white people. This did not mean that I loved black people; on the contrary, I despised them, possibly because they failed to produce Rembrandt. In effect, I hated and feared the world. And this meant, not only that I thus gave the world an alto-gether murderous power over me, but also that in such a self-destroying limbo I could never hope to write.

One writes out of one thing only—one's own experience. Everything depends on how relentlessly one forces from this experience the last drop, sweet or bitter, it can possibly give. This is the only real concern of the artist, to recreate out of the disorder of life that order which is art. The difficulty then, for me, of being a Negro writer was the fact that I was, in effect, prohibited from examining my own experience too closely by the tremendous demands and the very real dangers of my social situation.

I don't think the dilemma outlined above is uncommon. I do think, since writers work in the disastrously explicit me-dium of language, that it goes a little way towards explaining why, out of the enormous resources of Negro speech and life, and despite the example of Negro music, prose written by Negroes has been generally speaking so pallid and so harsh. I have not written about being a Negro at such length because I expect that to be my only subject, but only because it was the gate I had to unlock before I could hope to write about anything else. I don't think that the Negro problem in Amer-ica can be even discussed coherently without bearing in mind its context; its context being the history, traditions, customs, the moral assumptions and preoccupations of the country; in short, the general social fabric. Appearances to the contrary, no one in America escapes its effects and everyone in America bears some responsibility for it. I believe this the more firmly because it is the overwhelming tendency to speak of this problem as though it were a thing apart. But in the work of Faulkner, in the general attitude and certain specific passages in Robert Penn Warren, and, most significantly, in the advent of Ralph Ellison, one sees the beginnings—at least—of a more genuinely penetrating search. Mr. Ellison, by the way, is the first Negro novelist I have ever read to utilize in language, and brilliantly, some of the ambiguity and irony of Negro life.

About my interests: I don't know if I have any, unless the morbid desire to own a sixteen-millimeter camera and make experimental movies can be so classified. Otherwise, I love to eat and drink—it's my melancholy conviction that I've scarcely ever had enough to eat (this is because it's *impossible* to eat enough if you're worried about the next meal)—and I love to argue with people who do not disagree with me too profoundly, and I love to laugh. I do *not* like bohemia, or bohemians, I do not like people whose principal aim is pleasure, and I do not like people who are *earnest* about anything. I don't like people who like me because I'm a Negro; neither do I like people who find in the same accident grounds for contempt. I love America more than any other country in the world, and, exactly for this reason, I insist on the right to criticize her perpetually. I think all theories are suspect, that the finest principles may have to be modified, or may even be pulverized by the demands of life, and that one must find, therefore, one's own moral center and move through the world hoping that this center will guide one aright. I consider that I have many responsibilities, but none greater than this: to last, as Hemingway says, and get my work done.

I want to be an honest man and a good writer.

Part One

Everybody's Protest Novel

In *Uncle Tom's Cabin*, that cornerstone of American social protest fiction, St. Clare, the kindly master, remarks to his coldly disapproving Yankee cousin, Miss Ophelia, that, so far as he is able to tell, the blacks have been turned over to the devil for the benefit of the whites in this world—however, he adds thoughtfully, it may turn out in the next. Miss Ophelia's reaction is, at least, vehemently right-minded: "This is perfectly horrible!" she exclaims. "You ought to be ashamed of yourselves!"

Miss Ophelia, as we may suppose, was speaking for the author; her exclamation is the moral, neatly framed, and incontestable like those improving mottoes sometimes found hanging on the walls of furnished rooms. And, like these mottoes, before which one invariably flinches, recognizing an insupportable, almost an indecent glibness, she and St. Clare are terribly in earnest. Neither of them questions the medieval morality from which their dialogue springs: black, white, the devil, the next world—posing its alternatives between heaven and the flames—were realities for them as, of course, they were for their creator. They spurned and were terrified of the darkness, striving mightily for the light; and considered from this aspect, Miss Ophelia's exclamation, like Mrs. Stowe's novel, achieves a bright, almost a lurid significance, like the light from a fire which consumes a witch. This is the more striking as one considers the novels of Negro oppression written in our own, more enlightened day, all of which say only: "This is perfectly horrible! You ought to be ashamed of yourselves!" (Let us ignore, for the moment, those novels of oppression written by Negroes, which add only a raging, near-paranoiac postscript to this statement and actually reinforce, as I hope to make clear later, the principles which activate the oppression they decry.)

Uncle Tom's Cabin is a very bad novel, having, in its self-righteous, virtuous sentimentality, much in common with

Little Women. Sentimentality, the ostentatious parading of excessive and spurious emotion, is the mark of dishonesty, the inability to feel; the wet eyes of the sentimentalist betray his aversion to experience, his fear of life, his arid heart; and it is always, therefore, the signal of secret and violent inhumanity, the mask of cruelty. *Uncle Tom's Cabin*—like its multitudinous, hard-boiled descendants—is a catalogue of violence. This is explained by the nature of Mrs. Stowe's subject matter, her laudable determination to flinch from nothing in presenting the complete picture; an explanation which falters only if we pause to ask whether or not her picture is indeed complete; and what constriction or failure of perception forced her to so depend on the description of brutality—unmotivated, senseless—and to leave unanswered and unnoticed the only important question: what it was, after all, that moved her people to such deeds.

But this, let us say, was beyond Mrs. Stowe's powers; she was not so much a novelist as an impassioned pamphleteer; her book was not intended to do anything more than prove that slavery was wrong; was, in fact, perfectly horrible. This makes material for a pamphlet but it is hardly enough for a novel; and the only question left to ask is why we are bound still within the same constriction. How is it that we are so loath to make a further journey than that made by Mrs. Stowe, to discover and reveal something a little closer to the truth?

But that battered word, truth, having made its appearance here, confronts one immediately with a series of riddles and has, moreover, since so many gospels are preached, the unfortunate tendency to make one belligerent. Let us say, then, that truth, as used here, is meant to imply a devotion to the human being, his freedom and fulfillment; freedom which cannot be legislated, fulfillment which cannot be charted. This is the prime concern, the frame of reference; it is not to be confused with a devotion to Humanity which is too easily equated with a devotion to a Cause; and Causes, as we know, are notoriously bloodthirsty. We have, as it seems to me, in this most mechanical and interlocking of civilizations, attempted to lop this creature down to the status of a timesaving invention. He is not, after all, merely a member of a Society or a Group or a deplorable conundrum to be explained by Science. He is—and how old-fashioned the words sound!—something more than that, something resolutely indefinable, unpredictable. In overlooking, denying, evading his complexity—which is nothing more than the disquieting complexity of ourselves—we are diminished and we perish; only within this web of ambiguity, paradox, this hunger, danger, darkness, can we find at once ourselves and the power that will free us from ourselves. It is this power of revelation which is the business of the novelist, this journey toward a more vast reality which must take precedence over all other claims. What is today parroted as his Responsibility—which seems to mean that he must make formal declaration that he is involved in, and affected by, the lives of other people and to say something improving about this somewhat self-evident fact—is, when he believes it, his corruption and our loss; moreover, it is rooted in, interlocked with and intensifies this same mechanization. Both *Gentleman's Agreement* and *The Postman Always Rings Twice* exemplify this terror of the human being, the determination to cut him down to size. And in *Uncle Tom's Cabin* we may find foreshadowing of both: the formula created by the necessity to find a lie more palatable than the truth has been handed down and memorized and persists yet with a terrible power.

It is interesting to consider one more aspect of Mrs. Stowe's novel, the method she used to solve the problem of writing about a black man at all. Apart from her lively procession of field hands, house niggers, Chloe, Topsy, etc.—who are the stock, lovable figures presenting no problem—she has only three other Negroes in the book. These are the important ones and two of them may be dismissed immediately, since we have only the author's word that they are Negro and they are, in all other respects, as white as she can make them. The two are George and Eliza, a married couple with a wholly adorable child—whose quaintness, incidentally, and whose charm, rather put one in mind of a darky bootblack doing a buck and wing to the clatter of condescending coins. Eliza is a beautiful, pious hybrid, light enough to pass—the heroine of *Quality* might, indeed, be her reincarnation—differing from the genteel mistress who has overseered her education only in the respect that she is a servant. George is darker, but makes up for it by being a mechanical genius, and is, moreover, sufficiently un-Negroid to pass through town, a fugitive from his master, disguised as a Spanish gentleman, attracting no attention whatever beyond admiration. They are a race apart from Topsy. It transpires by the end of the novel, through one of those energetic, last-minute convolutions of the plot, that Eliza has some connection with French gentility. The figure from whom the novel takes its name, Uncle Tom, who is a figure of controversy yet, is jet-black, wooly-haired, illiterate; and he is phenomenally forbearing. He has to be; he is black; only through this forbearance can he survive or triumph. (*Cf.* Faulkner's preface to *The Sound and the Fury*: These others were not Compsons. They were black:—They endured.) His triumph is metaphysical, unearthly; since he is black, born without the light, it is only through humility, the incessant mortification of the flesh, that he can enter into communion with God or man. The virtuous rage of Mrs. Stowe is motivated by nothing so temporal as a concern for the relationship of men to one another—or, even, as she would have claimed, by a concern for their relationship to God—but merely by a panic of being hurled into the flames, of being caught in traffic with the devil. She embraced this merciless doctrine with all her heart, bargaining shamelessly before the throne of grace: God and salvation becoming her personal property, purchased with the coin of her virtue. Here, black equates with evil and white with grace; if, being mindful of the necessity of good works, she could not cast out the blacks—a wretched, huddled mass, apparently, claiming, like an obsession, her inner eye—she could not embrace them either without purifying them of sin. She must cover their intimidating nakedness, robe them in white, the garments of salvation; only thus could she herself be delivered from ever-present sin, only thus could she bury, as St. Paul demanded, "the carnal man, the man of the flesh." Tom, therefore, her only black man, has been robbed of his humanity and divested of his sex. It is the price for that darkness with which he has been branded.

Uncle Tom's Cabin, then, is activated by what might be called a theological terror, the terror of damnation; and the spirit that breathes in this book, hot, self-righteous, fearful, is not different from that spirit of medieval times which sought to exorcize evil by burning witches; and is not different from that terror which activates a lynch mob. One need not, indeed, search for examples so historic or so gaudy; this is a warfare waged daily in the heart, a warfare so vast, so relentless and so powerful that the interracial handshake or the interracial marriage can be as crucifying as the public hanging or the secret rape. This panic motivates our cruelty, this fear of the dark makes it impossible that our lives shall be other than superficial; this, interlocked with and feeding our glittering, mechanical, inescapable civilization which has put to death our freedom.

This, notwithstanding that the avowed aim of the American protest novel is to bring greater freedom to the oppressed. They are forgiven, on the strength of these good intentions, whatever violence they do to language, whatever excessive demands they make of credibility. It is, indeed, considered the sign of a frivolity so intense as to approach decadence to suggest that these books are both badly written and wildly improbable. One is told to put first things first, the good of society coming before niceties of style or characterization. Even if this were incontestable—for what exactly is the "good" of society?—it argues an insuperable confusion, since literature and sociology are not one and the same; it is impossible to discuss them as if they were. Our passion for categorization, life neatly fitted into pegs, has led to an unforeseen, paradoxical distress; confusion, a breakdown of meaning. Those categories which were meant to define and control the world for us have boomeranged us into chaos; in which limbo we whirl, clutching the straws of our definitions. The "protest" novel, so far from being disturbing, is an accepted and comforting aspect of the American scene, ramifying that framework we believe to be so necessary. Whatever unsettling questions are raised are evanescent, titillating; remote, for this has nothing to do with us, it is safely ensconced in the social arena, where, indeed, it has nothing to do with anyone, so that finally we receive a very definite thrill of virtue from the fact that we are reading such a book at all. This report from the pit reassures us of its reality and its darkness and of our own salvation; and "As long as such books are being published," an American liberal once said to me, "everything will be all right."

But unless one's ideal of society is a race of neatly analyzed, hard-working ciphers, one can hardly claim for the protest novels the lofty purpose they claim for themselves or share the present optimism concerning them. They emerge for what they are: a mirror of our confusion, dishonesty, panic, trapped and immobilized in the sunlit prison of the American dream. They are fantasies, connecting nowhere with reality, sentimental; in exactly the same sense that such movies as *The Best Years of Our Lives* or the works of Mr. James M. Cain are fantasies. Beneath the dazzling pyrotechnics of these current operas one may still discern, as the controlling force, the intense theological preoccupations of Mrs. Stowe, the sick vacuities of *The Rover Boys*. Finally, the aim of the protest novel becomes something very closely resembling the zeal of those alabaster missionaries to Africa to cover the nakedness of the natives, to hurry them into the pallid arms of Jesus and thence into slavery. The aim has now become to reduce all Americans to the compulsive, bloodless dimensions of a guy named Joe.

It is the peculiar triumph of society—and its loss—that it is able to convince those people to whom it has given inferior status of the reality of this decree; it has the force and the weapons to translate its dictum into fact, so that the allegedly inferior are actually made so, insofar as the societal realities are concerned. This is a more hidden phenomenon now than it was in the days of serfdom, but it is no less implacable. Now, as then, we find ourselves bound, first without, then within, by the nature of our categorization. And escape is not effected through a bitter railing against this trap; it is as though this very striving were the only motion needed to spring the trap upon us. We take our shape, it is true, within and against that cage of reality bequeathed us at our birth; and yet it is precisely through our dependence on this reality that we are most endlessly betrayed. Society is held together by our need; we bind it together with legend, myth, coercion, fearing that without it we will be hurled into that void, within which, like the earth before the Word was spoken, the foundations of society are hidden. From this void—ourselves—it is the function of society to protect us; but it is only this void, our unknown selves, demanding, forever, a new act of creation, which can save us—"from the evil that is in the world." With the same motion, at the same time, it is this toward which we endlessly struggle and from which, endlessly, we struggle to escape.

It must be remembered that the oppressed and the oppressor are bound together within the same society; they accept the same criteria, they share the same beliefs, they both alike depend on the same reality. Within this cage it is romantic, more, meaningless, to speak of a "new" society as the desire of the oppressed, for that shivering dependence on the props of reality which he shares with the *Herrenvolk* makes a truly "new" society impossible to conceive. What is meant by a new society is one in which inequalities will disappear, in which vengeance will be exacted; either there will be no oppressed at all, or the oppressed and the oppressor will change places. But, finally, as it seems to me, what the rejected desire is, is an elevation of status, acceptance within the present community. Thus, the African, exile, pagan, hurried off the auction block and into the fields, fell on his knees before that God in Whom he must now believe; who had made him, but not in His image. This tableau, this impossibility, is the heritage of the Negro in America: *Wash me*, cried the slave to his Maker, *and I shall be whiter, whiter than snow!* For black is the color of evil; only the robes of the saved are white. It is this cry, implacable on the air and in the skull, that he must live with. Beneath the widely published catalogue of brutality—bringing to mind, somehow, an image, a memory of church-bells burdening the air—is this reality which, in the same nightmare notion, he both flees and rushes to embrace. In America, now, this country devoted to the death of the paradox—which may, therefore, be put to death by one—his lot is as ambiguous as a tableau by Kafka. To flee or not, to move or not, it is all the same; his doom is written on his forehead, it is carried in his heart. In *Native Son*, Bigger Thomas stands on a Chicago street corner watching airplanes flown by white men racing against the sun and "Goddamn" he says, the bitterness bubbling up like blood, remembering a million indignities, the terrible, rat-infested house, the humiliation of home-relief, the intense, aimless, ugly bickering, hating it; hatred smoulders through these pages like sulphur fire. All of Bigger's life is controlled, defined by his hatred and his fear. And later, his fear drives him to murder and his hatred to rape; he dies, having come, through this violence, we are told, for the first time, to a kind of life, having for the first time redeemed his manhood. Below the surface of this novel there lies, as it seems to me, a continuation, a complement of that monstrous legend it was written to destroy. Bigger is Uncle Tom's descendant, flesh of his flesh, so exactly opposite a portrait that, when the books are placed together, it seems that the contemporary Negro novelist and the dead New England woman are locked together in a deadly, timeless battle; the one uttering merciless exhortations, the other shouting curses. And, indeed, within this web of lust and fury, black and white can only thrust and counter-thrust, long for each other's slow, exquisite death; death by torture, acid, knives and burning; the thrust, the counter-thrust, the longing making the heavier that cloud which blinds and suffocates them both, so that they go down into the pit together. Thus has the cage betrayed us all, this moment, our life, turned to nothing through our terrible attempts to insure it. For Bigger's tragedy is not that he is cold or black or hungry, not even that he is American, black; but that he has accepted a theology that denies him life, that he admits the possibility of his being sub-human and feels constrained, therefore, to battle for his humanity according to those brutal criteria bequeathed him at his birth. But our humanity is our burden, our life; we need not battle for it; we need only to do what is infinitely more difficult—that is, accept it. The failure of the protest novel lies in its rejection of life, the human being, the denial of his beauty, dread, power, in its insistence that it is his categorization alone which is real and which cannot be transcended.

Many Thousands Gone

IT IS ONLY in his music, which Americans are able to admire because a protective sentimentality limits their understanding of it, that the Negro in America has been able to tell his story. It is a story which otherwise has yet to be told and which no American is prepared to hear. As is the inevitable result of things unsaid, we find ourselves until today oppressed with a dangerous and reverberating silence; and the story is told, compulsively, in symbols and signs, in hieroglyphics; it is revealed in Negro speech and in that of the white majority and in their different frames of reference. The ways in which the Negro has affected the American psychology are betrayed in our popular culture and in our morality; in our estrangement from him is the depth of our estrangement from ourselves. We cannot ask: what do we *really* feel about him—such a question merely opens the gates on chaos. What we really feel about him is involved with all that we feel about everything, about everyone, about ourselves.

The story of the Negro in America is the story of America—or, more precisely, it is the story of Americans. It is not a very pretty story: the story of a people is never very pretty. The Negro in America, gloomily referred to as that shadow which lies athwart our national life, is far more than that. He is a series of shadows, self-created, intertwining, which now we helplessly battle. One may say that the Negro in America does not really exist except in the darkness of our minds.

This is why his history and his progress, his relationship to all other Americans, has been kept in the social arena. He is a social and not a personal or a human problem; to think of him is to think of statistics, slums, rapes, injustices, remote violence; it is to be confronted with an endless cataloguing of losses, gains, skirmishes; it is to feel virtuous, outraged, helpless, as though his continuing status among us were somehow analogous to disease—cancer, perhaps, or tuberculosis—which must be checked, even though it cannot be cured. In this arena the black man acquires quite another aspect from that which he has in life. We do not know what to do with him in life; if he breaks our sociological and sentimental image of him we are panic-stricken and we feel ourselves betrayed. When he violates this image, therefore, he stands in the greatest danger (sensing which, we uneasily suspect that he is very often playing a part for our benefit); and, what is not always so apparent but is equally true, we are then in some danger ourselves—hence our retreat or our blind and immediate retaliation.

Our dehumanization of the Negro then is indivisible from our dehumanization of ourselves: the loss of our own identity is the price we pay for our annulment of his. Time and our own force act as our allies, creating an impossible, a fruitless tension between the traditional master and slave. Impossible and fruitless because, literal and visible as this tension has become, it has nothing to do with reality.

Time has made some changes in the Negro face. Nothing has succeeded in making it exactly like our own, though the general desire seems to be to make it blank if one cannot make it white. When it has become blank, the past as thoroughly washed from the black face as it has been from ours, our guilt will be finished—at least it will have ceased to be visible, which we imagine to be much the same thing. But, paradoxically, it is we who prevent this from happening; since it is we, who, every hour that we live, reinvest the black face with our guilt; and we do this—by a further paradox, no less ferocious—helplessly, passionately, out of an unrealized need to suffer absolution.

Today, to be sure, we know that the Negro is not biologically or mentally inferior; there is no truth in those rumors of his body odor or his incorrigible sexuality; or no more truth than can be easily explained or even defended by the social sciences. Yet, in our most recent war, his blood was segregated as was, for the most part, his person. Up to today we are set at a division, so that he may not marry our daughters or our sisters, nor may he—for the most part—eat at our tables or live in our houses. Moreover, those who do, do so at the grave expense of a double alienation: from their own people, whose fabled attributes they must either deny or, worse, cheapen and bring to market; from us, for we require of them, when we accept them, that they at once cease to be Negroes and yet not fail to remember what being a Negro means—to remember, that is, what it means to us. The threshold of insult is higher or lower, according to the people involved, from the bootblack in Atlanta to the celebrity in New York. One must travel very far, among saints with nothing to gain or outcasts with nothing to lose, to find a place where it does not matter —and perhaps a word or a gesture or simply a silence will testify that it matters even there.

For it means something to be a Negro, after all, as it means something to have been born in Ireland or in China, to live where one sees space and sky or to live where one sees nothing but rubble or nothing but high buildings. We cannot escape our origins, however hard we try, those origins which contain the key—could we but find it—to all that we later become. What it means to be a Negro is a good deal more than this essay can discover; what it means to be a Negro in America can perhaps be suggested by an examination of the myths we perpetuate about him.

Aunt Jemima and Uncle Tom are dead, their places taken by a group of amazingly well-adjusted young men and women, almost as dark, but ferociously literate, well-dressed and scrubbed, who are never laughed at, who are not likely ever to set foot in a cotton or tobacco field or in any but the most modern of kitchens. There are others who remain, in our odd idiom, "underprivileged"; some are bitter and these come to grief; some are unhappy, but, continually presented with the evidence of a better day soon to come, are speedily becoming less so. Most of them care nothing whatever about race. They want only their proper place in the sun and the right to be left alone, like any other citizen of the republic. We may all breathe more easily. Before, however, our joy at the demise of Aunt Jemima and Uncle Tom approaches the indecent, we had better ask whence they sprang, how they lived? Into what limbo have they vanished?

However inaccurate our portraits of them were, these portraits do suggest, not only the conditions, but the quality of their lives and the impact of this spectacle on our consciences. There was no one more forbearing than Aunt Jemima, no one stronger or more pious or more loyal or more wise; there was, at the same time, no one weaker or more faithless or more vicious and certainly no one more immoral. Uncle Tom, trust-worthy and sexless, needed only to drop the title "Uncle" to become violent, crafty, and sullen, a menace to any white woman who passed by. They prepared our feast tables and our burial clothes; and, if we could boast that we understood them, it was far more to the point and far more true that they understood us. They were, moreover, the only people in the world who did; and not only did they know us better than we knew ourselves, but they knew us better than we knew them. This was the piquant flavoring to the national joke, it lay be-hind our uneasiness as it lay behind our benevolence: Aunt Jemima and Uncle Tom, our creations, at the last evaded us; they had a life—their own, perhaps a better life than ours—and they would never tell us what it was. At the point where we were driven most privately and painfully to conjecture what depths of contempt, what heights of indifference, what prod-igies of resilience, what untamable superiority allowed them so vividly to endure, neither perishing nor rising up in a body to wipe us from the earth, the image perpetually shattered and the word failed. The black man in our midst carried murder in his heart, he wanted vengeance. We carried murder too, we wanted peace.

In our image of the Negro breathes the past we deny, not dead but living yet and powerful, the beast in our jungle of statistics. It is this which defeats us, which continues to defeat us, which lends to interracial cocktail parties their rattling, genteel, nervously smiling air: in any drawing room at such a gathering the beast may spring, filling the air with flying things and an unenlightened wailing. Wherever the problem touches there is confusion, there is danger. Wherever the Ne-gro face appears a tension is created, the tension of a silence filled with things unutterable. It is a sentimental error, there-fore, to believe that the past is dead; it means nothing to say that it is all forgotten, that the Negro himself has forgotten it. It is not a question of memory. Oedipus did not remember the thongs that bound his feet; nevertheless the marks they left testified to that doom toward which his feet were leading him. The man does not remember the hand that struck him, the darkness that frightened him, as a child; nevertheless, the hand and the darkness remain with him, indivisible from himself forever, part of the passion that drives him wherever he thinks to take flight.

The making of an American begins at that point where he himself rejects all other ties, any other history, and himself adopts the vesture of his adopted land. This problem has been faced by all Americans throughout our history—in a way it *is* our history—and it baffles the immigrant and sets on edge the second generation until today. In the case of the Negro the past was taken from him whether he would or no; yet to forswear it was meaningless and availed him nothing, since his shameful history was carried, quite literally, on his brow. Shameful; for he was heathen as well as black and would never have discovered the healing blood of Christ had not we braved the jungles to bring him these glad tidings. Shameful; for, since our role as missionary had not been wholly disinterested, it was necessary to recall the shame from which we had delivered him in order more easily to escape our own. As he accepted the alabaster Christ and the bloody cross—in the bearing of which he would find his redemption, as, indeed, to our outraged astonishment, he sometimes did—he must, henceforth, accept that image we then gave him of himself: having no other and standing, moreover, in danger of death should he fail to accept the dazzling light thus brought into such darkness. It is this quite simple dilemma that must be borne in mind if we wish to comprehend his psychology.

However we shift the light which beats so fiercely on his head, or *prove*, by victorious social analysis, how his lot has changed, how we have both improved, our uneasiness refuses to be exorcized. And nowhere is this more apparent than in our literature on the subject—"problem" literature when written by whites, "protest" literature when written by Negroes—and nothing is more striking than the tremendous disparity of tone between the two creations. *Kingsblood Royal* bears, for example, almost no kinship to *If He Hollers Let Him Go*, though the same reviewers praised them both for what were, at bottom, very much the same reasons. These reasons may be suggested, far too briefly but not at all unjustly, by observing that the presupposition is in both novels exactly the same: black is a terrible color with which to be born into the world.

Now the most powerful and celebrated statement we have yet had of what it means to be a Negro in America is unquestionably Richard Wright's *Native Son*. The feeling which prevailed at the time of its publication was that such a novel, bitter, uncompromising, shocking, gave proof, by its very existence, of what strides might be taken in a free democracy; and its indisputable success, proof that Americans were now able to look full in the face without flinching the dreadful facts. Americans, unhappily, have the most remarkable ability to alchemize all bitter truths into an innocuous but piquant confection and to transform their moral contradictions, or public discussion of such contradictions, into a proud decoration, such as are given for heroism on the field of battle. Such a book, we felt with pride, could never have been written before—which was true. Nor could it be written today. It bears already the aspect of a landmark; for Bigger and his brothers have undergone yet another metamorphosis; they have been accepted in baseball leagues and by colleges hitherto exclusive; and they have made a most favorable appearance on the national screen. We have yet to encounter, nevertheless, a report so indisputably authentic, or one that can begin to challenge this most significant novel.

It is, in a certain American tradition, the story of an unremarkable youth in battle with the force of circumstance; that force of circumstance which plays and which has played so important a part in the national fables of success or failure. In this case the force of circumstance is not poverty merely but color, a circumstance which cannot be overcome, against which the protagonist battles for his life and loses. It is, on the surface, remarkable that this book should have enjoyed among Americans the favor it did enjoy; no more remarkable, however, than that it should have been compared, exuberantly, to Dostoevsky, though placed a shade below Dos Passos, Dreiser, and Steinbeck; and when the book is examined, its impact does not seem remarkable at all, but becomes, on the contrary, perfectly logical and inevitable.

We cannot, to begin with, divorce this book from the specific social climate of that time: it was one of the last of those angry productions, encountered in the late twenties and all through the thirties, dealing with the inequities of the social structure of America. It was published one year before our entry into the last world war—which is to say, very few years after the dissolution of the WPA and the end of the New Deal and at a time when bread lines and soup kitchens and bloody industrial battles were bright in everyone's memory. The rigors of that unexpected time filled us not only with a genuinely bewildered and despairing idealism—so that, because there at least was *something* to fight for, young men went off to die in Spain—but also with a genuinely bewildered self-consciousness. The Negro, who had been during the magnificent twenties a passionate and delightful primitive, now became, as one of the things we were most self-conscious about, our most oppressed minority. In the thirties, swallowing Marx whole, we discovered the Worker and realized—I should think with some relief—that the aims of the Worker and the aims of the Negro were one. This theorem—to which we shall return—seems now to leave rather too much out of account; it became, nevertheless, one of the slogans of the "class struggle" and the gospel of the New Negro.

As for this New Negro, it was Wright who became his most eloquent spokesman; and his work, from its beginning, is most clearly committed to the social struggle. Leaving aside the considerable question of what relationship precisely the artist bears to the revolutionary, the reality of man as a social being is not his only reality and that artist is strangled who is forced to deal with human beings solely in social terms; and who has, moreover, as Wright had, the necessity thrust on him of being the representative of some thirteen million people. It is a false responsibility (since writers are not congressmen) and impossible, by its nature, of fulfillment. The unlucky shepherd soon finds that, so far from being able to feed the hungry sheep, he has lost the wherewithal for his own nourishment: having not been allowed—so fearful was his burden, so present his audience!—to recreate his own experience. Further, the militant men and women of the thirties were not, upon examination, significantly emancipated from their antecedents, however bitterly they might consider themselves estranged or however gallantly they struggled to build a better world. However they might extol Russia, their concept of a better world was quite helplessly American and betrayed a certain thinness of imagination, a suspect reliance on suspect and badly digested formulae, and a positively fretful romantic haste. Finally, the relationship of the Negro to the Worker cannot be summed up, nor even greatly illuminated, by saying that their aims are one. It is true only insofar as they both desire better working conditions and useful only insofar as they unite their strength as workers to achieve these ends. Further than this we cannot in honesty go.

In this climate Wright's voice first was heard and the struggle which promised for a time to shape his work and give it purpose also fixed it in an ever more unrewarding rage. Recording his days of anger he has also nevertheless recorded, as no Negro before him had ever done, that fantasy Americans hold in their minds when they speak of the Negro: that fantastic and fearful image which we have lived with since the first slave fell beneath the lash. This is the significance of *Native Son* and also, unhappily, its overwhelming limitation.

Native Son begins with the *Brring!* of an alarm clock in the squalid Chicago tenement where Bigger and his family live. Rats live there too, feeding off the garbage, and we first encounter Bigger in the act of killing one. One may consider that the entire book, from that harsh *Brring!* to Bigger's weak "Good-by" as the lawyer, Max, leaves him in the death cell, is an extension, with the roles inverted, of this chilling metaphor. Bigger's situation and Bigger himself exert on the mind the same sort of fascination. The premise of the book is, as I take it, clearly conveyed in these first pages: we are confronting a monster created by the American republic and we are, through being made to share his experience, to receive illumination as regards the manner of his life and to feel both pity and horror at his awful and inevitable doom. This is an arresting and potentially rich idea and we would be discussing a very different novel if Wright's execution had been more perceptive and if he had not attempted to redeem a symbolical monster in social terms.

One may object that it was precisely Wright's intention to

create in Bigger a social symbol, revelatory of social disease and prophetic of disaster. I think, however, that it is this assumption which we ought to examine more carefully. Bigger has no discernible relationship to himself, to his own life, to his own people, nor to any other people—in this respect, perhaps, he is most American—and his force comes, not from his significance as a social (or anti-social) unit, but from his significance as the incarnation of a myth. It is remarkable that, though we follow him step by step from the tenement room to the death cell, we know as little about him when this journey is ended as we did when it began; and, what is even more remarkable, we know almost as little about the social dynamic which we are to believe created him. Despite the details of slum life which we are given, I doubt that anyone who has thought about it, disengaging himself from sentimentality, can accept this most essential premise of the novel for a moment. Those Negroes who surround him, on the other hand, his hard-working mother, his ambitious sister, his poolroom cronies, Bessie, might be considered as far richer and far more subtle and accurate illustrations of the ways in which Negroes are controlled in our society and the complex techniques they have evolved for their survival. We are limited, however, to Bigger's view of them, part of a deliberate plan which might not have been disastrous if we were not also limited to Bigger's perceptions. What this means for the novel is that a necessary dimension has been cut away; this dimension being the relationship that Negroes bear to one another, that depth of involvement and unspoken recognition of shared experience which creates a way of life. What the novel reflects—and at no point interprets—is the isolation of the Negro within his own group and the resulting fury of impatient scorn. It is this which creates its climate of anarchy and unmotivated and unapprehended disaster; and it is this climate, common to most Negro protest novels, which has led us all to believe that in Negro life there exists no tradition, no field of manners, no possibility of ritual or intercourse, such as may, for example, sustain the Jew even after he has left his father's house. But the fact is not that the Negro has no tradition but that there has as yet arrived no sensibility sufficiently profound and tough to make this tradition articulate. For a tradition expresses, after all, nothing more than the long and painful experience of a people; it comes out of the battle waged to maintain their integrity or, to put it more simply, out of their struggle to survive. When we speak of the Jewish tradition we are speaking of centuries of exile and persecution, of the strength which endured and the sensibility which discovered in it the high possibility of the moral victory.

This sense of how Negroes live and how they have so long endured is hidden from us in part by the very speed of the Negro's public progress, a progress so heavy with complexity, so bewildering and kaleidoscopic, that he dare not pause to conjecture on the darkness which lies behind him; and by the nature of the American psychology which, in order to apprehend or be made able to accept it, must undergo a metamorphosis so profound as to be literally unthinkable and which there is no doubt we will resist until we are compelled to achieve our own identity by the rigors of a time that has yet to come. Bigger, in the meanwhile, and all his furious kin, serve only to whet the notorious national taste for the sensational and to reinforce all that we now find it necessary to believe. It is not Bigger whom we fear, since his appearance among us makes our victory certain. It is the others, who smile, who go to church, who give no cause for complaint, whom we sometimes consider with amusement, with pity, even with affection—and in whose faces we sometimes surprise the merest arrogant hint of hatred, the faintest, withdrawn, speculative shadow of contempt—who make us uneasy; whom we cajole, threaten, flatter, fear; who to us remain unknown, though we are not (we feel with both relief and hostility and with bottomless confusion) unknown to them. It is out of our reaction to these hewers of wood and drawers of water that our image of Bigger was created.

It is this image, living yet, which we perpetually seek to evade with good works; and this image which makes of all our good works an intolerable mockery. The "nigger," black, benighted, brutal, consumed with hatred as we are consumed with guilt, cannot be thus blotted out. He stands at our shoulders when we give our maid her wages, it is his hand which we fear we are taking when struggling to communicate with the current "intelligent" Negro, his stench, as it were, which fills our mouths with salt as the monument is unveiled in honor of the latest Negro leader. Each generation has shouted behind him, *Nigger!* as he walked our streets; it is he whom we would rather our sisters did not marry; he is banished into the vast and wailing outer darkness whenever we speak of the "purity" of our women, of the "sanctity" of our homes, of "American" ideals. What is more, he knows it. He is indeed the "native son": he is the "nigger." Let us refrain from inquiring at the moment whether or not he actually exists; for we *believe* that he exists. Whenever we encounter him amongst us in the flesh, our faith is made perfect and his necessary and bloody end is executed with a mystical ferocity of joy.

But there is a complementary faith among the damned which involves their gathering of the stones with which those who walk in the light shall stone them; or there exists among the intolerably degraded the perverse and powerful desire to force into the arena of the actual those fantastic crimes of which they have been accused, achieving their vengeance and their own destruction through making the nightmare real. The American image of the Negro lives also in the Negro's heart; and when he has surrendered to this image life has no other possible reality. Then he, like the white enemy with whom he will be locked one day in mortal struggle, has no means save this of asserting his identity. This is why Bigger's murder of Mary can be referred to as an "act of creation" and why, once this murder has been committed, he can feel for the first time that he is living fully and deeply as a man was meant to live. And there is, I should think, no Negro living in America who has not felt, briefly or for long periods, with anguish sharp or dull, in varying degrees and to varying effect, simple, naked and unanswerable hatred; who has not wanted to smash any white face he may encounter in a day, to violate, out of motives of the cruelest vengeance, their women, to break the bodies of all white people and bring them low, as low as that dust into which he himself has been and is being trampled; no Negro, finally, who has not had to make his own precarious adjustment to the "nigger" who surrounds him and to the "nigger" in himself.

Yet the adjustment must be made—rather, it must be attempted, the tension perpetually sustained—for without this he has surrendered his birthright as a man no less than his birthright as a black man. The entire universe is then peopled only with his enemies, who are not only white men armed with rope and rifle, but his own far-flung and contemptible kinsmen. Their blackness is his degradation and it is their stupid and passive endurance which makes his end inevitable.

Bigger dreams of some black man who will weld all blacks together into a mighty fist, and feels, in relation to his family, that perhaps they had to live as they did precisely because none of them had ever done anything, right or wrong, which mattered very much. It is only he who, by an act of murder, has burst the dungeon cell. He has made it manifest that *he* lives and that his despised blood nourishes the passions of a man. He has forced his oppressors to see the fruit of that oppression: and he feels, when his family and his friends come to visit him in the death cell, that they should not be weeping or frightened, that they should be happy, *proud* that he has dared, through murder and now through his own imminent destruction, to redeem their anger and humiliation, that he has hurled into the spiritless obscurity of their lives the lamp of his passionate life and death. Henceforth, they may remember Bigger—who has died, as we may conclude, for them. But they do not feel this; they only know that he has murdered two women and precipitated a reign of terror; and that now he is to die in the electric chair. They therefore weep and are honestly frightened—for which Bigger despises them and wishes to "blot" them out. What is missing in his situation and in the representation of his psychology—which makes his situation false and his psychology incapable of development—is any revelatory apprehension of Bigger as one of the Negro's realities or as one of the Negro's roles. This failure is part of the previously noted failure to convey any sense of Negro life as a continuing and complex group reality. Bigger, who cannot function therefore as a reflection of the social illness, having, as it were, no society to reflect, likewise refuses to function on the loftier level of the Christ-symbol. His kinsmen are quite right to weep and be frightened, even to be appalled: for it is not his love for them or for himself which causes him to die, but his hatred and his self-hatred; he does not redeem the pains of a despised people, but reveals, on the contrary, nothing more than his own fierce bitterness at having been born one of them. In this also he is the "native son," his progress determinable by the speed with which the distance increases between himself and the auction-block and all that the auction-block implies. To have penetrated this phenomenon, this inward contention of love and hatred, blackness and whiteness, would have given him a stature more nearly human and an end more nearly tragic; and would have given us a document more profoundly and genuinely bitter and less harsh with an anger which is, on the one hand, exhibited and, on the other hand, denied.

Native Son finds itself at length so trapped by the American image of Negro life and by the American necessity to find the ray of hope that it cannot pursue its own implications. This is why Bigger must be at the last redeemed, to be received, if only by rhetoric, into that community of phantoms which is our tenaciously held ideal of the happy social life. It is the socially conscious whites who receive him—the Negroes being capable of no such objectivity—and we have, by way of illustration, that lamentable scene in which Jan, Mary's lover, forgives him for her murder; and, carrying the explicit burden of the novel, Max's long speech to the jury. This speech, which really ends the book, is one of the most desperate performances in American fiction. It is the question of Bigger's humanity which is at stake, the relationship in which he stands to all other Americans—and, by implication, to all people— and it is precisely this question which it cannot clarify, with which it cannot, in fact, come to any coherent terms. He is the monster created by the American republic, the present awful sum of generations of oppression; but to say that he is a monster is to fall into the trap of making him subhuman and he must, therefore, be made representative of a way of life which is real and human in precise ratio to the degree to which it seems to us monstrous and strange. It seems to me that this idea carries, implicitly, a most remarkable confession: that is, that Negro life is in fact as debased and impoverished as our theology claims; and, further, that the use to which Wright puts this idea can only proceed from the assumption— not entirely unsound—that Americans, who evade, so far as possible, all genuine experience, have therefore no way of assessing the experience of others and no way of establishing themselves in relation to any way of life which is not their own. The privacy or obscurity of Negro life makes that life capable, in our imaginations, of producing anything at all; and thus the idea of Bigger's monstrosity can be presented without fear of contradiction, since no American has the knowledge or authority to contest it and no Negro has the voice. It is an idea, which, in the framework of the novel, is dignified by the possibility it promptly affords of presenting Bigger as the herald of disaster, the danger signal of a more bitter time to come when not Bigger alone but all his kindred will rise, in the name of the many thousands who have perished in fire and flood and by rope and torture, to demand their rightful vengeance.

But it is not quite fair, it seems to me, to exploit the national innocence in this way. The idea of Bigger as a warning boomerangs not only because it is quite beyond the limit of probability that Negroes in America will ever achieve the means of wreaking vengeance upon the state but also because it cannot be said that they have any desire to do so. *Native Son* does not convey the altogether savage paradox of the American Negro's situation, of which the social reality which we prefer with such hopeful superficiality to study is but, as it were, the shadow. It is not simply the relationship of oppressed to oppressor, of master to slave, nor is it motivated merely by hatred; it is also, literally and morally, a *blood* relationship, perhaps the most profound reality of the American experience, and we cannot begin to unlock it until we accept how very much it contains of the force and anguish and terror of love.

Negroes are Americans and their destiny is the country's destiny. They have no other experience besides their experience on this continent and it is an experience which cannot be rejected, which yet remains to be embraced. If, as I believe, no American Negro exists who does not have his private Bigger Thomas living in the skull, then what most significantly fails to be illuminated here is the paradoxical adjustment which is perpetually made, the Negro being compelled to accept the fact that this dark and dangerous and unloved stranger is part of himself forever. Only this recognition sets him in any wise free and it is this, this necessary ability to contain and even, in the most honorable sense of the word, to *exploit* the "nigger," which lends to Negro life its high element of the ironic and which causes the most well-meaning of their American critics to make such exhilarating errors when attempting to understand them. To present Bigger as a warning is simply to reinforce the American guilt and fear concerning him, it is most forcefully to limit him to that previously mentioned social arena in which he has no human validity, it is simply to condemn him to death. For he has always been a warning, he represents the evil, the sin and suffering which we are compelled to reject. It is useless to say to the courtroom in which this heathen sits on trial that he is their responsibility, their creation, and his crimes are theirs; and that they ought, therefore, to allow him to live, to make articulate to himself behind the walls of prison the meaning of his existence. The meaning of his existence has already been most adequately expressed, nor does anyone wish, particularly not in the name of democracy, to think of it any more; as for the possibility of articulation, it is this possibility which above all others we most dread. Moreover, the courtroom, judge, jury, witnesses and spectators, recognize immediately that Bigger is their creation and they recognize this not only with hatred and fear and guilt and the resulting fury of self-righteousness but also with that morbid fullness of pride mixed with horror with which one regards the extent and power of one's wickedness. They know that death is his portion, that he runs to death; coming from darkness and dwelling in darkness, he must be, as often as he rises, banished, lest the entire planet be engulfed. And they know, finally, that they do not wish to forgive him and that he does not wish to be forgiven; that he dies, hating them, scorning that appeal which they cannot make to that irrecoverable humanity of his which cannot hear it; and that he *wants* to die because he glories in his hatred and prefers, like Lucifer, rather to rule in hell than serve in heaven.

For, bearing in mind the premise on which the life of such a man is based, *i.e.*, that black is the color of damnation, this is his only possible end. It is the only death which will allow him a kind of dignity or even, however horribly, a kind of beauty. To tell this story, no more than a single aspect of the story of the "nigger," is inevitably and richly to become involved with the force of life and legend, how each perpetually assumes the guise of the other, creating that dense, many-sided and shifting reality which is the world we live in and the world we make. To tell his story is to begin to liberate us from his image and it is, for the first time, to clothe this phantom with flesh and blood, to deepen, by our understanding of him and his relationship to us, our understanding of ourselves and of all men.

But this is not the story which *Native Son* tells, for we find here merely, repeated in anger, the story which we have told in pride. Nor, since the implications of this anger are evaded, are we ever confronted with the actual or potential significance of our pride; which is why we fall, with such a positive glow of recognition, upon Max's long and bitter summing up. It is addressed to those among us of good will and it seems to say that, though there are whites and blacks among us who hate each other, we will not; there are those who are betrayed by greed, by guilt, by blood lust, but not we; we will set our faces against them and join hands and walk together into that dazzling future when there will be no white or black. This is the dream of all liberal men, a dream not at all dishonorable, but, nevertheless, a dream. For, let us join hands on this mountain as we may, the battle is elsewhere. It proceeds far from us in the heat and horror and pain of life itself where all men are betrayed by greed and guilt and blood-lust and where no one's hands are clean. Our good will, from which we yet expect such power to transform us, is thin, passionless, strident: its roots, examined, lead us back to our forebears, whose assumption it was that the black man, to become truly human and acceptable, must first become like us. This assumption once accepted, the Negro in America can only acquiesce in the obliteration of his own personality, the distortion and debasement of his own experience, surrendering to those forces which reduce the person to anonymity and which make themselves manifest daily all over the darkening world.

Carmen Jones:
The Dark Is Light Enough

HOLLYWOOD'S peculiar ability to milk, so to speak, the cow and the goat at the same time—and then to peddle the results as ginger ale—has seldom produced anything more arresting than the 1955 production of *Carmen Jones*. In Hollywood, for example, immorality and evil (which are synonyms in that lexicon) are always vividly punished, though it is the way of the transgressor—hard perhaps but far from unattractive—which keeps us on the edge of our seats, and the transgressor himself (or herself) who engages all our sympathy. Similarly, in *Carmen Jones*, the implicit parallel between an amoral Gypsy and an amoral Negro woman is the entire root idea of the show; but at the same time, bearing in mind the distances covered since *The Birth of a Nation*, it is important that the movie always be able to repudiate any suggestion that Negroes are amoral—which it can only do, considering the role of the Negro in the national psyche, by repudiating any suggestion that Negroes are not white. With a story like *Carmen* interpreted by a Negro cast this may seem a difficult assignment, but Twentieth Century–Fox has brought it off. At the same time they have also triumphantly *not* brought it off, that is to say that the story *does* deal with amoral people, Carmen *is* a baggage, and it *is* a Negro cast.

This is made possible in the first place, of course, by the fact that *Carmen* is a "classic" or a "work of art" or something, therefore, sacrosanct and, luckily, quite old: it is as ludicrously unenlightened to accuse Mérimée and Bizet of having dirty minds as it is impossible to accuse them of being anti-Negro. (Though it *is* possible perhaps to accuse them of not knowing much and caring less about Gypsies.) In the second place the music helps, for it has assuredly never sounded so bald, or been sung so badly, or had less relevance to life, anybody's life, than in this production. The lyrics, too, in their way, help, being tasteless and vulgar in a way, if not to a degree, which cannot be called characteristic of Negroes. The movie's lifeless unreality is only occasionally threatened by

35

Pearl Bailey, who has, however, been forestalled by Mr.
Preminger's direction and is reduced—in a series of awful costumes, designed, it would appear, to camouflage her personality—to doing what is certainly the best that can be done
with an abomination called *Beat Out That Rhythm on a Drum*
and delivering her lines for the rest of the picture with such a
murderously amused disdain that one cannot quite avoid the
suspicion that she is commenting on the film. For a second
or so at a time she escapes the film's deadly inertia and in Miss
Bailey one catches glimpses of the imagination which might
have exploded this movie into something worth seeing.

But this movie, more than any movie I can remember
having seen, cannot afford, dare not risk, imagination. The
"sexiness," for example, of Dorothy Dandridge, who plays
Carmen, becomes quite clearly manufactured and even rather
silly the moment Pearl Bailey stands anywhere near her.* And
the moment one wishes that Pearl Bailey were playing Carmen
one understands that *Carmen Jones* is controlled by another
movie which Hollywood was studiously *not* making. For,
while it is amusing to parallel Bizet's amoral Gypsy with a
present-day, lower-class Negro woman, it is a good deal less
amusing to parallel the Bizet violence with the violence of the
Negro ghetto.

To avoid this—to exploit, that is, Carmen as a brown-
skinned baggage but to avoid even suggesting any of the motivations such a present-day Carmen might have—it was
helpful, first of all, that the script failed to require the services
of any white people. This seals the action off, as it were, in a
vacuum in which the spectacle of color is divested of its danger. The color itself then becomes a kind of vacuum which
each spectator will fill with his own fantasies. But *Carmen
Jones* does not inhabit the never-never land of such bogus but

*I have singled out Miss Bailey because the quality of her personality, forth-
right and wry, and with the authoritative ring of authenticity, highlights for
me the lack of any of these qualities, or any positive qualities at all, in the
movie itself. She is also the only performer with whose work I am more or
less familiar. Since even she is so thoroughly handicapped by the peculiar
necessities of *Carmen Jones*, I should like to make it clear that, in discussing
the rest of the cast, I am not trying to judge their professional competence,
which, on the basis of this movie—they do not even sing in their own voices—
it would be quite unfair to do.

rather entertaining works as *Stormy Weather* or *Cabin in the Sky*—in which at least one could listen to the music; *Carmen Jones* has moved into a stratosphere rather more interesting and more pernicious, in which even Negro speech is parodied out of its charm and liberalized, if one may so put it, out of its force and precision. The result is not that the characters sound like everybody else, which would be bad enough; the result is that they sound ludicrously false and affected, like ante-bellum Negroes imitating their masters. This is also the way they look, and also rather the way they are dressed, and the word that springs immediately to mind to describe the appallingly technicolored sets—an army camp, a room, and a street on Chicago's South Side, presumably, which Bigger Thomas would certainly fail to recognize—is "spotless." They could easily have been dreamed up by someone determined to prove that Negroes are as "clean" and as "modern" as white people and, I suppose, in one way or another, that is exactly how they *were* dreamed up.

And one is not allowed to forget for an instant that one is watching an opera (a word apparently synonymous in Mr. Preminger's mind with tragedy *and* fantasy), and the tone of *Carmen Jones* is stifling: a wedding of the blank, lofty solemnity with which Hollywood so often approaches "works of art" and the really quite helpless condescension with which Hollywood has always handled Negroes. The fact that one is watching a Negro cast interpreting *Carmen* is used to justify their remarkable vacuity, their complete improbability, their total divorce from anything suggestive of the realities of Negro life. On the other hand, the movie cannot possibly avoid depending very heavily on a certain quaintness, a certain lack of inhibition taken to be typical of Negroes, and further, the exigencies of the story—to say nothing of the images, which we will discuss in a moment—make it necessary to watch this movie, holding in the mind three disparate ideas: (1) that this is an opera having nothing to do with the present day, hence, nothing, *really*, to do with Negroes; but (2) the greater passion, that winning warmth (of which the movie exhibits not a trace), so typical of Negroes makes *Carmen* an ideal vehicle for their graduation into Art; and (3) these are *exceptional* Negroes, as American, that is, as you and me, interpreting lower-class Negroes of whom they, also, are very fond, an affection which is proven perhaps by the fact that everyone appears to undergo a tiny, strangling death before resolutely substituting "de" for "the."

A movie is, literally, a series of images, and what one *sees* in a movie can really be taken, beyond its stammering or misleading dialogue, as the key to what the movie is actually involved in saying. *Carmen Jones* is one of the first and most explicit—and far and away the most self-conscious—weddings of sex and color which Hollywood has yet turned out. (It will most certainly not be the last.) From this point of view the color wheel in *Carmen Jones* is very important. Dorothy Dandridge—Carmen—is a sort of taffy-colored girl, very obviously and vividly dressed, but really in herself rather more sweet than vivid. One feels—perhaps one is meant to feel—that here is a *very* nice girl making her way in movies by means of a bad-girl part; and the glow thus caused, especially since she is a colored girl, really must make up for the glow which is missing from the performance she is clearly working very hard at. Harry Belafonte is just a little darker and just as blankly handsome and fares very badly opposite her in a really offensive version of an already unendurable role. Olga James is Micaela, here called Cindy Lou, a much paler girl than Miss Dandridge but also much plainer, who is compelled to go through the entire movie in a kind of tearful stoop. Joe Adams is Husky Miller (Escamillo) and he is also rather taffy-colored, but since he is the second lead and by way of being the villain, he is not required to be as blank as Mr. Belafonte and there is therefore, simply in his presence, some fleeting hint of masculine or at least boyish force. For the rest, Pearl Bailey is quite dark and she plays, in effect, a floozie. The wicked sergeant who causes Joe to desert the army—in one of many wildly improbable scenes—and who has evil designs on Carmen is very dark indeed; and so is Husky Miller's trainer, who is, one is given to suppose, Miss Bailey's sugar-daddy. It is quite clear that these people do not live in the same world with Carmen, or Joe, or Cindy Lou. All three of the leads are presented as indefinably complex and tragic, not after money or rhinestones but something else which causes them to be misunderstood by the more earthy types around them. This something else is love, of course, and it is with the handling of this love story that the movie really goes to town.

It is true that no one in the original *Carmen*, least of all Carmen and her lover, are very clearly motivated; but there it scarcely matters because the opera is able to get by on a purely theatrical excitement, a sort of papier-mâché violence, and the intense, if finally incredible, sexuality of its heroine. The movie does not have any of this to work with, since here excitement or violence could only blow the movie to bits, and, while the movie certainly indicates that Carmen is a luscious lollipop, it is on rather more uncertain ground when confronted with the notion of how attractive *she* finds men, and it cannot, in any case, use this as a motivating factor. Carmen is thus robbed at a stroke of even her fake vitality and all her cohesiveness and has become, instead, a nice girl, if a little fiery, whose great fault—and, since this is a tragedy, also her triumph—is that she looks at "life," as her final aria states it, "straight in de eye." In lieu of sexuality the movie-makers have dreamed up some mumbo jumbo involving buzzards' wings, signs of the zodiac, and death-dealing cards, so that, it appears, Carmen ruins Joe because she loves him and decides to leave him because the cards tell her she is going to die. The fact that between the time she leaves him and the time he kills her she acquires some new clothes, and drinks—as one of her arias rather violently indicates she intends to—a great deal of champagne is simply a sign of her intense inner suffering.

Carmen has come a long way from the auction block, but Joe, of course, cannot be far behind. This Joe is a good, fine-looking boy who loves his Maw, has studied hard, and is going to be sent to flying school, and who is engaged to a girl who rather resembles his Maw, named Cindy Lou. His indifference to Carmen, who has all the other males in sight quivering with a passion never seen on land or sea, sets her ablaze; in a series of scenes which it is difficult to call erotic without adding that they are also infantile, she goes after him and he falls. Here the technicolored bodies of Dandridge and Belafonte, while the movie is being glum about the ruin of Joe's career and impending doom, are used for the maximum erotic effect. It is a sterile and distressing eroticism, however, because it is occurring in a vacuum between two mannequins who clearly are not involved in anything more serious than giving the customers a run for their money. One is not watching either tenderness or love, and one is certainly not watching the complex and consuming passion which leads to life or death—one is watching a timorous and vulgar misrepresentation of these things.

And it must be said that one of the reasons for this is that, while the movie-makers are pleased to have Miss Dandridge flouncing about in tight skirts and plunging necklines—which is not exactly sexuality, either—the Negro male is still too loaded a quantity for them to know quite how to handle. The result is that Mr. Belafonte is really not allowed to do anything more than walk around looking like a spaniel: *his* sexuality is really taken as given because Miss Dandridge wants him. It does not, otherwise, exist and he is not destroyed by his own sexual aggressiveness, which he is not allowed to have, but by the sexual aggressiveness of the girl—or, as it turns out, not even really by that, but by tea leaves. The only reason, finally, that the eroticism of *Carmen Jones* is more potent than, say, the eroticism of a Lana Turner vehicle is that *Carmen Jones* has Negro bodies before the camera and Negroes are associated in the public mind with sex. Since darker races always seem to have for lighter races an aura of sexuality, this fact is not distressing in itself. What is distressing is the conjecture this movie leaves one with as to what Americans take sex to be.

The most important thing about this movie—and the reason that, despite itself, it is one of the most important all-Negro movies Hollywood has yet produced—is that the questions it leaves in the mind relate less to Negroes than to the interior life of Americans. One wonders, it is true, if Negroes are really going to become the ciphers this movie makes them out to be; but, since they have until now survived public images even more appalling, one is encouraged to hope, for their sake and the sake of the Republic, that they will continue to prove themselves incorrigible. Besides, life does not produce ciphers like these: when people have become this empty they are not ciphers any longer, but monsters. The creation of such ciphers proves, however, that Americans are far from empty; they are, on the contrary, very deeply disturbed. And this disturbance is not the kind which can be eased by the doing of good works, but seems to have turned inward and shows every sign of becoming personal. This is one of the best things that can possibly happen. It can be taken to mean—among a great many other things—that the ferment which has resulted in as odd a brew as *Carmen Jones* can now be expected to produce something which will be more bitter on the tongue but sweeter in the stomach.

PART TWO

The Harlem Ghetto

HARLEM, physically at least, has changed very little in my parents' lifetime or in mine. Now as then the buildings are old and in desperate need of repair, the streets are crowded and dirty, there are too many human beings per square block. Rents are 10 to 58 per cent higher than anywhere else in the city; food, expensive everywhere, is more expensive here and of an inferior quality; and now that the war is over and money is dwindling, clothes are carefully shopped for and seldom bought. Negroes, traditionally the last to be hired and the first to be fired, are finding jobs harder to get, and, while prices are rising implacably, wages are going down. All over Harlem now there is felt the same bitter expectancy with which, in my childhood, we awaited winter: it is coming and it will be hard; there is nothing anyone can do about it.

All of Harlem is pervaded by a sense of congestion, rather like the insistent, maddening, claustrophobic pounding in the skull that comes from trying to breathe in a very small room with all the windows shut. Yet the white man walking through Harlem is not at all likely to find it sinister or more wretched than any other slum.

Harlem wears to the casual observer a casual face; no one remarks that—considering the history of black men and women and the legends that have sprung up about them, to say nothing of the ever-present policemen, wary on the street corners—the face is, indeed, somewhat excessively casual and may not be as open or as careless as it seems. If an outbreak of more than usual violence occurs, as in 1935 or in 1943, it is met with sorrow and surprise and rage; the social hostility of the rest of the city feeds on this as proof that they were right all along, and the hostility increases; speeches are made, committees are set up, investigations ensue. Steps are taken to right the wrong, without, however, expanding or demolishing the ghetto. The idea is to make it less of a social liability, a process about as helpful as make-up to a leper. Thus, we have the Boys' Club on West 134th Street, the playground at West 131st and Fifth Avenue; and, since Negroes will not be allowed to live in Stuyvesant Town, Metropolitan Life is thoughtfully erecting a housing project called Riverton in the center of Harlem; however, it is not likely that any but the professional class of Negroes—and not all of them—will be able to pay the rent.

Most of these projects have been stimulated by perpetually embattled Negro leaders and by the Negro press. Concerning Negro leaders, the best that one can say is that they are in an impossible position and that the handful motivated by genuine concern maintain this position with heartbreaking dignity. It is unlikely that anyone acquainted with Harlem seriously assumes that the presence of one playground more or less has any profound effect upon the psychology of the citizens there. And yet it is better to have the playground; it is better than nothing; and it will, at least, make life somewhat easier for parents who will then know that their children are not in as much danger of being run down in the streets. Similarly, even though the American cult of literacy has chiefly operated only to provide a market for the *Reader's Digest* and the *Daily News*, literacy is still better than illiteracy; so Negro leaders must demand more and better schools for Negroes, though any Negro who takes this schooling at face value will find himself virtually incapacitated for life in this democracy. Possibly the most salutary effect of all this activity is that it assures the Negro that he is not altogether forgotten: people *are* working in his behalf, however hopeless or misguided they may be; and as long as the water is troubled it cannot become stagnant.

The terrible thing about being a Negro leader lies in the term itself. I do not mean merely the somewhat condescending differentiation the term implies, but the nicely refined torture a man can experience from having been created and defeated by the same circumstances. That is, Negro leaders have been created by the American scene, which thereafter works against them at every point; and the best that they can hope for is ultimately to work themselves out of their jobs, to nag contemporary American leaders and the members of their own group until a bad situation becomes so complicated and so bad that it cannot be endured any longer. It is like needling a blister until it bursts. On the other hand, one cannot help observing that some Negro leaders and politicians are far more concerned with their careers than with the welfare of Negroes, and their dramatic and publicized battles are battles with the wind. Again, this phenomenon cannot be changed without a change in the American scene. In a land where, it is said, any citizen can grow up and become president, Negroes can be pardoned for desiring to enter Congress.

The Negro press, which supports any man, provided he is sufficiently dark and well-known—with the exception of certain Negro novelists accused of drawing portraits unflattering to the race—has for years received vastly confusing criticism based on the fact that it is helplessly and always exactly what it calls itself, that is, a press devoted entirely to happenings in or about the Negro world. This preoccupation can probably be forgiven in view of the great indifference and frequent hostility of the American white press. The Negro press has been accused of not helping matters much—as indeed, it has not, nor do I see how it could have. And it has been accused of being sensational, which it is; but this is a criticism difficult to take seriously in a country so devoted to the sensational as ours.

The best-selling Negro newspaper, I believe, is the *Amsterdam Star-News*, which is also the worst, being gleefully devoted to murders, rapes, raids on love-nests, interracial wars, any item—however meaningless—concerning prominent Negroes, and whatever racial gains can be reported for the week—all in just about that order. Apparently, this policy works well; it sells papers—which is, after all, the aim; in my childhood we never missed an edition. The day the paper came out we could hear, far down the street, the news vendor screaming the latest scandal and people rushing to read about it.

The *Amsterdam* has been rivaled, in recent years, by the *People's Voice*, a journal, modeled on *PM* and referred to as *PV*. *PV* is not so wildly sensational a paper as the *Amsterdam*, though its coverage is much the same (the news coverage of the Negro press is naturally pretty limited). *PV*'s politics are less murky, to the left of center (the *Amsterdam* is Republican, a political affiliation that has led it into some strange double-talk), and its tone, since its inception, has been ever more hopelessly militant, full of warnings, appeals, and open letters to the government—which, to no one's surprise, are not answered—and the same rather pathetic preoccupation with prominent Negroes and what they are doing. Columns signed by Lena Horne and Paul Robeson appeared in *PV* until several weeks ago, when both severed their connections with the paper. Miss Horne's column made her sound like an embittered Eleanor Roosevelt, and the only column of Robeson's I have read was concerned with the current witch-hunt in Hollywood, discussing the kind of movies under attack and Hollywood's traditional treatment of Negroes. It is personally painful to me to realize that so gifted and forceful a man as Robeson should have been tricked by his own bitterness and by a total inability to understand the nature of political power in general, or Communist aims in particular, into missing the point of his own critique, which is worth a great deal of thought: that there are a great many ways of being un-American, some of them nearly as old as the country itself, and that the House Un-American Activities Committee might find concepts and attitudes even more damaging to American life in a picture like *Gone With the Wind* than in the possibly equally romantic but far less successful *Watch on the Rhine.*

The only other newspapers in the field with any significant sale in Harlem are the Pittsburgh *Courier*, which has the reputation of being the best of the lot, and the *Afro-American*, which resembles the New York *Journal-American* in layout and type and seems to make a consistent if unsuccessful effort to be at once readable, intelligent, and fiery. The *Courier* is a high-class paper, reaching its peak in the handling of its society news and in the columns of George S. Schuyler, whose Olympian serenity infuriates me, but who, as a matter of fact, reflects with great accuracy the state of mind and the ambitions of the professional, well-to-do Negro who has managed to find a place to stand. Mr. Schuyler, who is remembered still for a satirical novel I have not read, called *Black No More*, is aided enormously in this position by a genteel white wife and a child-prodigy daughter—who is seriously regarded in some circles as proof of the incomprehensible contention that the mating of white and black is more likely to produce genius than any other combination. (The *Afro-American* recently ran a series of articles on this subject, "The Education of a Genius," by Mrs. Amarintha Work, who recorded in detail the development of her mulatto son, Craig.)

Ebony and *Our World* are the two big magazines in the field, *Ebony* looking and sounding very much like *Life*, and *Our World* being the black man's *Look*. *Our World* is a very strange, disorganized magazine indeed, sounding sometimes like a college newspaper and sometimes like a call to arms, but principally, like its more skillful brothers, devoted to the proposition that anything a white man can do a Negro can probably do better. *Ebony* digs feature articles out of such things as the "real" Lena Horne and Negro FBI agents, and it travels into the far corners of the earth for any news, however trivial, concerning any Negro or group of Negroes who are in any way unusual and/or newsworthy. The tone of both *Ebony* and *Our World* is affirmative; they cater to the "better class of Negro." *Ebony's* November 1947 issue carried an editoral entitled "Time To Count Our Blessings," which began by accusing Chester Himes (author of the novel *Lonely Crusade*) of having a color psychosis, and went on to explain that there are Negro racists also who are just as blind and dangerous as Bilbo, which is incontestably true, and that, compared to the millions of starving Europeans, Negroes are sitting pretty—which comparison, I hazard, cannot possibly mean anything to any Negro who has not seen Europe. The editorial concluded that Negroes had come a long way and that "as patriotic Americans" it was time "we" stopped singing the blues and realized just how bright the future was. These cheering sentiments were flanked—or underscored, if you will—by a photograph on the opposite page of an aging Negro farm woman carrying home a bumper crop of onions. It apparently escaped the editors of *Ebony* that the very existence of their magazine, and its table of contents for any month, gave the lie to this effort to make the best of a bad bargain.

The true *raison d'être* of the Negro press can be found in the letters-to-the-editor sections, where the truth about life among the rejected can be seen in print. It is the terrible dilemma of the Negro press that, having no other model, it models itself on the white press, attempting to emulate the same effortless, sophisticated tone—a tone its subject matter renders utterly unconvincing. It is simply impossible not to sing the blues, audibly or not, when the lives lived by Negroes are so inescapably harsh and stunted. It is not the Negro press that is at fault: whatever contradictions, inanities, and political infantilism can be charged to it can be charged equally to the American press at large. It is a black man's newspaper straining for recognition and a foothold in the white man's world. Matters are not helped in the least by the fact that the white man's world, intellectually, morally, and spiritually, has the meaningless ring of a hollow drum and the odor of slow death. Within the body of the Negro press all the wars and falsehoods, all the decay and dislocation and struggle of our society are seen in relief.

The Negro press, like the Negro, becomes the scapegoat for our ills. There is no difference, after all, between the *Amsterdam*'s handling of a murder on Lenox Avenue and the *Daily News'* coverage of a murder on Beekman Hill; nor is there any difference between the chauvinism of the two papers, except that the *News* is smug and the *Amsterdam* is desperate. Negroes live violent lives, unavoidably; a Negro press without violence is therefore not possible; and, further, in every act of violence, particularly violence against white men, Negroes feel a certain thrill of identification, a wish to have done it themselves, a feeling that old scores are being settled at last. It is no accident that Joe Louis is the most idolized man in Harlem. He has succeeded on a level that white America indicates is the only level for which it has any respect. We (Americans in general, that is) like to point to Negroes and to most of their activities with a kind of tolerant scorn; but it is ourselves we are watching, ourselves we are damning, or—condescendingly—bending to save.

I have written at perhaps excessive length about the Negro press, principally because its many critics have always seemed to me to make the irrational demand that the nation's most oppressed minority behave itself at all times with a skill and foresight no one ever expected of the late Joseph Patterson or ever expected of Hearst; and I have tried to give some idea of its tone because it seems to me that it is here that the innate

desperation is betrayed. As for the question of Negro advertising, which has caused so much comment, it seems to me
quite logical that any minority identified by the color of its
skin and the texture of its hair would eventually grow self-
conscious about these attributes and avoid advertising lotions
that made the hair kinkier and soaps that darkened the skin.
The American ideal, after all, is that everyone should be as
much alike as possible.

It is axiomatic that the Negro is religious, which is to say
that he stands in fear of the God our ancestors gave us and
before whom we all tremble yet. There are probably more
churches in Harlem than in any other ghetto in this city and
they are going full blast every night and some of them are
filled with praying people every day. This, supposedly, exem-
plifies the Negro's essential simplicity and good-will; but it is
actually a fairly desperate emotional business.

These churches range from the august and publicized Abyssinian Baptist Church on West 138th Street to resolutely un-
classifiable lofts, basements, store-fronts, and even private
dwellings. Nightly, Holyroller ministers, spiritualists, self-
appointed prophets and Messiahs gather their flocks together
for worship and for strength through joy. And this is not, as
Cabin in the Sky would have us believe, merely a childlike
emotional release. Their faith may be described as childlike,
but the end it serves is often sinister. It may, indeed, "keep
them happy"—a phrase carrying the inescapable inference that
the way of life imposed on Negroes makes them quite actively
unhappy—but also, and much more significantly, religion operates here as a complete and exquisite fantasy revenge: white
people own the earth and commit all manner of abomination
and injustice on it; the bad will be punished and the good
rewarded, for God is not sleeping, the judgment is not far off.
It does not require a spectacular degree of perception to realize that bitterness is here neither dead nor sleeping, and that
the white man, believing what he wishes to believe, has mis-
read the symbols. Quite often the Negro preacher descends
to levels less abstract and leaves no doubt as to what is on
his mind: the pressure of life in Harlem, the conduct of the
Italian-Ethiopian war, racial injustice during the recent war,
and the terrible possibility of yet another very soon. All these

topics provide excellent springboards for sermons thinly coated with spirituality but designed mainly to illustrate the injustice of the white American and anticipate his certain and long overdue punishment.

Here, too, can be seen one aspect of the Negro's ambivalent relation to the Jew. To begin with, though the traditional Christian accusation that the Jews killed Christ is neither questioned nor doubted, the term "Jew" actually operates in this initial context to include all infidels of white skin who have failed to accept the Savior. No real distinction is made: the preacher begins by accusing the Jews of having refused the light and proceeds from there to a catalog of their subsequent sins and the sufferings visited on them by a wrathful God. Though the notion of the suffering is based on the image of the wandering, exiled Jew, the context changes imperceptibly, to become a fairly obvious reminder of the trials of the Negro, while the sins recounted are the sins of the American republic.

At this point, the Negro identifies himself almost wholly with the Jew. The more devout Negro considers that he *is* a Jew, in bondage to a hard taskmaster and waiting for a Moses to lead him out of Egypt. The hymns, the texts, and the most favored legends of the devout Negro are all Old Testament and therefore Jewish in origin: the flight from Egypt, the Hebrew children in the fiery furnace, the terrible jubilee songs of deliverance: *Lord, wasn't that hard trials, great tribulations, I'm bound to leave this land!* The covenant God made in the beginning with Abraham and which was to extend to his children and to his children's children forever is a covenant made with these latter-day exiles also: as Israel was chosen, so are they. The birth and death of Jesus, which adds a non-Judaic element, also implements this identification. It is the covenant made with Abraham again, renewed, signed with his blood. ("Before Abraham was, I am.") Here the figure of Jesus operates as the intercessor, the bridge from earth to heaven; it was Jesus who made it possible, who made salvation free to all, "to the Jew first and afterwards the Gentile." The images of the suffering Christ and the suffering Jew are wedded with the image of the suffering slave, and they are one: the people that walked in darkness have seen a great light.

But if the Negro has bought his salvation with pain and the

New Testament is used to prove, as it were, the validity of the transformation, it is the Old Testament which is clung to and most frequently preached from, which provides the emotional fire and anatomizes the path of bondage; and which promises vengeance and assures the chosen of their place in Zion. The favorite text of my father, among the most earnest of ministers, was not "Father, forgive them, for they know not what they do," but "How can I sing the Lord's song in a strange land?"

This same identification, which Negroes, since slavery, have accepted with their mothers' milk, serves, in contemporary actuality, to implement an involved and specific bitterness. Jews in Harlem are small tradesmen, rent collectors, real estate agents, and pawnbrokers; they operate in accordance with the American business tradition of exploiting Negroes, and they are therefore identified with oppression and are hated for it. I remember meeting no Negro in the years of my growing up, in my family or out of it, who would really ever trust a Jew, and few who did not, indeed, exhibit for them the blackest contempt. On the other hand, this did not prevent their working for Jews, being utterly civil and pleasant to them, and, in most cases, contriving to delude their employers into believing that, far from harboring any dislike for Jews, they would rather work for a Jew than for anyone else. It is part of the price the Negro pays for his position in this society that, as Richard Wright points out, he is almost always acting. A Negro learns to gauge precisely what reaction the alien person facing him desires, and he produces it with disarming artlessness. The friends I had, growing up and going to work, grew more bitter every day; and, conversely, they learned to hide this bitterness and to fit into the pattern Gentile and Jew alike had fixed for them.

The tension between Negroes and Jews contains an element not characteristic of Negro-Gentile tension, an element which accounts in some measure for the Negro's tendency to castigate the Jew verbally more often than the Gentile, and which might lead one to the conclusion that, of all white people on the face of the earth, it is the Jew whom the Negro hates most. When the Negro hates the Jew *as a Jew* he does so partly because the nation does and in much the same painful fashion that he hates himself. It is an aspect of his humiliation whittled down to a manageable size and then transferred; it is the best form the Negro has for tabulating vocally his long record of grievances against his native land.

At the same time, there is a subterranean assumption that the Jew should "know better," that he has suffered enough himself to know what suffering means. An understanding is expected of the Jew such as none but the most naïve and visionary Negro has ever expected of the American Gentile. The Jew, by the nature of his own precarious position, has failed to vindicate this faith. Jews, like Negroes, must use every possible weapon in order to be accepted, and must try to cover their vulnerability by a frenzied adoption of the customs of the country; and the nation's treatment of Negroes is unquestionably a custom. The Jew has been taught—and, too often, accepts—the legend of Negro inferiority; and the Negro, on the other hand, has found nothing in his experience with Jews to counteract the legend of Semitic greed. Here the American white Gentile has two legends serving him at once: he has divided these minorities and he rules.

It seems unlikely that within this complicated structure any real and systematic cooperation can be achieved between Negroes and Jews. (This is in terms of the over-all social problem and is not meant to imply that individual friendships are impossible or that they are valueless when they occur.) The structure of the American commonwealth has trapped both these minorities into attitudes of perpetual hostility. They do not dare trust each other—the Jew because he feels he must climb higher on the American social ladder and has, so far as he is concerned, nothing to gain from identification with any minority even more unloved than he; while the Negro is in the even less tenable position of not really daring to trust anyone.

This applies, with qualifications and yet with almost no exceptions, even to those Negroes called progressive and "unusual." Negroes of the professional class (as distinct from professional Negroes) compete actively with the Jew in daily contact; and they wear anti-Semitism as a defiant proof of their citizenship; their positions are too shaky to allow them any real ease or any faith in anyone. They do not trust whites or each other or themselves; and, particularly and vocally, they do not trust Jews. During my brief days as a Socialist I spent more than one meeting arguing against anti-Semitism with a Negro college student, who was trying to get into civil service and was supporting herself meanwhile as a domestic. She was by no means a stupid girl, nor even a particularly narrow-minded one: she was all in favor of the millennium, even to working with Jews to achieve it; but she was not prepared ever to accept a Jew as a friend. It did no good to point out, as I did, that the exploitation of which she accused the Jews was American, not Jewish, that in fact, behind the Jewish face stood the American reality. And *my* Jewish friends in high school were not like that, I said, they had no intention of exploiting *me*, we did not hate each other. (I remember, as I spoke, being aware of doubt crawling like fog in the back of my mind.) This might all be very well, she told me, we were children now, with no need to earn a living. Wait until later, when your friends go into business and you try to get a job. You'll see!

It is this bitterness—felt alike by the inarticulate, hungry population of Harlem, by the wealthy on Sugar Hill, and by the brilliant exceptions ensconced in universities—which has defeated and promises to continue to defeat all efforts at interracial understanding. I am not one of the people who believe that oppression imbues a people with wisdom or insight or sweet charity, though the survival of the Negro in this country would simply not have been possible if this bitterness had been all he felt. In America, though, life seems to move faster than anywhere else on the globe and each generation is promised more than it will get: which creates, in each generation, a furious, bewildered rage, the rage of people who cannot find solid ground beneath their feet. Just as a mountain of sociological investigations, committee reports, and plans for recreational centers have failed to change the face of Harlem or prevent Negro boys and girls from growing up and facing, individually and alone, the unendurable frustration of being always, everywhere, inferior—until finally the cancer attacks the mind and warps it—so there seems no hope for better Negro-Jewish relations without a change in the American pattern.

Both the Negro and the Jew are helpless; the pressure of living is too immediate and incessant to allow time for understanding. I can conceive of no Negro native to this country who has not, by the age of puberty, been irreparably scarred by the conditions of his life. All over Harlem, Negro boys and girls are growing into stunted maturity, trying desperately to find a place to stand; and the wonder is not that so many are ruined but that so many survive. The Negro's outlets are desperately constricted. In his dilemma he turns first upon himself and then upon whatever most represents to him his own emasculation. Here the Jew is caught in the American crossfire. The Negro, facing a Jew, hates, at bottom, not his Jewishness but the color of his skin. It is not the Jewish tradition by which he has been betrayed but the tradition of his native land. But just as a society must have a scapegoat, so hatred must have a symbol. Georgia has the Negro and Harlem has the Jew.

Journey to Atlanta

THE PROGRESSIVE PARTY has not, so far as I can gather, made any very great impression in Harlem, and this is not so much despite as because of its campaign promises, promises rather too extravagant to be believed. It is considered a rather cheerful axiom that all Americans distrust politicians. (No one takes the further and less cheerful step of considering just what effect this mutual contempt has on either the public or the politicians, who have, indeed, very little to do with one another.) Of all Americans, Negroes distrust politicians most, or, more accurately, they have been best trained to expect nothing from them; more than other Americans, they are always aware of the enormous gap between election promises and their daily lives. It is true that the promises excite them, but this is not because they are taken as proof of good intentions. They are the proof of something more concrete than intentions: that the Negro situation is not static, that changes have occurred, and are occurring and will occur—this, in spite of the daily, dead-end monotony. It is this daily, dead-end monotony, though, as well as the wise desire not to be betrayed by too much hoping, which causes them to look on politicians with such an extraordinarily disenchanted eye.

This fatalistic indifference is something that drives the optimistic American liberal quite mad; he is prone, in his more exasperated moments, to refer to Negroes as political children, an appellation not entirely just. Negro liberals, being consulted, assure us that this is something that will disappear with "education," a vast, all-purpose term, conjuring up visions of sunlit housing projects, stacks of copybooks and a race of well-soaped, dark-skinned people who never slur their R's. Actually, this is not so much political irresponsibility as the product of experience, experience which no amount of education can quite efface. It is, as much as anything else, the reason the Negro vote is so easily bought and sold, the reason for that exclamation heard so frequently on Sugar Hill: "Our people never get anywhere."

"Our people" have functioned in this country for nearly a

century as political weapons, the trump card up the enemies' sleeve; anything promised Negroes at election time is also a threat levelled at the opposition; in the struggle for mastery the Negro is the pawn. It is inescapable that this is only possible because of his position in this country and it has very frequently seemed at least equally apparent that this is a position which no one, least of all the politician, seriously intended to change.

Since Negroes have been in this country their one major, devastating gain was their Emancipation, an emancipation no one regards any more as having been dictated by humanitarian impulses. All that has followed from that brings to mind the rather unfortunate image of bones thrown to a pack of dogs sufficiently hungry to be dangerous. If all this sounds rather deliberately grim, it is not through any wish to make the picture darker than it is; I would merely like to complete the picture usually presented by pointing out that no matter how many instances there have been of genuine concern and goodwill, nor how many hard, honest struggles have been carried on to improve the position of the Negro people, their position has not, in fact, changed so far as most of them are concerned.

Sociologists and historians, having the historical perspective in mind, may conclude that we are moving toward ever-greater democracy; but this is beyond the ken of a Negro growing up in any one of this country's ghettos. As regards Negro politicians, they are considered with pride as *politicians*, a pride much akin to that felt concerning Marian Anderson or Joe Louis: they have proven the worth of the Negro people and in terms, American terms, which no one can negate. But as no housewife expects Marian Anderson's genius to be of any practical aid in her dealings with the landlord, so nothing is expected of Negro representatives. The terrible thing, and here we have an American phenomenon in relief, is the fact that the Negro representative, by virtue of his position, is ever more removed from the people he ostensibly serves. Moreover, irrespective of personal integrity, his position—neatly and often painfully paradoxical—is utterly dependent on the continuing debasement of fourteen million Negroes; should the national ideals be put into practice tomorrow, countless prominent Negroes would lose their *raison d'être*.

Finally, we are confronted with the psychology and tradition of the country; if the Negro vote is so easily bought and sold, it is because it has been treated with so little respect; since no Negro dares seriously assume that any politician is concerned with the fate of Negroes, or would do much about it if he had the power, the vote must be bartered for what it will get, for whatever short-term goals can be managed. These goals are mainly economic and frequently personal, sometimes pathetic: bread or a new roof or five dollars, or, continuing up the scale, schools, houses or more Negroes in hitherto Caucasian jobs. The American commonwealth chooses to overlook what Negroes are never able to forget: they are not *really* considered a part of it. Like Aziz in *A Passage to India* or Topsy in *Uncle Tom's Cabin*, they know that white people, whatever their love for justice, have no love for them.

This is the crux of the matter; and the Progressive Party, with its extravagant claims, has, therefore, imposed on itself the considerable burden of proof. The only party within recent memory which made equally strident claims of fellowship were the Communists, who failed to survive this test; and the only politician of similar claims was, of course, Wallace's erstwhile master, Roosevelt, who did not after all, now that the magic of his voice is gone, succeed in raising the darker brother to the status of a citizen. This is the ancestry of the Wallace party, and it does not work wholly in its favor. It operates to give pause to even the most desperate and the most gullible.

It is, however, considered on one level, the level of short-term goals, with approval, since it does afford temporary work for Negroes, particularly those associated in any manner with the arts. The rather flippant question on 125th Street now is: "So? You working for Mr. Wallace these days?" For at least there is that: entertainers, personalities are in demand. To forestall lawsuits, I must explain that I am not discussing "names"—who are in rather a different position, too touchy and complex to analyze here—but the unknown, the struggling, endless armies of Negro boys and girls bent on, and as yet very far from, recognition. A segment of this army, a quartet called *The Melodeers*, made a trip to Atlanta under the auspices of the Progressive Party in August, a trip which lasted about eighteen days and which left them with no love for Mr. Wallace. Since this quartet included two of my brothers, I was given the details of the trip; indeed, David, the younger, kept a sort of journal for me—literally a blow-by-blow account.

Harlem is filled with churches and on Sundays it gives the impression of being filled with music. Quartets such as my brothers' travel from church to church in the fashion of circuit preachers, singing as much for the love of singing and the need for practice as for the rather indifferent sums collected for them which are then divided. These quartets have "battles of song," the winning team adding, of course, immensely to its prestige, the most consistent winners being the giants in this field. The aim of all these quartets, of course, is to branch out, to hit the big time and sing for a livelihood. The Golden Gate Quartet, judging at least from its music, had its roots here, and out of such a background came Sister Rosetta Tharpe, whom I heard, not quite ten years ago, plunking a guitar in a store-front church on Fifth Avenue. *The Melodeers* have not been singing very long and are very far from well-known, and the invitation to sing on tour with the Wallace party in the South seemed, whatever their misgivings about the Mason-Dixon line, too good an opportunity to pass up.

This invitation, by the way, seems to have been the brain-storm of a Clarence Warde, a Negro merchant seaman once employed as a cottage father in a corrective institution up-state; it was he in New York who acted as a go-between, arranging, since *The Melodeers* are minors, to be their legal guardian and manager on the road. An extended tour, such as was planned, met with some opposition from the parents, an opposition countered by the possible long-term benefits of the tour in so far as the boys' careers were concerned and, even more urgently, by the assurance that, at the very least, the boys would come home with a considerably larger sum of money than any of them were making on their jobs. (The political implications do not seem to have carried much weight.) A series of churches had been lined up for them pre-sumably throughout the South. "The understanding," writes David, "was that we were supposed to sing"; after which the

party was to take over to make speeches and circulate petitions. "The arrangement," David notes laconically, "sounded
very promising, so we decided to go."

And, indeed, they traveled South in splendor, in a Pullman,
to be exact, in which, since what David describes as a "Southern gentleman and wife" took exception to their presence,
they traveled alone.

At the Wallace headquarters in Atlanta they were introduced to a Mrs. Branson Price, a grey-haired white woman of
incurably aristocratic leanings who seems to have been the
directress of the party in that region. The graciousness of her
reception was only slightly marred by the fact that she was not
expecting singers and thought they were a new group of canvassers. She arranged for them to take rooms on Butler Street
at the YMCA. Here the first gap between promise and performance was made manifest, a gap, they felt, which was perhaps too trifling to make a fuss about. In New York they had
been promised comparative privacy, two to a room; but now,
it developed, they were to sleep in a dormitory. This gap, in
fact, it was the province of Mr. Warde to close, but whether
he was simply weary from the trip or overwhelmed by the
aristocratic Mrs. Price, he kept his mouth shut and, indeed,
did not open it again for quite some time.

When they returned to headquarters, somewhat irritated at
having had to wait three hours for the arrival of Louis Burner,
who had the money for their rooms, Mrs. Price suggested that
they go out canvassing. This was wholly unexpected, since no
one had mentioned canvassing in New York and, since, moreover, canvassers are voluntary workers who are not paid. Further, the oldest of them was twenty, which was not voting
age, and none of them knew anything about the Progressive
Party, nor did they care much. On the other hand, it is somewhat difficult to refuse a grey-haired, aristocratic lady who is
toiling day and night for the benefit of your people; and Mr.
Warde, who should have been their spokesman, had not yet
recovered his voice; so they took the petitions, which were
meant to put the Wallace party on the ballot, and began
knocking on doors in the Negro section of Atlanta. They were
sent out in pairs, white and black, a political device which

operates not only as the living proof of brotherhood, but which has the additional virtue of intimidating into passive silence the more susceptible beholder, who cannot, after all, unleash the impatient scorn he may feel with a strange, benevolent white man sitting in his parlor.

They canvassed for three days, during which time their expenses—$2.25 per man per day—were paid, but during which time they were doing no singing and making no money. On the third day they pointed out that this was not quite what they had been promised in New York, to be met with another suggestion from the invincible Mrs. Price: how would they like to sing on the sound-truck? They had not the faintest desire to sing on a sound-truck, especially when they had been promised a string of churches; however, the churches, along with Mr. Warde's vigor, seemed unavailable at the moment; they could hardly sit around Atlanta doing nothing; and so long as they worked with the party they were certain, at least, to be fed. "The purpose of our singing," David writes, "was to draw a crowd so the party could make speeches." Near the end of the singing and during the speeches, leaflets and petitions were circulated through the crowd.

David had not found Negroes in the South different in any important respect from Negroes in the North; except that many of them were distrustful and "they are always talking about the North; they have to let you know they know somebody in New York or Chicago or Detroit." Of the crowds that gathered—and, apparently, *The Melodeers* attracted great numbers—"many of these people couldn't read or write their names" and not many of them knew anything at all about the Progressive Party. But they did divine, as American Negroes must, what was expected of them; and they listened to the speeches and signed the petitions.

Becoming both desperate and impatient, *The Melodeers* began making engagements and singing on their own, stealing time from canvassing to rehearse. They made more appointments than they were able to keep; partly because the lack of money limited their mobility but also because the Party, discovering these clandestine appointments, moved in, demanding to be heard. Those churches which refused to make room for the Party were not allowed to hear the quartet, which thus lost its last hope of making any money. The quartet wondered what had happened to Mr. Warde. David's account all but ignores him until nearly the end of the trip, when his position during all this is perhaps given some illumination.

Things now began to go steadily worse. They got into an argument with the manager of the Y, who objected to their rehearsing, and moved to a private home, for which the Party paid 75¢ per man per day; and the Party, which was, one gathers, furiously retrenching, arranged for them to eat at Fraziers' Cafe, a Negro establishment on Hunter Street, for $1.25 per man per day. My correspondent notes that they had no choice of meals—"they served us what they liked"—which seems to have been mainly limp vegetables—and "we were as hungry when we walked out as we were when we walked in." On the other hand, they were allowed to choose their beverage: tea or coffee or soda pop.

Heaven only knows what prompted Mrs. Branson Price to give a party at this point. Perhaps the campaign was going extraordinarily well; perhaps Fraziers' Cafe, where the party was held, was in need of a little extra revenue as well as the knowledge that its adoption of the Party would help to bring about a better world; perhaps Mrs. Price merely longed to be a gracious hostess once again. In any case, on a Sunday night she gave a party to which everyone was invited. My brother, who at this point was much concerned with food, observed glumly, "We had ice-cream."

The quartet sat at a table by itself, robbed, however, of the presence of Mr. Warde, who was invited to sit at Mrs. Price's table: "she said it would be an honor," my correspondent notes, failing, however, to say for whom. "There was a man there called a *folk*-singer," says David with venom, "and, naturally, everybody had to hear some *folk* songs." Eventually, the folksy aspect of the evening was exhausted and the quartet was invited to sing. They sang four selections, apparently to everyone's delight for they had to be quite adamant about not singing a fifth. The strain of continual singing in the open air had done their voices no good and it had made one of them extremely hoarse. So they refused, over loud protests, and apologized. "This displeased Mrs. Price."

Indeed, it had. She was not in the least accustomed to having her suggestions, to say nothing of her requests, refused. Early Monday morning she called Mr. Warde to her office to inquire who those black boys thought they were? and determined to ship them all back that same day in a car. Mr. Warde, who, considering the honors of the evening before, must have been rather astounded, protested such treatment, to be warned that she might very well ship them off without a car; the six of them might very well be forced to take to the road. This is not a pleasant mode of traveling for a Negro in the North and no Negro in Atlanta, particularly no Northern Negro, is likely to get very far. Mr. Warde temporized: they could not leave on such short notice; for one thing, the boys had clothes at the cleaners which would not be ready for a while and which they could hardly afford to lose. Mrs. Price, every aristocratic vein pounding, did not wish to be concerned with such plebeian matters and, finally, losing all patience, commanded Mr. Warde to leave her office: Had he forgotten that he was in Georgia? Didn't he know better than sit in a white woman's office?

Mr. Warde, in whose bowels last night's bread of fellowship must have acquired the weight of rock, left the office. Then the quartet attempted to secure an audience; to be met with implacable refusal and the threat of the police. There were, incidentally, according to my brother, five Negro policemen in Atlanta at this time, who, though they were not allowed to arrest whites, would, of course, be willing, indeed, in their position, anxious, to arrest any Negro who seemed to need it. In Harlem, Negro policemen are feared even more than whites, for they have more to prove and fewer ways to prove it. The prospect of being arrested in Atlanta made them a little dizzy with terror: what might mean a beating in Harlem might quite possibly mean death here. "And at the same time," David says, "it was funny"; by which he means that the five policemen were faint prophecies of that equality which is the Progressive Party's goal.

They did not see Mrs. Price again; this was their severance from the Party, which now refused to pay any expenses; it was only the fact that their rent had been paid in advance which kept them off the streets. Food, however, remained a problem. Mr. Warde brought them a "couple of loaves of bread" and some jam; they sang one engagement. During this week Mrs. Price relented enough to get their clothes from the cleaners and send Mr. Warde, in custody of a white man who had been at the party, to the bus station for tickets. This man, whose resemblance to the Southern Gentleman of the Pullman is in no way diminished by his allegiance to Mr. Wallace, bought the tickets and threw them on the ground at Mr. Warde's feet, advising him not to show his black face in Georgia again.

The quartet, meanwhile, had gotten together six dollars doing odd jobs, which was enough, perhaps, for three of them to eat on the road. They split up, three leaving that Friday and the other two staying on about ten days longer, working for a construction company. Mr. Warde stopped off to visit his family, promising to see *The Melodeers* in New York, but he had not arrived as this was being written. *The Melodeers* laugh about their trip now, that good-natured, hearty laughter which is, according to white men, the peculiar heritage of Negroes, Negroes who were born with the fortunate ability to laugh all their troubles away. Somewhat surprisingly, they are not particularly bitter toward the Progressive Party, though they can scarcely be numbered among its supporters. "They're all the same," David tells me, "ain't none of 'em gonna do you no good; if you gonna be foolish enough to believe what they say, then it serves you good and right. Ain't none of 'em gonna do a thing for *me*."

Notes of a Native Son

O N THE 29TH OF JULY, in 1943, my father died. On the same day, a few hours later, his last child was born. Over a month before this, while all our energies were concentrated in waiting for these events, there had been, in Detroit, one of the bloodiest race riots of the century. A few hours after my father's funeral, while he lay in state in the undertaker's chapel, a race riot broke out in Harlem. On the morning of the 3rd of August, we drove my father to the graveyard through a wilderness of smashed plate glass.

The day of my father's funeral had also been my nineteenth birthday. As we drove him to the graveyard, the spoils of injustice, anarchy, discontent, and hatred were all around us. It seemed to me that God himself had devised, to mark my father's end, the most sustained and brutally dissonant of codas. And it seemed to me, too, that the violence which rose all about us as my father left the world had been devised as a corrective for the pride of his eldest son. I had declined to believe in that apocalypse which had been central to my father's vision; very well, life seemed to be saying, here is something that will certainly pass for an apocalypse until the real thing comes along. I had inclined to be contemptuous of my father for the conditions of his life, for the conditions of our lives. When his life had ended I began to wonder about that life and also, in a new way, to be apprehensive about my own.

I had not known my father very well. We had got on badly, partly because we shared, in our different fashions, the vice of stubborn pride. When he was dead I realized that I had hardly ever spoken to him. When he had been dead a long time I began to wish I had. It seems to be typical of life in America, where opportunities, real and fancied, are thicker than anywhere else on the globe, that the second generation has no time to talk to the first. No one, including my father, seems to have known exactly how old he was, but his mother had been born during slavery. He was of the first generation of free men. He, along with thousands of other Negroes, came North after 1919 and I was part of that generation which had never seen the landscape of what Negroes sometimes call the Old Country.

He had been born in New Orleans and had been a quite young man there during the time that Louis Armstrong, a boy, was running errands for the dives and honky-tonks of what was always presented to me as one of the most wicked of cities—to this day, whenever I think of New Orleans, I also helplessly think of Sodom and Gomorrah. My father never mentioned Louis Armstrong, except to forbid us to play his records; but there was a picture of him on our wall for a long time. One of my father's strong-willed female relatives had placed it there and forbade my father to take it down. He never did, but he eventually maneuvered her out of the house and when, some years later, she was in trouble and near death, he refused to do anything to help her.

He was, I think, very handsome. I gather this from photographs and from my own memories of him, dressed in his Sunday best and on his way to preach a sermon somewhere, when I was little. Handsome, proud, and ingrown, "like a toenail," somebody said. But he looked to me, as I grew older, like pictures I had seen of African tribal chieftains: he really should have been naked, with war-paint on and barbaric mementos, standing among spears. He could be chilling in the pulpit and indescribably cruel in his personal life and he was certainly the most bitter man I have ever met; yet it must be said that there was something else in him, buried in him, which lent him his tremendous power and, even, a rather crushing charm. It had something to do with his blackness, I think—he was very black—with his blackness and his beauty, and with the fact that he knew that he was black but did not know that he was beautiful. He claimed to be proud of his blackness but it had also been the cause of much humiliation and it had fixed bleak boundaries to his life. He was not a young man when we were growing up and he had already suffered many kinds of ruin; in his outrageously demanding and protective way he loved his children, who were black like him and menaced, like him; and all these things sometimes showed in his face when he tried, never to my knowledge with any success, to establish contact with any of us. When he took one of his children on his knee to play, the child always be-

came fretful and began to cry; when he tried to help one of
us with our homework the absolutely unabating tension which
emanated from him caused our minds and our tongues to
become paralyzed, so that he, scarcely knowing why, flew into
a rage and the child, not knowing why, was punished. If it
ever entered his head to bring a surprise home for his children,
it was, almost unfailingly, the wrong surprise and even the big
watermelons he often brought home on his back in the summertime led to the most appalling scenes. I do not remember,
in all those years, that one of his children was ever glad to see
him come home. From what I was able to gather of his early
life, it seemed that this inability to establish contact with other
people had always marked him and had been one of the things
which had driven him out of New Orleans. There was something in him, therefore, groping and tentative, which was
never expressed and which was buried with him. One saw it
most clearly when he was facing new people and hoping to
impress them. But he never did, not for long. We went from
church to smaller and more improbable church, he found
himself in less and less demand as a minister, and by the time
he died none of his friends had come to see him for a long
time. He had lived and died in an intolerable bitterness of
spirit and it frightened me, as we drove him to the graveyard
through those unquiet, ruined streets, to see how powerful
and overflowing this bitterness could be and to realize that
this bitterness now was mine.

When he died I had been away from home for a little over
a year. In that year I had had time to become aware of the
meaning of all my father's bitter warnings, had discovered the
secret of his proudly pursed lips and rigid carriage: I had discovered the weight of white people in the world. I saw that
this had been for my ancestors and now would be for me an
awful thing to live with and that the bitterness which had
helped to kill my father could also kill me.

He had been ill a long time—in the mind, as we now realized, reliving instances of his fantastic intransigence in the
new light of his affliction and endeavoring to feel a sorrow for
him which never, quite, came true. We had not known that
he was being eaten up by paranoia, and the discovery that his
cruelty, to our bodies and our minds, had been one of the

symptoms of his illness was not, then, enough to enable us to forgive him. The younger children felt, quite simply, relief that he would not be coming home anymore. My mother's observation that it was he, after all, who had kept them alive all these years meant nothing because the problems of keeping children alive are not real for children. The older children felt, with my father gone, that they could invite their friends to the house without fear that their friends would be insulted or, as had sometimes happened with me, being told that their friends were in league with the devil and intended to rob our family of everything we owned. (I didn't fail to wonder, and it made me hate him, what on earth we owned that anybody else would want.)

His illness was beyond all hope of healing before anyone realized that he was ill. He had always been so strange and had lived, like a prophet, in such unimaginably close communion with the Lord that his long silences which were punctuated by moans and hallelujahs and snatches of old songs while he sat at the living-room window never seemed odd to us. It was not until he refused to eat because, he said, his family was trying to poison him that my mother was forced to accept as a fact what had, until then, been only an unwilling suspicion. When he was committed, it was discovered that he had tuberculosis and, as it turned out, the disease of his mind allowed the disease of his body to destroy him. For the doctors could not force him to eat, either, and, though he was fed intravenously, it was clear from the beginning that there was no hope for him.

In my mind's eye I could see him, sitting at the window, locked up in his terrors; hating and fearing every living soul including his children who had betrayed him, too, by reaching towards the world which had despised him. There were nine of us. I began to wonder what it could have felt like for such a man to have had nine children whom he could barely feed. He used to make little jokes about our poverty, which never, of course, seemed very funny to us; they could not have seemed very funny to him, either, or else our all too feeble response to them would never have caused such rages. He spent great energy and achieved, to our chagrin, no small amount of success in keeping us away from the people who surrounded us, people who had all-night rent parties to which we listened when we should have been sleeping, people who cursed and drank and flashed razor blades on Lenox Avenue. He could not understand why, if they had so much energy to spare, they could not use it to make their lives better. He treated almost everybody on our block with a most uncharitable asperity and neither they, nor, of course, their children were slow to reciprocate.

The only white people who came to our house were welfare workers and bill collectors. It was almost always my mother who dealt with them, for my father's temper, which was at the mercy of his pride, was never to be trusted. It was clear that he felt their very presence in his home to be a violation: this was conveyed by his carriage, almost ludicrously stiff, and by his voice, harsh and vindictively polite. When I was around nine or ten I wrote a play which was directed by a young, white schoolteacher, a woman, who then took an interest in me, and gave me books to read and, in order to corroborate my theatrical bent, decided to take me to see what she somewhat tactlessly referred to as "real" plays. Theater-going was forbidden in our house, but, with the really cruel intuitiveness of a child, I suspected that the color of this woman's skin would carry the day for me. When, at school, she suggested taking me to the theater, I did not, as I might have done if she had been a Negro, find a way of discouraging her, but agreed that she should pick me up at my house one evening. I then, very cleverly, left all the rest to my mother, who suggested to my father, as I knew she would, that it would not be very nice to let such a kind woman make the trip for nothing. Also, since it was a schoolteacher, I imagine that my mother countered the idea of sin with the idea of "education," which word, even with my father, carried a kind of bitter weight.

Before the teacher came my father took me aside to ask *why* she was coming, what *interest* she could possibly have in our house, in a boy like me. I said I didn't know but I, too, suggested that it had something to do with education. And I understood that my father was waiting for me to say something—I didn't quite know what; perhaps that I wanted his protection against this teacher and her "education." I said none of these things and the teacher came and we went out. It was clear, during the brief interview in our living room, that my father was agreeing very much against his will and that he would have refused permission if he had dared. The fact that he did not dare caused me to despise him: I had no way of knowing that he was facing in that living room a wholly unprecedented and frightening situation.

Later, when my father had been laid off from his job, this woman became very important to us. She was really a very sweet and generous woman and went to a great deal of trouble to be of help to us, particularly during one awful winter. My mother called her by the highest name she knew: she said she was a "christian." My father could scarcely disagree but during the four or five years of our relatively close association he never trusted her and was always trying to surprise in her open, Midwestern face the genuine, cunningly hidden, and hideous motivation. In later years, particularly when it began to be clear that this "education" of mine was going to lead me to perdition, he became more explicit and warned me that my white friends in high school were not really my friends and that I would see, when I was older, how white people would do anything to keep a Negro down. Some of them could be nice, he admitted, but none of them were to be trusted and most of them were not even nice. The best thing was to have as little to do with them as possible. I did not feel this way and I was certain, in my innocence, that I never would.

But the year which preceded my father's death had made a great change in my life. I had been living in New Jersey, working in defense plants, working and living among southerners, white and black. I knew about the south, of course, and about how southerners treated Negroes and how they expected them to behave, but it had never entered my mind that anyone would look at me and expect *me* to behave that way. I learned in New Jersey that to be a Negro meant, precisely, that one was never looked at but was simply at the mercy of the reflexes the color of one's skin caused in other people. I acted in New Jersey as I had always acted, that is as though I thought a great deal of myself—I had to *act* that way—with results that were, simply, unbelievable. I had scarcely arrived before I had earned the enmity, which was extraordinarily ingenious, of all my superiors and nearly all my co-workers. In the beginning, to make matters worse, I simply did not know what was happening. I did not know what I had done, and I shortly began to wonder what *anyone* could possibly do, to bring about such unanimous, active, and unbearably vocal hostility. I knew about jim-crow but I had never experienced it. I went to the same self-service restaurant three times and stood with all the Princeton boys before the counter, waiting for a hamburger and coffee; it was always an extraordinarily long time before anything was set before me; but it was not until the fourth visit that I learned that, in fact, nothing had ever been set before me: I had simply picked something up. Negroes were not served there, I was told, and they had been waiting for me to realize that I was always the only Negro present. Once I was told this, I determined to go there all the time. But now they were ready for me and, though some dreadful scenes were subsequently enacted in that restaurant, I never ate there again.

It was the same story all over New Jersey, in bars, bowling alleys, diners, places to live. I was always being forced to leave, silently, or with mutual imprecations. I very shortly became notorious and children giggled behind me when I passed and their elders whispered or shouted—they really believed that I was mad. And it did begin to work on my mind, of course; I began to be afraid to go anywhere and to compensate for this I went places to which I really should not have gone and where, God knows, I had no desire to be. My reputation in town naturally enhanced my reputation at work and my working day became one long series of acrobatics designed to keep me out of trouble. I cannot say that these acrobatics succeeded. It began to seem that the machinery of the organization I worked for was turning over, day and night, with but one aim: to eject me. I was fired once, and contrived, with the aid of a friend from New York, to get back on the payroll; was fired again, and bounced back again. It took a while to fire me for the third time, but the third time took. There were no loopholes anywhere. There was not even any way of getting back inside the gates.

That year in New Jersey lives in my mind as though it were the year during which, having an unsuspected predilection for it, I first contracted some dread, chronic disease, the unfailing symptom of which is a kind of blind fever, a pounding in the skull and fire in the bowels. Once this disease is contracted, one can never be really carefree again, for the fever, without an instant's warning, can recur at any moment. It can wreck more important things than race relations. There is not a Negro alive who does not have this rage in his blood—one has the choice, merely, of living with it consciously or surrendering to it. As for me, this fever has recurred in me, and does, and will until the day I die.

My last night in New Jersey, a white friend from New York took me to the nearest big town, Trenton, to go to the movies and have a few drinks. As it turned out, he also saved me from, at the very least, a violent whipping. Almost every detail of that night stands out very clearly in my memory. I even remember the name of the movie we saw because its title impressed me as being so patly ironical. It was a movie about the German occupation of France, starring Maureen O'Hara and Charles Laughton and called *This Land Is Mine*. I remember the name of the diner we walked into when the movie ended: it was the "American Diner." When we walked in the counterman asked what we wanted and I remember answering with the casual sharpness which had become my habit: "We want a hamburger and a cup of coffee, what do you think we want?" I do not know why, after a year of such rebuffs, I so completely failed to anticipate his answer, which was, of course, "We don't serve Negroes here." This reply failed to discompose me, at least for the moment. I made some sardonic comment about the name of the diner and we walked out into the streets.

This was the time of what was called the "brown-out," when the lights in all American cities were very dim. When we re-entered the streets something happened to me which had the force of an optical illusion, or a nightmare. The streets were very crowded and I was facing north. People were moving in every direction but it seemed to me, in that instant, that all of the people I could see, and many more than that, were moving toward me, against me, and that everyone was white. I remember how their faces gleamed. And I felt, like a physical sensation, a *click* at the nape of my neck as though some interior string connecting my head to my body had been cut. I began to walk. I heard my friend call after me, but I ignored him. Heaven only knows what was going on in his mind, but he had the good sense not to touch me—I don't know what would have happened if he had—and to keep me in sight. I don't know what was going on in my mind, either; I certainly had no conscious plan. I wanted to do something to crush these white faces, which were crushing me. I walked for perhaps a block or two until I came to an enormous, glittering, and fashionable restaurant in which I knew not even the intercession of the Virgin would cause me to be served. I pushed through the doors and took the first vacant seat I saw, at a table for two, and waited.

I do not know how long I waited and I rather wonder, until today, what I could possibly have looked like. Whatever I looked like, I frightened the waitress who shortly appeared, and the moment she appeared all of my fury flowed towards her. I hated her for her white face, and for her great, astounded, frightened eyes. I felt that if she found a black man so frightening I would make her fright worth-while.

She did not ask me what I wanted, but repeated, as though she had learned it somewhere, "We don't serve Negroes here." She did not say it with the blunt, derisive hostility to which I had grown so accustomed, but, rather, with a note of apology in her voice, and fear. This made me colder and more murderous than ever. I felt I had to do something with my hands. I wanted her to come close enough for me to get her neck between my hands.

So I pretended not to have understood her, hoping to draw her closer. And she did step a very short step closer, with her pencil poised incongruously over her pad, and repeated the formula: ". . . don't serve Negroes here."

Somehow, with the repetition of that phrase, which was already ringing in my head like a thousand bells of a nightmare, I realized that she would never come any closer and that I would have to strike from a distance. There was nothing on the table but an ordinary watermug half full of water, and I picked this up and hurled it with all my strength at her. She ducked and it missed her and shattered against the mirror behind the bar. And, with that sound, my frozen blood abruptly thawed, I returned from wherever I had been, I *saw*, for the first time, the restaurant, the people with their mouths open, already, as it seemed to me, rising as one man, and I realized what I had done, and where I was, and I was frightened. I rose and began running for the door. A round, potbellied man grabbed me by the nape of the neck just as I reached the doors and began to beat me about the face. I kicked him and got loose and ran into the streets. My friend whispered, *"Run!"* and I ran.

My friend stayed outside the restaurant long enough to misdirect my pursuers and the police, who arrived, he told me, at once. I do not know what I said to him when he came to my room that night. I could not have said much. I felt, in the oddest, most awful way, that I had somehow betrayed him. I lived it over and over and over again, the way one relives an automobile accident after it has happened and one finds oneself alone and safe. I could not get over two facts, both equally difficult for the imagination to grasp, and one was that I could have been murdered. But the other was that I had been ready to commit murder. I saw nothing very clearly but I did see this: that my life, my *real* life, was in danger, and not from anything other people might do but from the hatred I carried in my own heart.

II

I had returned home around the second week in June—in great haste because it seemed that my father's death and my mother's confinement were both but a matter of hours. In the case of my mother, it soon became clear that she had simply made a miscalculation. This had always been her tendency and I don't believe that a single one of us arrived in the world, or has since arrived anywhere else, on time. But none of us dawdled so intolerably about the business of being born as did my baby sister. We sometimes amused ourselves, during those endless, stifling weeks, by picturing the baby sitting within in the safe, warm dark, bitterly regretting the necessity of becoming a part of our chaos and stubbornly putting it off as long as possible. I understood her perfectly and congratulated her on showing such good sense so soon. Death, however, sat as purposefully at my father's bedside as life stirred within my mother's womb and it was harder to understand why he so lingered in that long shadow. It seemed that he had bent, and for a long time, too, all of his energies towards dying. Now death was ready for him but my father held back.

All of Harlem, indeed, seemed to be infected by waiting. I had never before known it to be so violently still. Racial tensions throughout this country were exacerbated during the early years of the war, partly because the labor market brought together hundreds of thousands of ill-prepared people and partly because Negro soldiers, regardless of where they were born, received their military training in the south. What happened in defense plants and army camps had repercussions, naturally, in every Negro ghetto. The situation in Harlem had grown bad enough for clergymen, policemen, educators, politicians, and social workers to assert in one breath that there was no "crime wave" and to offer, in the very next breath, suggestions as to how to combat it. These suggestions always seemed to involve playgrounds, despite the fact that racial skirmishes were occurring in the playgrounds, too. Playground or not, crime wave or not, the Harlem police force had been augmented in March, and the unrest grew—perhaps, in fact, partly as a result of the ghetto's instinctive hatred of policemen. Perhaps the most revealing news item, out of the steady parade of reports of muggings, stabbings, shootings, assaults, gang wars, and accusations of police brutality, is the item concerning six Negro girls who set upon a white girl in the subway because, as they all too accurately put it, she was stepping on their toes. Indeed she was, all over the nation.

I had never before been so aware of policemen, on foot, on horseback, on corners, everywhere, always two by two. Nor had I ever been so aware of small knots of people. They were on stoops and on corners and in doorways, and what was striking about them, I think, was that they did not seem to be talking. Never, when I passed these groups, did the usual sound of a curse or a laugh ring out and neither did there seem to be any hum of gossip. There was certainly, on the other hand, occurring between them communication extraordinarily intense. Another thing that was striking was the unexpected diversity of the people who made up these groups.

Usually, for example, one would see a group of sharpies standing on the street corner, jiving the passing chicks; or a group of older men, usually, for some reason, in the vicinity of a barber shop, discussing baseball scores, or the numbers, or making rather chilling observations about women they had known. Women, in a general way, tended to be seen less often together—unless they were church women, or very young girls, or prostitutes met together for an unprofessional instant. But that summer I saw the strangest combinations: large, respectable, churchly matrons standing on the stoops or the corners with their hair tied up, together with a girl in sleazy satin whose face bore the marks of gin and the razor, or heavy-set, abrupt, no-nonsense older men, in company with the most disreputable and fanatical "race" men, or these same "race" men with the sharpies, or these sharpies with the churchly women. Seventh Day Adventists and Methodists and Spiritualists seemed to be hobnobbing with Holyrollers and they were all, alike, entangled with the most flagrant disbelievers; something heavy in their stance seemed to indicate that they had all, incredibly, seen a common vision, and on each face there seemed to be the same strange, bitter shadow.

The churchly women and the matter-of-fact, no-nonsense men had children in the Army. The sleazy girls they talked to had lovers there, the sharpies and the "race" men had friends and brothers there. It would have demanded an unquestioning patriotism, happily as uncommon in this country as it is undesirable, for these people not to have been disturbed by the bitter letters they received, by the newspaper stories they read, not to have been enraged by the posters, then to be found all over New York, which described the Japanese as "yellow-bellied Japs." It was only the "race" men, to be sure, who spoke ceaselessly of being revenged—how this vengeance was to be exacted was not clear—for the indignities and dangers suffered by Negro boys in uniform; but everybody felt a directionless, hopeless bitterness, as well as that panic which can scarcely be suppressed when one knows that a human being one loves is beyond one's reach, and in danger. This helplessness and this gnawing uneasiness does something, at length, to even the toughest mind. Perhaps the best way to sum all this up is to say that the people I knew felt, mainly, a peculiar kind of relief when they knew that their boys were being shipped out of the south, to do battle overseas. It was, perhaps, like feeling that the most dangerous part of a dangerous journey had been passed and that now, even if death should come, it would come with honor and without the complicity of their countrymen. Such a death would be, in short, a fact with which one could hope to live.

It was on the 28th of July, which I believe was a Wednesday, that I visited my father for the first time during his illness and for the last time in his life. The moment I saw him I knew why I had put off this visit so long. I had told my mother that I did not want to see him because I hated him. But this was not true. It was only that I *had* hated him and I wanted to hold on to this hatred. I did not want to look on him as a ruin: it was not a ruin I had hated. I imagine that one of the reasons people cling to their hates so stubbornly is because they sense, once hate is gone, that they will be forced to deal with pain.

We traveled out to him, his older sister and myself, to what seemed to be the very end of a very Long Island. It was hot and dusty and we wrangled, my aunt and I, all the way out, over the fact that I had recently begun to smoke and, as she said, to give myself airs. But I knew that she wrangled with me because she could not bear to face the fact of her brother's dying. Neither could I endure the reality of her despair, her unstated bafflement as to what had happened to her brother's life, and her own. So we wrangled and I smoked and from time to time she fell into a heavy reverie. Covertly, I watched her face, which was the face of an old woman; it had fallen in, the eyes were sunken and lightless; soon she would be dying, too.

In my childhood—it had not been so long ago—I had thought her beautiful. She had been quick-witted and quick-moving and very generous with all the children and each of her visits had been an event. At one time one of my brothers and myself had thought of running away to live with her. Now she could no longer produce out of her handbag some unexpected and yet familiar delight. She made me feel pity and revulsion and fear. It was awful to realize that she no longer caused me to feel affection. The closer we came to the hospital the more querulous she became and at the same time, naturally, grew more dependent on me. Between pity and guilt and fear I began to feel that there was another me trapped in my skull like a jack-in-the-box who might escape my control at any moment and fill the air with screaming.

She began to cry the moment we entered the room and she saw him lying there, all shriveled and still, like a little black monkey. The great, gleaming apparatus which fed him and would have compelled him to be still even if he had been able to move brought to mind, not beneficence, but torture; the tubes entering his arm made me think of pictures I had seen when a child, of Gulliver, tied down by the pygmies on that island. My aunt wept and wept, there was a whistling sound in my father's throat; nothing was said; he could not speak. I wanted to take his hand, to say something. But I do not know what I could have said, even if he could have heard me. He was not really in that room with us, he had at last really embarked on his journey; and though my aunt told me that he said he was going to meet Jesus, I did not hear anything except that whistling in his throat. The doctor came back and we left, into that unbearable train again, and home. In the morning came the telegram saying that he was dead. Then the house was suddenly full of relatives, friends, hysteria, and confusion and I quickly left my mother and the children to the care of those impressive women, who, in Negro communities at least, automatically appear at times of bereavement armed with lotions, proverbs, and patience, and an ability to cook. I went downtown. By the time I returned, later the same day, my mother had been carried to the hospital and the baby had been born.

III

For my father's funeral I had nothing black to wear and this posed a nagging problem all day long. It was one of those problems, simple, or impossible of solution, to which the mind insanely clings in order to avoid the mind's real trouble. I spent most of that day at the downtown apartment of a girl I knew, celebrating my birthday with whiskey and wondering what to wear that night. When planning a birthday celebration

one naturally does not expect that it will be up against competition from a funeral and this girl had anticipated taking me
out that night, for a big dinner and a night club afterwards.
Sometime during the course of that long day we decided that
we would go out anyway, when my father's funeral service
was over. I imagine *I* decided it, since, as the funeral hour
approached, it became clearer and clearer to me that I would
not know what to do with myself when it was over. The girl,
stifling her very lively concern as to the possible effects of the
whiskey on one of my father's chief mourners, concentrated
on being conciliatory and practically helpful. She found a
black shirt for me somewhere and ironed it and, dressed in
the darkest pants and jacket I owned, and slightly drunk, I
made my way to my father's funeral.

The chapel was full, but not packed, and very quiet. There
were, mainly, my father's relatives, and his children, and here
and there I saw faces I had not seen since childhood, the faces
of my father's one-time friends. They were very dark and solemn now, seeming somehow to suggest that they had known
all along that something like this would happen. Chief among
the mourners was my aunt, who had quarreled with my father
all his life; by which I do not mean to suggest that her mourning was insincere or that she had not loved him. I suppose
that she was one of the few people in the world who had, and
their incessant quarreling proved precisely the strength of the
tie that bound them. The only other person in the world, as
far as I knew, whose relationship to my father rivaled my
aunt's in depth was my mother, who was not there.

It seemed to me, of course, that it was a very long funeral.
But it was, if anything, a rather shorter funeral than most,
nor, since there were no overwhelming, uncontrollable expressions of grief, could it be called—if I dare to use the
word—successful. The minister who preached my father's
funeral sermon was one of the few my father had still been
seeing as he neared his end. He presented to us in his sermon
a man whom none of us had ever seen—a man thoughtful,
patient, and forbearing, a Christian inspiration to all who
knew him, and a model for his children. And no doubt the
children, in their disturbed and guilty state, were almost ready
to believe this; he had been remote enough to be anything

and, anyway, the shock of the incontrovertible, that it was really our father lying up there in that casket, prepared the mind for anything. His sister moaned and this grief-stricken moaning was taken as corroboration. The other faces held a dark, non-committal thoughtfulness. This was not the man they had known, but they had scarcely expected to be confronted with *him*; this was, in a sense deeper than questions of fact, the man they had not known, and the man they had not known may have been the real one. The real man, whoever he had been, had suffered and now he was dead: this was all that was sure and all that mattered now. Every man in the chapel hoped that when his hour came he, too, would be eulogized, which is to say forgiven, and that all of his lapses, greeds, errors, and strayings from the truth would be invested with coherence and looked upon with charity. This was perhaps the last thing human beings could give each other and it was what they demanded, after all, of the Lord. Only the Lord saw the midnight tears, only He was present when one of His children, moaning and wringing hands, paced up and down the room. When one slapped one's child in anger the recoil in the heart reverberated through heaven and became part of the pain of the universe. And when the children were hungry and sullen and distrustful and one watched them, daily, growing wilder, and further away, and running headlong into danger, it was the Lord who knew what the charged heart endured as the strap was laid to the backside; the Lord alone who knew what one *would* have said if one had had, like the Lord, the gift of the living word. It was the Lord who knew of the impossibility every parent in that room faced: how to prepare the child for the day when the child would be despised and how to *create* in the child—by what means?—a stronger antidote to this poison than one had found for oneself. The avenues, side streets, bars, billiard halls, hospitals, police stations, and even the playgrounds of Harlem—not to mention the houses of correction, the jails, and the morgue—testified to the potency of the poison while remaining silent as to the efficacy of whatever antidote, irresistibly raising the question of whether or not such an antidote existed; raising, which was worse, the question of whether or not an antidote was desirable; perhaps poison should be fought with poison. With these several schisms in the mind and with more terrors in the heart than could be named, it was better not to judge the man who had gone down under an impossible burden. It was better to remember: *Thou knowest this man's fall; but thou knowest not his wrassling.*

While the preacher talked and I watched the children— years of changing their diapers, scrubbing them, slapping them, taking them to school, and scolding them had had the perhaps inevitable result of making me love them, though I am not sure I knew this then—my mind was busily breaking out with a rash of disconnected impressions. Snatches of popular songs, indecent jokes, bits of books I had read, movie sequences, faces, voices, political issues—I thought I was going mad; all these impressions suspended, as it were, in the solution of the faint nausea produced in me by the heat and liquor. For a moment I had the impression that my alcoholic breath, inefficiently disguised with chewing gum, filled the entire chapel. Then someone began singing one of my father's favorite songs and, abruptly, I was with him, sitting on his knee, in the hot, enormous, crowded church which was the first church we attended. It was the Abyssinia Baptist Church on 138th Street. We had not gone there long. With this image, a host of others came. I had forgotten, in the rage of my growing up, how proud my father had been of me when I was little. Apparently, I had had a voice and my father had liked to show me off before the members of the church. I had forgotten what he had looked like when he was pleased but now I remembered that he had always been grinning with pleasure when my solos ended. I even remembered certain expressions on his face when he teased my mother—had he loved her? I would never know. And when had it all begun to change? For now it seemed that he had not always been cruel. I remembered being taken for a haircut and scraping my knee on the footrest of the barber's chair and I remembered my father's face as he soothed my crying and applied the stinging iodine. Then I remembered our fights, fights which had been of the worst possible kind because my technique had been silence.

I remembered the one time in all our life together when we had really spoken to each other.

It was on a Sunday and it must have been shortly before I left home. We were walking, just the two of us, in our usual silence, to or from church. I was in high school and had been doing a lot of writing and I was, at about this time, the editor of the high school magazine. But I had also been a Young Minister and had been preaching from the pulpit. Lately, I had been taking fewer engagements and preached as rarely as possible. It was said in the church, quite truthfully, that I was "cooling off."

My father asked me abruptly, "You'd rather write than preach, wouldn't you?"

I was astonished at his question—because it was a real question. I answered, "Yes."

That was all we said. It was awful to remember that that was all we had *ever* said.

The casket now was opened and the mourners were being led up the aisle to look for the last time on the deceased. The assumption was that the family was too overcome with grief to be allowed to make this journey alone and I watched while my aunt was led to the casket and, muffled in black, and shaking, led back to her seat. I disapproved of forcing the children to look on their dead father, considering that the shock of his death, or, more truthfully, the shock of death as a reality, was already a little more than a child could bear, but my judgment in this matter had been overruled and there they were, bewildered and frightened and very small, being led, one by one, to the casket. But there is also something very gallant about children at such moments. It has something to do with their silence and gravity and with the fact that one cannot help them. Their legs, somehow, seem *exposed*, so that it is at once incredible and terribly clear that their legs are all they have to hold them up.

I had not wanted to go to the casket myself and I certainly had not wished to be led there, but there was no way of avoiding either of these forms. One of the deacons led me up and I looked on my father's face. I cannot say that it looked like him at all. His blackness had been equivocated by powder and there was no suggestion in that casket of what his power had or could have been. He was simply an old man dead, and it was hard to believe that he had ever given anyone either joy or pain. Yet, his life filled that room. Further up the avenue his wife was holding his newborn child. Life and death so close together, and love and hatred, and right and wrong, said something to me which I did not want to hear concerning man, concerning the life of man.

After the funeral, while I was downtown desperately celebrating my birthday, a Negro soldier, in the lobby of the Hotel Braddock, got into a fight with a white policeman over a Negro girl. Negro girls, white policemen, in or out of uniform, and Negro males—in or out of uniform—were part of the furniture of the lobby of the Hotel Braddock and this was certainly not the first time such an incident had occurred. It was destined, however, to receive an unprecedented publicity, for the fight between the policeman and the soldier ended with the shooting of the soldier. Rumor, flowing immediately to the streets outside, stated that the soldier had been shot in the back, an instantaneous and revealing invention, and that the soldier had died protecting a Negro woman. The facts were somewhat different—for example, the soldier had not been shot in the back, and was not dead, and the girl seems to have been as dubious a symbol of womanhood as her white counterpart in Georgia usually is, but no one was interested in the facts. They preferred the invention because this invention expressed and corroborated their hates and fears so perfectly. It is just as well to remember that people are always doing this. Perhaps many of those legends, including Christianity, to which the world clings began their conquest of the world with just some such concerted surrender to distortion. The effect, in Harlem, of this particular legend was like the effect of a lit match in a tin of gasoline. The mob gathered before the doors of the Hotel Braddock simply began to swell and to spread in every direction, and Harlem exploded.

The mob did not cross the ghetto lines. It would have been easy, for example, to have gone over Morningside Park on the west side or to have crossed the Grand Central railroad tracks at 125th Street on the east side, to wreak havoc in white neighborhoods. The mob seems to have been mainly interested in something more potent and real than the white face, that is, in white power, and the principal damage done during the riot of the summer of 1943 was to white business establishments in Harlem. It might have been a far bloodier story, of course, if, at the hour the riot began, these establishments had still been open. From the Hotel Braddock the mob fanned out, east and west along 125th Street, and for the entire length of Lenox, Seventh, and Eighth avenues. Along each of these avenues, and along each major side street—116th, 125th, 135th, and so on—bars, stores, pawnshops, restaurants, even little luncheonettes had been smashed open and entered and looted—looted, it might be added, with more haste than efficiency. The shelves really looked as though a bomb had struck them. Cans of beans and soup and dog food, along with toilet paper, corn flakes, sardines, and milk tumbled every which way, and abandoned cash registers and cases of beer leaned crazily out of the splintered windows and were strewn along the avenues. Sheets, blankets, and clothing of every description formed a kind of path, as though people had dropped them while running. I truly had not realized that Harlem *had* so many stores until I saw them all smashed open; the first time the word *wealth* ever entered my mind in relation to Harlem was when I saw it scattered in the streets. But one's first, incongruous impression of plenty was countered immediately by an impression of waste. None of this was doing anybody any good. It would have been better to have left the plate glass as it had been and the goods lying in the stores.

It would have been better, but it would also have been intolerable, for Harlem had needed something to smash. To smash something is the ghetto's chronic need. Most of the time it is the members of the ghetto who smash each other, and themselves. But as long as the ghetto walls are standing there will always come a moment when these outlets do not work. That summer, for example, it was not enough to get into a fight on Lenox Avenue, or curse out one's cronies in the barber shops. If ever, indeed, the violence which fills Harlem's churches, pool halls, and bars erupts outward in a more direct fashion, Harlem and its citizens are likely to vanish in an apocalyptic flood. That this is not likely to happen is due to a great many reasons, most hidden and powerful among them the Negro's real relation to the white American. This relation prohibits, simply, anything as uncomplicated and satisfactory as pure hatred. In order really to hate white people, one has to blot so much out of the mind—and the heart—that this hatred itself becomes an exhausting and self-destructive pose. But this does not mean, on the other hand, that love comes easily: the white world is too powerful, too complacent, too ready with gratuitous humiliation, and, above all, too ignorant and too innocent for that. One is absolutely forced to make perpetual qualifications and one's own reactions are always canceling each other out. It is this, really, which has driven so many people mad, both white and black. One is always in the position of having to decide between amputation and gangrene. Amputation is swift but time may prove that the amputation was not necessary—or one may delay the amputation too long. Gangrene is slow, but it is impossible to be sure that one is reading one's symptoms right. The idea of going through life as a cripple is more than one can bear, and equally unbearable is the risk of swelling up slowly, in agony, with poison. And the trouble, finally, is that the risks are real even if the choices do not exist.

"But as for me and my house," my father had said, "we will serve the Lord." I wondered, as we drove him to his resting place, what this line had meant for him. I had heard him preach it many times. I had preached it once myself, proudly giving it an interpretation different from my father's. Now the whole thing came back to me, as though my father and I were on our way to Sunday school and I were memorizing the golden text: *And if it seem evil unto you to serve the Lord, choose you this day whom you will serve; whether the gods which your fathers served that were on the other side of the flood, or the gods of the Amorites, in whose land ye dwell: but as for me and my house, we will serve the Lord.* I suspected in these familiar lines a meaning which had never been there for me before. All of my father's texts and songs, which I had decided were meaningless, were arranged before me at his death like empty bottles, waiting to hold the meaning which life would give them for me. This was his legacy: nothing is ever escaped. That bleakly memorable morning I hated the unbelievable streets and the Negroes and whites who had, equally, made them that way. But I knew that it was folly, as my father would have said, this bitterness was folly. It was necessary to hold on to the things that mattered. The dead man mattered, the new life mattered; blackness and whiteness did not matter; to believe that they did was to acquiesce in one's own destruction. Hatred, which could destroy so much, never failed to destroy the man who hated and this was an immutable law.

It began to seem that one would have to hold in the mind forever two ideas which seemed to be in opposition. The first idea was acceptance, the acceptance, totally without rancor, of life as it is, and men as they are: in the light of this idea, it goes without saying that injustice is a commonplace. But this did not mean that one could be complacent, for the second idea was of equal power: that one must never, in one's own life, accept these injustices as commonplace but must fight them with all one's strength. This fight begins, however, in the heart and it now had been laid to my charge to keep my own heart free of hatred and despair. This intimation made my heart heavy and, now that my father was irrecoverable, I wished that he had been beside me so that I could have searched his face for the answers which only the future would give me now.

PART THREE

Encounter on the Seine: Black Meets Brown

IN PARIS nowadays it is rather more difficult for an American Negro to become a really successful entertainer than it is rumored to have been some thirty years ago. For one thing, champagne has ceased to be drunk out of slippers, and the frivolously colored thousand-franc note is neither as elastic nor as freely spent as it was in the 1920's. The musicians and singers who are here now must work very hard indeed to acquire the polish and style which will land them in the big time. Bearing witness to this eternally tantalizing possibility, performers whose eminence is unchallenged, like Duke Ellington or Louis Armstrong, occasionally pass through. Some of their ambitious followers are in or near the big time already; others are gaining reputations which have yet to be tested in the States. Gordon Heath, who will be remembered for his performances as the embattled soldier in Broadway's *Deep Are the Roots* some seasons back, sings ballads nightly in his own night club on the Rue L'Abbaye; and everyone who comes to Paris these days sooner or later discovers Chez Inez, a night club in the Latin Quarter run by a singer named Inez Cavanaugh, which specializes in fried chicken and jazz. It is at Chez Inez that many an unknown first performs in public, going on thereafter, if not always to greater triumphs, at least to other night clubs, and possibly landing a contract to tour the Riviera during the spring and summer.

In general, only the Negro entertainers are able to maintain a useful and unquestioning comradeship with other Negroes. Their nonperforming, colored countrymen are, nearly to a man, incomparably more isolated, and it must be conceded that this isolation is deliberate. It is estimated that there are five hundred American Negroes living in this city, the vast majority of them veterans studying on the G.I. Bill. They are studying everything from the Sorbonne's standard *Cours de Civilisation Française* to abnormal psychology, brain surgery, music, fine arts, and literature. Their isolation from each other is not difficult to understand if one bears in mind the axiom, unquestioned by American landlords, that Negroes are happy only when they are kept together. Those driven to break this pattern by leaving the U.S. ghettos not merely have effected a social and physical leave-taking but also have been precipitated into cruel psychological warfare. It is altogether inevitable that past humiliations should become associated not only with one's traditional oppressors but also with one's traditional kinfolk.

Thus the sight of a face from home is not invariably a source of joy, but can also quite easily become a source of embarrassment or rage. The American Negro in Paris is forced at last to exercise an undemocratic discrimination rarely practiced by Americans, that of judging his people, duck by duck, and distinguishing them one from another. Through this deliberate isolation, through lack of numbers, and above all through his own overwhelming need to be, as it were, forgotten, the American Negro in Paris is very nearly the invisible man.

The wariness with which he regards his colored kin is a natural extension of the wariness with which he regards all of his countrymen. At the beginning, certainly, he cherishes rather exaggerated hopes of the French. His white countrymen, by and large, fail to justify his fears, partly because the social climate does not encourage an outward display of racial bigotry, partly out of their awareness of being ambassadors, and finally, I should think, because they are themselves relieved at being no longer forced to think in terms of color. There remains, nevertheless, in the encounter of white Americans and Negro Americans the high potential of an awkward or an ugly situation.

The white American regards his darker brother through the distorting screen created by a lifetime of conditioning. He is accustomed to regard him either as a needy and deserving martyr or as the soul of rhythm, but he is more than a little intimidated to find this stranger so many miles from home. At first he tends instinctively, whatever his intelligence may belatedly clamor, to take it as a reflection on his personal honor and good-will; and at the same time, with that winning generosity, at once good-natured and uneasy, which characterizes Americans, he would like to establish communication, and sympathy, with his compatriot. "And how do *you* feel about it?" he would like to ask, "it" being anything—the Russians, Betty Grable, the Place de la Concorde. The trouble here is that any "it," so tentatively offered, may suddenly become loaded and vibrant with tension, creating in the air between the two thus met an intolerable atmosphere of danger.

The Negro, on the other hand, via the same conditioning which constricts the outward gesture of the whites, has learned to anticipate: as the mouth opens he divines what the tongue will utter. He has had time, too, long before he came to Paris, to reflect on the absolute and personally expensive futility of taking any one of his countrymen to task for his status in America, or of hoping to convey to them any of his experience. The American Negro and white do not, therefore, discuss the past, except in considerably guarded snatches. Both are quite willing, and indeed quite wise, to remark instead the considerably overrated impressiveness of the Eiffel Tower.

The Eiffel Tower has naturally long since ceased to divert the French, who consider that all Negroes arrive from America, trumpet-laden and twinkle-toed, bearing scars so unutterably painful that all of the glories of the French Republic may not suffice to heal them. This indignant generosity poses problems of its own, which, language and custom being what they are, are not so easily averted.

The European tends to avoid the really monumental confusion which might result from an attempt to apprehend the relationship of the forty-eight states to one another, clinging instead to such information as is afforded by radio, press, and film, to anecdotes considered to be illustrative of American life, and to the myth that we have ourselves perpetuated. The result, in conversation, is rather like seeing one's back yard reproduced with extreme fidelity, but in such a perspective that it becomes a place which one has never seen or visited, which never has existed, and which never can exist. The Negro is forced to say "Yes" to many a difficult question, and yet to deny the conclusion to which his answers seem to point. His past, he now realizes, has not been simply a series of ropes and bonfires and humiliations, but something vastly more complex, which, as he thinks painfully, "It was much worse than that," was also, he irrationally feels, something much better. As it is useless to excoriate his countrymen, it is galling now to be pitied as a victim, to accept this ready sympathy which is limited only by its failure to accept him as an American. He finds himself involved, in another language, in the same old battle: the battle for his own identity. To accept the reality of his being an American becomes a matter involving his integrity and his greatest hopes, for only by accepting this reality can he hope to make articulate to himself or to others the uniqueness of his experience, and to set free the spirit so long anonymous and caged.

The ambivalence of his status is thrown into relief by his encounters with the Negro students from France's colonies who live in Paris. The French African comes from a region and a way of life which—at least from the American point of view—is exceedingly primitive, and where exploitation takes more naked forms. In Paris, the African Negro's status, conspicuous and subtly inconvenient, is that of a colonial; and he leads here the intangibly precarious life of someone abruptly and recently uprooted. His bitterness is unlike that of his American kinsman in that it is not so treacherously likely to be turned against himself. He has, not so very many miles away, a homeland to which his relationship, no less than his responsibility, is overwhelmingly clear: His country must be given—or it must seize—its freedom. This bitter ambition is shared by his fellow colonials, with whom he has a common language, and whom he has no wish whatever to avoid; without whose sustenance, indeed, he would be almost altogether lost in Paris. They live in groups together, in the same neighborhoods, in student hotels and under conditions which cannot fail to impress the American as almost unendurable.

Yet what the American is seeing is not simply the poverty of the student but the enormous gap between the European and American standards of living. *All* of the students in the Latin Quarter live in ageless, sinister-looking hotels; they are all forced continually to choose between cigarettes and cheese at lunch.

It is true that the poverty and anger which the American Negro sees must be related to Europe and not to America.

Yet, as he wishes for a moment that he were home again, where at least the terrain is familiar, there begins to race within him, like the despised beat of the tom-tom, echoes of a past which he has not yet been able to utilize, intimations of a responsibility which he has not yet been able to face. He begins to conjecture how much he has gained and lost during his long sojourn in the American republic. The African before him has endured privation, injustice, medieval cruelty; but the African has not yet endured the utter alienation of himself from his people and his past. His mother did not sing "Sometimes I Feel Like a Motherless Child," and he has not, all his life long, ached for acceptance in a culture which pronounced straight hair and white skin the only acceptable beauty.

They face each other, the Negro and the African, over a gulf of three hundred years—an alienation too vast to be conquered in an evening's good-will, too heavy and too double-edged ever to be trapped in speech. This alienation causes the Negro to recognize that he is a hybrid. Not a physical hybrid merely: in every aspect of his living he betrays the memory of the auction block and the impact of the happy ending. In white Americans he finds reflected—repeated, as it were, in a higher key—his tensions, his terrors, his tenderness. Dimly and for the first time, there begins to fall into perspective the nature of the roles they have played in the lives and history of each other. Now he is bone of their bone, flesh of their flesh; they have loved and hated and obsessed and feared each other and his blood is in their soil. Therefore he cannot deny them, nor can they ever be divorced.

The American Negro cannot explain to the African what surely seems in himself to be a want of manliness, of racial pride, a maudlin ability to forgive. It is difficult to make clear that he is not seeking to forfeit his birthright as a black man, but that, on the contrary, it is precisely this birthright which he is struggling to recognize and make articulate. Perhaps it now occurs to him that in this need to establish himself in relation to his past he is most American, that this depthless alienation from oneself and one's people is, in sum, the American experience.

Yet one day he will face his home again; nor can he realistically expect to find overwhelming changes. In America, it is true, the appearance is perpetually changing, each generation greeting with short-lived exultation yet more dazzling additions to our renowned façade. But the ghetto, anxiety, bitterness, and guilt continue to breed their indescribable complex of tensions. What time will bring Americans is at last their own identity. It is on this dangerous voyage and in the same boat that the American Negro will make peace with himself and with the voiceless many thousands gone before him.

A Question of Identity

THE AMERICAN student colony in Paris is a social phenomenon so amorphous as to at once demand and defy the generality. One is far from being in the position of finding not enough to say—one finds far too much, and everything one finds is contradictory. What one wants to know at bottom, is what *they* came to find: to which question there are—at least—as many answers as there are faces at the café tables.

The assumed common denominator, which is their military experience, does not shed on this question as much light as one might hope. For one thing, it becomes impossible, the moment one thinks about it, to predicate the existence of a *common* experience. The moment one thinks about it, it becomes apparent that there is no such thing. That experience is a private, and a very largely speechless affair is the principal truth, perhaps, to which the colony under discussion bears witness—though the aggressively unreadable face which they, collectively, present also suggests the more disturbing possibility that experience may perfectly well be meaningless. This loaded speculation aside, it is certainly true that whatever this experience has done to them, or for them, whatever the effect has been, is, or will be, is a question to which no one has yet given any strikingly coherent answer. Military experience does not, furthermore, necessarily mean experience of battle, so that the student colony's common denominator reduces itself to nothing more than the fact that all of its members have spent some time in uniform. This is the common denominator of their entire generation, of which the majority is not to be found in Paris, or, for that matter, in Europe. One is at the outset, therefore, forbidden to assume that the fact of having surrendered to the necessary anonymity of uniform, or of having undergone the shock of battle, was enough to occasion this flight from home. The best that one can do by way of uniting these so disparate identities is simply to accept, without comment, the fact of their military experience, without questioning its extent; and, further, to suggest that they form, by virtue of their presence here, a somewhat unexpected minority. Unlike the majority of their fellows, who were simply glad to get back home, these have elected to tarry in the Old World, among scenes and people unimaginably removed from anything they have known. They are willing, apparently, at least for a season, to endure the wretched Parisian plumbing, the public baths, the Paris age, and dirt—to pursue some end, mysterious and largely inarticulate, arbitrarily summed up in the verb *to study*.

Arbitrarily, because, however hard the ex-GI is studying, it is very difficult to believe that it was only for this reason that he traveled so far. He is not, usually, studying anything which he couldn't study at home, in far greater comfort. (We are limiting ourselves, for the moment, to those people who are— more or less seriously—studying, as opposed to those, to be considered later, who are merely gold-bricking.) The people, for example, who are studying painting, which seems, until one looks around, the best possible subject to be studying here, are not studying, after all, with Picasso, or Matisse— they are studying with teachers of the same caliber as those they would have found in the States. They are treated by these teachers with the same highhandedness, and they accept their dicta with the very same measure of American salt. Nor can it be said that they produce canvases of any greater interest than those to be found along Washington Square, or in the cold-water flats of New York's lower east side. There is, *au contraire*, more than a little truth to the contention that the east side has a certain edge over Montparnasse, and this in spite of the justly renowned Paris light. If we tentatively use— purely by virtue of his numbers—the student painter as the nearest possible approach to a "typical" student, we find that his motives for coming to Paris are anything but clear. One is forced to suppose that it was nothing more than the legend of Paris, not infrequently at its most vulgar and superficial level. It was certainly no love for French tradition, whatever, indeed, in his mind, that tradition may be; and, in any case, since he is himself without a tradition, he is ill equipped to deal with the traditions of any other people. It was no love for their language, which he doesn't, beyond the most ines-capable necessities, speak; nor was it any love for their history, his grasp of French history being yet more feeble than his understanding of his own. It was no love for the monuments, cathedrals, palaces, shrines, for which, again, nothing in his experience prepares him, and to which, when he is not totally indifferent, he brings only the hurried bewilderment of the tourist. It was not even any particular admiration, or sympathy for the French, or, at least, none strong enough to bear the strain of actual contact. He may, at home, have admired their movies, in which case, confronting the reality, he tends to feel a little taken in. Those images created by Marcel Carné, for example, prove themselves treacherous precisely because they are so exact. The sordid French hotel room, so admirably detailed by the camera, speaking, in its quaintness, and distance, so beautifully of romance, undergoes a sea-change, becomes a room positively hostile to romance, once it is oneself, and not Jean Gabin, who lives there. This is the difference, simply, between what one desires and what the reality insists on— which difference we will not pursue except to observe that, since the reasons which brought the student here are so romantic, and incoherent, he has come, in effect, to a city which exists only in his mind. He cushions himself, so it would seem, against the shock of reality, by refusing for a very long time to recognize Paris at all, but clinging instead to its image. This is the reason, perhaps, that Paris for so long fails to make any mark on him; and may also be why, when the tension between the real and the imagined can no longer be supported, so many people undergo a species of breakdown, or take the first boat home.

For Paris is, according to its legend, the city where everyone loses his head, and his morals, lives through at least one *histoire d'amour*, ceases, quite, to arrive anywhere on time, and thumbs his nose at the Puritans—the city, in brief, where all become drunken on the fine old air of freedom. This legend, in the fashion of legends, has this much to support it, that it is not at all difficult to see how it got started. It is limited, as legends are limited, by being—literally—unlivable, and by referring to the past. It is perhaps not amazing, therefore, that this legend appears to have virtually nothing to do with the life of Paris itself, with the lives, that is, of the natives, to whom the city, no less than the legend, belong. The charm of this legend proves itself capable of withstanding the most improbable excesses of the French bureaucracy, the weirdest vagaries of the *concierge*, the fantastic rents paid for uncomfortable apartments, the discomfort itself, and, even, the great confusion and despair which is reflected in French politics—and in French faces. More, the legend operates to place all of the inconveniences endured by the foreigner, to say nothing of the downright misery which is the lot of many of the natives, in the gentle glow of the picturesque, and the absurd; so that, finally, it is perfectly possible to be enamored of Paris while remaining totally indifferent, or even hostile to the French. And this is made possible by the one person in Paris whom the legend seems least to affect, who is not living it at all, that is, the Parisian himself. He, with his impenetrable *politesse*, and with techniques unspeakably more direct, keeps the traveler at an unmistakable arm's length. Unlucky indeed, as well as rare, the traveler who thirsts to know the lives of the people—the people don't want him in their lives. Neither does the Parisian exhibit the faintest personal interest, or curiosity, concerning the life, or habits, of any stranger. So long as he keeps within the law, which, after all, most people have sufficient ingenuity to do, he may stand on his head, for all the Parisian cares. It is this arrogant indifference on the part of the Parisian, with its unpredictable effects on the traveler, which makes so splendid the Paris air, to say nothing whatever of the exhilarating effect it has on the Paris scene.

The American student lives here, then, in a kind of social limbo. He is allowed, and he gratefully embraces irresponsibility; and, at the same time, since he is an American, he is invested with power, whether or not he likes it, however he may choose to confirm or deny it. Though the students of any nation, in Paris, are allowed irresponsibility, few seem to need it as desperately as Americans seem to need it; and none, naturally, move in the same aura of power, which sets up in the general breast a perceptible anxiety, and wonder, and a perceptible resentment. This is the "catch," for the American, in the Paris freedom: that he becomes here a kind of revenant to Europe, the future of which continent, it may be, is in his hands. The problems proceeding from the distinction he thus finds thrust upon him might not, for a sensibility less definitively lonely, frame so painful a dilemma: but the American wishes to be liked *as a person*, an implied distinction which makes perfect sense to him, and none whatever to the European. What the American means is that he does not want to be confused with the Marshall Plan, Hollywood, the Yankee dollar, television, or Senator McCarthy. What the European, in a thoroughly exasperating innocence, assumes is that the American cannot, of course, be divorced from the so diverse phenomena which make up his country, and that he is willing, and able, to clarify the American conundrum. If the American cannot do this, his despairing aspect seems to say, who, under heaven, can? This moment, which instinctive ingenuity delays as long as possible, nevertheless arrives, and punctuates the Paris honeymoon. It is the moment, so to speak, when one leaves the Paris of legend and finds oneself in the real and difficult Paris of the present. At this moment Paris ceases to be a city dedicated to *la vie bohème*, and becomes one of the cities of Europe. At this point, too, it may be suggested, the legend of Paris has done its deadly work, which is, perhaps, so to stun the traveler with freedom that he begins to long for the prison of home—home then becoming the place where questions are not asked.

It is at this point, precisely, that many and many a student packs his bags for home. The transformation which can be effected, in less than a year, in the attitude and aspirations of the youth who has divorced himself from the crudities of main street in order to be married with European finesse is, to say the very least, astounding. His brief period of enchantment having ended, he cannot wait, it seems, to look again on his native land—the virtues of which, if not less crude, have also become, abruptly, *simple*, and *vital*. With the air of a man who has but barely escaped tumbling headlong into the bottomless pit, he tells you that he can scarcely wait to leave this city, which has been revealed to the eye of his maturity as old, dirty, crumbling, and dead. The people who were, when he arrived at Le Havre, the heirs of the world's richest culture, the possessors of the world's largest *esprit*, are really decadent, penurious, self-seeking, and false, with no trace of American spontaneity, and lacking in the least gratitude for American favors. Only America is alive, only Americans are doing anything worth mentioning in the arts, or in any other field of human activity: to America, only, the future belongs. Whereas, but only yesterday, to confess a fondness for anything American was to be suspected of the most indefensible jingoism, to suggest today that Europe is not all black is to place oneself under the suspicion of harboring treasonable longings. The violence of his embrace of things American is embarrassing, not only because one is not quite prepared to follow his admirable example, but also because it is impossible not to suspect that his present acceptance of his country is no less romantic, and unreal, than his earlier rejection. It is as easy, after all, and as meaningless, to embrace uncritically the cultural sterility of main street as it is to decry it. Both extremes avoid the question of whether or not main street is really sterile, avoid, in fact—which is the principal convenience of extremes—any questions about main street at all. What one vainly listens for in this cacophony of affirmation is any echo, however faint, of individual maturity. It is really quite impossible to be affirmative about anything which one refuses to question; one is doomed to remain inarticulate about anything which one hasn't, by an act of the imagination, made one's own. This so suddenly affirmative student is but changing the fashion of his innocence, nothing being more improbable than that he is now prepared, as he insists, to embrace his Responsibilities—the very word, in the face of his monumental aversion to experience, seems to shrink to the dimensions of a new, and rather sinister, frivolity.

The student, homeward bound, has only chosen, however, to flee down the widest road. Of those who remain here, the majority have taken roads more devious, and incomparably better hidden—so well hidden that they themselves are lost.

One very often finds in this category that student whose adaptation to French life seems to have been most perfect, and whose studies—of French art, or the drama, the language, or the history—give him the greatest right to be here. This student has put aside chewing gum forever, he eschews the T-shirt, and the crew cut, he can only with difficulty be prevailed upon to see an American movie, and it is so patent that he is *actually* studying that his appearance at the café tables is never taken as evidence of frivolity, but only as proof of his admirable passion to study the customs of the country. One assumes that he is living as the French live—which assumption, however, is immediately challenged by the suspicion that no American *can* live as the French live, even if one could find an American who wanted to. This student lives, nevertheless, with a French family, with whom he speaks French, and takes his meals; and he knows, as some students do not, that the Place de la Bastille no longer holds the prison. He has read, or is reading, all of Racine, Proust, Gide, Sartre, and authors more obscure—in the original, naturally. He regularly visits the museums, and he considers Arletty to be the most beautiful woman and the finest actress in the world. But the world, it seems, has become the French world: he is unwilling to recognize any other. This so severely cramps the American conversational style, that one looks on this student with awe, and some shame—he is so spectacularly getting out of his European experience everything it has to give. *He* has certainly made contact with the French, and isn't wasting his time in Paris talking to people he might perfectly well have met in America. His friends are French, in the classroom, in the bistro, on the boulevard, and, of course, at home—it is only that one is sometimes driven to wonder what on earth they find to talk about. This wonder is considerably increased when, in the rare conversations he condescends to have in English, one discovers that, certain picturesque details aside, he seems to know no more about life in Paris than everybody knew at home. His friends have, it appears, leaped unscathed from the nineteenth into the twentieth century, entirely undismayed by any of the reverses suffered by their country. This makes them a remarkable band indeed, but it is in vain that one attempts to discover anything more about them—their conversation being limited, one gathers, to remarks about French wine, witticisms concerning *l'amour*, French history, and the glories of Paris. The remarkably limited range of their minds is matched only by their perplexing definition of friendship, a definition which does not seem to include any suggestion of communication, still less of intimacy. Since, in short, the relationship of this perfectly adapted student to the people he now so strenuously adores is based simply on his unwillingness to allow them any of the human attributes with which his countrymen so confounded him at home, and since his vaunted grasp of their history reveals itself as the merest academic platitude, involving his imagination not at all, the extent of his immersion in French life impresses one finally as the height of artificiality, and, even, of presumption. The most curious thing about the passion with which he has embraced the Continent is that it seems to be nothing more or less than a means of safeguarding his American simplicity. He has placed himself in a kind of strongbox of custom, and refuses to see anything in Paris which can't be seen through a golden haze. He is thus protected against reality, or experience, or change, and has succeeded in placing beyond the reach of corruption values he prefers not to examine. Even his multitudinous French friends help him to do this, for it is impossible, after all, to be friends with a mob: they are simply a cloud of faces, bearing witness to romance.

Between these two extremes, the student who embraces Home, and the student who embraces The Continent—both embraces, as we have tried to indicate, being singularly devoid of contact, to say nothing of love—there are far more gradations than can be suggested here. The American in Europe is everywhere confronted with the question of his identity, and this may be taken as the key to all the contradictions one encounters when attempting to discuss him. Certainly, for the student colony one finds no other common denominator—this is all, really, that they have in common, and they are distinguished from each other by the ways in which they come to terms, or fail to come to terms with their confusion. This prodigious question, at home so little recognized, seems, germ-like, to be vivified in the European air, and to grow disproportionately, displacing previous assurances, and producing tensions and bewilderments entirely unlooked for. It is not, moreover, a question which limits itself to those who are, so to speak, in traffic with ideas. It confronts everyone, finding everyone unprepared; it is a question with implications not easily escaped, and the attempt to escape can precipitate disaster. Our perfectly adapted student, for example, should his strongbox of custom break, may find himself hurled into that coterie of gold-bricks who form such a spectacular element of the Paris scene that they are often what the Parisian has in the foreground of his mind when he wonderingly mutters, *C'est vraiment les Américains.* The great majority of this group, having attempted, on more or less personal levels, to lose or disguise their antecedents, are reduced to a kind of rubble of compulsion. Having cast off all previous disciplines, they have also lost the shape which these disciplines made for them and have not succeeded in finding any other. Their rejection of the limitations of American society has not set them free to function in any other society, and their illusions, therefore, remain intact: they have yet to be corrupted by the notion that society is never anything less than a perfect labyrinth of limitations. They are charmed by the reflection that Paris is more than two thousand years old, but it escapes them that the Parisian has been in the making just about that long, and that one does not, therefore, become Parisian by virtue of a Paris address. This little band of bohemians, as grimly single-minded as any evangelical sect, illustrate, by the very ferocity with which they disavow American attitudes, one of the most American of attributes, the inability to believe that time is real. It is this inability which makes them so romantic about the nature of society, and it is this inability which has led them into a total confusion about the nature of experience. Society, it would seem, is a flimsy structure, beneath contempt, designed by and for all the other people, and experience is nothing more than sensation—so many sensations, added up like arithmetic, give one the rich, full life. They thus lose what it was they so bravely set out to find, their own personalities, which, having been deprived of all nourishment, soon cease, in effect, to exist; and they arrive, finally, at a dangerous disrespect for the personalities of others. Though they persist in believing that their present shapelessness is freedom, it is observable that this present freedom is unable to endure either silence or privacy, and demands, for its ultimate expression, a rootless wandering among the cafés. Saint Germain des Près, the heart of the American colony, so far from having absorbed the American student, has been itself transformed, on spring, summer, and fall nights, into a replica, very nearly, of Times Square.

But if this were all one found in the American student

colony, one would hardly have the heart to discuss it. If the American found in Europe only confusion, it would obviously be infinitely wiser for him to remain at home. Hidden, however, in the heart of the confusion he encounters here is that which he came so blindly seeking: the terms on which he is related to his country, and to the world. This, which has so grandiose and general a ring, is, in fact, most personal—the American confusion seeming to be based on the very nearly unconscious assumption that it is possible to consider the person apart from all the forces which have produced him. This assumption, however, is itself based on nothing less than our history, which is the history of the total, and willing, alienation of entire peoples from their forebears. What is overwhelmingly clear, it seems, to everyone but ourselves is that this history has created an entirely unprecedented people, with a unique and individual past. It is, indeed, this past which has thrust upon us our present, so troubling role. It is the past lived on the American continent, as against that other past, irrecoverable now on the shores of Europe, which must sustain us in the present. The truth about that past is not that it is too brief, or too superficial, but only that we, having turned our faces so resolutely away from it, have never demanded from it what it has to give. It is this demand which the American student in Paris is forced, at length, to make, for he has otherwise no identity, no reason for being here, nothing to sustain him here. From the vantage point of Europe he discovers his own country. And this is a discovery which not only brings to an end the alienation of the American from himself, but which also makes clear to him, for the first time, the extent of his involvement in the life of Europe.

Equal in Paris

On the 19th of December, in 1949, when I had been living in Paris for a little over a year, I was arrested as a receiver of stolen goods and spent eight days in prison. My arrest came about through an American tourist whom I had met twice in New York, who had been given my name and address and told to look me up. I was then living on the top floor of a ludicrously grim hotel on the rue du Bac, one of those enormous dark, cold, and hideous establishments in which Paris abounds that seem to breathe forth, in their airless, humid, stone-cold halls, the weak light, scurrying chambermaids, and creaking stairs, an odor of gentility long long dead. The place was run by an ancient Frenchman dressed in an elegant black suit which was green with age, who cannot properly be described as bewildered or even as being in a state of shock, since he had really stopped breathing around 1910. There he sat at his desk in the weirdly lit, fantastically furnished lobby, day in and day out, greeting each one of his extremely impoverished and *louche* lodgers with a stately inclination of the head that he had no doubt been taught in some impossibly remote time was the proper way for a *propriétaire* to greet his guests. If it had not been for his daughter, an extremely hardheaded *tricoteuse*—the inclination of *her* head was chilling and abrupt, like the downbeat of an ax— the hotel would certainly have gone bankrupt long before. It was said that this old man had not gone farther than the door of his hotel for thirty years, which was not at all difficult to believe. He looked as though the daylight would have killed him.

I did not, of course, spend much of my time in this palace. The moment I began living in French hotels I understood the necessity of French cafés. This made it rather difficult to look me up, for as soon as I was out of bed I hopefully took notebook and fountain pen off to the upstairs room of the Flore, where I consumed rather a lot of coffee and, as evening approached, rather a lot of alcohol, but did not get much writing done. But one night, in one of the cafés of St. Germain des

Près, I was discovered by this New Yorker and only because we found ourselves in Paris we immediately established the illusion that we had been fast friends back in the good old U.S.A. This illusion proved itself too thin to support an evening's drinking, but by that time it was too late. I had committed myself to getting him a room in my hotel the next day, for he was living in one of the nest of hotels near the Gare St. Lazare, where, he said, the *propriétaire* was a thief, his wife a repressed nymphomaniac, the chambermaids "pigs," and the rent a crime. Americans are always talking this way about the French and so it did not occur to me that he meant what he said or that he would take into his own hands the means of avenging himself on the French Republic. It did not occur to me, either, that the means which he *did* take could possibly have brought about such dire results, results which were not less dire for being also comic-opera.

It came as the last of a series of disasters which had perhaps been made inevitable by the fact that I had come to Paris originally with a little over forty dollars in my pockets, nothing in the bank, and no grasp whatever of the French language. It developed, shortly, that I had no grasp of the French character either. I considered the French an ancient, intelligent, and cultured race, which indeed they are. I did not know, however, that ancient glories imply, at least in the middle of the present century, present fatigue and, quite probably, paranoia; that there is a limit to the role of the intelligence in human affairs; and that no people come into possession of a culture without having paid a heavy price for it. This price they cannot, of course, assess, but it is revealed in their personalities and in their institutions. The very word "institutions," from my side of the ocean, where, it seemed to me, we suffered so cruelly from the lack of them, had a pleasant ring, as of safety and order and common sense; one had to come into contact with these institutions in order to understand that they were also outmoded, exasperating, completely impersonal, and very often cruel. Similarly, the personality which had seemed from a distance to be so large and free had to be dealt with before one could see that, if it was large, it was also inflexible and, for the foreigner, full of strange, high, dusty rooms which could not be inhabited. One had, in short, to come into contact with an alien culture in order to understand that a culture was not a community basket-weaving project, nor yet an act of God; was something neither desirable nor undesirable in itself, being inevitable, being nothing more or less than the recorded and visible effects on a body of people of the vicissitudes with which they had been forced to deal. And their great men are revealed as simply another of these vicissitudes, even if, quite against their will, the brief battle of their great men with them has left them richer.

When my American friend left his hotel to move to mine, he took with him, out of pique, a bedsheet belonging to the hotel and put it in his suitcase. When he arrived at my hotel I borrowed the sheet, since my own were filthy and the chambermaid showed no sign of bringing me any clean ones, and put it on my bed. The sheets belonging to *my* hotel I put out in the hall, congratulating myself on having thus forced on the attention of the Grand Hôtel du Bac the unpleasant state of its linen. Thereafter, since, as it turned out, we kept very different hours—I got up at noon, when, as I gathered by meeting him on the stairs one day, he was only just getting in—my new-found friend and I saw very little of each other.

On the evening of the 19th I was sitting thinking melancholy thoughts about Christmas and staring at the walls of my room. I imagine that I had sold something or that someone had sent me a Christmas present, for I remember that I had a little money. In those days in Paris, though I floated, so to speak, on a sea of acquaintances, I knew almost no one. Many people were eliminated from my orbit by virtue of the fact that they had more money than I did, which placed me, in my own eyes, in the humiliating role of a free-loader; and other people were eliminated by virtue of the fact that they enjoyed their poverty, shrilly insisting that this wretched round of hotel rooms, bad food, humiliating concierges, and unpaid bills was the Great Adventure. It couldn't, however, for me, end soon enough, this Great Adventure; there was a real question in my mind as to which would end soonest, the Great Adventure or me. This meant, however, that there were many evenings when I sat in my room, knowing that I couldn't work there, and not knowing what to do, or whom to see. On this particular evening I went down and knocked on the American's door.

There were two Frenchmen standing in the room, who immediately introduced themselves to me as policemen; which did not worry me. I had got used to policemen in Paris bobbing up at the most improbable times and places, asking to see one's *carte d'identité*. These policemen, however, showed very little interest in my papers. They were looking for something else. I could not imagine what this would be and, since I knew I certainly didn't have it, I scarcely followed the conversation they were having with my friend. I gathered that they were looking for some kind of gangster and since I wasn't a gangster and knew that gangsterism was not, insofar as he had one, my friend's style, I was sure that the two policemen would presently bow and say *Merci, messieurs*, and leave. For by this time, I remember very clearly, I was dying to have a drink and go to dinner.

I did not have a drink or go to dinner for many days after this, and when I did my outraged stomach promptly heaved everything up again. For now one of the policemen began to exhibit the most vivid interest in me and asked, very politely, if he might see my room. To which we mounted, making, I remember, the most civilized small talk on the way and even continuing it for some moments after we were in the room in which there was certainly nothing to be seen but the familiar poverty and disorder of that precarious group of people of whatever age, race, country, calling, or intention which Paris recognizes as *les étudiants* and sometimes, more ironically and precisely, as *les nonconformistes*. Then he moved to my bed, and in a terrible flash, not quite an instant before he lifted the bedspread, I understood what he was looking for. We looked at the sheet, on which I read, for the first time, lettered in the most brilliant scarlet I have ever seen, the name of the hotel from which it had been stolen. It was the first time the word *stolen* entered my mind. I had certainly seen the hotel monogram the day I put the sheet on the bed. It had simply meant nothing to me. In New York I had seen hotel monograms on everything from silver to soap and towels. Taking things from New York hotels was practically a custom, though, I suddenly realized, I had never known anyone to take a *sheet*. Sadly, and without a word to me, the inspector took the sheet from the bed, folded it under his arm, and we started back downstairs. I understood that I was under arrest.

And so we passed through the lobby, four of us, two of us very clearly criminal, under the eyes of the old man and his daughter, neither of whom said a word, into the streets where a light rain was falling. And I asked, in French, "But is this very serious?"

For I was thinking, it is, after all, only a sheet, not even new.

"No," said one of them. "It's not serious."

"It's nothing at all," said the other.

I took this to mean that we would receive a reprimand at the police station and be allowed to go to dinner. Later on I concluded that they were not being hypocritical or even trying to comfort us. They meant exactly what they said. It was only that they spoke another language.

In Paris everything is very slow. Also, when dealing with the bureaucracy, the man you are talking to is never the man you have to see. The man you have to see has just gone off to Belgium, or is busy with his family, or has just discovered that he is a cuckold; he will be in next Tuesday at three o'clock, or sometime in the course of the afternoon, or possibly tomorrow, or, possibly, in the next five minutes. But if he is coming in the next five minutes he will be far too busy to be able to see you today. So that I suppose I was not really astonished to learn at the commissariat that nothing could possibly be done about us before The Man arrived in the morning. But no, we could not go off and have dinner and come back in the morning. Of course he knew that we *would* come back—that was not the question. Indeed, there was no question: we would simply have to stay there for the night. We were placed in a cell which rather resembled a chicken coop. It was now about seven in the evening and I relinquished the thought of dinner and began to think of lunch.

I discouraged the chatter of my New York friend and this left me alone with my thoughts. I was beginning to be frightened and I bent all my energies, therefore, to keeping my panic under control. I began to realize that I was in a country

I knew nothing about, in the hands of a people I did not understand at all. In a similar situation in New York I would have had some idea of what to do because I would have had some idea of what to expect. I am not speaking now of legality which, like most of the poor, I had never for an instant trusted, but of the temperament of the people with whom I had to deal. I had become very accomplished in New York at guessing and, therefore, to a limited extent manipulating to my advantage the reactions of the white world. But this was not New York. None of my old weapons could serve me here. I did not know what they saw when they looked at me. I knew very well what Americans saw when they looked at me and this allowed me to play endless and sinister variations on the role which they had assigned me; since I knew that it was, for them, of the utmost importance that they never be confronted with what, in their own personalities, made this role so necessary and gratifying to them, I knew that they could never call my hand or, indeed, afford to know what I was doing; so that I moved into every crucial situation with the deadly and rather desperate advantages of bitterly accumulated perception, of pride and contempt. This is an awful sword and shield to carry through the world, and the discovery that, in the game I was playing, I did myself a violence of which the world, at its most ferocious, would scarcely have been capable, was what had driven me out of New York. It was a strange feeling, in this situation, after a year in Paris, to discover that my weapons would never again serve me as they had.

It was quite clear to me that the Frenchmen in whose hands I found myself were no better or worse than their American counterparts. Certainly their uniforms frightened me quite as much, and their impersonality, and the threat, always very keenly felt by the poor, of violence, was as present in that commissariat as it had ever been for me in any police station. And I had seen, for example, what Paris policemen could do to Arab peanut vendors. The only difference here was that I did not understand these people, did not know what techniques their cruelty took, did not know enough about their personalities to see danger coming, to ward it off, did not know on what ground to meet it. That evening in the commissariat I was not a despised black man. They would simply have laughed at me if I had behaved like one. For them, I was an American. And here it was they who had the advantage, for that word, *Américain*, gave them some idea, far from inaccurate, of what to expect from me. In order to corroborate none of their ironical expectations I said nothing and did nothing—which was not the way any Frenchman, white or black, would have reacted. The question thrusting up from the bottom of my mind was not *what* I was, but *who*. And this question, since a *what* can get by with skill but a *who* demands resources, was my first real intimation of what humility must mean.

In the morning it was still raining. Between nine and ten o'clock a black Citroën took us off to the Ile de la Cité, to the great, gray Préfecture. I realize now that the questions I put to the various policemen who escorted us were always answered in such a way as to corroborate what I wished to hear. This was not out of politeness, but simply out of indifference—or, possibly, an ironical pity—since each of the policemen knew very well that nothing would speed or halt the machine in which I had become entangled. They knew I did not know this and there was certainly no point in their telling me. In one way or another I would certainly come out at the other side—for they also knew that being found with a stolen bedsheet in one's possession was not a crime punishable by the guillotine. (They had the advantage over me there, too, for there were certainly moments later on when I was not so sure.) If I did *not* come out at the other side—well, that was just too bad. So, to my question, put while we were in the Citroën—"Will it be over today?"—I received a *"Oui, bien sûr."* He was not lying. As it turned out, the *procès-verbal* was over that day. Trying to be realistic, I dismissed, in the Citroën, all thoughts of lunch and pushed my mind ahead to dinner.

At the Préfecture we were first placed in a tiny cell, in which it was almost impossible either to sit or to lie down. After a couple of hours of this we were taken down to an office, where, for the first time, I encountered the owner of the bedsheet and where the *procès-verbal* took place. This was simply an interrogation, quite chillingly clipped and efficient (so that there was, shortly, no doubt in one's own mind that one *should* be treated as a criminal), which was recorded by a secretary. When it was over, this report was given to us to sign. One had, of course, no choice but to sign it, even though my mastery of written French was very far from certain. We were being held, according to the law in France, incommunicado, and all my angry demands to be allowed to speak to my embassy or to see a lawyer met with a stony *"Oui, oui. Plus tard."* The *procès-verbal* over, we were taken back to the cell, before which, shortly, passed the owner of the bedsheet. He said he hoped we had slept well, gave a vindictive wink, and disappeared.

By this time there was only one thing clear: that we had no way of controlling the sequence of events and could not possibly guess what this sequence would be. It seemed to me, since what I regarded as the high point—the *procès-verbal*—had been passed and since the hotelkeeper was once again in possession of his sheet, that we might reasonably expect to be released from police custody in a matter of hours. We had been detained now for what would soon be twenty-four hours, during which time I had learned only that the official charge against me was *receleur*. My mental shifting, between lunch and dinner, to say nothing of the physical lack of either of these delights, was beginning to make me dizzy. The steady chatter of my friend from New York, who was determined to keep my spirits up, made me feel murderous; I was praying that some power would release us from this freezing pile of stone before the impulse became the act. And I was beginning to wonder what was happening in that beautiful city, Paris, which lived outside these walls. I wondered how long it would take before anyone casually asked, "But where's Jimmy? He hasn't been around"—and realized, knowing the people I knew, that it would take several days.

Quite late in the afternoon we were taken from our cells; handcuffed, each to a separate officer; led through a maze of steps and corridors to the top of the building; finger-printed; photographed. As in movies I had seen, I was placed against a wall, facing an old-fashioned camera, behind which stood one of the most completely cruel and indifferent faces I had ever seen, while someone next to me and, therefore, just outside my line of vision, read off in a voice from which all human feeling, even feeling of the most base description, had long since fled, what must be called my public characteristics—which, at that time and in that place, seemed anything but that. He might have been roaring to the hostile world secrets which I could barely, in the privacy of midnight, utter to myself. But he was only reading off my height, my features, my approximate weight, my color—that color which, in the United States, had often, odd as it may sound, been my salvation—the color of my hair, my age, my nationality. A light then flashed, the photographer and I staring at each other as though there was murder in our hearts, and then it was over. Handcuffed again, I was led downstairs to the bottom of the building, into a great enclosed shed in which had been gathered the very scrapings off the Paris streets. Old, old men, so ruined and old that life in them seemed really to prove the miracle of the quickening power of the Holy Ghost—for clearly their life was no longer their affair, it was no longer even their burden, they were simply the clay which had once been touched. And men not so old, with faces the color of lead and the consistency of oatmeal, eyes that made me think of stale *café-au-lait* spiked with arsenic, bodies which could take in food and water—any food and water—and pass it out, but which could not do anything more, except possibly, at midnight, along the riverbank where rats scurried, rape. And young men, harder and crueler than the Paris stones, older by far than I, their chronological senior by some five to seven years. And North Africans, old and young, who seemed the only living people in this place because they yet retained the grace to be bewildered. But they were not bewildered by being in this shed: they were simply bewildered because they were no longer in North Africa. There was a great hole in the center of this shed, which was the common toilet. Near it, though it was impossible to get very far from it, stood an old man with white hair, eating a piece of camembert. It was at this point, probably, that thought, for me, stopped, that physiology, if one may say so, took over. I found myself incapable of saying a word, not because I was afraid I would cry but because I was afraid I would vomit. And I did not think any longer of the city of Paris but my mind flew back to that home from which I had fled. I was sure that I would never see it any more. And it must have seemed to me that my flight from home was the cruelest trick I had ever played on myself, since it had led me here, down to a lower point than any I could ever in my life have imagined—lower, far, than anything I had seen in that Harlem which I had so hated and so loved, the escape from which had soon become the greatest direction of my life. After we had been here an hour or so a functionary came and opened the door and called out our names. And I was sure that *this* was my release. But I was handcuffed again and led out of the Préfecture into the streets—it was dark now, it was still raining—and before the steps of the Préfecture stood the great police wagon, doors facing me, wide open. The handcuffs were taken off, I entered the wagon, which was peculiarly constructed. It was divided by a narrow aisle, and on each side of the aisle was a series of narrow doors. These doors opened on a narrow cubicle, beyond which was a door which opened onto another narrow cubicle: three or four cubicles, each private, with a locking door. I was placed in one of them; I remember there was a small vent just above my head which let in a little light. The door of my cubicle was locked from the outside. I had no idea where this wagon was taking me and, as it began to move, I began to cry. I suppose I cried all the way to prison, the prison called Fresnes, which is twelve kilometers outside of Paris.

For reasons I have no way at all of understanding, prisoners whose last initial is A, B, or C are always sent to Fresnes; everybody else is sent to a prison called, rather cynically it seems to me, La Santé. I will, obviously, never be allowed to enter La Santé, but I was told by people who certainly seemed to know that it was infinitely more unbearable than Fresnes. This arouses in me, until today, a positive storm of curiosity concerning what I promptly began to think of as The Other Prison. My colleague in crime, occurring lower in the alphabet, had been sent there and I confess that the minute he was gone I missed him. I missed him because he was not French and because he was the only person in the world who knew that the story I told was true.

For, once locked in, divested of shoelaces, belt, watch, money, papers, nailfile, in a freezing cell in which both the window and the toilet were broken, with six other adventurers, the story I told of *l'affaire du drap de lit* elicited only the wildest amusement or the most suspicious disbelief. Among the people who shared my cell the first three days no one, it is true, had been arrested for anything much more serious—or, at least, not serious in my eyes. I remember that there was a boy who had stolen a knitted sweater from a *monoprix*, who would probably, it was agreed, receive a six-month sentence. There was an older man there who had been arrested for some kind of petty larceny. There were two North Africans, vivid, brutish, and beautiful, who alternated between gaiety and fury, not at the fact of their arrest but at the state of the cell. None poured as much emotional energy into the fact of their arrest as I did; they took it, as I would have liked to take it, as simply another unlucky happening in a very dirty world. For, though I had grown accustomed to thinking of myself as looking upon the world with a hard, penetrating eye, the truth was that they were far more realistic about the world than I, and more nearly right about it. The gap between us, which only a gesture I made could have bridged, grew steadily, during thirty-six hours, wider. I could not make any gesture simply because they frightened me. I was unable to accept my imprisonment as a fact, even as a temporary fact. I could not, even for a moment, accept my present companions as *my* companions. And they, of course, felt this and put it down, with perfect justice, to the fact that I was an American.

There was nothing to do all day long. It appeared that we would one day come to trial but no one knew when. We were awakened at seven thirty by a rapping on what I believe is called the Judas, that small opening in the door of the cell which allows the guards to survey the prisoners. At this rapping we rose from the floor—we slept on straw pallets and each of us was covered with one thin blanket—and moved to the door of the cell. We peered through the opening into the center of the prison, which was, as I remember, three tiers high, all gray stone and gunmetal steel, precisely that prison I had seen in movies, except that, in the movies, I had not known that it was cold in prison. I had not known that when one's shoelaces and belt have been removed one is, in the strangest way, demoralized. The necessity of shuffling and the necessity of holding up one's trousers with one hand turn one into a rag doll. And the movies fail, of course, to give one any idea of what prison food is like. Along the corridor, at seven-thirty, came three men, each pushing before him a great garbage can, mounted on wheels. In the garbage can of the first was the bread—this was passed to one through the small opening in the door. In the can of the second was the coffee. In the can of the third was what was always called *la soupe*, a pallid paste of potatoes which had certainly been bubbling on the back of the prison stove long before that first, so momentous revolution. Naturally, it was cold by this time and, starving as I was, I could not eat it. I drank the coffee—which was not coffee—because it was hot, and spent the rest of the day, huddled in my blanket, munching on the bread. It was not the French bread one bought in bakeries. In the evening the same procession returned. At ten-thirty the lights went out. I had a recurring dream, each night, a nightmare which always involved my mother's fried chicken. At the moment I was about to eat it came the rapping at the door. Silence is really all I remember of those first three days, silence and the color gray.

I am not sure now whether it was on the third or the fourth day that I was taken to trial for the first time. The days had nothing, obviously, to distinguish them from one another. I remember that I was very much aware that Christmas Day was approaching and I wondered if I was really going to spend Christmas Day in prison. And I remember that the first trial came the day before Christmas Eve.

On the morning of the first trial I was awakened by hearing my name called. I was told, hanging in a kind of void between my mother's fried chicken and the cold prison floor, *"Vous préparez. Vous êtes extrait"*—which simply terrified me, since I did not know what interpretation to put on the word *"extrait,"* and since my cellmates had been amusing themselves with me by telling terrible stories about the inefficiency of French prisons, an inefficiency so extreme that it had often happened that someone who was supposed to be taken out and tried found himself on the wrong line and was guillotined instead. The best way of putting my reaction to this is to say that, though I knew they were teasing me, it was simply not possible for me to totally *dis*believe them. As far as I was concerned, once in the hands of the law in France, anything could happen. I shuffled along with the others who were *extrait* to the center of the prison, trying, rather, to linger in the office, which seemed the only warm spot in the whole world, and found myself again in that dreadful wagon, and was carried again to the Ile de la Cité, this time to the Palais de Justice. The entire day, except for ten minutes, was spent in one of the cells, first waiting to be tried, then waiting to be taken back to prison.

For I was *not* tried that day. By and by I was handcuffed and led through the halls, upstairs to the courtroom where I found my New York friend. We were placed together, both stage-whisperingly certain that this was the end of our ordeal. Nevertheless, while I waited for our case to be called, my eyes searched the courtroom, looking for a face I knew, hoping, anyway, that there was someone there who knew *me*, who would carry to someone outside the news that I was in trouble. But there was no one I knew there and I had had time to realize that there was probably only one man in Paris who could help me, an American patent attorney for whom I had worked as an office boy. He could have helped me because he had a quite solid position and some prestige and would have testified that, while working for him, I had handled large sums of money regularly, which made it rather unlikely that I would stoop to trafficking in bedsheets. However, he was somewhere in Paris, probably at this very moment enjoying a snack and a glass of wine and as far as the possibility of reaching him was concerned, he might as well have been on Mars. I tried to watch the proceedings and to make my mind a blank. But the proceedings were not reassuring. The boy, for example, who had stolen the sweater *did* receive a six-month sentence. It seemed to me that all the sentences meted out that day were excessive; though, again, it seemed that all the people who were sentenced that day had made, or clearly were going to make, crime their career. This seemed to be the opinion of the judge, who scarcely looked at the prisoners or listened to them; it seemed to be the opinion of the prisoners, who scarcely bothered to speak in their own behalf; it seemed to be the opinion of the lawyers, state lawyers for the most part, who were defending them. The great impulse of the courtroom seemed to be to put these people where they could not be seen—and not because they were offended at the crimes, unless, indeed, they were offended that the crimes were so petty, but because they did not wish to know that their society could be counted on to produce, probably in greater and greater numbers, a whole body of people for whom crime was the only possible career. Any society inevitably produces its criminals, but a society at once rigid and unstable can do nothing whatever to alleviate the poverty of its lowest members, cannot present to the hypothetical young man at the crucial moment that so-well-advertised right path. And the fact, perhaps, that the French are the earth's least sentimental people and must also be numbered among the most proud aggravates the plight of their lowest, youngest, and unluckiest members, for it means that the idea of rehabilitation is scarcely real to them. I confess that this attitude on their part raises in me sentiments of exasperation, admiration, and despair, revealing as it does, in both the best and the worst sense, their renowned and spectacular hardheadedness.

Finally our case was called and we rose. We gave our names. At the point that it developed that we were American the proceedings ceased, a hurried consultation took place between the judge and what I took to be several lawyers. Someone called out for an interpreter. The arresting officer had forgotten to mention our nationalities and there was, therefore, no interpreter in the court. Even if our French had been better than it was we would not have been allowed to stand trial without an interpreter. Before I clearly understood what was happening, I was handcuffed again and led out of the courtroom. The trial had been set back for the 27th of December.

I have sometimes wondered if I would *ever* have got out of prison if it had not been for the older man who had been arrested for the mysterious petty larceny. He was acquitted that day and when he returned to the cell—for he could not be released until morning—he found me sitting numbly on the floor, having just been prevented, by the sight of a man, all blood, being carried back to *his* cell on a stretcher, from seizing the bars and screaming until they let me out. The sight of the man on the stretcher proved, however, that screaming would not do much for me. The petty-larceny man went around asking if he could do anything in the world outside for those he was leaving behind. When he came to me I, at first, responded, "No, nothing"—for I suppose I had by now retreated into the attitude, the earliest I remember, that of my father, which was simply (since I had lost his God) that nothing could help me. And I suppose I will remember with gratitude until I die the fact that the man now insisted: "*Mais, êtes-vous sûr?*" Then it swept over me that he was going *outside* and he instantly became my first contact since the Lord alone knew how long with the outside world. At the same time, I remember, I did not really believe that he would help me. There was no reason why he should. But I gave him the phone number of my attorney friend and my own name.

So, in the middle of the next day, Christmas Eve, I shuffled downstairs again, to meet my visitor. He looked extremely well fed and sane and clean. He told me I had nothing to worry about any more. Only not even he could do anything to make the mill of justice grind any faster. He would, however, send me a lawyer of his acquaintance who would defend me on the 27th, and he would himself, along with several other people, appear as a character witness. He gave me a package of Lucky Strikes (which the turnkey took from me on the way upstairs) and said that, though it was doubtful that there would be any celebration in the prison, he would see to it that I got a fine Christmas dinner when I got out. And this, somehow, seemed very funny. I remember being astonished at the discovery that I was actually laughing. I was, too, I imagine, also rather disappointed that my hair had not turned white, that my face was clearly not going to bear any marks of tragedy, disappointed at bottom, no doubt, to realize, facing him in that room, that far worse things had happened to most people and that, indeed, to paraphrase my mother, if this was the worst thing that ever happened to me I could consider myself among the luckiest people ever to be born. He injected—my visitor—into my solitary nightmare common sense, the world, and the hint of blacker things to come.

The next day, Christmas, unable to endure my cell, and feeling that, after all, the day demanded a gesture, I asked to be allowed to go to Mass, hoping to hear some music. But I found myself, for a freezing hour and a half, locked in exactly the same kind of cubicle as in the wagon which had first brought me to prison, peering through a slot placed at the level of the eye at an old Frenchman, hatted, overcoated, muffled, and gloved, preaching in this language which I did not understand, to this row of wooden boxes, the story of Jesus Christ's love for men.

The next day, the 26th, I spent learning a peculiar kind of game, played with match-sticks, with my cellmates. For, since I no longer felt that I would stay in this cell forever, I was beginning to be able to make peace with it for a time. On the 27th I went again to trial and, as had been predicted, the case against us was dismissed. The story of the *drap de lit*, finally told, caused great merriment in the courtroom, whereupon my friend decided that the French were "great." I was chilled by their merriment, even though it was meant to warm me. It could only remind me of the laughter I had often heard at home, laughter which I had sometimes deliberately elicited. This laughter is the laughter of those who consider themselves to be at a safe remove from all the wretched, for whom the pain of the living is not real. I had heard it so often in my native land that I had resolved to find a place where I would never hear it any more. In some deep, black, stony, and liberating way, my life, in my own eyes, began during that first year in Paris, when it was borne in on me that this laughter is universal and never can be stilled.

Stranger in the Village

FROM ALL available evidence no black man had ever set foot in this tiny Swiss village before I came. I was told before arriving that I would probably be a "sight" for the village; I took this to mean that people of my complexion were rarely seen in Switzerland, and also that city people are always something of a "sight" outside of the city. It did not occur to me—possibly because I am an American—that there could be people anywhere who had never seen a Negro.

It is a fact that cannot be explained on the basis of the inaccessibility of the village. The village is very high, but it is only four hours from Milan and three hours from Lausanne. It is true that it is virtually unknown. Few people making plans for a holiday would elect to come here. On the other hand, the villagers are able, presumably, to come and go as they please—which they do: to another town at the foot of the mountain, with a population of approximately five thousand, the nearest place to see a movie or go to the bank. In the village there is no movie house, no bank, no library, no theater; very few radios, one jeep, one station wagon; and, at the moment, one typewriter, mine, an invention which the woman next door to me here had never seen. There are about six hundred people living here, all Catholic—I conclude this from the fact that the Catholic church is open all year round, whereas the Protestant chapel, set off on a hill a little removed from the village, is open only in the summertime when the tourists arrive. There are four or five hotels, all closed now, and four or five *bistros*, of which, however, only two do any business during the winter. These two do not do a great deal, for life in the village seems to end around nine or ten o'clock. There are a few stores, butcher, baker, *épicerie*, a hardware store, and a money-changer—who cannot change travelers' checks, but must send them down to the bank, an operation which takes two or three days. There is something called the *Ballet Haus*, closed in the winter and used for God knows what, certainly not ballet, during the summer. There seems to be only one schoolhouse in the village, and this for the quite young children; I suppose this to mean that their older brothers and sisters at some point descend from these mountains in order to complete their education—possibly, again, to the town just below. The landscape is absolutely forbidding, mountains towering on all four sides, ice and snow as far as the eye can reach. In this white wilderness, men and women and children move all day, carrying washing, wood, buckets of milk or water, sometimes skiing on Sunday afternoons. All week long boys and young men are to be seen shoveling snow off the rooftops, or dragging wood down from the forest in sleds.

The village's only real attraction, which explains the tourist season, is the hot spring water. A disquietingly high proportion of these tourists are cripples, or semi-cripples, who come year after year—from other parts of Switzerland, usually—to take the waters. This lends the village, at the height of the season, a rather terrifying air of sanctity, as though it were a lesser Lourdes. There is often something beautiful, there is always something awful, in the spectacle of a person who has lost one of his faculties, a faculty he never questioned until it was gone, and who struggles to recover it. Yet people remain people, on crutches or indeed on deathbeds; and wherever I passed, the first summer I was here, among the native villagers or among the lame, a wind passed with me—of astonishment, curiosity, amusement, and outrage. That first summer I stayed two weeks and never intended to return. But I did return in the winter, to work; the village offers, obviously, no distractions whatever and has the further advantage of being extremely cheap. Now it is winter again, a year later, and I am here again. Everyone in the village knows my name, though they scarcely ever use it, knows that I come from America—though, this, apparently, they will never really believe: black men come from Africa—and everyone knows that I am the friend of the son of a woman who was born here, and that I am staying in their chalet. But I remain as much a stranger today as I was the first day I arrived, and the children shout *Neger! Neger!* as I walk along the streets.

It must be admitted that in the beginning I was far too shocked to have any real reaction. In so far as I reacted at all, I reacted by trying to be pleasant—it being a great part of the

American Negro's education (long before he goes to school) that he must make people "like" him. This smile-and-the-world-smiles-with-you routine worked about as well in this situation as it had in the situation for which it was designed, which is to say that it did not work at all. No one, after all, can be liked whose human weight and complexity cannot be, or has not been, admitted. My smile was simply another un-heard-of phenomenon which allowed them to see my teeth—they did not, really, see my smile and I began to think that, should I take to snarling, no one would notice any difference. All of the physical characteristics of the Negro which had caused me, in America, a very different and almost forgotten pain were nothing less than miraculous—or infernal—in the eyes of the village people. Some thought my hair was the color of tar, that it had the texture of wire, or the texture of cotton. It was jocularly suggested that I might let it all grow long and make myself a winter coat. If I sat in the sun for more than five minutes some daring creature was certain to come along and gingerly put his fingers on my hair, as though he were afraid of an electric shock, or put his hand on my hand, aston-ished that the color did not rub off. In all of this, in which it must be conceded there was the charm of genuine wonder and in which there was certainly no element of intentional unkindness, there was yet no suggestion that I was human: I was simply a living wonder.

I knew that they did not mean to be unkind, and I know it now; it is necessary, nevertheless, for me to repeat this to myself each time that I walk out of the chalet. The children who shout *Neger!* have no way of knowing the echoes this sound raises in me. They are brimming with good humor and the more daring swell with pride when I stop to speak with them. Just the same, there are days when I cannot pause and smile, when I have no heart to play with them; when, indeed, I mutter sourly to myself, exactly as I muttered on the streets of a city these children have never seen, when I was no bigger than these children are now: *Your* mother *was a nigger.* Joyce is right about history being a nightmare—but it may be the nightmare from which no one *can* awaken. People are trapped in history and history is trapped in them.

There is a custom in the village—I am told it is repeated in many villages—of "buying" African natives for the purpose of converting them to Christianity. There stands in the church all year round a small box with a slot for money, decorated with a black figurine, and into this box the villagers drop their francs. During the *carnaval* which precedes Lent, two village children have their faces blackened—out of which bloodless darkness their blue eyes shine like ice—and fantastic horsehair wigs are placed on their blond heads; thus disguised, they solicit among the villagers for money for the missionaries in Africa. Between the box in the church and the blackened children, the village "bought" last year six or eight African natives. This was reported to me with pride by the wife of one of the *bistro* owners and I was careful to express astonishment and pleasure at the solicitude shown by the village for the souls of black folk. The *bistro* owner's wife beamed with a pleasure far more genuine than my own and seemed to feel that I might now breathe more easily concerning the souls of at least six of my kinsmen.

I tried not to think of these so lately baptized kinsmen, of the price paid for them, or the peculiar price they themselves would pay, and said nothing about my father, who having taken his own conversion too literally never, at bottom, forgave the white world (which he described as heathen) for having saddled him with a Christ in whom, to judge at least from their treatment of him, they themselves no longer believed. I thought of white men arriving for the first time in an African village, strangers there, as I am a stranger here, and tried to imagine the astounded populace touching their hair and marveling at the color of their skin. But there is a great difference between being the first white man to be seen by Africans and being the first black man to be seen by whites. The white man takes the astonishment as tribute, for he arrives to conquer and to convert the natives, whose inferiority in relation to himself is not even to be questioned; whereas I, without a thought of conquest, find myself among a people whose culture controls me, has even, in a sense, created me, people who have cost me more in anguish and rage than they will ever know, who yet do not even know of my existence. The astonishment with which I might have greeted them, should they have stumbled into my African village a few hundred years ago, might have rejoiced their hearts. But the astonishment with which they greet me today can only poison mine.

And this is so despite everything I may do to feel differently, despite my friendly conversations with the *bistro* owner's wife, despite their three-year-old son who has at last become my friend, despite the *saluts* and *bonsoirs* which I exchange with people as I walk, despite the fact that I know that no individual can be taken to task for what history is doing, or has done. I say that the culture of these people controls me—but they can scarcely be held responsible for European culture. America comes out of Europe, but these people have never seen America, nor have most of them seen more of Europe than the hamlet at the foot of their mountain. Yet they move with an authority which I shall never have; and they regard me, quite rightly, not only as a stranger in their village but as a suspect latecomer, bearing no credentials, to everything they have—however unconsciously—inherited.

For this village, even were it incomparably more remote and incredibly more primitive, is the West, the West onto which I have been so strangely grafted. These people cannot be, from the point of view of power, strangers anywhere in the world; they have made the modern world, in effect, even if they do not know it. The most illiterate among them is related, in a way that I am not, to Dante, Shakespeare, Michelangelo, Aeschylus, Da Vinci, Rembrandt, and Racine; the cathedral at Chartres says something to them which it cannot say to me, as indeed would New York's Empire State Building, should anyone here ever see it. Out of their hymns and dances come Beethoven and Bach. Go back a few centuries and they are in their full glory—but I am in Africa, watching the conquerors arrive.

The rage of the disesteemed is personally fruitless, but it is also absolutely inevitable; this rage, so generally discounted, so little understood even among the people whose daily bread it is, is one of the things that makes history. Rage can only with difficulty, and never entirely, be brought under the domination of the intelligence and is therefore not susceptible to any arguments whatever. This is a fact which ordinary representatives of the *Herrenvolk*, having never felt this rage and being unable to imagine it, quite fail to understand. Also, rage cannot be hidden, it can only be dissembled. This dissembling deludes the thoughtless, and strengthens rage and adds, to rage, contempt. There are, no doubt, as many ways of coping with the resulting complex of tensions as there are black men in the world, but no black man can hope ever to be entirely liberated from this internal warfare—rage, dissembling, and contempt having inevitably accompanied his first realization of the power of white men. What is crucial here is that, since white men represent in the black man's world so heavy a weight, white men have for black men a reality which is far from being reciprocal; and hence all black men have toward all white men an attitude which is designed, really, either to rob the white man of the jewel of his naïveté, or else to make it cost him dear.

The black man insists, by whatever means he finds at his disposal, that the white man cease to regard him as an exotic rarity and recognize him as a human being. This is a very charged and difficult moment, for there is a great deal of will power involved in the white man's naïveté. Most people are not naturally reflective any more than they are naturally malicious, and the white man prefers to keep the black man at a certain human remove because it is easier for him thus to preserve his simplicity and avoid being called to account for crimes committed by his forefathers, or his neighbors. He is inescapably aware, nevertheless, that he is in a better position in the world than black men are, nor can he quite put to death the suspicion that he is hated by black men therefore. He does not wish to be hated, neither does he wish to change places, and at this point in his uneasiness he can scarcely avoid having recourse to those legends which white men have created about black men, the most usual effect of which is that the white man finds himself enmeshed, so to speak, in his own language which describes hell, as well as the attributes which lead one to hell, as being as black as night.

Every legend, moreover, contains its residuum of truth, and the root function of language is to control the universe by describing it. It is of quite considerable significance that black men remain, in the imagination, and in overwhelming numbers in fact, beyond the disciplines of salvation; and this despite the fact that the West has been "buying" African natives

for centuries. There is, I should hazard, an instantaneous necessity to be divorced from this so visibly unsaved stranger, in
whose heart, moreover, one cannot guess what dreams of vengeance are being nourished; and, at the same time, there are
few things on earth more attractive than the idea of the unspeakable liberty which is allowed the unredeemed. When, beneath the black mask, a human being begins to make himself
felt one cannot escape a certain awful wonder as to what kind
of human being it is. What one's imagination makes of other
people is dictated, of course, by the laws of one's own personality and it is one of the ironies of black-white relations
that, by means of what the white man imagines the black
man to be, the black man is enabled to know who the white
man is.

I have said, for example, that I am as much a stranger in
this village today as I was the first summer I arrived, but this
is not quite true. The villagers wonder less about the texture
of my hair than they did then, and wonder rather more about
me. And the fact that their wonder now exists on another level
is reflected in their attitudes and in their eyes. There are the
children who make those delightful, hilarious, sometimes
astonishingly grave overtures of friendship in the unpredictable fashion of children; other children, having been taught
that the devil is a black man, scream in genuine anguish as I
approach. Some of the older women never pass without a
friendly greeting, never pass, indeed, if it seems that they will
be able to engage me in conversation; other women look
down or look away or rather contemptuously smirk. Some of
the men drink with me and suggest that I learn how to ski—
partly, I gather, because they cannot imagine what I would
look like on skis—and want to know if I am married, and ask
questions about my *métier*. But some of the men have accused
le sale nègre—behind my back—of stealing wood and there is
already in the eyes of some of them that peculiar, intent,
paranoiac malevolence which one sometimes surprises in the
eyes of American white men when, out walking with their
Sunday girl, they see a Negro male approach.

There is a dreadful abyss between the streets of this village
and the streets of the city in which I was born, between the
children who shout *Neger!* today and those who shouted

Nigger! yesterday—the abyss is experience, the American experience. The syllable hurled behind me today expresses, above all, wonder: I am a stranger here. But I am not a stranger in America and the same syllable riding on the American air expresses the war my presence has occasioned in the American soul.

For this village brings home to me this fact: that there was a day, and not really a very distant day, when Americans were scarcely Americans at all but discontented Europeans, facing a great unconquered continent and strolling, say, into a marketplace and seeing black men for the first time. The shock this spectacle afforded is suggested, surely, by the promptness with which they decided that these black men were not really men but cattle. It is true that the necessity on the part of the settlers of the New World of reconciling their moral assumptions with the fact—and the necessity—of slavery enhanced immensely the charm of this idea, and it is also true that this idea expresses, with a truly American bluntness, the attitude which to varying extents all masters have had toward all slaves.

But between all former slaves and slave-owners and the drama which begins for Americans over three hundred years ago at Jamestown, there are at least two differences to be observed. The American Negro slave could not suppose, for one thing, as slaves in past epochs had supposed and often done, that he would ever be able to wrest the power from his master's hands. This was a supposition which the modern era, which was to bring about such vast changes in the aims and dimensions of power, put to death; it only begins, in unprecedented fashion, and with dreadful implications, to be resurrected today. But even had this supposition persisted with undiminished force, the American Negro slave could not have used it to lend his condition dignity, for the reason that this supposition rests on another: that the slave in exile yet remains related to his past, has some means—if only in memory—of revering and sustaining the forms of his former life, is able, in short, to maintain his identity.

This was not the case with the American Negro slave. He is unique among the black men of the world in that his past was taken from him, almost literally, at one blow. One wonders what on earth the first slave found to say to the first dark child he bore. I am told that there are Haitians able to trace their ancestry back to African kings, but any American Negro wishing to go back so far will find his journey through time abruptly arrested by the signature on the bill of sale which served as the entrance paper for his ancestor. At the time—to say nothing of the circumstances—of the enslavement of the captive black man who was to become the American Negro, there was not the remotest possibility that he would ever take power from his master's hands. There was no reason to suppose that his situation would ever change, nor was there, shortly, anything to indicate that his situation had ever been different. It was his necessity, in the words of E. Franklin Frazier, to find a "motive for living under American culture or die." The identity of the American Negro comes out of this extreme situation, and the evolution of this identity was a source of the most intolerable anxiety in the minds and the lives of his masters.

For the history of the American Negro is unique also in this: that the question of his humanity, and of his rights therefore as a human being, became a burning one for several generations of Americans, so burning a question that it ultimately became one of those used to divide the nation. It is out of this argument that the venom of the epithet *Nigger!* is derived. It is an argument which Europe has never had, and hence Europe quite sincerely fails to understand how or why the argument arose in the first place, why its effects are so frequently disastrous and always so unpredictable, why it refuses until today to be entirely settled. Europe's black possessions remained—and do remain—in Europe's colonies, at which remove they represented no threat whatever to European identity. If they posed any problem at all for the European conscience, it was a problem which remained comfortingly abstract: in effect, the black man, *as a man*, did not exist for Europe. But in America, even as a slave, he was an inescapable part of the general social fabric and no American could escape having an attitude toward him. Americans attempt until today to make an abstraction of the Negro, but the very nature of these abstractions reveals the tremendous effects the presence of the Negro has had on the American character.

When one considers the history of the Negro in America it is of the greatest importance to recognize that the moral beliefs of a person, or a people, are never really as tenuous as life—which is not moral—very often causes them to appear; these create for them a frame of reference and a necessary hope, the hope being that when life has done its worst they will be enabled to rise above themselves and to triumph over life. Life would scarcely be bearable if this hope did not exist. Again, even when the worst has been said, to betray a belief is not by any means to have put oneself beyond its power; the betrayal of a belief is not the same thing as ceasing to believe. If this were not so there would be no moral standards in the world at all. Yet one must also recognize that morality is based on ideas and that all ideas are dangerous—dangerous because ideas can only lead to action and where the action leads no man can say. And dangerous in this respect: that confronted with the impossibility of remaining faithful to one's beliefs, and the equal impossibility of becoming free of them, one can be driven to the most inhuman excesses. The ideas on which American beliefs are based are not, though Americans often seem to think so, ideas which originated in America. They came out of Europe. And the establishment of democracy on the American continent was scarcely as radical a break with the past as was the necessity, which Americans faced, of broadening this concept to include black men.

This was, literally, a hard necessity. It was impossible, for one thing, for Americans to abandon their beliefs, not only because these beliefs alone seemed able to justify the sacrifices they had endured and the blood that they had spilled, but also because these beliefs afforded them their only bulwark against a moral chaos as absolute as the physical chaos of the continent it was their destiny to conquer. But in the situation in which Americans found themselves, these beliefs threatened an idea which, whether or not one likes to think so, is the very warp and woof of the heritage of the West, the idea of white supremacy.

Americans have made themselves notorious by the shrillness and the brutality with which they have insisted on this idea, but they did not invent it; and it has escaped the world's notice that those very excesses of which Americans have been guilty imply a certain, unprecedented uneasiness over the idea's life and power, if not, indeed, the idea's validity. The idea of white supremacy rests simply on the fact that white men are the creators of civilization (the present civilization, which is the only one that matters; all previous civilizations are simply "contributions" to our own) and are therefore civilization's guardians and defenders. Thus it was impossible for Americans to accept the black man as one of themselves, for to do so was to jeopardize their status as white men. But not so to accept him was to deny his human reality, his human weight and complexity, and the strain of denying the overwhelmingly undeniable forced Americans into rationalizations so fantastic that they approached the pathological.

At the root of the American Negro problem is the necessity of the American white man to find a way of living with the Negro in order to be able to live with himself. And the history of this problem can be reduced to the means used by Americans—lynch law and law, segregation and legal acceptance, terrorization and concession—either to come to terms with this necessity, or to find a way around it, or (most usually) to find a way of doing both these things at once. The resulting spectacle, at once foolish and dreadful, led someone to make the quite accurate observation that "the Negro-in-America is a form of insanity which overtakes white men."

In this long battle, a battle by no means finished, the unforeseeable effects of which will be felt by many future generations, the white man's motive was the protection of his identity; the black man was motivated by the need to establish an identity. And despite the terrorization which the Negro in America endured and endures sporadically until today, despite the cruel and totally inescapable ambivalence of his status in his country, the battle for his identity has long ago been won. He is not a visitor to the West, but a citizen there, an American; as American as the Americans who despise him, the Americans who fear him, the Americans who love him—the Americans who became less than themselves, or rose to be greater than themselves by virtue of the fact that the challenge he represented was inescapable. He is perhaps the only black man in the world whose relationship to white men is more terrible, more subtle, and more meaningful than the relationship of bitter possessed to uncertain possessor. His survival depended, and his development depends, on his ability to turn his peculiar status in the Western world to his own advantage and, it may be, to the very great advantage of that world. It remains for him to fashion out of his experience that which will give him sustenance, and a voice.

The cathedral at Chartres, I have said, says something to the people of this village which it cannot say to me; but it is important to understand that this cathedral says something to me which it cannot say to them. Perhaps they are struck by the power of the spires, the glory of the windows; but they have known God, after all, longer than I have known him, and in a different way, and I am terrified by the slippery bottomless well to be found in the crypt, down which heretics were hurled to death, and by the obscene, inescapable gargoyles jutting out of the stone and seeming to say that God and the devil can never be divorced. I doubt that the villagers think of the devil when they face a cathedral because they have never been identified with the devil. But I must accept the status which myth, if nothing else, gives me in the West before I can hope to change the myth.

Yet, if the American Negro has arrived at his identity by virtue of the absoluteness of his estrangement from his past, American white men still nourish the illusion that there is some means of recovering the European innocence, of returning to a state in which black men do not exist. This is one of the greatest errors Americans can make. The identity they fought so hard to protect has, by virtue of that battle, undergone a change: Americans are as unlike any other white people in the world as it is possible to be. I do not think, for example, that it is too much to suggest that the American vision of the world—which allows so little reality, generally speaking, for any of the darker forces in human life, which tends until today to paint moral issues in glaring black and white—owes a great deal to the battle waged by Americans to maintain between themselves and black men a human separation which could not be bridged. It is only now beginning to be borne in on us—very faintly, it must be admitted, very slowly, and very much against our will—that this vision of the world is dangerously inaccurate, and perfectly useless. For it protects our moral high-mindedness at the terrible expense of weakening our grasp of reality. People who shut their eyes to reality simply invite their own destruction, and anyone who insists on remaining in a state of innocence long after that innocence is dead turns himself into a monster.

The time has come to realize that the interracial drama acted out on the American continent has not only created a new black man, it has created a new white man, too. No road whatever will lead Americans back to the simplicity of this European village where white men still have the luxury of looking on me as a stranger. I am not, really, a stranger any longer for any American alive. One of the things that distinguishes Americans from other people is that no other people has ever been so deeply involved in the lives of black men, and vice versa. This fact faced, with all its implications, it can be seen that the history of the American Negro problem is not merely shameful, it is also something of an achievement. For even when the worst has been said, it must also be added that the perpetual challenge posed by this problem was always, somehow, perpetually met. It is precisely this black-white experience which may prove of indispensable value to us in the world we face today. This world is white no longer, and it will never be white again.

NOBODY KNOWS MY NAME

More Notes of a Native Son

for my brothers,
George, Wilmer
and
David

Contents

Introduction 135

PART ONE   Sitting in the House . . .

1. The Discovery of What It Means To Be an
   American 137

2. Princes and Powers 143

3. Fifth Avenue, Uptown: A Letter from
   Harlem 170

4. East River, Downtown: Postscript to a Letter
   from Harlem 180

5. A Fly in Buttermilk 187

6. Nobody Knows My Name: A Letter from
   the South 197

7. Faulkner and Desegregation 209

8. In Search of a Majority 215

PART TWO   . . . With Everything on My Mind

9. Notes for a Hypothetical Novel 222

10. The Male Prison 231

11. The Northern Protestant 236

12. Alas, Poor Richard   I. Eight Men 247
                         II. The Exile 252
                         III. Alas, Poor Richard. . . 258

13. The Black Boy Looks at the White Boy . . . 269

Introduction

These essays were written over the last six years, in various places and in many states of mind. These years seemed, on the whole, rather sad and aimless to me. My life in Europe was ending, not because I had decided that it should, but because it became clearer and clearer—as I dealt with the streets, the climate, and the temperament of Paris, fled to Spain and Corsica and Scandinavia—that something had ended for me. I rather think now, to tell the sober truth, that it was merely my youth, first youth, anyway, that was ending and I hated to see it go. In the context of my life, the end of my youth was signaled by the reluctant realization that I had, indeed, become a writer; so far, so good: now I would have to go the distance.

In America, the color of my skin had stood between myself and me; in Europe, that barrier was down. Nothing is more desirable than to be released from an affliction, but nothing is more frightening than to be divested of a crutch. It turned out that the question of who I was was not solved because I had removed myself from the social forces which menaced me—anyway, these forces had become interior, and I had dragged them across the ocean with me. The question of who I was had at last become a personal question, and the answer was to be found in me.

I think that there is always something frightening about this realization. I know it frightened me—that was one of the reasons that I dawdled in the European haven for so long. And yet, I could not escape the knowledge, though God knows I tried, that if I was still in need of havens, my journey had been for nothing. Havens are high-priced. The price exacted of the haven-dweller is that he contrive to delude himself into believing that he has found a haven. It would seem, unless one looks more deeply at the phenomenon, that most people are able to delude themselves and get through their lives quite happily. But I still believe that the unexamined life is not worth living: and I know that self-delusion, in the service of no matter what small or lofty cause, is a price no writer can afford. His subject is himself and the world and it requires every ounce of stamina he can summon to attempt to look on himself and the world as they are.

What it came to for me was that I no longer needed to fear leaving Europe, no longer needed to hide myself from the high and dangerous winds of the world. The world was enormous and I could go anywhere in it I chose—including America: and I decided to return here because I was afraid to. But the question which confronted me, nibbled at me, in my stony Corsican exile was: Am I afraid of returning to America? Or am I afraid of journeying any further with myself? Once this question had presented itself it would not be appeased, it had to be answered.

"Be careful what you set your heart upon," someone once said to me, "for it will surely be yours." Well, I had said that I was going to be a writer, God, Satan, and Mississippi notwithstanding, and that color did not matter, and that I was going to be free. And, here I was, left with only myself to deal with. It was entirely up to me.

These essays are a very small part of a private logbook. The question of color takes up much space in these pages, but the question of color, especially in this country, operates to hide the graver questions of the self. That is precisely why what we like to call "the Negro problem" is so tenacious in American life, and so dangerous. But my own experience proves to me that the connection between American whites and blacks is far deeper and more passionate than any of us like to think. And, even in icy Sweden, I found myself talking with a man whose endless questioning has given him himself, and who reminded me of black Baptist preachers. The questions which one asks oneself begin, at last, to illuminate the world, and become one's key to the experience of others. One can only face in others what one can face in oneself. On this confrontation depends the measure of our wisdom and compassion. This energy is all that one finds in the rubble of vanished civilizations, and the only hope for ours.

JAMES BALDWIN

1. The Discovery of What It Means To Be an American

"IT IS a complex fate to be an American," Henry James observed, and the principal discovery an American writer makes in Europe is just how complex this fate is. America's history, her aspirations, her peculiar triumphs, her even more peculiar defeats, and her position in the world—yesterday and today—are all so profoundly and stubbornly unique that the very word "America" remains a new, almost completely undefined and extremely controversial proper noun. No one in the world seems to know exactly what it describes, not even we motley millions who call ourselves Americans.

I left America because I doubted my ability to survive the fury of the color problem here. (Sometimes I still do.) I wanted to prevent myself from becoming *merely* a Negro; or, even, merely a Negro writer. I wanted to find out in what way the *specialness* of my experience could be made to connect me with other people instead of dividing me from them. (I was as isolated from Negroes as I was from whites, which is what happens when a Negro begins, at bottom, to believe what white people say about him.)

In my necessity to find the terms on which my experience could be related to that of others, Negroes and whites, writers and non-writers, I proved, to my astonishment, to be as American as any Texas G.I. And I found my experience was shared by every American writer I knew in Paris. Like me, they had been divorced from their origins, and it turned out to make very little difference that the origins of white Americans were European and mine were African—they were no more at home in Europe than I was.

The fact that I was the son of a slave and they were the sons of free men meant less, by the time we confronted each

137

other on European soil, than the fact that we were both searching for our separate identities. When we had found these, we seemed to be saying, why, then, we would no longer need to cling to the shame and bitterness which had divided us so long.

It became terribly clear in Europe, as it never had been here, that we knew more about each other than any European ever could. And it also became clear that, no matter where our fathers had been born, or what they had endured, the fact of Europe had formed us both was part of our identity and part of our inheritance.

I had been in Paris a couple of years before any of this became clear to me. When it did, I, like many a writer before me upon the discovery that his props have all been knocked out from under him, suffered a species of breakdown and was carried off to the mountains of Switzerland. There, in that absolutely alabaster landscape, armed with two Bessie Smith records and a typewriter, I began to try to re-create the life that I had first known as a child and from which I had spent so many years in flight.

It was Bessie Smith, through her tone and her cadence, who helped me to dig back to the way I myself must have spoken when I was a pickaninny, and to remember the things I had heard and seen and felt. I had buried them very deep. I had never listened to Bessie Smith in America (in the same way that, for years, I would not touch watermelon), but in Europe she helped to reconcile me to being a "nigger."

I do not think that I could have made this reconciliation here. Once I was able to accept my role—as distinguished, I must say, from my "place"—in the extraordinary drama which is America, I was released from the illusion that I hated America.

The story of what can happen to an American Negro writer in Europe simply illustrates, in some relief, what can happen to any American writer there. It is not meant, of course, to imply that it happens to them all, for Europe can be very crippling, too; and, anyway, a writer, when he has made his first breakthrough, has simply won a crucial skirmish in a dangerous, unending and unpredictable battle. Still, the breakthrough is important, and the point is that an American writer, in order to achieve it, very often has to leave this country.

The American writer, in Europe, is released, first of all, from the necessity of apologizing for himself. It is not until he *is* released from the habit of flexing his muscles and proving that he is just a "regular guy" that he realizes how crippling this habit has been. It is not necessary for him, there, to pretend to be something he is not, for the artist does not encounter in Europe the same suspicion he encounters here. Whatever the Europeans may actually think of artists, they have killed enough of them off by now to know that they are as real—and as persistent—as rain, snow, taxes or businessmen.

Of course, the reason for Europe's comparative clarity concerning the different functions of men in society is that European society has always been divided into classes in a way that American society never has been. A European writer considers himself to be part of an old and honorable tradition—of intellectual activity, of letters—and his choice of a vocation does not cause him any uneasy wonder as to whether or not it will cost him all his friends. But this tradition does not exist in America.

On the contrary, we have a very deep-seated distrust of real intellectual effort (probably because we suspect that it will destroy, as I hope it does, that myth of America to which we cling so desperately). An American writer fights his way to one of the lowest rungs on the American social ladder by means of pure bull-headedness and an indescribable series of odd jobs. He probably *has* been a "regular fellow" for much of his adult life, and it is not easy for him to step out of that lukewarm bath.

We must, however, consider a rather serious paradox: though American society is more mobile than Europe's, it is easier to cut across social and occupational lines there than it is here. This has something to do, I think, with the problem of status in American life. Where everyone has status, it is also perfectly possible, after all, that no one has. It seems inevitable, in any case, that a man may become uneasy as to just what his status is.

But Europeans have lived with the idea of status for a long

time. A man can be as proud of being a good waiter as of being a good actor, and, in neither case, feel threatened. And this means that the actor and the waiter can have a freer and more genuinely friendly relationship in Europe than they are likely to have here. The waiter does not feel, with obscure resentment, that the actor has "made it," and the actor is not tormented by the fear that he may find himself, tomorrow, once again a waiter.

This lack of what may roughly be called social paranoia causes the American writer in Europe to feel—almost certainly for the first time in his life—that he can reach out to everyone, that he is accessible to everyone and open to everything. This is an extraordinary feeling. He feels, so to speak, his own weight, his own value.

It is as though he suddenly came out of a dark tunnel and found himself beneath the open sky. And, in fact, in Paris, I began to see the sky for what seemed to be the first time. It was borne in on me—and it did not make me feel melancholy—that this sky had been there before I was born and would be there when I was dead. And it was up to me, therefore, to make of my brief opportunity the most that could be made.

I was born in New York, but have lived only in pockets of it. In Paris, I lived in all parts of the city—on the Right Bank and the Left, among the bourgeoisie and among *les misérables*, and knew all kinds of people, from pimps and prostitutes in Pigalle to Egyptian bankers in Neuilly. This may sound extremely unprincipled or even obscurely immoral: I found it healthy. I love to talk to people, all kinds of people, and almost everyone, as I hope we still know, loves a man who loves to listen.

This perpetual dealing with people very different from myself caused a shattering in me of preconceptions I scarcely knew I held. The writer is meeting in Europe people who are not American, whose sense of reality is entirely different from his own. They may love or hate or admire or fear or envy this country—they see it, in any case, from another point of view, and this forces the writer to reconsider many things he had always taken for granted. This reassessment, which can be very painful, is also very valuable.

This freedom, like all freedom, has its dangers and its responsibilities. One day it begins to be borne in on the writer,
and with great force, that he is living in Europe as an American. If he were living there as a European, he would be living
on a different and far less attractive continent.

This crucial day may be the day on which an Algerian taxi-
driver tells him how it feels to be an Algerian in Paris. It may
be the day on which he passes a café terrace and catches a
glimpse of the tense, intelligent and troubled face of Albert
Camus. Or it may be the day on which someone asks him to
explain Little Rock and he begins to feel that it would be
simpler—and, corny as the words may sound, more honorable—to *go* to Little Rock than sit in Europe, on an American
passport, trying to explain it.

This is a personal day, a terrible day, the day to which his
entire sojourn has been tending. It is the day he realizes that
there are no untroubled countries in this fearfully troubled
world; that if he has been preparing himself for anything in
Europe, he has been preparing himself—for America. In short,
the freedom that the American writer finds in Europe brings
him, full circle, back to himself, with the responsibility for his
development where it always was: in his own hands.

Even the most incorrigible maverick has to be born somewhere. He may leave the group that produced him—he may
be forced to—but nothing will efface his origins, the marks of
which he carries with him everywhere. I think it is important
to know this and even find it a matter for rejoicing, as the
strongest people do, regardless of their station. On this acceptance, literally, the life of a writer depends.

The charge has often been made against American writers
that they do not describe society, and have no interest in it.
They only describe individuals in opposition to it, or isolated
from it. Of course, what the American writer is describing is
his own situation. But what is *Anna Karenina* describing if
not the tragic fate of the isolated individual, at odds with her
time and place?

The real difference is that Tolstoy was describing an old and
dense society in which everything seemed—to the people in
it, though not to Tolstoy—to be fixed forever. And the book

is a masterpiece because Tolstoy was able to fathom, and make us see, the hidden laws which really governed this society and made Anna's doom inevitable.

American writers do not have a fixed society to describe. The only society they know is one in which nothing is fixed and in which the individual must fight for his identity. This is a rich confusion, indeed, and it creates for the American writer unprecedented opportunities.

That the tensions of American life, as well as the possibilities, are tremendous is certainly not even a question. But these are dealt with in contemporary literature mainly compulsively; that is, the book is more likely to be a symptom of our tension than an examination of it. The time has come, God knows, for us to examine ourselves, but we can only do this if we are willing to free ourselves of the myth of America and try to find out what is really happening here.

Every society is really governed by hidden laws, by unspoken but profound assumptions on the part of the people, and ours is no exception. It is up to the American writer to find out what these laws and assumptions are. In a society much given to smashing taboos without thereby managing to be liberated from them, it will be no easy matter.

It is no wonder, in the meantime, that the American writer keeps running off to Europe. He needs sustenance for his journey and the best models he can find. Europe has what we do not have yet, a sense of the mysterious and inexorable limits of life, a sense, in a word, of tragedy. And we have what they sorely need: a new sense of life's possibilities.

In this endeavor to wed the vision of the Old World with that of the New, it is the writer, not the statesman, who is our strongest arm. Though we do not wholly believe it yet, the interior life is a real life, and the intangible dreams of people have a tangible effect on the world.

2. Princes and Powers

THE Conference of Negro-African Writers and Artists (*Le Congrès des Ecrivains et Artistes Noirs*) opened on Wednesday, September 19, 1956, in the Sorbonne's Amphitheatre Descartes, in Paris. It was one of those bright, warm days which one likes to think of as typical of the atmosphere of the intellectual capital of the Western world. There were people on the café terraces, boys and girls on the boulevards, bicycles racing by on their fantastically urgent errands. Everyone and everything wore a cheerful aspect, even the houses of Paris, which did not show their age. Those who were unable to pay the steep rents of these houses were enabled, by the weather, to enjoy the streets, to sit, unnoticed, in the parks. The boys and girls and old men and women who had nowhere at all to go and nothing whatever to do, for whom no provision had been made, or could be, added to the beauty of the Paris scene by walking along the river. The newspaper vendors seemed cheerful; so did the people who bought the newspapers. Even the men and women queueing up before bakeries—for there was a bread strike in Paris—did so as though they had long been used to it.

The conference was to open at nine o'clock. By ten o'clock the lecture hall was already unbearably hot, people choked the entrances and covered the wooden steps. It was hectic with the activity attendant upon the setting up of tape recorders, with the testing of ear-phones, with the lighting of flashbulbs. Electricity, in fact, filled the hall. Of the people there that first day, I should judge that not quite two-thirds were colored.

Behind the table at the front of the hall sat eight colored men. These included the American novelist Richard Wright; Alioune Diop, the editor of *Présence Africaine* and one of the principal organizers of the conference; poets Leopold Senghor, from Senegal, and Aimé Cesaire, from Martinique, and the poet and novelist Jacques Alexis, from Haiti. From Haiti, also, came the President of the conference, Dr. Price-Mars, a very old and very handsome man.

It was well past ten o'clock when the conference actually opened. Alioune Diop, who is tall, very dark and self-contained, and who rather resembles, in his extreme sobriety, an old-time Baptist minister, made the opening address. He referred to the present gathering as a kind of second Bandung. As at Bandung, the people gathered together here held in common the fact of their subjugation to Europe, or, at the very least, to the European vision of the world. Out of the fact that European well-being had been, for centuries, so crucially dependent on this subjugation had come that *racisme* from which all black men suffered. Then he spoke of the changes which had taken place during the last decade regarding the fate and the aspirations of non-European peoples, especially the blacks. "The blacks," he said, "whom history has treated in a rather cavalier fashion. I would even say that history has treated black men in a resolutely spiteful fashion were it not for the fact that this history with a large *H* is nothing more, after all, than the Western interpretation of the life of the world." He spoke of the variety of cultures the conference represented, saying that they were genuine cultures and that the ignorance of the West regarding them was largely a matter of convenience.

Yet, in speaking of the relation between politics and culture, he pointed out that the loss of vitality from which all Negro cultures were suffering was due to the fact that their political destinies were not in their hands. A people deprived of political sovereignty finds it very nearly impossible to recreate, for itself, the image of its past, this perpetual recreation being an absolute necessity for, if not, indeed, the definition of a living culture. And one of the questions, then, said Diop, which would often be raised during this conference was the question of assimilation. Assimilation was frequently but another name for the very special brand of relations between human beings which had been imposed by colonialism. These relations demanded that the individual, torn from the context to which he owed his identity, should replace his habits of feeling, thinking, and acting by another set of habits which belonged to the strangers who dominated him. He cited the example of certain natives of the Belgian Congo, who, *accablé des complexes*, wished for an assimilation so complete that they would no longer be distinguishable from white men. This, said Diop, indicated the blind horror which the spiritual heritage of Africa inspired in their breasts.

The question of assimilation could not, however, be posed this way. It was not a question, on the one hand, of simply being swallowed up, of disappearing in the maw of Western culture, nor was it, on the other hand, a question of rejecting assimilation in order to be isolated within African culture. Neither was it a question of deciding which African values were to be retained and which European values were to be adopted. Life was not that simple.

It was due to the crisis which their cultures were now undergoing that black intellectuals had come together. They were here to define and accept their responsibilities, to assess the riches and the promise of their cultures, and to open, in effect, a dialogue with Europe. He ended with a brief and rather moving reference to the fifteen-year struggle of himself and his confreres to bring about this day.

His speech won a great deal of applause. Yet, I felt that among the dark people in the hall there was, perhaps, some disappointment that he had not been more specific, more bitter, in a word, more demagogical; whereas, among the whites in the hall, there was certainly expressed in their applause a somewhat shame-faced and uneasy relief. And, indeed, the atmosphere was strange. No one, black or white, seemed quite to believe what was happening and everyone was tense with the question of which direction the conference would take. Hanging in the air, as real as the heat from which we suffered, were the great specters of America and Russia, of the battle going on between them for the domination of the world. The resolution of this battle might very well depend on the earth's non-European population, a population vastly outnumbering Europe's, and which had suffered such injustices at European hands. With the best will in the world, no one now living could undo what past generations had accomplished. The great question was what, exactly, *had* they accomplished: whether the evil, of which there had been so much, alone lived after them, whether the good, and there had been some, had been interred with their bones.

Of the messages from well-wishers which were read

immediately after Diop's speech, the one which caused the greatest stir came from America's W. E. B. Du Bois. "I am not present at your meeting," he began, "because the U.S. government will not give me a passport." The reading was interrupted at this point by great waves of laughter, by no means good-natured, and by a roar of applause, which, as it clearly could not have been intended for the State Department, was intended to express admiration for Du Bois' plain speaking. "Any American Negro traveling abroad today must either not care about Negroes or say what the State Department wishes him to say." This, of course, drew more applause. It also very neatly compromised whatever effectiveness the five-man American delegation then sitting in the hall might have hoped to have. It was less Du Bois' extremely ill-considered communication which did this than the incontestable fact that he had not been allowed to leave his country. It was a fact which could scarcely be explained or defended, particularly as one would have also had to explain just how the reasons for Du Bois' absence differed from those which had prevented the arrival of the delegation from South Africa. The very attempt at such an explanation, especially for people whose distrust of the West, however richly justified, also tends to make them dangerously blind and hasty, was to be suspected of "caring nothing about Negroes," of saying what the State Department "wished" you to say. It was a fact which increased and seemed to justify the distrust with which all Americans are regarded abroad, and it made yet deeper, for the five American Negroes present, that gulf which yawns between the American Negro and all other men of color. This is a very sad and dangerous state of affairs, for the American Negro is possibly the only man of color who can speak of the West with real authority, whose experience, painful as it is, also proves the vitality of the so transgressed Western ideals. The fact that Du Bois was not there and could not, therefore, be engaged in debate, naturally made the more seductive his closing argument: which was that, the future of Africa being socialist, African writers should take the road taken by Russia, Poland, China, etc., and not be "betrayed backward by the U.S. into colonialism."

When the morning session ended and I was spewed forth

with the mob into the bright courtyard, Richard Wright introduced me to the American delegation. And it seemed quite unbelievable for a moment that the five men standing with Wright (and Wright and myself) were defined, and had been brought together in this courtyard by our relation to the African continent. The chief of the delegation, John Davis, was to be asked just *why* he considered himself a Negro—he was to be told that he certainly did not look like one. He *is* a Negro, of course, from the remarkable legal point of view which obtains in the United States, but, more importantly, as he tried to make clear to his interlocutor, he was a Negro by choice and by depth of involvement—by experience, in fact. But the question of choice in such a context can scarcely be coherent for an African and the experience referred to, which produces a John Davis, remains a closed book for him. Mr. Davis might have been rather darker, as were the others—Mercer Cook, William Fontaine, Horace Bond, and James Ivy—and it would not have helped matters very much.

For what, at bottom, distinguished the Americans from the Negroes who surrounded us, men from Nigeria, Senegal, Barbados, Martinique—so many names for so many disciplines—was the banal and abruptly quite overwhelming fact that we had been born in a society, which, in a way quite inconceivable for Africans, and no longer real for Europeans, was open, and, in a sense which has nothing to do with justice or injustice, was free. It was a society, in short, in which nothing was fixed and we had therefore been born to a greater number of possibilities, wretched as these possibilities seemed at the instant of our birth. Moreover, the land of our forefathers' exile had been made, by that travail, our home. It may have been the popular impulse to keep us at the bottom of the perpetually shifting and bewildered populace; but we were, on the other hand, almost personally indispensable to each of them, simply because, without us, they could never have been certain, in such a confusion, where the bottom was; and nothing, in any case, could take away our title to the land which we, too, had purchased with our blood. This results in a psychology very different—at its best and at its worst—from the psychology which is produced by a sense of having been invaded and overrun, the sense of having no recourse whatever against

oppression other than overthrowing the machinery of the oppressor. We had been dealing with, had been made and man-
gled by, another machinery altogether. It had never been in
our interest to overthrow it. It had been necessary to make
the machinery work for our benefit and the possibility of its
doing so had been, so to speak, built in.

We could, therefore, in a way, be considered the connecting
link between Africa and the West, the most real and certainly
the most shocking of all African contributions to Western cultural life. The articulation of this reality, however, was another
matter. But it was clear that our relation to the mysterious
continent of Africa would not be clarified until we had found
some means of saying, to ourselves and to the world, more
about the mysterious American continent than had ever been
said before.

M. Lasebikan, from Nigeria, spoke that afternoon on the
tonal structure of Youriba poetry, a language spoken by five
million people in his country. Lasebikan was a very winning
and unassuming personality, dressed in a most arresting cos-
tume. What looked like a white lace poncho covered him from
head to foot; beneath this he was wearing a very subdued but
very ornately figured silk robe, which looked Chinese, and he
wore a red velvet toque, a sign, someone told me, that he was
a Mohammedan.

The Youriba language, he told us, had only become a written language in the middle of the last century and this had
been done by missionaries. His face expressed some sorrow at
this point, due, it developed, to the fact that this had not
already been accomplished by the Youriba people. However—
and his face brightened again—he lived in the hope that one
day an excavation would bring to light a great literature written by the Youriba people. In the meantime, with great good
nature, he resigned himself to sharing with us that literature
which already existed. I doubt that I learned much about the
tonal structure of Youriba poetry, but I found myself fascinated by the sensibility which had produced it. M. Lasebikan
spoke first in Youriba and then in English. It was perhaps
because he so clearly loved his subject that he not only succeeded in conveying the poetry of this extremely strange lan-

guage, he also conveyed something of the style of life out of which it came. The poems quoted ranged from the devotional to a poem which described the pounding of yams. And one somehow felt the loneliness and the yearning of the first and the peaceful, rhythmic domesticity of the second. There was a poem about the memory of a battle, a poem about a faithless friend, and a poem celebrating the variety to be found in life, which conceived of this variety in rather startling terms: "Some would have been great eaters, but they haven't got the food; some, great drinkers, but they haven't got the wine." Some of the poetry demanded the use of a marvelously ornate drum, on which were many little bells. It was not the drum it once had been, he told us, but despite whatever mishap had befallen it, I could have listened to him play it for the rest of the afternoon.

He was followed by Leopold Senghor. Senghor is a very dark and impressive figure in a smooth, bespectacled kind of way, and he is very highly regarded as a poet. He was to speak on West African writers and artists.

He began by invoking what he called the "spirit of Bandung." In referring to Bandung, he was referring less, he said, to the liberation of black peoples than he was saluting the reality and the toughness of their culture, which, despite the vicissitudes of their history, had refused to perish. We were now witnessing, in fact, the beginning of its renaissance. This renaissance would owe less to politics than it would to black writers and artists. The "spirit of Bandung" had had the effect of "sending them to school to Africa."

One of the things, said Senghor—perhaps *the* thing—which distinguishes Africans from Europeans is the comparative urgency of their ability to feel. *"Sentir c'est apercevoir"*: it is perhaps a tribute to his personal force that this phrase then meant something which makes the literal English translation quite inadequate, seeming to leave too great a distance between the feeling and the perception. The feeling and the perception, for Africans, is one and the same thing. This is the difference between European and African reasoning: the reasoning of the African is not compartmentalized, and, to illustrate this, Senghor here used the image of the bloodstream in which all things mingle and flow to and through the heart. He told us that the difference between the function of the arts in Europe and their function in Africa lay in the fact that, in Africa, the function of the arts is more present and pervasive, is infinitely less special, "is done by all, for all." Thus, art for art's sake is not a concept which makes any sense in Africa. The division between art and life out of which such a concept comes does not exist there. Art itself is taken to be perishable, to be made again each time it disappears or is destroyed. What is clung to is the spirit which makes art possible. And the African idea of this spirit is very different from the European idea. European art attempts to imitate nature. African art is concerned with reaching beyond and beneath nature, to contact, and itself become a part of *la force vitale*. The artistic image is not intended to represent the thing itself, but, rather, the reality of the force the thing contains. Thus, the moon is fecundity, the elephant is force.

Much of this made great sense to me, even though Senghor was speaking of, and out of, a way of life which I could only very dimly and perhaps somewhat wistfully imagine. It was the esthetic which attracted me, the idea that the work of art expresses, contains, and is itself a part of that energy which is life. Yet, I was aware that Senghor's thought had come into my mind translated. What he had been speaking of was something more direct and less isolated than the line in which my imagination immediately began to move. The distortions used by African artists to create a work of art are not at all the same distortions which have become one of the principal aims of almost every artist in the West today. (They are not the same distortions even when they have been copied from Africa.) And this was due entirely to the different situations in which each had his being. Poems and stories, in the only situation I know anything about, were never told, except, rarely, to children, and, at the risk of mayhem, in bars. They were written to be read, alone, and by a handful of people at that—there was really beginning to be something suspect in being read by more than a handful. These creations no more insisted on the actual presence of other human beings than they demanded the collaboration of a dancer and a drum. They could not be said to celebrate the society any more than the homage which Western artists sometimes receive can be said to have anything to do with society's celebration of a work of art. The only thing in Western life which seemed even faintly to approximate Senghor's intense sketch of the creative interdependence, the active, actual, joyful intercourse obtaining among African artists and what only a Westerner would call their public, was the atmosphere sometimes created among jazz musicians and their fans during, say, a jam session. But the ghastly isolation of the jazz musician, the neurotic intensity of his listeners, was proof enough that what Senghor meant when he spoke of social art had no reality whatever in Western life. He was speaking out of his past, which had been lived where art was naturally and spontaneously social, where artistic creation did not presuppose divorce. (Yet he was not there. Here he was, in Paris, speaking the adopted language in which he also wrote his poetry.)

Just what the specific relation of an artist to his culture says about that culture is a very pretty question. The culture which had produced Senghor seemed, on the face of it, to have a greater coherence as regarded assumptions, traditions, customs, and beliefs than did the Western culture to which it stood in so problematical a relation. And this might very well mean that the culture represented by Senghor was healthier than the culture represented by the hall in which he spoke. But the leap to this conclusion, than which nothing would have seemed easier, was frustrated by the question of just what health is in relation to a culture. Senghor's culture, for example, did not seem to need the lonely activity of the singular intelligence on which the cultural life—the moral life—of the West depends. And a really cohesive society, one of the attributes, perhaps, of what is taken to be a "healthy" culture, has, generally, and, I suspect, necessarily, a much lower level of tolerance for the maverick, the dissenter, the man who steals the fire, than have societies in which, the common ground of belief having all but vanished, each man, in awful and brutal isolation, is for himself, to flower or to perish. Or, not impossibly, to make real and fruitful again that vanished common ground, which, as I take it, is nothing more or less than the culture itself, endangered and rendered nearly inaccessible by the complexities it has, itself, inevitably created.

Nothing is more undeniable than the fact that cultures

vanish, undergo crises; are, in any case, in a perpetual state of change and fermentation, being perpetually driven, God knows where, by forces within and without. And one of the results, surely, of the present tension between the society represented by Senghor and the society represented by the Salle Descartes was just this perceptible drop, during the last decade, of the Western level of tolerance. I wondered what this would mean—for Africa, for us. I wondered just what effect the concept of art expressed by Senghor would have on that renaissance he had predicted and just what transformations this concept itself would undergo as it encountered the complexities of the century into which it was moving with such speed.

The evening debate rang perpetual changes on two questions. These questions—each of which splintered, each time it was asked, into a thousand more—were, first: What *is* a culture? This is a difficult question under the most serene circumstances—under which circumstances, incidentally, it mostly fails to present itself. (This implies, perhaps, one of the possible definitions of a culture, at least at a certain stage of its development.) In the context of the conference, it was a question which was helplessly at the mercy of another one. And the second question was this: Is it possible to describe as a culture what may simply be, after all, a history of oppression? That is, is this history and these present facts, which involve so many millions of people who are divided from each other by so many miles of the globe, which operates, and has operated, under such very different conditions, to such different effects, and which has produced so many different subhistories, problems, traditions, possibilities, aspirations, assumptions, languages, hybrids—is this history enough to have made of the earth's black populations anything that can legitimately be described as a culture? For what, beyond the fact that all black men at one time or another left Africa, or have remained there, do they really have in common?

And yet, it became clear as the debate wore on, that there *was* something which all black men held in common, something which cut across opposing points of view, and placed in the same context their widely dissimiliar experience. What they held in common was their precarious, their unutterably painful relation to the white world. What they held in common was the necessity to remake the world in their own image, to impose this image on the world, and no longer be controlled by the vision of the world, and of themselves, held by other people. What, in sum, black men held in common was their ache to come into the world as men. And this ache united people who might otherwise have been divided as to what a man should be.

Yet, whether or not this could properly be described as a *cultural* reality remained another question. Haiti's Jacques Alexis made the rather desperate observation that a cultural survey must have *something* to survey; but then seemed confounded, as, indeed, we all were, by the dimensions of the particular cultural survey in progress. It was necessary, for example, before one could relate the culture of Haiti to that of Africa, to know what the Haitian culture was. Within Haiti there were a great many cultures. Frenchmen, Negroes, and Indians had bequeathed it quite dissimilar ways of life; Catholics, voodooists, and animists cut across class and color lines. Alexis described as "pockets" of culture those related and yet quite specific and dissimilar ways of life to be found within the borders of any country in the world and wished to know by what alchemy these opposing ways of life became a national culture. And he wished to know, too, what relation national culture bore to national independence—was it possible, really, to speak of a national culture when speaking of nations which were not free?

Senghor remarked, apropos of this question, that one of the great difficulties posed by this problem of cultures within cultures, particularly within the borders of Africa herself, was the difficulty of establishing and maintaining contact with the people if one's language had been formed in Europe. And he went on, somewhat later, to make the point that the heritage of the American Negro was an African heritage. He used, as proof of this, a poem of Richard Wright's which was, he said, involved with African tensions and symbols, even though Wright himself had not been aware of this. He suggested that the study of African sources might prove extremely illuminating for American Negroes. For, he suggested, in the same way

that white classics exist—classic here taken to mean an enduring revelation and statement of a specific, peculiar, cultural
sensibility—black classics must also exist. This raised in my
mind the question of whether or not white classics *did* exist,
and, with this question, I began to see the implications of
Senghor's claim.

For, if white classics existed, in distinction, that is, to merely
French or English classics, these could only be the classics
produced by Greece and Rome. If *Black Boy*, said Senghor,
were to be analyzed, it would undoubtedly reveal the African
heritage to which it owed its existence; in the same way, I
supposed, that Dickens' *A Tale Of Two Cities*, would, upon
analysis, reveal its debt to Aeschylus. It did not seem very
important.

And yet, I realized, the question had simply never come up
in relation to European literature. It was not, now, the European necessity to go rummaging in the past, and through all
the countries of the world, bitterly staking out claims to its
cultural possessions.

Yet *Black Boy* owed its existence to a great many other factors, by no means so tenuous or so problematical; in so handsomely presenting Wright with his African heritage, Senghor
rather seemed to be taking away his identity. *Black Boy* is the
study of the growing up of a Negro boy in the Deep South,
and is one of the major American autobiographies. I had never
thought of it, as Senghor clearly did, as one of the major
African autobiographies, only one more document, in fact,
like one more book in the Bible, speaking of the African's
long persecution and exile.

Senghor chose to overlook several gaps in his argument, not
the least of which was the fact that Wright had not been in a
position, as Europeans had been, to remain in contact with
his hypothetical African heritage. The Greco-Roman tradition
had, after all, been *written down*; it was by this means that it
had kept itself alive. Granted that there was something African
in *Black Boy*, as there was undoubtedly something African in
all American Negroes, the great question of what this was,
and how it had survived, remained wide open. Moreover,
Black Boy had been written in the English language which
Americans had inherited from England, that is, if you like,

from Greece and Rome; its form, psychology, moral attitude, preoccupations, in short, its cultural validity, were all due to forces which had nothing to do with Africa. Or was it simply that we had been rendered unable to recognize Africa in it?— for, it seemed that, in Senghor's vast re-creation of the world, the footfall of the African would prove to have covered more territory than the footfall of the Roman.

Thursday's great event was Aimé Cesaire's speech in the afternoon, dealing with the relation between colonization and culture. Cesaire is a caramel-colored man from Martinique, probably around forty, with a great tendency to roundness and smoothness, physically speaking, and with the rather vaguely benign air of a schoolteacher. All this changes the moment he begins to speak. It becomes at once apparent that his curious, slow-moving blandness is related to the grace and patience of a jungle cat and that the intelligence behind those spectacles is of a very penetrating and demagogic order.

The cultural crisis through which we are passing today can be summed up thus, said Cesaire: that culture which is strongest from the material and technological point of view threatens to crush all weaker cultures, particularly in a world in which, distance counting for nothing, the technologically weaker cultures have no means of protecting themselves. All cultures have, furthermore, an economic, social, and political base, and no culture can continue to live if its political destiny is not in its own hands. "Any political and social regime which destroys the self-determination of a people also destroys the creative power of that people." When this has happened the culture of that people has been destroyed. And it is simply not true that the colonizers bring to the colonized a new culture to replace the old one, a culture not being something given to a people, but, on the contrary and by definition, something that they make themselves. Nor is it, in any case, in the nature of colonialism to wish or to permit such a degree of well-being among the colonized. The well-being of the colonized is desirable only insofar as this well-being enriches the dominant country, the necessity of which is simply to remain dominant. Now the civilizations of Europe, said Cesaire, speaking very clearly and intensely to a packed and attentive hall, evolved an economy based on capital and the capital was based on black labor; and thus, regardless of whatever arguments Europeans use to defend themselves, and in spite of the absurd palliatives with which they have sometimes tried to soften the blow, the fact, of their domination, in order to accomplish and maintain this domination—in order, in fact, to make money—they destroyed, with utter ruthlessness, everything that stood in their way, languages, customs, tribes, lives; and not only put nothing in its place, but erected, on the contrary, the most tremendous barriers between themselves and the people they ruled. Europeans never had the remotest intention of raising Africans to the Western level, of sharing with them the instruments of physical, political or economic power. It was precisely their intention, their necessity, to keep the people they ruled in a state of cultural anarchy, that is, simply in a barbaric state. "The famous inferiority complex one is pleased to observe as a characteristic of the colonized is no accident but something very definitely desired and deliberately inculcated by the colonizer." He was interrupted at this point—not for the first time—by long and prolonged applause.

"The situation, therefore, in the colonial countries, is tragic," Cesaire continued. "Wherever colonization is a fact the indigenous culture begins to rot. And, among these ruins, something begins to be born which is not a culture but a kind of subculture, a subculture which is condemned to exist on the margin allowed it by European culture. This then becomes the province of a few men, the elite, who find themselves placed in the most artificial conditions, deprived of any revivifying contact with the masses of the people. Under such conditions, this subculture has no chance whatever of growing into an active, living culture." And what, he asked, before this situation, can be done?

The answer would not be simple. "In every society there is always a delicate balance between the old and the new, a balance which is perpetually being re-established, which is re-established by each generation. Black societies, cultures, civilizations, will not escape this law." Cesaire spoke of the energy already proved by black cultures in the past, and, declining to believe that this energy no longer existed, declined

also to believe that the total obliteration of the existing culture
was a condition for the renaissance of black people. "In the
culture to be born there will no doubt be old and new elements. How these elements will be mixed is not a question
to which any individual can respond. The response must be
given by the community. But we can say this: that the response will be given, and not verbally, but in tangible facts,
and by action."

He was interrupted by applause again. He paused, faintly
smiling, and reached his peroration: "We find ourselves today
in a cultural chaos. And this is our role: to liberate the forces
which, alone, can organize from this chaos a new synthesis, a
synthesis which will deserve the name of a culture, a synthesis
which will be the reconciliation—*et dépassement*—of the old
and the new. We are here to proclaim the right of our people
to speak, to let our people, black people, make their entrance
on the great stage of history."

This speech, which was very brilliantly delivered, and which
had the further advantage of being, in the main, unanswerable
(and the advantage, also, of being very little concerned, at
bottom, with culture) wrung from the audience which heard
it the most violent reaction of joy. Cesaire had spoken for
those who could not speak and those who could not speak
thronged around the table to shake his hand, and kiss him. I
myself felt stirred in a very strange and disagreeable way. For
Cesaire's case against Europe, which was watertight, was also
a very easy case to make. The anatomizing of the great injustice which is the irreducible fact of colonialism was yet not
enough to give the victims of that injustice a new sense of
themselves. One may say, of course, that the very fact that
Cesaire had spoken so thrillingly, and in one of the great institutions of Western learning, invested them with this new
sense, but I do not think this is so. He had certainly played
very skillfully on their emotions and their hopes, but he had
not raised the central, tremendous question, which was, simply: What *had* this colonial experience made of them and what
were they now to do with it? For they were all, now, whether
they liked it or not, related to Europe, stained by European
visions and standards, and their relation to themselves, and to
each other, and to their past had changed. Their relation to

their poets had also changed, as had the relation of their poets to them. Cesaire's speech left out of account one of the great effects of the colonial experience: its creation, precisely, of men like himself. His real relation to the people who thronged about him now had been changed, by this experience, into something very different from what it once had been. What made him so attractive now was the fact that he, without having ceased to be one of them, yet seemed to move with the European authority. He had penetrated into the heart of the great wilderness which was Europe and stolen the sacred fire. And this, which was the promise of their freedom, was also the assurance of his power.

Friday's session began in a rather tense atmosphere and this tension continued throughout the day. Diop opened the session by pointing out that each speaker spoke only for himself and could not be considered as speaking for the conference. I imagined that this had something to do with Cesaire's speech of the day before and with some of its effects, among which, apparently, had been a rather sharp exchange between Cesaire and the American delegation.

This was the session during which it became apparent that there was a religious war going on at the conference, a war which suggested, in miniature, some of the tensions dividing Africa. A Protestant minister from the Cameroons, Pastor T. Ekollo, had been forced by the hostility of the audience the day before to abandon a dissertation in defense of Christianity in Africa. He was visibly upset still. "There will be Christians in Africa, even when there is not a white man there," he said, with a tense defiance, and added, with an unconsciously despairing irony to which, however, no one reacted, "supposing that to be possible." He had been asked how he could defend Christianity in view of what Christians had done in his country. To which his answer was that the doctrine of Christianity was of more moment than the crimes committed by Christians. The necessity which confronted Africans was to make Christianity real in their own lives, without reference to the crimes committed by others. The audience was extremely cold and hostile, forcing him again, in effect, from the floor. But I felt that this also had something to do with Pastor Ekollo's

rather petulant and not notably Christian attitude toward
them.

Dr. Marcus James, a priest of the Anglican church from
Jamaica, picked up where Ekollo left off. Dr. James is a round,
very pleasant-looking, chocolate-colored man, with spectacles.
He began with a quotation to the effect that, when the Christian arrived in Africa, he had the Bible and the African had
the land; but that, before long, the African had the Bible and
the Christian had the land. There was a great deal of laughter
at this, in which Dr. James joined. But the postscript to be
added today, he said, is that the African not only has the Bible
but has found in it a potential weapon for the recovery of his
land. The Christians in the hall, who seemed to be in the
minority, applauded and stomped their feet at this, but many
others now rose and left.

Dr. James did not seem to be distressed and went on to
discuss the relationship between Christianity and democracy.
In Africa, he said, there was none whatever. Africans do not,
in fact, believe that Christianity is any longer real for Europeans, due to the immense scaffolding with which they have
covered it, and the fact that this religion has no effect whatever on their conduct. There are, nevertheless, more than
twenty million Christians in Africa, and Dr. James believed
that the future of their country was very largely up to them.
The task of making Christianity real in Africa was made the
more difficult in that they could expect no help whatever from
Europe: "Christianity, as practiced by Europeans in Africa, is
a cruel travesty."

This bitter observation, which was uttered in sorrow, gained
a great deal of force from the fact that so genial a man had
felt compelled to make it. It made vivid, unanswerable, in a
way which rage could not have done, how little the West has
respected its own ideals in dealing with subject peoples, and
suggested that there was a price we would pay for this. He
speculated a little on what African Christianity might become,
and how it might contribute to the rebirth of Christianity
everywhere; and left his audience to chew on this momentous
speculation: Considering, he said, that what Africa wishes to
wrest from Europe is power, will it be necessary for Africa to
take the same bloody road which Europe has followed? Or

will it be possible for her to work out some means of avoiding this?

M. Wahal, from the Sudan, spoke in the afternoon on the role of the law in culture, using as an illustration the role the law had played in the history of the American Negro. He spoke at length on the role of French law in Africa, pointing out that French law is simply not equipped to deal with the complexity of the African situation. And what is even worse, of course, is that it makes virtually no attempt to do so. The result is that French law, in Africa, is simply a legal means of administering injustice. It is not a solution, either, simply to revert to African tribal custom, which is also helpless before the complexities of present-day African life. Wahal spoke with a quiet matter-of-factness, which lent great force to the ugly story he was telling, and he concluded by saying that the question was ultimately a political one and that there was no hope of solving it within the framework of the present colonial system.

He was followed by George Lamming. Lamming is tall, raw-boned, untidy, and intense, and one of his real distinctions is his refusal to be intimidated by the fact that he is a genuine writer. He proposed to raise certain questions pertaining to the quality of life to be lived by black people in that hypothetical tomorrow when they would no longer be ruled by whites. "The profession of letters is an untidy one," he began, looking as though he had dressed to prove it. He directed his speech to Aimé Cesaire and Jacques Alexis in particular, and quoted Djuna Barnes: "Too great a sense of identity makes a man feel he can do no wrong. And too little does the same." He suggested that it was important to bear in mind that the word Negro meant black—and meant nothing more than that; and commented on the great variety of heritages, experiences, and points of view which the conference had brought together under the heading of this single noun. He wished to suggest that the nature of power was unrelated to pigmentation, that bad faith was a phenomenon which was independent of race. He found—from the point of view of an untidy man of letters—something crippling in the obsession from which Negroes suffered as regards the existence and the attitudes of the Other—this Other being everyone who was not Negro. That black people faced great problems was surely not to be denied and yet the greatest problem facing us was what *we*, Negroes, would do among ourselves "when there was no longer any colonial horse to ride." He pointed out that this was the horse on which a great many Negroes, who were in what he called "the skin trade," hoped to ride to power, power which would be in no way distinguishable from the power they sought to overthrow.

Lamming was insisting on the respect which is due the private life. I respected him very much, not only because he raised this question, but because he knew what he was doing. He was concerned with the immensity and the variety of the experience called Negro; he was concerned that one should recognize this variety as wealth. He cited the case of Amos Tutuola's *The Palm-Wine Drinkard*, which he described as a fantasy, made up of legends, anecdotes, episodes, the product, in fact, of an oral story-telling tradition which disappeared from Western life generations ago. Yet "Tutuola really *does* speak English. It is *not* his second language." The English did not find the book strange. On the contrary, they were astonished by how truthfully it seemed to speak to them of their own experience. They felt that Tutuola was closer to the English than he could possibly be to his equivalent in Nigeria; and yet Tutuola's work could elicit this reaction only because, in a way which could never really be understood, but which Tutuola had accepted, he was closer to his equivalent in Nigeria than he would ever be to the English. It seemed to me that Lamming was suggesting to the conference a subtle and difficult idea, the idea that part of the great wealth of the Negro experience lay precisely in its double-edgedness. He was suggesting that all Negroes were held in a state of supreme tension between the difficult, dangerous relationship in which they stood to the white world and the relationship, not a whit less painful or dangerous, in which they stood to each other. He was suggesting that in the acceptance of this duality lay their strength, that in this, precisely, lay their means of defining and controlling the world in which they lived.

Lamming was interrupted at about this point, however, for it had lately been decided, in view of the great number of reports still to be read, to limit everyone to twenty minutes.

This quite unrealistic rule was not to be observed very closely, especially as regarded the French-speaking delegates. But Lamming put his notes in his pocket and ended by saying that if, as someone had remarked, silence was the only common language, politics, for Negroes, was the only common ground.

The evening session began with a film, which I missed, and was followed by a speech from Cheik Anta Diop, which, in sum, claimed the ancient Egyptian empire as part of the Negro past. I can only say that this question has never greatly exercised my mind, nor did M. Diop succeed in doing so—at least not in the direction he intended. He quite refused to remain within the twenty-minute limit and, while his claims of the deliberate dishonesty of all Egyptian scholars may be quite well founded for all I know, I cannot say that he convinced me. He was, however, a great success in the hall, second only, in fact, to Aimé Cesaire.

He was followed by Richard Wright. Wright had been acting as liaison man between the American delegation and the Africans and this had placed him in rather a difficult position, since both factions tended to claim him as their spokesman. It had not, of course, occurred to the Americans that he could be anything less, whereas the Africans automatically claimed him because of his great prestige as a novelist and his reputation for calling a spade a spade—particularly if the spade were white. The consciousness of his peculiar and certainly rather grueling position weighed on him, I think, rather heavily.

He began by confessing that the paper he had written, while on his farm in Normandy, impressed him as being, after the events of the last few days, inadequate. Some of the things he had observed during the course of the conference had raised questions in him which his paper could not have foreseen. He had not, however, rewritten his paper, but would read it now, exactly as it had been written, interrupting himself whenever what he had written and what he had since been made to feel seemed to be at variance. He was exposing, in short, his conscience to the conference and asking help of them in his confusion.

There was, first of all, he said, a painful contradiction in being at once a Westerner and a black man. "I see both worlds from another, and third, point of view." This fact had nothing to do with his will, his desire, or his choice. It was simply that he had been born in the West and the West had formed him.

As a black Westerner, it was difficult to know what one's attitude should be toward three realities which were inextricably woven together in the Western fabric. These were religion, tradition, and imperialism, and in none of these realities had the lives of black men been taken into account: their advent dated back to 1455, when the church had determined to rule all infidels. And it just so happened, said Wright, ironically, that a vast proportion of these infidels were black. Nevertheless, this decision on the part of the church had not been, despite the church's intentions, entirely oppressive, for one of the results of 1455 had, at length, been Calvin and Luther, who shook the authority of the church in insisting on the authority of the individual conscience. This might not, he said accurately, have been precisely their intention, but it had certainly been one of their effects. For, with the authority of the church shaken, men were left prey to many strange and new ideas, ideas which led, finally, to the discrediting of the racial dogma. Neither had this been foreseen, but what men imagine they are doing and what they are doing in fact are rarely the same thing. This was a perfectly valid observation which would, I felt, have been just as valid without the remarkable capsule history with which Wright imagined he supported it.

Wright then went on to speak of the effects of European colonialism in the African colonies. He confessed—bearing in mind always the great gap between human intentions and human effects—that he thought of it as having been, in many ways, liberating, since it smashed old traditions and destroyed old gods. One of the things that surprised him in the last few days had been the realization that most of the delegates to the conference did not feel as he did. He felt, nevertheless, that, though Europeans had not realized what they were doing in freeing Africans from the "rot" of their past, they had been accomplishing a good. And yet—he was not certain that he had the right to say that, having forgotten that Africans are not American Negroes and were not, therefore, as he somewhat mysteriously considered American Negroes to be, free from their "irrational" past.

In sum, Wright said, he felt that Europe had brought the Enlightenment to Africa and that "what was good for Europe was good for all mankind." I felt that this was, perhaps, a tactless way of phrasing a debatable idea, but Wright went on to express a notion which I found even stranger. And this was that the West, having created an African and Asian elite, should now "give them their heads" and "refuse to be shocked" at the "methods they will feel compelled to use" in unifying their countries. We had not, ourselves, used very pretty methods. Presumably, this left us in no position to throw stones at Nehru, Nasser, Sukarno, etc., should they decide, as they almost surely would, to use dictatorial methods in order to hasten the "social evolution." In any case, Wright said, these men, the leaders of their countries, once the new social order was established, would voluntarily surrender the "personal power." He did not say what would happen then, but I supposed it would be the second coming.

Saturday was the last day of the conference, which was scheduled to end with the invitation to the audience to engage with the delegates in the Euro-African dialogue. It was a day marked by much confusion and excitement and discontent—this last on the part of people who felt that the conference had been badly run, or who had not been allowed to read their reports. (They were often the same people.) It was marked, too, by rather a great deal of plain speaking, both on and off, but mostly off, the record. The hall was even more hot and crowded than it had been the first day and the photographers were back.

The entire morning was taken up in an attempt to agree on a "cultural inventory." This had to be done before the conference could draft those resolutions which they were, today, to present to the world. This task would have been extremely difficult even had there obtained in the black world a greater unity—geographical, spiritual, and historical—than is actually the case. Under the circumstances, it was an endeavor complicated by the nearly indefinable complexities of the word *culture*, by the fact that no coherent statement had yet been made concerning the relationship of black cultures to each other, and, finally, by the necessity, which had obtained throughout the conference, of avoiding the political issues.

The inability to discuss politics had certainly handicapped the conference, but it could scarcely have been run otherwise. The political question would have caused the conference to lose itself in a war of political ideologies. Moreover, the conference *was* being held in Paris, many of the delegates represented areas which belonged to France, most of them represented areas which were not free. There was also to be considered the delicate position of the American delegation, which had sat throughout the conference uncomfortably aware that they might at any moment be forced to rise and leave the hall.

The declaration of political points of view being thus prohibited, the "cultural" debate which raged in the hall that morning was in perpetual danger of drowning in the sea of the unstated. For, according to his political position, each delegate had a different interpretation of his culture, and a different idea of its future, as well as the means to be used to make that future a reality. A solution of a kind was offered by Senghor's suggestion that two committees be formed, one to take an inventory of the past, and one to deal with present prospects. There was some feeling that two committees were scarcely necessary. Diop suggested that one committee be formed, which, if necessary, could divide itself into two. Then the question arose as to just how the committee should be appointed, whether by countries or by cultural areas. It was decided, at length, that the committee should be set up on the latter basis, and should have resolutions drafted by noon. "It is by these resolutions," protested Mercer Cook, "that we shall make ourselves known. It cannot be done in an hour."

He was entirely right. At eleven-twenty a committee of eighteen members had been formed. At four o'clock in the afternoon they were still invisible. By this time, too, the most tremendous impatience reigned in the crowded hall, in which, today, Negroes by far outnumbered whites. At four-twenty-five the impatience of the audience erupted in whistles, cat-calls, and stamping of feet. At four-thirty, Alioune Diop arrived and officially opened the meeting. He tried to explain some of the difficulties such a conference inevitably encountered and assured the audience that the committee on resolutions would not be absent much longer. In the meantime, in their absence, and in the absence of Dr. Price-Mars, he proposed to read a few messages from well-wishers. But the audience was not really interested in these messages and was manifesting a very definite tendency to get out of hand again when, at four-fifty-five, Dr. Price-Mars entered. His arrival had the effect of calming the audience somewhat and, luckily, the committee on resolutions came in very shortly afterwards. At five-seven, Diop rose to read the document which had come one vote short of being unanimously approved.

As is the way with documents of this kind, it was carefully worded and slightly repetitious. This did not make its meaning less clear or diminish its importance.

It spoke first of the great importance of the cultural inventory here begun in relation to the various black cultures which had been "systematically misunderstood, underestimated, sometimes destroyed." This inventory had confirmed the pressing need for a re-examination of the history of these cultures (*"la verité historique"*) with a view to their re-evaluation. The ignorance concerning them, the errors, and the willful distortions, were among the great contributing factors to the crisis through which they now were passing, in relation to themselves and to human culture in general. The active aid of writers, artists, theologians, thinkers, scientists, and technicians was necessary for the revival, the rehabilitation, and the development of these cultures as the first step toward their integration in the active cultural life of the world. Black men, whatever their political and religious beliefs, were united in believing that the health and growth of these cultures could not possibly come about until colonialism, the exploitation of undeveloped peoples, and racial discrimination had come to an end. (At this point the conference expressed its regret at the involuntary absence of the South African delegation and the reading was interrupted by prolonged and violent applause.) All people, the document continued, had the right to be able to place themselves in fruitful contact with their national cultural values and to benefit from the instruction and education which could be afforded them within this framework. It spoke of the progress which had taken place in the world in the last few years and stated that this progress permitted one to hope for the general abolition of the colonial system and the total and universal end of racial discrimination, and ended: "Our conference, which respects the cultures of all countries and appreciates their contributions to the progress of civilization, engages all black men in the defense, the illustration, and the dissemination throughout the world of the national values of their people. We, black writers and artists, proclaim our brotherhood toward all men and expect of them (*'nous attendons d'eux'*) the manifestation of this same brotherhood toward our people."

When the applause in which the last words of this document were very nearly drowned had ended, Diop pointed out that this was not a declaration of war; it was, rather, he said, a declaration of love—for the culture, European, which had been of such importance in the history of mankind. But it had been very keenly felt that it was now necessary for black men to make the effort to define themselves *au lieu d'être toujours defini par les autres.* Black men had resolved "to take their destinies into their own hands." He spoke of plans for the setting up of an international association for the dissemination of black culture and, at five-twenty-two, Dr. Price-Mars officially closed the conference and opened the floor to the audience for the Euro-African dialogue.

Someone, a European, addressed this question to Aimé Cesaire: How, he asked, do you explain the fact that many Europeans—as well as many Africans, *bien entendu*—reject what is referred to as European culture? A European himself, he was far from certain that such a thing as a European culture existed. It was possible to be a European without accepting the Greco-Roman tradition. Neither did he believe in race. He wanted to know in what, exactly, this Negro-African culture consisted and, more, why it was judged necessary to save it. He ended, somewhat vaguely, by saying that, in his opinion, it was human values which had to be preserved, human needs which had to be respected and expressed.

This admirable but quite inadequate psychologist precipitated something of a storm. Diop tried to answer the first part of his question by pointing out that, in their attitudes toward their cultures, a great diversity of viewpoints also obtained among black men. Then an enormous, handsome, extremely impressive black man whom I had not remarked before, who was also named Cesaire, stated that the contemporary crisis of black cultures had been brought about by Europe's nineteenth- and twentieth-century attempts to impose their culture on other peoples. They did this without any recognition of the cultural validity of these peoples and thus aroused their resistance. In the case of Africa, where culture was fluid and largely unwritten, resistance had been most difficult. "Which is why," he said, "we are here. We are the most characteristic products of this crisis." And then a rage seemed to shake him, and he continued in a voice thick with fury, "Nothing will ever make us believe that our beliefs . . . are merely frivolous superstitions. No power will ever cause us to admit that we are lower than any other people." He then made a reference to the present Arab struggle against the French which I did not understand, and ended, "What we are doing is holding on to what is ours. Little," he added, sardonically, "but it belongs to us."

Aimé Cesaire, to whom the question had been addressed, was finally able to answer it. He pointed out, with a deliberate, mocking logic, that the rejection by a European of European culture was of the utmost unimportance. "Reject it or not, he is still a European, even his rejection is a European rejection. We do not choose our cultures, we belong to them." As to the speaker's implied idea of cultural relativity, and the progressive role this idea can sometimes play, he cited the French objection to this idea. It is an idea which, by making all cultures, as such, equal, undermines French justification for its presence in Africa. He also suggested that the speaker had implied that this conference was primarily interested in an idealistic reconstruction of the past. "But our attitude," said Cesaire, "toward colonialism and racial discrimination is very concrete. Our aims cannot be realized without this concreteness." And as for the question of race: "No one is suggesting that there is such a thing as a pure race, or that culture is a racial product. We are not Negroes by our own desire, but, in effect, because of Europe. What unites all Negroes is the injustices they have suffered at European hands."

The moment Cesaire finished, Cheik Anta Diop passionately demanded if it were a heresy from a Marxist point of view to try to hang onto a national culture. "Where," he asked, "is the European nation which, in order to progress, surrendered its past?"

There was no answer to this question, nor were there any further questions from the audience. Richard Wright spoke briefly, saying that this conference marked a turning point in the history of Euro-African relations: it marked, in fact, the beginning of the end of the European domination. He spoke of the great diversity of techniques and approaches now at the command of black people, with particular emphasis on the role the American Negro could be expected to play. Among black people, the American Negro was in the technological vanguard and this could prove of inestimable value to the developing African sovereignties. And the dialogue ended immediately afterward, at six-fifty-five, with Senghor's statement that this was the first of many such conferences, the first of many dialogues. As night was falling we poured into the Paris streets. Boys and girls, old men and women, bicycles, terraces, all were there, and the people were queueing up before the bakeries for bread.

3. Fifth Avenue, Uptown: A Letter from Harlem

THERE is a housing project standing now where the house in which we grew up once stood, and one of those stunted city trees is snarling where our doorway used to be. This is on the rehabilitated side of the avenue. The other side of the avenue—for progress takes time—has not been rehabilitated yet and it looks exactly as it looked in the days when we sat with our noses pressed against the windowpane, longing to be allowed to go "across the street." The grocery store which gave us credit is still there, and there can be no doubt that it is still giving credit. The people in the project certainly need it—far more, indeed, than they ever needed the project. The last time I passed by, the Jewish proprietor was still standing among his shelves, looking sadder and heavier but scarcely any older. Farther down the block stands the shoe-repair store in which our shoes were repaired until reparation became impossible and in which, then, we bought all our "new" ones. The Negro proprietor is still in the window, head down, working at the leather.

These two, I imagine, could tell a long tale if they would (perhaps they would be glad to if they could), having watched so many, for so long, struggling in the fishhooks, the barbed wire, of this avenue.

The avenue is elsewhere the renowned and elegant Fifth. The area I am describing, which, in today's gang parlance, would be called "the turf," is bounded by Lenox Avenue on the west, the Harlem River on the east, 135th Street on the north, and 130th Street on the south. We never lived beyond these boundaries; this is where we grew up. Walking along 145th Street—for example—familiar as it is, and similar, does not have the same impact because I do not know any of the people on the block. But when I turn east on 131st Street and Lenox Avenue, there is first a soda-pop joint, then a shoeshine "parlor," then a grocery store, then a dry cleaners', then the houses. All along the street there are people who watched me grow up, people who grew up with me, people I watched

170

grow up along with my brothers and sisters; and, sometimes in my arms, sometimes underfoot, sometimes at my shoulder—or on it—their children, a riot, a forest of children, who include my nieces and nephews.

When we reach the end of this long block, we find ourselves on wide, filthy, hostile Fifth Avenue, facing that project which hangs over the avenue like a monument to the folly, and the cowardice, of good intentions. All along the block, for anyone who knows it, are immense human gaps, like craters. These gaps are not created merely by those who have moved away, inevitably into some other ghetto; or by those who have risen, almost always into a greater capacity for self-loathing and self-delusion; or yet by those who, by whatever means—War II, the Korean war, a policeman's gun or billy, a gang war, a brawl, madness, an overdose of heroin, or, simply, unnatural exhaustion—are dead. I am talking about those who are left, and I am talking principally about the young. What are they doing? Well, some, a minority, are fanatical churchgoers, members of the more extreme of the Holy Roller sects. Many, many more are "moslems," by affiliation or sympathy, that is to say that they are united by nothing more—and nothing less—than a hatred of the white world and all its works. They are present, for example, at every Buy Black street-corner meeting—meetings in which the speaker urges his hearers to cease trading with white men and establish a separate economy. Neither the speaker nor his hearers can possibly do this, of course, since Negroes do not own General Motors or RCA or the A & P, nor, indeed, do they own more than a wholly insufficient fraction of anything else in Harlem (those who *do* own anything are more interested in their profits than in their fellows). But these meetings nevertheless keep alive in the participators a certain pride of bitterness without which, however futile this bitterness may be, they could scarcely remain alive at all. Many have given up. They stay home and watch the TV screen, living on the earnings of their parents, cousins, brothers, or uncles, and only leave the house to go to the movies or to the nearest bar. "How're you making it?" one may ask, running into them along the block, or in the bar. "Oh, I'm TV-ing it"; with the saddest, sweetest, most shame-faced of smiles, and from a great distance. This distance one is compelled to respect; anyone who has traveled so far will not easily be dragged again into the world. There are further retreats, of course, than the TV screen or the bar. There are those who are simply sitting on their stoops, "stoned," animated for a moment only, and hideously, by the approach of someone who may lend them the money for a "fix." Or by the approach of someone from whom they can purchase it, one of the shrewd ones, on the way to prison or just coming out.

And the others, who have avoided all of these deaths, get up in the morning and go downtown to meet "the man." They work in the white man's world all day and come home in the evening to this fetid block. They struggle to instill in their children some private sense of honor or dignity which will help the child to survive. This means, of course, that they must struggle, stolidly, incessantly, to keep this sense alive in themselves, in spite of the insults, the indifference, and the cruelty they are certain to encounter in their working day. They patiently browbeat the landlord into fixing the heat, the plaster, the plumbing; this demands prodigious patience; nor is patience usually enough. In trying to make their hovels habitable, they are perpetually throwing good money after bad. Such frustration, so long endured, is driving many strong, admirable men and women whose only crime is color to the very gates of paranoia.

One remembers them from another time—playing handball in the playground, going to church, wondering if they were going to be promoted at school. One remembers them going off to war—gladly, to escape this block. One remembers their return. Perhaps one remembers their wedding day. And one sees where the girl is now—vainly looking for salvation from some other embittered, trussed, and struggling boy—and sees the all-but-abandoned children in the streets.

Now I am perfectly aware that there are other slums in which white men are fighting for their lives, and mainly losing. I know that blood is also flowing through those streets and that the human damage there is incalculable. People are continually pointing out to me the wretchedness of white people in order to console me for the wretchedness of blacks. But an itemized account of the American failure does not console me and it should not console anyone else. That hundreds of thousands of white people are living, in effect, no better than the "niggers" is not a fact to be regarded with complacency. The social and moral bankruptcy suggested by this fact is of the bitterest, most terrifying kind.

The people, however, who believe that this democratic anguish has some consoling value are always pointing out that So-and-So, white, and So-and-So, black, rose from the slums into the big time. The existence—the public existence—of, say, Frank Sinatra and Sammy Davis, Jr., proves to them that America is still the land of opportunity and that inequalities vanish before the determined will. It proves nothing of the sort. The determined will is rare—at the moment, in this country, it is unspeakably rare—and the inequalities suffered by the many are in no way justified by the rise of a few. A few have always risen—in every country, every era, and in the teeth of regimes which can by no stretch of the imagination be thought of as free. Not all of these people, it is worth remembering, left the world better than they found it. The determined will is rare, but it is not invariably benevolent. Furthermore, the American equation of success with the big times reveals an awful disrespect for human life and human achievement. This equation has placed our cities among the most dangerous in the world and has placed our youth among the most empty and most bewildered. The situation of our youth is not mysterious. Children have never been very good at listening to their elders, but they have never failed to imitate them. They must, they have no other models. That is exactly what our children are doing. They are imitating our immorality, our disrespect for the pain of others.

All other slum dwellers, when the bank account permits it, can move out of the slum and vanish altogether from the eye of persecution. No Negro in this country has ever made that much money and it will be a long time before any Negro does. The Negroes in Harlem, who have no money, spend what they have on such gimcracks as they are sold. These include "wider" TV screens, more "faithful" hi-fi sets, more "powerful" cars, all of which, of course, are obsolete long before they are paid for. Anyone who has ever struggled with poverty knows how extremely expensive it is to be poor; and if one is a member of a captive population, economically speaking, one's feet have simply been placed on the treadmill forever. One is victimized, economically, in a thousand ways—rent, for example, or car insurance. Go shopping one day in Harlem—for anything—and compare Harlem prices and quality with those downtown.

The people who have managed to get off this block have only got as far as a more respectable ghetto. This respectable ghetto does not even have the advantages of the disreputable one—friends, neighbors, a familiar church, and friendly tradesmen; and it is not, moreover, in the nature of any ghetto to remain respectable long. Every Sunday, people who have left the block take the lonely ride back, dragging their increasingly discontented children with them. They spend the day talking, not always with words, about the trouble they've seen and the trouble—one must watch their eyes as they watch their children—they are only too likely to see. For children do not like ghettos. It takes them nearly no time to discover exactly why they are there.

The projects in Harlem are hated. They are hated almost as much as policemen, and this is saying a great deal. And they are hated for the same reason: both reveal, unbearably, the real attitude of the white world, no matter how many liberal speeches are made, no matter how many lofty editorials are written, no matter how many civil-rights commissions are set up.

The projects are hideous, of course, there being a law, apparently respected throughout the world, that popular housing shall be as cheerless as a prison. They are lumped all over Harlem, colorless, bleak, high, and revolting. The wide windows look out on Harlem's invincible and indescribable squalor: the Park Avenue railroad tracks, around which, about forty years ago, the present dark community began; the unrehabilitated houses, bowed down, it would seem, under the great weight of frustration and bitterness they contain; the dark, the ominous schoolhouses from which the child may emerge maimed, blinded, hooked, or enraged for life; and the churches, churches, block upon block of churches, niched in the walls like cannon in the walls of a fortress. Even if the administration of the projects were not so insanely humiliating (for example: one must report raises in salary to the management, which will then eat up the profit by raising one's rent; the management has the right to know who is staying in your apartment; the management can ask you to leave, at their discretion), the projects would still be hated because they are an insult to the meanest intelligence.

Harlem got its first private project, Riverton*—which is now, naturally, a slum—about twelve years ago because at that time Negroes were not allowed to live in Stuyvesant Town. Harlem watched Riverton go up, therefore, in the most violent bitterness of spirit, and hated it long before the builders arrived. They began hating it at about the time people began moving out of their condemned houses to make room for this additional proof of how thoroughly the white world despised them. And they had scarcely moved in, naturally, before they began smashing windows, defacing walls, urinating in the elevators, and fornicating in the playgrounds. Liberals, both white and black, were appalled at the spectacle. I was appalled by the liberal innocence—or cynicism, which comes out in practice as much the same thing. Other people were delighted to be able to point to proof positive that nothing could be done to better the lot of the colored people. They were, and are, right in one respect: that nothing can be done as long as they are treated like colored people. The people in Harlem know they are living there because white people do not think they are good enough to live anywhere else. No amount of "improvement" can sweeten this fact. Whatever money is now

*The inhabitants of Riverton were much embittered by this description; they have, apparently, forgotten how their project came into being; and have repeatedly informed me that I cannot possibly be referring to Riverton, but to another housing project which is directly across the street. It is quite clear, I think, that I have no interest in accusing any individuals or families of the depredations herein described: but neither can I deny the evidence of my own eyes. Nor do I blame anyone in Harlem for making the best of a dreadful bargain. But anyone who lives in Harlem and imagines that he has *not* struck this bargain, or that what he takes to be his status (in whose eyes?) protects him against the common pain, demoralization, and danger, is simply self deluded.

being earmarked to improve this, or any other ghetto, might as well be burnt. A ghetto can be improved in one way only: out of existence.

Similarly, the only way to police a ghetto is to be oppressive. None of the Police Commissioner's men, even with the best will in the world, have any way of understanding the lives led by the people they swagger about in twos and threes controlling. Their very presence is an insult, and it would be, even if they spent their entire day feeding gumdrops to children. They represent the force of the white world, and that world's real intentions are, simply, for that world's criminal profit and ease, to keep the black man corraled up here, in his place. The badge, the gun in the holster, and the swinging club make vivid what will happen should his rebellion become overt. Rare, indeed, is the Harlem citizen, from the most circumspect church member to the most shiftless adolescent, who does not have a long tale to tell of police incompetence, injustice, or brutality. I myself have witnessed and endured it more than once. The businessmen and racketeers also have a story. And so do the prostitutes. (And this is not, perhaps, the place to discuss Harlem's very complex attitude toward black policemen, nor the reasons, according to Harlem, that they are nearly all downtown.)

It is hard, on the other hand, to blame the policeman, blank, good-natured, thoughtless, and insuperably innocent, for being such a perfect representative of the people he serves. He, too, believes in good intentions and is astounded and offended when they are not taken for the deed. He has never, himself, done anything for which to be hated—which of us has?—and yet he is facing, daily and nightly, people who would gladly see him dead, and he knows it. There is no way for him not to know it: there are few things under heaven more unnerving than the silent, accumulating contempt and hatred of a people. He moves through Harlem, therefore, like an occupying soldier in a bitterly hostile country; which is precisely what, and where, he is, and is the reason he walks in twos and threes. And he is not the only one who knows why he is always in company: the people who are watching him know why, too. Any street meeting, sacred or secular, which he and his colleagues uneasily cover has as its explicit or im-

plicit burden the cruelty and injustice of the white domination. And these days, of course, in terms increasingly vivid and
jubilant, it speaks of the end of that domination. The white
policeman standing on a Harlem street corner finds himself at
the very center of the revolution now occurring in the world.
He is not prepared for it—naturally, nobody is—and, what is
possibly much more to the point, he is exposed, as few white
people are, to the anguish of the black people around him.
Even if he is gifted with the merest mustard grain of imagination, something must seep in. He cannot avoid observing
that some of the children, in spite of their color, remind him
of children he has known and loved, perhaps even of his own
children. He knows that he certainly does not want *his* children living this way. He can retreat from his uneasiness in only
one direction: into a callousness which very shortly becomes
second nature. He becomes more callous, the population becomes more hostile, the situation grows more tense, and the
police force is increased. One day, to everyone's astonishment,
someone drops a match in the powder keg and everything
blows up. Before the dust has settled or the blood congealed,
editorials, speeches, and civil-rights commissions are loud in
the land, demanding to know what happened. What happened
is that Negroes want to be treated like men.

Negroes want to be treated like men: a perfectly straight-
forward statement, containing only seven words. People who
have mastered Kant, Hegel, Shakespeare, Marx, Freud, and
the Bible find this statement utterly impenetrable. The idea
seems to threaten profound, barely conscious assumptions. A
kind of panic paralyzes their features, as though they found
themselves trapped on the edge of a steep place. I once tried
to describe to a very well-known American intellectual the
conditions among Negroes in the South. My recital disturbed
him and made him indignant; and he asked me in perfect
innocence, "Why don't all the Negroes in the South move
North?" I tried to explain what *has* happened, unfailingly,
whenever a significant body of Negroes move North. They do
not escape Jim Crow: they merely encounter another, not-
less-deadly variety. They do not move to Chicago, they move
to the South Side; they do not move to New York, they move
to Harlem. The pressure within the ghetto causes the ghetto

walls to expand, and this expansion is always violent. White people hold the line as long as they can, and in as many ways as they can, from verbal intimidation to physical violence. But inevitably the border which has divided the ghetto from the rest of the world falls into the hands of the ghetto. The white people fall back bitterly before the black horde; the landlords make a tidy profit by raising the rent, chopping up the rooms, and all but dispensing with the upkeep; and what has once been a neighborhood turns into a "turf." This is precisely what happened when the Puerto Ricans arrived in their thousands—and the bitterness thus caused is, as I write, being fought out all up and down those streets.

Northerners indulge in an extremely dangerous luxury. They seem to feel that because they fought on the right side during the Civil War, and won, they have earned the right merely to deplore what is going on in the South, without taking any responsibility for it; and that they can ignore what is happening in Northern cities because what is happening in Little Rock or Birmingham is worse. Well, in the first place, it is not possible for anyone who has not endured both to know which is "worse." I know Negroes who prefer the South and white Southerners, because "At least there, you haven't got to play any guessing games!" The guessing games referred to have driven more than one Negro into the narcotics ward, the madhouse, or the river. I know another Negro, a man very dear to me, who says, with conviction and with truth, "The spirit of the South is the spirit of America." He was born in the North and did his military training in the South. He did not, as far as I can gather, find the South "worse"; he found it, if anything, all too familiar. In the second place, though, even if Birmingham *is* worse, no doubt Johannesburg, South Africa, beats it by several miles, and Buchenwald was one of the worst things that ever happened in the entire history of the world. The world has never lacked for horrifying examples; but I do not believe that these examples are meant to be used as justification for our own crimes. This perpetual justification empties the heart of all human feeling. The emptier our hearts become, the greater will be our crimes. Thirdly, the South is not merely an embarrassingly backward region, but a part of this country, and what happens there concerns every one of us.

As far as the color problem is concerned, there is but one great difference between the Southern white and the Northerner: the Southerner remembers, historically and in his own psyche, a kind of Eden in which he loved black people and they loved him. Historically, the flaming sword laid across this Eden is the Civil War. Personally, it is the Southerner's sexual coming of age, when, without any warning, unbreakable taboos are set up between himself and his past. Everything, thereafter, is permitted him except the love he remembers and has never ceased to need. The resulting, indescribable torment affects every Southern mind and is the basis of the Southern hysteria.

None of this is true for the Northerner. Negroes represent nothing to him personally, except, perhaps, the dangers of carnality. He never sees Negroes. Southerners see them all the time. Northerners never think about them whereas Southerners are never really thinking of anything else. Negroes are, therefore, ignored in the North and are under surveillance in the South, and suffer hideously in both places. Neither the Southerner nor the Northerner is able to look on the Negro simply as a man. It seems to be indispensable to the national self-esteem that the Negro be considered either as a kind of ward (in which case we are told how many Negroes, comparatively, bought Cadillacs last year and how few, comparatively, were lynched), or as a victim (in which case we are promised that he will never vote in our assemblies or go to school with our kids). They are two sides of the same coin and the South will not change—*cannot* change—until the North changes. The country will not change until it re-examines itself and discovers what it really means by freedom. In the meantime, generations keep being born, bitterness is increased by incompetence, pride, and folly, and the world shrinks around us.

It is a terrible, an inexorable, law that one cannot deny the humanity of another without diminishing one's own: in the face of one's victim, one sees oneself. Walk through the streets of Harlem and see what we, this nation, have become.

4. East River, Downtown: Postscript to a Letter from Harlem

THE FACT that American Negroes rioted in the U.N. while Adlai Stevenson was addressing the Assembly shocked and baffled most white Americans. Stevenson's speech, and the spectacular disturbance in the gallery, were both touched off by the death, in Katanga, the day before, of Patrice Lumumba. Stevenson stated, in the course of his address, that the United States was "against" colonialism. God knows what the African nations, who hold 25 per cent of the voting stock in the U.N. were thinking—they may, for example, have been thinking of the U.S. abstention when the vote on Algerian freedom was before the Assembly—but I think I have a fairly accurate notion of what the Negroes in the gallery were thinking. I had intended to be there myself. It was my first reaction upon hearing of Lumumba's death. I was curious about the impact of this political assassination on Negroes in Harlem, for Lumumba had—has—captured the popular imagination there. I was curious to know if Lumumba's death, which is surely among the most sinister of recent events, would elicit from "our" side anything more than the usual, well-meaning rhetoric. And I was curious about the African reaction.

However, the chaos on my desk prevented my being in the U.N. gallery. Had I been there, I, too, in the eyes of most Americans, would have been merely a pawn in the hands of the Communists. The climate and the events of the last decade, and the steady pressure of the "cold" war, have given Americans yet another means of avoiding self-examination, and so it has been decided that the riots were "Communist" inspired. Nor was it long, naturally, before prominent Negroes rushed forward to assure the republic that the U.N. rioters do not represent the real feeling of the Negro community.

According, then, to what I take to be the prevailing view, these rioters were merely a handful of irresponsible, Stalinist-corrupted *provocateurs*.

I find this view amazing. It is a view which even a minimal effort at observation would immediately contradict. One has only, for example, to walk through Harlem and ask oneself two questions. The first question is: Would *I* like to live here? And the second question is: Why don't those who now live here move out? The answer to both questions is immediately obvious. Unless one takes refuge in the theory—however disguised—that Negroes are, somehow, different from white people, I do not see how one can escape the conclusion that the Negro's status in this country is not only a cruel injustice but a grave national liability.

Now, I do not doubt that, among the people at the U.N. that day, there were Stalinist and professional revolutionists acting out of the most cynical motives. Wherever there is great social discontent, these people are, sooner or later, to be found. Their presence is not as frightening as the discontent which creates their opportunity. What I find appalling—and really dangerous—is the American assumption that the Negro is so contented with his lot here that only the cynical agents of a foreign power can rouse him to protest. It is a notion which contains a gratuitous insult, implying, as it does, that Negroes can make no move unless they are manipulated. It forcibly suggests that the Southern attitude toward the Negro is also, essentially, the national attitude. When the South has trouble with its Negroes—when the Negroes refuse to remain in their "place"—it blames "outside" agitators and "Northern interference." When the nation has trouble with the Northern Negro, it blames the Kremlin. And this, by no means incidentally, is a very dangerous thing to do. We thus give credit to the Communists for attitudes and victories which are not theirs. We make of them the champions of the oppressed, and they could not, of course, be more delighted.

If, as is only too likely, one prefers not to visit Harlem and expose oneself to the anguish there, one has only to consider the two most powerful movements among Negroes in this country today. At one pole, there is the Negro student movement. This movement, I believe, will prove to be the very last attempt made by American Negroes to achieve acceptance in the republic, to force the country to honor its own ideals. The movement does not have as its goal the consumption of overcooked hamburgers and tasteless coffee at various sleazy lunch counters. Neither do Negroes, who have, largely, been produced by miscegenation, share the white man's helplessly hypocritical attitudes toward the time-honored and universal mingling. The goal of the student movement is nothing less than the liberation of the entire country from its most crippling attitudes and habits. The reason that it is important—of the utmost importance—for white people, here, to see the Negroes as people like themselves is that white people will not, otherwise, be able to see themselves as they are.

At the other pole is the Muslim movement, which daily becomes more powerful. The Muslims do not expect anything at all from the white people of this country. They do not believe that the American professions of democracy or equality have ever been even remotely sincere. They insist on the total separation of the races. This is to be achieved by the acquisition of land from the United States—land which is owed the Negroes as "back wages" for the labor wrested from them when they were slaves, and for their unrecognized and unhonored contributions to the wealth and power of this country. The student movement depends, at bottom, on an act of faith, an ability to see, beneath the cruelty and hysteria and apathy of white people, their bafflement and pain and essential decency. This is superbly difficult. It demands a perpetually cultivated spiritual resilience, for the bulk of the evidence contradicts the vision. But the Muslim movement has all the evidence on its side. Unless one supposes that the idea of black supremacy has virtues denied to the idea of white supremacy, one cannot possibly accept the deadly conclusions a Muslim draws from this evidence. On the other hand, it is quite impossible to argue with a Muslim concerning the actual state of Negroes in this country—the truth, after all, is the truth.

This is the great power a Muslim speaker has over his audience. His audience has not heard this truth—the truth about their daily lives—honored by anyone else. Almost anyone else, black or white, prefers to soften this truth, and point to a new day which is coming in America. But this day has been coming for nearly one hundred years. Viewed solely in the light of this country's moral professions, this lapse is inexcusable. Even more important, however, is the fact that there is desperately little in the record to indicate that white America ever seriously desired—or desires—to see this day arrive.

Usually, for example, those white people who are in favor of integration prove to be in favor of it later, in some other city, some other town, some other building, some other school. The arguments, or rationalizations, with which they attempt to disguise their panic cannot be respected. Northerners proffer their indignation about the South as a kind of badge, as proof of good intentions; never suspecting that they thus increase, in the heart of the Negro they are speaking to, a kind of helpless pain and rage—and pity. Negroes know how little most white people are prepared to implement their words with deeds, how little, when the chips are down, they are prepared to risk. And this long history of moral evasion has had an unhealthy effect on the total life of the country, and has eroded whatever respect Negroes may once have felt for white people.

We are beginning, therefore, to witness in this country a new thing. "I am not at all sure," states one prominent Negro, who is *not* a Muslim, "that I *want* to be integrated into a burning house." "I might," says another, "consider being integrated into something else, an American society more real and more honest—but *this*? No, thank you, man, who *needs* it?" And this searching disaffection has everything to do with the emergence of Africa: "At the rate things are going here, all of Africa will be free before we can get a lousy cup of coffee."

Now, of course, it is easy to say—and it is true enough, as far as it goes—that the American Negro deludes himself if he imagines himself capable of any loyalty other than his loyalty to the United States. He is an American, too, and he will survive or perish with the country. This seems an unanswerable argument. But, while I have no wish whatever to question the loyalty of American Negroes, I think this argument may be examined with some profit. The argument is used, I think, too often and too glibly. It obscures the effects of the passage of time, and the great changes that have taken place in the world.

In the first place, as the homeless wanderers of the twentieth century prove, the question of nationality no longer necessarily involves the question of allegiance. Allegiance, after all, has to work two ways; and one can grow weary of an allegiance which is not reciprocal. I have the right and the duty, for example, in my country, to vote; but it is my country's responsibility to protect my right to vote. People now approaching, or past, middle age, who have spent their lives in such struggles, have thereby acquired an understanding of America, and a belief in her potential which cannot now be shaken. (There are exceptions to this, however, W. E. B. Du Bois, for example. It is easy to dismiss him as a Stalinist; but it is more interesting to consider just why so intelligent a man became so disillusioned.) But I very strongly doubt that any Negro youth, now approaching maturity, and with the whole, vast world before him, is willing, say, to settle for Jim Crow in Miami, when he can—or, before the travel ban, *could*—feast at the welcome table in Havana. And he need not, to prefer Havana, have any pro-Communist, or, for that matter, pro-Cuban, or pro-Castro sympathies: he need merely prefer not to be treated as a second-class citizen.

These are extremely unattractive facts, but they *are* facts, and no purpose is served by denying them. Neither, as I have already tried to indicate, is any purpose served by pretending that Negroes who refuse to be bound by this country's peculiar attitudes are subversive. They have every right to refuse to be bound by a set of attitudes as useless now and as obsolete as the pillory. Finally, the time is forever behind us when Negroes could be expected to "wait." What is demanded now, and at once, is not that Negroes continue to adjust themselves to the cruel racial pressures of life in the United States but that the United States readjust itself to the facts of life in the present world.

One of these facts is that the American Negro can no longer, nor will he ever again, be controlled by white America's image of him. This fact has everything to do with the rise of Africa in world affairs. At the time that I was growing up, Negroes in this country were taught to be ashamed of Africa. They were taught it bluntly, as I was, for example, by being told that Africa had never contributed "anything" to civilization. Or one was taught the same lesson more obliquely, and even more effectively, by watching nearly naked, dancing, comic-opera, cannibalistic savages in the movies. They were nearly always all bad, sometimes funny, sometimes both. If one of them was good, his goodness was proved by his loyalty to the white man. A baffling sort of goodness, particularly as one's father, who certainly wanted one to be "good," was more than likely to come home cursing—cursing the white man. One's hair was always being attacked with hard brushes and combs and Vaseline: it was shameful to have "nappy" hair. One's legs and arms and face were always being greased, so that one would not look "ashy" in the wintertime. One was always being mercilessly scrubbed and polished, as though in the hope that a stain could thus be washed away— I hazard that the Negro children of my generation, anyway, had an earlier and more painful acquaintance with soap than any other children anywhere. The women were forever straightening and curling their hair, and using bleaching creams. And yet it was clear that none of this effort would release one from the stigma and danger of being a Negro; this effort merely increased the shame and rage. There was not, no matter where one turned, any acceptable image of oneself, no proof of one's existence. One had the choice, either of "acting just like a nigger" or of *not* acting just like a nigger— and only those who have tried it know how impossible it is to tell the difference.

My first hero was Joe Louis. I was ashamed of Father Divine. Haile Selassie was the first black emperor I ever saw— in a newsreel; he was pleading vainly with the West to prevent the rape of his country. And the extraordinary complex of tensions thus set up in the breast, between hatred of whites and contempt for blacks, is very hard to describe. Some of the most energetic people of my generation were destroyed by this interior warfare.

But none of this is so for those who are young now. The power of the white world to control their identities was crumbling as they were born; and by the time they were able to react to the world, Africa was on the stage of history. This could not but have an extraordinary effect on their own morale, for it meant that they were not merely the descendants of slaves in a white, Protestant, and puritan country: they were also related to kings and princes in an ancestral homeland, far away. And this has proved to be a great antidote to the poison of self-hatred.

It also signals, at last, the end of the Negro situation in this country, as we have so far known it. Any effort, from here on out, to keep the Negro in his "place" can only have the most extreme and unlucky repercussions. This being so, it would seem to me that the most intelligent effort we can now make is to give up this doomed endeavor and study how we can most quickly end this division in our house. The Negroes who rioted in the U.N. are but a very small echo of the black discontent now abroad in the world. If we are not able, and quickly, to face and begin to eliminate the sources of this discontent in our own country, we will never be able to do it on the great stage of the world.

5. A Fly in Buttermilk

YOU CAN take the child out of the country," my elders were fond of saying, "but you can't take the country out of the child." They were speaking of their own antecedents, I supposed; it didn't, anyway, seem possible that they could be warning me; I took myself out of the country and went to Paris. It was there I discovered that the old folks knew what they had been talking about: I found myself, willy-nilly, alchemized into an American the moment I touched French soil.

Now, back again after nearly nine years, it was ironical to reflect that if I had not lived in France for so long I would never have found it necessary—or possible—to visit the American South. The South had always frightened me. How deeply it had frightened me—though I had never seen it—and how soon, was one of the things my dreams revealed to me while I was there. And this made me think of the privacy and mystery of childhood all over again, in a new way. I wondered where children got their strength—the strength, in this case, to walk through mobs to get to school.

"You've got to remember," said an older Negro friend to me, in Washington, "that no matter what you see or how it makes you feel, it can't be compared to twenty-five, thirty years ago—you remember those photographs of Negroes hanging from trees?" I looked at him differently. *I* had seen the photographs—but *he* might have been one of them. "I remember," he said, "when conductors on streetcars wore pistols and had police powers." And he remembered a great deal more. He remembered, for example, hearing Booker T. Washington speak, and the day-to-day progress of the Scottsboro case, and the rise and bloody fall of Bessie Smith. These had been books and headlines and music for me but it now developed that they were also a part of my identity.

"You're just one generation away from the South, you know. You'll find," he added, kindly, "that people will be willing to talk to you . . . if they don't feel that you look down on them just because you're from the North."

187

The first Negro I encountered, an educator, didn't give me any opportunity to look down. He forced me to admit, at once, that I had never been to college; that Northern Negroes lived herded together, like pigs in a pen; that the campus on which we met was a tribute to the industry and determination of Southern Negroes. "Negroes in the South form a *community.*" My humiliation was complete with his discovery that I couldn't even drive a car. I couldn't ask him anything. He made me feel so hopeless an example of the general Northern spinelessness that it would have seemed a spiteful counter-attack to have asked him to discuss the integration problem which had placed his city in the headlines.

At the same time, I felt that there was nothing which bothered him more; but perhaps he did not really know what he thought about it; or thought too many things at once. His campus risked being very different twenty years from now. Its special function would be gone—and so would his position, arrived at with such pain. The new day a-coming was not for him. I don't think this fact made him bitter but I think it frightened him and made him sad; for the future is like heaven—everyone exalts it but no one wants to go there now. And I imagine that he shared the attitude, which I was to encounter so often later, toward the children who were helping to bring this future about: admiration before the general spectacle and skepticism before the individual case.

That evening I went to visit G., one of the "integrated" children, a boy of about fifteen. I had already heard something of his first day in school, the peculiar problems his presence caused, and his own extraordinary bearing.

He seemed extraordinary at first mainly by his silence. He was tall for his age and, typically, seemed to be constructed mainly of sharp angles, such as elbows and knees. Dark gingerbread sort of coloring, with ordinary hair, and a face disquietingly impassive, save for his very dark, very large eyes. I got the impression, each time that he raised them, not so much that they spoke but that they registered volumes; each time he dropped them it was as though he had retired into the library.

We sat in the living room, his mother, younger brother and

sister, and I, while G. sat on the sofa, doing his homework. The father was at work and the older sister had not yet come home. The boy had looked up once, as I came in, to say, "Good evening, sir," and then left all the rest to his mother.

Mrs. R. was a very strong-willed woman, handsome, quiet-looking, dressed in black. Nothing, she told me, beyond name-calling, had marked G.'s first day at school; but on the second day she received the last of several threatening phone calls. She was told that if she didn't want her son "cut to ribbons" she had better keep him at home. She heeded this warning to the extent of calling the chief of police.

"He told me to go on and send him. He said he'd be there when the cutting started. So I sent him." Even more remarkably perhaps, G. went.

No one cut him, in fact no one touched him. The students formed a wall between G. and the entrances, saying only enough, apparently, to make their intention clearly understood, watching him, and keeping him outside. (I asked him, "What did you feel when they blocked your way?" G. looked up at me, very briefly, with no expression on his face, and told me, "Nothing, sir.") At last the principal appeared and took him by the hand and they entered the school, while the children shouted behind them, "Nigger-lover!"

G. was alone all day at school.

"But I thought you already knew some of the kids there," I said. I had been told that he had friends among the white students because of their previous competition in a Soapbox Derby.

"Well, none of them are in his classes," his mother told me—a shade too quickly, as though she did not want to dwell on the idea of G.'s daily isolation.

"We don't have the same schedule," G. said. It was as though he were coming to his mother's rescue. Then, unwillingly, with a kind of interior shrug, "Some of the guys had lunch with me but then the other kids called them names." He went back to his homework.

I began to realize that there were not only a great many things G. would not tell me, there was much that he would never tell his mother.

"But nobody bothers you, anyway?"

"No," he said. "They just—call names. I don't let it bother me."

Nevertheless, the principal frequently escorts him through the halls. One day, when G. was alone, a boy tripped him and knocked him down and G. reported this to the principal. The white boy denied it but a few days later, while G. and the principal were together, he came over and said, "I'm sorry I tripped you; I won't do it again," and they shook hands. But it doesn't seem that this boy has as yet developed into a friend. And it is clear that G. will not allow himself to expect this.

I asked Mrs. R. what had prompted her to have her son reassigned to a previously all-white high school. She sighed, paused; then, sharply, "Well, it's not because I'm so anxious to have him around white people." Then she laughed. "I really don't know how I'd feel if I was to carry a white baby around who was calling me Grandma." G. laughed, too, for the first time. "White people say," the mother went on, "that that's all a Negro wants. I don't think they believe that themselves."

Then we switched from the mysterious question of what white folks believe to the relatively solid ground of what she, herself, knows and fears.

"You see that boy? Well, he's always been a straight-A student. He didn't hardly have to work at it. You see the way he's so quiet now on the sofa, with his books? Well, when he was going to —— High School, he didn't have no homework or if he did, he could get it done in five minutes. Then, there he was, out in the streets, getting into mischief, and all he did all day in school was just keep clowning to make the other boys laugh. He wasn't learning nothing and didn't nobody care if he *never* learned nothing and I could just see what was going to happen to him if he kept on like that."

The boy was very quiet.

"What were you learning in —— High?" I asked him.

"Nothing!" he exploded, with a very un-boyish laugh. I asked him to tell me about it.

"Well, the teacher comes in," he said, "and she gives you something to read and she goes out. She leaves some other student in charge . . ." ("You can just imagine how much reading gets done," Mrs. R. interposed.) "At the end of the period," G. continued, "she comes back and tells you something to read for the next day."

So, having nothing else to do, G. began amusing his classmates and his mother began to be afraid. G. is just about at the age when boys begin dropping out of school. Perhaps they get a girl into trouble; she also drops out; the boy gets work for a time or gets into trouble for a long time. I was told that forty-five girls had left school for the maternity ward the year before. A week or ten days before I arrived in the city eighteen boys from G.'s former high school had been sentenced to the chain gang.

"My boy's a good boy," said Mrs. R., "and I wanted to see him have a chance."

"Don't the teachers care about the students?" I asked. This brought forth more laughter. How could they care? How much could they do if they *did* care? There were too many children, from shaky homes and worn-out parents, in aging, inadequate plants. They could be considered, most of them, as already doomed. Besides, the teachers' jobs were safe. They were responsible only to the principal, an appointed official, whose judgment, apparently, was never questioned by his (white) superiors or confreres.

The principal of G.'s former high school was about seventy-five when he was finally retired and his idea of discipline was to have two boys beat each other—"under his supervision"—with leather belts. This once happened with G., with no other results than that his parents gave the principal a tongue-lashing. It happened with two boys of G.'s acquaintance with the result that, after school, one boy beat the other so badly that he had to be sent to the hospital. The teachers have themselves arrived at a dead end, for in a segregated school system they cannot rise any higher, and the students are aware of this. Both students and teachers soon cease to struggle.

"If a boy can wash a blackboard," a teacher was heard to say, "I'll promote him."

I asked Mrs. R. how other Negroes felt about her having had G. reassigned.

"Well, a lot of them don't like it," she said—though I gathered that they did not say so to her. As school time approached, more and more people asked her, "Are you going to send him?" "Well," she told them, "the man says the door is open and I feel like, yes, I'm going to go on and send him."

Out of a population of some fifty thousand Negroes, there had been only forty-five applications. People had said that they would send their children, had talked about it, had made plans; but, as the time drew near, when the application blanks were actually in their hands, they said, "I don't believe I'll sign this right now. I'll sign it later." Or, "I been thinking about this. I don't believe I'll send him right now."

"Why?" I asked. But to this she couldn't, or wouldn't, give me any answer.

I asked if there had been any reprisals taken against herself or her husband, if she was worried while G. was at school all day. She said that, no, there had been no reprisals, though some white people, under the pretext of giving her good advice, had expressed disapproval of her action. But she herself doesn't have a job and so doesn't risk losing one. Nor, she told me, had anyone said anything to her husband, who, however, by her own proud suggestion, is extremely close-mouthed. And it developed later that he was not working at his regular trade but at something else.

As to whether she was worried, "No," she told me; in much the same way that G., when asked about the blockade, had said, "Nothing, sir." In her case it was easier to see what she meant: she hoped for the best and would not allow herself, in the meantime, to lose her head. "I don't feel like nothing's going to happen," she said, soberly. "I *hope* not. But I know if anybody tries to harm me or any one of my children, I'm going to strike back with all my strength. I'm going to strike them in God's name."

G., in the meantime, on the sofa with his books, was preparing himself for the next school day. His face was as impassive as ever and I found myself wondering—again—how he managed to face what must surely have been the worst moment of his day—the morning, when he opened his eyes and realized that it was all to be gone through again. Insults, and incipient violence, teachers, and—exams.

"One among so many," his mother said, "that's kind of rough."

"Do you think you'll make it?" I asked him. "Would you rather go back to —— High?"

"No," he said, "I'll make it. I ain't going back."

"He ain't thinking about going back," said his mother—proudly and sadly. I began to suspect that the boy managed to support the extreme tension of his situation by means of a nearly fanatical concentration on his schoolwork; by holding in the center of his mind the issue on which, when the deal went down, others would be *forced* to judge him. Pride and silence were his weapons. Pride comes naturally, and soon, to a Negro, but even his mother, I felt, was worried about G.'s silence, though she was too wise to break it. For what was all this doing to him really?

"It's hard enough," the boy said later, still in control but with flashing eyes, "to keep quiet and keep walking when they call you nigger. But if anybody ever spits on me, I *know* I'll have to fight."

His mother laughs, laughs to ease them both, then looks at me and says, "I wonder sometimes what makes white folks so mean."

This is a recurring question among Negroes, even among the most "liberated"—which epithet is meant, of course, to describe the writer. The next day, with this question (more elegantly phrased) still beating in my mind, I visited the principal of G.'s new high school. But he didn't look "mean" and he wasn't "mean": he was a thin, young man of about my age, bewildered and in trouble. I asked him how things were working out, what he thought about it, what he thought would happen—in the long run, or the short.

"Well, I've got a job to do," he told me, "and I'm going to do it." He said that there hadn't been any trouble and that he didn't expect any. "Many students, after all, never see G. at all." None of the children have harmed him and the teachers are, apparently, carrying out their rather tall orders, which are to be kind to G. and, at the same time, to treat him like any other student.

I asked him to describe to me the incident, on the second day of school, when G.'s entrance had been blocked by the students. He told me that it was nothing at all—"It was a gesture more than anything else." He had simply walked out and spoken to the students and brought G. inside. "I've seen them do the same thing to other kids when they were kidding," he said. I imagine that he would like to be able to place this incident in the same cheerful if rowdy category, despite the shouts (which he does not mention) of "niggerlover!"

Which epithet does not, in any case, describe him at all.

"Why," I asked, "is G. the only Negro student here?" According to this city's pupil-assignment plan, a plan designed to allow the least possible integration over the longest possible period of time, G. was the only Negro student who qualified.

"And, anyway," he said, "I don't think it's right for colored children to come to white schools just *because* they're white."

"Well," I began, "even if you don't like it . . ."

"Oh," he said quickly, raising his head and looking at me sideways, "I never said I didn't like it."

And then he explained to me, with difficulty, that it was simply contrary to everything he'd ever seen or believed. He'd never dreamed of a mingling of the races; had never lived that way himself and didn't suppose that he ever would; in the same way, he added, perhaps a trifle defensively, that he only associated with a certain stratum of white people. But, "I've never seen a colored person toward whom I had any hatred or ill-will."

His eyes searched mine as he said this and I knew that he was wondering if I believed him.

I certainly did believe him; he impressed me as being a very gentle and honorable man. But I could not avoid wondering if he had ever really *looked* at a Negro and wondered about the life, the aspirations, the universal humanity hidden behind the dark skin. As I wondered, when he told me that race relations in his city were "excellent" and had not been strained by recent developments, how on earth he managed to hold on to this delusion.

I later got back to my interrupted question, which I phrased more tactfully.

"Even though it's very difficult for all concerned—this situation—doesn't it occur to you that the reason colored children wish to come to white schools isn't because they want to be with white people but simply because they want a better education?"

"Oh, I don't know," he replied, "it seems to me that colored schools are just as good as white schools." I wanted to ask him on what evidence he had arrived at this conclusion and also how they could possibly be "as good" in view of the kind of life they came out of, and perpetuated, and the dim prospects faced by all but the most exceptional or ruthless Negro students. But I only suggested that G. and his family, who certainly should have known, so thoroughly disagreed with him that they had been willing to risk G.'s present well-being and his future psychological and mental health in order to bring about a change in his environment. Nor did I mention the lack of enthusiasm evinced by G.'s mother when musing on the prospect of a fair grandchild. There seemed no point in making this man any more a victim of his heritage than he so gallantly was already.

"Still," I said at last, after a rather painful pause, "I should think that the trouble in this situation is that it's very hard for *you* to face a child and treat him unjustly because of something for which he is no more responsible than—than *you* are."

The eyes came to life then, or a veil fell, and I found myself staring at a man in anguish. The eyes were full of pain and bewilderment and he nodded his head. This was the impossibility which he faced every day. And I imagined that his tribe would increase, in sudden leaps and bounds was already increasing.

For segregation has worked brilliantly in the South, and, in fact, in the nation, to this extent: it has allowed white people, with scarcely any pangs of conscience whatever, to *create*, in every generation, only the Negro they wished to see. As the walls come down they will be forced to take another, harder look at the shiftless and the menial and will be forced into a wonder concerning them which cannot fail to be agonizing. It is not an easy thing to be forced to re-examine a way of life and to speculate, in a personal way, on the general injustice.

"What do you think," I asked him, "will happen? What do you think the future holds?"

He gave a strained laugh and said he didn't know. "I don't want to think about it." Then, "I'm a religious man," he said, "and I believe the Creator will always help us find a way to solve our problems. If a man loses that, he's lost everything he had." I agreed, struck by the look in his eyes.

"You're from the North?" he asked me, abruptly.

"Yes," I said.

"Well," he said, "you've got your troubles too."

"Ah, yes, we certainly do," I admitted, and shook hands and left him. I did not say what I was thinking, that our troubles were the same trouble and that, unless we were very swift and honest, what is happening in the South today will be happening in the North tomorrow.

6. Nobody Knows My Name: A Letter from the South

I walked down the street,
didn't have on no hat,
Asking everybody I meet,
Where's my man at?
— MA RAINEY

NEGROES in the North are right when they refer to the South as the Old Country. A Negro born in the North who finds himself in the South is in a position similar to that of the son of the Italian emigrant who finds himself in Italy, near the village where his father first saw the light of day. Both are in countries they have never seen, but which they cannot fail to recognize. The landscape has always been familiar; the speech is archaic, but it rings a bell; and so do the ways of the people, though their ways are not his ways. Everywhere he turns, the revenant finds himself reflected. He sees himself as he was before he was born, perhaps; or as the man he would have become, had he actually been born in this place. He sees the world, from an angle odd indeed, in which his fathers awaited his arrival, perhaps in the very house in which he narrowly avoided being born. He sees, in effect, his ancestors, who, in everything they do and are, proclaim his inescapable identity. And the Northern Negro in the South sees, whatever he or anyone else may wish to believe, that his ancestors are both white and black. The white men, flesh of his flesh, hate him for that very reason. On the other hand, there is scarcely any way for him to join the black community in the South: for both he and this community are in the grip of the immense illusion that their state is more miserable than his own.

This illusion owes everything to the great American illusion that our state is a state to be envied by other people: we are powerful, and we are rich. But our power makes us uncomfortable and we handle it very ineptly. The principal effect of our material well-being has been to set the children's teeth on edge. If we ourselves were not so fond of this illusion, we might understand ourselves and other peoples better than we do, and be enabled to help them understand us. I am very often tempted to believe that this illusion is all that is left of the great dream that was to have become America; whether this is so or not, this illusion certainly prevents us from making America what we say we want it to be.

But let us put aside, for the moment, these subversive speculations. In the fall of last year, my plane hovered over the rust-red earth of Georgia. I was past thirty, and I had never seen this land before. I pressed my face against the window, watching the earth come closer; soon we were just above the tops of trees. I could not suppress the thought that this earth had acquired its color from the blood that had dripped down from these trees. My mind was filled with the image of a black man, younger than I, perhaps, or my own age, hanging from a tree, while white men watched him and cut his sex from him with a knife.

My father must have seen such sights—he was very old when he died—or heard of them, or had this danger touch him. The Negro poet I talked to in Washington, much younger than my father, perhaps twenty years older than myself, remembered such things very vividly, had a long tale to tell, and counseled me to think back on those days as a means of steadying the soul. I was to remember that time, whatever else it had failed to do, nevertheless had passed, that the situation, whether or not it was better, was certainly no longer the same. I was to remember that Southern Negroes had endured things I could not imagine; but this did not really place me at such a great disadvantage, since they clearly had been unable to imagine what awaited them in Harlem. I remembered the Scottsboro case, which I had followed as a child. I remembered Angelo Herndon and wondered, again, whatever had become of him. I remembered the soldier in uniform blinded by an enraged white man, just after the Second World War. There had been many such incidents after the First War, which was one of the reasons I had been born in Harlem. I remembered Willie McGhee, Emmett Till, and the others. My younger brothers had visited Atlanta some years before. I remembered what they had told me about it. One of my brothers, in uniform, had had his front teeth kicked out by a white officer. I remembered my mother telling us how she had wept and prayed and tried to kiss the venom out of her suicidally embittered son. (She managed to do it, too; heaven only knows what she herself was feeling, whose father and brothers had lived and died down here.) I remembered myself as a very small boy, already so bitter about the pledge of allegiance that I could scarcely bring myself to say it, and never, never believed it.

I was, in short, but one generation removed from the South, which was now undergoing a new convulsion over whether black children had the same rights, or capacities, for education as did the children of white people. This is a criminally frivolous dispute, absolutely unworthy of this nation; and it is being carried on, in complete bad faith, by completely uneducated people. (We do not trust educated people and rarely, alas, produce them, for we do not trust the independence of mind which alone makes a genuine education possible.) Educated people, of any color, are so extremely rare that it is unquestionably one of the first tasks of a nation to open all of its schools to all of its citizens. But the dispute has actually nothing to do with education, as some among the eminently uneducated know. It has to do with political power and it has to do with sex. And this is a nation which, most unluckily, knows very little about either.

The city of Atlanta, according to my notes, is "big, wholly segregated, sprawling; population variously given as six hundred thousand or one million, depending on whether one goes beyond or remains within the city limits. Negroes 25 to 30 per cent of the population. Racial relations, on the record, can be described as fair, considering that this is the state of Georgia. Growing industrial town. Racial relations manipulated by the mayor and a fairly strong Negro middle class. This works mainly in the areas of compromise and concession and has very little effect on the bulk of the Negro population and none whatever on the rest of the state. No integration, pending or actual." Also, it seemed to me that the Negroes in Atlanta were "very vividly *city* Negroes"—they seemed less patient than their rural brethren, more dangerous, or at least more unpredictable. And: "Have seen one wealthy Negro section, very pretty, but with an unpaved road. . . . The section in which I am living is composed of frame houses in various stages of disrepair and neglect, in which two and three families live, often sharing a single toilet. This is the other side of the tracks; literally, I mean. It is located, as I am told is the case in many Southern cities, just beyond the underpass." Atlanta contains a high proportion of Negroes who own their own homes and exist, visibly anyway, independently of the white world. Southern towns distrust this class and do everything in their power to prevent its appearance. But it is a class which has a certain usefulness in Southern cities. There is an incipient war, in fact, between Southern cities and Southern towns— between the city, that is, and the state—which we will discuss later. Little Rock is an ominous example of this and it is likely—indeed, it is certain—that we will see many more such examples before the present crisis is over.

Before arriving in Atlanta I had spent several days in Charlotte, North Carolina. This is a bourgeois town, Presbyterian, pretty—if you like towns—and socially so hermetic that it contains scarcely a single decent restaurant. I was told that Negroes there are not even licensed to become electricians or plumbers. I was also told, several times, by white people, that "race relations" there were excellent. I failed to find a single Negro who agreed with this, which is the usual story of "race relations" in this country. Charlotte, a town of 165,000, was in a ferment when I was there because, of its 50,000 Negroes, four had been assigned to previously all-white schools, one to each school. In fact, by the time I got there, there were only three. Dorothy Counts, the daughter of a Presbyterian minister, after several days of being stoned and spat on by the mob—"spit," a woman told me, "was hanging from the hem of Dorothy's dress"—had withdrawn from Harding High. Several white students, I was told, had called—not called *on*—Miss Counts, to beg her to stick it out. Harry Golden, editor of *The Carolina Israelite*, suggested that the "hoodlum element" might not so have shamed the town and the nation if several of the town's leading businessmen had personally escorted Miss Counts to school.

I saw the Negro schools in Charlotte, saw, on street corners, several of their alumnae, and read about others who had been sentenced to the chain gang. This solved the mystery of just what made Negro parents send their children out to face mobs. White people do not understand this because they do not know, and do not want to know, that the alternative to this ordeal is nothing less than a lifelong ordeal. Those Negro parents who spend their days trembling for their children and the rest of their time praying that their children have not been too badly damaged inside, are not doing this out of "ideals" or "convictions" or because they are in the grip of a perverse desire to send their children where "they are not wanted." They are doing it because they want the child to receive the education which will allow him to defeat, possibly escape, and not impossibly help one day abolish the stifling environment in which they see, daily, so many children perish.

This is certainly not the purpose, still less the effect, of most Negro schools. It is hard enough, God knows, under the best of circumstances, to get an education in this country. White children are graduated yearly who can neither read, write, nor think, and who are in a state of the most abysmal ignorance concerning the world around them. But at least they are white. They are under the illusion—which, since they are so badly educated, sometimes has a fatal tenacity—that they can do whatever they want to do. Perhaps that is exactly what they *are* doing, in which case we had best all go down in prayer.

The level of Negro education, obviously, is even lower than the general level. The general level is low because, as I have said, Americans have so little respect for genuine intellectual effort. The Negro level is low because the education of Negroes occurs in, and is designed to perpetuate, a segregated society. This, in the first place, and no matter how much money the South boasts of spending on Negro schools, is utterly demoralizing. It creates a situation in which the Negro teacher is soon as powerless as his students. (There are exceptions among the teachers as there are among the students, but, in this country surely, schools have not been built for the exceptional. And, though white people often seem to expect Negroes to produce nothing but exceptions, the fact is that Negroes are really just like everybody else. Some of them are exceptional and most of them are not.)

The teachers are answerable to the Negro principal, whose power over the teachers is absolute but whose power with the school board is slight. As for this principal, he has arrived at the summit of his career; rarely indeed can he go any higher. He has his pension to look forward to, and he consoles himself, meanwhile, with his status among the "better class of Negroes." This class includes few, if any, of his students and by no means all of his teachers. The teachers, as long as they remain in this school system, and they certainly do not have much choice, can only aspire to become the principal one day. Since not all of them will make it, a great deal of the energy which ought to go into their vocation goes into the usual bitter, purposeless rivalry. They are underpaid and ill treated by the white world and rubbed raw by it every day; and it is altogether understandable that they, very shortly, cannot bear the sight of their students. The children know this; it is hard to fool young people. They also know why they are going to an overcrowded, outmoded plant, in classes so large that even the most strictly attentive student, the most gifted teacher cannot but feel himself slowly drowning in the sea of general helplessness.

It is not to be wondered at, therefore, that the violent distractions of puberty, occurring in such a cage, annually take their toll, sending female children into the maternity wards and male children into the streets. It is not to be wondered at that a boy, one day, decides that if all this studying is going to prepare him only to be a porter or an elevator boy—or his teacher—well, then, the hell with it. And there they go, with an overwhelming bitterness which they will dissemble all their lives, an unceasing effort which completes their ruin. They become the menial or the criminal or the shiftless, the Negroes whom segregation has produced and whom the South uses to prove that segregation is right.

In Charlotte, too, I received some notion of what the South means by "time to adjust." The NAACP there had been trying for six years before Black Monday to make the city fathers honor the "separate but equal" statute and do something about the situation in Negro schools. Nothing whatever was done. After Black Monday, Charlotte begged for "time": and what she did with this time was work out legal stratagems designed to get the least possible integration over the longest possible period. In August of 1955, Governor Hodges, a mod-

erate, went on the air with the suggestion that Negroes seg-
regate themselves voluntarily—for the good, as he put it, of
both races. Negroes seeming to be unmoved by this moderate
proposal, the Klan reappeared in the counties and was still
active there when I left. So, no doubt, are the boys on the
chain gang.

But "Charlotte," I was told, "is not the South." I was told,
"You haven't seen the South yet." Charlotte seemed quite
Southern enough for me, but, in fact, the people in Charlotte
were right. One of the reasons for this is that the South is not
the monolithic structure which, from the North, it appears to
be, but a most various and divided region. It clings to the
myth of its past but it is being inexorably changed, meanwhile,
by an entirely unmythical present: its habits and its self-interest
are at war. Everyone in the South feels this and this is why
there is such panic on the bottom and such impotence on the
top.

It must also be said that the racial setup in the South is not,
for a Negro, very different from the racial setup in the North.
It is the etiquette which is baffling, not the spirit. Segregation
is unofficial in the North and official in the South, a crucial
difference that does nothing, nevertheless, to alleviate the lot
of most Northern Negroes. But we will return to this question
when we discuss the relationship between the Southern cities
and states.

Atlanta, however, *is* the South. It is the South in this respect, that it has a very bitter interracial history. This is written
in the faces of the people and one feels it in the air. It was on
the outskirts of Atlanta that I first felt how the Southern landscape—the trees, the silence, the liquid heat, and the fact that
one always seems to be traveling great distances—seems designed for violence, seems, almost, to demand it. What passions cannot be unleashed on a dark road in a Southern night!
Everything seems so sensual, so languid, and so private. Desire
can be acted out here; over this fence, behind that tree, in the
darkness, there; and no one will see, no one will ever know.
Only the night is watching and the night was made for desire.
Protestantism is the wrong religion for people in such cli-
mates; America is perhaps the last nation in which such a
climate belongs. In the Southern night everything seems

possible, the most private, unspeakable longings; but then arrives the Southern day, as hard and brazen as the night was soft and dark. It brings what was done in the dark to light. It must have seemed something like this for those people who made the region what it is today. It must have caused them great pain. Perhaps the master who had coupled with his slave saw his guilt in his wife's pale eyes in the morning. And the wife saw his children in the slave quarters, saw the way his concubine, the sensual-looking black girl, looked at her—a woman, after all, and scarcely less sensual, but white. The youth, nursed and raised by the black Mammy whose arms had then held all that there was of warmth and love and desire, and still confounded by the dreadful taboos set up between himself and her progeny, must have wondered, after his first experiment with black flesh, where, under the blazing heavens, he could hide. And the white man must have seen his guilt written somewhere else, seen it all the time, even if his sin was merely lust, even if his sin lay in nothing but his power: in the eyes of the black man. He may not have stolen his woman, but he had certainly stolen his freedom—this black man, who had a body like his, and passions like his, and a ruder, more erotic beauty. How many times has the Southern day come up to find that black man, sexless, hanging from a tree!

It was an old black man in Atlanta who looked into my eyes and directed me into my first segregated bus. I have spent a long time thinking about that man. I never saw him again. I cannot describe the look which passed between us, as I asked him for directions, but it made me think, at once, of Shakespeare's "the oldest have borne most." It made me think of the blues: *Now, when a woman gets the blues, Lord, she hangs her head and cries. But when a man gets the blues, Lord, he grabs a train and rides.* It was borne in on me, suddenly, just why these men had so often been grabbing freight trains as the evening sun went down. And it was, perhaps, because I was getting on a segregated bus, and wondering how Negroes had borne this and other indignities for so long, that this man so struck me. He seemed to know what I was feeling. His eyes seemed to say that what I was feeling he had been feeling, at much higher pressure, all his life. But my eyes would never see the hell his eyes had seen. And this hell was, simply, that he had never in his life owned anything, not his wife, not his house, not his child, which could not, at any instant, be taken from him by the power of white people. This is what paternalism means. And for the rest of the time that I was in the South I watched the eyes of old black men.

Atlanta's well-to-do Negroes never take buses, for they all have cars. The section in which they live is quite far away from the poor Negro section. They own, or at least are paying for, their own homes. They drive to work and back, and have cocktails and dinner with each other. They see very little of the white world; but they are cut off from the black world, too.

Now, of course, this last statement is not literally true. The teachers teach Negroes, the lawyers defend them. The ministers preach to them and bury them, and others insure their lives, pull their teeth, and cure their ailments. Some of the lawyers work with the NAACP and help push test cases through the courts. (If anything, by the way, disproves the charge of "extremism" which has so often been made against this organization, it is the fantastic care and patience such legal efforts demand.) Many of the teachers work very hard to bolster the morale of their students and prepare them for their new responsibilities; nor did those I met fool themselves about the hideous system under which they work. So when I say that they are cut off from the black world, I am not sneering, which, indeed, I scarcely have any right to do. I am talking about their position as a class—*if* they are a class—and their role in a very complex and shaky social structure.

The wealthier Negroes are, at the moment, very useful for the administration of the city of Atlanta, for they represent there the potential, at least, of interracial communication. That this phrase is a euphemism, in Atlanta as elsewhere, becomes clear when one considers how astonishingly little has been communicated in all these generations. What the phrase almost always has reference to is the fact that, in a given time and place, the Negro vote is of sufficient value to force politicians to bargain for it. What interracial communication also refers to is that Atlanta is really growing and thriving, and because it wants to make even more money, it would like to prevent incidents that disturb the peace, discourage investments, and permit test cases, which the city of Atlanta would certainly lose, to come to the courts. Once this happens, as it certainly will one day, the state of Georgia will be up in arms and the present administration of the city will be out of power. I did not meet a soul in Atlanta (I naturally did not meet any members of the White Citizens' Council, not, anyway, to talk to) who did not pray that the present mayor would be re-elected. Not that they loved him particularly, but it is his administration which holds off the holocaust.

Now this places Atlanta's wealthy Negroes in a really quite sinister position. Though both they and the mayor are devoted to keeping the peace, their aims and his are not, and cannot be, the same. Many of those lawyers are working day and night on test cases which the mayor is doing his best to keep out of court. The teachers spend their working day attempting to destroy in their students—and it is not too much to say, in themselves—those habits of inferiority which form one of the principal cornerstones of segregation as it is practiced in the South. Many of the parents listen to speeches by people like Senator Russell and find themselves unable to sleep at night. They are in the extraordinary position of being compelled to work for the destruction of all they have bought so dearly—their homes, their comfort, the safety of their children. But the safety of their children is merely comparative; it is all that their comparative strength as a class has bought them so far; and they are not safe, really, as long as the bulk of Atlanta's Negroes live in such darkness. On any night, in that other part of town, a policeman may beat up one Negro too many, or some Negro or some white man may simply go berserk. This is all it takes to drive so delicately balanced a city mad. And the island on which these Negroes have built their handsome houses will simply disappear.

This is not at all in the interests of Atlanta, and almost everyone there knows it. Left to itself, the city might grudgingly work out compromises designed to reduce the tension and raise the level of Negro life. But it is not left to itself; it belongs to the state of Georgia. The Negro vote has no power in the state, and the governor of Georgia—that "third-rate man," Atlantans call him—makes great political capital out of keeping the Negroes in their place. When six Negro ministers attempted to create a test case by ignoring the segregation ordinance on the buses, the governor was ready to declare martial law and hold the ministers incommunicado. It was the mayor who prevented this, who somehow squashed all publicity, treated the ministers with every outward sign of respect, and it is his office which is preventing the case from coming into court. And remember that it was the governor of Arkansas, in an insane bid for political power, who created the present crisis in Little Rock—against the will of most of its citizens and against the will of the mayor.

This war between the Southern cities and states is of the utmost importance, not only for the South, but for the nation. The Southern states are still very largely governed by people whose political lives, insofar, at least, as they are able to conceive of life or politics, are dependent on the people in the rural regions. It might, indeed, be more honorable to try to guide these people out of their pain and ignorance instead of locking them within it, and battening on it; but it is, admittedly, a difficult task to try to tell people the truth and it is clear that most Southern politicians have no intention of attempting it. The attitude of these people can only have the effect of stiffening the already implacable Negro resistance, and this attitude is absolutely certain, sooner or later, to create great trouble in the cities. When a race riot occurs in Atlanta, it will not spread merely to Birmingham, for example. (Birmingham is a doomed city.) The trouble will spread to every metropolitan center in the nation which has a significant Negro population. And this is not only because the ties between Northern and Southern Negroes are still very close. It is because the nation, the entire nation, has spent a hundred years avoiding the question of the place of the black man in it.

That this has done terrible things to black men is not even a question. "Integration," said a very light Negro to me in Alabama, "has always worked very well in the South, after the sun goes down." "It's not miscegenation," said another Negro to me, "unless a black man's involved." Now, I talked to many Southern liberals who were doing their best to bring integration about in the South, but met scarcely a single

Southerner who did not weep for the passing of the old order. They were perfectly sincere, too, and, within their limits, they were right. They pointed out how Negroes and whites in the South had loved each other, they recounted to me tales of devotion and heroism which the old order had produced, and which, now, would never come again. But the old black men I looked at down there—those same black men that the Southern liberal had loved; for whom, until now, the Southern liberal—and not only the liberal—has been willing to undergo great inconvenience and danger—they were not weeping. Men do not like to be protected, it emasculates them. This is what black men know, it is the reality they have lived with; it is what white men do not want to know. It is not a pretty thing to be a father and be ultimately dependent on the power and kindness of some other man for the well-being of your house.

But what this evasion of the Negro's humanity has done to the nation is not so well known. The really striking thing, for me, in the South was this dreadful paradox, that the black men were stronger than the white. I do not know how they did it, but it certainly has something to do with that as yet unwritten history of the Negro woman. What it comes to, finally, is that the nation has spent a large part of its time and energy looking away from one of the principal facts of its life. This failure to look reality in the face diminishes a nation as it diminishes a person, and it can only be described as unmanly. And in exactly the same way that the South imagines that it "knows" the Negro, the North imagines that it has set him free. Both camps are deluded. Human freedom is a complex, difficult—and private—thing. If we can liken life, for a moment, to a furnace, then freedom is the fire which burns away illusion. Any honest examination of the national life proves how far we are from the standard of human freedom with which we began. The recovery of this standard demands of everyone who loves this country a hard look at himself, for the greatest achievements must begin somewhere, and they always begin with the person. If we are not capable of this examination, we may yet become one of the most distinguished and monumental failures in the history of nations.

7. Faulkner and Desegregation

Any real change implies the breakup of the world as one has always known it, the loss of all that gave one an identity, the end of safety. And at such a moment, unable to see and not daring to imagine what the future will now bring forth, one clings to what one knew, or thought one knew; to what one possessed or dreamed that one possessed. Yet, it is only when a man is able, without bitterness or self-pity, to surrender a dream he has long cherished or a privilege he has long possessed that he is set free—he has set himself free—for higher dreams, for greater privileges. All men have gone through this, go through it, each according to his degree, throughout their lives. It is one of the irreducible facts of life. And remembering this, especially since I am a Negro, affords me almost my only means of understanding what is happening in the minds and hearts of white Southerners today.

For the arguments with which the bulk of relatively articulate white Southerners of good will have met the necessity of desegregation have no value whatever as arguments, being almost entirely and helplessly dishonest, when not, indeed, insane. After more than two hundred years in slavery and ninety years of quasi-freedom, it is hard to think very highly of William Faulkner's advice to "go slow." "They don't mean go slow," Thurgood Marshall is reported to have said, "they mean don't go." Nor is the squire of Oxford very persuasive when he suggests that white Southerners, left to their own devices, will realize that their own social structure looks silly to the rest of the world and correct it of their own accord. It has looked silly, to use Faulkner's rather strange adjective, for a long time; so far from trying to correct it, Southerners, who seem to be characterized by a species of defiance most perverse when it is most despairing, have clung to it, at incalculable cost to themselves, as the only conceivable and as an absolutely sacrosanct way of life. They have never seriously conceded that their social structure was mad. They have insisted, on the contrary, that everyone who criticized it was mad.

Faulkner goes further. He concedes the madness and moral

209

wrongness of the South but at the same time he raises it to
the level of a mystique which makes it somehow unjust to
discuss Southern society in the same terms in which one
would discuss any other society. "Our position is wrong and
untenable," says Faulkner, "but it is not wise to keep an emotional people off balance." This, if it means anything, can only
mean that this "emotional people" have been swept "off balance" by the pressure of recent events, that is, the Supreme
Court decision outlawing segregation. When the pressure is
taken off—and not an instant before—this "emotional people" will presumably find themselves once again on balance
and will then be able to free themselves of an "obsolescence
in [their] own land" in their own way and, of course, in their
own time. The question left begging is what, in their history
to date, affords any evidence that they have any desire or capacity to do this. And it is, I suppose, impertinent to ask just
what Negroes are supposed to do while the South works out
what, in Faulkner's rhetoric, becomes something very closely
resembling a high and noble tragedy.

The sad truth is that whatever modifications have been effected in the social structure of the South since the Reconstruction, and any alleviations of the Negro's lot within it, are
due to great and incessant pressure, very little of it indeed
from within the South. That the North has been guilty of
Pharisaism in its dealing with the South does not negate the
fact that much of this pressure has come from the North. That
some—not nearly as many as Faulkner would like to believe—
Southern Negroes prefer, or are afraid of changing, the status
quo does not negate the fact that it is the Southern Negro
himself who, year upon year, and generation upon generation,
has kept the Southern waters troubled. As far as the Negro's
life in the South is concerned, the NAACP is the only organization which has struggled, with admirable single-mindedness
and skill, to raise him to the level of a citizen. For this reason
alone, and quite apart from the individual heroism of many
of its Southern members, it cannot be equated, as Faulkner
equates it, with the pathological Citizens' Council. One organization is working within the law and the other is working
against and outside it. Faulkner's threat to leave the "middle
of the road" where he has, presumably, all these years, been

working for the benefit of Negroes, reduces itself to a more or less up-to-date version of the Southern threat to secede from the Union.

Faulkner—among so many others!—is so plaintive concerning this "middle of the road" from which "extremist" elements of both races are driving him that it does not seem unfair to ask just what he has been doing there until now. Where is the evidence of the struggle he has been carrying on there on behalf of the Negro? Why, if he and his enlightened confreres in the South have been boring from within to destroy segregation, do they react with such panic when the walls show any signs of falling? Why—and how—does one move from the middle of the road where one was aiding Negroes into the streets—to shoot them?

Now it is easy enough to state flatly that Faulkner's middle of the road does not—cannot—exist and that he is guilty of great emotional and intellectual dishonesty in pretending that it does. I think this is why he clings to his fantasy. It is easy enough to accuse him of hypocrisy when he speaks of man being "indestructible because of his simple will to freedom." But he is not being hypocritical; he means it. It is only that Man is one thing—a rather unlucky abstraction in this case— and the Negroes he has always known, so fatally tied up in his mind with his grandfather's slaves, are quite another. He is at his best, and is perfectly sincere, when he declares, in *Harpers*, "To live anywhere in the world today and be against equality because of race or color is like living in Alaska and being against snow. We have already got snow. And as with the Alaskan, merely to live in armistice with it is not enough. Like the Alaskan, we had better use it." And though this seems to be flatly opposed to his statement (in an interview printed in *The Reporter*) that, if it came to a contest between the federal government and Mississippi, he would fight for Mississippi, "even if it meant going out into the streets and shooting Negroes," he means that, too. Faulkner means everything he says, means them all at once, and with very nearly the same intensity. This is why his statements demand our attention. He has perhaps never before more concretely expressed what it means to be a Southerner.

What seems to define the Southerner, in his own mind at

any rate, is his relationship to the North, that is to the rest of the Republic, a relationship which can at the very best be described as uneasy. It is apparently very difficult to be at once a Southerner and an American; so difficult that many of the South's most independent minds are forced into the American exile; which is not, of course, without its aggravating, circular effect on the interior and public life of the South. A Bostonian, say, who leaves Boston is not regarded by the citizenry he has abandoned with the same venomous distrust as is the Southerner who leaves the South. The citizenry of Boston do not consider that they have been abandoned, much less betrayed. It is only the American Southerner who seems to be fighting, in his own entrails, a peculiar, ghastly, and perpetual war with all the rest of the country. ("Didn't you say," demanded a Southern woman of Robert Penn Warren, "that you was born down here, used to live right near here?" And when he agreed that this was so: "Yes . . . but you never said where you living now!")

The difficulty, perhaps, is that the Southerner clings to two entirely antithetical doctrines, two legends, two histories. Like all other Americans, he must subscribe, and is to some extent controlled by the beliefs and the principles expressed in the Constitution; at the same time, these beliefs and principles seem determined to destroy the South. He is, on the one hand, the proud citizen of a free society and, on the other, is committed to a society which has not yet dared to free itself of the necessity of naked and brutal oppression. He is part of a country which boasts that it has never lost a war; but he is also the representative of a conquered nation. I have not seen a single statement of Faulkner's concerning desegregation which does not inform us that his family has lived in the same part of Mississippi for generations, that his great-grandfather owned slaves, and that his ancestors fought and died in the Civil War. And so compelling is the image of ruin, gallantry and death thus evoked that it demands a positive effort of the imagination to remember that slaveholding Southerners were not the only people who perished in that war. Negroes and Northerners were also blown to bits. American history, as opposed to Southern history, proves that Southerners were not the only slaveholders, Negroes were not even the only slaves.

And the segregation which Faulkner sanctifies by references to Shiloh, Chickamauga, and Gettysburg does not extend back that far, is in fact scarcely as old as the century. The "racial condition" which Faulkner will not have changed by "mere force of law or economic threat" was imposed by precisely these means. The Southern tradition, which is, after all, all that Faulkner is talking about, is not a tradition at all: when Faulkner evokes it, he is simply evoking a legend which contains an accusation. And that accusation, stated far more simply than it should be, is that the North, in winning the war, left the South only one means of asserting its identity and that means was the Negro.

"My people owned slaves," says Faulkner, "and the very obligation we have to take care of these people is morally bad." "This problem is . . . far beyond the moral one it is and still was a hundred years ago, in 1860, when many Southerners, including Robert Lee, recognized it as a moral one at the very instant they in turn elected to champion the underdog because that underdog was blood and kin and home." But the North escaped scot-free. For one thing, in freeing the slave, it established a moral superiority over the South which the South has not learned to live with until today; and this despite—or possibly because of—the fact that this moral superiority was bought, after all, rather cheaply. The North was no better prepared than the South, as it turned out, to make citizens of former slaves, but it was able, as the South was not, to wash its hands of the matter. Men who knew that slavery was wrong were forced, nevertheless, to fight to perpetuate it because they were unable to turn against "blood and kin and home." And when blood and kin and home were defeated, they found themselves, more than ever, committed: committed, in effect, to a way of life which was as unjust and crippling as it was inescapable. In sum, the North, by freeing the slaves of their masters, robbed the masters of any possibility of freeing themselves of the slaves.

When Faulkner speaks, then, of the "middle of the road," he is simply speaking of the hope—which was always unrealistic and is now all but smashed—that the white Southerner, with no coercion from the rest of the nation, will lift himself above his ancient, crippling bitterness and refuse to add to his already intolerable burden of blood-guiltiness. But this hope would seem to be absolutely dependent on a social and psychological stasis which simply does not exist. "Things have been getting better," Faulkner tells us, "for a long time. Only six Negroes were killed by whites in Mississippi last year, according to police figures." Faulkner surely knows how little consolation this offers a Negro and he also knows something about "police figures" in the Deep South. And he knows, too, that murder is not the worst thing that can happen to a man, black or white. But murder may be the worst thing a man can do. Faulkner is not trying to save Negroes, who are, in his view, already saved; who, having refused to be destroyed by terror, are far stronger than the terrified white populace; and who have, moreover, fatally, from his point of view, the weight of the federal government behind them. He is trying to save "whatever good remains in those white people." The time he pleads for is the time in which the Southerner will come to terms with himself, will cease fleeing from his conscience, and achieve, in the words of Robert Penn Warren, "moral identity." And he surely believes, with Warren, that "Then in a country where moral identity is hard to come by, the South, because it has had to deal concretely with a moral problem, may offer some leadership. And we need any we can get. If we are to break out of the national rhythm, the rhythm between complacency and panic."

But the time Faulkner asks for does not exist—and he is not the only Southerner who knows it. There is never time in the future in which we will work out our salvation. The challenge is in the moment, the time is always now.

8. In Search of a Majority:
An Address

I AM supposed to speak this evening on the goals of American society as they involve minority rights, but what I am really going to do is to invite you to join me in a series of speculations. Some of them are dangerous, some of them painful, all of them are reckless. It seems to me that before we can begin to speak of minority rights in this country, we've got to make some attempt to isolate or to define the majority.

Presumably the society in which we live is an expression—in some way—of the majority will. But it is not so easy to locate this majority. The moment one attempts to define this majority one is faced with several conundrums. Majority is not an expression of numbers, of numerical strength, for example. You may far outnumber your opposition and not be able to impose your will on them or even to modify the rigor with which they impose their will on you, i.e., the Negroes in South Africa or in some counties, some sections, of the American South. You may have beneath your hand all the apparatus of power, political, military, state, and still be unable to use these things to achieve your ends, which is the problem faced by de Gaulle in Algeria and the problem which faced Eisenhower when, largely because of his own inaction, he was forced to send paratroopers into Little Rock. Again, the most trenchant observers of the scene in the South, those who are embattled there, feel that the Southern mobs are not an expression of the Southern majority will. Their impression is that these mobs fill, so to speak, a moral vacuum and that the people who form these mobs would be very happy to be released from their pain, and their ignorance, if someone arrived to show them the way. I would be inclined to agree with this, simply from what we know of human nature. It is not my impression that people wish to become worse; they really wish to become better but very often do not know how. Most people assume the position, in a way, of the Jews in Egypt, who really wished to get to the Promised Land but were afraid of the rigors of the journey; and, of course, before you embark

215

on a journey the terrors of whatever may overtake you on that journey live in the imagination and paralyze you. It was through Moses, according to legend, that they discovered, by undertaking this journey, how much they could endure.

These speculations have led me a little bit ahead of myself. I suppose it can be said that there was a time in this country when an entity existed which could be called the majority, let's say a class, for the lack of a better word, which created the standards by which the country lived or which created the standards to which the country aspired. I am referring or have in mind, perhaps somewhat arbitrarily, the aristocracies of Virginia and New England. These were mainly of Anglo-Saxon stock and they created what Henry James was to refer to, not very much later, as our Anglo-American heritage, or Anglo-American connections. Now at no time did these men ever form anything resembling a popular majority. Their importance was that they kept alive and they bore witness to two elements of a man's life which are not greatly respected among us now: (1) the social forms, called manners, which prevent us from rubbing too abrasively against one another and (2) the interior life, or the life of the mind. These things were important; these things were realities for them and no matter how roughhewn or dark the country was then, it is important to remember that this was also the time when people sat up in log cabins studying very hard by lamplight or candlelight. That they were better educated than we are now can be proved by comparing the political speeches of that time with those of our own day.

Now, what I have been trying to suggest in all this is that the only useful definition of the word "majority" does not refer to numbers, and it does not refer to power. It refers to influence. Someone said, and said it very accurately, that what is honored in a country is cultivated there. If we apply this touchstone to American life we can scarcely fail to arrive at a very grim view of it. But I think we have to look grim facts in the face because if we don't, we can never hope to change them.

These vanished aristocracies, these vanished standard bearers, had several limitations, and not the least of these limitations was the fact that their standards were essentially nostalgic. They referred to a past condition; they referred to the achievements, the laborious achievements, of a stratified society; and what was evolving in America had nothing to do with the past. So inevitably what happened, putting it far too simply, was that the old forms gave way before the European tidal wave, gave way before the rush of Italians, Greeks, Spaniards, Irishmen, Poles, Persians, Norwegians, Swedes, Danes, wandering Jews from every nation under heaven, Turks, Armenians, Lithuanians, Japanese, Chinese, and Indians. Everybody was here suddenly in the melting pot, as we like to say, but without any intention of being melted. They were here because they had wanted to leave wherever they had been and they were here to make their lives, and achieve their futures, and to establish a new identity. I doubt if history has ever seen such a spectacle, such a conglomeration of hopes, fears, and desires. I suggest, also, that they presented a problem for the Puritan God, who had never heard of them and of whom they had never heard. Almost always as they arrived, they took their places as a minority, a minority because their influence was so slight and because it was their necessity to make themselves over in the image of their new and unformed country. There were no longer any universally accepted forms or standards, and since all the roads to the achievement of an identity had vanished, the problem of status in American life became and it remains today acute. In a way, status became a kind of substitute for identity, and because money and the things money can buy is the universally accepted symbol here of status, we are often condemned as materialists. In fact, we are much closer to being metaphysical because nobody has ever expected from things the miracles that we expect.

Now I think it will be taken for granted that the Irish, the Swedes, the Danes, etc., who came here can no longer be considered in any serious way as minorities; and the question of anti-Semitism presents too many special features to be profitably discussed here tonight. The American minorities can be placed on a kind of color wheel. For example, when we think of the American boy, we don't usually think of a Spanish, Turkish, a Greek, or a Mexican type, still less of an Oriental type. We usually think of someone who is kind of a cross between the Teuton and the Celt, and I think it is interesting to consider what this image suggests. Outrageous as this image is, in most cases, it is the national self-image. It is an image which suggests hard work and good clean fun and chastity and piety and success. It leaves out of account, of course, most of the people in the country, and most of the facts of life, and there is not much point in discussing those virtues it suggests, which are mainly honored in the breach. The point is that it has almost nothing to do with what or who an American really is. It has nothing to do with what life is. Beneath this bland, this conqueror-image, a great many unadmitted despairs and confusions, and anguish and unadmitted crimes and failures hide. To speak in my own person, as a member of the nation's most oppressed minority, the oldest oppressed minority, I want to suggest most seriously that before we can do very much in the way of clear thinking or clear doing as relates to the minorities in this country, we must first crack the American image and find out and deal with what it hides. We cannot discuss the state of our minorities until we first have some sense of what we are, who we are, what our goals are, and what we take life to be. The question is not what we can do now for the hypothetical Mexican, the hypothetical Negro. The question is what we really want out of life, for ourselves, what we think is real.

Now I think there is a very good reason why the Negro in this country has been treated for such a long time in such a cruel way, and some of the reasons are economic and some of them are political. We have discussed these reasons without ever coming to any kind of resolution for a very long time. Some of them are social, and these reasons are somewhat more important because they have to do with our social panic, with our fear of losing status. This really amounts sometimes to a kind of social paranoia. One cannot afford to lose status on this peculiar ladder, for the prevailing notion of American life seems to involve a kind of rung-by-rung ascension to some hideously desirable state. If this is one's concept of life, obviously one cannot afford to slip back one rung. When one slips, one slips back not a rung but back into chaos and no longer knows who he is. And this reason, this fear, suggests to me one of the real reasons for the status of the Negro in this country. In a way, the Negro tells us where the bottom is: *because he is there*, and *where* he is, beneath us, we know where the limits are and how far we must not fall. We must not fall beneath him. We must never allow ourselves to fall that low, and I am not trying to be cynical or sardonic. I think if one examines the myths which have proliferated in this country concerning the Negro, one discovers beneath these myths a kind of sleeping terror of some condition which we refuse to imagine. In a way, if the Negro were not here, we might be forced to deal within ourselves and our own personalities, with all those vices, all those conundrums, and all those mysteries with which we have invested the Negro race. Uncle Tom is, for example, if he is called uncle, a kind of saint. He is there, he endures, he will forgive us, and this is a key to that image. But if he is not uncle, if he is merely Tom, he is a danger to everybody. He will wreak havoc on the countryside. When he is Uncle Tom he has no sex—when he is Tom, he does—and this obviously says much more about the people who invented this myth than it does about the people who are the object of it.

If you have been watching television lately, I think this is unendurably clear in the faces of those screaming people in the South, who are quite incapable of telling you what it is they are afraid of. They do not really know what it is they are afraid of, but they know they are afraid of something, and they are so frightened that they are nearly out of their minds. And this same fear obtains on one level or another, to varying degrees, throughout the entire country. We would never, never allow Negroes to starve, to grow bitter, and to die in ghettos all over the country if we were not driven by some nameless fear that has nothing to do with Negroes. We would never victimize, as we do, children whose only crime is color and keep them, as we put it, in their place. We wouldn't drive Negroes mad as we do by accepting them in ball parks, and on concert stages, but not in our homes and not in our neighborhoods, and not in our churches. It is only too clear that even with the most malevolent will in the world Negroes can never manage to achieve one-tenth of the harm which we fear. No, it has everything to do with ourselves and this is one of the reasons that for all these generations we have disguised this problem in the most incredible jargon. One of the reasons we are so fond of sociological reports and research and investigational committees is because they hide something. As long as we can deal with the Negro as a kind of statistic, as something to be manipulated, something to be fled from, or something to be given something to, there is something we can avoid, and what we can avoid is what he really, really means to us. The question that still ends these discussions is an extraordinary question: Would you let your sister marry one? The question, by the way, depends on several extraordinary assumptions. First of all it assumes, if I may say so, that I *want* to marry your sister and it also assumes that if I asked your sister to marry me, she would immediately say yes. There is no reason to make either of these assumptions, which are clearly irrational, and the key to why these assumptions are held is not to be found by asking Negroes. The key to why these assumptions are held has something to do with some insecurity in the people who hold them. It is only, after all, too clear that everyone born is going to have a rather difficult time getting through his life. It is only too clear that people fall in love according to some principle that we have not as yet been able to define, to discover or to isolate, and that marriage depends entirely on the two people involved; so that this objection does not hold water. It certainly is not justification for segregated schools or for ghettos or for mobs. I suggest that the role of the Negro in American life has something to do with our concept of what God is, and from my point of view, this concept is not big enough. It has got to be made much bigger than it is because God is, after all, not anybody's toy. To be with God is really to be involved with some enormous, overwhelming desire, and joy, and power which you cannot control, which controls you. I conceive of my own life as a journey toward something I do not understand, which in the going toward, makes me better. I conceive of God, in fact, as a means of liberation and not a means to control others. Love does not begin and end the way we seem to think it does. Love is a battle, love is a war; love is a growing up. No one in the world—in the entire world—knows more—knows Americans better or, odd as this may sound, loves them more than the American Negro. This is because he has had to watch you, outwit you, deal with you, and bear you, and sometimes even bleed and die with you, ever since we got here, that is, since both of us, black and white, got here—and this is a wedding. Whether I like it or not, or whether you like it or not, we are bound together forever. We are part of each other. What is happening to every Negro in the country at any time is also happening to you. There is no way around this. I am suggesting that these walls—these artificial walls—which have been up so long to protect us from something we fear, must come down. I think that what we really have to do is to create a country in which there are no minorities—for the first time in the history of the world. The one thing that all Americans have in common is that they have no other identity apart from the identity which is being achieved on this continent. This is not the English necessity, or the Chinese necessity, or the French necessity, but they are born into a framework which allows them their identity. The necessity of Americans to achieve an identity is a historical and a present personal fact and this is the connection between you and me.

This brings me back, in a way, to where I started. I said that we couldn't talk about minorities until we had talked about majorities, and I also said that majorities had nothing to do with numbers or with power, but with influence, with moral influence, and I want to suggest this: that the majority for which everyone is seeking which must reassess and release us from our past and deal with the present and create standards worthy of what a man may be—this majority is you. No one else can do it. The world is before you and you need not take it or leave it as it was when you came in.

9. Notes for a Hypothetical Novel:
An Address

W E'VE been talking about writing for the last two days, which is a very reckless thing to do, so that I shall be absolutely reckless tonight and pretend that I'm writing a novel in your presence. I'm going to ramble on a little tonight about my own past, not as though it were my own past exactly, but as a subject for fiction. I'm doing this in a kind of halting attempt to relate the terms of my experience to yours; and to find out what specific principle, if any, unites us in spite of all the obvious disparities, some of which are superficial and some of which are profound, and most of which are entirely misunderstood. We'll come back to that, in any case, this misunderstanding, I mean, in a minute, but I want to warn you that I'm not pretending to be unbiased. I'm certain that there is something which unites all the Americans in this room, though I can't say what it is. But if I were to meet any one of you in some other country, England, Italy, France, or Spain, it would be at once apparent to everybody else, though it might not be to us, that we had something in common which scarcely any other people, or no other people could really share.

Let's pretend that I want to write a novel concerning the people or some of the people with whom I grew up, and since we are only playing let us pretend it's a very long novel. I want to follow a group of lives almost from the time they open their eyes on the world until some point of resolution, say, marriage, or childbirth, or death. And I want to impose myself on these people as little as possible. That means that I do not want to tell them or the reader what principle their lives illustrate, or what principle is activating their lives, but by examining their lives I hope to be able to make them convey to me and to the reader what their lives mean.

Now I know that this is not altogether possible. I mean that I know that my people are controlled by my point of view and that by the time I begin the novel I have some idea of what I want the novel to do, or to say, or to be. But just the same, whatever my point of view is and whatever my intentions, because I am an American writer my subject and my material inevitably has to be a handful of incoherent people in an incoherent country. And I don't mean incoherent in any light sense, and later on we'll talk about what I mean when I use that word.

Well, who are these people who fill my past and seem to clamor to be expressed? I was born on a very wide avenue in Harlem, and in those days that part of town was called The Hollow and now it's called Junkie's Hollow. The time was the 1920's, and as I was coming into the world there was something going on called The Negro Renaissance; and the most distinguished survivor of that time is Mr. Langston Hughes. This Negro Renaissance is an elegant term which means that white people had then discovered that Negroes could act and write as well as sing and dance and this Renaissance was not destined to last very long. Very shortly there was to be a depression and the artistic Negro, or the noble savage, was to give way to the militant or the new Negro; and I want to point out something in passing which I think is worth our time to look at, which is this: that the country's image of the Negro, which hasn't very much to do with the Negro, has never failed to reflect with a kind of frightening accuracy the state of mind of the country. This was the Jazz Age you will remember. It was the epoch of F. Scott Fitzgerald, Josephine Baker had just gone to France, Mussolini had just come to power in Italy, there was a peculiar man in Germany who was plotting and writing, and the lord knows what Lumumba's mother was thinking. And all of these things and a million more which are now known to the novelist, but not to his people, are to have a terrible effect on their lives.

There's a figure I carry in my mind's eye to this day and I don't know why. He can't really be the first person I remember, but he seems to be, apart from my mother and my father, and this is a man about as old perhaps as I am now who's coming up our street, very drunk, falling-down drunk, and it must have been a Saturday and I was sitting in the window. It must have been winter because I remember he had a black overcoat on—because his overcoat was open—and he's stumbling past one of those high, iron railings with spikes on top, and he falls and he bumps his head against one of these railings, and blood comes down his face, and there are kids behind him and they're tormenting him and laughing at him. And that's all I remember and I don't know why. But I only throw him in to dramatize this fact, that however solemn we writers, or myself, I, may sometimes sound, or how pontifical I may sometimes seem to be, on that level from which any genuine work of the imagination springs, I'm really, and we all are, absolutely helpless and ignorant. But this figure is important because he's going to appear in my novel. He can't be kept out of it. He occupies too large a place in my imagination.

And then, of course, I remember the church people because I was practically born in the church, and I seem to have spent most of the time that I was helpless sitting on someone's lap in the church and being beaten over the head whenever I fell asleep, which was usually. I was frightened of all those brothers and sisters of the church because they were all powerful, I thought they were. And I had one ally, my brother, who was a very undependable ally because sometimes I got beaten for things he did and sometimes he got beaten for things I did. But we were united in our hatred for the deacons and the deaconesses and the shouting sisters and of our father. And one of the reasons for this is that we were always hungry and he was always inviting those people over to the house on Sunday for an enormous banquet and we sat next to the ice-box in the kitchen watching all those hams, and chickens, and biscuits go down those righteous bellies, which had no bottom.

Now so far, in this hypothetical sketch of an unwritten and probably unwritable novel, so good. From what we've already sketched we can begin to anticipate one of those long, warm, toasty novels. You know, those novels in which the novelist is looking back on himself, absolutely infatuated with himself as a child and everything is in sentimentality. But I think we

ought to bring ourselves up short because we don't need another version of *A Tree Grows in Brooklyn* and we can do
without another version of *The Heart Is a Lonely Hunter*. This
hypothetical book is aiming at something more implacable
than that. Because no matter how ridiculous this may sound,
that unseen prisoner in Germany is going to have an effect on
the lives of these people. Two Italians are going to be executed presently in Boston, there's going to be something
called the Scottsboro case which will give the Communist
party hideous opportunities. In short, the social realities with
which these people, the people I remember, whether they
knew it or not, were really contending can't be left out of the
novel without falsifying their experience. And—this is very important—this all has something to do with the sight of that
tormented, falling down, drunken, bleeding man I mentioned
at the beginning. Who is he and what does he mean?

Well, then I remember, principally I remember, the boys
and girls in the streets. The boys and girls on the streets, at
school, in the church. I remember in the beginning I only
knew Negroes except for one Jewish boy, the only white boy
in an all-Negro elementary school, a kind of survivor of another day in Harlem, and there was an Italian fruit vendor
who lived next door to us who had a son with whom I fought
every campaign of the Italian-Ethiopian war. Because, remember that we're projecting a novel, and Harlem is in the course
of changing all the time, very soon there won't be any white
people there, and this is also going to have some effect on the
people in my story.

Well, more people now. There was a boy, a member of our
church, and he backslid, which means he achieved a sex life
and started smoking cigarettes, and he was therefore rejected
from the community in which he had been brought up, because Harlem is also reduced to communities. And I've always
believed that one of the reasons he died was because of this
rejection. In any case, eighteen months after he was thrown
out of the church he was dead of tuberculosis.

And there was a girl, who was a nice girl. She was a niece
of one of the deaconesses. In fact, she was my girl. We were
very young then, we were going to get married and we were
always singing, praying and shouting, and we thought we'd

live that way forever. But one day she was picked up in a nightgown on Lenox Avenue screaming and cursing and they carried her away to an institution where she still may be.

And by this time I was a big boy, and there were the friends of my brothers, my younger brothers and sisters. And I had danced to Duke Ellington, but they were dancing to Charlie Parker; and I had learned how to drink gin and whisky, but they were involved with marijuana and the needle. I will not really insist upon continuing this roster. I have not known many survivors. I know mainly about disaster, but then I want to remind you again of that man I mentioned in the beginning, who haunts the imagination of this novelist. The imagination of a novelist has everything to do with what happens to his material.

Now, we're a little beyond the territory of Betty Smith and Carson McCullers, but we are not quite beyond the territory of James T. Farrell or Richard Wright. Let's go a little bit farther. By and by I left Harlem. I left all those deaconesses, all those sisters, and all those churches, and all those tambourines, and I entered or anyway I encountered the white world. Now this white world which I was just encountering was, just the same, one of the forces that had been controlling me from the time I opened my eyes on the world. For it is important to ask, I think, where did these people I'm talking about come from and where did they get their peculiar school of ethics? What was its origin? What did it mean to them? What did it come out of? What function did it serve and why was it happening here? And why were they living where they were and what was it doing to them? All these things which sociologists think they can find out and haven't managed to do, which no chart can tell us. People are not, though in our age we seem to think so, endlessly manipulable. We think that once one has discovered that thirty thousand, let us say, Negroes, Chinese or Puerto Ricans or whatever have syphilis or don't, or are unemployed or not, that we've discovered something about the Negroes, Chinese or Puerto Ricans. But in fact, this is not so. In fact, we've discovered nothing very useful because people cannot be handled in that way.

Anyway, in the beginning I thought that the white world was very different from the world I was moving out of and I turned out to be entirely wrong. It seemed different. It seemed safer, at least the white people seemed safer. It seemed cleaner, it seemed more polite, and, of course, it seemed much richer from the material point of view. But I didn't meet anyone in that world who didn't suffer from the very same affliction that all the people I had fled from suffered from and that was that they didn't know who they were. They wanted to be something that they were not. And very shortly I didn't know who I was, either. I could not be certain whether I was really rich or really poor, really black or really white, really male or really female, really talented or a fraud, really strong or merely stubborn. In short, I had become an American. I had stepped into, I had walked right into, as I inevitably had to do, the bottomless confusion which is both public and private, of the American republic.

Now we've brought this hypothetical hero to this place, now what are we going to do with him, what does all of this mean, what can we make it mean? What's the thread that unites all these peculiar and disparate lives, whether it's from Idaho to San Francisco, from Idaho to New York, from Boston to Birmingham? Because there is something that unites all of these people and places. What does it mean to be an American? What nerve is pressed in you or me when we hear this word?

Earlier I spoke about the disparities and I said I was going to try and give an example of what I meant. Now the most obvious thing that would seem to divide me from the rest of my countrymen is the fact of color. The fact of color has a relevance objectively and some relevance in some other way, some emotional relevance and not only for the South. I mean that it persists as a problem in American life because it means something, it fulfills something in the American personality. It is here because the Americans in some peculiar way believe or think they need it. Maybe we can find out what it is that this problem fulfills in the American personality, what it corroborates and in what way this peculiar thing, until today, helps Americans to feel safe.

When I spoke about incoherence I said I'd try to tell you what I meant by that word. It's a kind of incoherence that occurs, let us say, when I am frightened, I am absolutely frightened to death, and there's something which is happening or about to happen that I don't want to face, or, let us say, which is an even better example, that I have a friend who has just murdered his mother and put her in the closet and I know it, but we're not going to talk about it. Now this means very shortly since, after all, I know the corpse is in the closet, and he knows I know it, and we're sitting around having a few drinks and trying to be buddy-buddy together, that very shortly, we can't talk about anything because we can't talk about that. No matter what I say I may inadvertently stumble on this corpse. And this incoherence which seems to afflict this country is analogous to that. I mean that in order to have a conversation with someone you have to reveal yourself. In order to have a real relationship with somebody you have got to take the risk of being thought, God forbid, "an oddball." You know, you have to take a chance which in some peculiar way we don't seem willing to take. And this is very serious in that it is not so much a writer's problem, that is to say, I don't want to talk about it from the point of view of a writer's problem, because, after all, you didn't ask me to become a writer, but it seems to me that the situation of the writer in this country is symptomatic and reveals, says something, very terrifying about this country. If I were writing hypothetically about a Frenchman I would have in a way a frame of reference and a point of view and in fact it is easier to write about Frenchmen, comparatively speaking, because they interest me so much less. But to try to deal with the American experience, that is to say to deal with this enormous incoherence, these enormous puddings, this shapeless thing, to try and make an American, well listen to them, and try to put that on a page. The truth about dialogue, for example, or the technical side of it, is that you try and make people say what they would say if they could and then you sort of dress it up to look like speech. That is to say that it's really an absolute height, people don't ever talk the way they talk in novels, but I've got to make you believe they do because I can't possibly do a tape recording.

But to try and find out what Americans mean is almost impossible because there are so many things they do not want to face. And not only the Negro thing which is simply the most obvious and perhaps the simplest example, but on the level of private life which is after all where we have to get to in order to write about anything and also the level we have to get to in order to live, it seems to me that the myth, the illusion, that this is a free country, for example, is disastrous. Let me point out to you that freedom is not something that anybody can be given; freedom is something people take and people are as free as they want to be. One hasn't got to have an enormous military machine in order to be unfree when it's simpler to be asleep, when it's simpler to be apathetic, when it's simpler, in fact, not to want to be free, to think that something else is more important. And I'm not using freedom now so much in a political sense as I'm using it in a personal sense. It seems to me that the confusion is revealed, for example, in those dreadful speeches by Eisenhower, those incredible speeches by Nixon, they sound very much, after all, like the jargon of the Beat generation, that is, in terms of clarity. Not a pin to be chosen between them, both levels, that is, the highest level presumably, the administration in Washington, and the lowest level in our national life, the people who are called "beatniks" are both involved in saying that something which is really on their heels does not exist. Jack Kerouac says "Holy, holy" and we say Red China does not exist. But it really does. I'm simply trying to point out that it's the symptom of the same madness.

Now, in some way, somehow, the problem the writer has which is, after all, his problem and perhaps not yours is somehow to unite these things, to find the terms of our connection, without which we will perish. The importance of a writer is continuous; I think it's socially debatable and usually socially not terribly rewarding, but that's not the point; his importance, I think, is that he is here to describe things which other people are too busy to describe. It is a function, let's face it, it's a special function. There is no democracy on this level. It's a very difficult thing to do, it's a very special thing to do and people who do it cannot by that token do many other things. But their importance is, and the importance of writers in this country now is this, that this country is yet to be discovered in any real sense. There is an illusion about America, a myth about America to which we are clinging which has nothing to do with the lives we lead and I don't believe that anybody in this country who has really thought about it or really almost anybody who has been brought up against it— and almost all of us have one way or another—this collision between one's image of oneself and what one actually is is always very painful and there are two things you can do about it, you can meet the collision head-on and try and become what you really are or you can retreat and try to remain what you thought you were, which is a fantasy, in which you will certainly perish. Now, I don't want to keep you any longer. But I'd like to leave you with this, I think we have some idea about reality which is not quite true. Without having anything whatever against Cadillacs, refrigerators or all the paraphernalia of American life, I yet suspect that there is something much more important and much more real which produces the Cadillac, refrigerator, atom bomb, and what produces it, after all, is something which we don't seem to want to look at, and that is the person. A country is only as good—I don't care now about the Constitution and the laws, at the moment let us leave these things aside—a country is only as strong as the people who make it up and the country turns into what the people want it to become. Now, this country is going to be transformed. It will not be transformed by an act of God, but by all of us, by you and me. I don't believe any longer that we can afford to say that it is entirely out of our hands. We made the world we're living in and we have to make it over.

10. *The Male Prison*

T HERE is something immensely humbling in this last document [*Madeleine* by André Gide] from the hand of a
writer whose elaborately graceful fiction very often impressed
me as simply cold, solemn and irritatingly pious, and whose
precise memoirs made me accuse him of the most exasperating
egocentricity. He does not, to be sure, emerge in *Madeleine*
as being less egocentric; but one is compelled to see this egocentricity as one of the conditions of his life and one of the
elements of his pain. Nor can I claim that reading *Madeleine*
has caused me to re-evaluate his fiction (though I care more
now for *The Immoralist* than I did when I read it several years
ago); it has only made me feel that such a re-evaluation must
be made. For, whatever Gide's shortcomings may have been,
few writers of our time can equal his devotion to a very high
ideal.

It seems to me now that the two things which contributed
most heavily to my dislike of Gide—or, rather, to the discomfort he caused me to feel—were his Protestantism and his homosexuality. It was clear to me that he had not got over his
Protestantism and that he had not come to terms with his
nature. (For I believed at one time—rather oddly, considering
the examples by which I was surrounded, to say nothing of
the spectacle I myself presented—that people *did* "get over"
their earliest impressions and that "coming to terms" with
oneself simply demanded a slightly more protracted stiffening
of the will.) It was his Protestantism, I felt, which made him
so pious, which invested all of his work with the air of an
endless winter, and which made it so difficult for me to care
what happened to any of his people.

And his homosexuality, I felt, was his own affair which he
ought to have kept hidden from us, or, if he needed to be so
explicit, he ought at least to have managed to be a little more
scientific—whatever, in the domain of morals, that word may
mean—less illogical, less romantic. He ought to have leaned
less heavily on the examples of dead, great men, of vanished
cultures, and he ought certainly to have known that the

examples provided by natural history do not go far toward illuminating the physical, psychological and moral complexities faced by men. If he were going to talk about homosexuality at all, he ought, in a word, to have sounded a little less *disturbed*.

This is not the place and I am certainly not the man to assess the work of André Gide. Moreover, I confess that a great deal of what I felt concerning his work I still feel. And that argument, for example, as to whether or not homosexuality is natural seems to me completely pointless—pointless because I really do not see what difference the answer makes. It seems clear, in any case, at least in the world we know, that no matter what encyclopedias of physiological and scientific knowledge are brought to bear the answer never can be Yes. And one of the reasons for this is that it would rob the normal—who are simply the many—of their very necessary sense of security and order, of their sense, perhaps, that the race is and should be devoted to outwitting oblivion—and will surely manage to do so.

But there are a great many ways of outwitting oblivion, and to ask whether or not homosexuality is natural is really like asking whether or not it was natural for Socrates to swallow hemlock, whether or not it was natural for St. Paul to suffer for the Gospel, whether or not it was natural for the Germans to send upwards of six million people to an extremely twentieth-century death. It does not seem to me that nature helps us very much when we need illumination in human affairs. I am certainly convinced that it is one of the greatest impulses of mankind to arrive at something higher than a natural state. How to be natural does not seem to me to be a problem—quite the contrary. The great problem is how to be—in the best sense of that kaleidoscopic word—a man.

This problem was at the heart of all Gide's anguish, and it proved itself, like most real problems, to be insoluble. He died, as it were, with the teeth of this problem still buried in his throat. What one learns from *Madeleine* is what it cost him, in terms of unceasing agony, to live with this problem at all. Of what it cost her, his wife, it is scarcely possible to conjecture. But she was not so much a victim of Gide's sexual nature—homosexuals do not choose women for their victims, nor is the difficulty of becoming a victim so great for a woman that she is compelled to turn to homosexuals for this—as she was a victim of his overwhelming guilt, which connected, it would seem, and most unluckily, with her own guilt and shame.

If this meant, as Gide says, that "the spiritual force of my love [for Madeleine] inhibited all carnal desire," it also meant that some corresponding inhibition in her prevented her from seeking carnal satisfaction elsewhere. And if there is scarcely any suggestion throughout this appalling letter that Gide ever really understood that he had married a woman or that he had any apprehension of what a woman was, neither is there any suggestion that she ever, in any way, insisted on or was able to believe in her womanhood and its right to flower.

Her most definite and also most desperate act is the burning of his letters—and the anguish this cost her, and the fact that in this burning she expressed what surely must have seemed to her life's monumental failure and waste, Gide characteristically (indeed, one may say, necessarily) cannot enter into and cannot understand. "They were my most precious belongings," she tells him, and perhaps he cannot be blamed for protecting himself against the knife of this dreadful conjugal confession. But: "It is the best of me that disappears," he tells us, *"and it will no longer counterbalance the worst."* (Italics mine.) He had entrusted, as it were, to her his purity, that part of him that was not carnal; and it is quite clear that, though he suspected it, he could not face the fact that it was only when her purity ended that her life could begin, that the key to her liberation was in his hands.

But if he had ever turned that key madness and despair would have followed for him, his world would have turned completely dark, the string connecting him to heaven would have been cut. And this is because then he could no longer have loved Madeleine as an ideal, as Emanuele, God-with-us, but would have been compelled to love her as a woman, which he could not have done except physically. And then he would have had to hate her, and at that moment those gates which, as it seemed to him, held him back from utter corruption would have been opened. He loved her as a woman, indeed, only in the sense that no man could have held the

place in Gide's dark sky which was held by Madeleine. She
was his Heaven who would forgive him for his Hell and help
him to endure it. As indeed she was and, in the strangest way
possible, did—by allowing him to feel guilty about *her* instead
of the boys on the *Piazza d'Espagne*—with the result that, in
Gide's work, both his Heaven and his Hell suffer from a certain lack of urgency.

Gide's relations with Madeleine place his relations with men
in rather a bleak light. Since he clearly could not forgive himself for his anomaly, he must certainly have despised them—
which almost certainly explains the fascination felt by Gide
and so many of his heroes for countries like North Africa. It
is not necessary to despise people who are one's inferiors—
whose inferiority, by the way, is amply demonstrated by the
fact that they appear to relish, without guilt, their sensuality.

It is possible, as it were, to have one's pleasure without
paying for it. But to have one's pleasure without paying for it
is precisely the way to find oneself reduced to a search for
pleasure which grows steadily more desperate and more grotesque. It does not take long, after all, to discover that sex is
only sex, that there are few things on earth more futile or
more deadening than a meaningless round of conquests. The
really horrible thing about the phenomenon of present-day
homosexuality, the horrible thing which lies curled like a
worm at the heart of Gide's trouble and his work and the
reason that he so clung to Madeleine, is that today's unlucky
deviate can only save himself by the most tremendous exertion
of all his forces from falling into an underworld in which he
never meets either men or women, where it is impossible to
have either a lover or a friend, where the possibility of genuine
human involvement has altogether ceased. When this possibility has ceased, so has the possibility of growth.

And, again: It is one of the facts of life that there are two
sexes, which fact has given the world most of its beauty, cost
it not a little of its anguish, and contains the hope and glory
of the world. And it is with this fact, which might better perhaps be called a mystery, that every human being born must
find some way to live. For, no matter what demons drive
them, men cannot live without women and women cannot
live without men. And this is what is most clearly conveyed

in the agony of Gide's last journal. However little he was able to understand it, or, more important perhaps, take upon himself the responsibility for it, Madeleine kept open for him a kind of door of hope, of possibility, the possibility of entering into communion with another sex. This door, which is the door to life and air and freedom from the tyranny of one's own personality, *must* be kept open, and none feel this more keenly than those on whom the door is perpetually threatening or has already seemed to close.

Gide's dilemma, his wrestling, his peculiar, notable and extremely valuable failure testify—which should not seem odd—to a powerful masculinity and also to the fact that he found no way to escape the prison of that masculinity. And the fact that he endured this prison with such dignity is precisely what ought to humble us all, living as we do in a time and country where communion between the sexes has become so sorely threatened that we depend more and more on the strident exploitation of externals, as, for example, the breasts of Hollywood glamour girls and the mindless grunting and swaggering of Hollywood he-men.

It is important to remember that the prison in which Gide struggled is not really so unique as it would certainly comfort us to believe, is not very different from the prison inhabited by, say, the heroes of Mickey Spillane. Neither can they get through to women, which is the only reason their muscles, their fists and their tommy guns have acquired such fantastic importance. It is worth observing, too, that when men can no longer love women they also cease to love or respect or trust each other, which makes their isolation complete. Nothing is more dangerous than this isolation, for men will commit any crimes whatever rather than endure it. We ought, for our own sakes, to be humbled by Gide's confession as he was humbled by his pain and make the generous effort to understand that his sorrow was not different from the sorrow of all men born. For, if we do not learn this humility, we may very well be strangled by a most petulant and unmasculine pride.

II. *The Northern Protestant*

I ALREADY knew that Bergman had just completed one movie, was mixing the sound for it, and was scheduled to begin another almost at once. When I called the Filmstaden, he himself, incredibly enough, came to the phone. He sounded tired but very pleasant, and told me he could see me if I came at once.

The Filmstaden is in a suburb of Stockholm called Rasunda, and is the headquarters of the Svensk Filmindustri, which is one of the oldest movie companies in the world. It was here that Victor Sjöström made those remarkable movies which, eventually (under the name of Victor Seastrom) carried him— briefly—to the arid plains of Hollywood. Here Mauritz Stiller directed *The Legend of Gösta Berling*, after which he and the star thus discovered, Garbo, also took themselves west—a disastrous move for Stiller and not, as it was to turn out, altogether the most fruitful move, artistically anyway, that Garbo could have made. Ingrid Bergman left here in 1939. (She is not related to Ingmar Bergman.) The Svensk Filmindustri is proud of these alumni, but they are prouder of no one, at the moment, than they are of Ingmar Bergman, whose films have placed the Swedish film industry back on the international map. And yet, on the whole, they take a remarkably steady view of the Bergman vogue. They realize that it *is* a vogue, they are bracing themselves for the inevitable reaction, and they hope that Bergman is doing the same. He is neither as great nor as limited as the current hue and cry suggests. But he is one of the very few genuine artists now working in films.

He is also, beyond doubt, the freest. Not for him the necessity of working on a shoestring, with unpaid performers, as has been the case with many of the younger French directors. He is backed by a film company; Swedish film companies usually own their laboratories, studios, rental distribution services, and theaters. If they did not they could scarcely afford to make movies at all, movies being more highly taxed in this tiny country than anywhere else in the world—except Denmark— and 60 per cent of the playing time in these company-owned theaters being taken up by foreign films. Nor can the Swedish film industry possibly support anything resembling the American star system. This is healthy for the performers, who never have to sit idly by for a couple of years, waiting for a fat part, and who are able to develop a range and flexibility rarely permitted even to the most gifted of our stars. And, of course, it's fine for Bergman because he is absolutely free to choose his own performers: if he wishes to work, say, with Geraldine Page, studio pressure will not force him into extracting a performance from Kim Novak. If it were not for this freedom we would almost certainly never have heard of Ingmar Bergman. Most of his twenty-odd movies were not successful when they were made, nor are they today his company's biggest moneymakers. (His vogue has changed this somewhat, but, as I say, no one expects this vogue to last.) "He wins the prizes and brings us the prestige," was the comment of one of his coworkers, "but it's So-and-So and So-and-So—" and here he named two very popular Swedish directors—"who can be counted on to bring in the money."

I arrived at the Filmstaden a little early; Bergman was still busy and would be a little late in meeting me, I was told. I was taken into his office to wait for him. I welcomed the opportunity of seeing the office without the man.

It is a very small office, most of it taken up by a desk. The desk is placed smack in front of the window—not that it could have been placed anywhere else; this window looks out on the daylight landscape of Bergman's movies. It was gray and glaring the first day I was there, dry and fiery. Leaves kept falling from the trees, each silent descent bringing a little closer the long, dark, Swedish winter. The forest Bergman's characters are always traversing is outside this window and the ominous carriage from which they have yet to escape is still among the properties. I realized, with a small shock, that the landscape of Bergman's mind was simply the landscape in which he had grown up.

On the desk were papers, folders, a few books, all very neatly arranged. Squeezed between the desk and the wall was a spartan cot; a brown leather jacket and a brown knitted cap were lying on it. The visitor's chair in which I sat was placed at an angle to the door, which proximity, each time that I was there, led to much bumping and scraping and smiling exchanges in Esperanto. On the wall were three photographs of Charlie Chaplin and one of Victor Sjöström.

Eventually, he came in, bareheaded, wearing a sweater, a tall man, economically, intimidatingly lean. He must have been the gawkiest of adolescents, his arms and legs still seeming to be very loosely anchored; something in his good-natured, self-possessed directness suggests that he would also have been among the most belligerently opinionated: by no means an easy man to deal with, in any sense, any relationship whatever, there being about him the evangelical distance of someone possessed by a vision. This extremely dangerous quality—authority—has never failed to incite the hostility of the many. And I got the impression that Bergman was in the habit of saying what he felt because he knew that scarcely anyone was listening.

He suggested tea, partly, I think, to give both of us time to become easier with each other, but also because he really needed a cup of tea before going back to work. We walked out of the office and down the road to the canteen.

I had arrived in Stockholm with what turned out to be the "flu" and I kept coughing and sneezing and wiping my eyes. After a while Bergman began to look at me worriedly and said that I sounded very ill.

I hadn't come there to talk about my health and I tried to change the subject. But I was shortly to learn that any subject changing to be done around Bergman is done by Bergman. He was not to be sidetracked.

"Can I do anything for you?" he persisted; and when I did not answer, being both touched and irritated by his question, he smiled and said, "You haven't to be shy. I know what it is like to be ill and alone in a strange city."

It was a hideously, an inevitably self-conscious gesture and yet it touched and disarmed me. I know that his concern, at bottom, had very little to do with me. It had to do with his memories of himself and it expressed his determination never to be guilty of the world's indifference.

He turned and looked out of the canteen window, at the brilliant October trees and the glaring sky, for a few seconds and then turned back to me.

"Well," he asked me, with a small laugh, "are you for me or against me?"

I did not know how to answer this question right away and he continued, "I don't care if you are or not. Well, that's not true. Naturally, I prefer—I would be happier—if you were *for* me. But I have to know."

I told him I was for him, which might, indeed, turn out to be my principal difficulty in writing about him. I had seen many of his movies—but did not intend to try to see them all—and I felt identified, in some way, with what I felt he was trying to do. What he saw when he looked at the world did not seem very different from what *I* saw. Some of his films seemed rather cold to me, somewhat too deliberate. For example, I had possibly heard too much about *The Seventh Seal* before seeing it, but it had impressed me less than some of the others.

"I cannot discuss that film," he said abruptly, and again turned to look out of the window. "I had to do it. I had to be free of that argument, those questions." He looked at me. "It's the same for you when you write a book? You just do it because you must and then, when you have done it, you are relieved, no?"

He laughed and poured some tea. He had made it sound as though we were two urchins playing a deadly and delightful game which must be kept a secret from our elders.

"Those questions?"

"Oh. God and the Devil. Life and Death. Good and Evil." He smiled. "*Those* questions."

I wanted to suggest that his being a pastor's son contributed not a little to his dark preoccupations. But I did not quite know how to go about digging into his private life. I hoped that we would be able to do it by way of the movies.

I began with: "The question of love seems to occupy you a great deal, too."

I don't doubt that it occupies you, too, was what he seemed to be thinking, but he only said, mildly, "Yes." Then, before I could put it another way, "You may find it a bit hard to talk to me. I really do not see much point in talking about my past work. And I cannot talk about work I haven't done yet."

I mentioned his great preoccupation with egotism, so many

of his people being centered on themselves, necessarily, and disastrously: Vogler in *The Magician*, Isak Borg in *Wild Strawberries*, the ballerina in *Summer Interlude*.

"I am very fond of *Summer Interlude*," he said. "It is my favorite movie.

"I don't mean," he added, "that it's my best. I don't know which movie is my best."

Summer Interlude was made in 1950. It is probably not Bergman's best movie—I would give that place to the movie which has been shown in the States as *The Naked Night*—but it is certainly among the most moving. Its strength lies in its portrait of the ballerina, uncannily precise and truthful, and in its perception of the nature of first love, which first seems to open the universe to us and then seems to lock us out of it. It is one of the group of films—including *The Waiting Women*, *Smiles of a Summer Night*, and *Brink of Life*—which have a woman, or women, at their center and in which the men, generally, are rather shadowy. But all the Bergman themes are in it: his preoccupation with time and the inevitability of death, the comedy of human entanglements, the nature of illusion, the nature of egotism, the price of art. These themes also run through the movies which have at their center a man: *The Naked Night* (which should really be called *The Clown's Evening*), *Wild Strawberries*, *The Face*, *The Seventh Seal*. In only one of these movies—*The Face*—is the male-female relation affirmed from the male point of view; as being, that is, a source of strength for the man. In the movies concerned with women, the male-female relation succeeds only through the passion, wit, or patience of the woman and depends on how astutely she is able to manipulate the male conceit. *The Naked Night* is the most blackly ambivalent of Bergman's films—and surely one of the most brutally erotic movies ever made—but it is essentially a study of the masculine helplessness before the female force. *Wild Strawberries* is inferior to it, I think, being afflicted with a verbal and visual rhetoric which is Bergman's most annoying characteristic. But the terrible assessments that the old Professor is forced to make in it prove that he is not merely the victim of his women: he is responsible for what his women have become.

We soon switched from Bergman's movies to the subject of Stockholm.

"It is not a city at all," he said, with intensity. "It is ridiculous of it to think of itself as a city. It is simply a rather larger village, set in the middle of some forests and some lakes. You wonder what it thinks it is doing there, looking so important."

I was to encounter in many other people this curious resistance to the idea that Stockholm could possibly become a city. It certainly seemed to be trying to become a city as fast as it knew how, which is, indeed, the natural and inevitable fate of any nation's principal commercial and cultural clearing house. But for Bergman, who is forty-one, and for people who are considerably younger, Stockholm seems always to have had the aspect of a village. They do not look forward to seeing it change. Here, as in other European towns and cities, people can be heard bitterly complaining about the "Americanization" which is taking place.

This "Americanization," so far as I could learn, refers largely to the fact that more and more people are leaving the countryside and moving into Stockholm. Stockholm is not prepared to receive these people, and the inevitable social tensions result, from housing problems to juvenile delinquency. Of course, there are juke boxes grinding out the inevitable rock-and-roll tunes, and there are, too, a few jazz joints which fail, quite, to remind one of anything in the States. And the ghost—one is tempted to call it the effigy—of the late James Dean, complete with uniform, masochistic girl friend, motorcycle, or (hideously painted) car, has made its appearance on the streets of Stockholm. These do not frighten me nearly as much as do the originals in New York, since they have yet to achieve the authentic American bewilderment or the inimitable American snarl. I ought to add, perhaps, that the American Negro remains, for them, a kind of *monstre sacré*, which proves, if anything does, how little they know of the phenomena which they feel compelled to imitate. They are unlike their American models in many ways: for example, they are not suffering from a lack of order but from an excess of it. Sexually, they are not drowning in taboos; they are anxious, on the contrary, to establish one or two.

But the people in Stockholm are right to be frightened. It is not Stockholm's becoming a city which frightens them. What frightens them is that the pressures under which everyone in this century lives are destroying the old simplicities. This is almost always what people really mean when they speak of Americanization. It is an epithet which is used to mask the fact that the entire social and moral structure that they have built is proving to be absolutely inadequate to the demands now being placed on it. The old cannot imagine a new one, or create it. The young have no confidence in the old; lacking which, they cannot find any standards in themselves by which to live. The most serious result of such a chaos, though it may not seem to be, is the death of love. I do not mean merely the bankruptcy of the concept of romantic love—it is entirely possible that this concept has had its day—but the breakdown of communication between the sexes.

Bergman talked a little about the early stages of his career. He came to the Filmstaden in 1944, when he wrote the script for *Torment*. This was a very promising beginning. But promising beginnings do not mean much, especially in the movies. Promise, anyway, was never what Bergman lacked. He lacked flexibility. Neither he nor anyone else I talked to suggested that he has since acquired much of this quality; and since he was young and profoundly ambitious and thoroughly untried, he lacked confidence. This lack he disguised by tantrums so violent that they are still talked about at the Filmstaden today. His exasperating allergies extended to such things as refusing to work with a carpenter, say, to whom he had never spoken but whose face he disliked. He has been known, upon finding guests at his home, to hide himself in the bathroom until they left. Many of these people never returned and it is hard, of course, to blame them. Nor was he, at this time in his life, particularly respectful of the feelings of his friends.

"He's improved," said a woman who has been working with him for the last several years, "but he was impossible. He could say the most terrible things, he could make you wish you were dead. Especially if you were a woman."

She reflected. "Then, later, he would come and apologize. One just had to accept it, that's all."

He was referred to in those days, without affection, as "the young one" or "the kid" or "the demon director." An American property whose movies, in spite of all this temperament, made no money at the box office, would have suffered, at best, the fate of Orson Welles. But Bergman went on working, as screen writer and director in films and as a director on the stage.

"I was an actor for a while," he says, "a terribly bad actor. But it taught me much."

It probably taught him a great deal about how to handle actors, which is one of his great gifts.

He directed plays for the municipal theaters of Hälsingborg, Göteborg, and Malmö, and is now working—or will be as soon as he completes his present film schedule—for the Royal Dramatic Theatre of Stockholm.

Some of the people I met told me that his work on stage is even more exciting than his work in films. They were the same people, usually, who were most concerned for Bergman's future when his present vogue ends. It was as though they were giving him an ace in the hole.

I did not interrogate Bergman on this point, but his record suggests that he is more attracted to films than to the theater. It would seem, too, that the theater very often operates for him as a kind of prolonged rehearsal or preparation for a film already embryonic in his consciousness. This is almost certainly the case with at least two of his theatrical productions. In 1954, he directed, for the municipal theater of Malmö, Franz Lehár's *The Merry Widow*. The next year he wrote and directed the elaborate period comedy, *Smiles of a Summer Night*, which beautifully utilizes—for Bergman's rather savage purposes—the atmosphere of romantic light opera. In 1956, he published his play *A Medieval Fresco*. This play was not produced, but it forms the basis for *The Seventh Seal*, which he wrote and directed the same year. It is safe, I think, to assume that the play will now never be produced, at least not by Bergman.

He has had many offers, of course, to work in other countries. I asked him if he had considered taking any of them.

He looked out of the window again. "I am home here," he said. "It took me a long time, but now I have all my instruments—everything—where I want them. I know my crew, my crew knows me, I know my actors."

I watched him. Something in me, inevitably, envied him for being able to love his home so directly and for being able to stay at home and work. And, in another way, rather to my surprise, I envied him not at all. Everything in a life depends on how that life accepts its limits: it would have been like envying him his language.

"If I were a violinist," he said after a while, "and I were invited to play in Paris—well, if the condition was that I could not bring my own violin but would have to play a French one—well, then, I could not go." He made a quick gesture toward the window. "This is my violin."

It was getting late. I had the feeling that I should be leaving, though he had not made any such suggestion. We got around to talking about *The Magician*.

"It doesn't have anything to do with hypnotism, does it?" I asked him.

"No. No, of course not."

"Then it's a joke. A long, elaborate metaphor for the condition of the artist—I mean, any time, anywhere, all the time—"

He laughed in much the same conspiratorial way he had laughed when talking about his reasons for doing *The Seventh Seal*. "Well, yes. He is always on the very edge of disaster, he is always on the very edge of great things. Always. Isn't it so? It is his element, like water is the element for the fish."

People had been interrupting us from the moment we sat down, and now someone arrived who clearly intended to take Bergman away with him. We made a date to meet early in the coming week. Bergman stood with me until my cab came and told the driver where I lived. I watched him, tall, bare-headed, and fearfully determined, as he walked away. I thought how there was something in the weird, mad, Northern Protestantism which reminded me of the visions of the black preachers of my childhood.

One of the movies which has made the most profound impression on Bergman is Victor Sjöström's *The Phantom Carriage*. It is based on a novel by Selma Lagerlöf which I have not read—and which, as a novel, I cannot imagine. But it makes great sense as a Northern fable; it has the atmosphere of a tale which has been handed down, for generations, from father to son. The premise of the movie is that whoever dies, in his sins, on New Year's Eve must drive Death's chariot throughout the coming year. The story that the movie tells is how a sinner—beautifully played by Sjöström himself—outwits Death. He outwits Death by virtue, virtue in the biblical, or, rather, in the New Testament sense: he outwits Death by opposing to this anonymous force his weak and ineradicable humanity.

Now this is, of course, precisely the story that Bergman is telling in *The Seventh Seal*. He has managed to utilize the old framework, the old saga, to speak of our condition in the world today and the way in which this loveless and ominous condition can be transcended. This ancient saga is part of his personal past and one of the keys to the people who produced him.

Since I had been so struck by what seemed to be our similarities, I amused myself, on the ride back into town, by projecting a movie, which, if I were a moviemaker, would occupy, among my own productions, the place *The Seventh Seal* holds among Bergman's. I did not have, to hold my films together, the Northern sagas; but I had the Southern music. From the African tom-toms, to Congo Square, to New Orleans, to Harlem—and, finally, all the way to Stockholm, and the European sectors of African towns. My film would begin with slaves, boarding the good ship *Jesus*: a white ship, on a dark sea, with masters as white as the sails of their ships, and slaves as black as the ocean. There would be one intransigent slave, an eternal figure, destined to appear, and to be put to death in every generation. In the hold of the slave ship, he would be a witch-doctor or a chief or a prince or a singer; and he would die, be hurled into the ocean, for protecting a black woman. Who would bear his child, however, and this child would lead a slave insurrection; and be hanged. During the Reconstruction, he would be murdered upon leaving Congress. He would be a returning soldier during the first World War, and be buried alive; and then, during the Depression, he would become a jazz musician, and go mad. Which would bring him up to our own day—what would his fate be now? What would I entitle this grim and vengeful fantasy? What would be happening, during all this time, to the descendants of the masters? It did not seem likely, after all, that I would ever be able to make of my past, on film, what Bergman had been able to make of his. In some ways, his past is easier to deal with: it was, at once, more remote and more present. Perhaps what divided the black Protestant from the white one was the nature of my still unwieldy, unaccepted bitterness. My hero, now, my tragic hero, would probably be a junkie—which, certainly, in one way, suggested the distance covered by America's dark generations. But it was in only one way, it was not the whole story; and it then occurred to me that my bitterness might be turned to good account if I should dare to envision the tragic hero for whom I was searching—as myself. All art is a kind of confession, more or less oblique. All artists, if they are to survive, are forced, at last, to tell the whole story, to vomit the anguish up. All of it, the literal and the fanciful. Bergman's authority seemed, then, to come from the fact that he was reconciled to this arduous, delicate, and disciplined self-exposure.

Bergman and his father had not got on well when Bergman was young.

"But how do you get along now?" I had asked him.

"Oh, now," he said, "we get on very well. I go to see him often."

I told him that I envied him. He smiled and said, "Oh, it is always like that—when such a battle is over, fathers and sons can be friends."

I did not say that such a reconciliation had probably a great deal to do with one's attitude toward one's past, and the uses to which one could put it. But I now began to feel, as I saw my hotel glaring up out of the Stockholm gloom, that what was lacking in my movie was the American despair, the search, in our country for authority. The blue-jeaned boys on the Stockholm streets were really imitations, so far; but the streets of my native city were filled with youngsters searching desperately for the limits which would tell them who they were, and create for them a challenge to which they could rise. What would a Bergman make of the American confusion? How would he handle a love story occurring in New York?

12. Alas, Poor Richard

UNLESS a writer is extremely old when he dies, in which case he has probably become a neglected institution, his death must always seem untimely. This is because a real writer is always shifting and changing and searching. The world has many labels for him, of which the most treacherous is the label of Success. But the man behind the label knows defeat far more intimately than he knows triumph. He can never be absolutely certain that he has achieved his intention.

This tension and authority—the authority of the frequently defeated—are in the writer's work, and cause one to feel that, at the moment of his death, he was approaching his greatest achievements. I should think that guilt plays some part in this reaction, as well as a certain unadmitted relief. Guilt, because of our failure in a relationship, because it is extremely difficult to deal with writers as people. Writers are said to be extremely egotistical and demanding, and they are indeed, but that does not distinguish them from anyone else. What distinguishes them is what James once described as a kind of "holy stupidity." The writer's greed is appalling. He wants, or seems to want, everything and practically everybody; in another sense, and at the same time, he needs no one at all; and families, friends, and lovers find this extremely hard to take. While he is alive, his work is fatally entangled with his personal fortunes and misfortunes, his personality, and the social facts and attitudes of his time. The unadmitted relief, then, of which I spoke has to do with a certain drop in the intensity of our bewilderment, for the baffling creator no longer stands between us and his works.

He does not, but many other things do, above all our own preoccupations. In the case of Richard Wright, dead in Paris at fifty-two, the fact that he worked during a bewildering and demoralizing era in Western history makes a proper assessment of his work more difficult. In *Eight Men*, the earliest story, "The Man Who Saw the Flood," takes place in the deep South and was first published in 1937. One of the two previously unpublished stories in the book, "Man, God Ain't Like That," begins in Africa, achieves its hideous resolution in Paris, and brings us, with an ironical and fitting grimness, to the threshold of the 1960's. It is because of this story, which is remarkable, and "Man of All Work," which is a masterpiece, that I cannot avoid feeling that Wright, as he died, was acquiring a new tone, and a less uncertain esthetic distance, and a new depth.

Shortly after we learned of Richard Wright's death, a Negro woman who was re-reading *Native Son* told me that it meant more to her now than it had when she had first read it. This, she said, was because the specific social climate which had produced it, or with which it was identified, seemed archaic now, was fading from our memories. Now, there was only the book itself to deal with, for it could no longer be read, as it had been read in 1940, as a militant racial manifesto. Today's racial manifestoes were being written very differently, and in many different languages; what mattered about the book now was how accurately or deeply the life of Chicago's South Side had been conveyed.

I think that my friend may prove to be right. Certainly, the two oldest stories in this book, "The Man Who Was Almost a Man," and "The Man Who Saw the Flood," both Depression stories, both occurring in the South, and both, of course, about Negroes, do not seem dated. Perhaps it is odd, but they did not make me think of the 1930's, or even, particularly, of Negroes. They made me think of human loss and helplessness. There is a dry, savage, folkloric humor in "The Man Who Was Almost a Man." It tells the story of a boy who wants a gun, finally manages to get one, and, by a hideous error, shoots a white man's mule. He then takes to the rails, for he would have needed two years to pay for the mule. There is nothing funny about "The Man Who Saw the Flood," which is as spare and moving an account as that delivered by Bessie Smith in "Backwater Blues."

It is strange to begin to suspect, now, that Richard Wright was never, really, the social and polemical writer he took himself to be. In my own relations with him, I was always exasperated by his notions of society, politics, and history, for they seemed to me utterly fanciful. I never believed that he had any real sense of how a society is put together. It had not occurred to me, and perhaps it had not occurred to him, that his major interests as well as his power lay elsewhere. Or perhaps it *had* occurred to me, for I distrusted his association with the French intellectuals, Sartre, de Beauvoir, and company. I am not being vindictive toward them or condescending toward Richard Wright when I say that it seemed to me that there was very little they could give him which he could use. It has always seemed to me that ideas were somewhat more real to them than people; but anyway, and this is a statement made with the very greatest love and respect, I always sensed in Richard Wright a Mississippi pickaninny, mischievous, cunning, and tough. This always seemed to be at the bottom of everything he said and did, like some fantastic jewel buried in high grass. And it was painful to feel that the people of his adopted country were no more capable of seeing this jewel than were the people of his native land, and were in their own way as intimidated by it.

Even more painful was the suspicion that Wright did not want to know this. The meaning of Europe for an American Negro was one of the things about which Richard Wright and I disagreed most vehemently. He was fond of referring to Paris as the "city of refuge"—which it certainly was, God knows, for the likes of us. But it was not a city of refuge for the French, still less for anyone belonging to France; and it would not have been a city of refuge for us if we had not been armed with American passports. It did not seem worthwhile to me to have fled the native fantasy only to embrace a foreign one. (Someone, some day, should do a study in depth of the role of the American Negro in the mind and life of Europe, and the extraordinary perils, different from those of America but not less grave, which the American Negro encounters in the Old World.)

But now that the storm of Wright's life is over, and politics is ended forever for him, along with the Negro problem and the fearful conundrum of Africa, it seems to have been the tough and intuitive, the genuine Richard Wright, who was being recorded all along. It now begins to seem, for example, that Wright's unrelentingly bleak landscape was not merely that of the Deep South, or of Chicago, but that of the world, of the human heart. The landscape does not change in any of these stories. Even the most good-natured performance this book contains, good-natured by comparison only, "Big Black Good Man," takes place in Copenhagen in the winter, and in the vastly more chilling confines of a Danish hotel-keeper's fears.

In "Man of All Work," a tight, raging, diamond-hard exercise in irony, a Negro male who cannot find a job dresses himself up in his wife's clothes and hires himself out as a cook. ("Who," he demands of his horrified, bedridden wife, "ever looks at us colored folks anyhow?") He gets the job, and Wright uses this incredible situation to reveal, with beautiful spite and accuracy, the private lives of the master race. The story is told entirely in dialogue, which perfectly accomplishes what it sets out to do, racing along like a locomotive and suggesting far more than it states.

The story, without seeming to, goes very deeply into the demoralization of the Negro male and the resulting fragmentization of the Negro family which occurs when the female is forced to play the male role of breadwinner. It is also a maliciously funny indictment of the sexual terror and hostility of American whites: and the horror of the story is increased by its humor.

"Man, God Ain't Like That," is a fable of an African's discovery of God. It is a far more horrible story than "Man of All Work," but it too manages its effects by a kind of Grand Guignol humor, and it too is an unsparing indictment of the frivolity, egotism, and wrong-headedness of white people—in this case, a French artist and his mistress. It too is told entirely in dialogue and recounts how a French artist traveling through Africa picks up an African servant, uses him as a model, and, in order to shock and titillate his jaded European friends, brings the African back to Paris with him.

Whether or not Wright's vision of the African sensibility will be recognized by Africans, I do not know. But certainly he has managed a frightening and truthful comment on the inexorably mysterious and dangerous relationships between ways of life, which are also ways of thought. This story and

"Man of All Work" left me wondering how much richer our extremely poor theater might now be if Wright had chosen to work in it.

But "The Man Who Killed a Shadow" is something else again; it is Wright at the mercy of his subject. His great forte, it now seems to me, was an ability to convey inward states by means of externals: "The Man Who Lived Underground," for example, conveys the spiritual horror of a man and a city by a relentless accumulation of details, and by a series of brief, sharply cut-off tableaus, seen through chinks and cracks and keyholes. The specifically sexual horror faced by a Negro cannot be dealt with in this way. "The Man Who Killed a Shadow" is a story of rape and murder, and neither the murderer nor his victim ever comes alive. The entire story seems to be occurring, somehow, beneath cotton. There are many reasons for this. In most of the novels written by Negroes until today (with the exception of Chester Himes' *If He Hollers Let Him Go*) there is a great space where sex ought to be; and what usually fills this space is violence.

This violence, as in so much of Wright's work, is gratuitous and compulsive. It is one of the severest criticisms than can be leveled against his work. The violence is gratuitous and compulsive because the root of the violence is never examined. The root is rage. It is the rage, almost literally the howl, of a man who is being castrated. I do not think that I am the first person to notice this, but there is probably no greater (or more misleading) body of sexual myths in the world today than those which have proliferated around the figure of the American Negro. This means that he is penalized for the guilty imagination of the white people who invest him with their hates and longings, and is the principal target of their sexual paranoia. Thus, when in Wright's pages a Negro male is found hacking a white woman to death, the very gusto with which this is done, and the great attention paid to the details of physical destruction reveal a terrible attempt to break out of the cage in which the American imagination has imprisoned him for so long.

In the meantime, the man I fought so hard and who meant so much to me, is gone. First America, then Europe, then

Africa failed him. He lived long enough to find all of the terms on which he had been born become obsolete; presently, all of his attitudes seemed to be historical. But as his life ended, he seems to me to have been approaching a new beginning. He had survived, as it were, his own obsolescence, and his imagination was beginning to grapple with that darkest of all dark strangers for him, the African. The depth thus touched in him brought him a new power and a new tone. He had survived exile on three continents and lived long enough to begin to tell the tale.

II. THE EXILE

I WAS far from imagining, when I agreed to write this memoir, that it would prove to be such a painful and difficult task. What, after all, can I really say about Richard . . . ? Everything founders in the sea of what might have been. We might have been friends, for example, but I cannot honestly say that we were. There might have been some way of avoiding our quarrel, our rupture; I can only say that I failed to find it. The quarrel having occurred, perhaps there might have been a way to have become reconciled. I think, in fact, that I counted on this coming about in some mysterious, irrevocable way, the way a child dreams of winning, by means of some dazzling exploit, the love of his parents.

However, he is dead now, and so we never shall be reconciled. The debt I owe him can now never be discharged, at least not in the way I hoped to be able to discharge it. In fact, the saddest thing about our relationship is that my only means of discharging my debt to Richard was to become a writer; and this effort revealed, more and more clearly as the years went on, the deep and irreconcilable differences between our points of view.

This might not have been so serious if I had been older when we met. . . . If I had been, that is, less uncertain of myself, and less monstrously egotistical. But when we met, I was twenty, a carnivorous age; he was then as old as I am now, thirty-six; he had been my idol since high school, and I, as the fledgling Negro writer, was very shortly in the position of his protégé. This position was not really fair to either of us. As writers we were about as unlike as any two writers could possibly be. But no one can read the future, and neither of us knew this then. We were linked together, really, because both of us were black. I had made my pilgrimage to meet him because he was the greatest black writer in the world for me. In *Uncle Tom's Children*, in *Native Son*, and, above all, in *Black Boy*, I found expressed, for the first time in my life, the sorrow, the rage, and the murderous bitterness which was eating up my life and the lives of those around me. His work was an immense liberation and revelation for me. He became my ally and my witness, and alas! my father.

I remember our first meeting very well. It was in Brooklyn; it was winter, I was broke, naturally, shabby, hungry, and scared. He appeared from the depths of what I remember as an extremely long apartment. Now his face, voice, manner, figure are all very sadly familiar to me. But they were a great shock to me then. It is always a shock to meet famous men. There is always an irreducible injustice in the encounter, for the famous man cannot possibly fit the image which one has evolved of him. My own image of Richard was almost certainly based on Canada Lee's terrifying stage portrait of Bigger Thomas. Richard was not like that at all. His voice was light and even rather sweet, with a Southern melody in it; his body was more round than square, more square than tall; and his grin was more boyish than I had expected, and more diffident. He had a trick, when he greeted me, of saying, "Hey, boy!" with a kind of pleased, surprised expression on his face. It was very friendly, and it was also, faintly, mockingly conspiratorial—as though we were two black boys, in league against the world, and had just managed to spirit away several loads of watermelon.

We sat in the living room and Richard brought out a bottle of bourbon and ice and glasses. Ellen Wright was somewhere in the back with the baby, and made only one brief appearance near the end of the evening. I did not drink in those days, did not know how to drink, and I was terrified that the liquor, on my empty stomach, would have the most disastrous consequences. Richard talked to me or, rather, drew me out on the subject of the novel I was working on then. I was so afraid of falling off my chair and so anxious for him to be interested in me, that I told him far more about the novel than I, in fact, knew about it, madly improvising, one jump ahead of the bourbon, on all the themes which cluttered up my mind. I am sure that Richard realized this, for he seemed to be amused by me. But I think he liked me. I know that I liked him, then, and later, and all the time. But I also know that, later on, he did not believe this.

He agreed, that night, to read the sixty or seventy pages I had done on my novel as soon as I could send them to him. I didn't dawdle, naturally, about getting the pages in the mail, and Richard commented very kindly and favorably on them, and his support helped me to win the Eugene F. Saxton Fellowship. He was very proud of me then, and I was puffed up with pleasure that he was proud, and was determined to make him prouder still.

But this was not to be, for, as so often happens, my first real triumph turned out to be the herald of my first real defeat. There is very little point, I think, in regretting anything, and yet I do, nevertheless, rather regret that Richard and I had not become friends by this time, for it might have made a great deal of difference. We might at least have caught a glimpse of the difference between my mind and his; and if we could have argued about it then, our quarrel might not have been so painful later. But we had not become friends mainly, indeed, I suppose, because of this very difference, and also because I really was too young to be his friend and adored him too much and was too afraid of him. And this meant that when my first wintry exposure to the publishing world had resulted in the irreparable ruin—carried out by me—of my first novel, I scarcely knew how to face anyone, let alone Richard. I was too ashamed of myself and I was sure that he was ashamed of me, too. This was utter foolishness on my part, for Richard knew far more about first novels and fledgling novelists than that; but I had been out for his approval. It simply had not occurred to me in those days that anyone *could* approve of me if I had tried for something and failed. The young think that failure is the Siberian end of the line,

banishment from all the living, and tend to do what I then did
—which was to hide.

I, nevertheless, did see him a few days before he went to
Paris in 1946. It was a strange meeting, melancholy in the way
a theater is melancholy when the run of the play is ended and
the cast and crew are about to be dispersed. All the relationships so laboriously created now no longer exist, seem never
to have existed; and the future looks gray and problematical
indeed. Richard's apartment—by this time, he lived in the Village, on Charles Street—seemed rather like that, dismantled,
everything teetering on the edge of oblivion; people rushing
in and out, friends, as I supposed, but alas, most of them were
merely admirers; and Richard and I seemed really to be at the
end of *our* rope, for he had done what he could for me, and
it had not worked out, and now he was going away. It seemed
to me that he was sailing into the most splendid of futures,
for he was going, of all places! to France, and he had been
invited there by the French government. But Richard did not
seem, though he was jaunty, to be overjoyed. There was a
striking sobriety in his face that day. He talked a great deal
about a friend of his, who was in trouble with the U.S. Im-
migration authorities, and was about to be, or already had
been, deported. Richard was not being deported, of course,
he was traveling to a foreign country as an honored guest;
and he was vain enough and young enough and vivid enough
to find this very pleasing and exciting. Yet he knew a great
deal about exile, all artists do, especially American artists, especially American Negro artists. He had endured already, liberals and literary critics to the contrary, a long exile in his own
country. He must have wondered what the real thing would
be like. And he must have wondered, too, what would be the
unimaginable effect on his daughter, who could now be raised
in a country which would not penalize her on account of her
color.

And that day was very nearly the last time Richard and I
spoke to each other without the later, terrible warfare. Two
years later, I, too, quit America, never intending to return.
The day I got to Paris, before I even checked in at a hotel, I
was carried to the Deux Magots, where Richard sat, with the
editors of *Zero* magazine. "Hey, boy!" he cried, looking more

surprised and pleased and conspiratorial than ever, and younger and happier. I took this meeting as a good omen, and I could not possibly have been more wrong.

I later became rather closely associated with *Zero* magazine, and wrote for them the essay called "Everybody's Protest Novel." On the day the magazine was published, and before I had seen it, I walked into the Brasserie Lipp. Richard was there, and he called me over. I will never forget that interview, but I doubt that I will ever be able to re-create it.

Richard accused me of having betrayed him, and not only him but all American Negroes by attacking the idea of protest literature. It simply had not occurred to me that the essay could be interpreted in that way. I was still in that stage when I imagined that whatever was clear to me had only to be pointed out to become immediately clear to everyone. I was young enough to be proud of the essay and, sad and incomprehensible as it now sounds, I really think that I had rather expected to be patted on the head for my original point of view. It had not occurred to me that this point of view, which I had come to, after all, with some effort and some pain, could be looked on as treacherous or subversive. Again, I had mentioned Richard's *Native Son* at the end of the essay because it was the most important and most celebrated novel of Negro life to have appeared in America. Richard thought that I had attacked it, whereas, as far as I was concerned, I had scarcely even criticized it. And Richard thought that I was trying to destroy his novel and his reputation; but it had not entered my mind that either of these *could* be destroyed, and certainly not by me. And yet, what made the interview so ghastly was not merely the foregoing or the fact that I could find no words with which to defend myself. What made it most painful was that Richard was right to be hurt, I was wrong to have hurt him. He saw clearly enough, far more clearly than I had dared to allow myself to see, what I had done: I had used his work as a kind of springboard into my own. His work was a road-block in my road, the sphinx, really, whose riddles I had to answer before I could become myself. I thought confusedly then, and feel very definitely now, that this was the greatest tribute I could have paid him. But it is not an easy tribute to bear and I do not know how I will take it when my time comes. For, finally, Richard was hurt because I had not given him credit for any human feelings or failings. And indeed I had not, he had never really been a human being for me, he had been an idol. And idols are created in order to be destroyed.

This quarrel was never really patched up, though it must be said that, over a period of years, we tried. "What do you mean, *protest!*" Richard cried. "*All* literature is protest. You can't name a single novel that isn't protest." To this I could only weakly counter that all literature might be protest but all protest was not literature. "Oh," he would say then, looking, as he so often did, bewilderingly juvenile, "here you come again with all that art for art's sake crap." This never failed to make me furious, and my anger, for some reason, always seemed to amuse him. Our rare, best times came when we managed to exasperate each other to the point of helpless hilarity. "Roots," Richard would snort, when I had finally worked my way around to this dreary subject, "what —— roots! Next thing you'll be telling me is that all colored folks have rhythm." Once, one evening, we managed to throw the whole terrifying subject to the winds, and Richard, Chester Himes, and myself went out and got drunk. It was a good night, perhaps the best I remember in all the time I knew Richard. For he and Chester were friends, they brought out the best in each other, and the atmosphere they created brought out the best in me. Three absolutely tense, unrelentingly egotistical, and driven people, free in Paris but far from home, with so much to be said and so little time in which to say it!

And time was flying. Part of the trouble between Richard and myself, after all, was that I was nearly twenty years younger and had never seen the South. Perhaps I can now imagine Richard's odyssey better than I could then, but it is only imagination. I have not, in my own flesh, traveled, and paid the price of such a journey, from the Deep South to Chicago to New York to Paris; and the world which produced Richard Wright has vanished and will never be seen again. Now, it seems almost in the twinkling of an eye, nearly twenty years have passed since Richard and I sat nervously over bourbon in his Brooklyn living room. These years have seen nearly all of the props of the Western reality knocked out from under it, all of the world's capitals have changed, the Deep South has changed, and Africa has changed.

For a long time, it seems to me, Richard was cruelly caught in this high wind. His ears, I think, were nearly deafened by the roar, all about him, not only of falling idols but of falling enemies. Strange people indeed crossed oceans, from Africa and America, to come to his door; and he really did not know who these people were, and they very quickly sensed this. Not until the very end of his life, judging by some of the stories in his last book, *Eight Men*, did his imagination really begin to assess the century's new and terrible dark stranger. Well, he worked up until the end, died, as I hope to do, in the middle of a sentence, and his work is now an irreducible part of the history of our swift and terrible time. Whoever He may be, and wherever you may be, may God be with you, Richard, and may He help me not to fail that argument which you began in me.

III. ALAS, POOR RICHARD

And my record's clear today, the church brothers and sisters used to sing, *for He washed my sins away, And that old account was settled long ago!* Well, so, perhaps it was, for them; they were under the illusion that they could read their records right. I am far from certain that I am able to read my own record at all, I would certainly hesitate to say that I am able to read it right. And, as for accounts, it is doubtful that I have ever really "settled" an account in my life.

Not that I haven't tried. In my relations with Richard, I was always trying to set the record "straight," to "settle" the account. This is but another way of saying that I wanted Richard to see me, not as the youth I had been when he met me, but as a man. I wanted to feel that he had accepted me, had accepted my right to my own vision, my right, as his equal, to disagree with him. I nourished for a long time the illusion that this day was coming. One day, Richard would turn to me, with the light of sudden understanding on his

face, and say, "Oh, *that's* what you mean." And then, so ran
the dream, a great and invaluable dialogue would have begun.
And the great value of this dialogue would have been not only
in its power to instruct all of you, and the ages. Its great value
would have been in its power to instruct me, its power to
instruct Richard: for it would have been nothing less than that
so universally desired, so rarely achieved reconciliation between spiritual father and spiritual son.

Now, of course, it is not Richard's fault that I felt this way.
But there is not much point, on the other hand, in dismissing
it as simply my fault, or my illusion. I had identified myself
with him long before we met: in a sense by no means metaphysical, his example had helped me to survive. He was black,
he was young, he had come out of the Mississippi nightmare
and the Chicago slums, and he was a writer. He proved it
could be done—proved it to me, and gave me an arm against
all those others who assured me it could *not* be done. And I
think I had expected Richard, on the day we met, somehow,
miraculously, to understand this, and to rejoice in it. Perhaps
that sounds foolish, but I cannot honestly say, not even now,
that I really think it is foolish. Richard Wright had a tremendous effect on countless numbers of people whom he never
met, multitudes whom he now will never meet. This means
that his responsibilities and his hazards were great. I don't
think that Richard ever thought of me as one of his responsibilities—*bien au contraire!*—but he certainly seemed, often
enough, to wonder just what he had done to deserve me.

Our reconciliation, anyway, never took place. This was a
great loss for me. But many of our losses have a compensating
gain. In my efforts to get through to Richard, I was forced
to begin to wonder exactly why he held himself so rigidly
against me. I could not believe—especially if one grants *my*
reading of our relationship—that it could be due only to my
criticism of his work. It seemed to me then, and it seems to
me now, that one really needs those few people who take
oneself and one's work seriously enough to be unimpressed
by the public hullabaloo surrounding the former or the un-
critical solemnity which menaces the latter from the instant
that, for whatever reason, it finds itself in vogue.

No, it had to be more than that—the more especially as his

attitude toward me had not, it turned out, been evolved for my particular benefit. It seemed to apply, with equal rigor, against a great many others. It applied against old friends, incontestably his equals, who had offended him, always, it turned out, in the same way: by failing to take his word for all the things he imagined, or had been led to believe, his word could cover. It applied against younger American Negroes who felt that Joyce, for example, not he, was the master; and also against younger American Negroes who felt that Richard did not know anything about jazz, or who insisted that the Mississippi and the Chicago he remembered were not precisely the Mississippi and the Chicago that they knew. It applied against Africans who refused to take Richard's word for Africa, and it applied against Algerians who did not feel that Paris was all that Richard had it cracked up to be. It applied, in short, against anyone who seemed to threaten Richard's system of reality. As time went on, it seemed to me that these people became more numerous and that Richard had fewer and fewer friends. At least, most of those people whom I had known to be friends of Richard's seemed to be saddened by him, and, reluctantly, to drift away. He's been away too long, some of them said. He's cut himself off from his roots. I resisted this judgment with all my might, more for my own sake than for Richard's, for it was far too easy to find this judgment used against myself. For the same reason I defended Richard when an African told me, with a small, mocking laugh, *I believe he thinks he's white.* I did *not* think I had been away too long: but I could not fail to begin, however unwillingly, to wonder about the uses and hazards of expatriation. I did not think I was white, either, or I did not *think* I thought so. But the Africans might think I did, and who could blame them? In their eyes, and in terms of my history, I could scarcely be considered the purest or most dependable of black men.

And I think that it was at about this point that I began to watch Richard as though he were a kind of object lesson. I could not help wondering if he, when facing an African, felt the same awful tension between envy and despair, attraction and revulsion. I had always been considered very dark, both Negroes and whites had despised me for it, and I had despised myself. But the Africans were much darker than I; I was a paleface among them, and so was Richard. And the disturbance thus created caused all of my extreme ambivalence about color to come floating to the surface of my mind. The Africans seemed at once simpler and more devious, more directly erotic and at the same time more subtle, and they were proud. If they had ever despised themselves for their color, it did not show, as far as I could tell. I envied them and feared them—feared that they had good reason to despise me. What did Richard feel? And what did Richard feel about other American Negroes abroad?

For example: one of my dearest friends, a Negro writer now living in Spain, circled around me and I around him for months before we spoke. One Negro meeting another at an all-white cocktail party, or at that larger cocktail party which is the American colony in Europe, cannot but wonder how the other got there. The question is: Is he for real? or is he kissing ass? Almost all Negroes, as Richard once pointed out, are almost always acting, but before a white audience—which is quite incapable of judging their performance: and even a "bad nigger" is, inevitably, giving something of a performance, even if the entire purpose of his performance is to terrify or blackmail white people.

Negroes know about each other what can here be called family secrets, and this means that one Negro, if he wishes, can "knock" the other's "hustle"—can give his game away. It is still not possible to overstate the price a Negro pays to climb out of obscurity—for it is a *particular* price, involved with being a Negro; and the great wounds, gouges, amputations, losses, scars, endured in such a journey cannot be calculated. But even this is not the worst of it, since he is really dealing with two hierarchies, one white and one black, the latter modeled on the former. The higher he rises, the less is his journey worth, since (unless he is extremely energetic and anarchic, a genuinely "bad nigger" in the most positive sense of the term) all he can possibly find himself exposed to is the grim emptiness of the white world—which does not live by the standards it uses to victimize him—and the even more ghastly emptiness of black people who wish they were white. Therefore, one "exceptional" Negro watches another "exceptional" Negro in order to find out if he knows how vastly successful and bitterly funny the hoax has been. Alliances, in the great cocktail party of the white man's world, are formed, almost purely, on this basis, for if both of you can laugh, you have a lot to laugh about. On the other hand, if only one of you can laugh, one of you, inevitably, is laughing at the other.

In the case of my new-found friend, Andy, and I, we were able, luckily, to laugh together. We were both baffled by Richard, but still respectful and fond of him—we accepted from Richard pronouncements and attitudes which we would certainly never have accepted from each other, or from anyone else—at the time Richard returned from wherever he had been to film *Native Son*. (In which, to our horror, later abundantly justified, he himself played Bigger Thomas.) He returned with a brainstorm, which he outlined to me one bright, sunny afternoon, on the terrace of the Royal St. Germain. He wanted to do something to protect the rights of American Negroes in Paris; to form, in effect, a kind of pressure group which would force American businesses in Paris, and American government offices, to hire Negroes on a proportional basis.

This seemed unrealistic to me. How, I asked him, in the first place, could one find out how many American Negroes there were in Paris? Richard quoted an approximate, semi-official figure, which I do not remember, but I was still not satisfied. Of this number, how many were looking for jobs? Richard seemed to feel that they spent most of their time being turned down by American bigots, but this was not really my impression. I am not sure I said this, though, for Richard often made me feel that the word "frivolous" had been coined to describe me. Nevertheless, my objections made him more and more impatient with me, and I began to wonder if I were not guilty of great disloyalty and indifference concerning the lot of American Negroes abroad. (I find that there is something helplessly sardonic in my tone now, as I write this, which also handicapped me on that distant afternoon. Richard, more than anyone I have ever known, brought this tendency to the fore in me. I always wanted to kick him, and say, "Oh, come off it, baby, ain't no white folks around now, let's tell it like it *is*.")

Still, most of the Negroes I knew had *not* come to Paris to look for work. They were writers or dancers or composers, they were on the G.I. Bill, or fellowships, or more mysterious shoestrings, or they worked as jazz musicians. I did not know anyone who doubted that the American hiring system remained in Paris exactly what it had been at home—but how was one to prove this, with a handful, at best, of problematical Negroes, scattered throughout Paris? Unlike Richard, I had no reason to suppose that any of them even *wanted* to work for Americans—my evidence, in fact, suggested that this was just about the last thing they wanted to do. But, even if they did, and even if they were qualified, how could one *prove* that So-and-So had not been hired by TWA *because* he was a Negro? I had found this almost impossible to do at home. Isn't this, I suggested, the kind of thing which ought to be done from Washington? Richard, however, was not to be put off, and he had made me feel so guilty that I agreed to find out how many Negroes were then working for the ECA.

There turned out to be two or three or four, I forget how many. In any case, we were dead, there being no way on earth to prove that there should have been six or seven. But we were all in too deep to be able to turn back now, and, accordingly, there was a pilot meeting of this extraordinary organization, quite late, as I remember, one evening, in a private room over a bistro. It was in some extremely inconvenient part of town, and we all arrived separately or by twos. (There was some vague notion, I think, of defeating the ever-present agents of the CIA, who certainly ought to have had better things to do, but who, quite probably, on the other hand, didn't.) We may have defeated pursuit on our way there, but there was certainly no way of defeating detection as we arrived: slinking casually past the gaping mouths and astounded eyes of a workingman's bistro, like a disorganized parade, some thirty or forty of us, through a back door, and up the stairs. My friend and I arrived a little late, perhaps a little drunk, and certainly on a laughing jag, for we felt that we had been trapped in one of the most improbable and old-fashioned of English melodramas.

But Richard was in his glory. He was on the platform above us, I think he was alone there; there were only Negroes in the room. The results of the investigations of others had proved no more conclusive than my own—one could certainly not, on the basis of our findings, attack a policy or evolve a strategy—but this did not seem to surprise Richard or, even, to disturb him. It was decided, since we could not be a pressure group, to form a fellowship club, the purpose of which would be to get to know the French, and help the French to get to know us. Given our temperaments, neither Andy nor myself felt any need to join a club for this, we were getting along just fine on our own; but, somewhat to my surprise, we did not know many of the other people in the room, and so we listened. If it were only going to be a social club, then, obviously, the problem, as far as we were concerned, was over.

Richard's speech, that evening, made a great impact on me. It frightened me. I felt, but suppressed the feeling, that he was being mightily condescending toward the people in the room. I suppressed the feeling because most of them did not, in fact, interest me very much; but I was still in that stage when I felt guilty about not loving every Negro that I met. Still, perhaps for this very reason, I could not help resenting Richard's aspect and Richard's tone. I do not remember how his speech began, but I will never forget how it ended. News of this get-together, he told us, had caused a great stir in Parisian intellectual circles. Everyone was filled with wonder (as well they might be) concerning the future of such a group. A great many white people had wished to be present, Sartre, de Beauvoir, Camus—"and," said Richard, "*my own wife*. But I told them, before I can allow you to come, we've got to prepare the Negroes to receive you!"

This revelation, which was uttered with a smile, produced the most strained, stunned, uneasy silence. I looked at Andy, and Andy looked at me. There was something terribly funny about it, and there was something not funny at all. I rather wondered what the probable response would have been had Richard dared make such a statement in, say, a Negro barber shop; rather wondered, in fact, what the probable response would have been had anyone else dared make such a statement to anyone in the room, under different circumstances. ("Nigger, I been receiving white folks all my life—prepare *who*? Who you think you going to *prepare*?") It seemed to me, in any case, that the preparation ought, at least, to be conceived of as mutual: there was no reason to suppose that Parisian intellectuals were more "prepared" to "receive" American Negroes than American Negroes were to receive them—rather, all things considered, the contrary.

This was the extent of my connection with the Franco-American Fellowship Club, though the club itself, rather anemically, seemed to drag on for some time. I do not know what it accomplished—very little, I should imagine; but it soon ceased to exist because it had never had any reason to come into existence. To judge from complaints I heard, Richard's interest in it, once it was—roughly speaking—launched, was minimal. He told me once that it had cost him a great deal of money—this referred, I think, to some disastrous project, involving a printer's bill, which the club had undertaken. It seemed, indeed, that Richard felt that, with the establishment of this club, he had paid his dues to American Negroes abroad, and at home, and forever; had paid his dues, and was off the hook, since they had once more proved themselves incapable of following where he led. For yet one or two years to come, young Negroes would cross the ocean and come to Richard's door, wanting his sympathy, his help, his time, his money. God knows it must have been trying. And yet, they could not possibly have taken up more of his time than did the dreary sycophants by whom, as far as I could tell, he was more and more surrounded. Richard and I, of course, drifted farther and farther apart—our dialogues became too frustrating and too acrid—but, from my helplessly sardonic distance, I could only make out, looming above what seemed to be an indescribably cacophonous parade of mediocrities, and a couple of the world's most empty and pompous black writers, the tough and loyal figure of Chester Himes. There was a noticeable chill in the love affair which had been going on between Richard and the French intellectuals. He had always made American intellectuals uneasy, and now they were relieved to discover that he bored them, and even more relieved to say so. By this time he had managed to estrange himself from almost all of the younger American Negro writers in Paris. They were often to be found in the same café, Richard compulsively playing the pin-ball machine, while they, spitefully and deliberately, refused to acknowledge his presence. Gone were the days when he had only to enter a café to be greeted with the American Negro equivalent of *"cher maître"* ("Hey, Richard, how you making it, my man? Sit down and tell me something"), to be seated at a table, while all the bright faces turned toward him. The brightest faces were now turned from him, and among these faces were the faces of the Africans and the Algerians. They did not trust him—and their distrust was venomous because they felt that he had promised them so much. When the African said to me *I believe he thinks he's white*, he meant that Richard cared more about his safety and comfort than he cared about the black condition. But it was to this condition, at least in part, that he owed his safety and comfort and power and fame. If one-tenth of the suffering which obtained (and obtains) among Africans and Algerians in Paris had been occurring in Chicago, one could not help feeling that Richard would have raised the roof. He never ceased to raise the roof, in fact, as far as the American color problem was concerned. But time passes quickly. The American Negroes had discovered that Richard did not really know much about the present dimensions and complexity of the Negro problem here, and, profoundly, did not want to know. And one of the reasons that he did not want to know was that his real impulse toward American Negroes, individually, was to despise them. They, therefore, dismissed his rage and his public pronouncements as an unmanly reflex; as for the Africans, at least the younger ones, they knew he did not know them and did not want to know them, and they despised *him*. It must have been extremely hard to bear, and it was certainly very frightening to watch. I could not help feeling: *Be careful. Time is passing for you, too, and this may be happening to you one day.*

For who has not hated his black brother? Simply *because* he is black, *because* he is brother. And who has not dreamed of violence? That fantastical violence which will drown in blood, wash away in blood, not only generation upon generation of horror, but which will also release one from the individual horror, carried everywhere in the heart. Which of us has overcome his past? And the past of a Negro is blood dripping down through leaves, gouged-out eyeballs, the sex torn from its socket and severed with a knife. But this past is not special to the Negro. This horror is also the past, and the everlasting potential, or temptation, of the human race. If we do not know this, it seems to me, we know nothing about ourselves, nothing about each other; to have accepted this is also to have found a source of strength—source of all our power. But one must first accept this paradox, with joy.

The American Negro has paid a hidden, terrible price for his slow climbing to the light; so that, for example, Richard was able, at last, to live in Paris exactly as he would have lived, had he been a white man, here, in America. This may seem desirable, but I wonder if it is. Richard paid the price such an illusion of safety demands. The price is a turning away from, an ignorance of, all of the powers of darkness. This sounds mystical, but it is not; it is a hidden fact. It is the failure of the moral imagination of Europe which has created the forces now determined to overthrow it. No European dreamed, during Europe's heyday, that they were sowing, in a dark continent, far away, the seeds of a whirlwind. It was not dreamed, during the Second World War, that Churchill's ringing words to the English were overheard by English slaves—who, now, coming in their thousands to the mainland, menace the English sleep. It is only now, in America, and it may easily be too late, that any of the anguish, to say nothing of the rage, with which the American Negro has lived so long begins, dimly, to trouble the public mind. The suspicion has been planted—and the principal effect, so far, here, has been panic—that perhaps the world is darker and therefore more real than we have allowed ourselves to believe.

Time brought Richard, as it has brought the American Negro, to an extraordinarily baffling and dangerous place. An American Negro, however deep his sympathies, or however bright his rage, ceases to be simply a black man when he faces a black man from Africa. When I say simply a black man, I do not mean that being a black man is simple, anywhere. But I am suggesting that one of the prices an American Negro pays—or can pay—for what is called his "acceptance" is a profound, almost ineradicable self-hatred. This corrupts every aspect of his living, he is never at peace again, he is out of touch with himself forever. And, when he faces an African, he is facing the unspeakably dark, guilty, erotic past which the

Protestant fathers made him bury—for their peace of mind, and for their power—but which lives in his personality and haunts the universe yet. What an African, facing an American Negro sees, I really do not yet know; and it is too early to tell with what scars and complexes the African has come up from the fire. But the war in the breast between blackness and whiteness, which caused Richard such pain, need not be a war. It is a war which just as it denies both the heights and the depths of our natures, takes, and has taken, visibly and invisibly, as many white lives as black ones. And, as I see it, Richard was among the most illustrious victims of this war. This is why, it seems to me, he eventually found himself wandering in a no-man's land between the black world and the white. It is no longer important to be white—thank heaven—the white face is no longer invested with the power of this world; and it is devoutly to be hoped that it will soon no longer be important to be black. The experience of the American Negro, if it is ever faced and assessed, makes it possible to hope for such a reconciliation. The hope and the effect of this fusion in the breast of the American Negro is one of the few hopes we have of surviving the wilderness which lies before us now.

13. The Black Boy Looks at the White Boy

I walked and I walked
Till I wore out my shoes.
I can't walk so far, but
Yonder come the blues.
　　　　　　—MA RAINEY

I FIRST met Norman Mailer about five years ago, in Paris, at the home of Jean Malaquais. Let me bring in at once the theme that will repeat itself over and over throughout this love letter: I was then (and I have not changed much) a very tight, tense, lean, abnormally ambitious, abnormally intelligent, and hungry black cat. It is important that I admit that, at the time I met Norman, I was extremely worried about my career; and a writer who is worried about his career is also fighting for his life. I was approaching the end of a love affair, and I was not taking it very well. Norman and I are alike in this, that we both tend to suspect others of putting us down, and we strike before we're struck. Only, our styles are very different: I am a black boy from the Harlem streets, and Norman is a middle-class Jew. I am not dragging my personal history into this gratuitously, and I hope I do not need to say that no sneer is implied in the above description of Norman. But these are the facts and in my own relationship to Norman they are crucial facts.

Also, I have no right to talk about Norman without risking a distinctly chilling self-exposure. I take him very seriously, he is very dear to me. And I think I know something about his journey from my black boy's point of view because my own journey is not really so very different, and also because I have spent most of my life, after all, watching white people and outwitting them, so that I might survive. I think that I know something about the American masculinity which most men of my generation do not know because they have not been menaced by it in the way that I have been. It is still true, alas, that to be an American Negro male is also to be a kind of

269

walking phallic symbol: which means that one pays, in one's own personality, for the sexual insecurity of others. The relationship, therefore, of a black boy to a white boy is a very complex thing.

There is a difference, though, between Norman and myself in that I think he still imagines that he has something to save, whereas I have never had anything to lose. Or, perhaps I ought to put it another way: the thing that most white people imagine that they can salvage from the storm of life is really, in sum, their innocence. It was this commodity precisely which I had to get rid of at once, literally, on pain of death. I am afraid that most of the white people I have ever known impressed me as being in the grip of a weird nostalgia, dreaming of a vanished state of security and order, against which dream, unfailingly and unconsciously, they tested and very often lost their lives. It is a terrible thing to say, but I am afraid that for a very long time the troubles of white people failed to impress me as being real trouble. They put me in mind of children crying because the breast has been taken away. Time and love have modified my tough-boy lack of charity, but the attitude sketched above was my first attitude and I am sure that there is a great deal of it left.

To proceed: two lean cats, one white and one black, met in a French living room. I had heard of him, he had heard of me. And here we were, suddenly, circling around each other. We liked each other at once, but each was frightened that the other would pull rank. He could have pulled rank on me because he was more famous and had more money and also because he was white; but I could have pulled rank on him precisely because I was black and knew more about that periphery he so helplessly maligns in *The White Negro* than he could ever hope to know. Already, you see, we were trapped in our roles and our attitudes: the toughest kid on the block was meeting the toughest kid on the block. I think that both of us were pretty weary of this grueling and thankless role, I know that I am; but the roles that we construct are constructed because we feel that they will help us to survive and also, of course, because they fulfill something in our personalities; and one does not, therefore, cease playing a role simply because one has begun to understand it. All roles are dangerous. The world tends to trap and immobilize you in the role you play; and it is not always easy—in fact, it is always extremely hard—to maintain a kind of watchful, mocking distance between oneself as one appears to be and oneself as one actually is.

I think that Norman was working on *The Deer Park* at that time, or had just finished it, and Malaquais, who had translated *The Naked and the Dead* into French, did not like *The Deer Park*. I had not then read the book; if I had, I would have been astonished that Norman could have expected Malaquais to like it. What Norman was trying to do in *The Deer Park*, and quite apart, now, from whether or not he succeeded, could only—it seems to me—baffle and annoy a French intellectual who seemed to me essentially rationalistic. Norman has many qualities and faults, but I have never heard anyone accuse him of possessing this particular one. But Malaquais' opinion seemed to mean a great deal to him—this astonished me, too; and there was a running, good-natured but astringent argument between them, with Malaquais playing the role of the old lion and Norman playing the role of the powerful but clumsy cub. And, I must say, I think that each of them got a great deal of pleasure out of the other's performance. The night we met, we stayed up very late, and did a great deal of drinking and shouting. But beneath all the shouting and the posing and the mutual showing off, something very wonderful was happening. I was aware of a new and warm presence in my life, for I had met someone I wanted to know, who wanted to know me.

Norman and his wife, Adele, along with a Negro jazz musician friend, and myself, met fairly often during the few weeks that found us all in the same city. I think that Norman had come in from Spain, and he was shortly to return to the States; and it was not long after Norman's departure that I left Paris for Corsica. My memory of that time is both blurred and sharp, and, oddly enough, is principally of Norman—confident, boastful, exuberant, and loving—striding through the soft Paris nights like a gladiator. And I think, alas, that I envied him: his success, and his youth, and his love. And this meant that though Norman really wanted to know me, and though I really wanted to know him, I hung back, held fire, danced, and lied. I was not going to come crawling out of my ruined house, all bloody, no, baby, sing no sad songs for *me*. And the great gap between Norman's state and my own had a terrible effect on our relationship, for it inevitably connected, not to say collided, with that myth of the sexuality of Negroes which Norman, like so many others, refuses to give up. The sexual battleground, if I may call it that, is really the same for everyone; and I, at this point, was just about to be carried off the battleground on my shield, if anyone could find it; so how could I play, in any way whatever, the noble savage?

At the same time, my temperament and my experience in this country had led me to expect very little from most American whites, especially, horribly enough, my friends: so it did not seem worthwhile to challenge, in any real way, Norman's views of life on the periphery, or to put him down for them. I was weary, to tell the truth. I had tried, in the States, to convey something of what it felt like to be a Negro and no one had been able to listen: they wanted their romance. And, anyway, the really ghastly thing about trying to convey to a white man the reality of the Negro experience has nothing whatever to do with the fact of color, but has to do with this man's relationship to his own life. He will face in your life only what he is willing to face in his. Well, this means that one finds oneself tampering with the insides of a stranger, to no purpose, which one probably has no right to do, and I chickened out. And matters were not helped at all by the fact that the Negro jazz musicians, among whom we sometimes found ourselves, who really liked Norman, did not for an instant consider him as being even remotely "hip" and Norman did not know this and I could not tell him. He never broke through to them, at least not as far I know; and they were far too "hip," if that is the word I want, even to consider breaking through to him. They thought he was a real sweet ofay cat, but a little frantic.

But we were far more cheerful than anything I've said might indicate and none of the above seemed to matter very much at the time. Other things mattered, like walking and talking and drinking and eating, and the way Adele laughed, and the way Norman argued. He argued like a young man, he argued to win: and while I found him charming, he may have found me exasperating, for I kept moving back before that short, prodding forefinger. I couldn't submit my arguments, or my real questions, for I had too much to hide. Or so it seemed to me then. I submit, though I may be wrong, that I was then at the beginning of a terrifying adventure, not too unlike the conundrum which seems to menace Norman now:

"I had done a few things and earned a few pence"; but the things I had written were behind me, could not be written again, could not be repeated. I was also realizing that all that the world could give me as an artist, it had, in effect, already given. In the years that stretched before me, all that I could look forward to, in that way, were a few more prizes, or a lot more, and a little more, or a lot more money. And my private life had failed—had failed, had failed. One of the reasons I had fought so hard, after all, was to wrest from the world fame and money and love. And here I was, at thirty-two, finding my notoriety hard to bear, since its principal effect was to make me more lonely; money, it turned out, was exactly like sex, you thought of nothing else if you didn't have it and thought of other things if you did; and love, as far as I could see, was over. Love seemed to be over not merely because an affair was ending; it would have seemed to be over under any circumstances; for it was the dream of love which was ending. I was beginning to realize, most unwillingly, all the things love could not do. It could not make me over, for example. It could not undo the journey which had made of me such a strange man and brought me to such a strange place.

But at that time it seemed only too clear that love had gone out of the world, and not, as I had thought once, because I was poor and ugly and obscure, but precisely because I was no longer any of these things. What point, then, was there in working if the best I could hope for was the Nobel Prize? And *how*, indeed, would I be able to keep on working if I could never be released from the prison of my egocentricity? By what act could I escape this horror? For horror it was, let us make no mistake about that.

And, beneath all this, which simplified nothing, was that sense, that suspicion—which is the glory and torment of every writer—that what was happening to me might be turned to good account, that I was trembling on the edge of great revelations, was being prepared for a very long journey, and might now begin, having survived my apprenticeship (but had I survived it?), a great work. I might really become a great writer. But in order to do this I would have to sit down at the typewriter again, alone—I would have to accept my despair: and I could not do it. It really does not help to be a strong-willed person or, anyway, I think it is a great error to misunderstand the nature of the will. In the most important areas of anybody's life, the will usually operates as a traitor. My own will was busily pointing out to me the most fantastically unreal alternatives to my pain, all of which I tried, all of which—luckily—failed. When, late in the evening or early in the morning, Norman and Adele returned to their hotel on the Quai Voltaire, I wandered through Paris, the underside of Paris, drinking, screwing, fighting—it's a wonder I wasn't killed. And then it was morning, I would somehow be home—usually, anyway—and the typewriter would be there, staring at me; and the manuscript of the new novel, which it seemed I would never be able to achieve, and from which clearly I was never going to be released, was scattered all over the floor.

That's the way it is. I think it is the most dangerous point in the life of any artist, his longest, most hideous turning; and especially for a man, an American man, whose principle is action and whose jewel is optimism, who must now accept what certainly then seems to be a gray passivity and an endless despair. It is the point at which many artists lose their minds, or commit suicide, or throw themselves into good works, or try to enter politics. For all of this is happening not only in the wilderness of the soul, but in the real world which accomplishes its seductions not by offering you opportunities to be wicked but by offering opportunities to be good, to be active and effective, to be admired and central and apparently loved.

Norman came on to America, and I went to Corsica. We wrote each other a few times. I confided to Norman that I was very apprehensive about the reception of *Giovanni's Room*, and he was good enough to write some very encouraging things about it when it came out. The critics had jumped on him with both their left feet when he published

The Deer Park—which I still had not read—and this created a kind of bond, or strengthened the bond already existing between us. About a year and several overflowing wastebaskets later, I, too, returned to America, not vastly improved by having been out of it, but not knowing where else to go; and one day, while I was sitting dully in my house, Norman called me from Connecticut. A few people were going to be there—for the weekend—and he wanted me to come, too. We had not seen each other since Paris.

Well, I wanted to go, that is, I wanted to see Norman; but I did not want to see any people, and so the tone of my acceptance was not very enthusiastic. I realized that he felt this, but I did not know what to do about it. He gave me train schedules and hung up.

Getting to Connecticut would have been no hassle if I could have pulled myself together to get to the train. And I was sorry, as I meandered around my house and time flew and trains left, that I had not been more honest with Norman and told him exactly how I felt. But I had not known how to do this, or it had not really occurred to me to do it, especially not over the phone.

So there was another phone call, I forget who called whom, which went something like this:

N: Don't feel you have to. I'm not trying to bug you.

J: It's not that. It's just—

N: You don't really want to come, do you?

J: I don't really feel up to it.

N: I understand. I guess you just don't like the Connecticut gentry.

J: Well—don't you ever come to the city?

N: Sure. We'll see each other.

J: I hope so. I'd like to see you.

N: Okay, till then.

And he hung up. I thought, I ought to write him a letter, but of course I did nothing of the sort. It was around this time I went South, I think; anyway, we did not see each other for a long time.

But I thought about him a great deal. The grapevine keeps all of us advised of the others' movements, so I knew when Norman left Connecticut for New York, heard that he had been present at this or that party and what he had said: usually something rude, often something penetrating, sometimes something so hilariously silly that it was difficult to believe he had been serious. (This was my reaction when I first heard his famous running-for-President remark. I dismissed it. I was wrong.) Or he had been seen in this or that Village spot, in which unfailingly there would be someone—out of spite, idleness, envy, exasperation, out of the bottomless, eerie, aimless hostility which characterizes almost every bar in New York, to speak only of bars—to put him down. I heard of a couple of fist-fights, and, of course, I was always encountering people who hated his guts. These people always mildly surprised me, and so did the news of his fights: it was hard for me to imagine that anyone could really dislike Norman, anyone, that is, who had encountered him personally. I knew of one fight he had had, forced on him, apparently, by a blow-hard Village type whom I considered rather pathetic. I didn't blame Norman for this fight, but I couldn't help wondering why he bothered to rise to such a shapeless challenge. It seemed simpler, as I was always telling myself, just to stay out of Village bars.

And people talked about Norman with a kind of avid glee, which I found very ugly. Pleasure made their saliva flow, they sprayed and all but drooled, and their eyes shone with that blood-lust which is the only real tribute the mediocre are capable of bringing to the extraordinary. Many of the people who claimed to be seeing Norman all the time impressed me as being, to tell the truth, pitifully far beneath him. But this is also true, alas, of much of my own entourage. The people who are in one's life or merely continually in one's presence reveal a great deal about one's needs and terrors. Also, one's hopes.

I was not, however, on the scene. I was on the road—not quite, I trust, in the sense that Kerouac's boys are; but I presented, certainly, a moving target. And I was reading Norman Mailer. Before I had met him, I had only read *The Naked and The Dead*, *The White Negro*, and *Barbary Shore*—I think this is right, though it may be that I only read *The White Negro* later and confuse my reading of that piece with some of my discussions with Norman. Anyway, I could not, with the best will in the world, make any sense out of *The White Negro* and, in fact, it was hard for me to imagine that this essay had been written by the same man who wrote the novels. Both *The Naked and The Dead* and (for the most part) *Barbary Shore* are written in a lean, spare, muscular prose which accomplishes almost exactly what it sets out to do. Even *Barbary Shore*, which loses itself in its last half (and which deserves, by the way, far more serious treatment than it has received) never becomes as downright impenetrable as *The White Negro* does.

Now, much of this, I told myself, had to do with my resistance to the title, and with a kind of fury that so antique a vision of the blacks should, at this late hour, and in so many borrowed heirlooms, be stepping off the A train. But I was also baffled by the passion with which Norman appeared to be imitating so many people inferior to himself, i.e., Kerouac, and all the other Suzuki rhythm boys. From them, indeed, I expected nothing more than their pablum-clogged cries of *Kicks!* and *Holy!* It seemed very clear to me that their glorification of the orgasm was but a way of avoiding all of the terrors of life and love. But Norman knew better, had to know better. *The Naked and The Dead, Barbary Shore,* and *The Deer Park* proved it. In each of these novels, there is a toughness and subtlety of conception, and a sense of the danger and complexity of human relationships which one will search for in vain, not only in the work produced by the aforementioned coterie, but in most of the novels produced by Norman's contemporaries. What in the world, then, was he doing, slumming so outrageously, in such a dreary crowd?

For, exactly because he knew better, and in exactly the same way that no one can become more lewdly vicious than an imitation libertine, Norman felt compelled to carry their *mystique* further than they had, to be more "hip," or more "beat," to dominate, in fact, their dreaming field; and since this *mystique* depended on a total rejection of life, and insisted on the fulfillment of an infantile dream of love, the *mystique* could only be extended into violence. No one is more dangerous than he who imagines himself pure in heart: for his purity, by definition, is unassailable.

But *why* should it be necessary to borrow the Depression language of deprived Negroes, which eventually evolved into jive and bop talk, in order to justify such a grim system of

delusions? Why malign the sorely menaced sexuality of Negroes in order to justify the white man's own sexual panic?
Especially as, in Norman's case, and as indicated by his work,
he has a very real sense of sexual responsibility, and, even, odd
as it may sound to some, of sexual morality, and a genuine
commitment to life. None of his people, I beg you to notice,
spend their lives on the road. They really become entangled
with each other, and with life. They really suffer, they spill real
blood, they have real lives to lose. This is no small achievement; in fact, it is absolutely rare. No matter how uneven one
judges Norman's work to be, all of it is genuine work. No
matter how harshly one judges it, it is the work of a genuine
novelist, and an absolutely first-rate talent.

Which makes the questions I have tried to raise—or, rather,
the questions which Norman Mailer irresistibly represents—
all the more troubling and terrible. I certainly do not know
the answers, and even if I did, this is probably not the place
to state them.

But I have a few ideas. Here is Kerouac, ruminating on what
I take to be the loss of the garden of Eden:

> At lilac evening I walked with every muscle aching among the
> lights of 27th and Welton in the Denver colored section, wishing I
> were a Negro, feeling that the best the white world had offered was
> not enough ecstasy for me, not enough life, joy, kicks, darkness, mu-
> sic, not enough night. I wished I were a Denver Mexican, or even a
> poor overworked Jap, anything but what I so drearily was, a "white
> man" disillusioned. All my life I'd had white ambitions. . . . I passed
> the dark porches of Mexican and Negro homes; soft voices were
> there, occasionally the dusky knee of some mysterious sensuous gal;
> and dark faces of the men behind rose arbors. Little children sat like
> sages in ancient rocking chairs.

Now, this is absolute nonsense, of course, objectively considered, and offensive nonsense at that: I would hate to be in
Kerouac's shoes if he should ever be mad enough to read this
aloud from the stage of Harlem's Apollo Theater.

And yet there is real pain in it, and real loss, however thin;
and it *is* thin, like soup too long diluted; thin because it does
not refer to reality, but to a dream. Compare it, at random,
with any old blues:

> Backwater blues done caused me
> To pack my things and go.
> 'Cause my house fell down
> And I can't live there no mo'.

"Man," said a Negro musician to me once, talking about Norman, "the only trouble with that cat is that he's white." This does not mean exactly what it says—or, rather, it *does* mean exactly what it says, and not what it might be taken to mean—and it is a very shrewd observation. What my friend meant was that to become a Negro man, let alone a Negro artist, one had to make oneself up as one went along. This had to be done in the not-at-all-metaphorical teeth of the world's determination to destroy you. The world had prepared no place for you, and if the world had its way, no place would ever exist. Now, this is true for everyone, but, in the case of a Negro, this truth is absolutely naked: if he deludes himself about it, he will die. This is not the way this truth presents itself to white men, who believe the world is theirs and who, albeit unconsciously, expect the world to help them in the achievement of their identity. But the world does not do this—for anyone; the world is not interested in anyone's identity. And, therefore, the anguish which can overtake a white man comes in the middle of his life, when he must make the almost inconceivable effort to divest himself of everything he has ever expected or believed, when he must take himself apart and put himself together again, walking out of the world, into limbo, or into what certainly looks like limbo. This cannot yet happen to any Negro of Norman's age, for the reason that his delusions and defenses are either absolutely impenetrable by this time, or he has failed to survive them. "I want to know how power works," Norman once said to me, "how it really works, in detail." Well, I know how power works, it has worked on me, and if I didn't know how power worked, I would be dead. And it goes without saying, perhaps, that I have simply never been able to afford myself any illusions concerning the manipulation of that power. My revenge, I decided very early, would be to achieve a power which outlasts kingdoms.

II

When I finally saw Norman again, I was beginning to suspect daylight at the end of my long tunnel, it was a summer day, I was on my way back to Paris, and I was very cheerful. We were at an afternoon party, Norman was standing in the kitchen, a drink in his hand, holding forth for the benefit of a small group of people. There seemed something different about him, it was the belligerence of his stance, and the really rather pontifical tone of his voice. I had only seen him, remember, in Malaquais' living room, which Malaquais indefatigably dominates, and on various terraces and in various dives in Paris. I do not mean that there was anything unfriendly about him. On the contrary, he was smiling and having a ball. And yet—he was leaning against the refrigerator, rather as though he had his back to the wall, ready to take on all comers.

Norman has a trick, at least with me, of watching, somewhat ironically, as you stand on the edge of the crowd around him, waiting for his attention. I suppose this ought to be exasperating, but in fact I find it rather endearing, because it is so transparent and because he gets such a bang out of being the center of attention. So do I, of course, at least some of the time.

We talked, bantered, a little tensely, made the usual, doomed effort to bring each other up to date on what we had been doing. I did not want to talk about my novel, which was only just beginning to seem to take shape, and, therefore, did not dare ask him if he were working on a novel. He seemed very pleased to see me, and I was pleased to see him, but I also had the feeling that he had made up his mind about me, adversely, in some way. It was as though he were saying, Okay, so now I know who *you* are, baby.

I was taking a boat in a few days, and I asked him to call me.

"Oh, no," he said, grinning, and thrusting that forefinger at me, "*you* call me."

"That's fair enough," I said, and I left the party and went on back to Paris. While I was out of the country, Norman published *Advertisements for Myself*, which presently crossed the ocean to the apartment of James Jones. Bill Styron was also in Paris at that time, and one evening the three of us sat in Jim's living room, reading aloud, in a kind of drunken, masochistic fascination, Norman's judgment of our personalities and our work. Actually, I came off best, I suppose; there was less about me, and it was less venomous. But the condescension infuriated me; also, to tell the truth, my feelings were hurt. I felt that if that was the way Norman felt about me, he should have told me so. He had said that I was incapable of saying "F——— you" to the reader. My first temptation was to send him a cablegram which would disabuse him of that notion, at least insofar as one reader was concerned. But then I thought, No, I would be cool about it, and fail to react as he so clearly wanted me to. Also, I must say, his judgment of myself seemed so wide of the mark and so childish that it was hard to stay angry. I wondered what in the world was going on in his mind. Did he really suppose that he had now become the builder and destroyer of reputations,

And of *my* reputation?

We met in the Actors' Studio one afternoon, after a performance of *The Deer Park*—which I deliberately arrived too late to see, since I really did not know how I was going to react to Norman, and didn't want to betray myself by clobbering his play. When the discussion ended, I stood, again on the edge of the crowd around him, waiting. Over someone's shoulder, our eyes met, and Norman smiled.

"We've got something to talk about," I told him.

"I figured that," he said, smiling.

We went to a bar, and sat opposite each other. I was relieved to discover that I was not angry, not even (as far as I could tell) at the bottom of my heart. But, "Why did you write those things about me?"

"Well, I'll tell you about that," he said—Norman has several accents, and I think this was his Texas one—"I sort of figured you had it coming to you."

"Why?"

"Well, I think there's some truth in it."

"Well, if you felt that way, why didn't you ever say so—to me?"

"Well, I figured if this was going to break up our friendship, something else would come along to break it up just as fast."

I couldn't disagree with that.

"You're the only one I kind of regret hitting so hard," he said, with a grin. "I think I—probably—wouldn't say it quite that way now."

With this, I had to be content. We sat for perhaps an hour, talking of other things and, again, I was struck by his stance: leaning on the table, shoulders hunched, seeming, really, to roll like a boxer's, and his hands moving as though he were dealing with a sparring partner. And we were talking of physical courage, and the necessity of never letting another guy get the better of you.

I laughed. "Norman, I can't go through the world the way you do because I haven't got your shoulders."

He grinned, as though I were his pupil. "But you're a pretty tough little mother, too," he said, and referred to one of the grimmer of my Village misadventures, a misadventure which certainly proved that I had a dangerously sharp tongue, but which didn't really prove anything about my courage. Which, anyway, I had long ago given up trying to prove.

I did not see Norman again until Provincetown, just after his celebrated brush with the police there, which resulted, according to Norman, in making the climate of Provincetown as "mellow as Jello." The climate didn't seem very different to me—dull natives, dull tourists, malevolent policemen; I certainly, in any case, would never have dreamed of testing Norman's sanguine conclusion. But we had a great time, lying around the beach, and driving about, and we began to be closer than we had been for a long time.

It was during this Provincetown visit that I realized, for the first time, during a long exchange Norman and I had, in a kitchen, at someone else's party, that Norman was really fascinated by the nature of political power. But, though he said so, I did not really believe that he was fascinated by it as a possibility for himself. He was then doing the great piece on the Democratic convention which was published in *Esquire*, and I put his fascination down to that. I tend not to worry about writers as long as they are working—which is not as romantic as it may sound—and he seemed quite happy with his wife, his family, himself. I declined, naturally, to rise at dawn, as he apparently often did, to go running or swimming or boxing, but Norman seemed to get a great charge out of these admirable pursuits and didn't put me down too hard for my comparative decadence.

He and Adele and the two children took me to the plane one afternoon, the tiny plane which shuttles from Provincetown to Boston. It was a great day, clear and sunny, and that was the way I felt: for it seemed to me that we had all, at last, re-established our old connection.

And then I heard that Norman was running for mayor, which I dismissed as a joke and refused to believe until it became hideously clear that it was not a joke at all. I was furious. I thought, You son of a bitch, you're copping out. You're one of the very few writers around who might really become a great writer, who might help to excavate the buried consciousness of this country, and you want to settle for being the lousy mayor of New York. *It's not your job.* And I don't at all mean to suggest that writers are not responsible to and for—in any case, always for—the social order. I don't, for that matter, even mean to suggest that Norman would have made a particularly bad Mayor, though I confess that I simply cannot see him in this role. And there is probably some truth in the suggestion, put forward by Norman and others, that the shock value of having such a man in such an office, or merely running for such an office, would have had a salutary effect on the life of this city—particularly, I must say, as relates to our young people, who are certainly in desperate need of adults who love them and take them seriously, and whom they can respect. (Serious citizens may not respect Norman, but young people do, and do not respect the serious citizens; and their instincts are quite sound.)

But I do not feel that a writer's responsibility can be discharged in this way. I do not think, if one is a writer, that one escapes it by trying to become something else. One does *not* become something else: one becomes nothing. And what is crucial here is that the writer, however unwillingly, always, somewhere, knows this. There is no structure he can build strong enough to keep out this self-knowledge. What *has* happened, however, time and time again, is that the fantasy structure the writer builds in order to escape his central responsibility operates not as his fortress, but his prison, and he perishes within it. Or: the structure he has built becomes so stifling, so lonely, so false, and acquires such a violent and dangerous life of its own, that he can break out of it only by bringing the entire structure down. With a great crash, inevitably, and on his own head, and on the heads of those closest to him. It is like smashing the windows one second before one asphyxiates; it is like burning down the house in order, at last, to be free of it. And this, I think, really, to touch upon it lightly, is the key to the events at that monstrous, baffling, and so publicized party. Nearly everyone in the world—or nearly everyone, at least, in this extraordinary city—was there: policemen, Mafia types, the people whom we quaintly refer to as "beatniks," writers, actors, editors, politicians, and gossip columnists. It must be admitted that it was a considerable achievement to have brought so many unlikely types together under one roof; and, in spite of everything, I can't help wishing that I had been there to witness the mutual bewilderment. But the point is that no politician would have dreamed of giving such a party in order to launch his mayoralty campaign. Such an imaginative route is not usually an attribute of politicians. In addition, the price one pays for pursuing any profession, or calling, is an intimate knowledge of its ugly side. It is scarcely worth observing that political activity is often, to put it mildly, pungent, and I think that Norman, perhaps for the first time, really doubted his ability to deal with such a world, and blindly struck his way out of it. We do not, in this country now, have much taste for, or any real sense of, the extremes human beings can reach; time will improve us in this regard; but in the meantime the general fear of experience is one of the reasons that the American writer has so peculiarly difficult and dangerous a time.

One can never really see into the heart, the mind, the soul of another. Norman is my very good friend, but perhaps I do not really understand him at all, and perhaps everything I have tried to suggest in the foregoing is false. I do not think so, but it may be. One thing, however, I am certain is *not* false, and that is simply the fact of his being a writer, and the incalculable potential he as a writer contains. His work, after all, is all that will be left when the newspapers are yellowed, all the gossip columnists silenced, and all the cocktail parties over, and when Norman and you and I are dead. I know that this point of view is not terribly fashionable these days, but I think we *do* have a responsibility, not only to ourselves and to our own time, but to those who are coming after us. (I refuse to believe that no one is coming after us.) And I suppose that this responsibility can only be discharged by dealing as truthfully as we know how with our present fortunes, these present days. So that my concern with Norman, finally, has to do with how deeply he has understood these last sad and stormy events. If he has understood them, then he is richer and we are richer, too; if he has not understood them, we are all much poorer. For, though it clearly needs to be brought into focus, he has a real vision of ourselves as we are, and it cannot be too often repeated in this country now, that, where there is no vision, the people perish.

THE FIRE NEXT TIME

"God gave Noah the rainbow sign,
No more water, the fire next time!"

for James
James
Luc James

Contents

MY DUNGEON SHOOK: *Letter to My
Nephew on the One Hundredth
Anniversary of the Emancipation* 291

DOWN AT THE CROSS: *Letter from a
Region in My Mind* 296

My Dungeon Shook

Letter to My Nephew
on the One Hundredth Anniversary
of the Emancipation

Dear James:

I HAVE begun this letter five times and torn it up five times. I keep seeing your face, which is also the face of your father and my brother. Like him, you are tough, dark, vulnerable, moody—with a very definite tendency to sound truculent because you want no one to think you are soft. You may be like your grandfather in this, I don't know, but certainly both you and your father resemble him very much physically. Well, he is dead, he never saw you, and he had a terrible life; he was defeated long before he died because, at the bottom of his heart, he really believed what white people said about him. This is one of the reasons that he became so holy. I am sure that your father has told you something about all that. Neither you nor your father exhibit any tendency towards holiness: you really *are* of another era, part of what happened when the Negro left the land and came into what the late E. Franklin Frazier called "the cities of destruction." You can only be destroyed by believing that you really are what the white world calls a *nigger*. I tell you this because I love you, and please don't you ever forget it.

I have known both of you all your lives, have carried your Daddy in my arms and on my shoulders, kissed and spanked him and watched him learn to walk. I don't know if you've known anybody from that far back; if you've loved anybody that long, first as an infant, then as a child, then as a man, you gain a strange perspective on time and human pain and effort. Other people cannot see what I see whenever I look into your father's face, for behind your father's face as it is today are all those other faces which were his. Let him laugh and I see a cellar your father does not remember and a house he does not remember and I hear in his present laughter his laughter as a child. Let him curse and I remember him falling down the cellar steps, and howling, and I remember, with pain, his tears, which my hand or your grandmother's so easily wiped away. But no one's hand can wipe away those tears he sheds invisibly today, which one hears in his laughter and in his speech and in his songs. I know what the world has done to my brother and how narrowly he has survived it. And I know, which is much worse, and this is the crime of which I accuse my country and my countrymen, and for which neither I nor time nor history will ever forgive them, that they have destroyed and are destroying hundreds of thousands of lives and do not know it and do not want to know it. One can be, indeed one must strive to become, tough and philosophical concerning destruction and death, for this is what most of mankind has been best at since we have heard of man. (But remember: *most* of mankind is not *all* of mankind.) But it is not permissible that the authors of devastation should also be innocent. It is the innocence which constitutes the crime.

Now, my dear namesake, these innocent and well-meaning people, your countrymen, have caused you to be born under conditions not very far removed from those described for us by Charles Dickens in the London of more than a hundred years ago. (I hear the chorus of the innocents screaming, "No! This is not true! How *bitter* you are!"—but I am writing this letter to *you*, to try to tell you something about how to handle *them*, for most of them do not yet really know that you exist. I *know* the conditions under which you were born, for I was there. Your countrymen were *not* there, and haven't made it yet. Your grandmother was also there, and no one has ever accused her of being bitter. I suggest that the innocents check with her. She isn't hard to find. Your countrymen don't know that *she* exists, either, though she has been working for them all their lives.)

Well, you were born, here you came, something like fifteen years ago; and though your father and mother and grandmother, looking about the streets through which they were carrying you, staring at the walls into which they brought you, had every reason to be heavyhearted, yet they were not. For here you were, Big James, named for me—you were a big baby, I was not—here you were: to be loved. To be loved, baby, hard, at once, and forever, to strengthen you against the loveless world. Remember that: I know how black it looks today, for you. It looked bad that day, too, yes, we were trembling. We have not stopped trembling yet, but if we had not loved each other none of us would have survived. And now you must survive because we love you, and for the sake of your children and your children's children.

This innocent country set you down in a ghetto in which, in fact, it intended that you should perish. Let me spell out precisely what I mean by that, for the heart of the matter is here, and the root of my dispute with my country. You were born where you were born and faced the future that you faced because you were black and *for no other reason*. The limits of your ambition were, thus, expected to be set forever. You were born into a society which spelled out with brutal clarity, and in as many ways as possible, that you were a worthless human being. You were not expected to aspire to excellence: you were expected to make peace with mediocrity. Wherever you have turned, James, in your short time on this earth, you have been told where you could go and what you could do (and *how* you could do it) and where you could live and whom you could marry. I know your countrymen do not agree with me about this, and I hear them saying, "You exaggerate." They do not know Harlem, and I do. So do you. Take no one's word for anything, including mine—but trust your experience. Know whence you came. If you know whence you came, there is really no limit to where you can go. The details and symbols of your life have been deliberately constructed to make you believe what white people say about you. Please try to remember that what they believe, as well as what they do and cause you to endure, does not testify to your inferiority but to their inhumanity and fear. Please try to be clear, dear James, through the storm which rages about your youthful head today, about the reality which lies behind the words *acceptance* and *integration*. There is no reason for you to try to become like white people and there is no basis whatever for their impertinent assumption that *they* must accept *you*. The really terrible thing, old buddy, is that *you* must accept *them*. And I mean that very seriously. You must accept them and accept them with love. For these innocent people have no other hope. They are, in effect, still trapped in a history which they do not understand; and until they understand it, they cannot be released from it. They have had to believe for many years, and for innumerable reasons, that black men are inferior to white men. Many of them, indeed, know better, but, as you will discover, people find it very difficult to act on what they know. To act is to be committed, and to be committed is to be in danger. In this case, the danger, in the minds of most white Americans, is the loss of their identity. Try to imagine how you would feel if you woke up one morning to find the sun shining and all the stars aflame. You would be frightened because it is out of the order of nature. Any upheaval in the universe is terrifying because it so profoundly attacks one's sense of one's own reality. Well, the black man has functioned in the white man's world as a fixed star, as an immovable pillar: and as he moves out of his place, heaven and earth are shaken to their foundations. You, don't be afraid. I said that it was intended that you should perish in the ghetto, perish by never being allowed to go behind the white man's definitions, by never being allowed to spell your proper name. You have, and many of us have, defeated this intention; and, by a terrible law, a terrible paradox, those innocents who believed that your imprisonment made them safe are losing their grasp of reality. But these men are your brothers—your lost, younger brothers. And if the word *integration* means anything, this is what it means: that we, with love, shall force our brothers to see themselves as they are, to cease fleeing from reality and begin to change it. For this is your home, my friend, do not be driven from it; great men have done great things here, and will again, and we can make America what America must become. It will be hard, James, but you come from sturdy, peasant stock, men who picked cotton and dammed rivers and built railroads, and, in the teeth of the most terrifying odds, achieved an unassailable and monumental dignity. You come from a long line of great poets, some of the greatest poets since Homer. One of them said, *The very time I thought I was lost, My dungeon shook and my chains fell off.*

You know, and I know, that the country is celebrating one hundred years of freedom one hundred years too soon. We cannot be free until they are free. God bless you, James, and Godspeed.

Your uncle,
James

Down at the Cross

Letter from a Region in My Mind

Take up the White Man's burden—
Ye dare not stoop to less—
Nor call too loud on Freedom
To cloak your weariness;
By all ye cry or whisper,
By all ye leave or do,
The silent, sullen peoples
Shall weigh your Gods and you.

—Kipling

Down at the cross where my Saviour died,
Down where for cleansing from sin I cried,
There to my heart was the blood applied,
Singing glory to His name!

—Hymn

I UNDERWENT, during the summer that I became fourteen, a prolonged religious crisis. I use the word "religious" in the common, and arbitrary, sense, meaning that I then discovered God, His saints and angels, and His blazing Hell. And since I had been born in a Christian nation, I accepted this Deity as the only one. I supposed Him to exist only within the walls of a church—in fact, of *our* church—and I also supposed that God and safety were synonymous. The word "safety" brings us to the real meaning of the word "religious" as we use it. Therefore, to state it in another, more accurate way, I became, during my fourteenth year, for the first time in my life, afraid—afraid of the evil within me and afraid of the evil without. What I saw around me that summer in Harlem was what I had always seen; nothing had changed. But now, without any warning, the whores and pimps and racketeers on the Avenue had become a personal menace. It had not before occurred to me that I could become one of them, but now I realized that we had been produced by the same circumstances. Many of my comrades were clearly headed for the Avenue, and my father said that I was headed that way, too. My friends began to drink and smoke, and embarked—at first avid, then groaning—on their sexual careers. Girls, only slightly older than I was, who sang in the choir or taught Sunday school, the children of holy parents, underwent, before my eyes, their incredible metamorphosis, of which the most bewildering aspect was not their budding breasts or their rounding behinds but something deeper and more subtle, in their eyes, their heat, their odor, and the inflection of their voices. Like the strangers on the Avenue, they became, in the twinkling of an eye, unutterably different and fantastically *present*. Owing to the way I had been raised, the abrupt discomfort that all this aroused in me and the fact that I had no idea what my voice or my mind or my body was likely to do next caused me to consider myself one of the most depraved people on earth. Matters were not helped by the fact that these holy girls seemed rather to enjoy my terrified lapses, our grim, guilty, tormented experiments, which were at once as chill and joyless as the Russian steppes and hotter, by far, than all the fires of Hell.

Yet there was something deeper than these changes, and less definable, that frightened me. It was real in both the boys and the girls, but it was, somehow, more vivid in the boys. In the case of the girls, one watched them turning into matrons before they had become women. They began to manifest a curious and really rather terrifying single mindedness. It is hard to say exactly how this was conveyed: something implacable in the set of the lips, something farseeing (seeing what?) in the eyes, some new and crushing determination in the walk, something peremptory in the voice. They did not tease us, the boys, any more; they reprimanded us sharply, saying, "You better be thinking about your soul!" For the girls also saw the evidence on the Avenue, knew what the price would be, for them, of one misstep, knew that they had to be protected and that we were the only protection there was. They understood that they must act as God's decoys, saving the souls of the boys for Jesus and binding the bodies of the boys in marriage. For this was the beginning of our burning time, and "It is better," said St. Paul—who elsewhere, with a most unusual and stunning exactness, described himself as a "wretched man"—"to marry than to burn." And I began to feel in the boys a curious, wary, bewildered despair, as though they were now settling in for the long, hard winter of life. I did not know then what it was that I was reacting to; I put it to myself that they were letting themselves go. In the same way that the girls were destined to gain as much weight as their mothers, the boys, it was clear, would rise no higher than their fathers. School began to reveal itself, therefore, as a child's game that one could not win, and boys dropped out of school and went to work. My father wanted me to do the same. I refused, even though I no longer had any illusions about what an education could do for me; I had already encountered too many college-graduate handymen. My friends were now "downtown," busy, as they put it, "fighting the man." They began to care less about the way they looked, the way they dressed, the things they did; presently, one found them in twos and threes and fours, in a hallway, sharing a jug of wine or a bottle of whiskey, talking, cursing, fighting, sometimes weeping: lost, and unable to say what it was that oppressed them, except that they knew it was "the man"— the white man. And there seemed to be no way whatever to remove this cloud that stood between them and the sun, between them and love and life and power, between them and whatever it was that they wanted. One did not have to be very bright to realize how little one could do to change one's situation; one did not have to be abnormally sensitive to be worn down to a cutting edge by the incessant and gratuitous humiliation and danger one encountered every working day, all day long. The humiliation did not apply merely to working days, or workers; I was thirteen and was crossing Fifth Avenue on my way to the Forty-second Street library, and the cop in the middle of the street muttered as I passed him, "Why don't you niggers stay uptown where you belong?" When I was ten, and didn't look, certainly, any older, two policemen amused themselves with me by frisking me, making comic (and terrifying) speculations concerning my ancestry and probable sexual prowess, and for good measure, leaving me flat on my back in one of Harlem's empty lots. Just before and then during the Second World War, many of my friends fled into the service, all to be changed there, and rarely for the better, many to be ruined, and many to die. Others fled to other states and

cities—that is, to other ghettos. Some went on wine or whiskey or the needle, and are still on it. And others, like me, fled
into the church.

For the wages of sin were visible everywhere, in every wine-
stained and urine-splashed hallway, in every clanging ambu-
lance bell, in every scar on the faces of the pimps and their
whores, in every helpless, newborn baby being brought into
this danger, in every knife and pistol fight on the Avenue, and
in every disastrous bulletin: a cousin, mother of six, suddenly
gone mad, the children parcelled out here and there; an indestructible aunt rewarded for years of hard labor by a slow,
agonizing death in a terrible small room; someone's bright
son blown into eternity by his own hand; another turned rob-
ber and carried off to jail. It was a summer of dreadful speculations and discoveries, of which these were not the worst.
Crime became real, for example—for the first time—not as *a*
possibility but as *the* possibility. One would never defeat one's
circumstances by working and saving one's pennies; one
would never, by working, acquire that many pennies, and,
besides, the social treatment accorded even the most successful Negroes proved that one needed, in order to be free,
something more than a bank account. One needed a handle,
a lever, a means of inspiring fear. It was absolutely clear that
the police would whip you and take you in as long as they
could get away with it, and that everyone else—housewives,
taxi-drivers, elevator boys, dishwashers, bartenders, lawyers,
judges, doctors, and grocers—would never, by the operation
of any generous human feeling, cease to use you as an outlet
for his frustrations and hostilities. Neither civilized reason nor
Christian love would cause any of those people to treat you
as they presumably wanted to be treated; only the fear of your
power to retaliate would cause them to do that, or to seem
to do it, which was (and is) good enough. There appears to
be a vast amount of confusion on this point, but I do not
know many Negroes who are eager to be "accepted" by white
people, still less to be loved by them; they, the blacks, simply
don't wish to be beaten over the head by the whites every
instant of our brief passage on this planet. White people in
this country will have quite enough to do in learning how to
accept and love themselves and each other, and when they

have achieved this—which will not be tomorrow and may very well be never—the Negro problem will no longer exist, for it will no longer be needed.

People more advantageously placed than we in Harlem were, and are, will no doubt find the psychology and the view of human nature sketched above dismal and shocking in the extreme. But the Negro's experience of the white world cannot possibly create in him any respect for the standards by which the white world claims to live. His own condition is overwhelming proof that white people do not live by these standards. Negro servants have been smuggling odds and ends out of white homes for generations, and white people have been delighted to have them do it, because it has assuaged a dim guilt and testified to the intrinsic superiority of white people. Even the most doltish and servile Negro could scarcely fail to be impressed by the disparity between his situation and that of the people for whom he worked; Negroes who were neither doltish nor servile did not feel that they were doing anything wrong when they robbed white people. In spite of the Puritan-Yankee equation of virtue with well-being, Negroes had excellent reasons for doubting that money was made or kept by any very striking adherence to the Christian virtues; it certainly did not work that way for black Christians. In any case, white people, who had robbed black people of their liberty and who profited by this theft every hour that they lived, had no moral ground on which to stand. They had the judges, the juries, the shotguns, the law—in a word, power. But it was a criminal power, to be feared but not respected, and to be outwitted in any way whatever. And those virtues preached but not practiced by the white world were merely another means of holding Negroes in subjection.

It turned out, then, that summer, that the moral barriers that I had supposed to exist between me and the dangers of a criminal career were so tenuous as to be nearly nonexistent. I certainly could not discover any principled reason for not becoming a criminal, and it is not my poor, God-fearing parents who are to be indicted for the lack but this society. I was icily determined—more determined, really, than I then knew—never to make my peace with the ghetto but to die and go to Hell before I would let any white man spit on me,

before I would accept my "place" in this republic. I did not
intend to allow the white people of this country to tell me
who I was, and limit me that way, and polish me off that way.
And yet, of course, at the same time, I *was* being spat on and
defined and described and limited, and could have been polished off with no effort whatever. Every Negro boy—in my
situation during those years, at least—who reaches this point
realizes, at once, profoundly, because he wants to live, that he
stands in great peril and must find, with speed, a "thing," a
gimmick, to lift him out, to start him on his way. *And it does
not matter what the gimmick is.* It was this last realization that
terrified me and—since it revealed that the door opened on
so many dangers—helped to hurl me into the church. And,
by an unforeseeable paradox, it was my career in the church
that turned out, precisely, to be my gimmick.

For when I tried to assess my capabilities, I realized that I
had almost none. In order to achieve the life I wanted, I had
been dealt, it seemed to me, the worst possible hand. I could
not become a prizefighter—many of us tried but very few succeeded. I could not sing. I could not dance. I had been well
conditioned by the world in which I grew up, so I did not
yet dare take the idea of becoming a writer seriously. The only
other possibility seemed to involve my becoming one of the
sordid people on the Avenue, who were not really as sordid
as I then imagined but who frightened me terribly, both because I did not want to live that life and because of what they
made me feel. Everything inflamed me, and that was bad
enough, but I myself had also become a source of fire and
temptation. I had been far too well raised, alas, to suppose
that any of the extremely explicit overtures made to me that
summer, sometimes by boys and girls but also, more alarmingly, by older men and women, had anything to do with my
attractiveness. On the contrary, since the Harlem idea of seduction is, to put it mildly, blunt, whatever these people saw
in me merely confirmed my sense of my depravity.

It is certainly sad that the awakening of one's senses should
lead to such a merciless judgment of oneself—to say nothing
of the time and anguish one spends in the effort to arrive at
any other—but it is also inevitable that a literal attempt to
mortify the flesh should be made among black people like

those with whom I grew up. Negroes in this country—and Negroes do not, strictly or legally speaking, exist in any other—are taught really to despise themselves from the moment their eyes open on the world. This world is white and they are black. White people hold the power, which means that they are superior to blacks (intrinsically, that is: God decreed it so), and the world has innumerable ways of making this difference known and felt and feared. Long before the Negro child perceives this difference, and even longer before he understands it, he has begun to react to it, he has begun to be controlled by it. Every effort made by the child's elders to prepare him for a fate from which they cannot protect him causes him secretly, in terror, to begin to await, without knowing that he is doing so, his mysterious and inexorable punishment. He must be "good" not only in order to please his parents and not only to avoid being punished by them; behind their authority stands another, nameless and impersonal, infinitely harder to please, and bottomlessly cruel. And this filters into the child's consciousness through his parents' tone of voice as he is being exhorted, punished, or loved; in the sudden, uncontrollable note of fear heard in his mother's or his father's voice when he has strayed beyond some particular boundary. He does not know what the boundary is, and he can get no explanation of it, which is frightening enough, but the fear he hears in the voices of his elders is more frightening still. The fear that I heard in my father's voice, for example, when he realized that I really *believed* I could do anything a white boy could do, and had every intention of proving it, was not at all like the fear I heard when one of us was ill or had fallen down the stairs or strayed too far from the house. It was another fear, a fear that the child, in challenging the white world's assumptions, was putting himself in the path of destruction. A child cannot, thank Heaven, know how vast and how merciless is the nature of power, with what unbelievable cruelty people treat each other. He reacts to the fear in his parents' voices because his parents hold up the world for him and he has no protection without them. I defended myself, as I imagined, against the fear my father made me feel by remembering that he was very old-fashioned. Also, I prided myself on the fact that I already knew how to outwit him. To defend oneself against a fear is simply to insure that one will, one day, be conquered by it; fears must be faced. As for one's wits, it is just not true that one can live by them—not, that is, if one wishes really to live. That summer, in any case, all the fears with which I had grown up, and which were now a part of me and controlled my vision of the world, rose up like a wall between the world and me, and drove me into the church.

As I look back, everything I did seems curiously deliberate, though it certainly did not seem deliberate then. For example, I did not join the church of which my father was a member and in which he preached. My best friend in school, who attended a different church, had already "surrendered his life to the Lord," and he was very anxious about my soul's salvation. (I wasn't, but any human attention was better than none.) One Saturday afternoon, he took me to his church. There were no services that day, and the church was empty, except for some women cleaning and some other women praying. My friend took me into the back room to meet his pastor—a woman. There she sat, in her robes, smiling, an extremely proud and handsome woman, with Africa, Europe, and the America of the American Indian blended in her face. She was perhaps forty-five or fifty at this time, and in our world she was a very celebrated woman. My friend was about to introduce me when she looked at me and smiled and said, "Whose little boy are you?" Now this, unbelievably, was precisely the phrase used by pimps and racketeers on the Avenue when they suggested, both humorously and intensely, that I "hang out" with them. Perhaps part of the terror they had caused me to feel came from the fact that I unquestionably wanted to be *somebody's* little boy. I was so frightened, and at the mercy of so many conundrums, that inevitably, that summer, *someone* would have taken me over; one doesn't, in Harlem, long remain standing on any auction block. It was my good luck—perhaps—that I found myself in the church racket instead of some other, and surrendered to a spiritual seduction long before I came to any carnal knowledge. For when the pastor asked me, with that marvellous smile, "Whose little boy are you?" my heart replied at once, "Why, yours."

The summer wore on, and things got worse. I became more

guilty and more frightened, and kept all this bottled up inside me, and naturally, inescapably, one night, when this woman had finished preaching, everything came roaring, screaming, crying out, and I fell to the ground before the altar. It was the strangest sensation I have ever had in my life—up to that time, or since. I had not known that it was going to happen, or that it could happen. One moment I was on my feet, singing and clapping and, at the same time, working out in my head the plot of a play I was working on then; the next moment, with no transition, no sensation of falling, I was on my back, with the lights beating down into my face and all the vertical saints above me. I did not know what I was doing down so low, or how I had got there. And the anguish that filled me cannot be described. It moved in me like one of those floods that devastate counties, tearing everything down, tearing children from their parents and lovers from each other, and making everything an unrecognizable waste. All I really remember is the pain, the unspeakable pain; it was as though I were yelling up to Heaven and Heaven would not hear me. And if Heaven would not hear me, if love could not descend from Heaven—to wash me, to make me clean—then utter disaster was my portion. Yes, it does indeed mean something—something unspeakable—to be born, in a white country, an Anglo-Teutonic, antisexual country, black. You very soon, without knowing it, give up all hope of communion. Black people, mainly, look down or look up but do not look at each other, not at you, and white people, mainly, look away. And the universe is simply a sounding drum; there is no way, no way whatever, so it seemed then and has sometimes seemed since, to get through a life, to love your wife and children, or your friends, or your mother and father, or to be loved. The universe, which is not merely the stars and the moon and the planets, flowers, grass, and trees, but *other people*, has evolved no terms for your existence, has made no room for you, and if love will not swing wide the gates, no other power will or can. And if one despairs—as who has not?—of human love, God's love alone is left. But God—and I felt this even then, so long ago, on that tremendous floor, unwillingly—is white. And if His love was so great, and if He loved all His children, why were we, the blacks, cast down so

far? Why? In spite of all I said thereafter, I found no answer
on the floor—not *that* answer, anyway—and I was on the floor
all night. Over me, to bring me "through," the saints sang
and rejoiced and prayed. And in the morning, when they
raised me, they told me that I was "saved."

Well, indeed I was, in a way, for I was utterly drained and
exhausted, and released, for the first time, from all my guilty
torment. I was aware then only of my relief. For many years,
I could not ask myself why human relief had to be achieved
in a fashion at once so pagan and so desperate—in a fashion
at once so unspeakably old and so unutterably new. And by
the time I was able to ask myself this question, I was also able
to see that the principles governing the rites and customs of
the churches in which I grew up did not differ from the principles governing the rites and customs of other churches,
white. The principles were Blindness, Loneliness, and Terror,
the first principle necessarily and actively cultivated in order
to deny the two others. I would love to believe that the principles were Faith, Hope, and Charity, but this is clearly not
so for most Christians, or for what we call the Christian world.

I was saved. But at the same time, out of a deep, adolescent
cunning I do not pretend to understand, I realized immediately that I could not remain in the church merely as another
worshipper. I would have to give myself something to do, in
order not to be too bored and find myself among all the
wretched unsaved of the Avenue. And I don't doubt that I
also intended to best my father on his own ground. Anyway,
very shortly after I joined the church, I became a preacher—
a Young Minister—and I remained in the pulpit for more than
three years. My youth quickly made me a much bigger drawing card than my father. I pushed this advantage ruthlessly,
for it was the most effective means I had found of breaking
his hold over me. That was the most frightening time of my
life, and quite the most dishonest, and the resulting hysteria
lent great passion to my sermons—for a while. I relished the
attention and the relative immunity from punishment that my
new status gave me, and I relished, above all, the sudden right
to privacy. It had to be recognized, after all, that I was still a
schoolboy, with my schoolwork to do, and I was also expected
to prepare at least one sermon a week. During what we may

call my heyday, I preached much more often than that. This
meant that there were hours and even whole days when I
could not be interrupted—not even by my father. I had immobilized him. It took rather more time for me to realize that
I had also immobilized myself, and had escaped from nothing
whatever.

The church was very exciting. It took a long time for me
to disengage myself from this excitement, and on the blindest,
most visceral level, I never really have, and never will. There
is no music like that music, no drama like the drama of the
saints rejoicing, the sinners moaning, the tambourines racing,
and all those voices coming together and crying holy unto the
Lord. There is still, for me, no pathos quite like the pathos of
those multicolored, worn, somehow triumphant and transfig-
ured faces, speaking from the depths of a visible, tangible,
continuing despair of the goodness of the Lord. I have never
seen anything to equal the fire and excitement that sometimes,
without warning, fill a church, causing the church, as Lead-
belly and so many others have testified, to "rock." Nothing
that has happened to me since equals the power and the glory
that I sometimes felt when, in the middle of a sermon, I knew
that I was somehow, by some miracle, really carrying, as they
said, "the Word"—when the church and I were one. Their
pain and their joy were mine, and mine were theirs—they surrendered their pain and joy to me, I surrendered mine to
them—and their cries of "Amen!" and "Hallelujah!" and
"Yes, Lord!" and "Praise His name!" and "Preach it,
brother!" sustained and whipped on my solos until we all became equal, wringing wet, singing and dancing, in anguish
and rejoicing, at the foot of the altar. It was, for a long time,
in spite of—or, not inconceivably, because of—the shabbiness
of my motives, my only sustenance, my meat and drink. I
rushed home from school, to the church, to the altar, to be
alone there, to commune with Jesus, my dearest Friend, who
would never fail me, who knew all the secrets of my heart.
Perhaps He did, but I didn't, and the bargain we struck, actually, down there at the foot of the cross, was that He would
never let me find out.

He failed His bargain. He was a much better Man than I
took Him for. It happened, as things do, imperceptibly, in

many ways at once. I date it—the slow crumbling of my faith, the pulverization of my fortress—from the time, about a year after I had begun to preach, when I began to read again. I justified this desire by the fact that I was still in school, and I began, fatally, with Dostoevski. By this time, I was in a high school that was predominantly Jewish. This meant that I was surrounded by people who were, by definition, beyond any hope of salvation, who laughed at the tracts and leaflets I brought to school, and who pointed out that the Gospels had been written long after the death of Christ. This might not have been so distressing if it had not forced me to read the tracts and leaflets myself, for they were indeed, unless one believed their message already, impossible to believe. I remember feeling dimly that there was a kind of blackmail in it. People, I felt, ought to love the Lord *because* they loved Him, and not because they were afraid of going to Hell. I was forced, reluctantly, to realize that the Bible itself had been written by men, and translated by men out of languages I could not read, and I was already, without quite admitting it to myself, terribly involved with the effort of putting words on paper. Of course, I had the rebuttal ready: These men had all been operating under divine inspiration. *Had* they? *All* of them? And I also knew by now, alas, far more about divine inspiration than I dared admit, for I knew how I worked myself up into my own visions, and how frequently—indeed, incessantly—the visions God granted to me differed from the visions He granted to my father. I did not understand the dreams I had at night, but I knew that they were not holy. For that matter, I knew that my waking hours were far from holy. I spent most of my time in a state of repentance for things I had vividly desired to do but had not done. The fact that I was dealing with Jews brought the whole question of color, which I had been desperately avoiding, into the terrified center of my mind. I realized that the Bible had been written by white men. I knew that, according to many Christians, I was a descendant of Ham, who had been cursed, and that I was therefore predestined to be a slave. This had nothing to do with anything I was, or contained, or could become; my fate had been sealed forever, from the beginning of time. And it seemed, indeed, when one looked out over Christendom, that this was what Christendom effectively believed. It was certainly the way it behaved. I remembered the Italian priests and bishops blessing Italian boys who were on their way to Ethiopia.

Again, the Jewish boys in high school were troubling because I could find no point of connection between them and the Jewish pawnbrokers and landlords and grocery-store owners in Harlem. I knew that these people were Jews—God knows I was told it often enough—but I thought of them only as white. Jews, as such, until I got to high school, were all incarcerated in the Old Testament, and their names were Abraham, Moses, Daniel, Ezekiel, and Job, and Shadrach, Meshach, and Abednego. It was bewildering to find them so many miles and centuries out of Egypt, and so far from the fiery furnace. My best friend in high school was a Jew. He came to our house once, and afterward my father asked, as he asked about everyone, "Is he a Christian?"—by which he meant "Is he saved?" I really do not know whether my answer came out of innocence or venom, but I said coldly, "No. He's Jewish." My father slammed me across the face with his great palm, and in that moment everything flooded back—all the hatred and all the fear, and the depth of a merciless resolve to kill my father rather than allow my father to kill me—and I knew that all those sermons and tears and all that repentance and rejoicing had changed nothing. I wondered if I was expected to be glad that a friend of mine, or anyone, was to be tormented forever in Hell, and I also thought, suddenly, of the Jews in another Christian nation, Germany. They were not so far from the fiery furnace after all, and my best friend might have been one of them. I told my father, "He's a better Christian than you are," and walked out of the house. The battle between us was in the open, but that was all right; it was almost a relief. A more deadly struggle had begun.

Being in the pulpit was like being in the theatre; I was behind the scenes and knew how the illusion was worked. I knew the other ministers and knew the quality of their lives. And I don't mean to suggest by this the "Elmer Gantry" sort of hypocrisy concerning sensuality; it was a deeper, deadlier, and more subtle hypocrisy than that, and a little honest sensuality, or a lot, would have been like water in an extremely bitter desert. I knew how to work on a congregation until the last dime was surrendered—it was not very hard to do—and I knew where the money for "the Lord's work" went. I knew, though I did not wish to know it, that I had no respect for the people with whom I worked. I could not have said it then, but I also knew that if I continued I would soon have no respect for myself. And the fact that I was "the young Brother Baldwin" increased my value with those same pimps and racketeers who had helped to stampede me into the church in the first place. They still saw the little boy they intended to take over. They were waiting for me to come to my senses and realize that I was in a very lucrative business. They knew that I did not yet realize this, and also that I had not yet begun to suspect where my own needs, *coming up* (they were very patient), could drive me. They themselves did know the score, and they knew that the odds were in their favor. And, really, I knew it, too. I was even lonelier and more vulnerable than I had been before. And the blood of the Lamb had not cleansed me in any way whatever. I was just as black as I had been the day that I was born. Therefore, when I faced a congregation, it began to take all the strength I had not to stammer, not to curse, not to tell them to throw away their Bibles and get off their knees and go home and organize, for example, a rent strike. When I watched all the children, their copper, brown, and beige faces staring up at me as I taught Sunday school, I felt that I was committing a crime in talking about the gentle Jesus, in telling them to reconcile themselves to their misery on earth in order to gain the crown of eternal life. Were only Negroes to gain this crown? Was Heaven, then, to be merely another ghetto? Perhaps I might have been able to reconcile myself even to this if I had been able to believe that there was any loving-kindness to be found in the haven I represented. But I had been in the pulpit too long and I had seen too many monstrous things. I don't refer merely to the glaring fact that the minister eventually acquires houses and Cadillacs while the faithful continue to scrub floors and drop their dimes and quarters and dollars into the plate. I really mean that there was no love in the church. It was a mask for hatred and self-hatred and despair. The transfiguring power of the Holy Ghost ended when the service ended, and salvation stopped at the church door. When we were told to love everybody, I had thought that that meant *everybody*. But no. It applied only to those who believed as we did, and it did not apply to white people at all. I was told by a minister, for example, that I should never, on any public conveyance, under any circumstances, rise and give my seat to a white woman. White men never rose for Negro women. Well, that was true enough, in the main—I saw his point. But what was the point, the purpose, of *my* salvation if it did not permit me to behave with love toward others, no matter how they behaved toward me? What others did was their responsibility, for which they would answer when the judgment trumpet sounded. But what *I* did was *my* responsibility, and I would have to answer, too—unless, of course, there was also in Heaven a special dispensation for the benighted black, who was not to be judged in the same way as other human beings, or angels. It probably occurred to me around this time that the vision people hold of the world to come is but a reflection, with predictable wishful distortions, of the world in which they live. And this did not apply only to Negroes, who were no more "simple" or "spontaneous" or "Christian" than anybody else—who were merely more oppressed. In the same way that we, for white people, were the descendants of Ham, and were cursed forever, white people were, for us, the descendants of Cain. And the passion with which we loved the Lord was a measure of how deeply we feared and distrusted and, in the end, hated almost all strangers, always, and avoided and despised ourselves.

But I cannot leave it at that; there is more to it than that. In spite of everything, there was in the life I fled a zest and a joy and a capacity for facing and surviving disaster that are very moving and very rare. Perhaps we were, all of us—pimps, whores, racketeers, church members, and children—bound together by the nature of our oppression, the specific and peculiar complex of risks we had to run; if so, within these limits we sometimes achieved with each other a freedom that was close to love. I remember, anyway, church suppers and outings, and, later, after I left the church, rent and waistline parties where rage and sorrow sat in the darkness and did not stir, and we ate and drank and talked and laughed and danced and forgot all about "the man." We had the liquor, the chicken, the music, and each other, and had no need to pretend to be what we were not. This is the freedom that one hears in some gospel songs, for example, and in jazz. In all jazz, and especially in the blues, there is something tart and ironic, authoritative and double-edged. White Americans seem to feel that happy songs are *happy* and sad songs are *sad*, and that, God help us, is exactly the way most white Americans sing them—sounding, in both cases, so helplessly, defenselessly fatuous that one dare not speculate on the temperature of the deep freeze from which issue their brave and sexless little voices. Only people who have been "down the line," as the song puts it, know what this music is about. I think it was Big Bill Broonzy who used to sing "I Feel So Good," a really joyful song about a man who is on his way to the railroad station to meet his girl. She's coming home. It is the singer's incredibly moving exuberance that makes one realize how leaden the time must have been while she was gone. There is no guarantee that she will stay this time, either, as the singer clearly knows, and, in fact, she has not yet actually arrived. Tonight, or tomorrow, or within the next five minutes, he may very well be singing "Lonesome in My Bedroom," or insisting, "Ain't we, ain't we, going to make it all right? Well, if we don't today, we will tomorrow night." White Americans do not understand the depths out of which such an ironic tenacity comes, but they suspect that the force is sensual, and they are terrified of sensuality and do not any longer understand it. The word "sensual" is not intended to bring to mind quivering dusky maidens or priapic black studs. I am referring to something much simpler and much less fanciful. To be sensual, I think, is to respect and rejoice in the force of life, of life itself, and to be *present* in all that one does, from the effort of loving to the breaking of bread. It will be a great day for America, incidentally, when we begin to eat bread again, instead of the blasphemous and tasteless foam rubber that we have substituted for it. And I am not being frivolous now, either. Something very sinister happens to the people of a country when they begin to distrust their own reactions as deeply as they do here, and become as joyless as they have become. It is this individual uncertainty on the part of white American men and women, this inability to renew themselves at the fountain of their own lives, that makes the discussion, let alone elucidation, of any conundrum—that is, any reality—so supremely difficult. The person who distrusts himself has no touchstone for reality—for this touchstone can be only oneself. Such a person interposes between himself and reality nothing less than a labyrinth of attitudes. And these attitudes, furthermore, though the person is usually unaware of it (is unaware of so much!), are historical and public attitudes. They do not relate to the present any more than they relate to the person. Therefore, whatever white people do not know about Negroes reveals, precisely and inexorably, what they do not know about themselves.

White Christians have also forgotten several elementary historical details. They have forgotten that the religion that is now identified with their virtue and their power—"God is on our side," says Dr. Verwoerd—came out of a rocky piece of ground in what is now known as the Middle East before color was invented, and that in order for the Christian church to be established, Christ had to be put to death, by Rome, and that the real architect of the Christian church was not the disreputable, sun-baked Hebrew who gave it his name but the mercilessly fanatical and self-righteous St. Paul. The energy that was buried with the rise of the Christian nations must come back into the world; nothing can prevent it. Many of us, I think, both long to see this happen and are terrified of it, for though this transformation contains the hope of liberation, it also imposes a necessity for great change. But in order to deal with the untapped and dormant force of the previously subjugated, in order to survive as a human, moving, moral weight in the world, America and all the Western nations will be forced to reëxamine themselves and release themselves from many things that are now taken to be sacred, and to discard nearly all the assumptions that have been used to justify their lives and their anguish and their crimes so long.

"The white man's Heaven," sings a Black Muslim minister, "is the black man's Hell." One may object—possibly—that this puts the matter somewhat too simply, but the song is true, and it has been true for as long as white men have ruled the world. The Africans put it another way: When the white man came to Africa, the white man had the Bible and the African had the land, but now it is the white man who is being, reluctantly and bloodily, separated from the land, and the African who is still attempting to digest or to vomit up the Bible. The struggle, therefore, that now begins in the world is extremely complex, involving the historical role of Christianity in the realm of power—that is, politics—and in the realm of morals. In the realm of power, Christianity has operated with an unmitigated arrogance and cruelty—necessarily, since a religion ordinarily imposes on those who have discovered the true faith the spiritual duty of liberating the infidels. This particular true faith, moreover, is more deeply concerned about the soul than it is about the body, to which fact the flesh (and the corpses) of countless infidels bears witness. It goes without saying, then, that whoever questions the authority of the true faith also contests the right of the nations that hold this faith to rule over him—contests, in short, their title to his land. The spreading of the Gospel, regardless of the motives or the integrity or the heroism of some of the missionaries, was an absolutely indispensable justification for the planting of the flag. Priests and nuns and school-teachers helped to protect and sanctify the power that was so ruthlessly being used by people who were indeed seeking a city, but not one in the heavens, and one to be made, very definitely, by captive hands. The Christian church itself—again, as distinguished from some of its ministers—sanctified and rejoiced in the conquests of the flag, and encouraged, if it did not formulate, the belief that conquest, with the resulting relative well-being of the Western populations, was proof of the favor of God. God had come a long way from the desert—but then so had Allah, though in a very different direction. God, going north, and rising on the wings of power, had become white, and Allah, out of power, and on the dark side of Heaven, had become—for all practical purposes, anyway—black. Thus, in the realm of morals the role of Christianity has been, at best, ambivalent. Even leaving out of account the remarkable arrogance that assumed that the ways and morals of others were inferior to those of Christians, and that they therefore had every right, and could use any means, to change them, the collision between cultures—and the schizophrenia in the mind

of Christendom—had rendered the domain of morals as chart-
less as the sea once was, and as treacherous as the sea still is.
It is not too much to say that whoever wishes to become a
truly moral human being (and let us not ask whether or not
this is possible; I think we must *believe* that it is possible) must
first divorce himself from all the prohibitions, crimes, and hy-
pocrisies of the Christian church. If the concept of God has
any validity or any use, it can only be to make us larger, freer,
and more loving. If God cannot do this, then it is time we
got rid of Him.

I had heard a great deal, long before I finally met him, of
the Honorable Elijah Muhammad, and of the Nation of Islam
movement, of which he is the leader. I paid very little attention to what I heard, because the burden of his message did
not strike me as being very original; I had been hearing variations of it all my life. I sometimes found myself in Harlem
on Saturday nights, and I stood in the crowds, at 125th Street
and Seventh Avenue, and listened to the Muslim speakers. But
I had heard hundreds of such speeches—or so it seemed to
me at first. Anyway, I have long had a very definite tendency
to tune out the moment I come anywhere near either a pulpit
or a soapbox. What these men were saying about white people
I had often heard before. And I dismissed the Nation of Islam's demand for a separate black economy in America, which
I had also heard before, as willful, and even mischievous, nonsense. Then two things caused me to begin to listen to the
speeches, and one was the behavior of the police. After all, I
had seen men dragged from their platforms on this very corner
for saying less virulent things, and I had seen many crowds
dispersed by policemen, with clubs or on horseback. But the
policemen were doing nothing now. Obviously, this was not
because they had become more human but because they were
under orders and because they were afraid. And indeed they
were, and I was delighted to see it. There they stood, in twos
and threes and fours, in their Cub Scout uniforms and with
their Cub Scout faces, totally unprepared, as is the way with
American he-men, for anything that could not be settled with
a club or a fist or a gun. I might have pitied them if I had

not found myself in their hands so often and discovered, through ugly experience, what they were like when *they* held the power and what they were like when *you* held the power. The behavior of the crowd, its silent intensity, was the other thing that forced me to reassess the speakers and their message. I sometimes think, with despair, that Americans will swallow whole any political speech whatever—we've been doing very little else, these last, bad years—so it may not mean anything to say that this sense of integrity, after what Harlem, especially, has been through in the way of demagogues, was a very startling change. Still, the speakers had an air of utter dedication, and the people looked toward them with a kind of intelligence of hope on their faces—not as though they were being consoled or drugged but as though they were being jolted.

Power was the subject of the speeches I heard. We were offered, as Nation of Islam doctrine, historical and divine proof that all white people are cursed, and are devils, and are about to be brought down. This has been revealed by Allah Himself to His prophet, the Honorable Elijah Muhammad. The white man's rule will be ended forever in ten or fifteen years (and it must be conceded that all present signs would seem to bear witness to the accuracy of the prophet's statement). The crowd seemed to swallow this theology with no effort—all crowds do swallow theology this way, I gather, in both sides of Jerusalem, in Istanbul, and in Rome—and, as theology goes, it was no more indigestible than the more familiar brand asserting that there is a curse on the sons of Ham. No more, and no less, and it had been designed for the same purpose; namely, the sanctification of power. But very little time was spent on theology, for one did not need to prove to a Harlem audience that all white men were devils. They were merely glad to have, at last, divine corroboration of their experience, to hear—and it was a tremendous thing to hear—that they had been lied to for all these years and generations, and that their captivity was ending, for God was black. Why were they *hearing* it now, since this was not the first time it had been said? I had heard it many times, from various prophets, during all the years that I was growing up. Elijah Muhammad himself has now been carrying the same message for more than thirty years; he is not an overnight sensation, and we owe his ministry, I am told, to the fact that when he was a child of six or so, his father was lynched before his eyes. (So much for states' rights.) And now, suddenly, people who have never before been able to hear this message hear it, and believe it, and are changed. Elijah Muhammad has been able to do what generations of welfare workers and committees and resolutions and reports and housing projects and playgrounds have failed to do: to heal and redeem drunkards and junkies, to convert people who have come out of prison and to keep them out, to make men chaste and women virtuous, and to invest both the male and the female with a pride and a serenity that hang about them like an unfailing light. He has done all these things, which our Christian church has spectacularly failed to do. How has Elijah managed it?

Well, in a way—and I have no wish to minimize his peculiar role and his peculiar achievement—it is not he who has done it but time. Time catches up with kingdoms and crushes them, gets its teeth into doctrines and rends them; time reveals the foundations on which any kingdom rests, and eats at those foundations, and it destroys doctrines by proving them to be untrue. In those days, not so very long ago, when the priests of that church which stands in Rome gave God's blessing to Italian boys being sent out to ravage a defenseless black country—which until that event, incidentally, had not considered itself to be black—it was not possible to believe in a black God. To entertain such a belief would have been to entertain madness. But time has passed, and in that time the Christian world has revealed itself as morally bankrupt and politically unstable. The Tunisians were quite right in 1956—and it was a very significant moment in Western (and African) history—when they countered the French justification for remaining in North Africa with the question "Are the *French* ready for self-government?" Again, the terms "civilized" and "Christian" begin to have a very strange ring, particularly in the ears of those who have been judged to be neither civilized nor Christian, when a Christian nation surrenders to a foul and violent orgy, as Germany did during the Third Reich. For the crime of their ancestry, millions of people in the middle of the twentieth century, and in the heart of Europe—God's citadel—

were sent to a death so calculated, so hideous, and so prolonged that no age before this enlightened one had been able to imagine it, much less achieve and record it. Furthermore, those beneath the Western heel, unlike those within the West, are aware that Germany's current role in Europe is to act as a bulwark against the "uncivilized" hordes, and since power is what the powerless want, they understand very well what we of the West want to keep, and are not deluded by our talk of a freedom that we have never been willing to share with them. From my own point of view, the fact of the Third Reich alone makes obsolete forever any question of Christian superiority, except in technological terms. White people were, and are, astounded by the holocaust in Germany. They did not know that they could act that way. But I very much doubt whether black people were astounded—at least, in the same way. For my part, the fate of the Jews, and the world's indifference to it, frightened me very much. I could not but feel, in those sorrowful years, that this human indifference, concerning which I knew so much already, would be my portion on the day that the United States decided to murder its Negroes systematically instead of little by little and catch-as-catch-can. I was, of course, authoritatively assured that what had happened to the Jews in Germany could not happen to the Negroes in America, but I thought, bleakly, that the German Jews had probably believed similar counsellors, and, again, I could not share the white man's vision of himself for the very good reason that white men in America do not behave toward black men the way they behave toward each other. When a white man faces a black man, especially if the black man is helpless, terrible things are revealed. I know. I have been carried into precinct basements often enough, and I have seen and heard and endured the secrets of desperate white men and women, which they knew were safe with me, because even if I should speak, no one would believe me. And they would not believe me precisely because they would know that what I said was true.

The treatment accorded the Negro during the Second World War marks, for me, a turning point in the Negro's relation to America. To put it briefly, and somewhat too simply, a certain hope died, a certain respect for white Americans faded. One began to pity them, or to hate them. You must put yourself in the skin of a man who is wearing the uniform of his country, is a candidate for death in its defense, and who is called a "nigger" by his comrades-in-arms and his officers; who is almost always given the hardest, ugliest, most menial work to do; who knows that the white G.I. has informed the Europeans that he is subhuman (so much for the American male's sexual security); who does not dance at the U.S.O. the night white soldiers dance there, and does not drink in the same bars white soldiers drink in; and who watches German prisoners of war being treated by Americans with more human dignity than he has ever received at their hands. And who, at the same time, as a human being, is far freer in a strange land than he has ever been at home. *Home!* The very word begins to have a despairing and diabolical ring. You must consider what happens to this citizen, after all he has endured, when he returns—home: search, in his shoes, for a job, for a place to live; ride, in his skin, on segregated buses; see, with his eyes, the signs saying "White" and "Colored," and especially the signs that say "White Ladies" and "Colored *Women*"; look into the eyes of his wife; look into the eyes of his son; listen, with his ears, to political speeches, North and South; imagine yourself being told to "wait." And all this is happening in the richest and freest country in the world, and in the middle of the twentieth century. The subtle and deadly change of heart that might occur in you would be involved with the realization that a civilization is not destroyed by wicked people; it is not necessary that people be wicked but only that they be spineless. I and two Negro acquaintances, all of us well past thirty, and looking it, were in the bar of Chicago's O'Hare Airport several months ago, and the bartender refused to serve us, because, he said, we looked too young. It took a vast amount of patience not to strangle him, and great insistence and some luck to get the manager, who defended his bartender on the ground that he was "new" and had not yet, presumably, learned how to distinguish between a Negro boy of twenty and a Negro "boy" of thirty-seven. Well, we were served, finally, of course, but by this time no amount of Scotch would have helped us. The bar was very crowded, and our altercation had been extremely noisy; not one customer in the bar had done anything to help us. When it was over, and the three of us stood at the bar trembling with rage and frustration, and drinking—and trapped, now, in the airport, for we had deliberately come early in order to have a few drinks and to eat—a young white man standing near us asked if we were students. I suppose he thought that this was the only possible explanation for our putting up a fight. I told him that he hadn't wanted to talk to us earlier and we didn't want to talk to him now. The reply visibly hurt his feelings, and this, in turn, caused me to despise him. But when one of us, a Korean War veteran, told this young man that the fight we had been having in the bar had been his fight, too, the young man said, "I lost my conscience a long time ago," and turned and walked out. I know that one would rather not think so, but this young man is typical. So, on the basis of the evidence, had everyone else in the bar lost *his* conscience. A few years ago, I would have hated these people with all my heart. Now I pitied them, pitied them in order not to despise them. And this is not the happiest way to feel toward one's countrymen.

But, in the end, it is the threat of universal extinction hanging over all the world today that changes, totally and forever, the nature of reality and brings into devastating question the true meaning of man's history. We human beings now have the power to exterminate ourselves; this seems to be the entire sum of our achievement. We have taken this journey and arrived at this place in God's name. This, then, is the best that God (the white God) can do. If that is so, then it is time to replace Him—replace Him with what? And this void, this despair, this torment is felt everywhere in the West, from the streets of Stockholm to the churches of New Orleans and the sidewalks of Harlem.

God is black. All black men belong to Islam; they have been chosen. And Islam shall rule the world. The dream, the sentiment is old; only the color is new. And it is this dream, this sweet possibility, that thousands of oppressed black men and women in this country now carry away with them after the Muslim minister has spoken, through the dark, noisome ghetto streets, into the hovels where so many have perished. The white God has not delivered them; perhaps the Black God will.

While I was in Chicago last summer, the Honorable Elijah Muhammad invited me to have dinner at his home. This is a stately mansion on Chicago's South Side, and it is the headquarters of the Nation of Islam movement. I had not gone to Chicago to meet Elijah Muhammad—he was not in my thoughts at all—but the moment I received the invitation, it occurred to me that I ought to have expected it. In a way, I owe the invitation to the incredible, abysmal, and really cowardly obtuseness of white liberals. Whether in private debate or in public, any attempt I made to explain how the Black Muslim movement came about, and how it has achieved such force, was met with a blankness that revealed the little connection that the liberals' attitudes have with their perceptions or their lives, or even their knowledge—revealed, in fact, that they could deal with the Negro as a symbol or a victim but had no sense of him as a man. When Malcolm X, who is considered the movement's second-in-command, and heir apparent, points out that the cry of "violence" was not raised, for example, when the Israelis fought to regain Israel, and, indeed, is raised only when black men indicate that they will fight for *their* rights, he is speaking the truth. The conquests of England, every single one of them bloody, are part of what Americans have in mind when they speak of England's glory. In the United States, violence and heroism have been made synonymous except when it comes to blacks, and the only way to defeat Malcolm's point is to concede it and then ask oneself why this is so. Malcolm's statement is *not* answered by references to the triumphs of the N.A.A.C.P., the more particularly since very few liberals have any notion of how long, how costly, and how heartbreaking a task it is to gather the evidence that one can carry into court, or how long such court battles take. Neither is it answered by references to the student sit-in movement, if only because not all Negroes are students and not all of them live in the South. I, in any case, certainly refuse to be put in the position of denying the truth of Malcolm's statements simply because I disagree with his conclusions, or in order to pacify the liberal conscience. Things are as bad as the Muslims say they are—in fact, they are worse, and the Muslims do not help matters—but there *is* no reason that black men should be expected to be more patient, more forbearing, more farseeing than whites; indeed, quite the contrary. The real reason that non-violence is considered to be a virtue in Negroes—I am not speaking now of its racial value, another matter altogether—is that white men do not want their lives, their self-image, or their property threatened. One wishes they would say so more often. At the end of a television program on which Malcolm X and I both appeared, Malcolm was stopped by a white member of the audience who said, "I have a thousand dollars and an acre of land. What's going to happen to me?" I admired the directness of the man's question, but I didn't hear Malcolm's reply, because I was trying to explain to someone else that the situation of the Irish a hundred years ago and the situation of the Negro today cannot very usefully be compared. Negroes were brought here in chains long before the Irish ever thought of leaving Ireland; what manner of consolation is it to be told that emigrants arriving here—voluntarily—long after you did have risen far above you? In the hall, as I was waiting for the elevator, someone shook my hand and said, "Goodbye, Mr. James Baldwin. We'll soon be addressing you as Mr. James X." And I thought, for an awful moment, My God, if this goes on much longer, you probably will. Elijah Muhammad had seen this show, I think, or another one, and he had been told about me. Therefore, late on a hot Sunday afternoon, I presented myself at his door.

I was frightened, because I had, in effect, been summoned into a royal presence. I was frightened for another reason, too. I knew the tension in me between love and power, between pain and rage, and the curious, the grinding way I remained extended between these poles—perpetually attempting to choose the better rather than the worse. But this choice was a choice in terms of a personal, a private better (I was, after all, a writer); what was its relevance in terms of a social worse? Here was the South Side—a million in captivity—stretching from this doorstep as far as the eye could see. And they didn't even read; depressed populations don't have the time or energy to spare. The affluent populations, which should have been their help, didn't, as far as could be discovered, read, either—they merely bought books and devoured them, but not in order to learn: in order to learn new attitudes. Also, I knew that once I had entered the house, I couldn't smoke or drink, and I felt guilty about the cigarettes in my pocket, as I had felt years ago when my friend first took me into his church. I was half an hour late, having got lost on the way here, and I felt as deserving of a scolding as a schoolboy.

The young man who came to the door—he was about thirty, perhaps, with a handsome, smiling face—didn't seem to find my lateness offensive, and led me into a large room. On one side of the room sat half a dozen women, all in white; they were much occupied with a beautiful baby, who seemed to belong to the youngest of the women. On the other side of the room sat seven or eight men, young, dressed in dark suits, very much at ease, and very imposing. The sunlight came into the room with the peacefulness one remembers from rooms in one's early childhood—a sunlight encountered later only in one's dreams. I remember being astounded by the quietness, the ease, the peace, the taste. I was introduced, they greeted me with a genuine cordiality and respect—and the respect increased my fright, for it meant that they expected something of me that I knew in my heart, for their sakes, I could not give—and we sat down. Elijah Muhammad was not in the room. Conversation was slow, but not as stiff as I had feared it would be. They kept it going, for I simply did not know which subjects I could acceptably bring up. They knew more about me, and had read more of what I had written, than I had expected, and I wondered what they made of it all, what they took my usefulness to be. The women were carrying on their own conversation, in low tones; I gathered that they were not expected to take part in male conversations. A few women kept coming in and out of the room, apparently making preparations for dinner. We, the men, did not plunge deeply into any subject, for, clearly, we were all waiting for the appearance of Elijah. Presently, the men, one by one, left the room and returned. Then I was asked if I would like to wash, and I, too, walked down the hall to the bathroom. Shortly after I came back, we stood up, and Elijah entered.

I do not know what I had expected to see. I had read some

of his speeches, and had heard fragments of others on the radio and on television, so I associated him with ferocity. But, no—the man who came into the room was small and slender, really very delicately put together, with a thin face, large, warm eyes, and a most winning smile. Something came into the room with him—his disciples' joy at seeing him, his joy at seeing them. It was the kind of encounter one watches with a smile simply because it is so rare that people enjoy one another. He teased the women, like a father, with no hint of that ugly and unctuous flirtatiousness I knew so well from other churches, and they responded like that, with great freedom and yet from a great and loving distance. He had seen me when he came into the room, I knew, though he had not looked my way. I had the feeling, as he talked and laughed with the others, whom I could only think of as his children, that he was sizing me up, deciding something. Now he turned toward me, to welcome me, with that marvellous smile, and carried me back nearly twenty-four years, to that moment when the pastor had smiled at me and said, "Whose little boy are you?" I did not respond now as I had responded then, because there are some things (not many, alas!) that one cannot do twice. But I knew what he made me feel, how I was drawn toward his peculiar authority, how his smile promised to take the burden of my life off my shoulders. *Take your burdens to the Lord and leave them there.* The central quality in Elijah's face is pain, and his smile is a witness to it—pain so old and deep and black that it becomes personal and particular only when he smiles. One wonders what he would sound like if he could sing. He turned to me, with that smile, and said something like "I've got a lot to say to *you*, but we'll wait until we sit *down*." And I laughed. He made me think of my father and me as we might have been if we had been friends.

In the dining room, there were two long tables; the men sat at one and the women at the other. Elijah was at the head of our table, and I was seated at his left. I can scarcely remember what we ate, except that it was plentiful, sane, and simple—so sane and simple that it made me feel extremely decadent, and I think that I drank, therefore, two glasses of milk. Elijah mentioned having seen me on television and said that it seemed to him that I was not yet brainwashed and was trying to become myself. He said this in a curiously unnerving way, his eyes looking into mine and one hand half hiding his lips, as though he were trying to conceal bad teeth. But his teeth were not bad. Then I remembered hearing that he had spent time in prison. I suppose that I *would* like to become myself, whatever that may mean, but I knew that Elijah's meaning and mine were not the same. I said yes, I was trying to be me, but I did not know how to say more than that, and so I waited.

Whenever Elijah spoke, a kind of chorus arose from the table, saying "Yes, that's right." This began to set my teeth on edge. And Elijah himself had a further, unnerving habit, which was to ricochet his questions and comments off someone else on their way to you. Now, turning to the man on his right, he began to speak of the white devils with whom I had last appeared on TV: What had they made *him* (me) feel? I could not answer this and was not absolutely certain that I was expected to. The people referred to had certainly made me feel exasperated and useless, but I did not think of them as devils. Elijah went on about the crimes of white people, to this endless chorus of "Yes, that's right." Someone at the table said, "The white man sure *is* a devil. He proves that by his own actions." I looked around. It was a very young man who had said this, scarcely more than a boy—very dark and sober, very bitter. Elijah began to speak of the Christian religion, of Christians, in the same soft, joking way. I began to see that Elijah's power came from his single-mindedness. There is nothing calculated about him; he means every word he says. The real reason, according to Elijah, that I failed to realize that the white man was a devil was that I had been too long exposed to white teaching and had never received true instruction. "The so-called American Negro" is the only reason Allah has permitted the United States to endure so long; the white man's time was up in 1913, but it is the will of Allah that this lost black nation, the black men of this country, be redeemed from their white masters and returned to the true faith, which is Islam. Until this is done—and it will be accomplished very soon—the total destruction of the white man is being delayed. Elijah's mission is to return "the so-called

Negro" to Islam, to separate the chosen of Allah from this doomed nation. Furthermore, the white man knows his history, knows himself to be a devil, and knows that his time is running out, and all his technology, psychology, science, and "tricknology" are being expended in the effort to prevent black men from hearing the truth. This truth is that at the very beginning of time there was not one white face to be found in all the universe. Black men ruled the earth and the black man was perfect. This is the truth concerning the era that white men now refer to as prehistoric. They want black men to believe that they, like white men, once lived in caves and swung from trees and ate their meat raw and did not have the power of speech. But this is not true. Black men were never in such a condition. Allah allowed the Devil, through his scientists, to carry on infernal experiments, which resulted, finally, in the creation of the devil known as the white man, and later, even more disastrously, in the creation of the white woman. And it was decreed that these monstrous creatures should rule the earth for a certain number of years—I forget how many thousand, but, in any case, their rule now is ending, and Allah, who had never approved of the creation of the white man in the first place (who knows him, in fact, to be not a man at all but a devil), is anxious to restore the rule of peace that the rise of the white man totally destroyed. There is thus, by definition, no virtue in white people, and since they are another creation entirely and can no more, by breeding, become black than a cat, by breeding, can become a horse, there is no hope for them.

There is nothing new in this merciless formulation except the explicitness of its symbols and the candor of its hatred. Its emotional tone is as familiar to me as my own skin; it is but another way of saying that *sinners shall be bound in Hell a thousand years.* That sinners have always, for American Negroes, been white is a truth we needn't labor, and every American Negro, therefore, risks having the gates of paranoia close on him. In a society that is entirely hostile, and, by its nature, seems determined to cut you down—that has cut down so many in the past and cuts down so many every day—it begins to be almost impossible to distinguish a real from a fancied injury. One can very quickly cease to attempt this distinction, and, what is worse, one usually ceases to attempt it without realizing that one has done so. All doormen, for example, and all policemen have by now, for me, become exactly the same, and my style with them is designed simply to intimidate them before they can intimidate me. No doubt I am guilty of some injustice here, but it is irreducible, since I cannot risk assuming that the humanity of these people is more real to them than their uniforms. Most Negroes cannot risk assuming that the humanity of white people is more real to them than their color. And this leads, imperceptibly but inevitably, to a state of mind in which, having long ago learned to expect the worst, one finds it very easy to believe the worst. The brutality with which Negroes are treated in this country simply cannot be overstated, however unwilling white men may be to hear it. In the beginning—and neither can this be overstated—a Negro just cannot *believe* that white people are treating him as they do; he does not know what he has done to merit it. And when he realizes that the treatment accorded him has nothing to do with anything he has done, that the attempt of white people to destroy him—for that is what it is—is utterly gratuitous, it is not hard for him to think of white people as devils. For the horrors of the American Negro's life there has been almost no language. The privacy of his experience, which is only beginning to be recognized in language, and which is denied or ignored in official and popular speech—hence the Negro idiom—lends credibility to any system that pretends to clarify it. And, in fact, the truth about the black man, as a historical entity and as a human being, *has* been hidden from him, deliberately and cruelly; the power of the white world is threatened whenever a black man refuses to accept the white world's definitions. So every attempt is made to cut that black man down—not only was made yesterday but is made today. Who, then, is to say with authority where the root of so much anguish and evil lies? Why, then, is it not possible that all things began with the black man and that he was perfect—especially since this is precisely the claim that white people have put forward for themselves all these years? Furthermore, it is now absolutely clear that white people are a minority in the world—so severe a minority that they now look rather more like an invention—and that they cannot possibly hope to rule it any longer. If this is so, why is it not also possible that they achieved their original dominance by stealth and cunning and bloodshed and in opposition to the will of Heaven, and not, as they claim, by Heaven's will? And if *this* is so, then the sword they have used so long against others can now, without mercy, be used against them. Heavenly witnesses are a tricky lot, to be used by whoever is closest to Heaven at the time. And legend and theology, which are designed to sanctify our fears, crimes, and aspirations, also reveal them for what they are.

I said, at last, in answer to some other ricocheted questions, "I left the church twenty years ago and I haven't joined anything since." It was my way of saying that I did not intend to join their movement, either.

"And what are you now?" Elijah asked.

I was in something of a bind, for I really could not say—could not allow myself to be stampeded into saying—that I was a Christian. "I? Now? Nothing." This was not enough. "I'm a writer. I like doing things alone." I heard myself saying this. Elijah smiled at me. "I don't, anyway," I said, finally, "think about it a great deal."

Elijah said, to his right, "I think he ought to think about it *all* the deal," and with this the table agreed. But there was nothing malicious or condemnatory in it. I had the stifling feeling that *they* knew I belonged to them but knew that I did not know it yet, that I remained unready, and that they were simply waiting, patiently, and with assurance, for me to discover the truth for myself. For where else, after all, could I go? I was black, and therefore a part of Islam, and would be saved from the holocaust awaiting the white world whether I would or no. My weak, deluded scruples could avail nothing against the iron word of the prophet.

I felt that I was back in my father's house—as, indeed, in a way, I was—and I told Elijah that *I* did not care if white and black people married, and that I had many white friends. I would have no choice, if it came to it, but to perish with them, for (I said to myself, but not to Elijah), "I love a few people and they love me and some of them are white, and isn't love more important than color?"

Elijah looked at me with great kindness and affection, great pity, as though he were reading my heart, and indicated, skeptically, that I *might* have white friends, or think I did, and they *might* be trying to be decent—now—but their time was up. It was almost as though he were saying, "They had their chance, man, and they goofed!"

And I looked around the table. I certainly had no evidence to give them that would outweigh Elijah's authority or the evidence of their own lives or the reality of the streets outside. Yes, I knew two or three people, white, whom I would trust with my life, and I knew a few others, white, who were struggling as hard as they knew how, and with great effort and sweat and risk, to make the world more human. But how could I say this? One cannot argue with anyone's experience or decision or belief. All my evidence would be thrown out of court as irrelevant to the main body of the case, for I could cite only exceptions. The South Side proved the justice of the indictment; the state of the world proved the justice of the indictment. Everything else, stretching back throughout recorded time, was merely a history of those exceptions who had tried to change the world and had failed. Was this true? *Had* they failed? How much depended on the point of view? For it would seem that a certain category of exceptions never failed to make the world worse—that category, precisely, for whom power is more real than love. And yet power *is* real, and many things, including, very often, love, cannot be achieved without it. In the eeriest way possible, I suddenly had a glimpse of what white people must go through at a dinner table when they are trying to prove that Negroes are not subhuman. I had almost said, after all, "Well, take my friend Mary," and very nearly descended to a catalogue of those virtues that gave Mary the right to be alive. And in what hope? That Elijah and the others would nod their heads solemnly and say, at least, "Well, *she's* all right—but the *others!*"

And I looked again at the young faces around the table, and looked back at Elijah, who was saying that no people in history had ever been respected who had not owned their land. And the table said, "Yes, that's right." I could not deny the truth of this statement. For everyone else has, *is*, a nation, with a specific location and a flag—even, these days, the Jew. It is only "the so-called American Negro" who remains trapped, disinherited, and despised, in a nation that has kept him in bondage for nearly four hundred years and is still unable to recognize him as a human being. And the Black Muslims, along with many people who are not Muslims, no longer wish for a recognition so grudging and (should it ever be achieved) so tardy. Again, it cannot be denied that this point of view is abundantly justified by American Negro history. It is galling indeed to have stood so long, hat in hand, waiting for Americans to grow up enough to realize that you do not threaten them. On the other hand, how is the American Negro now to form himself into a separate nation? For this—and not only from the Muslim point of view—would seem to be his only hope of not perishing in the American backwater and being entirely and forever forgotten, as though he had never existed at all and his travail had been for nothing.

Elijah's intensity and the bitter isolation and disaffection of these young men and the despair of the streets outside had caused me to glimpse dimly what may now seem to be a fantasy, although, in an age so fantastical, I would hesitate to say precisely what a fantasy is. Let us say that the Muslims were to achieve the possession of the six or seven states that they claim are owed to Negroes by the United States as "back payment" for slave labor. Clearly, the United States would never surrender this territory, on any terms whatever, unless it found it impossible, for whatever reason, to hold it—unless, that is, the United States were to be reduced as a world power, exactly the way, and at the same degree of speed, that England has been forced to relinquish her Empire. (It is simply not true—and the state of her ex-colonies proves this—that England "always meant to go.") If the states were Southern states—and the Muslims seem to favor this—then the borders of a hostile Latin America would be raised, in effect, to, say, Maryland. Of the American borders on the sea, one would face toward a powerless Europe and the other toward an untrustworthy and non-white East, and on the North, after Canada, there would be only Alaska, which is a Russian border. The effect of this would be that the white people of the United States and Canada would find themselves marooned on a hostile continent, with the rest of the white world probably unwilling and certainly unable to come to their aid. All this is not, to my mind, the most imminent of possibilities, but if I were a Muslim, this is the possibility that I would find myself holding in the center of my mind, and driving toward. And if I were a Muslim, I would not hesitate to utilize—or, indeed, to exacerbate—the social and spiritual discontent that reigns here, for, at the very worst, I would merely have contributed to the destruction of a house I hated, and it would not matter if I perished, too. One has been perishing here so long!

And what were they thinking around the table? "I've come," said Elijah, "to give you something which can never be taken away from you." How solemn the table became then, and how great a light rose in the dark faces! This is the message that has spread through streets and tenements and prisons, through the narcotics wards, and past the filth and sadism of mental hospitals to a people from whom everything has been taken away, including, most crucially, their sense of their own worth. People cannot live without this sense; they will do anything whatever to regain it. This is why the most dangerous creation of any society is that man who has nothing to lose. You do not need ten such men—one will do. And Elijah, I should imagine, has had nothing to lose since the day he saw his father's blood rush out—rush down, and splash, so the legend has it, down through the leaves of a tree, on him. But neither did the other men around the table have anything to lose. "Return to your true religion," Elijah has written. "Throw off the chains of the slavemaster, the devil, and return to the fold. Stop drinking his alcohol, using his dope—protect your women—and forsake the filthy swine." I remembered my buddies of years ago, in the hallways, with their wine and their whiskey and their tears; in hallways still, frozen on the needle; and my brother saying to me once, "If Harlem didn't have so many churches and junkies, there'd be blood flowing in the streets." *Protect your women:* a difficult thing to do in a civilization sexually so pathetic that the white man's masculinity depends on a denial of the masculinity of the blacks. *Protect your women:* in a civilization that emasculates the male and abuses the female, and in which, moreover, the male is forced to depend on the female's bread-winning power. *Protect your women:* in the teeth of the white man's boast "We figure we're doing you folks a favor by pumping some white blood into your kids," and while facing the Southern shotgun and the Northern billy. Years ago, we used to say, "*Yes*, I'm black, goddammit, and I'm beautiful!"—in defiance, into the void. But now—now—African kings and heroes have come into the world, out of the past, the past that can now be put to the uses of power. And black has *become* a beautiful color—not because it is loved but because it is feared. And this urgency on the part of American Negroes is *not to be forgotten!* As they watch black men elsewhere rise, the promise held out, at last, that they may walk the earth with the authority with which white men walk, protected by the power that white men shall have no longer, is enough, and more than enough, to empty prisons and pull God down from Heaven. It has happened before, many times, before color was invented, and the hope of Heaven has always been a metaphor for the achievement of this particular state of grace. The song says, "I know my robe's going to fit me well. I tried it on at the gates of Hell."

It was time to leave, and we stood in the large living room, saying good night, with everything curiously and heavily unresolved. I could not help feeling that I had failed a test, in their eyes and in my own, or that I had failed to heed a warning. Elijah and I shook hands, and he asked me where I was going. Wherever it was, I would be driven there—"because, when we invite someone here," he said, "we take the responsibility of protecting him from the white devils until he gets wherever it is he's going." I was, in fact, going to have a drink with several white devils on the other side of town. I confess that for a fraction of a second I hesitated to give the address— the kind of address that in Chicago, as in all American cities, identified itself as a white address by virtue of its location. But I did give it, and Elijah and I walked out onto the steps, and one of the young men vanished to get the car. It was very strange to stand with Elijah for those few moments, facing those vivid, violent, so problematical streets. I felt very close to him, and really wished to be able to love and honor him as a witness, an ally, and a father. I felt that I knew something of his pain and his fury, and, yes, even his beauty. Yet precisely because of the reality and the nature of those streets—because of what he conceived as his responsibility and what I took to be mine—we would always be strangers, and possibly, one day, enemies. The car arrived—a gleaming, metallic, grossly American blue—and Elijah and I shook hands and said good night once more. He walked into his mansion and shut the door.

The driver and I started on our way through dark, murmuring—and, at this hour, strangely beautiful—Chicago, along the lake. We returned to the discussion of the land. How were we—Negroes—to get this land? I asked this of the dark boy who had said earlier, at the table, that the white man's actions proved him to be a devil. He spoke to me first of the Muslim temples that were being built, or were about to be built, in various parts of the United States, of the strength of the Muslim following, and of the amount of money that is annually at the disposal of Negroes—something like twenty billion dollars. "That alone shows you how strong we are," he said. But, I persisted, cautiously, and in somewhat different terms, this twenty billion dollars, or whatever it is, depends on the total economy of the United States. What happens when the Negro is no longer a part of this economy? Leaving aside the fact that in order for this to happen the economy of the United States will itself have had to undergo radical and certainly disastrous changes, the American Negro's spending power will obviously no longer be the same. On what, then, will the economy of this separate nation be based? The boy gave me a rather strange look. I said hurriedly, "I'm not saying it *can't* be done—I just want to know *how* it's to be done." I was thinking, In order for this to happen, your entire frame of reference will have to change, and you will be forced to surrender many things that you now scarcely know you have. I didn't feel that the things I had in mind, such as the pseudo-elegant heap of tin in which we were riding, had any very great value. But life would be very different without them, and I wondered if he had thought of this.

How can one, however, dream of power in any other terms than in the symbols of power? The boy could see that freedom depended on the possession of land; he was persuaded that, in one way or another, Negroes must achieve this possession. In the meantime, he could walk the streets and fear nothing, because there were millions like him, coming soon, now, to power. He was held together, in short, by a dream—though it is just as well to remember that some dreams come true—and was united with his "brothers" on the basis of their color. Perhaps one cannot ask for more. People always seem to band together in accordance to a principle that has nothing to do with love, a principle that releases them from personal responsibility.

Yet I could have hoped that the Muslim movement had been able to inculcate in the demoralized Negro population a truer and more individual sense of its own worth, so that Negroes in the Northern ghettos could begin, in concrete terms, and at whatever price, to change their situation. But in order to change a situation one has first to see it for what it is: in the present case, to accept the fact, whatever one does with it thereafter, that the Negro has been formed by this nation, for better or for worse, and does not belong to any other—not to Africa, and certainly not to Islam. The paradox—and a fearful paradox it is—is that the American Negro can have no future anywhere, on any continent, as long as he is unwilling to accept his past. To accept one's past—one's history—is not the same thing as drowning in it; it is learning how to use it. An invented past can never be used; it cracks and crumbles under the pressures of life like clay in a season of drought. How can the American Negro's past be used? The unprecedented price demanded—and at this embattled hour of the world's history—is the transcendence of the realities of color, of nations, and of altars.

"Anyway," the boy said suddenly, after a very long silence, "things won't ever again be the way they used to be. I know *that*."

And so we arrived in enemy territory, and they set me down at the enemy's door.

No one seems to know where the Nation of Islam gets its money. A vast amount, of course, is contributed by Negroes, but there are rumors to the effect that people like Birchites and certain Texas oil millionaires look with favor on the movement. I have no way of knowing whether there is any truth to the rumors, though since these people make such a point of keeping the races separate, I wouldn't be surprised if for this smoke there was some fire. In any case, during a recent Muslim rally, George Lincoln Rockwell, the chief of the American Nazi party, made a point of contributing about twenty dollars to the cause, and he and Malcolm X decided that, racially speaking, anyway, they were in complete agreement. The glorification of one race and the consequent debasement of another—or others—always has been and always will be a recipe for murder. There is no way around this. If one is permitted to treat any group of people with special disfavor because of their race or the color of their skin, there is no limit to what one will force them to endure, and, since the entire race has been mysteriously indicted, no reason not to attempt to destroy it root and branch. This is precisely what the Nazis attempted. Their only originality lay in the means they used. It is scarcely worthwhile to attempt remembering how many times the sun has looked down on the slaughter of the innocents. I am very much concerned that American Negroes achieve their freedom here in the United States. But I am also concerned for their dignity, for the health of their souls, and must oppose any attempt that Negroes may make to do to others what has been done to them. I think I know—we see it around us every day—the spiritual wasteland to which that road leads. It is so simple a fact and one that is so hard, apparently, to grasp: *Whoever debases others is debasing himself.* That is not a mystical statement but a most realistic one, which is proved by the eyes of any Alabama sheriff—and I would not like to see Negroes ever arrive at so wretched a condition.

Now, it is extremely unlikely that Negroes will ever rise to power in the United States, because they are only approximately a ninth of this nation. They are not in the position of the Africans, who are attempting to reclaim their land and break the colonial yoke and recover from the colonial experience. The Negro situation is dangerous in a different way, both for the Negro qua Negro and for the country of which he forms so troubled and troubling a part. The American Negro is a unique creation; he has no counterpart anywhere, and no predecessors. The Muslims react to this fact by referring to the Negro as "the so-called American Negro" and substituting for the names inherited from slavery the letter "X." It is a fact that every American Negro bears a name that originally belonged to the white man whose chattel he was. I am called Baldwin because I was either sold by my African tribe or kidnapped out of it into the hands of a white Christian named Baldwin, who forced me to kneel at the foot of the cross. I am, then, both visibly and legally the descendant of slaves in a white, Protestant country, and this is what it means to be an American Negro, this is who he is—a kidnapped pagan, who was sold like an animal and treated like one, who was once defined by the American Constitution as "three-fifths" of a man, and who, according to the Dred Scott decision, had no rights that a white man was bound to respect. And today, a hundred years after his technical emancipation, he remains—with the possible exception of the American Indian—the most despised creature in his country. Now, there is simply no possibility of a real change in the Negro's situation without the most radical and far-reaching changes in the American political and social structure. And it is clear that white Americans are not simply unwilling to effect these changes; they are, in the main, so slothful have they become, unable even to envision them. It must be added that the Negro himself no longer believes in the good faith of white Americans—if, indeed, he ever could have. What the Negro *has* discovered, and on an international level, is that power to intimidate which he has always had privately but hitherto could manipulate only privately—for private ends often, for limited ends always. And therefore when the country speaks of a "new" Negro, which it has been doing every hour on the hour for decades, it is not really referring to a change in the Negro, which, in any case, it is quite incapable of assessing, but only to a new difficulty in keeping him in his place, to the fact that it encounters him (again! again!) barring yet another door to its spiritual and social ease. This is probably, hard and odd as it may sound, the most important thing that one human being can do for another—it is certainly *one* of the most important things; hence the torment and necessity of love—and this is the enormous contribution that the Negro has made to this otherwise shapeless and undiscovered country. Consequently, white Americans are in nothing more deluded than in supposing that Negroes could ever have imagined that white people would "give" them anything. It is rare indeed that people give. Most people guard and keep; they suppose that it is they themselves and what they identify with themselves that they are guarding and keeping, whereas what they are actually guarding and keeping is their system of reality and what they assume themselves to be. One can give nothing whatever without giving oneself—that is to say, risking oneself. If one cannot risk oneself, then one is simply incapable of giving. And, after all, one can give freedom only by setting someone free. This, in the case of the Negro, the American republic has never become sufficiently mature to do. White Americans have contented themselves with gestures that are now described as "tokenism." For hard example, white Americans congratulate themselves on the 1954 Supreme Court decision outlawing segregation in the schools; they suppose, in spite of the mountain of evidence that has since accumulated to the contrary, that this was proof of a change of heart—or, as they like to say, progress. Perhaps. It all depends on how one reads the word "progress." Most of the Negroes I know do not believe that this immense concession would ever have been made if it had not been for the competition of the Cold War, and the fact that Africa was clearly liberating herself and therefore had, for political reasons, to be wooed by the descendants of her former masters. Had it been a matter of love or justice, the 1954 decision would surely have occurred sooner; were it not for the realities of power in this difficult era, it might very well not have occurred yet. This seems an extremely harsh way of stating the case—ungrateful, as it were—but the evidence that supports this way of stating it is not easily refuted. I myself do not think that it can be refuted at all. In any event, the sloppy and fatuous nature of American good will can never be relied upon to deal with hard problems. These have been dealt with, when they have been dealt with at all, out of necessity—and in political terms, anyway, necessity means concessions made in order to stay on top. I think this is a fact, which it serves no purpose to deny, *but, whether it is a fact or not, this is what the black population of the world, including black Americans, really believe.* The word "independence" in Africa and the word "integration" here are almost equally meaningless; that is, Europe has not yet left Africa, and black men here are not yet free. And both of these last statements are undeniable facts, related facts, containing the gravest implications for us all. The Negroes of this country may never be able to rise to power, but they are very well placed indeed to precipitate chaos and ring down the curtain on the American dream.

This has everything to do, of course, with the nature of that dream and with the fact that we Americans, of whatever color, do not dare examine it and are far from having made it a reality. There are too many things we do not wish to know about ourselves. People are not, for example, terribly anxious to be equal (equal, after all, to what and to whom?) but they love the idea of being superior. And this human truth has an especially grinding force here, where identity is almost impossible to achieve and people are perpetually attempting to find their feet on the shifting sands of status. (Consider the history of labor in a country in which, spiritually speaking, there are no workers, only candidates for the hand of the boss's daughter.) Furthermore, I have met only a very few people—and most of these were not Americans—who had any real desire to be free. Freedom is hard to bear. It can be objected that I am speaking of political freedom in spiritual terms, but the political institutions of any nation are always menaced and are ultimately controlled by the spiritual state of that nation. We are controlled here by our confusion, far more than we know, and the American dream has therefore become something much more closely resembling a nightmare, on the private, domestic, and international levels. Privately, we cannot stand our lives and dare not examine them; domestically, we take no responsibility for (and no pride in) what goes on in our country; and, internationally, for many millions of people, we are an unmitigated disaster. Whoever doubts this last statement has only to open his ears, his heart, his mind, to the testimony of—for example—any Cuban peasant or any Spanish poet, and ask himself what *he* would feel about us if *he* were the victim of our performance in pre-Castro Cuba or in Spain. We defend our curious role in Spain by referring to the Russian menace and the necessity of protecting the free world. It has not occurred to us that we have simply been mesmerized by Russia, and that the only real advantage Russia has in what we think of as a struggle between the East and the West is the moral history of the Western world. Russia's secret weapon is the bewilderment and despair and hunger of millions of people of whose existence we are scarcely aware. The Russian Communists are not in the least concerned about these people. But our ignorance and indecision have had the effect, if not of delivering them into Russian hands, of plunging them very deeply in the Russian shadow, for which effect—and it is hard to blame them—the most articulate among them, and the most oppressed as well, distrust us all the more. Our power and our fear of change help bind these people to their misery and bewilderment, and insofar as they find this state intolerable we are intolerably menaced. For if they find their state intolerable, but are too heavily oppressed to change it, they are simply pawns in the hands of larger powers, which, in such a context, are always unscrupulous, and when, eventually, they do change their situation—as in Cuba—we are menaced more than ever, by the vacuum that succeeds all violent upheavals. We should certainly know by now that it is one thing to overthrow a dictator or repel an invader and quite another thing really to achieve a revolution. Time and time and time again, the people discover that they have merely betrayed themselves into the hands of yet another Pharaoh, who, since he was necessary to put the broken country together, will not let them go. Perhaps, people being the conundrums that they are, and having so little desire to shoulder the burden of their lives, this is what will always happen. But at the bottom of my heart I do not believe this. I think that people can be better than that, and I know that people can be better than they are. We are capable of bearing a great burden, once we discover that the burden is reality and arrive where reality is. Anyway, the point here is that we are living in an age of revolution, whether we will or no, and that America is the only Western nation with both the power and, as I hope to suggest, the experience that may help to make these revolutions real and minimize the human damage. Any attempt we make to oppose these outbursts of energy is tantamount to signing our death warrant.

Behind what we think of as the Russian menace lies what

we do not wish to face, and what white Americans do not face
when they regard a Negro: reality—the fact that life is tragic.
Life is tragic simply because the earth turns and the sun inexorably rises and sets, and one day, for each of us, the sun
will go down for the last, last time. Perhaps the whole root
of our trouble, the human trouble, is that we will sacrifice all
the beauty of our lives, will imprison ourselves in totems,
taboos, crosses, blood sacrifices, steeples, mosques, races,
armies, flags, nations, in order to deny the fact of death, which
is the only fact we have. It seems to me that one ought to
rejoice in the *fact* of death—ought to decide, indeed, to *earn*
one's death by confronting with passion the conundrum of
life. One is responsible to life: It is the small beacon in that
terrifying darkness from which we come and to which we shall
return. One must negotiate this passage as nobly as possible,
for the sake of those who are coming after us. But white
Americans do not believe in death, and this is why the darkness of my skin so intimidates them. And this is also why the
presence of the Negro in this country can bring about its
destruction. It is the responsibility of free men to trust and to
celebrate what is constant—birth, struggle, and death are constant, and so is love, though we may not always think so—
and to apprehend the nature of change, to be able and willing
to change. I speak of change not on the surface but in the
depths—change in the sense of renewal. But renewal becomes
impossible if one supposes things to be constant that are
not—safety, for example, or money, or power. One clings then
to chimeras, by which one can only be betrayed, and the entire
hope—the entire possibility—of freedom disappears. And by
destruction I mean precisely the abdication by Americans of
any effort really to be free. The Negro can precipitate this
abdication because white Americans have never, in all their
long history, been able to look on him as a man like themselves. This point need not be labored; it is proved over and
over again by the Negro's continuing position here, and his
indescribable struggle to defeat the stratagems that white
Americans have used, and use, to deny him his humanity.
America could have used in other ways the energy that both
groups have expended in this conflict. America, of all the
Western nations, has been best placed to prove the uselessness

and the obsolescence of the concept of color. But it has not dared to accept this opportunity, or even to conceive of it as an opportunity. White Americans have thought of it as their shame, and have envied those more civilized and elegant European nations that were untroubled by the presence of black men on their shores. This is because white Americans have supposed "Europe" and "civilization" to be synonyms—which they are not—and have been distrustful of other standards and other sources of vitality, especially those produced in America itself, and have attempted to behave in all matters as though what was east for Europe was also east for them. What it comes to is that if we, who can scarcely be considered a white nation, persist in thinking of ourselves as one, we condemn ourselves, with the truly white nations, to sterility and decay, whereas if we could accept ourselves *as we are*, we might bring new life to the Western achievements, and transform them. The price of this transformation is the unconditional freedom of the Negro; it is not too much to say that he, who has been so long rejected, must now be embraced, and at no matter what psychic or social risk. He is *the* key figure in his country, and the American future is precisely as bright or as dark as his. And the Negro recognizes this, in a negative way. Hence the question: Do I really *want* to be integrated into a burning house?

White Americans find it as difficult as white people elsewhere do to divest themselves of the notion that they are in possession of some intrinsic value that black people need, or want. And this assumption—which, for example, makes the solution to the Negro problem depend on the speed with which Negroes accept and adopt white standards—is revealed in all kinds of striking ways, from Bobby Kennedy's assurance that a Negro can become President in forty years to the unfortunate tone of warm congratulation with which so many liberals address their Negro equals. It is the Negro, of course, who is presumed to have become equal—an achievement that not only proves the comforting fact that perseverance has no color but also overwhelmingly corroborates the white man's sense of his own value. Alas, this value can scarcely be corroborated in any other way; there is certainly little enough in the white man's public or private life that one should desire to imitate. White men, at the bottom of their hearts, know this. Therefore, a vast amount of the energy that goes into what we call the Negro problem is produced by the white man's profound desire not to be judged by those who are not white, not to be seen as he is, and at the same time a vast amount of the white anguish is rooted in the white man's equally profound need to be seen as he is, to be released from the tyranny of his mirror. All of us know, whether or not we are able to admit it, that mirrors can only lie, that death by drowning is all that awaits one there. It is for this reason that love is so desperately sought and so cunningly avoided. Love takes off the masks that we fear we cannot live without and know we cannot live within. I use the word "love" here not merely in the personal sense but as a state of being, or a state of grace—not in the infantile American sense of being made happy but in the tough and universal sense of quest and daring and growth. And I submit, then, that the racial tensions that menace Americans today have little to do with real antipathy—on the contrary, indeed—and are involved only symbolically with color. These tensions are rooted in the very same depths as those from which love springs, or murder. The white man's unadmitted—and apparently, to him, unspeakable—private fears and longings are projected onto the Negro. The only way he can be released from the Negro's tyrannical power over him is to consent, in effect, to become black himself, to become a part of that suffering and dancing country that he now watches wistfully from the heights of his lonely power and, armed with spiritual traveller's checks, visits surreptitiously after dark. How can one respect, let alone adopt, the values of a people who do not, on any level whatever, live the way they say they do, or the way they say they should? I cannot accept the proposition that the four-hundred-year travail of the American Negro should result merely in his attainment of the present level of the American civilization. I am far from convinced that being released from the African witch doctor was worthwhile if I am now—in order to support the moral contradictions and the spiritual aridity of my life—expected to become dependent on the American psychiatrist. It is a bargain I refuse. The only thing white people have that black people need, or should want, is power—and no one holds power forever. White people cannot, in the generality, be taken as models of how to live. Rather, the white man is himself in sore need of new standards, which will release him from his confusion and place him once again in fruitful communion with the depths of his own being. And I repeat: The price of the liberation of the white people is the liberation of the blacks—the total liberation, in the cities, in the towns, before the law, and in the mind. Why, for example—especially knowing the family as I do—I should *want* to marry your sister is a great mystery to me. But your sister and I have every right to marry if we wish to, and no one has the right to stop us. If she cannot raise me to her level, perhaps I can raise her to mine.

In short, we, the black and the white, deeply need each other here if we are really to become a nation—if we are really, that is, to achieve our identity, our maturity, as men and women. To create one nation has proved to be a hideously difficult task; there is certainly no need now to create two, one black and one white. But white men with far more political power than that possessed by the Nation of Islam movement have been advocating exactly this, in effect, for generations. If this sentiment is honored when it falls from the lips of Senator Byrd, then there is no reason it should not be honored when it falls from the lips of Malcolm X. And any Congressional committee wishing to investigate the latter must also be willing to investigate the former. They are expressing exactly the same sentiments and represent exactly the same danger. There is absolutely no reason to suppose that white people are better equipped to frame the laws by which I am to be governed than I am. It is entirely unacceptable that I should have no voice in the political affairs of my own country, for I am not a ward of America; I am one of the first Americans to arrive on these shores.

This past, the Negro's past, of rope, fire, torture, castration, infanticide, rape; death and humiliation; fear by day and night, fear as deep as the marrow of the bone; doubt that he was worthy of life, since everyone around him denied it; sorrow for his women, for his kinfolk, for his children, who needed his protection, and whom he could not protect; rage, hatred, and murder, hatred for white men so deep that it often turned against him and his own, and made all love, all trust, all joy impossible—this past, this endless struggle to achieve and reveal and confirm a human identity, human authority, yet contains, for all its horror, something very beautiful. I do not mean to be sentimental about suffering—enough is certainly as good as a feast—but people who cannot suffer can never grow up, can never discover who they are. That man who is forced each day to snatch his manhood, his identity, out of the fire of human cruelty that rages to destroy it knows, if he survives his effort, and even if he does not survive it, something about himself and human life that no school on earth—and, indeed, no church can teach. He achieves his own authority, and that is unshakable. This is because, in order to save his life, he is forced to look beneath appearances, to take nothing for granted, to hear the meaning behind the words. If one is continually surviving the worst that life can bring, one eventually ceases to be controlled by a fear of what life can bring; whatever it brings must be borne. And at this level of experience one's bitterness begins to be palatable, and hatred becomes too heavy a sack to carry. The apprehension of life here so briefly and inadequately sketched has been the experience of generations of Negroes, and it helps to explain how they have endured and how they have been able to produce children of kindergarten age who can walk through mobs to get to school. It demands great force and great cunning continually to assault the mighty and indifferent fortress of white supremacy, as Negroes in this country have done so long. It demands great spiritual resilience not to hate the hater whose foot is on your neck, and an even greater miracle of perception and charity not to teach your child to hate. The Negro boys and girls who are facing mobs today come out of a long line of improbable aristocrats—the only genuine aristocrats this country has produced. I say "this country" because their frame of reference was totally American. They were hewing out of the mountain of white supremacy the stone of their individuality. I have great respect for that unsung army of black men and women who trudged down back lanes and entered back doors, saying "Yes, sir" and "No, Ma'am" in order to acquire a new roof for the schoolhouse, new books, a new chemistry lab, more beds for the dormitories, more dormitories. They did not like saying "Yes, sir" and "No Ma'am," but the country was in no hurry to educate Negroes, these black men and women knew that the job had to be done, and they put their pride in their pockets in order to do it. It is very hard to believe that they were in any way inferior to the white men and women who opened those back doors. It is very hard to believe that those men and women, raising their children, eating their greens, crying their curses, weeping their tears, singing their songs, making their love, as the sun rose, as the sun set, were in any way inferior to the white men and women who crept over to share these splendors after the sun went down. But we must avoid the European error; we must not suppose that, because the situation, the ways, the perceptions of black people so radically differed from those of whites, they were racially superior. I am proud of these people not because of their color but because of their intelligence and their spiritual force and their beauty. The country should be proud of them, too, but, alas, not many people in this country even know of their existence. And the reason for this ignorance is that a knowledge of the role these people played—and play—in American life would reveal more about America to Americans than Americans wish to know.

The American Negro has the great advantage of having never believed that collection of myths to which white Americans cling: that their ancestors were all freedom-loving heroes, that they were born in the greatest country the world has ever seen, or that Americans are invincible in battle and wise in peace, that Americans have always dealt honorably with Mexicans and Indians and all other neighbors or inferiors, that American men are the world's most direct and virile, that American women are pure. Negroes know far more about white Americans than that; it can almost be said, in fact, that they know about white Americans what parents—or, anyway, mothers—know about their children, and that they very often regard white Americans that way. And perhaps this attitude, held in spite of what they know and have endured, helps to explain why Negroes, on the whole, and until lately, have allowed themselves to feel so little hatred. The tendency has really been, insofar as this was possible, to dismiss white people as the slightly mad victims of their own brainwashing.

One watched the lives they led. One could not be fooled about that; one watched the things they did and the excuses that they gave themselves, and if a white man was really in trouble, deep trouble, it was to the Negro's door that he came. And one felt that if one had had that white man's worldly advantages, one would never have become as bewildered and as joyless and as thoughtlessly cruel as he. The Negro came to the white man for a roof or for five dollars or for a letter to the judge; the white man came to the Negro for love. But he was not often able to give what he came seeking. The price was too high; he had too much to lose. And the Negro knew this, too. When one knows this about a man, it is impossible for one to hate him, but unless he becomes a man—becomes equal—it is also impossible for one to love him. Ultimately, one tends to avoid him, for the universal characteristic of children is to assume that they have a monopoly on trouble, and therefore a monopoly on *you*. (Ask any Negro what he knows about the white people with whom he works. And then ask the white people with whom he works what they know about *him*.)

How can the American Negro past be used? It is entirely possible that this dishonored past will rise up soon to smite all of us. There are some wars, for example (if anyone on the globe is still mad enough to go to war), that the American Negro will not support, however many of his people may be coerced—and there is a limit to the number of people any government can put in prison, and a rigid limit indeed to the practicality of such a course. A bill is coming in that I fear America is not prepared to pay. "The problem of the twentieth century," wrote W. E. B. Du Bois around sixty years ago, "is the problem of the color line." A fearful and delicate problem, which compromises, when it does not corrupt, all the American efforts to build a better world—here, there, or anywhere. It is for this reason that everything white Americans think they believe in must now be reëxamined. What one would not like to see again is the consolidation of peoples on the basis of their color. But as long as we in the West place on color the value that we do, we make it impossible for the great unwashed to consolidate themselves according to any other principle. Color is not a human or a personal reality; it

is a political reality. But this is a distinction so extremely hard
to make that the West has not been able to make it yet. And
at the center of this dreadful storm, this vast confusion, stand
the black people of this nation, who must now share the fate
of a nation that has never accepted them, to which they were
brought in chains. Well, if this is so, one has no choice but
to do all in one's power to change that fate, and at no matter
what risk—eviction, imprisonment, torture, death. For the
sake of one's children, in order to minimize the bill that *they*
must pay, one must be careful not to take refuge in any delusion—and the value placed on the color of the skin is always
and everywhere and forever a delusion. I know that what I
am asking is impossible. But in our time, as in every time, the
impossible is the least that one can demand—and one is, after
all, emboldened by the spectacle of human history in general,
and American Negro history in particular, for it testifies to
nothing less than the perpetual achievement of the impossible.

When I was very young, and was dealing with my buddies
in those wine- and urine-stained hallways, something in me
wondered, *What will happen to all that beauty?* For black people, though I am aware that some of us, black and white, do
not know it yet, are very beautiful. And when I sat at Elijah's
table and watched the baby, the women, and the men, and
we talked about God's—or Allah's—vengeance, I wondered,
when that vengeance was achieved, *What will happen to all
that beauty then?* I could also see that the intransigence and
ignorance of the white world might make that vengeance inevitable—a vengeance that does not really depend on, and
cannot really be executed by, any person or organization, and
that cannot be prevented by any police force or army: historical vengeance, a cosmic vengeance, based on the law that we
recognize when we say, "Whatever goes up must come
down." And here we are, at the center of the arc, trapped in
the gaudiest, most valuable, and most improbable water wheel
the world has ever seen. Everything now, we must assume, is
in our hands; we have no right to assume otherwise. If we—
and now I mean the relatively conscious whites and the relatively conscious blacks, who must, like lovers, insist on, or
create, the consciousness of the others—do not falter in our
duty now, we may be able, handful that we are, to end the

racial nightmare, and achieve our country, and change the history of the world. If we do not now dare everything, the fulfillment of that prophecy, re-created from the Bible in song by a slave, is upon us: *God gave Noah the rainbow sign, No more water, the fire next time!*

NO NAME IN THE STREET

for
  Berdis Baldwin
    and
  Beauford Delaney
    and
  Rudy Lombard
    and
  Jerome

His remembrance shall perish from the earth
and He shall have no name in the street.
He shall be driven from light into darkness,
and chased out of the world.
Job 18:17–18

Take Me to the Water

If I had-a- my way
I'd tear this building down.
Great God, then, if I had-a- my way
If I had-a- my way, little children,
I'd tear this building down.
—SLAVE SONG

Just a little while to stay here,
Just a little while to stay.
—TRADITIONAL

T HAT *is* a good idea," I heard my mother say. She was staring at a wad of black velvet, which she held in her hand, and she carefully placed this bit of cloth in a closet. We can guess how old I must have been from the fact that for years afterward I thought that an "idea" was a piece of black velvet.

Much, much, much has been blotted out, coming back only lately in bewildering and untrustworthy flashes. I must have been about five, I should think, when I made my connection between ideas and velvet, but I may have been younger; this may have been the same year that my father had me circumcised, a terrifying event which I scarcely remember at all; or I may think I was five because I remember tugging at my mother's skirts once and watching her face while she was telling someone else that she was twenty-seven. This meant, for me, that she was virtually in the grave already, and I tugged a little harder at her skirts. I already knew, for some reason, or had given myself some reason to believe, that she had been twenty-two when I was born. And, though I can't count today, I could count when I was little.

I was the only child in the house—or houses—for a while, a halcyon period which memory has quite repudiated; and if I remember myself as tugging at my mother's skirts and staring up into her face, it was because I was so terrified of the man we called my father; who did not arrive on *my* scene, really, until I was more than two years old. I have written both too much and too little about this man, whom I did not understand till he was past understanding. In my first memory of him, he is standing in the kitchen, drying the dishes. My mother had dressed me to go out, she is taking me someplace, and it must be winter, because I am wearing, in my memory, one of those cloth hats with a kind of visor, which button under the chin—a Lindbergh hat, I think. I am apparently in my mother's arms, for I am staring at my father over my mother's shoulder, we are near the door; and my father smiles. This may be a memory, I think it is, but it may be a fantasy. One of the very last times I saw my father on his feet, I was staring at him over my mother's shoulder—she had come rushing into the room to separate us—and my father was not smiling and neither was I.

His mother, Barbara, lived in our house, and she had been born in slavery. She was so old that she never moved from her bed. I remember her as pale and gaunt and she must have worn a kerchief because I don't remember her hair. I remember that she loved me; she used to scold her son about the way he treated me; and he was a little afraid of her. When she died, she called me into the room to give me a present—one of those old, round, metal boxes, usually with a floral design, used for candy. *She* thought it was full of candy and *I* thought it was full of candy, but it wasn't. After she died, I opened it and it was full of needles and thread.

This broke my heart, of course, but her going broke it more because I had loved her and depended on her. I knew—children *must* know—that she would always protect me with all her strength. So would my mother, too, I knew that, but my mother's strength was only to be called on in a desperate emergency. It did not take me long, nor did the children, as they came tumbling into this world, take long to discover that our mother paid an immense price for standing between us and our father. He had ways of making her suffer quite beyond our ken, and so we soon learned to depend on each other and became a kind of wordless conspiracy to protect *her*. (We were all, absolutely and mercilessly, united against our father.) We soon realized, anyway, that she scarcely belonged to us: she was always in the hospital, having another baby. Between his merciless children, who were terrified of him, the pregnancies, the births, the rats, the murders on Lenox Avenue, the whores who lived downstairs, his job on Long Island—to which he went every morning, wearing a Derby or a Homburg, in a black suit, white shirt, dark tie, looking like the preacher he was, and with his black lunchbox in his hand—and his unreciprocated love for the Great God Almighty, it is no wonder our father went mad. We, on the other hand, luckily, on the whole, for our father, and luckily indeed for our mother, simply took over each new child and made it ours. I want to avoid generalities as far as possible; it will, I hope, become clear presently that what I am now attempting dictates this avoidance; and so I will not say that children love miracles, but I will say that I think we did. A newborn baby is an extraordinary event; and I have never seen two babies who looked or even sounded remotely alike. Here it is, this breathing miracle who could not live an instant without you, with a skull more fragile than an egg, a miracle of eyes, legs, toenails, and (especially) lungs. It gropes in the light like a blind thing—it *is*, for the moment, blind—what can it make of what it sees? It's got a little hair, which it's going to lose, it's got no teeth, it pees all over you, it belches, and when it's frightened or hungry, quite without knowing what a miracle it's accomplishing, it exercises its lungs. You watch it discover it has a hand; then it discovers it has toes. Presently, it discovers it has *you*, and since it has already decided it wants to live, it gives you a toothless smile when you come near it, gurgles or giggles when you pick it up, holds you tight by the thumb or the eyeball or the hair, and, having already opted against solitude, howls when you put it down. You begin the extraordinary journey of beginning to know and to control this creature. You know the sound—the meaning—of one cry from another; without knowing that you know it. You know when it's hungry—that's one sound. You know when it's wet—that's another sound. You know when it's angry. You know when it's bored. You know when it's frightened. You know when it's suffering. You come or you go or you sit still according to the sound the baby makes. And you watch over it where I was born, even in your sleep, because rats love the odor of newborn babies and are much, much bigger.

By the time it has managed to crawl under every bed, nearly suffocate itself in every drawer, nearly strangle itself with string, somehow, God knows how, trapped itself behind the radiator, been pulled back, by one leg, from its suicidal investigation of the staircase, and nearly poisoned itself with everything—*its* hand being quicker than *your* eye—it can possibly get into its mouth, you have either grown to love it or you have left home.

I, James, in August. George, in January. Barbara, in August. Wilmer, in October, David, in December. Gloria, Ruth, Elizabeth, and (when we thought it was over!) Paula Maria, named by me, born on the day our father died, all in the summertime.

The youngest son of the New Orleans branch of the family—family, here, is used loosely and has to be; we knew almost nothing about this branch, which knew nothing about us; Daddy, the great good friend of the Great God Almighty, had simply fled the South, leaving a branch behind. As I have said, he was the son of a slave, and his youngest daughter, by his first marriage, is my mother's age and his youngest son is nine years older than I. This boy, who did not get along with his father, was my elder brother, as far as I then knew, and he sometimes took me with him here and there. He took me into the Coney Island breakers on his back one day, teaching me to swim, and somehow ducked beneath me, playing, or was carried away from me for a moment, terrified, caught me and brought me above the waves. In the time that his body vanished beneath me and the waters rolled over my head, I still remember the slimy sea water and the blinding green—it was not green; it was all the world's snot and vomit; it entered into me; when my head was abruptly lifted out of the water, when I felt my brother's arms and saw his worried face—his eyes looking steadily into mine with the intense and yet impersonal anxiety of a surgeon, the sky above me not yet in focus, my lungs failing to deliver the mighty scream I had nearly burst with in the depths, my four or five or six-year-old legs kicking—and my brother slung me over his shoulder like a piece of meat, or a much beloved child, and strode up out of the sea with me, with me! he had saved me, after all,

I learned something about the terror and the loneliness and the depth and the height of love.

Not so very much later, this brother, who was in his teens, fooling around with girls or shooting dice with his friends, who knows, came home late, which was forbidden in our Baptist house, and had a terrible fight with his Daddy and left the house and never came back. He swore that he never would come back, that his Daddy would never see him again. And he never did come back, not while Daddy was still alive. Daddy wrote, but his son never answered. When I became a young minister, I was asked to write him, and I did—sometimes my father dictated the letters to me. And the boy answered me, sometimes, but he never answered his father and never mentioned him. Daddy slowly began to realize that he was never going to see that son, who was his darling, the apple of his eye, anymore, and this broke his heart and destroyed his will and helped him into the madhouse and the grave— my only intimation, perhaps, during all those years, that he was human. The son came home, when his father died, to help me bury him. Then he went away again, and I didn't see him until I had to go to California on a Civil Rights gig, and he met me at the airport. By then, I was thirty-nine and he was nearly fifty, I had made his disowned father's name famous, and I had left home in exactly the same way he did, for more or less the same reasons, and when I was seventeen.

Since Martin's death, in Memphis, and that tremendous day in Atlanta, something has altered in me, something has gone away. Perhaps even more than the death itself, the manner of his death has forced me into a judgment concerning human life and human beings which I have always been reluctant to make—indeed, I can see that a great deal of what the knowledgeable would call my life-style is dictated by this reluctance. Incontestably, alas, most people are not, in action, worth very much; and yet, every human being is an unprecedented miracle. One tries to treat them as the miracles they are, while trying to protect oneself against the disasters they've become. This is not very different from the act of faith demanded by all those marches and petitions while Martin was still alive. One could scarcely be deluded by Americans anymore, one scarcely dared expect anything from the great, vast, blank generality; and yet one was compelled to demand of Americans—and for their sakes, after all—a generosity, a clarity, and a nobility which they did not dream of demanding of themselves. Part of the error was irreducible, in that the marchers and petitioners were forced to suppose the existence of an entity which, when the chips were down, could not be located—*i.e.*, there *are* no American people yet: but to this speculation (or desperate hope) we shall presently return. Perhaps, however, the moral of the story (and the hope of the world) lies in what one demands, not of others, but of oneself. However that may be, the failure and the betrayal are in the record book forever, and sum up, and condemn, forever, those descendants of a barbarous Europe who arbitrarily and arrogantly reserve the right to call themselves Americans.

The mind is a strange and terrible vehicle, moving according to rigorous rules of its own; and my own mind, after I had left Atlanta, began to move backward in time, to places, people, and events I thought I had forgotten. Sorrow drove it there, I think, sorrow, and a certain kind of bewilderment, triggered, perhaps, by something which happened to me in connection with Martin's funeral.

When Martin was murdered, I was based in Hollywood, working—working, in fact, on the screen version of *The Autobiography of Malcolm X*. This was a difficult assignment, since I had known Malcolm, after all, crossed swords with him, worked with him, and held him in that great esteem which is not easily distinguishable, if it is distinguishable at all, from love. (The Hollywood gig did not work out because I did not wish to be a party to a second assassination: but we will also return to Hollywood, presently.)

Very shortly before his death, I had to appear with Martin at Carnegie Hall, in New York. Having been on the Coast so long, I had nothing suitable to wear for my Carnegie Hall gig, and so I rushed out, got a dark suit, got it fitted, and made my appearance. Something like two weeks later, I wore this same suit to Martin's funeral; returned to Hollywood; presently, had to come East again, on business. I ran into Leonard Lyons one night, and I told him that I would never be able to wear that suit again. Leonard put this in his column. I went back to Hollywood.

Weeks later, either because of a Civil Rights obligation, or because of Columbia Pictures, I was back in New York. On my desk in New York were various messages—and it must be said that my sister, Gloria, who worked for me then, is extremely selective, not to say brutal, about the messages she leaves on my desk. I don't see, simply, most of the messages I get. I couldn't conceivably live with them. No one could—as Gloria knows. However, my best friend, black, when I had been in junior high school, when I was twelve or thirteen, had been calling and calling and calling. The guilt of the survivor is a real guilt—as I was now to discover. In a way that I may never be able to make real for my countrymen, or myself, the fact that I had "made it"—that is, had been seen on television, and at Sardi's, could (presumably!) sign a check anywhere in the world, could, in short, for the length of an entrance, a dinner, or a drink, intimidate headwaiters by the use of a name which had not been mine when I was born and which love had compelled me to make my own—meant that I had betrayed the people who had produced me. Nothing could be more unutterably paradoxical: to have thrown in your lap what you never dreamed of getting, and, in sober, bitter truth, could never have dreamed of having, and that at the price of an assumed betrayal of your brothers and your sisters! One is always disproving the accusation in action as futile as it is inevitable.

I had not seen this friend—who could scarcely, any longer, be called a friend—in many years. I was brighter, or more driven than he—not my fault!—and, though neither of us knew it then, our friendship really ended during my ministry and was deader than my hope of heaven by the time I left the pulpit, the church, and home. Hindsight indicates, obviously, that this particular rupture, which was, of necessity, exceedingly brutal and which involved, after all, the deliberate repudiation of everything and everyone that had given me an identity until that moment, must have left some scars. The current of my life meant that I did not see this person very often, but I was always terribly guilty when I did. I was guilty because I had nothing to say to him, and at one time I had told him everything, or nearly everything. I was guilty because he was just another post-office worker, and we had dreamed such tremendous futures for ourselves. I was guilty because he and his family had been very nice to me during an awful time in my life and now none of that meant anything to me. I was guilty because I knew, at the bottom of my heart, that I judged this unremarkable colored man very harshly, far more harshly than I would have done if he were white, and I knew this to be unjust as well as sinister. I was furious because he thought my life was easy and I thought my life was hard, and I yet had to see that by his lights, certainly, and by any ordinary yardstick, my life was enviable compared to his. And if, as I kept saying, it was not my fault, it was not *his* fault, either. You can certainly see why I tended to avoid my old school chum.

But I called him, of course. I thought that he probably needed money, because that was the only thing, by now, that I could possibly hope to give him. But, no. He, or his wife, or a relative, had read the Leonard Lyons column and knew that I had a suit I wasn't wearing, and—as he remembered in one way and I in quite another—he was just my size.

Now, for me, that suit was drenched in the blood of all the crimes of my country. If I had said to Leonard, somewhat melodramatically, no doubt, that I could never wear it again, I was, just the same, being honest. I simply could not put it on, or look at it, without thinking of Martin, and Martin's end, of what he had meant to me, and to so many. I could not put it on without a bleak, pale, cold wonder about the future. I could not, in short, live with it, it was too heavy a garment. Yet—it was only a suit, worn, at most, three times. It was not a very expensive suit, but it was still more expensive than any my friend could buy. He could not afford to have suits in his closet which he didn't wear, he couldn't afford to throw suits away—he couldn't, in short, afford my elegant despair. Martin was dead, but *he* was living, he needed a suit, and—I was just his size. He invited me for dinner that evening, and I said that I would bring him the suit.

The American situation being what it is, and American taxi drivers being what they mostly are, I have, in effect, been forbidden to expose myself to the quite tremendous hazards of getting a cab to stop for me in New York, and have been forced to hire cars. Naturally, the car which picked me up on that particular guilty evening was a Cadillac limousine about seventy-three blocks long, and, naturally, the chauffeur was white. Neither did he want to drive a black man through Harlem to the Bronx, but American democracy has always been at the mercy of the dollar: the chauffeur may not have liked the gig, but he certainly wasn't about to lose the bread. Here we were, then, this terrified white man and myself, trapped in this leviathan, eyed bitterly, as it passed, by a totally hostile population. But it was not the chauffeur which the population looked on with such wry contempt: I held the suit over my arm, and was tempted to wave it: *I'm only taking a suit to a friend!*

I knew how they felt about black men in limousines—unless they were popular idols—and I couldn't blame them, and I knew that I could never explain. We found the house, and, with the suit over my arm, I mounted the familiar stairs.

I was no longer the person my friend and his family had known and loved—I was a stranger now, and keenly aware of it, and trying hard to act, as it were, normal. But nothing *can* be normal in such a situation. They *had* known me, and they *had* loved me; but now they couldn't be blamed for feeling *He thinks he's too good for us now.* I certainly didn't feel that, but I had no conceivable relationship to them anymore—that shy, pop-eyed thirteen year old my friend's mother had scolded and loved was no more. *I* was not the same, but *they* were, as though they had been trapped, preserved, in that moment in time. They seemed scarcely to have grown any older, my friend and his mother, and they greeted me as they had greeted me years ago, though I was now well past forty and felt every hour of it. My friend and I remained alike only in that neither of us had gained any weight. His face was as boyish as ever, and his voice; only a touch of grey in his hair proved that we were no longer at P.S. 139. And my life came with me into their small, dark, unspeakably respectable, incredibly hard-won rooms like the roar of champagne and the odor of brimstone. They still believed in the Lord, but I had quarreled with Him, and offended Him, and walked out of

His house. They didn't smoke, but they knew (from seeing me on television) that I did, and they had placed about the room, in deference to me, those hideous little ash trays which can hold exactly one cigarette butt. And there was a bottle of whiskey, too, and they asked me if I wanted steak or chicken; for, in my travels, I might have learned not to like fried chicken anymore. I said, much relieved to be able to tell the truth, that I preferred chicken. I gave my friend the suit.

My friend's stepdaughter is young, considers herself a militant, and we had a brief argument concerning Bill Styron's *Nat Turner*, which I suggested that she read before condemning. This rather shocked the child, whose militancy, like that of many, tends to be a matter of indigestible fury and slogans and quotations. It rather checked the company, which had not imagined that I and a black militant could possibly disagree about anything. But what was most striking about our brief exchange was that it obliquely revealed how little the girl respected her stepfather. She appeared not to respect him at all. This was not revealed by anything she said to him, but by the fact that she said nothing to him. She barely looked at him. He didn't count.

I always think that this is a terrible thing to happen to a man, especially in his own house, and I am always terribly humiliated for the man to whom it happens. Then, of course, you get angry at the man for allowing it to happen.

And *how* had it happened? He had never been the brightest boy in the world, nobody is, but he had been energetic, active, funny, wrestling, playing handball, cheerfully submitting to being tyrannized by me, even to the extent of kneeling before the altar and having his soul saved—my insistence had accomplished that. I looked at him and remembered his sweating and beautiful face that night as he wrestled on the church floor and we prayed him through. I remembered his older brother, who had died in Sicily, in battle for the free world—he had barely had time to see Sicily before he died and had assuredly never seen the free world. I remembered the day he came to see me to tell me that his sister, who had been very ill, had died. We sat on the steps of the tenement, he was looking down as he told me, one finger making a circle on the step, and his tears splashed on the wood. We were children then, his sister had not been much older, and he was the youngest and now the only boy. But this was not *how* it had happened, although I thought I could see, watching his widowed mother's still very handsome face watching him, how her human need might have held and trapped and frozen him. She had been sewing in the garment center all the years I knew them, rushing home to get supper on the table before her husband got home from *his* job; at night, and on Sundays, he was a deacon; and God knows, or should, where his energy came from. When I began working for the garment center, I used to see her, from time to time, rushing to catch the bus, in a crowd of black and Puerto Rican ladies.

And, yes, we had all loved each other then, and I had had great respect for my friend, who was handsomer than I, and more athletic, and more popular, and who beat me in every game I was foolish enough to play with him. I had gone my way and life had accomplished its inexorable mathematic—and what in the world was I by now but an aging, lonely, sexually dubious, politically outrageous, unspeakably erratic freak? his old friend. And what was *he* now? he worked for the post office and was building a house next door to his mother, in, I think, Long Island. They, too, then, had made it. But what I could not understand was how nothing seemed to have touched this man. We are living through what our church described as "these last and evil days," through wars and rumors of wars, to say the least. He could, for example, have known something about the anti-poverty program if only because his wife was more or less involved in it. He should have known something about the then raging school battle, if only because his stepdaughter was a student; and she, whether or not she had thought her position through, was certainly involved. She may have hoped, at one time, anyway, for his clarity and his help. But, no. He seemed as little touched by the cataclysm in his house and all around him as he was by the mail he handled every day. I found this unbelievable, and, given my temperament and our old connection, maddening. We got into a battle about the war in Vietnam. I probably really should not have allowed this to happen, but it was partly the stepdaughter's prodding. And I was astounded that my friend would defend this particular racist folly. What for? for his job at the post office? And the answer came back at once, alas—yes. For his job at the post office. I told him that Americans had no business at all in Vietnam; and that black people certainly had no business there, aiding the slave master to enslave yet more millions of dark people, and also identifying themselves with the white American crimes: we, the blacks, are going to need our allies, for the Americans, odd as it may sound at the moment, will presently have none. It wasn't, I said, hard to understand why a black boy, standing, futureless, on the corner, would decide to join the Army, nor was it hard to decipher the slave master's reasons for hoping that he wouldn't live to come home, with a gun; but it wasn't necessary, after all, to defend it: to defend, that is, one's murder and one's murderers. "Wait a minute," he said, "let me stand up and tell you what I think we're trying to do there." "*We?*" I cried, "what motherfucking *we*? You stand up, motherfucker, and I'll kick you in the ass!"

He looked at me. His mother conveyed—but the good Lord knows I had hurt her—that she didn't want that language in her house, and that I had never talked that way before. And I love the lady. I had meant no disrespect. I stared at my friend, my old friend, and felt millions of people staring at us both. I tried to make a kind of joke out of it all. But it was too late. The way they looked at me proved that I had tipped my hand. And *this* hurt *me*. They should have known me better, or at least enough, to have known that I meant what I said. But the general reaction to famous people who hold difficult opinions is that they can't really mean it. It's considered, generally, to be merely an astute way of attracting public attention, a way of making oneself interesting: one marches in Montgomery, for example, merely (in my own case) to sell one's books. Well. There is nothing, then, to be said. There went the friendly fried chicken dinner. There went the loving past. I watched the mother watching me, wondering what had happened to her beloved Jimmy, and giving me up: her sourest suspicions confirmed. In great weariness I poured myself yet another stiff drink, by now definitively condemned, and lit another cigarette, they watching me all the while for symptoms of cancer, and with a precipice at my feet.

For that bloody suit was *their* suit, after all, it had been bought *for* them, it had even been bought *by* them: *they* had created Martin, he had not created them, and the blood in which the fabric of that suit was stiffening was theirs. The distance between us, and I had never thought of this before, was that they did not know this, and I now dared to realize that I loved them more than they loved me. And I do not mean that my love was greater: who dares judge the inexpressible expense another pays for his life? who knows how much one is loved, by whom, or what that love may be called on to do? No, the way the cards had fallen meant that I had to face more about them than they could know about me, knew their rent, whereas they did not know mine, and was condemned to make them uncomfortable. For, on the other hand, they certainly wanted that freedom which they thought was mine—that frightening limousine, for example, or the power to give away a suit, or my increasingly terrifying trans-Atlantic journeys. How can one say that freedom is taken, not given, and that no one is free until all are free? and that the price is high.

My friend tried on the suit, a perfect fit, and they all admired him in it, and I went home.

Well. Time passes and passes. It passes backward and it passes forward and it carries you along, and no one in the whole wide world knows more about time than this: it is carrying you through an element you do not understand into an element you will not remember. Yet, *something* remembers— it can even be said that something avenges: the trap of our century, and the subject now before us.

I left home—Harlem—in 1942. I returned, in 1946, to do, with a white photographer, one of several unpublished efforts; had planned to marry, then realized that I couldn't—or shouldn't, which comes to the same thing—threw my wedding rings into the Hudson River, and left New York for Paris, in 1948. By this time, of course, I was mad, as mad as my dead father. If I had not gone mad, I could not have left.

I starved in Paris for a while, but I learned something: for one thing, I fell in love. Or, more accurately, I realized, and accepted for the first time that love was not merely a general, human possibility, nor merely the disaster it had so often, by then, been for me—according to me—nor was it something that happened to other people, like death, nor was it merely a mortal danger: it was among *my* possibilities, for here it was, breathing and belching beside me, and it was the key to life. Not merely the key to *my* life, but to life itself. My falling in love is in no way the subject of this book, and yet honesty compels me to place it among the details, for I think—I know—that my story would be a very different one if love had not forced me to attempt to deal with myself. It began to pry open for me the trap of color, for people do not fall in love according to their color—this may come as news to noble pioneers and eloquent astronauts, to say nothing of most of the representatives of most of the American states—and when lovers quarrel, as indeed they inevitably do, it is not the degree of their pigmentation that they are quarreling about, nor can lovers, on any level whatever, use color as a weapon. This means that one must accept one's nakedness. And nakedness has no color: this can come as news only to those who have never covered, or been covered by, another naked human being.

In any case, the world changes then, and it changes forever. Because you love one human being, you see everyone else very differently than you saw them before—perhaps I only mean to say that you begin to *see*—and you are both stronger and more vulnerable, both free and bound. Free, paradoxically, because, now, you have a home—your lover's arms. And bound: to that mystery, precisely, a bondage which liberates you into something of the glory and suffering of the world.

I had come to Paris with no money and this meant that in those early years I lived mainly among *les misérables*—and, in Paris, *les misérables* are Algerian. They slept four or five or six to a room, and they slept in shifts, they were treated like dirt, and they scraped such sustenance as they could off the filthy, unyielding Paris stones. The French called them lazy because they appeared to spend most of their time sitting around, drinking tea, in their cafés. But they were not lazy. They were mostly unable to find work, and their rooms were freezing. (French students spent most of their time in cafés, too, for the same reason, but no one called them lazy.) The Arab cafés were warm and cheap, and they were together there. They could not, in the main, afford the French cafés, nor in the main, were they welcome there. And, though they spoke French, and had been, in a sense, produced by France, they were not at home in Paris, no more at home than I, though for a different reason. They remembered, as it were, an opulence, opulence of taste, touch, water, sun, which I had barely dreamed of, and they had not come to France to stay. One day they were going home, and they knew exactly where home was. They, thus, held something within them which they would never surrender to France. But on my side of the ocean, or so it seemed to me then, we had surrendered everything, or had had everything taken away, and there was no place for us to go: we *were* home. The Arabs were together in Paris, but the American blacks were alone. The Algerian poverty was absolute, their stratagems grim, their personalities, for me, unreadable, their present bloody and their future certain to be more so: and yet, after all, their situation was far more coherent than mine. I will not say that I envied them, for I didn't, and the directness of their hunger, or hungers, intimidated me; but I respected them, and as I began to discern what their history had made of them, I began to suspect, somewhat painfully, what my history had made of me.

The French were still hopelessly slugging it out in Indo-China when I first arrived in France, and I was living in Paris when Dien Bien Phu fell. The Algerian rug-sellers and peanut vendors on the streets of Paris then had obviously not the remotest connection with this most crucial of the French reverses; and yet the attitude of the police, which had always been menacing, began to be yet more snide and vindictive. This puzzled me at first, but it shouldn't have. This is the way people react to the loss of empire—for the loss of an empire also implies a radical revision of the individual identity—and I was to see this over and over again, not only in France. The Arabs were not a part of Indo-China, but they *were* part of an empire visibly and swiftly crumbling, and part of a history which was achieving, in the most literal and frightening sense, its *dénouement*—was revealing itself, that is, as being not at all the myth which the French had made of it—and the French authority to rule over them was being more hotly contested with every hour. The challenged authority, unable to justify itself and not dreaming indeed of even attempting to do so, simply increased its force. This had the interesting result of revealing how frightened the French authority had become, and many a North African then resolved, *coûte que coûte*, to bring the French to another Dien Bien Phu.

Something else struck me, which I was to watch more closely in my own country. The French were hurt and furious that their stewardship should be questioned, especially by those they ruled, and if, in this, they were not very original, they were exceedingly intense. After all, as they continually pointed out, there had been nothing in those colonies before they got there, nothing at all; or what meagre resources of mineral or oil there might have been weren't doing the natives any good because the natives didn't even know that they were there, or what they were there for. Thus, the exploitation of the colony's resources was done for the good of the natives; and so vocal could the French become as concerns what they had brought into their colonies that it would have been the height of bad manners to have asked what they had brought out. (I was later to see something of how this fair exchange worked when I visited Senegal and Guinea.)

It was strange to find oneself, in another language, in another country, listening to the same old song and hearing oneself condemned in the same old way. The French (for example) had always had excellent relations with their natives, and they had a treasurehouse of anecdotes to prove it. (I never found any natives to corroborate the anecdotes, but, then, I have never met an African who did not loathe Dr. Schweitzer.) They cited the hospitals built, and the schools—I was to see some of these later, too. Every once in a while someone might be made uneasy by the color of my skin, or an expression on my face, or I might say something to make him uneasy, or I might, arbitrarily (there was no reason to suppose that they wanted me), claim kinship with the Arabs. Then, I was told, with a generous smile, that I was different: *le noir Americain est très évolué, voyons!* But the Arabs were not like me, they were not "civilized" like me. It was something of a shock to hear myself described as civilized, but the accolade thirsted for so long had, alas, been delivered too late, and I was fascinated by one of several inconsistencies. I have never heard a Frenchman describe the United States as civilized, not even those Frenchmen who like the States. Of course, I think the truth is that the French do not consider that the world contains any nation as civilized as France. But, leaving that aside, if so crude a nation as the United States could produce so gloriously civilized a creature as myself, how was it that the French, armed with centuries of civilized grace, had been unable to civilize the Arab? I thought that this was a very cunning question, but I was wrong, because the answer was so simple: the Arabs did not wish to be civilized. Oh, it was not possible for an American to understand these people as the French did; after all, they had got on well together for nearly one hundred and thirty years. But they had, the Arabs, their customs, their dialects, languages, tribes, regions, another religion, or, perhaps, many religions—and the French were not *raciste*, like the Americans, they did not believe in destroying indigenous cultures. And then, too, the Arab was always hiding something; you couldn't guess what he was thinking and couldn't trust what he was saying. And they had a different attitude toward women, they were very brutal with them, in a word they were rapists, and they stole, and they carried knives. But the French had endured this for more than a hundred years and were willing to endure it for a hundred years more, in spite of the fact that Algeria was a great drain on the national pocketbook and the fact that any Algerian—due to the fact that Algeria was French, was, in fact, a French *département*, and was damn well going to stay that way—was free to come to Paris at any time and jeopardize the economy and prowl the streets and prey on French women. In short, the record of French generosity was so exemplary that it was impossible to believe that the children could seriously be bent on revolution.

Impossible for a Frenchman, perhaps, but not for me. I had watched the police, one sunny afternoon, beat an old, one-armed Arab peanut vendor senseless in the streets, and I had watched the unconcerned faces of the French on the café terraces, and the congested faces of the Arabs. Yes, I could believe it: and here it came.

Not without warning, and not without precedent: but only poets, since they must excavate and recreate history, have ever learned anything from it.

I returned to New York in 1952, after four years away, at the height of the national convulsion called McCarthyism. This convulsion did not surprise me, for I don't think that it was possible for Americans to surprise me anymore; but it was very frightening, in many ways, and for many reasons. I realized, for one thing, that I was saved from direct—or, more accurately, public—exposure to the American Inquisitors only by my color, my obscurity, and my comparative youth: or, in other words, by the lack, on their parts, of any imagination. I was just a shade too young to have had any legally recognizable political history. A boy of thirteen is a minor, and, in the eyes of the Republic, if he is black, and lives in a black ghetto, he was born to carry packages; but, in fact, at thirteen, I had been a convinced fellow traveler. I marched in one May Day parade, carrying banners, shouting, *East Side, West Side, all around the town, We want the landlords to tear the slums down!* I didn't know anything about Communism, but I knew a lot about slums. By the time I was nineteen, I was a Trotskyite, having learned a great deal by then, if not about Communism, at least about Stalinists. The convulsion was the more ironical for me in that I had been an anti-Communist when America and Russia were allies. I had nearly been murdered on 14th Street, one evening, for putting down too loudly, in the presence of patriots, that memorable contribution to the War effort, the Warner Brothers production of *Mission To Moscow.* The very same patriots now wanted to burn the film and hang the filmmakers, and Warners, during the McCarthy era, went to no little trouble to explain their film away. Warners was abject, and so was nearly everybody else, it was a foul, ignoble time: and my contempt for most American intellectuals, and/or liberals dates from what I observed of their manhood then. I say most, not all, but the exceptions constitute a remarkable pantheon, even, or, rather, especially those who did not survive the flames into which their lives and their reputations were hurled. I had come home to a city in which nearly everyone was gracelessly scurrying for shelter, in which friends were throwing their friends to the wolves, and justifying their treachery by learned discourses (and tremendous tomes) on the treachery of the Comintern. Some of the things written during those years, justifying, for example, the execution of the Rosenbergs, or the crucifixion of Alger Hiss (and the beatification of Whittaker Chambers) taught me something about the irresponsibility and cowardice of the liberal community which I will never forget. Their performance, then, yet more than the combination of ignorance and arrogance with which this community has always protected itself against the deepest implications of black suffering, persuaded me that brilliance without passion is nothing more than sterility. It must be remembered, after all, that I did not begin meeting these people at the point that they began to meet *me*: I had been delivering their packages and emptying their garbage and taking their tips for years. (And they don't tip well.) And what I watched them do to each other during the McCarthy era was, in some ways, worse than anything they had ever done to me, for I, at least, had never been mad enough to depend on their devotion. It seemed very clear to me that they were lying about their motives and were being blackmailed by their guilt; were, in fact, at bottom, nothing more than the respectable issue of various immigrants, struggling to hold on to what they had acquired. For, intellectual activity, according to me, is, and must be, disinterested—the truth *is* a two-edged sword—and if one is not willing to be pierced by that sword, even to the extreme of dying on it, then all of one's intellectual activity is a masturbatory delusion and a wicked and dangerous fraud.

I made such motions as I could to understand what was happening, and to keep myself afloat. But I had been away too long. It was not only that I *could* not readjust myself to life in New York—it was also that I *would* not: I was never going to be anybody's nigger again. But I was now to discover that the world has more than one way of keeping you a nigger, has evolved more than one way of skinning the cat; if the hand slips here, it tightens there, and now I was offered, gracefully indeed, membership in the club. I had lunch at some elegant bistros, dinner at some exclusive clubs. I tried to be understanding about my countrymen's concern for difficult me, and unruly mine—and I really *was* trying to be understanding, though not without some bewilderment, and, eventually, some malice. I began to be profoundly uncomfortable. It was a strange kind of discomfort, a terrified apprehension that I had lost my bearings. I did not altogether understand what I was hearing. I did not trust what I heard myself saying. In very little that I heard did I hear anything that reflected anything which *I* knew, or had endured, of life. My mother and my father, my brothers and my sisters were not present at the tables at which I sat down, and no one in the company had ever heard of them. My own beginnings, or instincts, began to shift as nervously as the cigarette smoke that wavered around my head. I was not trying to hold on to my wretchedness. On the contrary, if my poverty was coming, at last, to an end, so much the better, and it wasn't happening a moment too soon—and yet, I felt an increasing chill, as though the rest of my life would have to be lived in silence.

I think it may have been my own obsession with the McCarthy phenomenon which caused me to suspect the impotence and narcissism of so many of the people whose names I had respected. I had never had any occasion to judge them, as it were, intimately. For me, simply, McCarthy was a coward and a bully, with no claim to honor, nor any claim to honorable attention. For me, emphatically, there were *not* two sides to this dubious coin, and, as to his baleful and dangerous effect, there could be no *question* at all. Yet, they spent hours debating whether or not McCarthy was an enemy of domestic liberties. I couldn't but wonder what conceivable further proof they were awaiting: I thought of German Jews sitting around debating whether or not Hitler was a threat to their lives until the debate was summarily resolved for them by a knocking at the door. Nevertheless, this learned, civilized, intellectual-liberal debate cheerfully raged in its vacuum, while every hour brought more distress and confusion—and dishonor—to the country they claimed to love. The pretext for all this, of course, was the necessity of "containing" Communism, which, they unblushingly informed me, was a threat to the "free" world. I did not say to what extent this free world menaced me, and millions like me. But I wondered how the justification of blatant and mindless tyranny, on any level, could operate in the interests of liberty, and I wondered what interior, unspoken urgencies of these people made necessary so thoroughly unattractive a delusion. I wondered what they really felt about human life, for they were so choked and cloaked with formulas that they no longer seemed to have any connection with it. They were all, for a while anyway, very proud of me, of course, proud that I had been able to crawl up to their level and been "accepted." What *I* might think of *their* level, how *I* might react to this "acceptance," or what this acceptance might cost me, were not among the questions which racked them in the midnight hour. One wondered, indeed, if anything could ever disturb their sleep. They walked the same streets I walked, after all, rode the same subways, must have seen the same increasingly desperate and hostile boys and girls, must, at least occasionally, have passed through the garment center. It is true that even those who taught at Columbia never saw Harlem, but, on the other hand, everything that New York has become, in 1971, was visibly and swiftly beginning to happen in 1952: one had only to take a bus from the top of the city and ride through it to see how it was darkening and deteriorating, how human bewilderment and hostility rose, how human contact was endangered and dying. Of course, these liberals were not, as I was, forever being found by the police in the "wrong" neighborhood, and so could not have had first-hand knowledge of how gleefully a policeman translates his orders from above. But they had no right not to know that; if they did not know that, they knew nothing and had no right to speak as though they were responsible actors in their society; for their complicity with the patriots of that hour meant that the policeman was acting on *their* orders, too.

No, I couldn't hack it. When my first novel was finally sold, I picked up my advance and walked straight to the steamship office and booked passage back to France.

I place it here, though it occurred during a later visit: I found myself in a room one night, with my liberal friends, after a private showing of the French film, *The Wages of Fear*. The question on the floor was whether or not this film should be shown in the United States. The reason for the question was that the film contained unflattering references to American oil companies. I do not know if I said anything, or not; I rather doubt that I could have said much. I felt as paralyzed, fascinated, as a rabbit before a snake. I had, in fact, already seen the film in France. It had not occurred to me, or to anyone I knew, that the film was even remotely anti-American: by no stretch of the imagination could this be considered the film's *motif*. Yet, here were the autumn patriots, hotly discussing the dangers of a film which dared to suggest that American oil interests didn't give a shit about human life. There was a French woman in the room, tight-mouthed, bitter, far from young. She may or may not have been the widow of a Vichyite General, but her sympathies were in that region: and I will never forget her saying, looking straight at me, "We always knew that you, the Americans, would realize, one day, that you fought on the wrong side!"

I was ashamed of myself for being in that room: but, I must say, too, that I was glad, glad to have been a witness, glad to have come far enough to have heard the devil speak. That woman gave me something, I will never forget her, and I walked away from the welcome table.

Yet, hope—the hope that we, human beings, can be better than we are—dies hard; perhaps one can no longer live if one allows that hope to die. But it is also hard to see what one sees. One sees that most human beings are wretched, and, in one way or another, become wicked: because they are so wretched. And one's turning away, then, from what I have called the welcome table is dictated by some mysterious vow one scarcely knows one's taken—never to allow oneself to fall so low. Lower, perhaps, much lower, to the very dregs: but never there.

When I came back to Paris at the end of the summer, most of the Arab cafés I knew had been closed. My favorite money-changer and low-life guide, a beautiful stone hustler, had disappeared, no one knew—or no one said—where. Another cat had had his eyes put out—some said by the police, some said by his brothers, because he was a police informer. In a sense, that beautiful, blinded boy who had been punished either as a traitor to France or as a traitor to Algeria, sums up the Paris climate in the years immediately preceding the revolution. One was either French, or Algerian; one could not be both.

There began, now, a time of rumor unlike anything I had ever been through before. In a way, I was somewhat insulated against what was happening to the Algerians, or was aware of it from a certain distance, because what was happening to the Algerians did not appear to be happening to the blacks. I was still operating, unconsciously, within the American framework, and, in that framework, since Arabs are paler than blacks, it is the blacks who would have suffered most. But the blacks, from Martinique and Senegal, and so on, were as visible and vivid as they had always been, and no one appeared to molest them or to pay them any particular attention at all. Not only was I operating within the American frame of reference, I was also a member of the American colony, and we were, in general, slow to pick up on what was going on around us.

Nevertheless, I began to realize that I could not find *any* of the Algerians I knew, not one; and since I could not find one, there was no way to ask about the others. They were in none of the dives we had frequented, they had apparently abandoned their rooms, their cafés, as I have said, were closed, and they were no longer to be seen on the Paris sidewalks, changing money, or selling their rugs, their peanuts, or themselves. We heard that they had been placed in camps around Paris, that they were being tortured there, that they were being murdered. No one wished to believe any of this, it made us exceedingly uncomfortable, and we felt that we should do something, but there was nothing we could do. We began to realize that there *had* to be some truth to these pale and cloudy rumors: one woman told me of seeing an Algerian hurled by the proprietor of a café in Pigalle *through* the café's *closed* plate-glass door. If she had not witnessed a murder, she had certainly witnessed a murder attempt. And, in fact, Algerians *were* being murdered in the streets, and corraled into prisons, and being dropped into the Seine, like flies.

Not only Algerians. Everyone in Paris, in those years, who was not, resoundingly, from the north of Europe was suspected of being Algerian; and the police were on every street corner, sometimes armed with machine guns. Turks, Greeks,

Spaniards, Jews, Italians, American blacks, and Frenchmen from Marseilles, or Nice, were all under constant harassment, and we will never know how many people having not the remotest connection with Algeria were thrown into prison, or murdered, as it were, by accident. The son of a world-famous actor, and an actor himself, swarthy, and speaking no French—rendered speechless indeed by the fact that the policeman had a gun leveled at him—was saved only by the fact that he was close enough to his hotel to shout for the night porter, who came rushing out and identified him. Two young Italians, on holiday, did not fare so well: speeding merrily along on their Vespa, they failed to respond to a policeman's order to halt, whereupon the policeman fired, and the holiday came to a bloody end. Everyone one knew was full of stories like these, which eventually began to appear in the press, and one had to be careful how one moved about in the fabulous city of light.

I had never, thank God—and certainly not once I found myself living there—been even remotely romantic about Paris. I may have been romantic about London—because of Charles Dickens—but the romance lasted for exactly as long as it took me to carry my bags out of Victoria Station. My journey, or my flight, had not been *to* Paris, but simply *away* from America. For example, I had seriously considered going to work on a kibbutz in Israel, and I ended up in Paris almost literally by closing my eyes and putting my finger on a map. So I was not as demoralized by all of this as I would certainly have been if I had ever made the error of considering Paris the most civilized of cities and the French as the least primitive of peoples. I knew too much about the French Revolution for that. I had read too much Balzac for that. Whenever I crossed la place de la Concorde, I heard the tumbrils arriving, and the roar of the mob, and where the obelisk now towers, I saw—and see— *la guillotine*. Anyone who has ever been at the mercy of the people, then, knows something awful about us, will forever distrust the popular patriotism, and avoids even the most convivial of mobs.

Still, my flight had been dictated by my hope that I could find myself in a place where I would be treated more humanely than my society had treated me at home, where my risks would be more personal, and my fate less austerely sealed. And Paris had done this for me: by leaving me completely alone. I lived in Paris for a long time without making a single French friend, and even longer before I saw the inside of a French home. This did not really upset me, either, for Henry James had been here before me and had had the generosity to clue me in. Furthermore, for a black boy who had grown up on Welfare and the chicken-shit goodwill of American liberals, this total indifference came as a great relief and, even, as a mark of respect. If I could make it, I could make it; so much the better. And if I couldn't, I couldn't—so much the worse. I didn't want any help, and the French certainly didn't give me any—they let me do it myself; and for that reason, even knowing what I know, and unromantic as I am, there will always be a kind of love story between myself and that odd, unpredictable collection of bourgeois chauvinists who call themselves *la France.*

Or, in other words, my reasons for coming to France, and the comparative freedom of my life in Paris, meant that my attitude toward France was very different from that of any Algerian. He, and his brothers, were, in fact, being murdered by my hosts. And Algeria, after all, is a part of Africa, and France, after all, is a part of Europe: that Europe which invaded and raped the African continent and slaughtered those Africans whom they could not enslave—that Europe from which, in sober truth, Africa has yet to liberate herself. The fact that I had never seen the Algerian casbah was of no more relevance before this unanswerable panorama than the fact that the Algerians had never seen Harlem. The Algerian and I were both, alike, victims of this history, and I was still a part of Africa, even though I had been carried out of it nearly four hundred years before.

The question of my identity had never before been so crucially allied with the reality—the doom—of the moral choice. The irreducible inconvenience of the moral choice is that it is, by definition, arbitrary—though it sounds so grandiose—and, on the surface, unreasonable, and has no justification but (or in) itself. My reaction, in the present instance, was unreasonable on its face, not only because of my ignorance of the Arab world, but also because I could not affect their destiny in any degree. And yet, their destiny was somehow tied to mine, their battle was not theirs alone but was my battle also, and it began to be a matter of my honor not to attempt to avoid this loaded fact.

And, furthermore—though this was truer in principle than it was in fact, as I had had occasion to learn—my life in Paris was to some extent protected by the fact that I carried a green passport. This passport proclaimed that I was a free citizen of a free country, and was not, therefore, to be treated as one of Europe's uncivilized, black possessions. This same passport, on the other side of the ocean, underwent a sea change and proclaimed that I was not an African prince, but a domestic nigger and that no foreign government would be offended if my corpse were to be found clogging up the sewers. I had never had occasion to reflect before on the brilliance of the white strategy: blacks didn't know each other, could barely speak to each other, and, therefore, could scarcely trust each other—and therefore, wherever we turned, we found ourselves in the white man's territory, and at the white man's mercy. Four hundred years in the West had certainly turned me into a Westerner—there was no way around that. But four hundred years in the West had also failed to bleach me—there was no way around *that*, either—and my history in the West had, for its daily effect, placed me in such mortal danger that I had fled, all the way around the corner, to France. And if I had fled, to Israel, a state created for the purpose of protecting Western interests, I would have been in yet a tighter bind: on which side of Jerusalem would I have decided to live? In 1948, no African nation, as such, existed, and could certainly neither have needed, nor welcomed, a penniless black American, with the possible exception of Liberia. But, even with black overseers, I would not have lasted long on the Firestone rubber plantation.

I have said that I was almost entirely ignorant of the details of the Algerian-French complexity, but I was endeavoring to correct this ignorance; and one of the ways in which I was going about it compelled me to keep a file of the editorial pronouncements made by M. Albert Camus in the pages of the French political newspaper, *Combat*. Camus had been born in Oran, which is the scene of his first novel, *The Stranger*. He could be described, perhaps, as a radical humanist; he was young, he was lucid, and it was not illogical to assume that he would bring—along with the authority of knowing the land of his birth—some of these qualities to bear on his apprehension of the nature of the French-Algerian conflict.

I have never esteemed this writer as highly as do so many others. I was struck by the fact that, for Camus, the European humanism appeared to expire at the European gates: so that Camus, who was dedicated to liberty, in the case of Europeans, could only speak of "justice" in the case of Algeria. And yet, he must surely have known, must have seen with his own eyes, some of the results of French "justice" in Algeria. ("A legal means," said an African recipient, "of administering injustice.") Given the precepts upon which he based his eloquent discourses concerning the problems of individual liberty, he must have seen that what the battle of Algiers was really about was the fact that the French refused to give the Algerians the right to be wrong; refused to allow them, so to speak, that "existentialist" situation, of which the French, for a season, were so enamored; or, more accurately, did not even dare imagine that the Algerian situation could be "existentialist"; precisely because the French situation was so extreme. There was no way for him not to have known that Algeria was French only insofar as French power had decreed it to be French. It existed on the European map only insofar as European power had placed it there. It is power, not justice, which keeps rearranging the map, and the Algerians were not fighting the French for justice (of which, indeed, they must have had their fill by that time) but for the power to determine their own destinies.

It was during this time that Camus translated and directed, for the Mathurin Theatre, in Paris, William Faulkner's *Requiem for a Nun*, and an American magazine asked me to review it. I would almost certainly not have seen this production otherwise, for I had seen the play in New York, and I had read the book, and had found Faulkner's fable to be a preposterous bore. But I trotted off to the Mathurin Theatre to see it, taking along a gallant lady friend. And we suffered through this odd and interminable account of the sins of a white Southern lady, and her cardboard husband, and the nigger-whore-dope fiend maid, Nancy. Nancy, in order to arrest her mistress's headlong flight to self-destruction—to bring her to her senses—murders the white lady's infant. This may seem an odd way of healing the sick, but Nancy is, in fact, the Christ figure, and has taken her mistress's sins on herself.

Why? Nancy has enough sins of her own, which on the whole would seem to be rather more interesting, and the lady she takes such drastic means of saving is too dull, and much, much too talkative—in a word, too unreal—to warrant such concern.

The key to a tale is to be found in who tells it; and so I thought I could see why Faulkner may have needed to believe in a black forgiveness, furthermore, which, if one stands aside from what Faulkner wishes us to make of it, can scarcely be distinguished from the bloodiest, most classical Old Testament revenge. What Faulkner wishes us to believe, and what he wishes to believe, is at war with what he, fatally, suspects. He suspects that black Nancy may have murdered white Temple's white baby out of pure, exasperated hatred. In life, in any case, it would scarcely matter: Nancy's forgiveness, or Nancy's revenge, result, anyway, in infanticide; and it is this tension between hope and terror, this panic-stricken inability to read the meaning of the event, which condemns the play to an insupportable turgidity. I could see why Faulkner needed Nancy: but why did Camus need Faulkner? On what ground did they meet, the mind of the great, aging, Mississippi novelist, and the mind of the young writer from Oran?

Neither of them could accurately, or usefully, be described as racists, in spite of Faulkner's declared intention of shooting Negroes in the streets if he found this necessary for the salvation of the state of Mississippi. This statement had to be read as an excess of patriotism, unlikely, in Faulkner's case, to lead to any further action. The mischief of the remark lay in the fact that it certainly encouraged others to such action. And Faulkner's portraits of Negroes, which lack a system of nuances that, perhaps, only a black writer can see in black life—for Faulkner could see Negroes only as they related to him, not as they related to each other—are nevertheless made vivid by the torment of their creator. He is seeking to exorcise a history which is also a curse. He wants the old order, which came into existence through unchecked greed and wanton murder, to redeem itself without further bloodshed—without, that is, any further menacing itself—and without coercion. This, old orders never do, less because they would not than because they cannot. They cannot because they have always existed in relation to a force which they have had to subdue. This subjugation is the key to their identity and the triumph and justification of their history, and it is also on this continued subjugation that their material well-being depends. One may see that the history, which is now indivisible from oneself, has been full of errors and excesses; but this is not the same thing as seeing that, for millions of people, this history—oneself—has been nothing but an intolerable yoke, a stinking prison, a shrieking grave. It is not so easy to see that, for millions of people, life itself depends on the speediest possible demolition of this history, even if this means the leveling, or the destruction of its heirs. And whatever this history may have given to the subjugated is of absolutely no value, since they have never been free to reject it; they will never even be able to assess it until they are free to take from it what they need, and to add to history the monumental fact of their presence. The South African coal miner, or the African digging for roots in the bush, or the Algerian mason working in Paris, not only have no reason to bow down before Shakespeare, or Descartes, or Westminster Abbey, or the cathedral at Chartres: they have, once these monuments intrude on their attention, no honorable access to them. Their apprehension of this history cannot fail to reveal to them that they have been robbed, maligned, and rejected: to bow down before that history is to accept that history's arrogant and unjust judgment.

This is why, ultimately, all attempts at dialogue between the subdued and subduer, between those placed within history and those dispersed outside, break down. One may say, indeed, that until this hour such a dialogue has scarcely been attempted: the subdued and the subduer do not speak the same language. What has passed for dialogue has usually involved one of "our" niggers, or, say, an *évolué* from Dakar. The "evolved," or civilized one is almost always someone educated by, and for, France, and some of "our" niggers, proving how well they have been educated, become spokesmen for "black" capitalism—a concept demanding yet more faith and infinitely more in schizophrenia than the concept of the Virgin Birth. Dakar is a French city on the West African coast, and a representative from Dakar is not necessarily a man from Senegal. He is much more likely to be a spiritual citizen of France, in which event he cannot possibly convey the actual needs of his part of Africa, or of Africa. And when such a dialogue truly erupts, it cannot avoid the root question of the possession of the land, and the exploitation of the land's resources. At that point, the cultural pretensions of history are revealed as nothing less than a mask for power, and thus it happens that, in order to be rid of Shell, Texaco, Coca-Cola, the Sixth Fleet, and the friendly American soldier whose mission it is to protect these investments, one finally throws Balzac and Shakespeare—and Faulkner and Camus—out with them. Later, of course, one may welcome them back, but on one's own terms, and, absolutely, on one's own land.

When the pagan and the slave spit on the cross and pick up the gun, it means that the halls of history are about to be invaded once again, destroying and dispersing the present occupants. These, then, can call only on their history to save them—that same history which, in the eyes of the subjugated, has already condemned them. Therefore, Faulkner hoped that American blacks would have the generosity to "go slow"—would allow white people, that is, the time to save themselves, as though they had not had more than enough time already, and as though their victims still believed in white miracles—and Camus repeated the word "justice" as though it were a magical incantation to which all of Africa would immediately respond. American blacks could not "go slow" because they had made a rendezvous with history for the purpose of taking their children out of history's hands. And Camus' "justice" was a concept forged and betrayed in Europe, in exactly the same way as the Christian church has betrayed and dishonored and blasphemed that Saviour in whose name they have slaughtered millions and millions and millions of people. And if this mighty objection seems trivial, it can only be because of the total hardening of the heart and the coarsening of the conscience among those people who believed that their power has given them the exclusive right to history. If the Christians do not believe in their Saviour (who has certainly, furthermore, failed to save them) why, then, wonder the unredeemed, should I abandon my gods for yours? For I *know* my gods are real: they have enabled me to withstand you.

In the fall of 1956, I was covering, for *Encounter* (or for the CIA) the first International Conference of Black Writers and Artists, at the Sorbonne, in Paris. One bright afternoon, several of us, including the late Richard Wright, were meandering up the Boulevard St.-Germain, on the way to lunch. Much, if not most of the group was African, and all of us (though some only legally) were black. Facing us, on every newspaper kiosk on that wide, tree-shaded boulevard, were photographs of fifteen-year-old Dorothy Counts being reviled and spat upon by the mob as she was making her way to school in Charlotte, North Carolina. There was unutterable pride, tension, and anguish in that girl's face as she approached the halls of learning, with history, jeering, at her back.

It made me furious, it filled me with both hatred and pity, and it made me ashamed. Some one of us should have been there with her! I dawdled in Europe for nearly yet another year, held by my private life and my attempt to finish a novel, but it was on that bright afternoon that I knew I was leaving France. I could, simply, no longer sit around in Paris discussing the Algerian and the black American problem. Everybody else was paying their dues, and it was time I went home and paid mine.

I took a boat home in the summer of 1957, intending to go South as soon as I could get the bread together. This meant, in my case, as soon as I could get an assignment. This was not so easy in 1957, and I was stuck in New York for a discouragingly long time. And now I had to begin to arrive at some kind of *modus vivendi* with New York—for here I was, home again, for the first time in nine years—to stay. *To stay:* if this thought chilled me, it also relieved me. It was only here, after all, that I would be able to find out what my journey had meant to me, or what it had made of me.

And I began to see New York in a different way, seeing beneath the formlessness, in the detail of a cornice, the shape of a window, the movement of stone steps—*stoep*, say the Dutch, and we say, *stoop*—beneath the nearly invincible and despairing noise, the sound of many tongues, all struggling for dominance. Since I was here to stay, I had to examine it, learn it all over again, and try to find out if I had ever loved it. But the question contained, or so I suspected, its own melancholy answer. If I had ever loved New York, that love had, literally, been beaten out of me; if I had ever loved it, my life could never have depended on so long an absence and so deep a divorce; or, if I had ever loved it, I would have been glad, not frightened, to be back in my home town. No, I didn't love it, at least not any more, but I was going to have to survive it. In order to survive it, I would have to watch it. And, though I had nightmares about that Southland which I had never seen, I was terribly anxious to get there, perhaps to corroborate the nightmare, but certainly to get out of what was once described to me as "the great unfinished city."

Finally, I got my assignment, and I went South. Something began, for me, tremendous. I met some of the noblest, most beautiful people a man can hope to meet, and I saw some beautiful and some terrible things. I was old enough to recognize how deep and strangling were my fears, how manifold and mighty my limits: but no one can demand more of life than that life do him the honor to demand that he learn to live with his fears, and learn to live, every day, both within his limits and beyond them.

I must add, for the benefit of my so innocent and criminal countrymen, that, today, fifteen years later, the photograph of Angela Davis has replaced the photograph of Dorothy Counts. These two photographs would appear to sum up the will of the Americans—heirs of all the ages—in relation to the blacks.

There comes floating up to me, out of a life I lived long ago—during the cybernetics craze, the Wilhelm Reich misapprehension, the Karen Horney precisions, that time, predating Sartre, when many of my friends vanished into the hills, or into anarchies called communes, or into orgone boxes, never to be seen, and certainly never to make love again—the memory of a young white man, beautiful, Jewish, American, who ate his wife's afterbirth, frying it in a frying pan. He did this because—who knows?—Wilhelm Reich, according to him, had ordered it. He comes floating up to me because, though he never knew it, I loved him, and the silence between us was the precise indication of how deeply something in me responded to, and is still bewildered by, his trouble. I remember his face when he told me about it, long after his courageous culinary effort. By this effort, he made his wife and child a part of himself. The question which has remained in my mind, no doubt, is why so extreme an effort should have been needed to prove a fact which should have been so obvious and so joyous. By the time he told me, he had lost both the wife and the child, was virtually adopting another one, black, this time, and, though he was younger than I, and I am speaking of a long time ago, had, emotionally, it seemed to me, ceased to exist. I got the impression that he had hurried himself through a late and tormented adolescence into an early middle age, with an almost audible sigh of relief, having encountered only theorems along the way: and, though he did not know it, was now helplessly and hopelessly in love with a small black boy, not more than ten. I do not mean to suggest that he had sexual designs on the boy. It might, indeed, have been better for him if he had, however outrageous that may sound—it would, at least, have landed him in deep emotional trouble and brought to the fore the question of his honor: I mean that he appeared to be able to love only the helpless. I have not seen this man in many years, and I hope that everything I say here has since been proven false. I hope, in short, that he has been able to live. But I have always been struck, in America, by an emotional poverty so bottomless, and a terror of human life, of human touch, so deep, that virtually no American appears able to achieve any viable, organic connection between his public stance and his private life. This is what makes them so baffling, so moving, so exasperating, and so untrustworthy. "Only connect," Henry James has said. Perhaps only an American writer would have been driven to say it, his very existence being so threatened by the failure, in most American lives, of the most elementary and crucial connections.

This failure of the private life has always had the most devastating effect on American public conduct, and on black-
white relations. If Americans were not so terrified of their
private selves, they would never have needed to invent and
could never have become so dependent on what they still call
"the Negro problem." This problem, which they invented in
order to safeguard their purity, has made of them criminals
and monsters, and it is destroying them; and this not from
anything blacks may or may not be doing but because of the
role a guilty and constricted white imagination has assigned
to the blacks. That the scapegoat pays for the sins of others
is well known, but this is only legend, and a revealing one at
that. In fact, however the scapegoat may be made to suffer,
his suffering cannot purify the sinner; it merely incriminates
him the more, and it seals his damnation. The scapegoat,
eventually, is released, to death: his murderer continues to live.
The suffering of the scapegoat has resulted in seas of blood,
and yet not one sinner has been saved, or changed, by this
despairing ritual. Sin has merely been added to sin, and guilt
piled upon guilt. In the private chambers of the soul, the
guilty party is identified, and the accusing finger, there, is not
legend, but consequence, not fantasy, but the truth. People
pay for what they do, and, still more, for what they have allowed themselves to become. And they pay for it very simply:
by the lives they lead. The crucial thing, here, is that the sum
of these individual abdications menaces life all over the world.
For, in the generality, as social and moral and political and
sexual entities, white Americans are probably the sickest and
certainly the most dangerous people, of any color, to be found
in the world today. I may not have realized this before my
first journey South. But, once I found myself there, I recognized that the South was a riddle which could be read only
in the light, or the darkness, of the unbelievable disasters
which had overtaken the private life.

I say, "riddle": not the riddle of what this unhappy people
claim, madly enough, as their "folk" ways. I had been a nigger
for a long time. I was not struck by their wickedness, for that
wickedness was but the spirit and the history of America.
What struck me was the unbelievable dimension of their sorrow. I felt as though I had wandered into hell. But, it must

also be said that, if they were in hell, some among them were beginning to recognize what fuel, in themselves, fed the flames. Their sorrow placed them far beyond, exactly, as at that hour, it seemed to have placed them far beneath, their compatriots—who did not yet know that sorrow existed, and who imagined that hell was a condition to which others were sentenced. For this reason, and I am not the only black man who will say this, I have more faith in Southerners than I will ever have in Northerners: the mighty and pious North could never, after all, have acquired its wealth without utilizing, brutally, and consciously, those "folk" ways, and locking the South within them. And when this country's absolutely inescapable disaster levels it, it is in the South and not in the North that the rebirth will begin.

I went, first, if memory serves, to Charlotte, North Carolina, where I met, among others, *The Carolina Israelite.* I went to Little Rock, where I met, among others, Mr. and Mrs. Bates. I went to Atlanta, where I met, among others, Reverend Martin Luther King, Jr. I went to Birmingham. I went to Montgomery. I went to Tuskegee. I don't know how long I was on the road. The canvas suitcase I had carried down was so full of contraband by the time I lugged it, on one shoulder, up, that it burst in the middle of Grand Central Station, scattering underground secrets all over the floor: no one, luckily, exhibited the remotest curiosity. I managed to get it all together, tied the suitcase together with the belt from my trousers, and got up the stairs, into the city. I collapsed in the home of a friend who lived in what was not yet known as the East Village—when I had been a tenant, it was known as the Lower East Side—and, re-living my trip, surrendered to my nightmares, and, as far as the city was concerned, vanished. I could not take it on, I could not move out of that cold-water flat. I kept meaning to, I kept putting it off: for five days. I had called my sister, Gloria, from the station, so she knew that I was back in New York, but she did not know where. Therefore, my family and friends were searching for me in every Village street and bar and were considering the dubious and desperate extreme of calling the police. But, finally, I surfaced, fully conscious of how irresponsible I had been, and more than a little shaken by the realization that it had been a kind of retrospective terror which had paralyzed me so long. While in the South I had suppressed my terror well enough, in any case, to function; but when the pressure came off, a kind of wonder of terror overcame me, making me as useless as a snapped rubber band. This worried me exceedingly. I sensed in it a pattern which I was never, in fact, thoroughly to overcome. I will never forget the weary face of a black friend who had been searching for me for days, meeting me on Sixth Avenue as I was on my repentant way to the subway. He saw me as he turned from Waverly Place onto the avenue at the same time that I saw him. He stood stock-still as I was forced to walk toward him. A small, unwilling smile tugged at the corners of his lips. Then, I was in front of him and Lonnie said, "Well, *I'm* not going to curse you out. You've done it to yourself already." And he bought me a drink, and I went uptown to my sister's house, where I was sleeping on the couch in those days.

In the church, the preacher says, after an apparently meaningless anecdote, "I have said all that to say"—this: I doubt that I really knew much about terror before I went South. I do not mean, merely, though I very well might, that visceral reaction produced by the realization that one is facing one's own death. Then, as now, a Northern policeman, black or white, a white co-worker, or a black one, the colorless walls of precinct basements, the colorless handcuffs, the colorless future, are quite enough to introduce into one's life the stunning realization that that life can be ended at any moment. Furthermore, this terror can produce its own antidote: an overwhelming pride and rage, so that, whether or not one is ready to die, one gives every appearance of being willing to die. And at that moment, in fact, since retreat means accepting a death far worse, one *is* willing to die, hoping merely (God's last small mercy) to drag one's murderer along.

Not many among the redeemed have any sense of this passion, which they describe, without knowing how profoundly they are describing themselves, as suicidal. They mean that it is suicidal to contend with a force obviously, or apparently, greater than oneself and that they would never dream of doing such a thing. They also mean that they, by definition, by their numbers, are the greater force, and they never suspect to what merciless level of contempt this oblique and arrogant confession exposes them. A man who knows that he is facing death, or, more accurately, who knows that it is, after all, he, himself, who has insisted on and brought about this moment, may, involuntarily, helplessly, shout or weep, or even piss or shit in his pants, where he stands. But he will not turn back. To turn back is no longer among his possibilities: that is why he may shout or weep and his stink may then fill the air. He has brought himself to this moment, and this is *he*—if only for a moment—*he*; and the others are beneath him, and anonymous forever because they value their manhood less than he.

But the terror I am speaking of has little to do with one's specific fears for oneself: it relates to Dante's *I would not have believed that death had undone so many.*

I arrived in Little Rock, for example, during the famous—then famous, now all but forgotten—school convulsion. This convulsion, it is to be remembered, had apparently to do with the question of the integration or education of black children—integration and education are not synonyms, though Americans appear to think so. I am a city boy. My life began in the Big City, and had to be slugged out, toe to toe, on the city pavements. This meant that I was badly prepared for an entity like Little Rock, which, while it was certainly not yet a city, was, equally certainly, no longer a town. For that matter, it was not, geographically speaking, Southern. It was Southern only in truth, in terms of what its history had made of it, which is to say, ultimately, that it was Southern by choice. It was Southern, therefore, to put it brutally, because of the history of America—the United States of America: and small black boys and girls were now paying for this holocaust. They were attempting to go to school. They were attempting to get an education, in a country in which education is a synonym for indoctrination, if you are white, and subjugation, if you are black. It was rather as though small Jewish boys and girls, in Hitler's Germany, insisted on getting a German education in order to overthrow the Third Reich. Here they were, nevertheless, scrubbed and shining, in their never-to-be-forgotten stiff little dresses, in their never-to-be-forgotten little blue suits, facing an army, facing a citizenry, facing white fathers, facing white mothers, facing the progeny of these co-citizens, facing the white past, to say nothing of the white present: small soldiers, armed with stiff, white dresses, and long or short dark blue pants, entering a leper colony, and young enough to believe that the colony could be healed, and saved. They paid a dreadful price, those children, for their missionary work among the heathen.

My terror involved my realization of the nature of the heathen. I did not meet any of my official murderers, not during that first journey. I met the Negro's friends. Thus, I was forced to recognize that, so long as your friend thinks of you as a Negro, you do not have a friend, and neither does he— your friend. You have become accomplices. Everything between you depends on what he cannot say to you, and what you will not say to him. And one of you is listening. If one of you is listening, to all those things, precisely, which are not being said, the intensity of this attention can scarcely be described as the attention one friend brings to another. If one of you is listening, both of you are plotting, though, perhaps, only one of you knows it. Both of you may be plotting to escape, but, since very different avenues appear to be open to each of you, you are plotting your escape from each other.

I have written elsewhere about those early days in the South, but from a distance more or less impersonal. I have never, for example, written about my unbelieving shock when I realized that I was being groped by one of the most powerful men in one of the states I visited. He had got himself sweating drunk in order to arrive at this despairing titillation. With his wet eyes staring up at my face, and his wet hands groping for my cock, we were both, abruptly, in history's asspocket. It was very frightening—not the gesture itself, but the abjectness of it, and the assumption of a swift and grim complicity: as my identity was defined by his power, so was my humanity to be placed at the service of his fantasies. If the lives of those children were in those wet, despairing hands, if their future was to be read in those wet, blind eyes, there was reason to tremble. This man, with a phone call, could prevent or provoke a lynching. This was one of the men you called (or had a friend call) in order to get your brother off the prison farm. A phone call from him might prevent your brother from being dug up, later, during some random archaeological expedition. Therefore, one had to be friendly: but the price for this was your cock.

This will sound an exaggerated statement to Americans, who will suppose it to refer, merely, to sexual (or sectional) abnormality. This supposition misses the point: which is double-edged. The slave knows, however his master may be deluded on this point, that he is called a slave because his manhood has been, or can be, or will be taken from him. To be a slave means that one's manhood is engaged in a dubious battle indeed, and this stony fact is not altered by whatever devotion some masters and some slaves may have arrived at in relation to each other. In the case of American slavery, the black man's right to his women, as well as to his children, was simply taken from him, and whatever bastards the white man begat on the bodies of black women took their condition from the condition of their mother: blacks were not the only stallions on the slave-breeding farms! And one of the many results of this loveless, money-making conspiracy was that, in giving the masters every conceivable sexual and commercial license, it also emasculated them of any human responsibility—to their women, to their children, to their wives, or to themselves. The results of this blasphemy resound in this country, on every private and public level, until this hour. When the man grabbed my cock, I didn't think of him as a faggot, which, indeed, if having a wife and children, house, cars, and a respectable and powerful standing in the community, mean anything, he wasn't: I watched his eyes, thinking, with great sorrow, *The unexamined life is not worth living.* The despair among the loveless is that they must narcoticize themselves before they can touch any human being at all. They, then, fatally, touch the wrong person, not merely because they have gone blind, or have lost the sense of touch, but because they no longer have any way of knowing that any loveless touch is a violation, whether one is touching a woman or a man. When the loveless come to power, or when sexual despair comes to power, the sexuality of the object is either a threat or a fantasy. That most men will choose women to debase is not a matter of rejoicing either for the chosen women or anybody else; brutal truth, furthermore, forces the observation, particularly if one is a black man, that this choice is by no means certain.

That men have an enormous need to debase other men—and only because they are *men*—is a truth which history forbids us to labor. And it is absolutely certain that white men, who invented the nigger's big black prick, are still at the mercy of this nightmare, and are still, for the most part, doomed, in one way or another, to attempt to make this prick their own: so much for the progress which the Christian world has made from that jungle in which it is their clear intention to keep black men treed forever.

Every black man walking in this country pays a tremendous price for walking: for men are not women, and a man's balance depends on the weight he carries between his legs. All men, however they may face or fail to face it, however they may handle, or be handled by it, know something about each other, which is simply that a man without balls is not a man; that the word *genesis* describes the male, involves the phallus, and refers to the seed which gives life. When one man can no longer honor this in another man—and this remains true even if that man is his lover—he has abdicated from a man's estate, and, hard upon the heels of that abdication, chaos arrives. It was something like this that I began to see, watching black men in the South and watching white men watching them. For that marvelously mocking, salty authority with which black men walked was dictated by the tacit and shared realization of the price each had paid to be able to walk at all. Their fights came out of that, their laughter came out of that, their curses, their tears, their decisions, their so menaced loves, their courage, and even their cowardice—and perhaps especially the stunning and unexpected changes they could play on these so related strings—their music, their dancing: it all came from the center. "No," said an elderly black man, standing in front of his barber shop, "I don't believe I'll join this voting registration drive. You see, I only cut the white folks' hair in here, and they'll close me up." He was very tall; as he said this, he seemed to be looking up at me, a physical impossibility; he had been bowing so long, my brother said, that his head would never be straight on his neck again. Yet, there he stood, a gnarled old tree, and the authority of his response made it impossible to question his decision: he may have been planning to cut a white man's throat one day. If I had been white, I certainly would never have allowed him anywhere near *me* with a razor in his hand. Most white men, by comparison, seemed to be barely shuffling along, and one always doubted whatever they said, because one realized that they doubted it themselves. As far as personal authority went, one could imagine that their shriveled faces were an exact indication of how matters were with them below the belt. And the women were worse—proof, if proof were needed: nowhere in the world have I encountered women so blighted, and blighted so soon. It began to seem to me, indeed, not entirely frivolously, that the only thing which prevented the South from being an absolutely homosexual community was, precisely, the reverberating absence of men.

One could not be in any Southern community for long and not be confronted with the question of what a man is, should do, or become. The world in which we live is, after all, a reflection of the desires and activities of men. We are responsible for the world in which we find ourselves, if only because we are the only sentient force which can change it. What brought this question to the front of my mind, of course, was the fact that so many of the black men I talked to in the South in those years were—I can find no other word for them— heroic. I don't want to be misunderstood as having fallen into an easy chauvinism when I say that: but I don't see how any observer of the Southern scene in those years can have arrived at any other judgment. Their heroism was to be found less in large things than in small ones, less in public than in private. Some of the men I am thinking of could be very impressive publicly, too, and responsible for large events; but it was not this which impressed me. What impressed me was how they went about their daily tasks, in the teeth of the Southern terror. The first time I saw Reverend Shuttlesworth, for example, he came strolling across the parking lot of the motel where I was staying, his hat perched precariously between the back of his skull and the nape of his neck, alone. It was late at night, and Shuttlesworth was a marked man in Birmingham. He came up into my room, and, while we talked, he kept walking back and forth to the window. I finally realized that he was keeping an eye on his car—making sure that no one put a bomb in it, perhaps. As he said nothing about this, however, naturally I could not. But I was worried about his driving home alone, and, as he was leaving, I could not resist saying something to this effect. And he smiled—smiled as though I were a novice, with much to learn, which was true, and as though he would be glad to give me a few pointers, which, indeed, not much later on, he did—and told me he'd be all right and went downstairs and got into his car, switched on the motor and drove off into the soft Alabama night. There was no hint of defiance or bravado in his manner. Only, when I made my halting observation concerning his safety, a shade of sorrow crossed his face, deep, impatient, dark; then it was gone. It was the most impersonal anguish I had ever seen on a man's face. It was as though he were wrestling with the mighty fact that the danger in which he stood was as nothing compared to the spiritual horror which drove those who were trying to destroy him. They endangered him, but they doomed themselves.

I had never seen this horror, this poverty, before, though I had worked among Southerners, years before, when I was working for the Army, during the war. It was very frightening, disagreeable, and dangerous, but I was not, after all, in their territory—in a sense, or at least as they resentfully supposed, they were in mine. Also, I could, in a sense, protect myself against their depredations and the fear that they inspired in me by considering them, quite honestly, as mad. And I was too young for the idea of my death or destruction really to have taken hold of my mind. It is hard for anyone under twenty to realize that death has already assigned him a number, which is going to come up one day.

But I was not in my territory now. I was in territory absolutely hostile and exceedingly strange, and I was old enough to realize that I could be destroyed. It was lucky, oddly enough, that I had been out of the country for so long and had come South from Paris, in effect, instead of from New York. If I had not come from Paris, I would certainly have attempted to draw on my considerable kit of New York survival tricks, with what results I cannot imagine, for they would certainly not have worked in the South. But I had so far forgotten all my New York tricks as to have been unable to use them in New York, and now I was simply, helplessly, nakedly, an odd kind of foreigner and could only look on the scene that way. And this meant that, exactly like a foreigner, I was more fascinated than frightened.

There was more than enough to fascinate. In the Deep South—Florida, Georgia, Alabama, Mississippi, for example—there is the great, vast, brooding, welcoming and blood-stained land, beautiful enough to astonish and break the heart. The land seems nearly to weep beneath the burden of this civilization's unnameable excrescences. The people and the children wander blindly through their forest of billboards, antennae, Coca-Cola bottles, gas stations, drive-ins, motels, beer cans, music of a strident and invincible melancholy, stilted wooden porches, snapping fans, aggressively blue-jeaned buttocks, strutting crotches, pint bottles, condoms, in the weeds, rotting automobile corpses, brown as beetles, earrings flashing in the gloom of bus stops: over all there seems to hang a miasma of lust and longing and rage. Every Southern city seemed to me to have been but lately rescued from the swamps, which were patiently waiting to reclaim it. The people all seemed to remember their time under water, and to be both dreading and anticipating their return to that freedom from responsibility. Every black man, whatever his style, had been scarred, as in some tribal rite; and every white man, though white men, mostly, had no style, had been maimed. And, everywhere, the women, the most fearfully mistreated creatures of this region, with narrowed eyes and pursed lips—lips turned inward on a foul aftertaste—watched and rocked and waited. Some of them reminded me of a moment in my adolescent life when a church sister, not much older than I, who had been my girl friend, went mad, and was incarcerated. I went to visit her, in the women's wing of the asylum, and, coming out into the courtyard, stood there for a moment to catch my breath. Something, eventually, made me turn my head. Then I realized that I was standing in the sight of hundreds of incarcerated women. Behind those bars and windows, I don't know how many pairs of female eyes were riveted on the one male in that courtyard. I could dimly see their faces at the windows all up and down that wall; and they did not make a sound. For a moment I thought that I would never be able to persuade my feet to carry me away from that unspeakable, despairing, captive avidity.

My first night in Montgomery, I, like a good reporter, decided to investigate the town a little. I had been warned to be very careful how I moved about in the South after dark—indeed, I had been told not to move at all; but it was a pleasant evening, night just beginning to fall: suppertime. I walked a ways, past dark porches which were mostly silent, yet one felt a presence, or presences, sitting deep in the dark, sometimes silhouetted—but rarely—in the light from an open door, or one saw the ember of a cigarette, or heard a child's voice. It was very peaceful, and, though it may sound odd, I was very glad that I had come South. In spite of all that could have divided us, and in spite of the fact that some of them looked on me with an inevitable suspicion, I felt very much at home among the dark people who lived where I, if so much had not been disrupted, would logically have been born. I felt, beneath everything, a profound acceptance, an unfamiliar peace, almost as though, after despairing and debilitating journeys, I had, at last, come home. If there was, in this, some illusion, there was also some truth. In the years in Paris, I had never been homesick for anything American—neither waffles, ice cream, hot dogs, baseball, majorettes, movies, nor the Empire State Building, nor Coney Island, nor the Statue of Liberty, nor the *Daily News*, nor Times Square. All of these things had passed out of me as naturally and simply as taking a leak, and even less self-consciously. They might never have existed for me, and it made absolutely no difference to me if I never saw them again. But I had missed my brothers and my sisters, and my mother—*they* made a difference. I wanted to be able to see them, and to see their children. I hoped that they wouldn't forget me. I missed Harlem Sunday mornings and fried chicken and biscuits, I missed the music, I missed the style—that style possessed by no other people in this world. I missed the way the dark face closes, the way dark eyes watch, and the way, when a dark face opens, a light seems to go on everywhere. I missed my brothers especially—missed David's grin and George's solemnity and Wilmer's rages, missed, in short, my connections, missed the life which had produced me and nourished me and paid for me. Now, though I was a stranger, I was home.

The racial dividing lines of Southern towns are baffling and treacherous for a stranger, for they are not as clearly marked as in the North—or not as clearly marked for *him*. I passed a porch with dark people; on the corner about a block away there was a restaurant. When I reached the corner, I entered the restaurant.

I will never forget it. I don't know if I can describe it. Everything abruptly froze into what, even at that moment, struck me as a kind of Marx Brothers parody of horror. Every white face turned to stone: the arrival of the messenger of death could not have had a more devastating effect than the appearance in the restaurant doorway of a small, unarmed, utterly astounded black man. I had realized my error as soon as I opened the door: but the absolute terror on all these white faces—I swear that not a soul moved—paralyzed me. They stared at me, I stared at them.

The spell was broken by one of those women, produced, I hope, only in the South, with a face like a rusty hatchet, and eyes like two rusty nails—nails left over from the Crucifixion. She rushed at me as though to club me down, and she barked—for it was not a human sound: "What you want, boy? What you want in here?" And then, a decontaminating gesture, "Right around there, boy. Right around there."

I had no idea what she was talking about. I backed out the door.

"Right around there, boy," said a voice behind me.

A white man had appeared out of nowhere, on the sidewalk which had been empty not more than a second before. I stared at him blankly. He watched me steadily, with a kind of suspended menace.

My first shock had subsided. I really had not had time to feel either fear or anger. Now, both began to rise in me. I knew I had to get off this street.

He had pointed to a door, and I knew immediately that he was pointing to the colored entrance.

And this was a dreadful moment—as brief as lightning, and far more illuminating. I realized that this man thought that he was being kind; and he was, indeed, being as kind as can be expected from a guide in hell. I realized that I must not speak to him, must not involve myself with him in any way whatever. I wasn't hungry anymore, but I certainly couldn't say *that*. Not only because this would have forced both of us to go further, into what confrontation I dared not think, but because of my Northern accent. It was the first time I realized that this accent was going to be a very definite liability; since I certainly couldn't change it, I was going to have to find some way of turning it into some kind of asset. But not at this very flaming moment, on this dark and empty street.

I saved my honor, hopefully, by reflecting, *Well, this is what you came here for. Hit it*—and I tore my eyes from his face and walked through the door he had so kindly pointed out.

I found myself in a small cubicle, with one electric light, and a counter, with, perhaps, four or five stools. On one side of the cubicle was a window. This window more closely resembled a cage-wire mesh, and an opening in the mesh. I was, now, in the back of the restaurant, though no one in the restaurant could see me. I was behind the restaurant counter, behind the hatchet-faced woman, who had her back to me, serving the white customers at the counter. I was nearly close enough to touch them, certainly close enough to touch her, close enough to kill them all, but they couldn't see me, either.

Hatchet-Face now turned to me, and said, "What you want?" This time, she did not say, "boy": it was no longer necessary.

I told her I wanted a hamburger and a cup of coffee, which I didn't; but I wanted to see how those on my side of the mesh were served; and I wondered if she had to wash her hands each time, before she served the white folks again. Possibly not: for the hamburger came in paper, and the coffee in a paper cup.

I had all I could do to be silent as I paid her, and she turned away. I sat down on one of the stools, and a black man came in, grunted a greeting to me, went to the window, ordered, paid, sat down, and began to eat. I sat there for a while, thinking that I'd certainly asked for one hell of a gig. I wasn't sorry I'd come—I was never, in fact, ever to be sorry about that, and, until the day I die, I will always consider myself among the greatly privileged because, however inadequately, I was there. But I could see that the difficulties were not going to be where I had confidently placed them—in others—but in me. I was far from certain that I was equipped to get through a single day down here, and if I could not so equip myself then I would be a menace to all that others were trying to do, and a betrayal of their vast travail. They had been undergoing and overcoming for a very long time without me, after all, and they hadn't asked me to come: my role was to do a story and avoid becoming one. I watched the patient man as he ate, watched him with both wonder and respect. If he could do that, then the people on the other side of the mesh were right to be frightened—if he could do that, he could do anything and when he walked through the mesh there would be nothing to stop him. But *I* couldn't do it yet; my stomach was as tight as a black rubber ball. I took my hamburger and walked outside and dropped it into the weeds. The dark silence of the streets now frightened me a little, and I walked back to my hotel.

My hotel was a very funky black joint, so poverty stricken and for so long, that no one had anything to hide, or lose—not that they had stopped trying: they failed in the first endeavor as monotonously as they succeeded in the second. Life still held out the hope of what Americans, helplessly and honestly enough, call a "killing" and what blacks, revealingly enough, call a "hit." There seemed to be music all the time, someone was dancing all the time. It would have seemed, from a casual view, that this hotel was the gathering place for all the dregs of the town and that was true enough. But, since these dregs included the entire black society, it was a very various and revealing truth. Lodging for transient blacks, or entertainment for the locals, is a severely circumscribed matter in the Deep South, so that, for example, if one is not staying with friends or relatives, one stays in a hotel like mine, or, if one's friends or relatives decide to buy you a drink, they will bring you to the bar of this hotel. I liked it very much. I liked watching staid Baptist ministers and their plump, starched wives seated but a table away from the town's loose and fallen ladies and their unstarched men. I thought it healthy, because it reduced the possibilities of self-delusion—especially in those years. The Man had everybody in the same bag, and for the same reason, no matter what kind of suit he was wearing, or what kind of car he drove. And the people treated each other, it seemed to me, with rather more respect than was typical of New York, where, of course, the opportunities for self-delusion were, comparatively, so much greater.

Where whiskey was against the law, you simply bought your whiskey from the law enforcers. I did it, many times, all over the South, at first simply to find out if what I had been told was true—to see it with my own eyes and to pay the man with my own hands—and then, later, because life on the road began to run me ragged. It was almost impossible to get anything but bourbon, and the very smell of bourbon is still associated in my mind with the mean little eyes of deputy sheriffs and the holster on the hip and the ominous trees which line the highways. Nor can you get a meal anywhere in the South without being confronted with "grits"; a pale, lumpy, tasteless kind of porridge which the Southerner insists is a delicacy but which I believe they ingest as punishment for their sins. "What? you don't want no grits?" asks the wide-eyed waitress; not hostile yet, merely baffled. She moves away and spreads the word all over the region: "You see that man there? Well, he don't *eat* no grits"—and you are, suddenly, a marked man.

It is not difficult to become a marked man in the South—all you have to do, in fact, is go there. The Montgomery airport, for example, was, in those years, a brave little shack, set down, defiantly, in limbo. It was being guarded, on the morning of my first arrival, by three more or less senior citizens, metallic of color and decidedly sparing of speech. I was the only thing, of any color, to descend from that plane that morning, and they stood at the gate and watched me as I crossed the field. I was carrying my typewriter, which suddenly seemed very heavy. I was frightened. The way they watched me frightened me. Their silence frightened me. Martin Luther King, Jr., had promised to have a car meet me at the airport. There was no car in sight, but I had the phone number of the Montgomery Improvement Association—if I could find a phone, if I could get past the men at the wire. It was eerie and instructive to realize that, though these were human beings like myself, I could not expect them to respond to any human request from me. There was nothing but space behind me, and those three men before me: I could do nothing but walk toward them. Three grown men: and what was the point of this pathetic, boys-together, John Wayne stance? Here I was, after all, having got on a plane with the intention of coming here. The plane had landed and here I was—and what did they suppose they could do about it now? short, of course, of murdering every black passenger who arrived, or bombing the airport. But these alternatives, however delectable, could not lightly be undertaken. I walked past them and into the first phone booth I saw, not checking to see, and not caring whether I had entered the white or the black waiting room. I had resolved to avoid incidents, if possible, but it was already clear that it wouldn't always be possible. By the time I got my number, they watching me all the while, the MIA car drove up. And if the eyes of those men had had the power to pulverize that car, it would have been done, exactly as, in the Bible, the wicked city is leveled—I had never in all my life seen such a concentrated, malevolent poverty of spirit.

The Montgomery blacks were marching then, remember, and were in the process of bringing the bus company to its knees. What had begun in Montgomery was beginning to happen all over the South. The student sit-in movement has yet to begin. No one has yet heard of James Foreman or James Bevel. We have only begun to hear of Martin Luther King, Jr. Malcolm X has yet to be taken seriously. No one, except their parents, has ever heard of Huey Newton or Bobby Seale or Angela Davis. Emmett Till had been dead two years. Bobby Hutton and Jonathan Jackson have just mastered their first words, and, with someone holding them by the hand, are discovering how much fun it is to climb up and down the stairs. Oh, pioneers!—I got into the car, and we drove into town: the cradle of the Confederacy, the whitest town this side of Casablanca, and one of the most wretched on the face of the earth. And wretched because no one in authority in the town, the state, or the nation, had the force or the courage or the love to attempt to correct the manners or redeem the souls of those three desperate men, standing before that dismal airport, imagining that they were holding back a flood.

But how can I suggest any of the quality of some of those

black men and women in the South then?—for it is important that I try. I can't name the names; sometimes because I can't remember them, or never knew them; and sometimes for other reasons. They were, the men, mostly preachers, or small tradesmen—this last word describes, or must be taken to suggest, a multitude of indescribable efforts—or professionals, such as teachers, or dentists, or lawyers. Because the South is, or certainly was then, so closed a community, their colors struck the light—the eye—far more vividly than these same colors strike one in the North: the prohibition, precisely, of the social mingling revealed the extent of the sexual amalgamation. Girls the color of honey, men nearly the color of chalk, hair like silk, hair like cotton, hair like wire, eyes blue, grey, green, hazel, black, like the gypsy's, brown like the Arab's, narrow nostrils, thin, wide lips, thin lips, every conceivable variation struck along incredible gamuts—it was not in the Southland that one could hope to keep a secret! And the niggers, of course, didn't try, though they knew their white brothers and sisters and papas, and watched them, daily, strutting around in their white skins. And sometimes shoveled garbage for their kith and kin, and sometimes went, hat in hand, looking for a job, or on more desperate errands. But: they could do it, knowing what they knew. And white men couldn't bear it—knowing that they knew: it is not only in the Orient that white is the color of death.

I remember the Reverend S., for example, a small, pale man, with hair resembling charred popcorn, and his tiny church, in a tiny town, where every black man was owned by a white man. In democratic parlance, of course, one says that every black man *worked* for a white man, and the democratic myth wishes us to believe that they worked together as men, and respected and honored and loved each other as men. But the democratic circumlocution pretends a level of liberty which does not exist and cannot exist until slavery in America comes to an end: in those towns, in those days, to speak only of the towns, and only of those days, a black man who displeased his employers was not going to eat for very long, which meant that neither he, nor his wife, nor children, were intended to live for very long. Yet, here he was, the Reverend S., every Sunday, in his pulpit, with his wife and children in the church, and bullet holes in the church basement, urging the people to move, to march, and to vote. For we believed, in those days, or made ourselves believe, that the black move to the registrar's office would be protected from Washington. I remember a Reverend D., who was also a grocer, and the night he described to me his conversion to nonviolence. A black grocer in the Deep South must also, like all grocers everywhere, purchase somewhere, somehow, the beans he places on his shelves to sell. This means that a black grocer who is one of the guiding spirits of a voting registration drive and who is also, virtually, a one-man car pool, can find remaining in business, to say nothing of his skin, an exceedingly strenuous matter. This was a big, cheerful man, as strong as an ox and stubborn as a mule, a fly not destined for the fly-paper, and he stayed in business. It cost him something. Bombing was not yet the great Southern sport which it was to become: they simply hurled bricks through his windows. He armed himself and his sons and they sat in the dark store night after night, waiting for their co-citizens—who, knowing they were armed, did not appear. And then, one morning, after the long night, the Reverend D. decided that this was no way for a man or a woman or a child to live. He may, of course, by this time, have been forced to change his mind again, but he was the first person to make the concept of nonviolence real to me: for it entered, then, precisely, the realm of individual and, above all, private choice and I saw, for the first time, how difficult a choice it could be.

To Be Baptized

I told Jesus it would be all right
If He changed my name.
—TRADITIONAL

ALL OF the Western nations have been caught in a lie, the lie of their pretended humanism; this means that their history has no moral justification, and that the West has no moral authority. Malcolm, yet more concretely than Frantz Fanon—since Malcolm operated in the Afro-American idiom, and referred to the Afro-American situation—made the nature of this lie, and its implications, relevant and articulate to the people whom he served. He made increasingly articulate the ways in which this lie, given the history and the power of the Western nations, had become a global problem, menacing the lives of millions. "Vile as I am," states one of the characters in Dostoevski's *The Idiot*, "I don't believe in the wagons that bring bread to humanity. For the wagons that bring bread to humanity, without any moral basis for conduct, may coldly exclude a considerable part of humanity from enjoying what is brought; so it has been already." Indeed. And so it is now. Dostoevski's personage was speaking of the impending proliferation of railways, and the then prevalent optimism (which was perfectly natural) as to the uplifting effect this conquest of distance would have on the life of man. But Dostoevski saw that the rise of this power would "coldly exclude a considerable part of humanity." Indeed, it was on this exclusion that the rise of this power inexorably depended; and now the excluded—"so it has been already"—whose lands have been robbed of the minerals, for example, which go into the building of railways and telegraph wires and TV sets and jet airliners and guns and bombs and fleets, must attempt, at exorbitant cost, to buy their manufactured resources back— which is not even remotely possible, since they must attempt this purchase with money borrowed from their exploiters. If they attempt to work out their salvation—their autonomy— on terms dictated by those who have excluded them, they are in a delicate and dangerous position, and if they refuse, they are in a desperate one: it is hard to know which case is worse. In both cases, they are confronted with the relentless necessities of human life, and the rigors of human nature. Anyone, for example, who has worked in, or witnessed, any of the "anti-poverty" programs in the American ghetto has an instant understanding of "foreign aid" in the "underdeveloped" nations. In both locales, the most skillful adventurers improve their material lot; the most dedicated of the natives are driven mad or inactive—or underground—by frustration; while the misery of the hapless, voiceless millions is increased—and not only that: their reaction to their misery is described to the world as criminal. Nowhere is this grisly pattern clearer than it is in America today, but what America is doing within her borders, she is doing around the world. One has only to remember that American investments cannot be considered safe wherever the population cannot be considered tractable; with this in mind, consider the American reaction to the Jew who boasts of sending arms to Israel, and the probable fate of an American black who wishes to stage a rally for the purpose of sending arms to black South Africa.

America proves, certainly, if any nation ever has, that man cannot live by bread alone; on the other hand, men can scarcely begin to react to this principle until they—and, still more, their children—have enough bread to eat. Hunger has no principles, it simply makes men, at worst, wretched, and, at best, dangerous. Also, it must be remembered—it cannot be overstated—that those centuries of oppression are also the history of a system of thought, so that both the ex-man who considers himself master and the ex-man who is treated like a mule suffer from a particular species of schizophrenia, in which each contains the other, in which each longs to be the other: "What connects a slave to his master," observes David Caute, in his novel, *The Decline of the West*, "is more tragic than that which separates them."

It is true that political freedom is a matter of power and has nothing to do with morality; and if one had ever hoped to find a way around this principle, the performance of power at bay, which is the situation of the Western nations, and the very definition of the American crisis, has dashed this hope to pieces. Moreover, as habits of thought reinforce and sustain the habits of power, it is not even remotely possible for the excluded to become included, for this inclusion means, precisely, the end of the *status quo*—or would result, as so many of the wise and honored would put it, in a mongrelization of the races.

But for power truly to feel itself menaced, it must somehow sense itself in the presence of another power—or, more accurately, an energy—which it has not known how to define and therefore does not really know how to control. For a very long time, for example, America prospered—or seemed to prosper: this prosperity cost millions of people their lives. Now, not even the people who are the most spectacular recipients of the benefits of this prosperity are able to endure these benefits: they can neither understand them nor do without them, nor can they go beyond them. Above all, they cannot, or dare not, assess or imagine the price paid by their victims, or subjects, for this way of life, and so they cannot afford to know why the victims are revolting. They are forced, then, to the conclusion that the victims—the barbarians—are revolting against all established civilized values—which is both true and not true—and, in order to preserve these values, however stifling and joyless these values have caused their lives to be, the bulk of the people desperately seek out representatives who are prepared to make up in cruelty what both they and the people lack in conviction.

This is a formula for a nation's or a kingdom's decline, for no kingdom can maintain itself by force alone. Force does not work the way its advocates seem to think it does. It does not, for example, reveal to the victim the strength of his adversary. On the contrary, it reveals the weakness, even the panic of his adversary, and this revelation invests the victim with patience. Furthermore, it is ultimately fatal to create too many victims. The victor can do nothing with these victims, for they do not belong to him, but—to the victims. They belong to the people he is fighting. The people know this, and as inexorably as the roll call—the honor roll—of victims expands, so does their will become inexorable: they resolve that these dead, their brethren, shall not have died in vain. When this point is reached, however long the battle may go on, the victor can never be the victor: on the contrary, all his energies, his entire life, are bound up in a terror he cannot articulate, a mystery he cannot read, a battle he cannot win—he has simply become the prisoner of the people he thought to cow, chain, or murder into submission.

Power, then, which can have no morality in itself, is yet dependent on human energy, on the wills and desires of human beings. When power translates itself into tyranny, it means that the principles on which that power depended, and which were its justification, are bankrupt. When this happens, and it is happening now, power can only be defended by thugs and mediocrities—and seas of blood. The representatives of the *status quo* are sickened and divided, and dread looking into the eyes of their young; while the excluded begin to realize, having endured everything, that they *can* endure everything. They do not know the precise shape of the future, but they know that the future belongs to them. They realize this— paradoxically—by the failure of the moral energy of their oppressors and begin, almost instinctively, to forge a new morality, to create the principles on which a new world will be built.

My sister, Paula, and my brother, David, and I lived together in London for a while in 1968. London was very peaceful, partly because we hardly ever went out. The house was big, so that we were not on top of each other, and all of us could cook. Besides, going out was hazardous. London was reacting to its accelerating racial problem and compounding the disaster by denying that it had one. My famous face created a certain kind of hazard—or hazards: for example, I remember a girl sitting next to me in a cinema suddenly *seeing* me in the light from the match with which she was lighting her cigarette. She stared and shook—I could not tell whether she was about to cry *Rape!* or ask for an autograph. In the event, she moved away. My dusky tribe had the same troubles, without the tremendous pause.

Nevertheless, London was still far from being as hysterical and dangerous as New York. Eventually, of course, black Englishmen, Indians, students, conscientious objectors, and CIA infiltrators—no doubt—tracked me down, as we had known was inevitable. Dick Gregory came to town and we shared a platform before part of London's black community. A British columnist told his readers before or during this time that he wished I would either "drop dead or shut up"; and on King's Road, near our house, British hippies paraded one day, carrying banners, one of which read, "Keep Britain Black." I felt myself in London on borrowed time, for sometime before, the Home Office, as I learned when I landed at Heathrow Airport, had declared me *persona non grata* in Britain. They had let me land, finally, but it took awhile. (They had thrown Stokely out about a week before.) I thought of the late Lorraine Hansberry's statement (to me) concerning the solidarity of the Western powers, and the impossibility, for such as we, of hoping for political asylum anywhere in the West. I thought of Robert Williams, who had not intended and almost surely never desired, to go East. And I thought of Malcolm.

Alex Haley wrote *The Autobiography of Malcolm X*. Months before the foregoing, in New York, he and Elia Kazan and I had agreed to do it as a play—and I still wish we had. We were vaguely aware that Hollywood was nibbling for a book, but, as Hollywood is always nibbling, it occurred to no one, certainly not to me, to take these nibbles seriously. It simply was not a subject which Hollywood could manage, and I didn't see any point in talking to them about it. But the book was sold to an independent producer, named Marvin Worth, who would produce it for Columbia Pictures. By this time, I was already in London; and I was also on the spot. For, while I didn't believe Hollywood could do it, I didn't quite see, since they declared themselves sincerely and seriously willing to attempt it, how I could duck the challenge. What it came to, in fact, was an enormous question: to what extent was I prepared again to gamble on the good faith of my countrymen?

In that time, now so incredibly far behind us, when the Black Muslims meant to the American people exactly what the Black Panthers mean today, and when they were described in exactly the same terms by that High Priest, J. Edgar Hoover, and when many of us believed or made ourselves believe that the American state still contained within itself the power of self-confrontation, the power to change itself in the direction of honor and knowledge and freedom, or, as Malcolm put it, "to atone," I first met Malcolm X. Perhaps it says a great deal about the black American experience, both negatively and positively, that so many should have believed so hard, so long, and paid such a price for believing: but what this betrayed belief says about white Americans is very accurately and abjectly summed up by the present, so-called Nixon Administration.

I had heard a great deal about Malcolm, as had everyone else, and I was a little afraid of him, as was everyone else, and I was further handicapped by having been out of the country for so long. When I returned to America, I again went South, and thus, imperceptibly, found myself mainly on the road. I saw Malcolm before I met him. I had just returned from someplace like Savannah, I was giving a lecture somewhere in New York, and Malcolm was sitting in the first or second row of the hall, bending forward at such an angle that his long arms nearly caressed the ankles of his long legs, staring up at me. I very nearly panicked. I knew Malcolm only by legend, and this legend, since I was a Harlem street boy, I was sufficiently astute to distrust. I distrusted the legend because we, in Harlem, have been betrayed so often. Malcolm might be the torch white people claimed he was—though, in general, white America's evaluations of these matters would be laughable and even pathetic did not these evaluations have such wicked results—or he might be the hustler I remembered from my pavements. On the other hand, Malcolm had no reason to trust me, either—and so I stumbled through my lecture, with Malcolm never taking his eyes from my face.

It must be remembered that in those great days I was considered to be an "integrationist"—this was never, quite, my own idea of myself—and Malcolm was considered to be a "racist in reverse." This formulation, in terms of power—and power is the arena in which racism is acted out—means absolutely nothing: it may even be described as a cowardly formulation. The powerless, by definition, can never be "racists," for they can never make the world pay for what they feel or fear except by the suicidal endeavor which makes them fanatics or revolutionaries, or both; whereas, those in power can be urbane and charming and invite you to those homes which they know you will never own. The powerless must do their own dirty work. The powerful have it done for them.

Anyway: somewhat later, I was the host, or moderator, for a radio program starring Malcolm X and a sit-in student from the Deep South. I was the moderator because both the radio station and I were afraid that Malcolm would simply eat the boy alive. I didn't want to be there, but there was no way out of it. I had come prepared to throw various camp stools under the child, should he seem wobbly; to throw out the life-line whenever Malcolm should seem to be carrying the child beyond his depth. Never has a moderator been less needed. Malcolm understood that child and talked to him as though he were talking to a younger brother, and with that same watchful attention. What most struck me was that he was not at all trying to proselytize the child: he was trying to make him think. He was trying to do for the child what he supposed, for too long a time, that the Honorable Elijah had done for him. But I did not think of that until much later. I will never forget Malcolm and that child facing each other, and Malcolm's extraordinary gentleness. And that's the truth about Malcolm: he was one of the gentlest people I have ever met. And I am sure that the child remembers him that way. That boy, by the way, battling so valiantly for civil rights, might have been, for all I can swear to, Stokely Carmichael or Huey Newton or Bobby Seale or Rap Brown or one of my nephews. That's how long or how short—*oh, pioneers!*—the apprehension of betrayal takes: "If you are an American citizen," Malcolm asked the boy, "why have you got to fight for your rights as a citizen? To be a citizen means that you have the rights of a citizen. If you haven't got the rights of a citizen, then you're not a citizen." "It's not as simple as that," the boy said. "Why not?" asked Malcolm.

I was, in some way, in those years, without entirely realizing it, the Great Black Hope of the Great White Father. I was *not* a racist—so I thought; Malcolm *was* a racist, so *he* thought. In fact, we were simply trapped in the same situation, as poor Martin was later to discover (who, in those days, did not talk to Malcolm and was a little nervous with me). As the GBH of the GWF, anyway, I appeared on a television program, along with Malcolm and several other hopes, including Mr. George S. Schuyler. It was pretty awful. If I had ever hoped to become a racist, Mr. Schuyler dashed my hopes forever, then and there. I can scarcely discuss this program except to say that Malcolm and I very quickly dismissed Mr. Schuyler and virtually everyone else, and, as the old street rats and the heirs of Baptist ministers, played the program off each other.

Nothing could have been more familiar to me than Malcolm's style in debate. I had heard it all my life. It was vehemently non-stop and Malcolm was young and looked younger; this caused his opponents to suppose that Malcolm was reckless. Nothing could have been less reckless, more calculated, even to those loopholes he so often left dangling. These were not loopholes at all, but hangman's knots, as whoever rushed for the loophole immediately discovered. Whenever this happened, the strangling interlocutor invariably looked to me, as being the more "reasonable," to say something which would loosen the knot. Mr. Schuyler often *did* say something, but it was always the wrong thing, giving Malcolm yet another opportunity. All I could do was elaborate on some of Malcolm's points, or modify, or emphasize, or seem to try to clarify, but there was no way I could disagree with him. The others were discussing the past or the future, or a country which may once have existed, or one which may yet be brought into existence—Malcolm was speaking of the bitter and unanswerable present. And it was too important that this be heard for anyone to attempt to soften it. It was important, of course, for white people to hear it, if they were still able to hear; but it was of the utmost importance for black people to hear it, for the sake of their morale. It was important for them to know that there was someone like them, in public life, telling the truth about their condition. Malcolm considered himself to be the spiritual property of the people who produced him. He did not consider himself to be their saviour, he was far too modest for that, and gave that role to another; but he considered himself to be their servant and in order not to betray that trust, he was willing to die, and died. Malcolm was not a racist, not even when he thought he was. His intelligence was more complex than that; furthermore, if he had been a racist, not many in this racist country would have considered him dangerous. He would have sounded familiar and even comforting, his familiar rage confirming the reality of white power and sensuously inflaming a bizarre species of guilty eroticism without which, I am beginning to believe, most white Americans of the more or less liberal persuasion cannot draw a single breath. What made him unfamiliar and dangerous was not his hatred for white people but his love for blacks, his apprehension of the horror of the black condition, and the reasons for it, and his determination so to work on their hearts and minds that they would be enabled to see their condition and change it themselves.

For this, after all, not only were no white people needed; they posed, *en bloc*, the very greatest obstacle to black self-knowledge and had to be considered a menace. But white people have played so dominant a role in the world's history for so long that such an attitude toward them constitutes the most disagreeable of novelties; and it may be added that, though they have never learned how to live with the darker brother, they do not look forward to having to learn how to live without him. Malcolm, finally, was a genuine revolutionary, a virile impulse long since fled from the American way of life—in himself, indeed, he was a kind of revolution, both in the sense of a return to a former principle, and in the sense of an upheaval. It is pointless to speculate on his probable fate had he been legally white. Given the white man's options, it is probably just as well for all of us that he was legally black. In some church someday, so far unimagined and unimaginable, he will be hailed as a saint. Of course, this day waits on the workings of the temporal power which Malcolm understood, at last, so well. Rome, for example, has just desanctified some saints and invented, if one dares to use so utilitarian a word in relation to so divine an activity, others, and the Pope has been to Africa, driven there, no doubt, however belatedly, by his concern for the souls of black folk: who dares imagine the future of such a litany as *black like me*! Malcolm, anyway, had this much in common with all real saints and prophets, he had the power, if not to drive the money-changers from the temple, to tell the world what they were doing there.

For reasons I will never understand, on the day that I realized that a play based on *The Autobiography* was not going to be done, that sooner or later I would have to say yes or no to the idea of doing a movie, I flew to Geneva. I will never know why I flew to Geneva, which is far from being my favorite town. I will never know how it is that I arrived there with no toilet articles whatever, no toothbrush, no toothpaste, no razor, no hairbrush, no comb, and virtually no clothes. Furthermore, I have a brother-in-law and a sister-in-law living in Geneva of whom I'm very fond and it didn't even occur to me that they were there. All that I seem to have brought with me is *The Autobiography*. And I sat in the hotel bedroom all the weekend long, with the blinds drawn, reading and re-reading—or, rather, endlessly traversing—the great jungle of Malcolm's book.

The problems involved in a cinematic translation were clearly going to be formidable, and wisdom very strongly urged that I have nothing to do with it. It could not possibly bring me anything but grief. I still would have much preferred to have done it as a play, but that possibility was gone. I had grave doubts and fears about Hollywood. I had been there before, and I had not liked it. The idea of Hollywood doing a truthful job on Malcolm could not but seem preposterous. And yet—I didn't want to spend the rest of my life thinking: *It could have been done if you hadn't been chicken.* I felt that Malcolm would never have forgiven me for that. He had trusted me in life and I believed he trusted me in death, and that trust, as far as I was concerned, was my obligation.

From Geneva, I eventually went to London, to join my brother and sister. It was from London that I wired Kazan to say that the play was off, and I was doing the movie. This was only to take K. off the hook, for I wired no one else, had made no agreement to do the movie, and was very troubled and uncertain in my own mind.

Sometime during all this, through William Styron, I learned that a friend of mine, black, was in prison in Hamburg, Germany, charged with murder. This was William A. (Tony) Maynard, Jr., who had worked for me for some time, several years before, as bodyguard and chauffeur and man Friday. He had been arrested by Interpol and was being held in a Hamburg prison, from which he would probably be extradited to the

States. The murder had been committed in New York's Greenwich Village in April of 1967. Tony knew Bill Styron because he had often driven me to Bill's house in Connecticut, and his letter to Bill, since he knew Bill to be rather more stationary than I, was a way of alerting me, and any other friends he had outside, of his desperate situation.

I did not doubt his innocence. Tony is a big man and can be very loud, is far from discreet, and has done his share of street fighting: but it is hard to imagine him killing anybody, especially, as was claimed, with a sawed-off shotgun. No one who knows Tony can believe that he would ever so lower himself as to be seen with so inelegant a weapon. For he has, in fact, a kind of pantherlike, street-boy elegance—he walks something like a cat—and a tricky, touchy, dangerous pride, which, in the years we worked together, kept him in all kinds of fruitless trouble; and he had a taste for white women (who had a taste for him) which made him, especially given his aggressively virile good looks, particularly unattractive to the NYPD. I had not seen Tony in some years. We had worked together in civil rights demonstrations and rallies, but, after the bombing of the Birmingham Sunday school—a much underrated event in this country's shameful history, and one which had a devastating effect on all black people—we had had a serious disagreement concerning the strategy needed to handle a rent strike, and had, thereafter, gone our separate ways. But I still considered him a friend. I wrote to him and I flew from London to Hamburg to visit him.

That winter, the beginning of 1968, London was cold, but damp and grey. Hamburg was frosty and dry as a bone, and blinding with ice and snow; and the sun, which never came to London, loitered in Hamburg all day long: *über alles*. Germans say that Hamburg is the German city which most resembles London. It is hard to know, from their tone, whether they are bragging or complaining, and it did not really remind me of London, lacking London's impressive sprawl; yet, it did confirm my ancient sense of the British and the Germans as cousins. Hamburg looks like a city built only for the purposes of affairs of state—an extraordinary sequence of stony façades. It makes one think of trumpets; there should be at least six trumpeters on every roof. The people are as friendly as people are in London, and in the same way: with a courtesy as final as the raised drawbridge and as unsettling as the deep moat at one's feet. Behind the façade, of course, lives the city, furtive, paranoiac, puritanical, obsessed and in love with what it imagines to be sin—and also with what it imagines to be joy, it being difficult in Western culture to distinguish between these two. The prison was not far from my hotel, and I eventually acquired enough of a sense of direction to be able to walk from one castle to another. All the time I spent in Hamburg was spent between these two fixed points. The hotel was called The Four Seasons; because of the Maynard case, I once called Senator Javits from there; and ran into Pierre Salinger in the lobby once, he on his way out, I on my way in. If he had not been rushing out and if I had known him better, I might have tried to discuss the case with him. I needed help and advice and I have always rather liked Mr. Salinger. But I am not very good at buttonholing people, and besides I have learned that it frightens them.

It is not an easy matter to be allowed to visit a prisoner. Without the really extraordinary cooperation of my German publishers, I could never have managed it at all. But manage it we did, and so the day came when I was deposited in the waiting room of the prison at Holstenglacis.

The prison is part of a complex of intimidating structures, scattered over quite a large area—a little like the complex on l'Ile de la Cité in Paris, or the complex on Center Street in New York—but it resembles neither of them. It is more medieval than either, and gives the impression of being far more isolated—though, as I say, I could walk to it from my exceedingly fashionable hotel. Yet, the streets were torn up all around it—men at work; I learned to walk from there because taxis seemed never to come anywhere near it; there was a tramline, but I did not know how to use it, and it also seemed to skirt the prison. The only people I ever saw around there were clearly connected with the prison, or were visitors; you could tell the lawyers by their briefcases and their slightly chastened air of self-importance. To visit the prisoner, one had, of course, to have a pass. I am not, legally, related to Tony by blood, and my only pretext to have the right to visit (a right later to be taken from me) was that I was the only friend he had in Germany, and I had traveled quite a long way to see him. This was all arranged between my publishers and the lawyer, and I will never quite know how it was done. But the lawyer rang the bell, anyway, one frosty afternoon, before the great door, which opened and let us in. Then, I was deposited in the waiting room, and before me, at the height of two or three steps, was the great barred door which led to the interior of the prison. There were two or three people in the room with me. One man silently offered me a cigarette and, silently, I took it. The smoke between us, then, was all that we could manage of communion.

I was frightened in a way very hard to describe. The fact that this was the fabled Germany of the Third Reich, and this was a German prison, certainly had something to do with it. I was not so much afraid to see him as I was afraid of what might have happened to him—in him—the way one feels when about to see a loved one who has encountered great misfortune. One does not know what is left of the person. Human help often arrives too late, and if the person has really turned his face to the wall, no human being can help. The great barred door had opened often, letting people in or out; then, I was called or beckoned, and mounted the stone steps, standing before the bars; the turnkey smiled at me as he turned the key in the lock. Then I was led into another wait-ing room, narrow, two long benches on either side of a long table. The prisoners sat on one side, their visitors on the other. The guard stood at the door. Tall, and thinner than I had ever seen him, his high cheekbones pushing out of his skin, his hair too long, wearing clothes he hated, and with his eyes both wet and blazing, Tony stood and smiled. We held each other a moment, and sat down, facing each other, and Tony grinned: I saw that he hadn't turned his face to the wall.

"Hey—!" he said, "how you doing?"

The room was very crowded, and I hardly knew what to say. It would be hard to discuss his case.

"Upon my soul," said Tony, "I didn't do it."

I was glad he said it, though he didn't have to say it.

"Upon my soul," I said, "we'll get you out."

*

Between the night and the morning of April 3–4, in 1967, a Marine, Michael E. Kroll, was murdered on West 3rd Street, in Greenwich Village. He was killed, according to the newspaper stories, as a result of his intervention in a heated argument which a young sailor, Michael Crist, was having with two men, one white and one black. The black man is described as being about five feet, eight inches, and about twenty years old. (Tony was then twenty-seven, and is over six feet tall.) The two men, the black and the white, then walked away, but Kroll and the sailor apparently followed them and another argument ensued, which ended when the black man produced a sawed-off shotgun from beneath his jacket and shot the Marine in the head, killing him instantly. Then, the two men ran away. The claim was that all this happened because the black man had made an indecent proposal to the sailor.

"Can you see me doing that?" Tony asked. His face was extraordinarily vivid with the scorn he felt for so much of the human race. "Since when have I even *talked*"—his face convulsed as though he were vomiting—"to punks like that?"

And, truly, anyone knowing Tony, and hearing such a description of his conduct, would have been forced to the conclusion that Tony had suddenly gone mad. Tony barely spoke when spoken to by strangers—when we worked together, it was his unending complaint that I was "too nice to these mothers"; he treated nearly everyone not within his immediate entourage with a bored, patient contempt. It was impossible to imagine the arrogant Tony walking through Village streets accosting strangers. As for the indecent proposal, the only way *that* could be explained was for the sailor to have mistaken a curse for an invitation. But it was difficult to imagine Tony speaking to him at all, and also hard to imagine that the sailor would have accosted him. Tony looks dangerous. And Tony could not have engaged in such conduct even if he were drunk, for the very good reason that he could not *get* drunk—long before he got drunk, he got sick. In short, in order to believe any of this, it would be necessary to invent a Tony whom no one knew.

But that, of course, would pose no difficulty for the police or the jury or the judge.

*

"Before I left New York"—this is another black friend of mine speaking to me, in Paris, many years ago—"well, you know, I was living with this white chick and we went around together, naturally, and we used to have coffee late at night, or early in the morning in this joint on Sheridan Square. And the neighborhood people didn't like it, and the cops didn't like it. And sometimes the cops would come in and give us a very rough time—making wisecracks, asking me for my draft card, and wanting to know where I lived, and all. You see, they didn't really *do* anything. We weren't bothering anybody and we weren't on dope, or anything, and although her family didn't *like* the situation, still, she was white, and the cops didn't know what her family might do if they really got rough with their daughter. Her family was respectable and had some money. But if *they* didn't do anything, you can just imagine the effect they had on the people—they were telling the people that it was all right to go ahead and beat the shit out of us. One of the cops saw me one day when I was alone, and he said, 'I'm going to get you.' Just like that, looking me in the eye. I started dreaming about that cop. He never spoke to me again, just looked at me like that every time we passed each other on the street. I knew he meant it. If I hung around too long, he'd find a way. And so I got some change together, and I hauled ass."

I knew a blond girl in the Village a long time ago, and, eventually, we never walked out of the house together. She was far safer walking the streets alone than when walking with me—a brutal and humiliating fact which thoroughly destroyed whatever relationship this girl and I might have been able to achieve. This happens all the time in America, but Americans have yet to realize what a sinister fact this is, and what it says about them. When we walked out in the evening, then, she would leave ahead of me, alone. I would give her about five minutes, and then I would walk out alone, taking another route, and meet her on the subway platform. We would not acknowledge each other. We would get into the same subway car, sitting at opposite ends of it, and walk, separately, through the streets of the free and the brave, to wherever we were going—a friend's house, or the movies. There was only one restaurant, eventually, in which we ever ate together, and it was run by a black woman. We were fighting for our lives, and we were very young. As for the police, our protectors, we would never have dreamed of calling one. Our connection caused us to be menaced by the police in ways indescribable and nearly inconceivable; and the police egged on the populace, stood laughing and talking while we were spit on, and cursed. When with a girl, I never ran, I couldn't: except once, when a girl I had been sleeping with slapped me in the face in the middle of Washington Square Park. She was pulling rank, she was crying *Rape!*—and then I ran. I still remember the day and the hour, and the sunlight, the faces of the people, and the girl's face—she had short red hair—and I will never forgive that girl. I am astonished until today that I have both my eyes and most of my teeth and functioning kidneys and my sexual equipment: but small black boys have the advantage of being able to curl themselves into knots, and roll with the kicks and the punches. Of course, I was a target for the police. I was black and visible and helpless and the word was out to "get" me, and so, soon, I, too, hauled ass. And the prisons of this country are full of boys like the boy I was.

"All right," cried Tony, with tears in his eyes, "I'm twenty-eight, and I'm a criminal, right? I've got a record—now they can do anything they want!"

Tony had been arrested about four years earlier, as a civil rights demonstrator—that stays on the books; then on a narcotics charge; then charged with stealing an overcoat—"I was running a business—who's going to steal an overcoat out of his own shop!"—and then charged with stealing a car. He was prosecuted only on the car-theft charge, which has since been dropped. Nevertheless, the car-theft charge marked the most important turning point of his life. He was held for something like two months—this was after the murder, and long before he was connected with it—and then released on bail. But a thoroughly shaken Tony, having been assured by the police that they would "get" him, jumped bail and went to Germany. He had been there before and had been happy there. His flight turned out to be his greatest error: but he could not have supposed that he would be arrested in Germany for having been accused of stealing a car—particularly as Tony's brand of arrogance causes him to act as if his private knowledge of his innocence constitutes irrefutable public proof. With his lofty *I would never do a thing like that*, he dismisses the accusation and is affronted—and surprised—when others do not take him at what he supposes to be his sacred word. And, in fact, almost the very first thing he did in Germany was to register his presence with the American Embassy and give them his address—unlikely conduct indeed for anyone supposing himself to be suspected of murder.

The murder occurred in April. The alleged car theft took place before the murder, but Tony was indicted on the car-theft charge well after the murder occurred, sometime in May. He was in jail for about two months and then released on bail. He arrived in Hamburg on October 22. On October 25, a Detective Hanst, in New York, swore out a complaint which declared that "as a result of information received and investigation made," Maynard was guilty of homicide. On October 27, a Judge Weaver, in New York, cabled the Hamburg chief of police demanding Maynard's arrest. It is not until October 31 that the deposition on which the entire case rests makes its appearance. This is signed by a certain Dennis Morris, whose address is in Brooklyn, and he identifies Tony Maynard by means of a passport-size snapshot. His deposition reads: "That on the morning of April 3, 1967 [but the crime is alleged to have taken place on the morning of the fourth] I was on West 4th Street, near Sixth Avenue, in the city, county, and state of New York, and saw a man, now known to me as Wm. A. Maynard, Jr., whose photograph on which I have placed my initials appears below and is part hereof, shoot and kill a man now known to me as Michael E. Kroll. I then saw said Wm. A. Maynard, Jr. run away from the scene of the crime."

This document, to say nothing of the date of its appearance, strikes me as extraordinary. It appears six days after Hanst's warrant and four days after Judge Weaver's cable—to say nothing of the fact that this authoritative identification of the murderer, by means of a photograph, occurs seven months after the event. Dennis Morris has made no appearance until this moment, and no one knows anything about him. The logical eyewitness, Crist, who was locked in an eyeball to eyeball confrontation with the murderer, has entirely disappeared. (He is to reappear during Tony's trial, armed with a most engaging reason for having been away so long.) In any case, Maynard had been under police surveillance for months, during which time the police were presumably investigating the murder, presumably picking up blacks and whites by the scores, and placing them in line-ups, and it seems never to have occurred to them to connect Maynard with the murder. Incidentally, the white assailant disappears completely and forever from this investigation, as though he had never existed.

That, roughly, was the case until that moment, as it could be reconstructed from Germany. Time was to reveal several unnerving details, but this outline never changed. It was to prove important, later, that during this time Tony had been involved with two white women, one of whom, Giselle Nicole, claiming extreme police harassment, disappeared. The other, Mary Quinn, he married. They did not live happily ever after, and Mary Quinn's subsequent conduct was scarcely that of a loving wife.

According to the treaty between Germany and America, two classes of prisoners are not subject to extradition: political prisoners, and those facing the death penalty. Tony wanted to fight the extradition proceedings, for he was certain that he would be murdered on the way back home. This fear may strike the ordinary American as preposterous, in spite of what they themselves know concerning the violence which is the heritage and the scourge of their country. I could not, of course, agree with Tony, but I didn't find his terror, which was exceedingly controlled and therefore very moving, in the least preposterous. But I had no remote notion how to go about fighting his extradition. Ironically, the very greatest obstacle lay in the fact that New York had abolished the death penalty. The plea could be made, then, only on political grounds. I agree with the Black Panther position concerning black prisoners: not one of them has ever had a fair trial, for not one of them has ever been tried by a jury of his peers. White middle-class America is always the jury, and they know

absolutely nothing about the lives of the people on whom
they sit in judgment: and this fact is not altered, on the contrary it is rendered more implacable by the presence of one or
two black faces in the jury box.

But it would be difficult indeed to convey to a German
court the political implications of a black man's arrest: difficult
if not impossible to convey, especially to a nation "friendly"
to the United States, to what extent black Americans are political prisoners. Muhammad Ali, formerly Cassius Clay, is a
vivid example of what can happen to a black man who obeys
the American injunction, *be true to your faith*, but his press
has been so misleading that he is also an unwieldy and intimidating example. Muhammad Ali is one of the best of the "bad
niggers" and has been publicly hanged like one, but since I
had to avoid the religious issue, which had nothing to do with
Tony's case, I could not cite him as an example. Neither was
the Maynard case likely to interest civil rights organizations,
or the NAACP; it was, in fact, simply another example of a
black hustler being thrown into jail. The complex of reasons
dictating such a fate could scarcely be articulated in a letter to
the German court. There was also the enormous and delicate
problem of publicity. Though I had no choice in the matter,
for I certainly couldn't abandon him, I was terrified that my
presence in the case would work strongly to Tony's disadvantage. I intended to fight the extradition proceedings as hard
as I knew how, but I knew how unlikely it was that we would
win. In the event that we lost, Tony would be brought to trial
and any publicity prior to that trial could certainly be considered prejudicial. On the other hand, both Tony and my
German editor felt that an appeal to the press would work
strongly in Tony's favor. It is really rather awful to find oneself
in a position in which any move one makes may result in
irreparable harm to another, and I was torn in two by this
question for some time. But the question was brutally taken
out of my hands.

One dark, Gothic evening, much delayed by the fact that
we had spent hours trying to arrive at a strategy—no easy
matter if one's strategy must be dictated by the laws of two
different countries, and the psychology of two not so very
different peoples—the German lawyer, my German editor,

and myself, arrived at the door of the Holstenglacis prison. *We* were rattled because, though we were not exactly late, we knew that we were arriving at just about the time that prisoners were due to be taken upstairs for meals; and, furthermore, again a trick accomplished by my German publishers, by this time Tony and I no longer met in the public waiting room, but in another, smaller and private, where we could smoke, where we could talk. This was an enormous concession, and being late could possibly mean losing it.

Only the lawyer and I had passes to enter. My German editor—Fritz Raddadtz, an anti-Nazi German, who has the scars to prove it—had no right to enter at all. But the guard who opened the door also seemed rattled and, without examining anybody's pass, led us all into the room in which he knew I always awaited Tony.

And there we waited, for quite some time. Another rattled functionary appeared, explaining that Tony was not in his cell and could not be seen that night. My German editor, smelling a rat—I didn't, yet, and the lawyer seemed bewildered—pointed out that Tony, in his cell or not, was, nevertheless, somewhere in the prison, and that we were perfectly prepared to wait in this room until morning, or for weeks, if it came to that: that we would not, in short, leave until we saw Tony. The rattled functionary disappeared again. Then, after quite a long while, they brought in the birthday boy.

Someone had goofed in that prison, very badly; after this visit, heads surely rolled. Tony had been beaten, and beaten very hard; his cheekbones had disappeared and one of his eyes was crooked; he looked swollen above the neck, and he took down his shirt collar, presently, to show us the swelling on his shoulders. And he was weeping, trying not to—I had seen him with tears in his eyes, but I had never seen him weeping.

But when I say that heads surely rolled and that someone had goofed, I do not mean that they goofed because they beat him. They goofed because they let us see him. No one would have taken my word for this beating, or our lawyer's word. But Fritz knows what it means to be beaten in prison. And he, therefore, not only alerted the German press, but armed with the weight of one of the most powerful of German publishing houses, sued the German state. So, there it was, after all, anyway, in the newspapers, and I, too, had to meet the press.

"I've got a religious medallion," Tony said—he has become a kind of Muslim, or, at least, an anti-Christian—"and the guard told me the other day that they were going to let me have it back again. Because they took it, you know. And I wanted it back. It means a lot to me—I'm not about to kill myself with it, I'm not about to kill myself. So, when the guard walked in, I asked him for it because he said he would bring it to me Friday night." (And this was Friday.) "Well, I don't know, he jumped salty and he walked out. And I started beating on the door of my cell, trying to make him come back, to listen to me, at least to explain to me *why* I couldn't have it, after he'd promised. And then the door opened and fifteen men walked in and they beat me up—fifteen men!"

The headline on one of the German newspapers, which, incongruously or cunningly enough also has beneath the headline an old photograph of myself, laughing, is: "Tony Never Lies"! This means at least two things, for it is not humanly possible for it to mean what it says. It means that Tony has never lied to me, though I have frequently watched him attempt to delude me into his delusions: but we human beings do this with each other all the time. Friends and lovers are able, sometimes, not always, to resist and correct the delusions. But it also means something exceedingly difficult to capture, which is that some people are liars, and some people are not. We will return to this speculation later. Somewhere in the Bible there is the chilling observation: *Ye are liars, and the truth's not in you.*

I had been in London when Malcolm was murdered. The sister who worked for me then, Gloria, had the habit, whenever she decided that it was time to get me out of town, of simply arbitrarily picking up an invitation, it scarcely mattered to where, and putting me on a plane; so, for example, we once found ourselves in the midnight sun of Helsinki. This time, we were the guests of my British publishers, in London, and we were staying at the Hilton. On this particular night, we were free and we had decided to treat ourselves to a really fancy, friendly dinner. There we were, at the table, all dressed up, and we'd ordered everything, and we were having a very nice time with each other. The headwaiter came, and said there was a phone call for me, and Gloria rose to take it. She was very strange when she came back—she didn't say anything, and I began to be afraid to ask her anything. Then, nibbling at something she obviously wasn't tasting, she said, "Well, I've got to tell you because the press is on its way over here. They've just killed Malcolm X."

The British press said that I accused innocent people of this murder. What I tried to say then, and will try to repeat now, is that whatever hand pulled the trigger did not buy the bullet. That bullet was forged in the crucible of the West, that death was dictated by the most successful conspiracy in the history of the world, and its name is white supremacy.

Years and years and years ago, a black friend of mine killed himself partly because of what he had been forced to endure at the hands of his countrymen because he was in love with a white girl. I had been away and didn't know that he was dead. I came out of the subway one evening, at West 4th Street, just as the train came in on the other side of the platform. A man I knew came running down the steps to catch this train. He saw me, and he yelled, "Did you hear what happened to Gene?" "No," I cried, "what happened?" "He's dead," shouted the hurrying man, and the subway doors closed and the train pulled out of the station.

When George Bernard Shaw wrote *Saint Joan*, he had the immense advantage of having never known her. He had never seen her walk, never heard her talk, could never have been haunted by any of those infinitesimal, inimitable tones, turns, tics, quirks, which are different in every human being, and which make love and death such inexorably private affairs. He had the advantage of the historical panorama: the forces responsible for Joan's death, as well as the ways in which she herself was responsible, were ranged as clearly as chessmen on a chessboard. The forces responsible for that death, and the forces released by it, had had a long time to make themselves felt, and, while Joan was a riddle for her time, she was not a riddle by the time Shaw got around to her: the riddle could be read in her effect in time. She had been safely burned, and somewhat more thoughtfully canonized and no longer posed any conceivable threat to anyone alive. She was, as Shaw points out, one of the world's first nationalists and terrified, equally, the feudal landlords and the princes of the church by refusing to concede their validity. They had no choice but to burn her, which did not, of course, by the merest iota, alter the exactness of her prophecy or the inevitability of their fate.

But it is a very different matter to attempt to deal with the present, in the present, and with a contemporary, younger than oneself, hideously dead too soon, and one who became, furthermore, long before he died, a much disputed legend. And there is, since his death, a Malcolm, virtually, for every persuasion. People who hated him, people who despised him, people who feared him, and people who, in their various ways and degrees, according to their various lights and darknesses, loved him, all claim him now. It is easy to claim him now, just as it was easy for the church to claim Saint Joan.

But, though this storm of human voices creates a great difficulty, it does not create the greatest one.

The greatest difficulty is to accept the fact that the man is dead. It is one thing to *know* that a friend is dead and another thing to accept, within oneself, that unanswering silence: that not many of us are able to accept the reality of death is both an obvious and a labyrinthine statement. The imagination, then, which has been assigned the job of recreating and interpreting a life one witnessed and loved simply kicks like a stalled motor, refuses to make contact, and will not get the vehicle to move. One no longer knows if one ever really knew the person, but, what's worse, that no longer makes any difference: one's stuck with whatever it is one thought one knew, with whatever filtered through the complex screen of one's limitations. That's one's legacy, that's all there is: and now only that work which is love and that love which is work will allow one to come anywhere near obeying the dictum laid down by the great Ray Charles, and—tell the truth.

Every new environment, particularly if one knows that one must make the effort to accustom oneself to working in it, risks being more than a little traumatic. One finds oneself nervously examining one's new surroundings, searching for the terms of the adjustment; therefore, in the beginning, I made a somewhat too conscious effort to be pleased by Hollywood. There was the sky, after all, which New Yorkers seldom see, and there was space, which New Yorkers have forgotten, there was the mighty and dramatic Pacific, there were the hills. Some very valuable and attractive people had lived and functioned here for years, I reminded myself, and there was really no reason why I could not—so I insisted to myself. I had a few friends and acquaintances here already, scattered from Watts to Baldwin Hills to Mulholland Drive, and I was sure they'd be happy if I decided to stay. If I were going to be in Hollywood for months, there was no point in raising the odds against me by hating it, or despising it; besides, such an attitude seemed too obvious a defense against my fear of it. As hotels go, the Beverly Hills is more congenial than most, and certainly everyone there was very nice to me. And so I tried—too hard—to look about me with wonder, and be pleased. But I was already in trouble, and the odds against the venture were very long odds indeed.

I was actually in the Beverly Hills until more permanent lodging could be found. This was not easy, since it involved finding someone to take care of me—to keep house, cook, and drive. *I* was no help, since I was still, at the beginning of 1968, committed to various fund-raising functions in the East, and, more particularly, to the question of a lawyer for Tony Maynard, who had been extradited from Germany and placed in the Tombs, in New York. He had been extradited very shortly after I left Hamburg, so speedily indeed that I was unable to fly from the Coast to meet him in New York, as I had promised. I had engaged, at his suggestion, a lawyer named S. J. Siegel, a very sharp, spry old man, who must have been close to eighty, and who was to teach me a great deal about criminal lawyers. Part of the irreducible conflict which was to drive both Columbia and myself up the wall was already implicit during those early days at the Beverly Hills hotel. The conflict was simply between my life as a writer and my life as—not spokesman exactly, but as public witness to the situation of black people. I had to play both roles: there was nothing anyone, including myself, could do about it. This was an unprecedented situation for Columbia, which, after all, had me under exclusive contract and didn't really like my dashing off, making public appearances. It was an unprecedented situation for me, too, since I had never before been under exclusive contract, and had always juggled my conflicting schedules as best I could. I had lived with my two roles for a long time, and had even, insofar as this is ever true, begun to get used to them—I accepted, anyway, that the dichotomy wasn't likely to end soon. But it didn't make the Hollywood scene any easier. It wasn't a matter of wiping the slate clean of existing commitments and then vanishing behind the typewriter, nor was it even a matter of keeping outside commitments to a minimum, though I tried: events were moving much faster than that, creating perpetual crises and making ever new demands. Columbia couldn't but be concerned about the time and energy I expended on matters remote from the scenario. On the other hand, I couldn't really regret it, since it seemed to me that in this perpetual and bitter ferment I was learning something which kept me in touch with reality and would deepen the truth of the scenario.

But I anticipate. People have their environments: the Beverly Hills Hotel was not mine. For no reason that I could easily name, its space, its opulence, its shapelessness, depressed and frightened me. The people in the bar, the lounge, the halls, the walks, the swimming pools, the shops, seemed as rootless as I, seemed unreal. In spite—perhaps because of— all my efforts to feel relaxed and free and at home (for America *is* my home!) I began to feel unreal—almost as though I were playing an unworthy part in a cheap, unworthy drama. I, who have spent half my life in hotels, sometimes woke up in the middle of the night, terrified, wondering where I was. But, though I scarcely realized it, and might even have been ashamed to admit it to myself, I think that this had partly to do with the fact that I was the only black person in the hotel. I must stress that in no way whatever did anyone in the hotel ever make me feel this, nor, indeed, did I ever consciously feel it—it's only now, in looking back, that I suspect it had to be partly that. My presence in the hotel was absolutely unquestioned, even by people who did not know who I was, or who thought I was Sammy Davis. It was simply taken for granted that I would not have been in the hotel if I had not belonged there. This, irrationally enough, got to me—*did* I belong there? In any case, thousands of black people, miles away, did *not* belong there, though some of them sometimes came to visit me there. (People had to come and get me, or come to visit me, because I do not drive.) The drive from Beverly Hills to Watts and back again is a long and loaded drive—I sometimes felt as though my body were being stretched across those miles. I don't think I felt anything so trivial as guilt, guilt at what appeared to be my comparative good fortune. I knew more about comparative fortunes than that, but I felt a stunning helplessness. These two worlds would never meet, and that fact prefigured disaster for my countrymen, and me. It caused me to look about me with an intensity of wonder which had no pleasure in it. Perhaps even more than the drive from Beverly Hills to Watts, the effect of this ruthless division was summed up for me by a visit I received from a young, very bright black man whom I had met years before, in Boston, after a lecture. Then, he had been very bright indeed, eager, full of ideas for his future, and the future of black people. A few years later, I had run across him, briefly, in Helsinki—he was studying, and seeing the world. Beautiful, I had thought then, make it, baby—it's wonderful to see a black cat at large in the world. Alas, to be at large in the world is also distinctly to risk being lost in it, and now, one afternoon, I received a message from a Prince of Abyssinia and I forget how many other territories, he was downstairs. In spite of the exotic titles, I recognized the domestic name, and I had him sent up. Here he came, then, a piteous, mad, unutterably moving wreck; he could scarcely have passed his thirtieth birthday. He wanted me to deposit ten thousand dollars in one of the many bank accounts he had around the world. He had a map, and a list of the banks, his patrons, and his titles, all impeccably handwritten. When confronting madness, it is usually best to hold one's peace, and so I do not know what I could have said. I did not question his titles, or his fortune, but indicated that I did not have ten thousand dollars. He took this with very good grace, had another drink, and bade me farewell—he had a pressing appointment with a fellow potentate. It was dark when he left, and black people—or white people, for that matter—walking in Beverly Hills do not walk far unnoticed. I almost started to call him a cab, but his regal bearing forbade it, and I then realized that there was nothing I could do.

I, of course, will always believe that this boy would not have been so quickly broken on the wheel of life if he had not been born black, in America. Many of my countrymen will not agree with me and will accuse me of special pleading. Neither they, nor I, can hope to come anywhere near the truth of the matter, so long as a man's color exerts so powerful a force on his fate. In the long meantime, I can only say that the authority of my countrymen in these matters is not equal to my own, since I know what black Americans endure—know it in my own flesh and spirit, know it by the human wreckage through which I have passed.

Therefore, my desire to be seduced, charmed, was a hope poisoned by despair: for better or for worse, it simply was not in me to make a separate peace. It was a symptom of how bitterly weary I was of wandering, how I hoped to find a resting place, reconciliation, in the land where I was born. But everything that might have charmed me merely reminded me of how many were excluded, how many were suffering and groaning and dying, not far from a paradise which was itself but another circle of hell. Everything that charmed me reminded me of someplace else, someplace where I could walk and talk, someplace where I was freer than I was at home, someplace where I could live without the stifling mask—made me homesick for a liberty I had never tasted here, and without which I could never live or work. In America, I was free only in battle, never free to rest—and he who finds no way to rest cannot long survive the battle.

Watts doesn't immediately look like a slum, if you come from New York; but it does if you drive from Beverly Hills. I have said that it is a very long drive, long and increasingly ugly; then one is in the long, flat streets of Watts, low, flat houses on either side. For a New Yorker, where the filth is piled so high that the light can never break through, Watts looks, at first, like a fine place to raise a child. There are little patches of yard, which can be enclosed by a fence, and a tree to which one can attach a swing, and space for a barbecue pit.

But, then, one looks again and sees how spare, shabby, and dark the houses are. One sees that garbage collection is scarcely more efficient here than it is in Harlem. One walks the long street and sees all that one sees in the East: the shabby pool halls, the shabby bars, the boarded-up doors and windows, the plethora of churches and lodges and liquor stores, the shining automobiles, the wine bottles in the gutter, the garbage-strewn alleys, and the young people, boys and girls, in the streets. Over it all hangs a miasma of fury and frustration, a perceptible darkening, as of storm clouds, of rage and despair, and the girls move with a ruthless, defiant dignity, and the boys move against the traffic as though they are moving against the enemy. The enemy is not there, of course, but his soldiers are, in patrol cars, armed.

And yet—I have been to Watts to give high-school lectures, for example, and these despised, maligned, and menaced children have an alertness, an eagerness, and a depth which I certainly did not find in—or failed to elicit from—students at many splendid universities. The future leaders of this country (in principle, anyway) do not impress me as being the intellectual equals of the most despised among us. I am not being vindictive when I say that, nor am I being sentimental or chauvinistic; and indeed the reason that this would be so is a very simple one. It is only very lately that white students, in the main, have had any reason to question the structure into which they were born; it is the very lateness of the hour, and their bewildered resentment—their sense of having been betrayed—which is responsible for their romantic excesses; and a young, white revolutionary remains, in general, far more romantic than a black one. For it is a very different matter, and results in a very different intelligence, to grow up under the necessity of questioning everything—everything, from the question of one's identity to the literal, brutal question of how to save one's life in order to begin to live it. White children, in the main, and whether they are rich or poor, grow up with a grasp of reality so feeble that they can very accurately be described as deluded—about themselves and the world they live in. White people have managed to get through entire lifetimes in this euphoric state, but black people have not been so lucky: a black man who sees the world the way John Wayne, for example, sees it would not be an eccentric patriot, but a raving maniac. The reason for this, at bottom, is that the doctrine of white supremacy, which still controls most white people, is itself a stupendous delusion: but to be born black in America is an immediate, a mortal challenge. People who cling to their delusions find it difficult, if not impossible, to learn anything worth learning: a people under the necessity of creating themselves must examine everything, and soak up learning the way the roots of a tree soak up water. A people still held in bondage must believe that *Ye shall know the truth, and the truth shall make ye free.*

But, of course, what black people are also learning as they learn is the truth about white people: and that's the rub. Actually, black people have known the truth about white people for a long time, but now there is no longer any way for the truth to be hidden. The whole world knows it. The truth which frees black people will also free white people, but this is a truth which white people find very difficult to swallow.

They need desperately to be released, for one thing, from the necessity of lying all the time. I remember visiting a correctional school in Watts where the boys were being taught a "useful" trade. I visited some of the shops—they were being taught to make wooden frames for hassocks—nonsense like that. The boys knew it was a bullshit trip, the teachers knew it, the principal, escorting me through the school, knew it. He looked ashamed of himself, and he should have been ashamed. The truth is that this country does not know what to do with its black population now that the blacks are no longer a source of wealth, are no longer to be bought and sold and bred, like cattle; and they especially do not know what to do with young black men, who pose as devastating a threat to the economy as they do to the morals of young white cheerleaders. It is not at all accidental that the jails and the army and the needle claim so many, but there are still too many prancing about for the public comfort. Americans will, of course, deny, with horror, that they are dreaming of anything like "the final solution"—those Americans, that is, who are likely to be asked:

what goes on in the great, vast, private hinterland of the American heart can only be guessed at by observing the way the country goes these days. Some pale, compelling nightmare—an overwhelming collection of private nightmares—is responsible for the irresponsible ferocity of the Omnibus Crime Control and Safe Streets Act. Some vindictive terror on the part of the people made possible the Government's indefensible and obscene performance in Chicago. Something has gone violently wrong in a nation when the government dares attempt to muzzle the press—a press already quite supine enough—and to intimidate reporters by the use of the subpoena. Black men have been burned alive in this country more than once—many men now living have seen it with their own eyes; black men and boys are being murdered here today, in cold blood, and with impunity; and it is a very serious matter when the government which is sworn to protect the interests of all American citizens publicly and unabashedly allies itself with the enemies of black men. Let us tell it like it is: the rhetoric of a Stennis, a Maddox, a Wallace, historically and actually, has brought death to untold numbers of black people and it was meant to bring death to them. This is absolutely true, no matter who denies it—no black man can possibly deny it. Now, in the interest of the public peace, it is the Black Panthers who are being murdered in their beds, by the dutiful and zealous police. But, for a policeman, all black men, especially young black men, are probably Black Panthers and all black women and children are probably allied with them: just as, in a Vietnamese village, the entire population, men, women, children, are considered as probable Vietcong. In the village, as in the ghetto, those who were not dangerous before the search-and-destroy operation assuredly become so afterward, for the inhabitants of the village, like the inhabitants of the ghetto, realize that they are identified, judged, menaced, murdered, solely because of the color of their skin. This is as curious a way of waging a war for a people's freedom as it is of maintaining the domestic public peace.

The ghetto, beleaguered, betrayed by Washington, by the total lack of vision of the men in Washington, determined to outwit, withstand, survive, this present, overwhelming danger, yet lacks a focus, a rallying point, a spokesman. And many of us looked at each other and sighed, saying, *Lord, we really need Malcolm now.*

Hollywood, or a segment of it, at least, was becoming increasingly active on the question of civil rights—now, I thought, sourly, and somewhat unjustly, that the question had been rendered moribund. Just the same, there was a groundswell to replace the toothsome, grimly folksy mayor, Sam Yorty, who had been in office since 1911, with someone who had heard of the twentieth century, in this case, Tom Bradley, a Negro. People like Jack Lemmon, Jean Seberg, Robert Culp, and France Nuyen were actively supporting Martin Luther King, pledging money and getting others to pledge, and some were helping to raise money for a projected Malcolm X Foundation.

Marlon Brando was very much in the forefront of all this. He had a strong interest in the Black Panthers and was acquainted with many of them. On April 6, Eldridge Cleaver was wounded, and Bobby Hutton was killed, in Oakland, in what the police describe as a "shoot-out." Marlon called me to say that he was going up to Oakland. I wanted to go with him, but Martin Luther King had been murdered two days before, and, to tell the truth, I was in a state resembling shock. I can't describe this, or defend it, and I won't dwell on it. Marlon flew up to Oakland to deliver the eulogy for seventeen-year-old Bobby Hutton, shot down, exactly, by the dutiful police, like a mad dog in the streets. The Oakland Police Force was outraged, naturally, and I think they threatened to sue him, probably for defamation of character. The Grand Jury had judged their shooting of an unarmed, black adolescent as "justifiable homicide": the names of these jurors, many of whom can claim as their intimates eminent judges and lawyers, could scarcely have been found on the Master Panel if it were supposed that they were capable of bringing in any other verdict.

(I went to Oakland to visit the house where Hutton was killed, and Cleaver wounded. The house where the Panthers were is wedged between two houses just like it. There are windows on either side of the house, facing the alley; facing the street, there is only an enormous garage door, from which, needless to say, no one could hope to shoot, and live. The house, particularly the basement, where the people were, looks like something from a search-and-destroy operation. The warehouse across the street, where the cops were, doesn't have a scratch on it: so much for the official concept of a shoot-out. When I was there, there were flowers on a rock, marking the spot where Bobby fell: the people of the neighborhood had made of the place a shrine.)

I think it was in March, but it may have been somewhat earlier, that Martin Luther King came to town, to speak in a private dwelling in the Hollywood hills to raise money for the Southern Christian Leadership Conference. I had not seen Martin in quite some time, and I looked forward to seeing him in a setting where we might be able to talk a little bit before he had to dash off and grab some sleep before catching the next plane. For years, most of us had seen each other only at airports, or, wearily, marching, marching.

It always seems—unfairly enough, perhaps, in many cases—incongruous and suspect when relatively wealthy and certainly very worldly people come together for the express purpose of declaring their allegiance to a worthy cause and with the intention of parting with some of their money. I think that someone like myself can scarcely avoid a certain ambivalence before such a spectacle—someone like myself being someone significantly and crucially removed from the world which produced these people. In my own experience, genuine, disinterested compassion or conviction are very rare; yet, it is as well to remember that, rare as these are, they are real, they exist. Giving these people the benefit of the necessary doubt—assuming, that is, for example, that if they were called to serve on a Grand Jury investigating the legal murder of a black, they would have the courage to vote their conscience instead of their class—I would hazard that, in the case of most people in gatherings such as these, their presence is due to a vivid, largely incoherent uneasiness. They are nagged by a sense that something is terribly wrong, and that they must do what they can to put it right: but much of their quality, or lack of it, depends on what they perceive to be wrong. They do not, in any case, know what to do—who does? it may be asked—and so they give their money and their allegiance to whoever appears to be doing what they feel should be done. Their fatal temptation, to which, mostly, they appear to succumb, is to assume that they are, then, off the hook. But, on the other hand, always assuming that they are serious, the crucial lack in their perception is that they do not quite see where, when the chips are down, their allegiance is likely to land them—*à la lanterne!* or to recantation: they do not know how ruthless and powerful is the evil that lives in the world. Years before, for example, I remember having an argument—a most melancholy argument—with a friend of mine concerning our relation to Martin. It was shortly after our celebrated and stormy meeting with Bobby Kennedy, and I was very low. I said that we could petition and petition and march and march and raise money and give money until we wore ourselves out and the stars began to moan: none of this endeavor would or could reach the core of the matter, it would change nobody's fate. The thirty thousand dollars raised tonight would be gone in bail bonds in the morning, and so it would continue until we dropped. Nothing would ever reach the conscience of the people of this nation—it was a dream to suppose that the people of any nation had a conscience. Some individuals within the nation might, and the nation always saw to it that these people came to a bad, if not a bloody end. Nothing we could do would prevent, at last, an open confrontation. And where, then, when the chips were down, would we stand?

We were seated near a fireplace, and my friend's face was very thoughtful. He looked over at me, almost as though he were seeing me for the first time.

"You really believe that, don't you?"

I said, "I wish I didn't. But I'm afraid I do."

"Well," he said, at last, "if you're black, you don't have to worry too much about where you stand. They've got *that* covered, I believe."

Indeed, they do. And, therefore, people like the people in the Hollywood hills can be looked on as the highly problematical leaven in the loaf. Instinctively, when speaking before them, one attempts to fan into a blaze, or at least into positive heat, their somewhat chilled apprehension of life. In attempting to lessen the distance between them and oneself, one is also, unconsciously and inevitably, suggesting that they lessen the distance between themselves and their deepest hopes and fears and desires; even that they dispense with that middleman they call doctor, who is one of their greatest, most infantile self-indulgences. One senses sometimes in their still faces an intense, speculative hesitation. Bobby Seale insists that one of the things that most afflict white people is their disastrous concept of God; they have never accepted the dark gods, and their fear of the dark gods, who live in them at least as surely as the white God does, causes them to distrust life. It causes them, profoundly, to be fascinated by, and more than a little frightened of the lives led by black people: it is this tension which makes them problematical. But, on the other hand, it must be becoming increasingly clear to some, at least, that all of us are standing in the same deep shadow, a shadow which can only be lifted by human courage and honor. Many still hope to keep their honor and their safety, too. No one can blame them for this hope, it is impossible indeed not to share it: but when queried as to the soundness of such a hope, for a people caught in a civilization in crisis, history fails to give any very sanguine answers.

Eventually, Martin arrived, in a light blue suit, accompanied by Andrew Young, and they both looked very tired. We were very glad to see each other. We sat down in a relatively secluded corner and tried to bring each other up to date.

Alas, it would never be possible for us to bring each other up to date. We had first met during the last days of the Montgomery bus boycott—and how long ago was that? It was senseless to say, eight years, ten years ago—it was longer ago than time can reckon. Martin and I had never got to know each other well, circumstances, if not temperament, made that impossible, but I had much respect and affection for him, and I think Martin liked me, too. I told him what I was doing in Hollywood, and both he and Andrew, looking perhaps a trifle dubious, wished me well. I don't remember whether it was on this evening that we arranged to appear together a few weeks later at Carnegie Hall, or if this had already been arranged. Presently, Marlon, very serious, and even being, as I remember, a little harsh with the assembled company—wanting to make certain that they understood the utter gravity of our situation, and the speed with which the time for peaceful change was running out—took the floor, and introduced Dr. Martin Luther King, Jr.

As our situation had become more complex, Martin's speeches had become simpler and more concrete. As I remember, he spoke very simply that evening on the work of the Southern Christian Leadership Conference, what had been done, what was being done, and the enormity of the tasks that lay ahead. But I remember his tone more than his words. He spoke very humbly, as one of many workers, speaking to his co-workers. I think he made everyone in that room feel that whatever they were doing, whatever they could do, was important, was of the utmost importance. He did not flatter them—very subtly, he challenged them, challenged them to live up to their moral obligations. The room was quite remarkable when he finished—still, thoughtful, grateful: perhaps, in the most serious sense of that weary phrase, profoundly honored.

And yet—how striking to compare his tone that night with what it had been not many years before! Not many years before, we had all marched on Washington. Something like two hundred and fifty thousand people had come to the nation's capital to petition their government for a redress of grievances. They had come from all over the nation, in every condition, in every conceivable attire, and in all kinds of vehicles. Even a skeptic like myself, with every reason to doubt that the petition would, or could, be heard, or acted on, could not fail to respond to the passion of so many people, gathered together, for that purpose, in that place. Their passion made one forget that a terrified Washington had bolted its doors and fled, that many politicians had been present only because they had been afraid not to be, that John Lewis, then of SNCC, had been forced to tone down his speech because of the insuperable arrogance of a Boston archbishop, that the administration had done everything in its power to prevent the March, even to finding out if I, who had nothing whatever to do with the March as organized, would use my influence to try to prevent it. (I said that such influence as I had, which wasn't much, would certainly not be used against the March, and, perhaps to prove this, I led the March on Washington from the American Church, in Paris, to the American Embassy, and brought back from Paris a scroll bearing about a thousand names. I wonder where it is now.)

In spite of all that one knew, and feared, it was a very stirring day, and one very nearly dared, in spite of all that one knew, to hope—to hope that the need and the passion of the people, so nakedly and vividly, and with such dignity revealed, would not be, once again, betrayed. (The People's Republic of China had sent a telegram in our support, which was repudiated by Roy Wilkins, who said, in effect, that we would be glad to accept such a telegram on the day that the Chinese were allowed to petition *their* government for redress of grievances, as we were petitioning ours. I had an uneasy feeling that we might live to hear this boast ring somewhat mockingly in our ears.)

But Martin had been quite moving that day. Marlon (carrying a cattle prod, for the purpose of revealing the depravity of the South) and Sidney Poitier and Harry Belafonte, Charlton Heston, and some others of us had been called away to do a Voice of America show for Ed Murrow, and so we watched and listened to Martin on television. All of us were very silent in that room, listening to Martin, feeling the passion of the people flowing up to him and transforming him, transforming us. Martin finished with one hand raised: "Free at last, free at last, praise God Almighty, I'm free at last!" That day, for a moment, it almost seemed that we stood on a height, and could see our inheritance; perhaps we could make the kingdom real, perhaps the beloved community would not forever remain that dream one dreamed in agony. The people quietly dispersed at nightfall, as had been agreed. Sidney Poitier took us out to dinner that night, in a very, very quiet Washington. The people had come to their capitol, had made themselves known, and were gone: no one could any longer doubt that their suffering was real. Ironically enough, after Washington, I eventually went on the road, on a lecture tour which carried me to Hollywood. So I was in Hollywood when, something like two weeks later, my phone rang, and a nearly hysterical, white, female CORE worker told me that a

Sunday school in Birmingham had been bombed, and that four young black girls had been blown into eternity. That was the first answer we received to our petition.

The original plans for the March on Washington had been far from polite: the original plan had been to lie down on airport runways, to block the streets and offices, to immobilize the city completely, and to remain as long as we had to, to force the government to recognize the urgency and the justice of our demands. Malcolm was very caustic about the March on Washington, which he described as a sell-out. I think he was right. Martin, five years later, was five years wearier and five years sadder, and still petitioning. But the impetus was gone, because the people no longer believed in their petitions, no longer believed in their government. The reasoning behind the March on Washington, as it eventually evolved—or as it was, in Malcolm's words, "diluted"—was that peaceful assembly would produce the best results. But, five years later, it was very hard to believe that the frontal assault, as planned, on the capitol, could possibly have produced more bloodshed, or more despair. Five years later, it seemed clear that we had merely postponed, and not at all to our advantage, the hour of dreadful reckoning.

Martin and Andrew and I said good night to each other, and promised to meet in New York.

Siegel, the first lawyer I engaged for Tony, was a refugee from *Bleak House*, and I wish I'd met him in those pages and not in life. Spry, as I have said, white-haired, cunning, with a kind of old-fashioned, phony courtliness, he was eventually to make me think of vultures. He had been a criminal lawyer for a long time, practically since birth, and he had, I was told, a "good" reputation. But I was to discover that to have a "good" reputation as a criminal lawyer does not necessarily reflect any credit on said lawyer's competence or dedication; still less does it indicate that he has any interest in his clients: the term seems to refer almost exclusively to the lawyer's ability to wheel and deal and to his influence with other lawyers and judges, and district attorneys. A criminal lawyer's reputation—except, of course, for the one or two titans in the field—would appear to depend on his standing in this club.

The fate of his client depends, to put it brutally, on the client's money: one may say, generally, that, if a poor man in trouble with the law receives justice, one can suppose heavenly intervention.

A poor man is always an isolated man, in the sense that his intimates are as ignorant and as helpless as he. Tony has been in prison since October 27, 1967, and remains in prison still. He had been brought to trial once in all that time; the trial resulted in a hung jury. A citizen more favorably placed than Tony would never have been treated in this way. It would appear, for example, that Tony's constitutional rights were violated at the very moment he was arrested because of the means used to identify him. This question has never been brought up, though Tony has insisted on it time and again. The police are very sensitive about being accused of violating a suspect's constitutional rights—they are, indeed, as sensitive to any and all criticism as aging beauty queens—and would never have arrested Tony in the way that they did if they had not been certain that his accusation could never be heard. Tony had almost nothing going for him, except his devoted sister, Valerie, and me. But neither Valerie nor I are equipped to deal with the world into which we found ourselves so suddenly plunged, and I found myself severely handicapped in this battle by being forced to fight it from three thousand miles away.

This meant that there was a vacuum where Tony's witness should have been. This would not have been so if the system worked differently, or if it were served by different people. But the system works as it works, and it attracts the people it attracts. The poor, the black, and the ignorant become the stepping stones of careers; for the people who make up this remarkable club are judged by their number of arrests and convictions. These matter far more than justice, if justice can be said to matter at all. It is clearly much easier to drag some ignorant wretch to court and burden him with whatever crimes one likes than it is to undergo the inconvenience and possible danger of finding out what actually happened, and who is actually guilty. In my experience, the defenders of the public peace do not care who is guilty. I have been arrested by the New York police, for example, and charged guilty before the judge, and had the charge entered in the record, without anyone asking me how I chose to plead, and without being allowed to speak. (I had the case thrown out of court, and if I'd had any means, I would have sued the city. The judge, when asked to explain his oversight, said that the court was crowded that day, and that the traffic noises, coming in from the streets, distracted him.)

In Tony Maynard's case, the question of justice is simply mocked when one considers that no attempt appears to have been made to discover the white assailant, and also by the fact that Tony has been asked to plead guilty and promised a light sentence if he would so plead. I know this to be a fact because, during Tony's trial, while the jury was out—and the jury was out much longer than anyone expected it to be—Galena, the D.A. who was prosecuting Tony, took me aside, in the presence of Tony's sister, Valerie, and the second lawyer I engaged for Tony, Selig Lenefsky, to ask me to use my influence to persuade Tony to accept the deal. He also told me that they would "get" him, anyway. Lenefsky and Galena are partners now, a perfectly normal development, which enhances the respectful trust and affection with which the poor regard their protectors.

But I anticipate. My absence from New York meant that there was virtually no pressure on Siegel, and Siegel, as far as I could discover, did nothing whatever. Most of his correspondence with me mentions money. I had paid him a retainer, and I wasn't trying to beat him out of his fee; but I was naturally reluctant, especially as time wore on, with no progress being made, to continue throwing good money after bad. This led, really, to a stalemate, and Valerie and I found ourselves thoroughly at a loss. I wanted to fire Siegel, but on what basis would I hire the next lawyer? No one I knew knew anything about criminal lawyers; the lawyers I knew dismissed them as a "scurvy breed." I thought of Melvin Belli, but he operates in California; I thought of Louis Nizer, and, in fact, tried to see him: but I knew I couldn't pay the fee for either of these lawyers. I thought of publicity, but it is not so easy to get publicity for a case which is, alas, so unremarkable. I didn't feel that my unsupported testimony would mean very much, and I couldn't get the groundswell going which might lead to a public hue and cry. I couldn't work at it full time because I was under contract in California and had to get back there. And, furthermore, I now had to finish that screenplay, if only to collect my fee: what price justice indeed!

Val and I would meet in Siegel's office, to learn that the trial had been postponed again, but that this might be all to the good because it meant that Judge So-and-So instead of Judge What-not would be sitting—at least, he would try to make certain that it was Judge What-not instead of Judge So-and-So. He, Siegel, was on friendly terms with Judge What-not, he'd call him later in the evening. And he would smile in a very satisfied way, as though to say, You see how I'm putting myself out for you, how much I take your interests to heart. No, his private investigators had failed to locate Dennis Morris. (Morris is the unknown who identified Tony by means of a photograph.) Morris had disappeared. No one seemed to know where he was. No, there was no word about the whereabouts of Michael Crist, either. All of this took time and money—and he would light a cigar, his bright blue eyes watching me expectantly.

Well, what in the world could we say to this terrifying old man? How could we know whether he had spoken to a single person, or made the remotest phone call on Tony's behalf? We could spend the rest of our lives in this office, while Tony was perishing in jail, and never know. He didn't care about Tony, but we hadn't expected him to—we had supposed that he cared about something else. What? his honor as a criminal lawyer? Probably—which proved what fools we were. His honor as a criminal lawyer was absolutely unassailable, he was a lifetime member of the club. We had no way whatever of lighting a fire under his ass and making him do what we were paying him to do. He didn't need us. There were thousands like us, yes, and black like us, who would keep him in cigars forever, turning over their nickels and dimes to get their loved ones out of trouble. And sometimes he would get them out— he had no objection to getting people out of trouble. But it was a lottery; it depended on whose number came up; and he certainly wasn't bucking the machine. Day after day after day, we would leave him and go to the Tombs, and I would see Tony: who was bearing up fantastically well; I'd not have believed he could be so tough. Seeing him, I felt guilty, frustrated, and helpless, felt time flowing through my hands like water. Val would be waiting for me when I came down, we might walk around a bit, and then I would leave her with the others, who were waiting for the six o'clock visit.

Whoever wishes to know who is in prison in this country has only to go to the prisons and watch who comes to visit. We spent hours and hours, days and days, eternities, down at the Tombs, Val and I, and, later, my brother, David. I suppose there must have been white visitors; it stands, so to speak, to reason, but they were certainly overwhelmed by the dark, dark mass. Black, and Puerto Rican matrons, black, and Puerto Rican girls, black, and Puerto Rican boys, black, and Puerto Rican men: such are the fish trapped in the net called justice. Bewilderment, despair, and poverty roll through the halls like a smell: the visitors have come, looking for a miracle. The miracle will be to find someone who really cares about the people in prison. But no one can afford to care. The prison is overcrowded, the calendars full, the judges busy, the lawyers ambitious, and the cops zealous. What does it matter if someone gets trapped here for a year or two, gets ruined here, goes mad here, commits murder or suicide here? It's too bad, but that's the way the cookie crumbles sometimes.

I do not claim that everyone in prison here is innocent, but I do claim that the law, as it operates, is guilty, and that the prisoners, therefore, are all unjustly imprisoned. Is it conceivable, after all, that any middle-class white boy—or, indeed, almost any white boy—would have been arrested on so grave a charge as murder, with such flimsy substantiation, and forced to spend, as of this writing, three years in prison? What force, precisely, is operating when a prisoner is advised, requested, ordered, intimidated, or forced, to confess to a crime he has not committed, and promised a lighter sentence for so perjuring and debasing himself? Does the law exist for the purpose of furthering the ambitions of those who have sworn to uphold the law, or is it seriously to be considered as a moral, unifying force, the health and strength of a nation? The trouble with these questions, of course, is that they sound rhetorical, and have the effect of irritating the reader, who does not wish to be told that the administration of justice in this country is a wicked farce. Well, if one really wishes to know how justice is administered in a country, one does not question the policemen, the lawyers, the judges, or the protected members of the middle class. One goes to the unprotected—those, precisely, who need the law's protection most!—and listens to their testimony. Ask any Mexican, any Puerto Rican, any black man, any poor person—ask the wretched how they fare in the halls of justice, and then you will know, not whether or not the country is just, but whether or not it has any love for justice, or any concept of it. It is certain, in any case, that ignorance, allied with power, is the most ferocious enemy justice can have.

I saw Martin in New York, and we did our Carnegie Hall gig. Everything I had was dirty, and I had to rush out and buy a dark suit for the occasion. After two or three murderously crowded days, I was on the plane again, flying West. Each time I left New York, I felt that I had heartlessly abandoned Valerie and Tony, and was always tempted to abandon the script instead, and see the battle in New York through. But I knew, of course, that I couldn't do that; in a way they were the same battle: yet, I couldn't help wondering if I were destined to lose them both.

There is a day in Palm Springs that I will remember forever, a bright day. I had moved there from the Beverly Hills Hotel, into a house the producer had found for me. Billy Dee Williams had come to town, and he was staying at the house; and a lot of the day had been spent with a very bright, young, lady reporter, who was interviewing me about the film version of Malcolm. I felt very confident that day—I was never to feel so confident again—and I talked very freely to the reporter. (Too freely, Marvin Worth, the producer, was to tell me later.) I had decided to lay my cards on the table and to state, as clearly as I could, what I felt the movie was about and how I intended to handle it. I thought that this might make things simpler later on, but I was wrong about that. The studio and I were at loggerheads, really, from the moment I stepped off the plane. Anyway, I had opted for candor, or a reasonable facsimile of same, and sounded as though I were in charge of the film, as, indeed, by my lights, for that moment, certainly, I had to be. I was really in a difficult position because, by both temperament and experience, I tend to work alone, and I dread making announcements concerning my work. But I was in a very public position, and I thought that I had better make my own announcements rather than have them made for me. The studio, on the other hand, did not want me making announcements of any kind at all. So there we were, and this particular tension, since it got to the bloody heart of the matter—the question of by whose vision, precisely, this film was to be controlled—was not to be resolved until I finally threw up my hands and walked away.

I very much wanted Billy Dee for Malcolm, and since no one else had any other ideas, I didn't see why this couldn't work out. In brutal Hollywood terms, Poitier is the only really big, black box-office star, and this fact, especially since Marvin had asked me to "keep an eye out" for an actor, gave me, as I considered it, a free hand. To tell the bitter truth, from the very first days we discussed it, I had never had any intention of allowing the Columbia brass to cast this part: I was determined to take my name off the production if I were overruled. Call this bone-headed stupidity, or insufferable arrogance, or what you will—I had made my decision, and once I had made it, nothing could make me waver, and nothing could make me alter it. If there were errors in my concept of the film, and if I made errors in the execution, well, then, I would have to pay for my errors. But one can learn from one's errors. What one cannot survive is allowing other people to make your errors for you, discarding your own vision, in which, at least, you believe, for someone else's vision, in which you do *not* believe.

Anyway, all that shit had yet to hit the fan. This day, the girl, and Billy, and I had a few drinks by the swimming pool. Walter, my cook-chauffeur, was about to begin preparing supper. The girl got up to leave, and we walked her to her car, and came back to the swimming pool, jubilant.

The phone had been brought out to the pool, and now it rang. Billy was on the other side of the pool, doing what I took to be African improvisations to the sound of Aretha Franklin. And I picked up the phone.

It was David Moses. It took awhile before the sound of his voice—I don't mean the *sound* of his voice, something *in* his voice—got through to me.

He said, "Jimmy—? Martin's just been shot," and I don't think I said anything, or felt anything. I'm not sure I knew who *Martin* was. Yet, though I know—or I think—the record player was still playing, silence fell. David said, "He's not dead yet"—*then* I knew who Martin was—"but it's a head wound—so—"

I don't remember what I said; obviously, I must have said something. Billy and Walter were watching me. I told them what David had said.

I hardly remember the rest of that evening at all, it's retired into some deep cavern in my mind. We must have turned on the television set, if we had one, I don't remember. But we must have had one. I remember weeping, briefly, more in helpless rage than in sorrow, and Billy trying to comfort me. But I really don't remember that evening at all. Later, Walter told me that a car had prowled around the house all night.

The very last time I saw Medgar Evers, he stopped at his house on the way to the airport so I could autograph my books for him and his wife and children. I remember Myrilie Evers standing outside, smiling, and we waved, and Medgar drove to the airport and put me on the plane. He grinned that kind of country boy preacher's grin of his, and we said we'd see each other soon.

Months later, I was in Puerto Rico, working on the last act of my play. My host and hostess, and my friend, Lucien, and I, had spent a day or so wandering around the island, and now we were driving home. It was a wonderful, bright, sunny day, the top to the car was down, we were laughing and talking, and the radio was playing. Then the music stopped, and a voice announced that Medgar Evers had been shot to death in the carport of his home, and his wife and children had seen that big man fall.

No, I can't describe it. I've thought of it often, or been haunted by it often. I said something like, "That's a friend of mine—!" but no one in the car really knew who he was, or what he had meant to me, and to so many people. For some reason, I didn't see him: I saw Myrilie, and the children. They were quite small children. The blue sky seemed to descend like a blanket, and the speed of the car, the wind against my face, seemed stifling, as though the elements were determined to stuff something down my throat, to fill me with something I could never contain. And I couldn't say anything, I couldn't cry; I just remembered his face, a bright, blunt, handsome face, and his weariness, which he wore like his skin, and the way he said *ro-aad* for road, and his telling me how the tatters of clothes from a lynched body hung, flapping, in the tree for days, and how he had to pass that tree every day. Medgar. Gone.

I went to Atlanta alone, I do not remember why. I wore the suit I had bought for my Carnegie Hall appearance with Martin. I seem to have had the foresight to have reserved a hotel room, for I vaguely remember stopping in the hotel and talking to two or three preacher type looking men, and we started off in the direction of the church. We had not got far before it became very clear that we would never get anywhere near it. We went in this direction and then in that direction, but the press of people choked us off. I began to wish that I had not come incognito, and alone, for now that I was in Atlanta, I wanted to get inside the church. I lost my companions and sort of squeezed my way, inch by inch, closer to the church. But, directly between me and the church, there was an impassable wall of people. Squeezing my way up to this point, I had considered myself lucky to be small; but now my size worked against me, for, though there were people on the church steps who knew me, whom I knew, they could not possibly see me, and I could not shout. I squeezed a few more inches and asked a very big man ahead of me please to let me through. He moved, and said, "Yeah, let me see you get through this big Cadillac." It was true—there it was, smack in front of me, big as a house. I saw Jim Brown at a distance, but he didn't see me. I leaned up on the car, making frantic signals, and, finally, someone on the church steps did see me and came to the car and sort of lifted me over. I talked to Jim Brown for a minute, and then somebody led me into the church and I sat down.

The church was packed, of course, incredibly so. Far in the front, I saw Harry Belafonte sitting next to Coretta King. I had interviewed Coretta years ago, when I was doing a profile on her husband. We had got on very well; she had a nice, free laugh. Ralph David Abernathy sat in the pulpit. I remembered him from years ago, sitting in his shirtsleeves in the house in Montgomery, big, black, and cheerful, pouring some cool soft drink, and, later, getting me settled in a nearby hotel. In the pew directly before me sat Marlon Brando, Sammy Davis, Eartha Kitt—covered in black, looking like a lost ten-year-old girl—and Sidney Poitier, in the same pew, or nearby. Marlon saw me and nodded. The atmosphere was black, with a tension indescribable—as though something, perhaps the heavens, perhaps the earth, might crack. Everyone sat very still.

The actual service sort of washed over me, in waves. It wasn't that it seemed unreal; it was the most real church service I've ever sat through in my life, or ever hope to sit through; but I have a childhood hangover thing about not weeping in public, and I was concentrating on holding myself together. I did not want to weep for Martin; tears seemed futile. But I may also have been afraid, and I could not have been the only one, that if I began to weep, I would not be able to stop. There was more than enough to weep for, if one was to weep—so many of us, cut down, so soon. Medgar, Malcolm, Martin: and their widows, and their children. Reverend Ralph David Abernathy asked a certain sister to sing a song which Martin had loved—"once more," said Ralph David, "for Martin and for me," and he sat down.

The long, dark sister, whose name I do not remember, rose, very beautiful in her robes, and in her covered grief, and began to sing. It was a song I knew: "My Heavenly Father Watches Over Me." The song rang out as it might have over dark fields, long ago; she was singing of a covenant a people had made, long ago, with life, and with that larger life which ends in revelation and which moves in love.

He guides the eagle through the pathless air.

She stood there, and she sang it. How she bore it, I do not know; I think I have never seen a face quite like that face that afternoon. She was singing it for Martin, and for us.

> *And surely, He*
> *Remembers me.*
> *My heavenly Father watches over me.*

At last, we were standing, and filing out, to walk behind Martin, home. I found myself between Marlon and Sammy.

I had not been aware of the people when I had been pressing past them to get to the church. But, now, as we came out, and I looked up the road, I saw them. They were all along the road, on either side, they were on all the roofs, on either side. Every inch of ground, as far as the eye could see, was black with black people, and they stood in silence. It was the silence that undid me. I started to cry, and I stumbled, and Sammy grabbed my arm. We started to walk.

A week or so later, Billy and I were having a few drinks in some place like The Factory, I think, and one of the young Hollywood producers came over to the table to insist that the Martin Luther King story should be done at once, and that I should write it. I said that I couldn't, because I was tied up with Malcolm. (I also thought that it was a terrible idea, but I didn't bother to say so.)

Well, if I couldn't, what black writer could? He asked me to give him some names, and I did. But he shook his head, finally, and said, No, I was the only one who could do it.

I was still not reacting very quickly. But Billy got mad.

"You don't really mean any of that crap," he said, "about Jimmy being the greatest, and all that. That's bullshit. You mean that Jimmy's a commercial name, and if you get that name on a marquee linked with Martin Luther King's name, you'll make yourself some bread. That's what *you* mean."

Billy spoke the truth, but it's hard to shame the devil.

In February, the Panthers in Oakland gave a birthday party for the incarcerated Huey Newton. They asked me to "host" this party, and so I flew to Oakland. The birthday party was, of course, a rally to raise money for Huey's defense, and it was a way of letting the world know that the sorely beleaguered Panthers had no intention of throwing in the towel. It was also a way of letting the world—and Huey—know how much they loved and honored the very young man who, along with Bobby Seale, had organized The Black Panther Party for Self Defense, in the spring of 1966. That was the original name of the Party, and the name states very succinctly the need which brought the Party into existence.

It is a need which no black citizen of the ghetto has to have spelled out. When, as white cops are fond of pointing out to me, ghetto citizens "ask for more cops, not less," what they are asking for is more police protection: for crimes committed by blacks against blacks have never been taken very seriously. Furthermore, the prevention of crimes such as these is not the reason for the policeman's presence. That black people need protection *against* the police is indicated by the black community's reaction to the advent of the Panthers. Without community support, the Panthers would have been merely another insignificant street gang. It was the reaction of the black community which triggered the response of the police: these young men, claiming the right to bear arms, dressed deliberately in guerrilla fashion, standing nearby whenever a black man was accosted by a policeman to inform the black man of his rights and insisting on the right of black people to self defense, were immediately marked as "trouble-makers."

But white people seem affronted by the black distrust of white policemen, and appear to be astonished that a black man, woman, or child can have any reason to fear a white cop. One of the jurors challenged by Charles Garry during the *voir dire* proceedings before Huey's trial had this to say:

"As I said before, that I feel, and it is my opinion that racism, bigotry, and segregation is something that we have to wipe out of our hearts and minds, and not on the street. I have had an opinion that—and been taught never to resist a police officer, that we have courts of law in which to settle—no matter how much I thought I was in the right, the police officer would order me to do something, I would do it expecting if I thought I was right in what I was doing, that I could get justice in the courts"—And, in response to Garry's question, "Assuming the police officer pulled a gun and shot you, what would you do about it?" the prospective juror, at length, replied, "Let me say this. I do not believe a police officer will do that."

This is a fairly vivid and accurate example of the American piety at work. The beginning of the statement is revealing indeed: "——racism, bigotry, and segregation is something we have to wipe out of our hearts and minds and not on the street." One can wonder to whom the "we" here refers, but there isn't any question as to the object of the tense, veiled accusation contained in "not on the street." Whoever the "we" is, it is probably not the speaker—to leave it at that: but the anarchy and danger *"on the street"* are the fault of the blacks. Unnecessarily: for the police are honorable, and the courts are just.

It is no accident that Americans cling to this dream. It involves American self-love on some deep, disastrously adolescent level. And Americans are very carefully and deliberately conditioned to believe this fantasy: by their politicians, by the news they get and the way they read it, by the movies, and the television screen, and by every aspect of the popular culture. If I learned nothing else in Hollywood, I learned how abjectly the purveyors of the popular culture are manipulated. The brainwashing is so thorough that blunt, brutal reality stands not a chance against it; the revelation of corruption in high places, as in the recent "scandals" in New Jersey, for example, has no effect whatever on the American complacency; nor have any of our recent assassinations had any more effect than to cause Americans to arm—thus proving their faith in the law!—and double-lock their doors. No doubt, behind these locked doors, with their weapons handy, they switch on the tube and watch The F.B.I., or some similarly reassuring fable. It means nothing, therefore, to say to so thoroughly insulated a people that the forces of crime and the forces of law and order work hand in hand in the ghetto, bleeding it day and night. It means nothing to say that, in the eyes of the black and the poor certainly, the principal distinction between a policeman and a criminal is to be found in their attire. A criminal can break into one's house without warning, at will, and harass or molest everyone in the house, and even commit murder, and so can a cop, and they do; whoever operates whatever hustle in the ghetto without paying off the cops does not stay in business long; and it will be remembered—Malcolm certainly remembered it—that the dope trade flourished in the ghetto for years without ever being seriously molested. Not until white boys and girls began to be hooked—not until the plague in the ghetto spread outward, as plagues do—was there any public uproar. As long as it was only the niggers who were killing themselves and paying white folks handsomely for the privilege, the forces of law and order were silent. The very structure of the ghetto is a nearly irresistible temptation to criminal activity of one kind or another: it is a very rare man who does not victimize the helpless. There is no pressure on the landlord to be responsible for the upkeep of his property: the only pressure on him is to collect his rent; that is, to bleed the ghetto. There is no pressure on the butcher to be honest: if he can sell bad meat at a profit, why should he not do so? buying cheap and selling dear is what made this country great. If the storekeeper can sell, on the installment plan, a worthless "bedroom suite" for six or seven times its value, what is there to prevent him from doing so, and who will ever hear, or credit, his customer's complaint? in the unlikely event that the customer has any notion of where to go to complain. And the ghetto is a goldmine for the insurance companies. A dime a week, for five or ten or twenty years, is a lot of money, but rare indeed is the funeral paid for by the insurance. I myself do not know of any. Some member of my family had been carrying insurance at a dime a week for years and we finally persuaded her to drop it and cash in the policy—which was now worth a little over two hundred dollars. And let me state candidly, and I know, in this instance, that I do not speak only for myself, that every time I hear the black people of this country referred to as "shiftless" and "lazy," every time it is implied that the blacks deserve their condition here (look at the Irish! look at the Poles! Yes. Look at them.) I think of all the pain and sweat with which these greasy dimes were earned, with what trust they were given, in order to make the difficult passage somewhat easier for the living, in order to show honor to the dead, and I then have no compassion whatever for this country, or my countrymen.

Into this maelstrom, this present elaboration of the slave quarters, this rehearsal for a concentration camp, we place, armed, not for the protection of the ghetto but for the protection of American investments there, some blank American boy who is responsible only to some equally blank elder patriot—Andy Hardy and his pious father. Richard Harris, in his New Yorker article, *The Turning Point*, observes that "Back in 1969, a survey of three hundred police departments around the country had revealed that less than one percent required any college training. Three years later, a pilot study ordered by the President showed that most criminals were mentally below average, which suggested that that policemen who failed to stop or find them might not be much above it."

The white cop in the ghetto is as ignorant as he is frightened, and his entire concept of police work is to cow the natives. He is not compelled to answer to these natives for anything he does; whatever he does, he knows that he will be protected by his brothers, who will allow nothing to stain the honor of the force. When his working day is over, he goes home and sleeps soundly in a bed miles away—miles away from the niggers, for that is the way he really thinks of black people. And he is assured of the rightness of his course and the justice of his bigotry every time Nixon, or Agnew, or Mitchell—or the Governor of the State of California—open their mouths.

Watching the Northern reaction to the Black Panthers, observing the abject cowardice with which the Northern populations allow them to be menaced, jailed, and murdered, and all this with but the faintest pretense to legality, can fill one with great contempt for that emancipated North which, but only yesterday, was so full of admiration and sympathy for the heroic blacks in the South. Luckily, many of us were skeptical of the righteous Northern sympathy then, and so we are not overwhelmed or disappointed now. Luckily, many of us have always known, as one of my brothers put it to me something like twenty-four years ago, that "the spirit of the South is the spirit of America." Now, exactly like the Germans at the time of the Third Reich, though innocent men are being harassed, jailed, and murdered, in all the Northern cities, the citizens know nothing, and wish to know nothing, of what is happening around them. Yet the advent of the Panthers was as inevitable as the arrival of that day in Montgomery, Alabama, when Mrs. Rosa Parks refused to stand up on that bus and give her seat to a white man. That day had been coming for a very long time; danger upon danger, and humiliation upon humiliation, had piled intolerably high and gave Mrs. Parks her platform. If Mrs. Parks had merely had a headache that day, and if the community had had no grievances, there would have been no bus boycott and we would never have heard of Martin Luther King.

Just so with the Panthers: it was inevitable that the fury would erupt, that a black man, openly, in the sight of all his fellows, should challenge the policeman's gun, and not only that, but the policeman's right to be in the ghetto at all, and that man happened to be Huey. It is not conceivable that the challenge thus thrown down by this rather stubby, scrubbed-looking, gingerbread-colored youth could have had such repercussions if he had not been articulating the rage and repudiating the humiliation of thousands, more, millions of men.

Huey, on that day, the day which prompted Bobby Seale to describe Huey as "the baddest motherfucker in history," restored to the men and women of the ghetto their honor. And, for this reason, the Panthers, far from being an illegal or a lawless organization, are a great force for peace and stability in the ghetto. But, as this suggests an unprecedented measure of autonomy for the ghetto citizens, no one in authority is prepared to face this overwhelmingly obvious fact. White America remains unable to believe that black America's grievances are real; they are unable to believe this because they cannot face what this fact says about themselves and their country; and the effect of this massive and hostile incomprehension is to increase the danger in which all black people live here, especially the young. No one is more aware of this than the Black Panther leadership. This is why they are so anxious to create work and study programs in the ghetto—everything from hot lunches for school children to academic courses in high schools and colleges to the content, format, and distribution of the Black Panther newspapers. All of these are antidotes to the demoralization which is the scourge of the ghetto, are techniques of self-realization. This is also why they are taught to bear arms—not, like most white Americans, because they fear their neighbors, though indeed they have the most to fear, but in order, this time, to protect *their* lives, *their* women and children, *their* homes, rather than the life and property of an Uncle Sam who has rarely been able to treat his black nephews with more than a vaguely benign contempt. For the necessity, now, which I think nearly all black people see in different ways, is the creation and protection of a nucleus which will bring into existence a new people.

The Black Panthers made themselves visible—made themselves targets, if you like—in order to hip the black community to the presence of a new force in its midst, a force working toward the health and liberation of the community. It was a force which set itself in opposition to that force which uses people as things and which grinds down men and women and children, not only in the ghetto, into an unrecognizable powder. They announced themselves especially as a force for the rehabilitation of the young—the young who were simply perishing, in and out of schools, on the needle, in the Army, or in prison. The black community recognized this energy almost at once and flowed toward it and supported it; a people's most valuable asset is the well-being of their young. Nothing more thoroughly reveals the actual intentions of this country, domestically and globally, than the ferocity of the repression, the storm of fire and blood which the Panthers have been forced to undergo merely for declaring themselves as men—men who want "land, bread, housing, education, clothing, justice, and peace." The Panthers thus became the native Vietcong, the ghetto became the village in which the Vietcong were hidden, and in the ensuing search-and-destroy operations, everyone in the village became suspect.

Under such circumstances, the creation of a new people may seem as unlikely as fashioning the proverbial bricks without straw. On the other hand, though no one appears to learn very much from history, the rulers of empires assuredly learn the least. This unhappy failing will prove to be especially aggravated in the case of the American rulers, who have never heard of history and who have never read it, who do not know what the passion of a people can withstand or what it can accomplish, or how fatal is the moment, for the kingdom, when the passion is driven underground. They do not, for that matter, yet realize that they have already been forced to do two deadly things. They have been forced to reveal their motives, themselves, in all their unattractive nakedness; hence the reaction of the blacks, on every level, to the "Nixon Administration," which is of a stunning, unprecedented unanimity. The administration, increasingly, can rule only by fear: the fears of the people who elected them, and the fear that the administration can inspire. In spite of the tear gas, mace, clubs, helicopters, bugged installations, spies, *provocateurs*, tanks, machine guns, prisons, and detention centers, this is a shaky foundation. And they have helped to create a new pantheon of black heroes. Black babies will be born with new names hereafter and will have a standard to which to aspire new in this country, new in the world. The great question is what this will cost. The great effort is to minimize the damage. While I was on the Coast, Eldridge Cleaver and Bobby Seale and David Hilliard were still free, Fred Hampton and Mark Clark were still alive. Now, every day brings a new setback, frequently a bloody one. The government is absolutely determined to wipe the Black Panthers from the face of the earth: which is but another way of saying that it is absolutely determined to keep the nigger in his place. But this merciless and bloody repression, which is carried out, furthermore, with a remarkable contempt for the sensibilities and intelligence of the black people of this nation—for who can believe the police reports?—causes almost all blacks to realize that neither the government, the police, nor the populace are able to distinguish between a Black Panther, a black school child, or a black lawyer. And this reign of terror is creating a great problem in prisons all over this country. "Now, look," said a harassed prison official to Bobby Seale, "you got a lot of notoriety. We don't want no organizing here, or nothing else. We ain't got no Panthers, we ain't got no Rangers, we ain't got no Muslims. All we got is in-mates." All he's got is trouble. All he's got is black people who know why they're in prison, and not all of them can be kept in solitary. These blacks have unforgiving relatives, to say nothing of unforgiving children, at every level of American life. The government cannot afford to trust a single black man in this country, nor can they penetrate any black's disguise, or apprehend how devious and tenacious black patience can be, and any black man that they

appear to trust is useless to them, for he will never be trusted
by the blacks. It is true that our weapons do not appear to be
very formidable, but, then, they never have. Then, as now,
our greatest weapon is silence. As black poet Robert E. Hay-
den puts it in his poem to Harriet Tubman, "Runagate, Runagate": *Mean mean mean to be free.*

I first met Huey in San Francisco, shortly before his fateful
encounter with Officers Frey and Heanes. This encounter
took place at 5 A.M., in Oakland, on October 28, 1967—on
the same day, oddly enough, that Tony Maynard, halfway
across the world, was also being arrested for murder.

I had been in San Francisco with my sister, Gloria, I to hide
out in a friend's house, working, and she to look after me,
and also, poor girl, to rest. It had been a hard, embattled year
and we were simply holding our breath, waiting for it to end.
We hoped, with that apprehension refugees must feel when
they are approaching a border, that the passage would be un-
noticeable and that no further disasters would whiten the
bleaching year.

A very old friend of mine, a black lady—old in the sense of
friendship, indeterminate as to age—made a big West Indian
dinner for us in her apartment, and it was also on this evening
that I first met Eldridge Cleaver. I'd heard a lot about Cleaver,
but all that I knew of Huey Newton was that poster of him
in that elaborate chair, as the Black Panthers' Minister of Defense. I talked to him very little that evening. He and Gloria
talked, and, as I remember, they scarcely talked to anyone else.
I was very impressed by Huey—by his youth, his intelligence,
and by a kind of vivid anxiety of hope in him which made his
face keep changing as lights failed or flared within. Gloria was
impressed by his manners. She had expected, I know, an intolerant, rabble-rousing type who might address her, sneer-
ingly, as "sister," and put her down for not wearing a natural,
and give her an interminable, intolerable, and intolerant lecture on the meaning of "black." "I am *tired*," Gloria sometimes said, "of these middle-class, college-educated *darkies*
who never saw a rat or a roach in their lives and who never
starved or worked a day—who just turned black last *week*—
coming and telling *me* what it means to be black." Huey

wasn't and isn't like that at all. Huey talks a lot—he has a lot
to talk about—but Huey listens.

Anyway, the two of them got on famously. Before we
parted, Huey gave me several Black Panther newspapers (the
beginning of *my* file on the Panthers, Mr. Mitchell) and he
and Eldridge and I promised to keep in touch, and to see
each other soon.

I was very much impressed by Eldridge, too—it's impossible not to be impressed by him—but I felt a certain constraint
between us. I felt that he didn't like me—or not exactly that:
that he considered me a rather doubtful quantity. I'm used to
this, though I can't claim to like it. I knew he'd written about
me in *Soul On Ice*, but I hadn't yet read it. Naturally, when I
did read it, I didn't like what he had to say about me at all.
But, eventually—especially as I admired the book, and felt him
to be valuable and rare—I thought I could see why he felt
impelled to issue what was, in fact, a warning: he was being
a zealous watchman on the city wall, and I do not say that
with a sneer. He seemed to feel that I was a dangerously odd,
badly twisted, and fragile reed, of too much use to the Establishment to be trusted by blacks. I felt that he used my public
reputation against me both naïvely and unjustly, and I also felt
that I was confused in his mind with the unutterable debasement of the male—with all those faggots, punks, and sissies,
the sight and sound of whom, in prison, must have made him
vomit more than once. Well, I certainly hope I know more
about myself, and the intention of my work than that, but I
am an odd quantity. So is Eldridge; so are we all. It is a pity
that we won't, probably, ever have the time to attempt to
define once more the relationship of the odd and disreputable
artist to the odd and disreputable revolutionary; for the revolutionary, however odd, is rarely disreputable in the same
way that an artist can be. These two seem doomed to stand
forever at an odd and rather uncomfortable angle to each
other, and they both stand at a sharp and not always comfortable angle to the people they both, in their different fashions, hope to serve. But I think that it is just as well to
remember that the people are one mystery and that the person
is another. Though I know what a very bitter and delicate and
dangerous conundrum this is, it yet seems to me that a failure

to respect the person so dangerously limits one's perception of the people that one risks betraying them and oneself, either by sinking to the apathy of cynical disappointment, or rising to the rage of knowing, better than the people do, what the people want. Ultimately, the artist and the revolutionary function as they function, and pay whatever dues they must pay behind it because they are both possessed by a vision, and they do not so much follow this vision as find themselves driven by it. Otherwise, they could never endure, much less embrace, the lives they are compelled to lead. And I think we need each other, and have much to learn from each other, and, more than ever, now.

Huey and I were supposed to meet again one afternoon, but something happened and Huey couldn't make it. Shortly thereafter Gloria and I returned to New York; eventually we received a phone call from a friend, telling us what had happened to Huey. Gloria's reaction was, first—"That nice boy!" and then a sombre, dry, bitter, "At least he isn't dead."

Many months later, I went to see him, with Charles Garry, his lawyer, and some other journalists, in the Alameda County Courthouse. I remember it as being a hot day; the little room in which we sat was very crowded. Huey looked somewhat thinner and paler than when we had first met, but he was very good-natured and lucid.

Huey is a hard man to describe. People surrounded by legend rarely look the parts they've been assigned, but, in Huey's case, the Great Casting Director decided to blow everybody's mind. Huey looks like the cleanest, most scrubbed, most well-bred of adolescents—everybody's favorite baby-sitter. He is old-fashioned in the most remarkable sense, in that he treats everyone with respect, especially his elders. One can see him—almost—a few years hence working quietly for a law firm, say, able but not distinguished, with a pretty wife and a couple of sturdy children, smoking a pipe, living peacefully in a more or less integrated suburb. I say "almost" because the moment one tries to place him in any ordinary, respectable setting something goes wrong with the picture, leaving a space where one had thought to place Huey. There is in him a dedication as gentle as it is unyielding, absolutely single-minded. I began to realize this when I realized that Huey was always listening and always watching. No doubt he can be fooled, he's human, though he certainly can't be fooled easily; but it would be a very great mistake to try to lie to him. Those eyes take in everything, and behind the juvenile smile, he keeps a complicated scoreboard. It has to be complicated. That day, for example, he was dealing with the press, with photographers, with his lawyer, with me, with prison regulations, with his notoriety in the prison, with the latest pronouncements of Police Chief Gain, with the shape of the terror speedily engulfing his friends and co-workers, and he was also, after all, at that moment, standing in the shadow of the gas chamber.

Anyone, under such circumstances, can be pardoned for being rattled or even rude, but Huey was beautiful, and spoke with perfect candor of what was on his mind. Huey believes, and I do, too, in the necessity of establishing a form of socialism in this country—what Bobby Seale would probably call a "Yankee-Doodle type" socialism. This means an indigenous socialism, formed by, and responding to, the real needs of the American people. This is not a doctrinaire position, no matter how the Panthers may seem to glorify Mao or Che or Fanon. (It may perhaps be noted that these men have something to say to the century, after all, and may be read with profit, and are not, as public opinion would seem to have it, merely more subtle, or more dangerous, heroin peddlers.) The necessity for a form of socialism is based on the observation that the world's present economic arrangements doom most of the world to misery; that the way of life dictated by these arrangements is both sterile and immoral; and, finally, that there is no hope for peace in the world so long as these arrangements obtain.

But not only does the world make its arrangements slowly, and submit to any change only with the greatest reluctance; the idea of a genuine socialism in America, of all places, is an utterly intolerable idea, and those in power, as well as the bulk of the people, will resist so tremendous a heresy with all the force at their command; for which reason, precisely, Huey sits in prison and the blacks of the nation walk in danger. Watching Huey, I wondered what force sustained him, and lent him his bright dignity—then I suddenly did not wonder. The very fact that the odds are so great, and the journey, barely begun, so dangerous means that there is no time to waste, and it invests every action with an impersonal urgency. It may, for example, seem nothing to feed hot lunches to children at school, but it must be done, for the sake of the health and morale of the child, for the sake of the health and morale of his elders. It may seem nothing to establish a Liberation school, or to insist that all adult Panther members take Political Education classes, but that school, and those classes, can be very potent antidotes to the tranquilizers this country hands out as morality, truth, and history. A needle, or a piece of bread are nothing, but it is very important that all Panther members are forbidden to steal or take even that much from the people: and it changes a person when he conceives of himself, in Huey's words, as "an ox to be ridden by the people." To study the economic structure of this country, to know which hands control the wealth, and to which end, seems an academic exercise—and yet it is necessary, all of it is necessary, for discipline, for knowledge, and for power. Since the blacks are so seriously outnumbered, it is possible to dismiss these passionate exercises as mere acts of faith, preposterous to everyone but the believer: but no one in power appears to find the Panthers even remotely preposterous. On the contrary, they have poured out on these black, defenseless, outnumbered heads a storm of retribution so unspeakably vindictive as to have attracted the wondering and skeptical notice of the world—which does not accept the American version of reality as gospel; and they apparently consider the Panthers so dangerous that nations—or, rather, governments—friendly to the United States have refused to allow individual Panthers to land on their shores, much to the displeasure of their already restive and distinctly crucial student populations. This is to sum up the effect of the Panthers negatively, but this effect reveals volumes about America, and our role in the world. Those who rule in this country now—as distinguished, it must be said, from governing it—are determined to smash the Panthers in order to hide the truth of the American black situation. They want to hide this truth from black people—by making it impossible for them to respond to it—and they would like to hide it from the world; and not, alas, because they are ashamed of it but because they have no intention of changing it. They cannot afford to change it. They would not know how to go about changing it, even if their imaginations were capable of encompassing the concept of black freedom. But this concept lives in their imaginations, and in the popular imagination, only as a nightmare. Blacks have never been free in this country, never was it intended that they should be free, and the spectre of so dreadful a freedom—the idea of a license so bloody and abandoned—conjures up another, unimaginable country, a country in which no decent, God-fearing white man or woman can live. A civilized country is, by definition, a country dominated by whites, in which the blacks clearly know their place. This is really the way the generality of white Americans feel, and they consider—quite rightly, as far as any concern for their interest goes—that it is they who, now, at long last, are being represented in Washington. And, of course, any real commitment to black freedom in this country would have the effect of reordering all our priorities, and altering all our commitments, so that, for horrendous example, we would be supporting black freedom fighters in South Africa and Angola, and would not be allied with Portugal, would be closer to Cuba than we are to Spain, would be supporting the Arab nations instead of Israel, and would never have felt compelled to follow the French into Southeast Asia. But such a course would forever wipe the smile from the face of that friend we all rejoice to have at Chase Manhattan. The course we *are* following is bound to have the same effect, and with dreadful repercussions, but to hint such things now is very close to treason. In spite of our grim situation, and even facing the possibility that the Panthers may be smashed and driven underground, they—that is, the black people here—yet have more going for them than did those outnumbered Christians, running through the catacombs: and digging the grave, as Malcolm put it, of the mighty Roman empire.

In this place, and more particularly, in this time, generations appear to flower, flourish, and wither with the speed of light. I don't think that this is merely the inevitable reflection of middle age: I suspect that there really has been some radical alteration in the structure, the nature, of time. One may say that there are no clear images; everything seems superimposed on, and at war with something else. There are no clear vistas: the road that seems to pull one forward into the future is also pulling one backward into the past. I felt, anyway, kaleidoscopic, fragmented, walking through the streets of San Francisco, trying to decipher whatever it was that my own consciousness made of all the elements in which I was entangled, and which were all tangled up in me. In spite of the fact that my reasons for being in San Francisco were rather chilling, there were compensations. Looking into Huey's face, even though he was in jail, had been a kind of compensation— at least I knew that he was holding on. Talking to Charles Garry, because he is intelligent, honest, and vivid, and devoted to Huey, had been a compensation, and meeting Huey's brother, Melvin, and simply walking through the streets of San Francisco, by far my favorite town—my favorite American town.

I had first been in San Francisco at the height of the civil rights movement, first on an *Esquire* junket, then on a lecture tour. There had been no flower children here then, only earnest, eager students anxious to know what they could "do." Would black people take it amiss if the white kids came into the neighborhood, and—fraternized is probably the only word—with the kids in the pool halls, the bars, the soda fountains? Would black people take it amiss if some of them were to visit a black church? Could they invite members of the black congregation to their white churches, or would the black people feel uncomfortable? Wouldn't it be a good idea if the black and white basketball teams played each other? And there wouldn't be any trouble about the dance afterward, because all the fellows would invite their own dates. Did I think they should go south to work on voting registration this summer, or should they stay home and work in their own communities? Some of them wanted to get a discussion started on open housing—on Proposition Fourteen—and would I come and speak and answer questions? What do you do about older people who are *very nice, really*, but who just—well, who just don't seem to understand the issues—what do you say to them, what do you do? And the black kids: It's another way of life—you have to understand that. *Yeah*, a whole lot of black people are going to put you down, you have to understand *that*. Man, I know my mother don't really want to come to your church. We got more life in *our* church. Mr. B., Brother Malcolm says that no people in history have ever been respected who did not own their own land. What do you say about that, and how are we going to *get* the land? My parents think I shouldn't be sitting in and demonstrating and all that, that I should be getting an education first. What do you think about that? Mr. B., what do you say to an older black man who just feels discouraged about everything? Mr. B., what are we going to do about the dope traffic in the ghetto? Mr. B., do you think black people should join the Army? Mr. B., do you think the Muslims are right and we should be a separate state? Mr. B., have you ever been to Africa? Mr. B., don't you think the first thing our people need is unity? How can we trust those white people in Washington? they don't really care about black people. Mr. B., what do you think of integration? Don't you think it might just be a trap, to brainwash black people? I come to the conclusion that the man just ain't never going to do right. He a devil, just like Malcolm says he is. I told my teacher I wasn't going to salute the flag no more— don't you think I was right? You mean, if we have a dance after the basketball game, all the brothers is going to have to dance with the *same girl* all night? What about the white guys? Oh, they can dance with *your* girl. Laughter, embarrassment, bewildered ill-feeling. Mr. B., What do *you* think of intermarriage?

Real questions can be absurdly phrased, and probably can be answered only by the questioner, and, at that, only in time. But real questions, especially from the young, are very moving and I will always remember the faces of some of those children. Though the questions facing them were difficult, they appeared, for the most part, to like the challenge. It is true that the white students seemed to look on the black students with some apprehension and some bewilderment, and they also revealed how deeply corrupted they were by the doctrine of white supremacy in many unconscious ways. But the black students, though they were capable of an elaborate, deliberate, and overpowering condescension, seemed, for the most part, to have their tongue in their cheek and exhibited very little malice or venom—toward the students: they felt toward their white elders a passionate contempt.

What seemed most to distress the white students—distress may be too strong a word; what rendered them thoughtful and uneasy—was the unpromising nature of their options. It was not that they had compared their options with those of the black student and been upset by the obvious, worldly injustice. On the contrary, they seemed to feel, some dimly and some desperately, that the roles which they, as whites, were expected to play were not very meaningful, and perhaps—therefore—not very honorable. I remember one boy who was already set to become an executive at one of the major airlines—for him, he joked, bleakly, the sky would be the limit. But he wondered if he could "hold on" to himself, if he could retain the respect of some of the people who respected him now. What he meant was that he hoped not to be programmed out of all meaningful human existence, and, clearly, he feared the worst. He, like many students, was being forced to choose between treason and irrelevance. Their moral obligations to the darker brother, if they were real, and if they were really to be acted on, placed them in conflict with all that they had loved and all that had given them an identity, rendered their present uncertain and their future still more so, and even jeopardized their means of staying alive. They were far from judging or repudiating the American state as oppressive or immoral—they were merely profoundly uneasy. They were aware that the blacks looked on the white commitment very skeptically indeed, and they made it clear that they did not depend on the whites. They could not depend on the whites until the whites had a clearer sense of what they had let themselves in for. And what the white students had not expected to let themselves in for, when boarding the Freedom Train, was the realization that the black situation in America was but one aspect of the fraudulent nature of American life. They had not expected to be forced to judge their parents, their elders, and their antecedents, so harshly, and they had not realized how cheaply, after all, the rulers of the republic held their white lives to be. Coming to the defense of the rejected and destitute, they were confronted with the extent of their own alienation, and the unimaginable dimensions of their own poverty. They were privileged and secure only so long as they did, in effect, what they were told: but they had been raised to believe that they were free.

I next came to San Francisco at the time of the flower children, when everyone, young and not so young, was freaking out on whatever came to hand. The flower children were all up and down the Haight-Ashbury section of San Francisco—and they might have been everywhere else, too, but for the vigilance of the cops—with their long hair, their beads, their robes, their fancied resistance, and, in spite of a shrewd, hard skepticism as unnerving as it was unanswerable, really tormented by the hope of love. The fact that their uniforms and their jargon precisely represented the distances they had yet to cover before arriving at that maturity which makes love possible—or no longer possible—could not be considered their fault. They had been born into a society in which nothing was harder to achieve, in which perhaps nothing was more scorned and feared than the idea of the soul's maturity. Their flowers had the validity, at least, of existing in direct challenge to the romance of the gun; their gentleness, however specious, was nevertheless a direct repudiation of the American adoration of violence. Yet they looked—alas—doomed. They seemed to sense their doom. They really were flower children, having opted out on the promises and possibilities offered them by the shining and now visibly perishing republic. I could not help feeling, watching them, knowing them to be idealistic, fragmented, and impotent, that, exactly as the Third Reich had had first to conquer the German opposition before getting around to the Jews, and then the rest of Europe, my republic, which, unhappily, I was beginning to think of as the Fourth Reich, would be forced to plow under the flower children—in all their variations—before getting around to the blacks and then the rest of the world.

The blacks, for the most part, were not to be found with the flower children. In the eerie American way, they walked the same streets, were to be found in the same neighborhoods, were the targets of the very same forces, seemed to bear each other no ill will—on the contrary indeed, especially from the point of view of the forces watching them—and yet they seemed to have no effect on each other, and they certainly were not together. The blacks were not putting their trust in flowers. They were putting their trust in guns.

An historical wheel had come full circle. The descendants of the cowboys, who had slaughtered the Indians, the issue of those adventurers who had enslaved the blacks, wished to lay down their swords and shields. But these could be laid down only at Sambo's feet, and this was why they could not be together: I felt like a lip-reader watching the communication of despair.

It was appalling, anyway, with or without flowers, to find so many children in the streets. In benighted, incompetent Africa, I had never encountered an orphan: the American streets resembled nothing so much as one vast, howling, unprecedented orphanage. It has been vivid to me for many years that what we call a race problem here is not a race problem at all: to keep calling it that is a way of avoiding the problem. The problem is rooted in the question of how one treats one's flesh and blood, especially one's children. The blacks are the despised and slaughtered children of the great Western house—nameless and unnameable bastards. This is a fact so obvious, so speedily verifiable, that it would seem pure insanity to deny it, and yet the life of the entire country is predicated on this denial, this monstrous and pathetic lie. For many generations, many a white American has gone—sometimes shrieking—to his grave, knowing that his own son, the issue of his loins, was denied, and sometimes murdered by him. Many a white American woman has gone through life carrying the knowledge that she is responsible for the slaughter of her lover, and also for the destruction of that love's issue. *Ye are liars and the truth's not in you:* it cannot be pretty to be forced, with every day the good Lord sends, to tell so many lies about everything. It demands a tremendous effort of the will and an absolute surrender of the personality to act on the lies one tells oneself. It is not true that people become liars without knowing it. A liar always knows he is lying, and that is why liars travel in packs: in order to be reassured that the judgment day will never come for them. They need each other for the well-being, the health, the perpetuation of their lie. They have a tacit agreement to guard each other's secrets, for they have the same secret. That is why all liars are cruel and filthy minded—one's merely got to listen to their dirty jokes, to what they think is funny, which is also what they think is real.

The flower children seemed completely aware that the blacks were their denied brothers, seemed even to be patiently waiting for the blacks to recognize that they had repudiated the house. For it seemed to have struck the flower children—I judged this from their conduct, from what seemed to be their blind and moving need to become organic, autonomous, loving and joyful creatures; their desire to connect love, joy, and eroticism, so that all flowed together as one—that they were themselves the issue of a dirty joke, the dirty joke which has always been hidden at the heart of the legend of the Virgin birth. They were in the streets in the hope of becoming whole. They had taken the first step—they had said, No. Whether or not they would be able to take the second step, the harder step—of saying, Yes, and then going for their own most private broke—was a question which much exercised my mind, as indeed it seemed to exercise the minds, very loosely speaking, of all the tourists and policemen in the area. When the heir of a great house repudiates the house, the house cannot continue, unless it looks to alien blood to save it; and here were the heirs and heiresses of all the ages, in the streets, along with that blood always considered to be most alien, never lawfully to be mixed with that of the sons and daughters of the great house.

I seemed to observe in some of the eyes that watched them that same bright, paranoid, flinching bewilderment I have seen in the eyes of some white Americans when they encounter a black man abroad. In the latter case, one sometimes had the feeling that they were ducking a blow—that they had encountered their deadliest enemy on a lonely mountain road. The eyes seemed to say, *I didn't do it! Let me pass!* and in such a moment one recognized the fraudulent and expedient nature of the American innocence which has always been able to persuade itself that it does not know what it knows too well. Or, it was exactly like watching someone who finds himself caught in a lie: for a black man abroad is no longer one of "our" niggers, is a stranger, not to be controlled by anything his countrymen think or say or do. In a word, he is free and thus discovers how little equipped his countrymen are to behold him in that state. In San Francisco, the eyes that watched seemed to feel that the children were deliberately giving away family secrets in the hope of egging on the blacks to destroy the family. And that is precisely what they *were* doing—helplessly, unconsciously, out of a profound desire to be saved, to live. But the blacks already knew the family secrets and had no interest in them. Nor did they have much confidence in these troubled white boys and girls. The black trouble was of a different order, and blacks had to be concerned with much more than their own private happiness or unhappiness. They had to be aware that this troubled white person might suddenly decide not to be in trouble and go home— and when he went home, he would be the enemy. Therefore, it was best not to speak too freely to anyone who spoke too freely to you, especially not on the streets of a nation which probably has more hired informers working for it, here and all over the world, than any nation in history. True rebels, after all, are as rare as true lovers, and, in both cases, to mistake a fever for a passion can destroy one's life.

The black and white confrontation, whether it be hostile, as in the cities and the labor unions, or with the intention of forming a common front and creating the foundations of a new society, as with the students and the radicals, is obviously crucial, containing the shape of the American future and the only potential of a truly valid American identity. No one knows precisely how identities are forged, but it is safe to say that identities are not invented: an identity would seem to be arrived at by the way in which the person faces and uses his experience. It is a long drawn-out and somewhat bewildering and awkward process. When I was young, for example, it was an insult to be called black. The blacks have now taken over this once pejorative term and made of it a rallying cry and a badge of honor and are teaching their children to be proud that they are black. It is true that the children are as vari-colored—tea, coffee, chocolate, mocha, honey, eggplant coated with red pepper, red pepper dipped in eggplant—as it is possible for a people to be; black people, here, are no more uniformly black than white people are physically white; but

the shades of color, which have been used for so long to distress and corrupt our minds and set us against each other,
now count, at least in principle, for nothing. Black is a tremendous spiritual condition, one of the greatest challenges
anyone alive can face—this is what the blacks are saying.
Nothing is easier, nor, for the guilt-ridden American, more
inevitable, than to dismiss this as chauvinism in reverse. But,
in this, white Americans are being—it is a part of their
fate—inaccurate. To be liberated from the stigma of blackness
by embracing it is to cease, forever, one's interior agreement
and collaboration with the authors of one's degradation. It
abruptly reduces the white enemy to a contest merely physical,
which he can win only physically. White men have killed black
men for refusing to say, "Sir": but it was the corroboration
of their worth and their power that they wanted, and not the
corpse, still less the staining blood. When the black man's
mind is no longer controlled by the white man's fantasies, a
new balance or what may be described as an unprecedented
inequality begins to make itself felt: for the white man no
longer knows who he is, whereas the black man knows them
both. For if it is difficult to be released from the stigma of
blackness, it is clearly at least equally difficult to surmount the
delusion of whiteness. And as the black glories in his new-
found color, which is *his* at last, and asserts, not always with
the very greatest politeness, the unanswerable validity and
power of his being—even in the shadow of death—the white
is very often affronted and very often made afraid. He has his
reasons, after all, not only for being weary of the entire concept of color, but fearful as to what may be made of this
concept once it has fallen, as it were, into the wrong hands.
And one may indeed be wary, but the point is that it was
inevitable that black and white should arrive at this dizzying
height of tension. Only when we have passed this moment
will we know what our history has made of us.

Many white people appear to live in a state of carefully repressed terror in relation to blacks. There is something curious
and paradoxical about this terror, which is involved not only
with the common fear of death, but with a sense of its being
considered utterly irrelevant whether one is breathing or not.
I think that this has something to do with the fact that,

whereas white men have killed black men for sport, or out of terror or out of the intolerable excess of terror called hatred, or out of the necessity of affirming their identity as white men, none of these motives appear necessarily to obtain for black men: it is not necessary for a black man to hate a white man, or to have any particular feelings about him at all, in order to realize that he must kill him. Yes, we have come, or are coming to this, and there is no point in flinching before the prospect of this exceedingly cool species of fratricide—which prospect white people, after all, have brought on themselves. Of course, whenever a black man discusses violence he is said to be "advocating" it. This is very far indeed from my intention, if only because I have no desire whatever to see a generation perish in the streets. But the shape and extent of whatever violence may come is not in the hands of people like myself, but in the hands of the American people, who are at present among the most dishonorable and violent people in the world. I am merely trying to face certain blunt, human facts. I do not carry a gun and do not consider myself to be a violent man: but my life has more than once depended on the gun in a brother's holster. I know that when certain powerful and blatant enemies of black people are shoveled, at last, into the ground I may feel a certain pity that they spent their lives so badly, but I certainly do not mourn their passing, nor, when I hear that they are ailing, do I pray for their recovery. I know what I would do if I had a gun and someone had a gun pointed at my brother, and I would not count ten to do it and there would be no hatred in it, nor any remorse. People who treat other people as less than human must not be surprised when the bread they have cast on the waters comes floating back to them, poisoned.

I'm black and I'm proud: yet, I suppose that the most accurate term, now, for this history, this particular and peculiar danger, as well as for all persons produced out of it and struggling in it, is: Afro-American. Which is but a wedding, however, of two confusions, an arbitrary linking of two undefined and currently undefinable proper nouns. I mean that, in the case of Africa, Africa is still chained to Europe, and exploited by Europe, and Europe and America are chained together; and as long as this is so, it is hard to speak of Africa except as a cradle and a potential. Not until the many millions of people on the continent of Africa control their land and their resources will the African personality flower or genuinely African institutions flourish and reveal Africa as she is. But it is striking that that part of the North American continent which calls itself, arrogantly enough, *America* poses as profound and dangerous a mystery for human understanding as does the fabled dark continent of Africa. The terms in which the mystery is posed, as well as the mysteries themselves, are very different. Yet, when one places the mysteries side by side—ponders the history and possible future of Africa, and the history and possible future of America—something is illuminated of the nature, the depth and the tenacity of the great war between black and white life styles here. Something is suggested of the nature of fecundity, the nature of sterility, and one realizes that it is by no means a simple matter to know which is which: the one can very easily resemble the other. Questions louder than drums begin beating in the mind, and one realizes that what is called civilization lives first of all in the mind, has the mind above all as its province, and that the civilization, or its rudiments, can continue to live long after its externals have vanished—they can never entirely vanish from the mind. These questions—they are too vague for questions, this excitement, this discomfort—concern the true nature of any inheritance and the means by which that inheritance is handed down. There is a reason, after all, that some people wish to colonize the moon, and others dance before it as before an ancient friend. And the extent to which these apprehensions, instincts, relations, are modified by the passage of time, or the accumulation of inventions, is a question that no one seems able to answer. All men, clearly, are primitive, but it can be doubted that all men are primitive in the same way; and if they are not, it can only be because, in that absolutely unassailable privacy of the soul, they do not worship the same gods. Both continents, Africa and America, be it remembered, were "discovered"—what a wealth of arrogance that little word contains!—with devastating results for the indigenous populations, whose only human use thereafter was as the source of capital for white people. On both continents the white and the dark gods met in combat, and it is on the outcome of this combat that the future of both continents depends.

To be an Afro-American, or an American black, is to be in the situation, intolerably exaggerated, of all those who have ever found themselves part of a civilization which they could in no wise honorably defend—which they were compelled, indeed, endlessly to attack and condemn—and who yet spoke out of the most passionate love, hoping to make the kingdom new, to make it honorable and worthy of life. Whoever is part of whatever civilization helplessly loves some aspects of it, and some of the people in it. A person does not lightly elect to oppose his society. One would much rather be at home among one's compatriots than be mocked and detested by them. And there is a level on which the mockery of the people, even their hatred, is moving because it is so blind: it is terrible to watch people cling to their captivity and insist on their own destruction. I think black people have always felt this about America, and Americans, and have always seen, spinning above the thoughtless American head, the shape of the wrath to come.

Epilogue:
Who Has Believed Our Report?

THIS BOOK has been much delayed by trials, assassinations, funerals, and despair. Nor is the American crisis, which is part of a global, historical crisis, likely to resolve itself soon. An old world is dying, and a new one, kicking in the belly of its mother, time, announces that it is ready to be born. This birth will not be easy, and many of us are doomed to discover that we are exceedingly clumsy midwives. No matter, so long as we accept that our responsibility is to the newborn: the acceptance of responsibility contains the key to the necessarily evolving skill.

This book is not finished—can never be finished, by me. As of this writing, I am waiting to hear the fate of Tony Maynard, whose last address was Attica. Though the cops have been buried, with much patriotic grief, the blacks are still waiting to hear who is alive or dead. Mr. Nixon has congratulated Mr. Rockefeller, who has congratulated the police: so much for that. As to the effect of all this—and so much more!—on the Black Panther leadership and on black or non-white people, in this country, and all over the world, time will give a sufficiently authoritative answer. People, even if they are so thoughtless as to be born black, do not come into this world merely to provide mink coats and diamonds for chattering, trivial, pale matrons, or genocidal opportunities for their unsexed, unloved, and, finally, despicable men—oh, pioneers!

There will be bloody holding actions all over the world, for years to come: but the Western party is over, and the white man's sun has set. Period.

Angela Davis is still in danger. George Jackson has joined his beloved baby brother, Jon, in the royal fellowship of death. And one may say that Mrs. Georgia Jackson and the alleged mother of God have, at last, found something in common. Now, it is the Virgin, the alabaster Mary, who must embrace the despised black mother whose children are also the issue of the Holy Ghost.

New York, San Francisco, Hollywood, London,
Istanbul, St. Paul de Vence, 1967–1971.

THE DEVIL FINDS WORK

An Essay

For
    PAULA-MARIA,
        on her birthday,
and
    JOHN LATHAM
and
    brother, DAVID MOSES

I

Congo Square

For our God is a consuming fire.
Hebrews 12:29

JOAN CRAWFORD's straight, narrow, and lonely back. We are following her through the corridors of a moving train. She is looking for someone, or she is trying to escape from someone. She is eventually intercepted by, I think, Clark Gable.

I am fascinated by the movement on, and of, the screen, that movement which is something like the heaving and swelling of the sea (though I have not yet been to the sea): and which is also something like the light which moves on, and especially beneath, the water.

I am about seven. I am with my mother, or my aunt. The movie is *Dance, Fools, Dance*.

I don't remember the film. A child is far too self-centered to relate to any dilemma which does not, somehow, relate to him—to his own evolving dilemma. The child escapes into what he would like his situation to be, and I certainly did not wish to be a fleeing fugitive on a moving train; and, also, with quite another part of my mind, I was aware that Joan Crawford was a white lady. Yet, I remember being sent to the store sometime later, and a colored woman, who, to me, looked exactly like Joan Crawford, was buying something. She was so incredibly beautiful—she seemed to be wearing the sunlight, rearranging it around her from time to time, with a movement of one hand, with a movement of her head, and with her smile—that, when she paid the man and started out of the store, I started out behind her. The storekeeper, who knew me, and others in the store who knew my mother's little boy (and who also knew my Miss Crawford!) laughed and called me back. Miss Crawford also laughed and looked down at me with so beautiful a smile that I was not even embarrassed. Which was rare for me.

479

Tom Mix, on his white horse. Actually, it was Tom Mix's hat, a shadow in the shadow of the hat, a kind of rocky background (which, again, was always moving) and the white horse. Tom Mix was a serial. Every Saturday, then, if memory serves, we left Tom Mix and some bleakly interchangeable girl in the most dreadful danger—or, rather, we left the hat and the shadow of the hat and the white horse: for the horse was not interchangeable and the serial could not have existed without it.

The Last of the Mohicans: Randolph Scott (a kind of fifteenth-rate Gary Cooper) and Binnie Barnes (a kind of funky Geraldine Fitzgerald), Heather Angel (a somewhat more bewildered Olivia de Havilland) and Philip Reed (a precursor of Anthony Quinn). Philip Reed was the Indian, Uncas, whose savage, not to say slavish adoration of Miss Angel's fine blonde frame drives her over a cliff, headlong, to her death. She has chosen death before dishonor, which made perfect sense. The erring Uncas eventually pays for his misguided lust with his life, and a tremulous, wet-eyed, brave couple, Randolph Scott and Binnie Barnes, eventually, hand in hand, manage to make it out of the wilderness. Into America, or back to England, I really do not remember, and I don't suppose that it matters.*

20,000 Years in Sing Sing: Spencer Tracy and Bette Davis. By this time, I had been taken in hand by a young white schoolteacher, a beautiful woman, very important to me. I was between ten and eleven. She had directed my first play and endured my first theatrical tantrums and had then decided to escort me into the world. She gave me books to read and talked to me about the books, and about the world: about Spain, for example, and Ethiopia, and Italy, and the German Third Reich; and took me to see plays and films, plays and films to which no one else would have dreamed of taking a ten-year-old boy. I loved her, of course, and absolutely, with a child's love; didn't understand half of what she said, but remembered it; and it stood me in good stead later. It is certainly partly because of her, who arrived in my terrifying life so soon, that I never really managed to hate white people—

---

*The novel, which I read much later, is not my favorite novel, and, on some other day, I may detail my quarrel with it; but it is far more honest and courageous than the film.

though, God knows, I have often wished to murder more than one or two. But Bill Miller—her name was Orilla, we called her Bill—was not white for me in the way, for example, that Joan Crawford was white, in the way that the landlords and the storekeepers and the cops and most of my teachers were white. She didn't baffle me that way and she never frightened me and she never lied to me. I never felt her pity, either, in spite of the fact that she sometimes brought us old clothes (because she worried about our winters) and cod-liver oil, especially for me, because I seemed destined, then, to be carried away by whooping cough.

I was a child, of course, and, therefore, unsophisticated. I don't seem ever to have had any innate need (or, indeed, any innate ability) to distrust people: and so I took Bill Miller as she was, or as she appeared to be to me. Yet, the difference between Miss Miller and other white people, white people as they lived in my imagination, and also as they were in life, had to have had a profound and bewildering effect on my mind. Bill Miller was not at all like the cops who had already beaten me up, she was not like the landlords who called me nigger, she was not like the storekeepers who laughed at me. I had found white people to be unutterably menacing, terrifying, mysterious—wicked: and they were mysterious, in fact, to the extent that they were wicked: the unfathomable question being, precisely, this one: what, under heaven, or beneath the sea, or in the catacombs of hell, could cause any people to act as white people acted? From Miss Miller, therefore, I began to suspect that white people did not act as they did because they were white, but for some other reason, and I began to try to locate and understand the reason. She, too, anyway, was treated like a nigger, especially by the cops, and she had no love for landlords.

My father said, during all the years I lived with him, that I was the ugliest boy he had ever seen, and I had absolutely no reason to doubt him. But it was not my father's hatred of *my* frog-eyes which hurt me, this hatred proving, in time, to be rather more resounding than real: I have my mother's eyes. When my father called me ugly, he was not attacking me so much as he was attacking my mother. (No doubt, he was also attacking my real, and unknown, father.) And I loved my mother. I knew that she loved me, and I sensed that she was paying an enormous price for me. I was a boy, and so I didn't really too much care that my father thought me hideous. (So I said to myself—this judgment, nevertheless, was to have a decidedly terrifying effect on my life.) But I thought that he must have been stricken blind (or was as mysteriously wicked as white people, a paralyzing thought) if he was unable to see that my mother was absolutely beyond any question the most beautiful woman in the world.

So, here, now, was Bette Davis, on that Saturday afternoon, in close-up, over a champagne glass, pop-eyes popping. I was astounded. I had caught my father, not in a lie, but in an infirmity. For, here, before me, after all, was a *movie star: white:* and if she was white and a movie star, she was *rich:* and she was *ugly.* I felt exactly the same way I felt, just before this moment, or just after, when I was in the street, playing, and I saw an old, very black, and very drunk woman stumbling up the sidewalk, and I ran upstairs to make my mother come to the window and see what I had found: *You see? You see? She's uglier than you, Mama! She's uglier than me!* Out of bewilderment, out of loyalty to my mother, probably, and also because I sensed something menacing and unhealthy (for me, certainly) in the face on the screen, I gave Davis's skin the dead-white greenish cast of something crawling from under a rock, but I was held, just the same, by the tense intelligence of the forehead, the disaster of the lips: and when she moved, she moved just like a nigger. Eventually, from a hospital bed, she murders someone, and Tracy takes the weight, to Sing Sing. In his arms, Davis cries and cries, and the movie ends. "What's going to happen to her now?" I asked Bill Miller. "We don't know," said Bill, conveying to me, nevertheless, that she would probably never get over it, that people pay for what they do.

I had not yet heard Bessie Smith's *"why they call this place the Sing Sing?/Come stand here by this rock pile, and listen to these hammers ring,"* and it would be seven years before I would begin working for the railroad. It was to take a longer time than that before I would cry; a longer time than that before I would cry in anyone's arms; and a long long long long time before I would begin to realize what I myself was doing with my enormous eyes—or vice versa. This had nothing to with Davis, the actress, or with all those hang-ups I didn't yet know I had: I had discovered that my infirmity might not be my doom: my infirmity, or infirmities, might be forged into weapons.

For, I was not only considered by my father to be ugly. I was considered by everyone to be "strange," including my poor mother, who didn't, however, beat me for it. Well, if I was "strange"—and I knew that I must be, otherwise people would not have treated me so strangely, and I would not have been so miserable—perhaps I could find a way to use my strangeness. A "strange" child, anyway, dimly and fearfully apprehends that the years are not likely to make him less strange. Therefore, if he wishes to live, he must calculate, and I knew that I had to live. I very much wanted my mother to be happy and to be proud of me, and I very much loved my brothers and my sisters, who, in a sense, were all I had. My father showed no favoritism, he did not beat me worse than the others because I was not his son. (I didn't know this then, anyway, none of the children did, and by the time we all found out, it became just one more detail of the peculiar journey we had made in company with each other.) I knew, too, that my mother depended on me. I was not always dependable, for no child can be, but I tried: and I knew that I might have to prepare myself to be, one day, the actual head of my family. I did not actually do this, either, for we were all forced to take on our responsibilities each for the other, and to discharge them in our different ways. The eldest can be, God knows, as much a burden as a help, and is doomed to be something of a mystery for those growing up behind him—a mystery when not, indeed, an intolerable exasperation. *I*, nevertheless, was the eldest, a responsibility I did not intend to fail, and my first conscious calculation as to how to go about defeating the world's intentions for me and mine began on that Saturday afternoon in what we called *the movies*, but which was actually my first entrance into the cinema of my mind.

I read *Uncle Tom's Cabin* over and over and over again— this is the first book I can remember having read—and then I read *A Tale of Two Cities*—over and over and over again.

Bill Miller takes me to see *A Tale of Two Cities*, at the Lincoln, on 135th Street. I am twelve.

I did not yet know that virtually every black community in America contains a movie house, or, sometimes, in those days, an actual theater, called the Lincoln, or the Booker T. Washington, nor did I know why; any more than I knew why The Cotton Club was called The Cotton Club. I knew about Lincoln only that he had freed the slaves (in the South, which made the venture remote from me) and then had been shot, dead, in a theater, by an actor; and a movie I was never to see, called *The Prisoner of Shark Island*, had something to do with the murder of Lincoln. How I knew this, I do not remember precisely. But I know that I read everything I could get my hands on, including movie advertisements, and *Uncle Tom's Cabin* had had a tremendous impact on me, and I certainly reacted to the brutal conjunction of the words, *prisoner*, and *shark*, and *island*. I may have feared becoming a prisoner or feared that I was one already; had never seen a shark—I hoped: but I was certainly trapped on an island. And, in any case, the star of this film, Warner Baxter, later, but during the same era, made a film with the female star of *A Tale of Two Cities*, called *Slave Ship*: which I did not see, either.

I knew about Booker T. Washington less than I knew about my father's mother, who had been born a slave, and who died in our house when I was little: a child cannot make the connection between *slave* and *grandmother*, and it was to take me a while (mainly because I had discovered the Schomburg collection at the 135th Street Library) to read *Up From Slavery*: but, when I read it, I no longer knew which way was up. As for The Cotton Club, I knew only that it was a dance hall which gave out free Thanksgiving dinners every Thanksgiving (!) for which my brother, George, and I, stood in line. Which means that I knew that I was poor, and knew that I was black, but did not yet know what being black really meant, what it meant, that is, in the history of my country, and in my own history. Bill could instruct me as to how poverty came about and what it meant and what it did, and, also, what it was meant to do: but she could not instruct me as to blackness, except obliquely, feeling that she had neither the right nor the authority, and also knowing that I was certain to find out.

Thus, she tried to suggest to me the extent to which the world's social and economic arrangements are responsible for (and to) the world's victims. But a victim may or may not have a color, just as he may or may not have virtue: a difficult, not to say unpopular notion, for nearly everyone prefers to be defined by his status, which, unlike his virtue, is ready to wear.

The 1936 Metro-Goldwyn-Mayer production of *A Tale of Two Cities* ends with this enormity sprawled across the screen:

I am the resurrection and the life, saith the Lord: he that believeth in me, though he were dead, yet shall he live: and he that believeth in me shall never die.

I had lived with this text all my life, which made encountering it on the screen of the Lincoln Theater absolutely astounding: and I had lived with the people of *A Tale of Two Cities* for very nearly as long. I had no idea what *Two Cities* was really about, any more than I knew what *Uncle Tom's Cabin* was really about, which was why I had read them both so obsessively: they had something to tell me. It was this particular child's way of circling around the question of what it meant to be a nigger. It was the reason that I was reading Dostoevsky, a writer—or, rather, for me, a messenger—whom I would have had to understand, obviously, even less: my relentless pursuit of *Crime and Punishment* made my father (vocally) and my mother (silently) consider the possibility of brain fever. I was intrigued, but not misled, by the surface of these novels—Sydney Carton's noble renunciation of his life on the spectacular guillotine, Tom's forbearance before Simon Legree, the tracking down of Raskolnikov: the time of my time was to reduce all these images to the angel dancing on the edge of the junkie's needle: I did not believe in any of these people so much as I believed in their situation, which I suspected, dreadfully, to have something to do with my own.

And it had clearly escaped everyone's notice that I had already been bull-whipped through the Psalms of David and The Book of Job, to say nothing of the arrogant and loving Isaiah, the doomed Ezekiel, and the helplessly paranoiac Saint Paul: such a forced march, designed to prepare the mind for conciliation and safety, can also prepare it for subversion and danger. For, I was on Job's side, for example, *though He slay me, yet will I trust Him*, and *I will maintain mine own ways before Him*—You will not talk to *me* from the safety of your whirlwind, never—and, yet, something in me, out of the unbelievable pride and sorrow and beauty of my father's face, caused me to understand—I did not understand, perhaps I still do not understand, and never will—caused me to begin to accept the fatality and the inexorability of that voice out of the whirlwind, for if one is not able to live with so crushing and continuing a mystery, one is not able to live.

The pride and sorrow and beauty of my father's face: for that man I called my father really *was* my father in every sense except the biological, or literal one. He formed me, and he raised me, and he did not let me starve: and he gave me something, however harshly, and however little I wanted it, which prepared me for an impending horror which he could not prevent. This is not a Western idea, but fathers and sons arrive at that relationship only by claiming that relationship: that is, by paying for it. If the relationship of father to son could really be reduced to biology, the whole earth would blaze with the glory of fathers and sons. (But to pursue this further carries us far beyond the confines of the present discussion.)

In the novel, *A Tale of Two Cities*, it had been Madame Defarge who most struck me. I recognized that unrelenting hatred, for it was all up and down my streets, and in my father's face and voice. The wine cask, *shattered like a walnut shell*, shattered every Saturday night on the corner of our street, and, yes, Dickens was right, the gutters turned a bright and then a rusty red. I understood the knitted registers as hope and fate, for I knew that everything (including my own name) had long been written in The Book: *you may run on a great long time but great God Almighty's going to cut you down!* I understood the meaning of the rose in the turban of Madame Defarge as she sits knitting in the wine shop, the flower in the headdress meant to alert the neighborhood to the presence of a spy. We lived by such signals, and long before it was safe to say *there is a rose in Spanish Harlem!*

When, at last, in the film, the people rise and fill the streets and alleys and hurl themselves onto the drawbridge of the Bastille, I was tremendously stirred and frightened. I did not really know who these people were, or why they were in the streets—they were white: and a white mob can be in no way reassuring to a black boy (even though, or if, he cannot say why). If, in the novel, it was Madame Defarge who most held me, in the film two images and one moment stand out, even from this distance. The first is a long climb up an outside staircase, in Paris, when Lucie Manette and Dr. Lorry and Ernest Defarge go to retrieve Lucie's father, Dr. Manette: for I knew about staircases. The second is when the carriage of the Marquis races headlong through a provincial village. We are confronted with the speeding wheels of the carriage, the relentless hooves of the horses, and a small, running, ragged boy, trying to get out of the way. He is knocked down, he is run over, he is killed: and I knew something about that. The moment that most stands out, for me, is that moment in the tumbril, near the end of the film, when the seamstress (Isabel Jewell) recognizes that Sydney Carton (Ronald Colman) is dying in his friend's stead. I knew nothing about *that*, but I had been taught *greater love hath no man than this*, and something in me believed it. Yet, when Bill whispered to me, during the scene of the storming of the Bastille, "Every time somebody drops from the drawbridge, they die," though I watched the people dropping off the drawbridge like so many dead cockroaches being swept into the dust pan, I was also aware that Bill was not telling me that Metro-Goldwyn-Mayer was murdering all these people, any more than that that guillotine was really going to chop off Ronald Colman's head. The guillotine was going to chop off *Sydney Carton's* head: my first director was instructing me in the discipline and power of make-believe.

For, while believing it all, and *really* believing it, I still knew that Madame Defarge was really an actress named Blanche Yurka, and that Lucie Manette was really an English girl, named Elizabeth Allan. Something implacable in the set of Yurka's mouth probably reminded me of my grandmother, and I knew that Elizabeth Allan–Lucie Manette reminded me of my music teacher, a Miss Taub, with whom I was desperately in love. When Lucie Manette and Charles Darnay are torn from each other's arms in the courtroom, tears rose to my eyes, for I knew something about *that*: yet, at the very same time, I also knew that Charles Darnay was really an actor, named Donald Woods. This was the first time in my life, after all, that I had seen a *screen rendition* (so the ads and the press put it) of a novel, which, considering my age, I could claim to know. And I felt very close to the actors, who had not betrayed the friends I had lived with for nearly as long as I had lived with the people of *Uncle Tom's Cabin.*

I had read *Uncle Tom's Cabin* compulsively, the book in one hand, the newest baby on my hipbone. I was trying to find out something, sensing something in the book of some immense import for me: which, however, I knew I did not really understand.

My mother got scared. She hid the book. The last time she hid it, she hid it on the highest shelf above the bathtub. I was somewhere around seven or eight. God knows how I did it, but I somehow climbed up and dragged the book down. Then, my mother, as she herself puts it, "didn't hide it anymore," and, indeed, from that moment, though in fear and trembling, began to let me go.

I understood, as Bill had intended me to, something of revolution—understood, that is, something of the universal and inevitable human ferment which explodes into what is called a revolution. *Revolution:* the word had a solemn, dreadful ring: what was going on in Spain was a *revolution*. It was said that Roosevelt had saved America: from a *revolution*. Revolution was the only hope of the American working class—the *proletariat*; and world-wide revolution was the only hope of the world. I could understand (or, rather, accept) all this, as it were, negatively. I could not see where I fit in this formulation, and I did not see where blacks fit. I don't think that I ever dared pose this question to Bill, partly because I hadn't yet really accepted, or understood, that *I* was black and also because I knew (and didn't want her to know, although, of course, she did) how much my father distrusted and disliked her. My father was certainly a proletarian, but I had been sent downtown often to pay his union dues, and I knew how much he hated these greasy, slimy men—also proletarian—whom he called, quite rightly, robbers.

In the film, I was not overwhelmed by the guillotine. The guillotine had been very present for me in the novel because

I already wanted, and for very good reasons, to lop off heads. But: once begun, how to distinguish one head from another, and how, where, and for what reason, would the process stop? Beneath the resonance of the word, *revolution*, thundered the word, *revenge*. But: *vengeance is mine, saith the Lord:* a hard saying, the identity of *the Lord* becoming, with the passage of time, either a private agony or an abstract question. And, to put it as simply as it can be put, unless one can conceive of (and endure) an abstract life, there can be no abstract questions. A question is a threat, the door which slams shut, or swings open: on another threat.

I was haunted, for example, by Alexandre Manette's doc ument, in *A Tale of Two Cities*, describing the murder of a peasant boy—who, dying, speaks: *I say, we were so robbed, and hunted, and were made so poor, that our father told us it was a dreadful thing to bring a child into this world, and that what we should most pray for was that our women might be barren and our miserable race die out!* (*I had never before,* observes Dr. Manette, *seen the sense of being oppressed, bursting forth like a fire.*)

Dickens has not seen it at all. The wretched of the earth do not decide to become extinct, they resolve, on the contrary, to multiply: life is their only weapon against life, life is all that they have. This is why the dispossessed and starving will never be convinced (though some may be coerced) by the population-control programs of the civilized. I have watched the dispossessed and starving laboring in the fields which others own, with their transistor radios at their ear, all day long: so they learn, for example, along with equally weighty matters, that the Pope, one of the heads of the civilized world, forbids to the civilized that abortion which is being, literally, forced on them, the wretched. The civilized have created the wretched, quite coldly and deliberately, and do not intend to change the *status quo*; are responsible for their slaughter and enslavement; rain down bombs on defenseless children whenever and wherever they decide that their "vital interests" are menaced, and think nothing of torturing a man to death: these people are not to be taken seriously when they speak of the "sanctity" of human life, or the "conscience" of the civilized world. There is a "sanctity" involved with bringing a child into this world: it is better than bombing one out of it. Dreadful indeed it is to see a starving child, but the answer to that is not to prevent the child's arrival but to restructure the world so that the child can live in it: so that the "vital interest" of the world becomes nothing less than the life of the child. However—I could not have said any of this then, nor is so absurd a notion about to engulf the world now. But we were all starving children, after all, and none of our fathers, even at their most embittered and enraged, had ever suggested that we "die out." It was not *we* who were supposed to *die out*: this was, of all notions, the most forbidden, and we learned this from the cradle. Every trial, every beating, every drop of blood, every tear, were meant to be used by us for a day that was coming—for a day that was certainly coming, absolutely certainly, certainly coming: not for us, perhaps, but for our children. The children of the despised and rejected are menaced from the moment they stir in the womb, and are therefore sacred in a way that the children of the saved are not. And the children know it, which is how they manage to raise their children, and why they will not be persuaded—by their children's murderers, after all—to cease having children.

But I was haunted, too, by the fact that it is Dr. Manette's testimony, written in prison, and recuperated by Ernest Defarge upon the storming of the Bastille, which dooms his son-in-law to death. The Defarges seize and hide this document in order to use it against the son-in-law at the latter's trial: at which trial, Dr. Manette is chief witness for the defense—or, in other words, in fact, his son-in-law's only hope.

Manette wrote his testimony in agony and silence, never expecting to see his daughter again, and unable, of course, to imagine that his daughter would marry one of the descendants of the house which had condemned him to a living death. His testimony ends: *them and their descendants, to the last of their race, I . . . denounce them to Heaven and to earth.* His son-in-law is the descendant of the "race" which had imprisoned him, and the "last" of that race, denounced by him, is flesh of his flesh, his granddaughter. Which connected for me, horribly, with the testimony of Madame Defarge, sister of the murdered boy: *that brother was my brother, that father was my father, those dead are my dead and that summons to answer for*

all those things descends to me! Her husband reluctantly agrees
that this is so, whereupon Madame Defarge says, *Then tell
wind and fire where to stop, but don't tell me!*

I understood *that*: I had seen it in the face, heard it in the
voice of many a black man or woman, sweeping the pavement,
wrestling with the garbage cans, men and women whose children were dying faster than those MGM extras dropping from
the drawbridge. *If I love you, I love you, and I don't give a
damn. You my nigger, nigger, if you don't* get *no bigger. I will
cut your* dick *off, I will cut your balls* out. *I ain't* got *to do
nothing but stay black and die and I'm black already! Honey.
Don't be like that. Honey. Don't do me like that. We in this shit
together, and you need me and I need you, now ain't that so?
Who going to take care of us if we don't take care of each other?*

I feared, feared—like a thief in the night, as one of my
brothers would put it—to connect all this with my father and
mother and everyone I knew, and with myself, and to connect
all this with black Uncle Tom: no more than I had wished to
be that fleeing fugitive on that moving train did I desire to
endure his destiny or meet his end. Uncle Tom really believed
vengeance is mine, saith the Lord, for he believed in the Lord,
as I flattered myself I did not: this inconvenient faith (described, furthermore, by a white woman) obscured the fact
that Tom allowed himself to be murdered for refusing to dis-
close the road taken by a runaway slave. Because Uncle Tom
would not take vengeance into his own hands, he was not a
hero for me. Heroes, as far as I could then see, were white,
and not merely because of the movies but because of the land
in which I lived, of which movies were simply a reflection: I
despised and feared those heroes because they *did* take vengeance into their own hands. They thought that vengeance
was theirs to take. This difficult coin did not cease to spin, it
had neither heads nor tails: for what white people took into
their hands could scarcely even be called vengeance, it was
something less and something more. The Scottsboro boys, for
example—for the Scottsboro Case has begun—were certainly
innocent of anything requiring vengeance. My father's youngest son by his first marriage, nine years older than I, who had
vanished from our lives, might have been one of those boys,
now being murdered by my fellow Americans on the basis of

the rape charge delivered by two white whores: and I was reading Angelo Herndon's *Let Me Live*. Yes. I understood *that*: my countrymen were my enemy, and I had already begun to hate them from the bottom of my heart.

Angelo Herndon was a young, black labor organizer in the Deep South, railroaded to prison, who lived long enough, at least, to write a book about it—the George Jackson of the era. No one resembling him, or anyone resembling any of the Scottsboro Boys, nor anyone resembling my father, has yet made an appearance on the American cinema scene. Perhaps to compensate for this, Bill now takes me to see Sylvia Sidney and Henry Fonda in the Walter Wanger production of Fritz Lang's *You Only Live Once*. I, also, either with her or without her, I don't remember, see the Warner Brothers production (or *screen rendition*, which pompous formulation I adored) of a novel I had read, Ward Greene's *Death in the Deep South*, brought to the screen by (I think) Mervyn LeRoy, as *They Won't Forget*, starring Claude Rains; and Samuel Goldwyn's production of William Wyler's *Dead End*, again starring Sylvia Sidney. Who also starred in the film version of a play Bill took me to see, the WPA Living Newspaper production,—*one third of a nation*—.

It is not entirely true that no one from the world I knew had yet made an appearance on the American screen: there were, for example, Stepin Fetchit and Willie Best and Manton Moreland, all of whom, rightly or wrongly, I loathed. It seemed to me that they lied about the world I knew, and debased it, and certainly I did not know anybody like them— as far as I could tell; for it is also possible that their comic, bug-eyed terror contained the truth concerning a terror by which I hoped never to be engulfed.

Yet, I had no reservations at all concerning the terror of the black janitor in *They Won't Forget*. I think that it was a black actor named Clinton Rosewood who played this part, and he looked a little like my father. He is terrified because a young white girl, in this small Southern town, has been raped and murdered, and her body has been found on the premises of which he is the janitor. (Lana Turner, in her first movie, is the raped and murdered girl, which is, perhaps, a somewhat cu-

rious beginning for so gold-plated a career.) The role of the
janitor is small, yet the man's face hangs in my memory until
today: and the film's icy brutality both scared me and
strengthened me. The Southern politician (Rains) needs an
issue on which to be re-elected. He decides, therefore, that to
pin the rape and murder of the white girl on a black man is
insufficiently sensational. He very coldly frames a white
Northern schoolteacher for this crime, and brings about his
death at the hands of a lynch mob. (And I knew that this was
exactly what would have happened to Bill, if such a mob had
ever got its hands on her.) Unlike the later *Ox-Bow Incident*,
in which a similar lynching is partially redeemed by the reading of a letter, which, presumably, will cause the members of
the mob to repent the horror of what they have done and
resolve to become better men and women, and also unlike the
later *Intruder in the Dust*, which suggests the same hopeful
improbability, *They Won't Forget* ends with the teacher dead
and the politician triumphantly re-elected. As he watches the
widow walk down the courthouse steps, he mutters, seeming,
almost, to stifle a yawn, *I wonder if he really did it, after all.*

And, yes: I was beginning to understand *that.*

Sylvia Sidney was the only American film actress who reminded me of a colored girl, or woman—which is to say that
she was the only American film actress who reminded me of
reality. All of the others, without exception, were white, and,
even when they moved me (like Margaret Sullavan or Bette
Davis or Carole Lombard) they moved me from that distance.
Some instinct caused me profoundly to distrust the sense of
life they projected: this sense of life could certainly never, in
any case, be used by me, and, while *His* eye might be on the
sparrow, mine had to be on the hawk. And, similarly, while I
admired Edward G. Robinson and James Cagney (and, on a
more demanding level, Fredric March), the only actor of the
era with whom I identified was Henry Fonda. I was not alone.
A black friend of mine, after seeing Henry Fonda in *The
Grapes of Wrath*, swore that Fonda had colored blood. You
could tell, he said, by the way Fonda walked down the road
at the end of the film: *white men don't walk like that!* and he

imitated Fonda's stubborn, patient, wide-legged hike away
from the camera. My reaction to Sylvia Sidney was certainly
due, in part, to the kind of film she appeared in during that
era—*Fury; Mary Burns, Fugitive; You and Me; Street Scene* (I
was certain, even, that I knew the meaning of the title of a
film she made with Gene Raymond, which I never saw, *Behold
My Wife*). It was almost as though she and I had a secret: she
seemed to know something I knew. *Every street in New York
ends in a river:* this is the legend which begins the film, *Dead
End*, and I was enormously grateful for it. I had never thought
of that before. Sylvia Sidney, facing a cop in this film, pulling
her black hat back from her forehead: *One of you lousy cops
gave me that.* She was always being beaten up, victimized,
weeping, and she should have been drearier than Tom Mix's
girl friends. But I always believed her—in a way, she reminded
me of Bill, for I had seen Bill facing hostile cops. Bill took us
on a picnic downtown once, and there was supposed to be
ice cream waiting for us at a police station. The cops didn't
like Bill, didn't like the fact that we were colored kids, and
didn't want to give up the ice cream. I don't remember anything Bill said. I just remember her face as she stared at the
cop, clearly intending to stand there until the ice cream all
over the world melted or until the earth's surface froze, and
she got us our ice cream, saying, *Thank you,* I remember, as
we left. *You Only Live Once* was the most powerful movie I
had seen until that moment. The only other film to hit me as
hard, at that time of my life, was *The Childhood of Maxim
Gorky*, which, for me, had not been about white people. Similarly, while *20,000 Years in Sing Sing* had concerned the trials
of a finally somewhat improbable white couple, *You Only Live
Once* came much much closer to home.

It is the top of 1937. I am not yet thirteen.

Fury, MGM, 1936, is, I believe, Lang's first American film.
It is meant to be a study of mob violence, on which level it
is indignant, sincere, and inept. Since the mob separates the
lovers almost at the beginning of the film, the film works as
a love story only intermittently, and to the extent that one
responds to the lovers (Sylvia Sidney and Spencer Tracy). It
is an exceedingly uneasy and uneven film, with both the lovers

and the mob placed, really, in the German Third Reich, which Lang has not so much fled as furiously repudiated, and to which he is still reacting. (The railroad station at which the lovers separate is heavy with menace, and the train which carries Sidney away to go to work in another town is rather like the train to a bloody destination unknown.) Lang's is the *fury* of the film: but his grasp of the texture of American life is still extremely weak: he has not yet really left Germany. His fury, nevertheless, manages to convey something of the idle, aimless, compulsive wickedness of idle, terrified, aimless people, who can come together only as a mob: but his hatred of these people also makes them, at last, unreal. God knows what Lang had already seen, in Germany.

By the time of *You Only Live Once*, Lang had found his American feet. He never succeeded quite so brilliantly again. Considering the speed with which we moved from the New Deal to World War II, to Yalta, to the Marshall Plan, the Truman Doctrine, to Korea, and the House Un-American Activities Committee, this may not be his fault.

(One of the last of his films, entitled *Beyond a Reasonable Doubt*, starring Joan Fontaine, Dana Andrews, and Sydney Blackmer, is an utterly shameless apology for American justice, the work of a defeated man. But, children, yes, it be's that way sometimes.)

Lang's concern, or obsession, was with the fact and the effect of human loneliness, and the ways in which we are all responsible for the creation, and the fate, of the isolated monster: whom we isolate because we recognize him as living within us. This is what his great German film, *M*, which launched Peter Lorre, is all about. In the American context, there being no way for him to get to the *nigger*, he could use only that other American prototype, the criminal, *le gangster*. The premise of *You Only Live Once* is that Eddie Taylor (Henry Fonda) is an ex-convict who wants to go "straight": but the society will not allow him to live down, or redeem, his criminal past. This apparently banal situation is thrust upon us with so heavy a hand that one is forced—as I was, even so long ago—to wonder if one is resisting the film or resisting the truth. But, however one may wish to defend oneself against Lang's indictment of the small, faceless people, always available for any public ceremony and absent forever from any private one, who *are* society, one is left defenseless before his study of the result, which is the isolation and the doom of the lovers.

Very early in the film we meet the earnest and popular prison chaplain—a priest: we meet him as he pitches the ball to the men who are playing baseball in the prison courtyard. It is a curiously loaded moment, a disturbing image: perhaps only an exiled German, at that period of our history, would have dreamed of so connecting games and slaughter, thus foreshadowing the fate of the accomplice, who is, in this case, the priest. The film does not suggest that the priest's popularity has anything to do with the religious instruction he, presumably, brings to the men—his popularity is due to his personal qualities, which include a somewhat overworked cheerfulness: and his function, at bottom, is to prepare the men for death. His role, also, is to make the prison more bearable, both for the men in the courtyard and the guard behind the machine gun in the tower. And he is, also, of course, to prepare these men for their eventual freedom beyond these walls—which freedom, according to Lang's savage and elaborately articulated vision, does not and probably cannot exist.

The film has a kind of claustrophobic physicality—Sidney is first seen, for example, behind a desk, trapped, and Lang forces us to concentrate on her maneuvers to free herself, smiling all the way. (She's trapped behind her desk by a telephone and by an apple vendor who has come to City Hall, where Sidney works, to complain that policemen eat his apples for free.) The first reunion of the lovers takes place with bars between them: it takes a moment before they realize that the gate is open, the man is being set free. There is a marvelous small moment in the flop house, with Fonda pacing the room the way he paced the cell, and pausing at the window to listen to the Salvation Army Band outside, singing, *if you love your mother, meet her in the skies.* I cannot imagine any native-born white American daring to use, so laconically, a banality so nearly comic in order to capture so deep a distress.

The genuine indignation which informs this film is a quality which was very shortly to disappear out of the American cinema, and severely to be menaced in American life. In a way, we were all niggers in the thirties. I do not know if that really made us more friendly with each other—at bottom, I doubt that, for more would remain of that friendliness today—but it was harder then, and riskier, to attempt a separate peace, and benign neglect was not among our possibilities. The Okies, of *The Grapes of Wrath*, were still crossing the plains in their jalopy and had not yet arrived in California, there, every single one of them, to encounter running water, and to become cops. Neither Steinbeck nor Dos Passos had yet said, *my country, right or wrong*, nor did anyone suppose that they ever could—but they did; and Hemingway was as vocal concerning the Spanish revolution as he was to be silent concerning the Cuban one.

There is that moment in the film, in prison, when Fonda whispers to Sidney, through jail-house glass, *Get me a gun.* Sidney says, *I can't get you a gun. You'll kill somebody!* and Fonda says, *What do you think they're going to do to me?*

I understood *that*: it was a real question. I was living with that question.

It is the priest who covers for the trapped and weary girl when she attempts to smuggle a gun into the prison, and it is the priest whom Fonda murders, with a gun. And I wondered about that, the well-meaning accomplice and his fate: he is murdered because Fonda does not believe him, even though he is, in fact, speaking the truth. But the prisoner has no way of knowing with whom the priest is playing ball at the moment and so dares not risk believing him. This dread is underscored by the film's last line, delivered (in the dying prisoner's memory) by the priest: *the gates are open*. I knew damn well that the gates were *not* open, and, by this time, in any case, the lovers were dead.

Dead End, on the other hand, left me cold, and so did *Street Scene*, for the same reason: my streets were funkier and more dangerous than that. I had seen the gangster, Baby-Face Martin (Humphrey Bogart), in *my* streets, with his one-hundred-dollar suits, and his silk shirts, and his hat: sometimes he was a pimp and sometimes he was a preacher and often he was both: but Baby-Face always had the same taste in women, boys, and cars. I knew no one like the heroine, Drina (Sylvia Sidney), except certain high-yellow bitches, whose concern for their younger brother, if they had any concern, would long before have forced them to hit the block, hit the road, or hit a clean old banker, and steal the keys to the long old highway; or, in other words, the severity of the social situation which *Dead End* so romanticizes (somewhat like its direct descendant, *West Side Story*) utterly precludes the innocence of its heroine. Much closer to the truth are the gangster, his broken mother, and his broken girl—yes: I had seen *that*. The script is unable to face the fact that it is merely another version of that brutal fantasy known as the American success story: this helpless dishonesty is revealed by the script's resolution. I was by no means certain that I approved of the hero's decision to inform on Baby-Face, to turn him over to the police, and bring about his death. In my streets, we never called the cops, and whoever turned anyone in to the cops was a pariah. I did not believe, though the film insists on it, that the hero (Joel McCrea) turned in the gangster in order to save the children. I had never seen any children saved that way. In my own experience, on the contrary, and not only because I was watching Bill, I had observed that those who really wished to save the children became themselves, immediately, the target of the police. I could believe—though the film pretends that this consideration never entered the hero's mind—that the hero turned in the gangster in order to collect the reward money: that reward money which will allow the hero and heroine to escape from the stink of the children: for I had certainly seen attempts at *that*. Should the hero and heroine take the younger brother with them into that so celebrated American mainstream, the boy, having no friends, and finding, therefore, no resonance, no corroboration of himself anywhere, will become either a derelict, or the most monstrous of patriots. Or, perhaps (trying to escape and atone, or, perhaps, simply trying to live) the boy will become a kind of revolutionary, a superior and dedicated gangster: for there is a reason that the heroes of the poor resemble so little (and yet so closely resemble!) the heroes of the rich. I do not wish to be misunderstood as suggesting, for example, that the late

Adam Clayton Powell was in any way whatever a bandit, but that is what the white world called him. Harlem's position, therefore, as concerned Adam, was that Adam might have his faults, but that he was certainly a better man than any of his accusers, his accusers being on our backs: and that is why Harlem never abandoned him. Of course, I could not have said any of that then, either. I knew about Adam only that he was the son of "old" Adam, the pastor of Abyssinian Baptist Church, of which church we had been members when I was little; and that he had been instrumental, in the wake of the 1935 Harlem riot, in getting black people hired—for the first time—in the stores on 125th Street where we spent so much of our money—the word, "money," here being meant to convey the image of black fistfuls of nickels and dimes.

In any case, the happy resolution of *Dead End* could mean nothing to me, since, even with some money, black people could move only into black neighborhoods: which is not to be interpreted as meaning that we wished to move into white neighborhoods. We wished, merely, to be free to move. At the time that I am speaking of we had not yet even begun to move across the river, into the Bronx.

Bill takes me to see my first play, the Orson Welles production of *Macbeth*, with an all-black cast, at the Lafayette Theater, on 132nd Street and Seventh Avenue, in Harlem.

I do not remember if I had already read *Macbeth*. My impression is that I read the play when Bill told me she was taking me to see it. In any case, before the curtain rose, I knew the play by heart.

I don't think that the name, *Shakespeare*, meant very much to me in those years. I was not yet intimidated by the name—that was to come later. I had read a play which took place in Scotland. Bill had not warned me—she may not have known—that Welles had transposed the play to Haiti.

I am still about twelve or thirteen. I can be fairly certain about all this, because my life changed so violently when I entered the church, and I entered the church around the time of fourteen. When I entered the church, I ceased going to the theater. It took me awhile to realize that I was working in one.

There is an enormous difference between the stage and the screen: but I may never be able to be articulate as concerns this difference because the first time I ever really saw black actors at work was on the stage: and it is important to emphasize that the people I was watching were black, like me. Nothing that I had seen before had prepared me for this—which is a melancholy comment indeed, but I cannot be blamed for an ignorance which an entire republic had deliberately inculcated.

The distance between oneself—the audience—and a screen performer is an absolute: a paradoxical absolute, masquerading as intimacy. No one, for example, will ever really know whether Katharine Hepburn or Bette Davis or Humphrey Bogart or Spencer Tracy or Clark Gable—or John Wayne—can, or could, really act, or not, nor does anyone care: acting is not what they are required to do. Their acting ability, so far from being what attracts their audience, can often be what drives their audience away. One does not go to see them act: one goes to watch them *be*. One does not go to see Humphrey Bogart, *as Sam Spade*: one goes to see Sam Spade, *as Humphrey Bogart*. I don't wish, here, to belabor a point to which we shall, presently, and somewhat elaborately, be compelled to return: but, *no one*, I read somewhere, a long time ago, *makes his escape personality black*. That the movie star is an "escape" personality indicates one of the irreducible dangers to which the moviegoer is exposed: the danger of surrendering to the corroboration of one's fantasies as they are thrown back from the screen. The danger is as great for the performer: Bette Davis may have longed, all these years, to play Mrs. Alving, in *Ghosts*, and Spencer Tracy may have carried with him to the grave an unfulfilled *King Lear*—nobody was about to let them try it, for fear that their public would feel themselves betrayed. This is one of the reasons that Joan Crawford, for example, doesn't like the film *Rain*, in which she starred. God knows that it's not a very good picture, but Crawford didn't write the abysmal script. She made the mistake, and very honorably, after all, of trying to be Miss Sadie Thompson instead of Miss Joan Crawford, and the kids didn't like that at all.

For the tension in the theater is a very different, and very particular tension: this tension between the real and the imagined *is* the theater, and this is why the theater will always remain a necessity. One is not in the presence of shadows, but responding to one's flesh and blood: in the theater, we are re-creating each other. Clearly, now, when speaking of the theater, I am not referring to those desperate and debilitating commercial ventures on which Broadway embarks each season, or those grim "revivals" of stillborn plays of which London is so fond, or those "adaptations" of American monstrosities which have been the rage of Paris for so long. Nor, in the present instance, is the term, "one's flesh and blood" meant to refer, merely, to the spectacle of a black boy seeing, for the first time in his life, living black actors on a living stage: we are *all* each other's flesh and blood.

This is a truth which it is very difficult for the theater to deny, and when it attempts to do so the same thing happens to the theater as happens to the church: it becomes sterile and irrelevant, a blasphemy, and the true believer goes elsewhere—carrying, as it happens, the church and the theater with him, and leaving the form behind. For, the church and the theater are carried within us and it is we who create them, out of our need and out of an impulse more mysterious than our desire. If this seems to be saying that the life of the theater and the life of the church are dependent on maverick freak poets and visionaries, I can only point out that these difficult creatures are *also* our flesh and blood, and are also created by our need and out of an impulse more mysterious than our desire.

In the darkened Lafayette Theater—that moment when the house lights dim in the theater is not at all like the dimming of the house lights in the movies—I watched the narrow, horizontal ribbon of light which connects the stage curtain to the floor of the stage, and which also separates them. That narrow ribbon of light then contains a mystery. That mystery may contain the future—you are, yourself, suspended, as mortal as that ribbon. No one can possibly know what is about to happen: it is happening, each time, for the first time, for the only time. For this reason, although I did not know this, I had never before, in the movies, been aware of the audience: in the movies, we knew what was going to happen, and, if we wanted to, we could stay there all afternoon, seeing it happen over and over again.

But I was aware of the audience now. Everyone seemed to be waiting, as I was waiting. The curtain rose.

Between three and four years later, that is, around the time that I was seventeen, my best friend, Emile, took me to a movie at the Irving Place Theater, a Russian movie, since America and Russia were allies then. My friend is a Jew—an American Jew, of Spanish descent: he was then, and is today, one of the most honest and honorable people I have ever known. He took me to the movie because he was trying to help me leave the church. I had not been to a film, or a theater from the time of my conversion, which came hard upon the heels of *Macbeth*.

At this time of my life, Emile was the only friend I had who knew to what extent my ministry tormented me. I knew that I could not stay in the pulpit. I could not make my peace with that particular lie—a lie, in any case, for me. I did not want to become Baby-Face Martin—I could see that coming, and, indeed, it demanded no spectacular perception, since I found myself surrounded by what I was certain to become. But neither did I know how to leave—to jump: it could not be explained to my brothers and sisters, or my mother, and my father had begun his descent into the valley. Emile took me to this film, of which I remember only a close-up of a tambourine. I played the tambourine, in church: the tambourine on the screen might as well have been Gabriel's trumpet. I collapsed, weeping, terrified, and Emile led me out. He walked me up to Herald Square. It was night. He talked to me; he tried to make me see something—tried to do something only a friend can do: and challenged me, thus:

Even if what I was preaching was gospel, I had no right to preach it if I no longer believed it. To stay in the church merely because I was afraid of leaving it was unutterably far beneath me, and too despicable a cowardice for him to support in any friend of his. Therefore, on the coming Sunday, he would buy two tickets to a Broadway matinee and meet me on the steps of the 42nd Street Library, at two o'clock in the afternoon. He knew that I spent all day Sunday in church—the point, precisely, of the challenge. If I were not on the steps of the library (in the bookshelves of which so much of my trouble had begun!) then he would be ashamed of me and never speak to me again, and I would be ashamed of myself.

(I cannot resist observing that this still seems to me a quite extraordinary confrontation between two adolescents, one white and one black: but, then, I had never forgotten Bill's quiet statement, when I went down to her house on 12th Street to tell her that I had been "saved" and would not be going to the movies, or the theater anymore—which meant that I would not be seeing her anymore: *I've lost a lot of respect for you.* Perhaps, in the intervening time, I had lost a lot of respect for myself.)

But beneath all this, as under a graveyard pallor, or the noonday sun, lay the fact that the leap demanded that I commit myself to the clear impossibility of becoming a writer, and attempting to save my family that way. I do not think I said this. I think Emile knew it.

I had hoped for a reprieve, hoped, on the marked Sunday, to get away, unnoticed: but I was the "young" Brother Baldwin, and I sat in the front row, and the pastor did not begin his sermon until about a quarter past one. Well. At one thirty, I—*tip-toed*—out. The further details of my departure do not concern us here: that was how I left the church.

I am fairly certain that the matinee, that Sunday, was *Native Son* (also directed by Orson Welles) at the St. James Theatre. We were in the balcony, and I remember standing up, abruptly and unwisely, when the play ended, and nearly falling headlong from the balcony to the pit. I did not know that I had been hit so hard: I will not forget Canada Lee's performance as long as I live.

Canada Lee was Bigger Thomas, but he was also Canada Lee: his physical presence, like the physical presence of Paul Robeson, gave me the right to live. He was not at the mercy of my imagination, as he would have been, on the screen: he was on the stage, in flesh and blood, and I was, therefore, at the mercy of *his* imagination.

For that long-ago *Macbeth* had both terrified and exhilarated me. I knew enough to know that the actress (the colored lady!) who played Lady Macbeth might very well be a janitor, or a janitor's wife, when the play closed, or when the curtain came down. Macbeth was a nigger, just like me, and I saw the witches in church, every Sunday, and all up and down the block, all week long, and Banquo's face was a familiar face. At the same time, the majesty and torment on that stage were real: indeed they revealed the play, *Macbeth*. They *were* those people and that torment was a torment I recognized, those were real daggers, it was real blood, and those crimes resounded and compounded, as real crimes do: I did not have to ask, *what happens to them now?* And, if niggers have rhythm, these niggers had the beat—*tomorrow and tomorrow and tomorrow*, and—*thou shalt be King hereafter!* It is not accidental that I was carrying around the plot of a play in my head, and looking, with a new wonder (and a new terror) at everyone around me, when I suddenly found myself on the floor of the church, one Sunday, crying holy unto the Lord. Flesh and blood had proved to be too much for flesh and blood.

For, they were themselves, these actors—these people were themselves. They could *be* Macbeth only because they were themselves: my first real apprehension of the mortal challenge. Here, nothing corroborated any of my fantasies: flesh and blood was being challenged by flesh and blood. It is said that the camera cannot lie, but rarely do we allow it to do anything else, since the camera sees what you point it at: the camera sees what you want it to see. The language of the camera is the language of our dreams.

2

Who Saw Him Die?
I, Said The Fly

If religion was a thing
money could buy,
The rich would live,
and the poor would die.
Traditional

I *Shall Spit on Your Graves* is a French look at the black
American problem. It is, also, an utterly cynical use of the
name of Boris Vian, the young Frenchman who wrote the
novel on which the film is emphatically *not* based. (I am told
that Vian never saw the completed film. During the first
screening of the film, he had a heart attack, and died. The
story may be apocryphal, but I can well believe it.)

Vian himself points out, somewhat savagely, that *I Shall Spit
on Your Graves* is not a very good novel: he was enraged (and
enlightened) by the vogue it had in France. This vogue was
due partly to the fact that it was presented as Vian's translation
of an American novel. But this vogue was due also to Vian
himself, who was one of the most striking figures of a long-
ago Saint-Germain des Pres. I am speaking of the immediate
post-war years. Paris was then on bicycles: there were few cars,
and gas (along with milk, cheese, and butter) was rationed.
Juliette Greco was in the process of becoming famous in *Le
Tabou*, and was often to be seen driving an ancient automobile: she was the envy of the neighborhood. Sydney Bechet
and Claude Luter were playing together at *Le Vieux Colom-
bier*; Kenny Clarke was soon to arrive. There were jam sessions
over a theater in rue Fontaine which lasted until dawn, and
sometimes until noon, at one of which jam sessions I first
heard Annie Ross.

I was sitting at the Café Flore one afternoon when an enormous car, with baggage piled on the roof, stopped before the
café. A large woman opened the car door, leaned out, and
yelled, "Is Jean-Paul Sartre here today?" The waiter said,

"No, madame," whereupon the car door slammed, and the car drove off. Camus's hour had yet so savagely to strike: and both men eventually disappeared from the Flore. The curious, and, on the whole, rather obvious doctrine of *l'existentialisme* flourished, and the word *négritude*, though it was beginning to be muttered, had yet to be heard. *I Shall Spit on Your Graves*, and Vian himself, and a tense, even rather terrified wonder about Americans, were part of this ferment: and, further, the straight-laced French (who had not yet heard of Jean Genet, and who remain absolutely impervious to Rimbaud and Baudelaire) considered the novel pornographic.

One of the reasons—perhaps *the* reason—that the novel was considered pornographic is that it is concerned with the vindictive sexual aggression of one black man against many white women. (At that moment in time, the black G.I. in Europe was a genuinely disturbing conundrum.) The novel takes place in America, and the black man looks like a white man—this double remove liberating both fantasy and hope, which is, perhaps, at bottom, what pornography is all about. This is certainly what that legend created by Rudolph Valentino, in *The Sheik*, is all about, as is made clear by his fan mail—poor boy!—and this fantasy and hope contain the root appeal of *Tarzan (King of The Apes!)*. Both the Sheik and Tarzan are white men who look and act like black men—act like black men, that is, according to the white imagination which has created them: one can eat one's cake without having it, or one can have one's cake without eating it.

What informs Vian's book, however, is not sexual fantasy, but rage and pain: that rage and pain which Vian (almost alone) was able to hear in the black American musicians, in the bars, dives, and cellars, of the Paris of those years. In his book, a black man who can "cross the line" sets out to avenge the murder of his younger, darker brother; and the primary tool of this vengeance is—his tool. Vian would have known something of this from Faulkner, and from Richard Wright, and from Chester Himes, but he *heard* it in the music, and, indeed, he saw it in the streets. Vian's character is eventually uncovered, but not before he has seduced and murdered two of the richest and most attractive white women he can find. He is caught, and hanged—hung, like a horse, his sex, according to Vian, mocking his murderers to the last. Vian did not know that this particular nigger would almost certainly have been castrated: which is but another and deadlier way for white men to be mocked by the terror and fury by which they are engulfed upon the discovery that the black man is a man: "it hurt," says T. E. Lawrence, in *Seven Pillars of Wisdom*, "that they [the negroes] should possess exact counterparts of all our bodies."

Vian's social details, as concerns American life, are all askew, but he had the sense to frame his story in such a way as to prevent these details from intruding. And he gets some things right, for example, the idle, self-centered, spoiled, erotic dreaming of a certain category of American youth: there are moments which bring to mind *Rebel Without a Cause*. For these children, the passage of time can mean only the acceleration of hostility and despair. In spite of the book's naïveté, Vian cared enough about his subject to force one into a confrontation with a certain kind of anguish. The book's power comes from the fact that he forces you to see this anguish from the undisguised viewpoint of his foreign, alienated own.

The film is quite another matter, having, for one thing, no viewpoint whatever except that from the window of the Stock Exchange. The film takes place, so we are endlessly informed, in Trenton: which is, in the film, a small, unbelievably unattractive town, just outside of Paris, on the road to New Orleans. In fact, it begins in (I guess) New Orleans, with a black boy, playing a harmonica, sitting on an immense bale of cotton which is being hoisted to the dock. The boy jumps off the bale of cotton, still playing his harmonica, starts walking; is grabbed around the neck by his affectionate, older, light white brother; and, alas, the film begins. The young black boy, who would appear to be about thirteen, seems to have been playing around with a white girl. (We do not, thank heaven, meet her.) His older brother warns him to be careful. Harmonica says that he will be. The brothers separate, and we next see and hear Harmonica in the cool of the evening (not yet in the heat of the night) unconcernedly walking along a deserted country road. Headlights flash behind him; white men leap out of their cars, the boy turns to face them; and the next time we see him, he is hanging from a tree.

His older light white brother cuts him down and carries him to where the darkies are assembled, beginning to moan—the darkies, that is. The older light white brother vows vengeance, over the Christian plea for forgiveness of the old black preacher, to whom he appears—though certainly not physically—to be related. He puts his brother's body on a table in the cabin, while the darkies watch; douses it with kerosene, while the darkies watch, and moan; lights a match, setting his brother, the cabin, and, presumably, the entire neighborhood aflame, while the darkies keep moaning; and, sensibly enough, leaves.

There follows a somewhat opaque episode, involving the French idea of a drunken, cowardly Southerner—an idea which is not absolutely inaccurate, bearing in mind that *New* Orleans is found in the state of *Louisiana*, for very precise reasons, and leaving aside the Haitian adventure, and to go, for the moment, no further than that—from whom our hero, indisputably *évolué*, needs credentials for Trenton: a city to be found, he has been told, in the North. For he is going North, he is going to "cross the line," and he is, in effect, blackmailing the Southern drunkard into being his accomplice. There is a great deal of unsuspenseful business with a loaded shotgun, but our hero gets the letter, throws the loaded shotgun toward the arms of his drunken friend, gets into his car, and drives off. (None of this paranoia is in Vian's book.) Our hero takes what is, in effect, his letter of racial credit to an aging bookstore owner in Trenton, and so we meet the far from merry maidens of our hero's grim desire.

Vian's book has a certain weary, misogynistic humor—the chicks fuck like rabbits, or minks, and our hero gets a certain charge, or arrives at the mercy of a nearly unbearable ecstasy, out of his private knowledge that they are being fucked by a nigger: he is committing the crime for which his brother was murdered, he is fucking these cunts with his brother's prick. And he comes three times, so to speak, each time he comes, once for his brother, and once for the "little death" of the orgasms to which he always brings the ladies, and, uncontrollably, for the real death to which he is determined to bring them. This intersection, where life disputes with death, is very vivid in the book: and it does not, of course, exist in the film.

In the book, one believes that the hero loved his brother, and to such a depth indeed that he is deliberately destroying his own sexuality—his hope of love—in order to keep faith with his destroyed brother: *the mortification of the flesh*. One may object that this is not exactly what Paul or Peter or The Bank of the Holy Ghost meant to say, but, incontestably, this is what has been accomplished: that the use of one's own body in the act of love is considered a crime against the Holy Ghost. No greater blasphemy against the human being can be imagined. One may remark that the hero's vengeance is not at all what the brother would have wanted, for his brother, but the younger brother is not there to speak for himself. The younger brother lives only in the memory of his older brother, and in the unanswerable light of an unforgivable crime.

This relentless need for something much deeper than revenge comes close to the truth of many lives, black and white: but revenge is not among the human possibilities. Revenge is a human dream. There is no way of conveying to the corpse the reasons you have made him one—you have the corpse, and you are, thereafter, at the mercy of a fact which missed the truth, which means that the corpse has you. On the other hand, the corpse doesn't want his murderer, either, and one is under the iron obligation not to allow oneself to be turned into one. The key is contained in the question of where the power lies—power, literally, and power on a more dreadful level—and Vian's anecdote pivots on the geometry of destruction and self-destruction. This is a delicate tightrope stretched taut and high, above unimaginable chasms, coming close to the truth of many black lives: many have fallen, but many have not. There is, indeed, far beyond and beneath the truth of Vian's anecdote, another truth, a truth which drags us into the icy and fiery center of a mystery: how have we endured? But the key word, there, is *we*.

In the film there is no brother, there are no brothers, there are no women, no passion, and no pain: there is the guilty, furtive, European notion of sex, a notion which obliterates any possibility of communion, or any hope of love. There is also the European dream of America—which, after all, is how we *got* America: a dream full of envy, guilt, condescension, and terror, a dream which began as an adventure in real estate.

That song which Europe let out of its heart so long ago, to be sung on ships, and to cross all that water, is now coming back to Europe, perhaps to drive Europe mad: the return of the song will certainly render Europe obsolete, and return the North American wilderness—yet to be conquered!—to a truth which has nothing to do with Europe.

The Birth of a Nation is based on a novel I will almost certainly never read, *The Clansman*, by a certain Thomas Dixon, who achieved it sometime after the Civil War. He did not, oddly enough, write the 1952 film, *Storm Warning*, also about the Klan, starring Ginger Rogers, Steve Cochran, Ronald Reagan, and Doris Day. Unlike, and quite unjustly, *Storm Warning* (possibly because the Ginger Rogers film speaks courageously for the Union, and against the Confederacy), *The Birth of a Nation* is known as one of the great classics of the American cinema: and indeed it is.

It is impossible to do justice to the story, such story as attempts to make an appearance being immediately submerged by the tidal wave of the plot; and, in Griffith's handling of this fable, anyway, the key is to be found in the images. The film cannot be called dishonest: it has the Niagara force of an obsession.

A story is impelled by the necessity to reveal: the aim of the story is revelation, which means that a story can have nothing—at least not deliberately—to hide. This also means that a story resolves nothing. The resolution of a story must occur in us, with what we make of the questions with which the story leaves us. A plot, on the other hand, must come to a resolution, prove a point: a plot must answer all the questions which it pretends to pose. *In the Heat of the Night*, for example, turns on a plot, a plot designed to camouflage exceedingly bitter questions; it can be said, for *The Defiant Ones*, that it attempts to tell a story. The Book of Job is a story, the proof being that the details of Job's affliction never, for an instant, obscure Job from our view. This story has no resolution. We end where we began: everything Job has lost has been returned to him. And, yet, we are not quite where we began. We do not know what that voice out of the whirlwind will thunder next time—and we know that there will certainly be a next time. Job is not the same, nor are we: Job's story has changed Job forever, and illuminated us. By contrast, the elaborate anecdote of Joseph and his brothers turns on a plot, the key to which is that coat of many colors. That coat is meant to blind us to the fact that the anecdote of Joseph and his brothers, so far from being a record of brotherly love and forgiveness, is an absolutely deadly study of frustrated fratricide and frustrated (although elaborately disguised) revenge. When Joseph feeds his brothers, it is not an act of love: he could just as easily have let them starve, which they, very logically, expected him to do. They, just as logically, expected him to die when they threw him into the pit. Having done the unexpected once, Joseph can do it twice: *here is the brother who was thrown into a pit by you, my brothers, and left alone there, to die!—help yourself, there's plenty.* Neither Joseph, nor, more importantly, perhaps, his brothers, have got past that day. It is an act which cannot be forgotten, any more than the branding iron on the skin can be forgotten. And, if it cannot be forgotten, which is to say undone, then it will certainly, in one way or another, be repeated: therefore, it cannot be forgiven: a grave matter, if one accepts my central premise, which is that all men are brothers.

Similarly, *The Birth of a Nation* is really an elaborate justification of mass murder. The film cannot possibly admit this, which is why we are immediately placed at the mercy of a plot labyrinthine and preposterous—as follows:

The gallant South, on the edge of the great betrayal by the Northern brethren: this is the pastoral and yet doom-laden weight of the early images. Two brothers, robust, two sisters, fair, a handsome house, a loving and united family, and happy, loyal slaves.

Unhappily, however, for the South, and for us all, a certain eminent Southern politician has a mulatto slave mistress—a house nigger, whose cot he shares when the sun goes down: she does not share his bed, to which he returns shortly before the sun comes up: and the baleful effect of this carnal creature on the eminent Southern politician helps bring about the ruin of the South. I cannot tell you exactly *how* she brings about so devastating a fate, and I defy anyone to tell *me*: but she does. Without attempting to track my way through any more of what we will call the pre-plot: the War comes. The South is shamefully defeated—or, not so much defeated, it would appear, as betrayed: by the influence of the mulattoes. For the previously noted eminent and now renegade Southern politician has also, as it turns out, a mulatto protégé (we do not know how this happened, but we are allowed to suspect the worst) and this mulatto protégé is maneuvered into the previously all-white Congress of the United States. At which point the Carpetbaggers arrive, and the movie begins. For the film is concerned with the Reconstruction, and how the birth of the Ku Klux Klan overcame that dismal and mistaken chapter in our—American—history.

The first image of the film is of the African slave's arrival. The image and the title both convey the European terror before the idea of the black and white, red and white, saved and pagan, confrontation. I think that it was Freud who suggested that the presence of the black man in America foreshadowed America's doom—which America, if it could not civilize these savages, would deserve: it is certainly the testimony of such disparate witnesses as William Faulkner and Isadora Duncan. For Marx and Engels, the presence of the black man in America was simply a useful crowbar for the liberation of whites: an idea which has had its issue in the history of American labor unions. The Founding Fathers shared this view, eminently, Thomas Jefferson, and The Great Emancipator freed those slaves he could not reach, in order to create, hopefully, a fifth column behind the Confederate lines. This ambivalence contains the key to American literature—in a way, it can be said to *be* American literature—all the way from *The Scarlet Letter* to *The Big Sleep*. In any case, what Europe really felt about the black presence in America is revealed by the stratagems the European-Americans have used, and use, to avoid it: that is, by American history, or the actual, present condition of any American city.

The first image, then, of *The Birth of a Nation* is immensely and unconsciously revealing. Were it not for their swarthy color—or not even that, so many immigrants having been transformed into white men only upon arrival, and, as it were, by decree—were it not for the title preceding the image: they would look exactly like European passengers, huddled, silent, patient, and hopeful, in the shadow of the Statue of Liberty. (*Give us your poor!* Many of the poor, not only in America, but all over the world, are beginning to find that these famous lines have a somewhat sinister ring.) These slaves look as though they *want* to enter the Promised Land, and are regarding their imminent masters in the hope of being bought.

This is not exactly the way blacks looked, of course, as they entered America, nor were they yet covered by European clothes. Blacks got here nearly as naked as the day they were born, and were sold that way, every inch of their anatomy exposed and examined, teeth to testicles, breast to bottom. That's how darkies were born: more to the point, here, it is certainly how mulattoes were born.

For, the most striking thing about the merciless plot on which *The Birth of a Nation* depends is that, although the legend of the nigger controls it the way the day may be controlled by threat of rain, there are really no niggers in it. The plot is entirely controlled by the image of the mulatto, and there are two of them, one male and one female. All of the energy of the film is siphoned off into these two dreadful and improbable creatures. It might have made sense—that is, might have made a story—if these two mulattoes had been related to each other, or to the renegade politician, whose wards they are: but, no, he seems to have dreamed them up (they *are* like creatures in a nightmare *someone* is having) and they are related to each other only by their envy of white people. The renegade politician, I should already have told you—but this is one of the difficulties of trying to follow a plot—is also the heroine's father. This fact brings about his belated enlightenment, the final victory of the Klan, the film's denouement, and a double wedding.

I am leaving a great deal out, but, in any case, the renegade politician is brought brutally to his senses when his mulatto ward, now a rising congressman, so far forgets himself as to offer himself in marriage to the renegade politician's beautiful daughter, Miss Lillian Gish. The Klan rides out in fury, making short work of the ruffian, and others like him. The niggers are last seen, heads averted and eyes down, returning to their cabins—none of which have been burned, apparently, there being no point in burning empty cabins—and the South rises triumphantly to its feet.

It is not clear what happens to the one presumably remaining mulatto, the female. Neither of the two mulattoes had any sexual interest in the other; given what we see of their charms, this is quite understandable. Both are driven by a hideous lust for whites, she for the master, he for the maid: they are, at least, thank heaven, heterosexual, due, probably, to their lack of imagination.

Their lust for the whites, however, is of such a nature that it suffers from all the manifestations of hysterical hatred. And this is not quite so understandable, except in the gaudy light of the film's intention. The film presents us, after all, with the spectacle of a noble people, brought to such a pass that even their loyal slaves are subverted. For the sake of the dignity of this temporarily defeated people, and out of a vivid and loving concern for their betrayed and endangered slaves, the violated social order must, at all costs, be re-established. And it *is* re-established by the vision and heroism of the noblest among these noble. The disaster which they must overcome (and, in future, avert) has been brought about, not through any fault of their own, and not because of any defection among their slaves, but by the weak and misguided among them who have given the mulattoes ideas above their station.

But how did so ungodly a creature as the mulatto enter this Eden, and where did he come from?

The film cannot concern itself with this inconvenient and impertinent question, any more than can Governor Wallace, or the bulk of his confreres, North or South. We need not pursue it, except to observe that almost all mulattoes, and especially at that time, were produced by white men, and rarely indeed by an act of love. The mildest possible word is coercion: which is why white men invented the crime of rape, with the specific intention (and effect) of castrating and hanging the nigger. Neither did black men fasten on the word, *mulatto*, to describe the issue of their own loins. But white men did—as follows:

The root of the word, *mulatto*, is Spanish, according to Webster, from *mulo*, a mule. The word refers to: (1) a person, one of whose parents is Negro and the other Caucasian, or white; and (2) popularly, any person with mixed Negro and Caucasian ancestry.

A mule is defined as (1) the offspring of a donkey and a horse, especially the offspring of a jackass and a mare—*mules are usually sterile*. And, a further definition: in biology, a hybrid, *especially a sterile hybrid*. (Italics mine.)

The idea of producing a child, on condition, and under the guarantee, that the child cannot reproduce must, after all, be relatively rare: no matter how dim a view one may take of the human race. It argues an extraordinary spiritual condition, or an unspeakable spiritual poverty: to produce a child with the intention of using it to gain a lease on limbo, or, failing that, on purgatory: to produce a child with the extinction of the child as one's hope of heaven. *Mulatto:* for that outpost of Christianity, that segment of the race which called itself white, which found itself stranded among the heathen on the North American continent, under the necessity of destroying all evidence of sin, including, if need be, those children who were proof of abandonment to savage, heathen passion, and under the absolute necessity of preserving its idea of itself by any means necessary, the use of the word, *mulatto*, was by no means inadvertent. It is one of the keys to American history, present, and past. Americans are still destroying their own children: and, infanticide being but a step away from genocide, not only theirs. If we do not know where the mulatto came from, we certainly know where a multitude went, dispatched by their own fathers, and we know where multitudes are, until today, plotting death, plotting life, groaning in the chains in which their fathers have bound them.

Our fathers, indeed, for here we all are: and we encounter an invitation to discover the essential decency of this history (this is known as progress) in the person of the Sheriff in a film made some fifty-odd years later, *In the Heat of the Night.*

This film has no mulattoes: unless one wishes to examine, with a certain rigor, the roles played by some of the townspeople: we will return to this speculation: and, apart from the brief cotton-picking sequence, seen from the window of the Sheriff's moving car, it is hard to locate the niggers. (This, also, is progress.) The man who lodges the black detective comes close to being a nigger. The lady who arranges abortions is dark indeed, but is clearly passing—through; and Mr. Virgil Tibbs comes from freedom-loving Philadelphia, the city of brotherly love. To this haven, he will return, if he lives. But we know that he *will* live. The star of a film is rarely put to death, and certainly not *this* star, and certainly not in this film.

The entire burden, therefore, of such suspense as the film may claim to have falls squarely on the shoulders of the Sheriff (Rod Steiger). The life of Virgil Tibbs (Sidney Poitier) is endangered precisely to the extent that we are concerned about the salvation of the Sheriff's soul. One ought, indeed, I suppose, to be concerned about the soul of any descendant of *The Birth of a Nation*, and the Sheriff is certainly such a descendant, as is the film itself. On the other hand, it is difficult to sustain such a concern when the concern is not reciprocal, and if this concern demands one's complicity in a lie: which state of affairs, having gone beyond progress, is sometimes called brotherhood, the achievement of which state of grace is exactly what *In the Heat of the Night* imagines itself to be about.

The film is breathtaking, not to say vertiginous, in the speed with which it moves from one preposterous proposition to another. We are asked to believe that a grown black man, who knows the South, and who, being a policeman, must know something about his colleagues, both South and North, would elect to change trains in a Southern backwater at that hour of the early morning and sit alone in the waiting room; that the Sheriff imagines that he needs a confession from this black Northern vagrant, and so elects to converse with him before locking him up, turning him over to his deputies, and closing the case. (Of course, it is suggested, at that moment— and quite helplessly, the truth of the white and black male meeting living far beneath the moment of this manipulated scene—that the Sheriff is being something of a sadist, and is playing cat and mouse.) And the film betrays itself, in the early sequences, in quite a curious way. One might suppose, after all, since the film was made *after* the 1964 Civil Rights Act, that the Sheriff might be concerned about the pressure which might be brought to bear by the Federal Government: but this possibility, astoundingly enough, does not appear to enter his mind. He reacts to the fact that the black man makes more money than he does: which has the effect of eliciting our sympathy for this doubly poor white man. Virgil's continued presence on the case is due entirely to the reaction of the widow of the murdered man; this man, conveniently enough (as concerns the necessities of the plot) was in the process of bringing new industry to the town when he was murdered. As the man's widow, she now has the power to transfer this potential wealth to another town, which she will do if Virgil is not allowed to continue his investigation of her husband's murder. This convolution of the plot really demands a separate essay: it contains so many oblique and unconscious confessions concerning the roles of money, sex, marriage, greed, and guilt and power. In any case, the widow, having done her bit, disappears, and the town is stuck with Virgil. So is the Sheriff: and the Sheriff just don't know, now, if he glad or if he bad: but he got to do his best to look bad.

What kind of people are you? the widow cries out at one point in the film: as well she might. There is something really stunning—cunning is too loaded a word—in the casting of this film. Poitier's presence gives the film its only real virility, and so emphatically indeed that the emotional climate of the film is that of a mysteriously choked and baffled—and yet compulsive—act of contrition. This virility is not in the least compromised by the fact that he has no woman, visibly: on the contrary, it is thus reinforced, since we know that he is saving himself for Philadelphia, where *"they call me Mr. Tibbs!"* The wealth of his health is presented in very powerful contrast to the poverty and infirmity of the white men by whom he is surrounded, and is the only genuinely positive element the film contains. It coats the film lightly, so to speak, with a kind of desperately boyish, unadmitted anguish. But that the film cannot or dare not pursue the implications of this sorrow is made very clear in that choked and opaque scene between the black detective and the Sheriff, in the latter's living room, over bourbon. The chief deputy, Sam (Warren Oates), in terms of the weights and balances of the film has the best assignment, his role allowing him to be absolutely truthful, though never deep. Sam drives his patrol car, each night, off his route to watch a naked girl through the windows of her house. She is to be found thus, apparently, every night, at the hour that Sam drives by: and, so far as the film informs us, this is their only connection—a rather horrifying thought, when one considers how much of the truth it contains, for lives like that, and in such a town.

The girl is a poor white, and is as marked by this misfortune as are the mulattoes of *The Birth of a Nation*, and she has a poor white brother, who appears to know nothing at all about his sister. There is the white boy, picked up for the murder after Virgil Tibbs's credentials have been established, and Virgil has agreed to remain on the case, or been coerced into doing so: this boy first hates, then learns to love the black cop who clears him, and saves his life. And there is the waiter in the diner, who refuses to serve Virgil Tibbs. This is an utterly grotesque creature, as hysterical as *Nation*'s mulatto maid, presented as being virtually biologically inferior to everyone else. He, it turns out, is the lover of the exhibitionistic girl—a circumstance which one does not believe for a moment, not even in that sleepy little town—and he is the father of the child she is expecting. He is, also, the murderer. He committed the murder because (I think) he needed money for an abortion. The climactic scene, anyway, takes place outside the establishment of the lady who deals in abortions. This is an exciting scene indeed, but before I try to deal with this excitement, there are a couple of other scenes we should consider.

One is the scene in the hothouse of the wealthy horticulturist, who is presented as being one of the most powerful men of the region. In this scene, Tibbs exhibits a somewhat unexpected knowledge of varieties of plant life. This allows his host to make clear his racial bias. ("These plants are delicate. They like the nigras. They need care.") One thing leads to another, so to speak, and, eventually, the wealthy horticulturist slaps Tibbs in the face. Under the eyes of the Sheriff, Tibbs slaps him back. The wealthy host is astonished that the Sheriff does not shoot Tibbs on the spot: the Sheriff, furious that anyone should suppose him capable of so base an action, throws his chewing gum on the ground (of the powerful host) and stalks out, after Virgil. The wealthy landowner ("There was a day when I could have had you shot!") looks on in

disbelief, and we leave him weeping, possibly because his day
has passed. End of joke.

Then, there is the scene with the lady who deals in abortions. I have described this lady somewhat rudely; she may
have passed through the West Indies, or Africa, and, at that,
speedily; but she surely do not come from around here. She
appears to be looking for a home, and, from the way Virgil
Tibbs treats her, no wonder—I would, too. Demanding to
know who, in the town, is paying for an abortion, he informs
her (speaking of the prison sentence with which he is threatening her) that "there's white time and black time—and ain't
nothing worse than black time!" The lady who deals in abortions appears to be utterly astounded and downcast by this
news and rolls her eyes toward (I suppose) her suitcase. But
she is saved by the arrival of the exhibitionistic girl: who, seeing Virgil Tibbs (they have met before), runs out into the
night.

Virgil runs after her (while the lady who deals in abortions
flees into the back room, to pack, and book passage to Canada, or Algeria) and picks up the fleeing poor white chick in
his arms. In this unlucky posture he is found as headlights
flash, before, and behind, and all around him, and white men
leap out of their cars: into the heat of the night.

This is the penultimate, exciting scene. One of the white
men is the poor white brother of the poor white girl, and,
naturally, he intends to lynch the nigger, whose black hands
are still on the body of his white sister. With great presence
of mind, Mr. Tibbs drops the sister and points to the real
killer, who has the money for the abortion in his pocket. The
attention of the murderous mob is thus distracted, naturally,
from the nigger and the white chick to this creep, who
promptly shoots the brother, dead: end of exciting scene.

There remains the obligatory, fade-out kiss. I am aware that
men do not kiss each other in American films, nor, for the
most part, in America, nor do the black detective and the
white Sheriff kiss here. But the obligatory, fade-out kiss, in
the classic American film, did not really speak of love, and,
still less, of sex: it spoke of reconciliation, of all things now
becoming possible. It was a device desperately needed among
a people for whom so much had to be made possible. And,

no matter how inept one must judge this film to be, in spite of its absolutely appalling distance from reality, in spite of my own helplessly sardonic tone when discussing it, and even in spite of the fact that the effect of such a film is to increase and not lessen white confusion and complacency, and black rage and despair, I still do not wish to be guilty of the gratuitous injustice of seeming to impute base motives to the people responsible for its existence. Our situation would be far more coherent if it were possible to categorize, or dismiss, *In the Heat of the Night* so painlessly. No: the film helplessly conveys—without confronting—the anguish of people trapped in a legend. They cannot live within this legend; neither can they step out of it. The film gave me the impression, according to my notes the day I saw it, of "something strangling, alive, struggling to get out." And I certainly felt this during the final scene, when the white Sheriff takes the black detective's bag as they walk to the train. It is not that the creators of the film were inspired by base motives, but that they could not understand their motives, nor be responsible for the effect of their exceedingly complex motives, in action. (All motives are complex, and it is just as well to remember this: including, or perhaps especially, one's own.) The history which produces such a film cannot, after all, be swiftly understood, nor can the effects of this history be easily resolved. Nor can this history be blamed on any single individual; but, at the same time, no one can be let off the hook. It is a terrible thing, simply, to be trapped in one's history, and attempt, in the same motion (and in this, our life!) to accept, deny, reject, and redeem it—and, also, on whatever level, to profit from it. And: with one's head in the fetid jaws of this lion's mouth, attempt to love and be loved, and raise one's children, and pay the rent, and wrestle with one's mortality. In the final scene at the station, there is something choked and moving, something sensed through a thick glass, dimly, in the Sheriff's sweet, boyish, Southern injunction, to Virgil, "take care, you hear?" and something equally choked and rigid in the black detective's reaction. It reminded me of nothing so much as William Blake's *Little Black Boy*—that remote, that romantic, and that hopeless. Virgil Tibbs goes to where they call him *Mister*, far away, presumably, from South Street, and the

Sheriff has gone back to the niggers, who are really his only assignment. And nothing, alas, has been made possible by this obligatory, fade-out kiss, this preposterous adventure: except that white Americans have been encouraged to continue dreaming, and black Americans have been alerted to the necessity of waking up. People who cannot escape thinking of themselves as white are poorly equipped, if equipped at all, to consider the meaning of black: people who know so little about themselves can face very little in another: and one dare hope for nothing from friends like these. This cruel observation is implicit in the script: for what would have happened to our Mr. Tibbs, or, indeed, to our Sheriff, had the widow demanded the black man's blood as the price for the wealth she was bringing into the town? Who, among that manly crew, would have resisted the widow's might? The people of *In the Heat of the Night* can be considered moving and pathetic only if one has the luxury of the assurance that one will never be at their mercy. And that no one in the world has the luxury of this assurance is beginning to be clear: all over the world.

In *The Birth of a Nation*, the Sheriff would have been an officer of the Klan. The widow would, secretly, have been sewing Klan insignia. The murdered man (whether or not he was her husband) would have been a carpetbagger. Sam would have been a Klan deputy. The troublesome poor whites would have been mulattoes. And Virgil Tibbs would have been the hunted, not the hunter. It is impossible to pretend that this state of affairs has really altered: a black man, in any case, had certainly best not believe everything he sees in the movies.

In 1942, Bette Davis, under the direction of John Huston, delivered a ruthlessly accurate (and much underrated) portrait of a Southern girl, in the Warner Brothers production of Ellen Glasgow's novel, *In This, Our Life*. She thus became, and, indeed, remained, the toast of Harlem because her prison scene with the black chauffeur was cut when the movie came uptown. The uproar in Harlem was impressive, and I think that the scene was reinserted; in any case, either uptown or downtown, I saw it. Davis appeared to have read, and grasped, the script—which must have made her rather lonely—and she certainly understood the role. Her performance had the effect, rather, of exposing and shattering the film, so that she played in a kind of vacuum: much the same thing was to happen, later, to Sidney Poitier, with his creation of Noah Cullen, in *The Defiant Ones*.

In *In This, Our Life*, Davis is a spoiled Southern girl, guilty of murder in a hit-and-run automobile accident, and she has blamed this crime on her black chauffeur. (An actor named Ernest Anderson: Hattie McDaniel played his mother.) But he has steadfastly denied having had the car that night. She, armed with her wealth, her color, and her sex, goes to the prison to persuade him to corroborate her story: and what she uses, through jailhouse bars, is her sex. She will pay, for the chauffeur's silence, any price he demands. Indeed, the price is implicit in the fact that she knows he knows that she is guilty: she can have no secrets from him now.

Blacks are often confronted, in American life, with such devastating examples of the white descent from dignity; devastating not only because of the enormity of the white pretensions, but because this swift and graceless descent would seem to indicate that white people have no principles whatever. At the beginning of the Attica uprising, for example, a white guard was heard pleading with a black prisoner: "You can have anything you want," the guard is reported to have said. "You can have *me*. Just don't send me out there."

In the film, the black chauffeur simply does not trust the white girl to keep her end of the bargain—which would involve using her power to save his life—and is far too proud, anyway, to strike such a bargain. But the offer has been made, and the truth about the woman revealed.

The blacks have a song which says, *I can't believe what you say, because I see what you do*. No American film, relating to blacks, can possibly incorporate this observation. This observation—set to music, as are so many black observations—denies, simply, the validity of the legend which is responsible for these films: films which exist for the sole purpose of perpetuating the legend.

Black men, after all, have been the lovers, and victims, of women like the woman in *In This, Our Life*: and these women have also been the victims of black men: and sometimes they have loved each other: and sometimes had to live in hell to pay for it. Even the most thoughtless, even the most deluded black person knows more about his life than the image he is offered as the justification of it. Black men know something about white sheriffs. They know, for one thing, that the sheriff is no freer to become friends with them than they are to become friends with the sheriff: For example:

A white taxi driver once drove me from the airport in Birmingham, Alabama, to the Gaston Motel. This is a long, dark, tree-lined drive, and the taxi driver was breaking the law: for a white taxi driver is not—or was not, it is hard to be accurate concerning the pace of my country's progress—allowed to pick up a black fare. That this was not a wicked man is proven, perhaps, by the fact that I am still here. But I was in his cab only because the idea of waiting another hour at the airport (sitting on my typewriter, which I never carried South again) was too frightening. I had had no choice but to gamble on him. Yet, I could not be at ease about his motives in breaking the law for a black, Northern journalist. It was perfectly possible, after all, that he had no intention of driving me to the Gaston Motel (which had already been bombed three times) but to my death. And there was no way for this thought not to have entered my mind: I would have had to be mindless not to have thought it. And what was he thinking? For, I felt that he wanted to talk to me, and I certainly wanted to talk to him. But neither of us could manage it. It was not his fault, and it was not my fault. We could find no way out of our common trouble, for we had been forbidden—and on pain of death—to trust, or to use, our common humanity, that confrontation and acceptance which is all that can save another human being.

Blacks know something about black cops, too, even those called Mister, in Philadelphia. They know that their presence on the force doesn't change the force or the judges or the lawyers or the bondsmen or the jails. They know the black cop's mother and his father, they may have met the sister, and they know the younger, or the older brother, who may be a bondsman, or a junkie, or a student, in limbo, at Yale. They know how much the black cop has to prove, and how limited are his means of proving it: where I grew up, black cops were yet more terrifying than white ones.

I think that it was T. S. Eliot who observed that the people cannot bear very much reality. This may be true enough, as far as it goes, so much depending on what the word "people" brings to mind: I think that we bear a little more reality than we might wish. In any case, in order for a person to bear his life, he needs a valid re-creation of that life, which is why, as Ray Charles might put it, blacks chose to sing the blues. This is why *Raisin in the Sun* meant so much to black people—on the stage: the film is another matter. In the theater, a current flowed back and forth between the audience and the actors: flesh and blood corroborating flesh and blood—as we say, testifying. The filmed play, which is all, alas, that *Raisin* is on film, simply stayed up there, on that screen. The unimaginative rigidity of the film locked the audience out of it. Furthermore, the people in *Raisin* are not the people one goes to the movies to see. The root argument of the play is really far more subtle than either its detractors or the bulk of its admirers were able to see.

The Defiant Ones, on the other hand, *is* a film, with people we are accustomed to seeing in the movies. Well: all except one. The irreducible difficulty of this genuinely well-meaning film is that no one, clearly, was able to foresee what Poitier would do with his role—nor was anyone, thereafter, able to undo it—and his performance, which lends the film its only real distinction, also, paradoxically, smashes it to pieces. There is no way to believe both Noah Cullen *and* the story. With the best will in the world, it is virtually impossible to watch Tony Curtis while Sidney is on the screen, or, with the possible exception of Lon Chaney, Jr., anyone else. It is impossible to accept the premise of the story, a premise based on the profound American misunderstanding of the nature of the hatred between black and white. There is a hatred—certainly: though I am now using this word with great caution, and only in the light of the effects, or the results, of hatred. But the hatred is not equal on both sides, for it does not have the same roots. This is, perhaps, a very subtle argument, but black men do not have the same reason to hate white men as white men have to hate blacks. The root of the white man's hatred is terror, a bottomless and nameless terror, which focuses on the black, surfacing, and concentrating on this dread figure, an entity which lives only in his mind. But the root of the black man's hatred is rage, and he does not so much hate white men as simply want them out of his way, and, more than that, out of his children's way. When the white man begins to have in the black man's mind the weight that the black man has in the white man's mind, that black man is going mad. And when he goes under, he does not go under screaming in terror: he goes under howling with rage. A black man knows that two men chained together have to learn to forage, eat, fart, shit, piss, and tremble, and sleep together: they are indispensable to each other, and anything can happen between them, and anyone who has been there knows this. No black man, in such a situation, and especially knowing what Poitier conveys so vividly Noah Cullen knows, would rise to the bait proffered by this dimwitted poor white child, whose only real complaint is that he is a bona-fide mediocrity who failed to make it in the American rat-race. But many, no better than he, and many much worse, make it every day, all the way to Washington: sometimes, indeed, via Hollywood. It is a species of cowardice, grave indeed, to pretend that black men do not know this. And it is a matter of the most disastrous sentimentality to attempt to bring black men into the white American nightmare, and on the same terms, moreover, which make life for white men all but intolerable.

It is this which black audiences resented about *The Defiant Ones*: that Sidney was in company far beneath him, and that the unmistakable truth of his performance was being placed at the mercy of a lie. Liberal white audiences applauded when Sidney, at the end of the film, jumped off the train in order not to abandon his white buddy. The Harlem audience was outraged, and yelled, *Get back on the train, you fool!* And yet, even at that, recognized, in Sidney's face, at the very end, as he sings "Sewing Machine," something noble, true, and terrible, something out of which we come: I have heard exasperated black voices mutter, more than once, *Lord, have mercy on these children, have* mercy—! *they just don't* know.

There is an image in *The Defiant Ones* which suggests the truth it can neither face nor articulate; and there is a sequence which gives the film completely away. The image occurs when the little boy has been disarmed, and, accidentally, knocked unconscious. The two fugitives are anxiously trying to revive him.

When the boy comes to, he looks up and sees Sidney's black face over him: and we see this face from the boy's point of view, and as the boy sees it: black, unreadable, not quite in focus—and, with a moving, and, as I take it, deliberate irony, this image is the single most beautiful image in the film. The boy screams in terror, and turns to the white man for protection; and the white man assures him that he needs no protection from the black man he was cursing when the boy came along.

We are trembling on the edge of confession here, for, of course, the way the little boy sees the black face is exactly the way the man sees it. It is a presence vaguely, but mightily threatening, partly because of its strangeness and privacy, but also because of its beauty: that beauty which lives so tormentedly in the eye of the white beholder. The film cannot pursue this perception, or suspicion, without bringing into focus the question of white maturity, or white masculinity. This is not the ostensible subject of *The Defiant Ones.* Yet, the dilemma with which we are confronted in the film can only begin to be unlocked on that level, precisely, which the film is compelled to avoid.

In the next sequence, they go along to the home of the boy's mother, who lives alone with her child. The husband, or the father, has been long gone. This sequence is crucial, containing the only justification for the ending of the film, and it deserves a little scrutiny.

The woman who now enters the picture has already been abandoned; and, in quite another sense, once she sees the white boy, is anxious to *be* abandoned. She has the tools which allow the two men to destroy the manacles and break the chain which has bound them together for so long.

The logic of actuality would now strongly indicate, given their situation, and what we have seen of their relationship, that they separate. For one thing, each fugitive is safer without the other, and, for another, the woman clearly wishes to be alone with the white boy. She feeds them both, first asking the white boy if he wants her to feed the black one. He says that he does, and they eat. It is unlikely that Noah Cullen would have sat still for this scene, and even more unlikely that he would obligingly fall asleep at the table while the white boy and the woman make love.

Of course, what the film is now attempting to say—consciously—is that the ordeal of the black man and the white man has brought them closer together than they ever imagined they could be. The fact, and the effect, of this particular ordeal is being offered as a metaphor for the ordeal of black-white relations in America, an ordeal, the film is saying, which has brought us closer together than we know. But the only level on which this can be said to be true is that level of human experience—that depth—of which Americans are most terrified. The complex of conflicting terrors which the black-white connection engenders is suggested by the turgidity of the action which ends this film.

For, when the morning comes, the white boy has elected to throw in his lot with the woman, which means that Noah, after all, is to brave the swamps, and ride the rails, alone.

Noah accepts this, with a briefly mocking bitterness, and he goes. The white boy and the woman begin preparing for their journey. The white boy is worried about his black buddy; though it is difficult to guess at what point, precisely, he begins to think of Noah as his buddy; and wonders, aloud, if he'll be all right. Whereupon, the woman tells him that she has deliberately given Noah instructions which will lead him to his death: that he will never get out of the swamps alive.

It is absolutely impossible to locate the woman's motive for conveying this information. Once Noah has walked out of her door, he is long gone, simply, and can pose no threat. It cannot conceivably matter to her whether he lives, or dies: he has left their lives, in any case, never to return. If she, for whatever reason, has found a means to make certain that he dies, it is impossible to believe that she would risk telling her newfound lover this. She does not know enough about him. The woman is presented as a kind of pathetic, unthinking racist. But she cannot be so unthinking (no woman is) as to take for granted that the man she met last night will approve of being made, in fact, her accomplice in murder. After all, she knows only that the man she met last night ordered her to feed the black boy: and the white boy who orders you to feed his black boy may not be willing to authorize you to kill him. This is not only *what every woman knows*, it is, more crucially, what every white Southern woman knows.

It would appear, however, that this revelation on the part of the woman has the effect of opening our white hero's eyes to the bottomless evil of racial hatred, and, after a stormy scene—a scene quite remarkably unconvincing—and, after the little boy has shot him in the shoulder, our hero lights out for the swamps, and Noah. He finds Noah, and they head for the train—Lord, that Hollywood train, forever coming round the bend!—but the gunshot wound slows the white boy up. Noah refuses to leave him—*you're dragging on the chain!* he cries, stretching out his arm. They get to the train, the black man jumps on, but the white boy can't make it, and the black man jumps off the train, it is hard, indeed, to say why.

Well. He jumps off the train in order to reassure white people, to make them know that they are not hated; that, though they have made human errors, they have done nothing for which to be hated. Well, blacks may or may not hate whites, and when they do, as I have tried to indicate, it's in their fashion. Whites may or may not deserve to be hated, depending on how one manipulates one's reserves of energy, and what one makes of history: in any case, the reassurance is false, the need ignoble, and the question, in this context, absolutely irrelevant. The question operates to hide the question: for what has actually happened, at the end of *The Defiant Ones*, is that a white male and a white female have come together, but are menaced by the presence of the black man. The white woman, therefore, eliminates the black man, so that she and the white man can be alone together. But the white man cannot endure this rupture—from what one must, here, perhaps, call his other, better, worse, or deeper self—and so rejects the white woman, crashing through the swamps, and braving death, in order to regain his black buddy. And his black buddy is waiting for him, and, eventually, takes him in his arms. The white boy has given up his woman. The black man has given up his hope of freedom: and what are we to make of such rigorous choices, so rigorously arrived at?

The choices do not involve, for example, that seismographic shudder which the word, *homosexual,* until today, produces in the American mind, or soul: I doubt that Americans will ever be able to face the fact that the word, homosexual, is not a noun. The root of this word, as Americans use it—or, as this word uses Americans—simply involves a terror of any human touch, since any human touch can change you. A black man and a white man can come together only in the absence of women: which is, simply, the American legend of masculinity brought to its highest pressure, and revealed, as it were, in black and white.

In black and white: the late James Edwards, and Lloyd Bridges, in the long-ago *Home of the Brave,* love each other, as friends must, and as men do. But the fact that one is black and one is white eliminates the possibility of the female presence, according, that is, to the American theology: *may the best man win!* In the black-white context, this elicits, simply, white paranoia: it is hard to imagine anything more abjectly infantile, or anything more tragic.

The film takes place in the heat of the jungles of the Second World War. The white boy loses his life immediately after a quarrel with the black boy. The quarrel is intense. The black boy imagines—hears, though the word is not spoken—that the white boy, his buddy, is about to call him nigger, or an approximation thereof. The nature of the military crisis forces them, at that precise moment, to separate: the white boy does not join them on the beach, where the boats are waiting to rescue our people from the Japanese. The black boy crawls back through the jungle, to find his dying friend, who dies in his arms. Then, guilt paralyzes him, physically, and he undergoes psychotherapy (the central action of the film) and, cured, able to walk, walks into the sunset with another victim, a white, one-armed veteran, to start a business—one dare not say a life—together. The doomed connect, again without women: *Coward,* says the one-armed white victim to that definitive victim, the black, *take my coward's hand.*

Okay. But why is the price of what should, after all, be a simple human connection so high? Is it really necessary to lose a woman, an arm, or one's mind, in order to say hello? And, let's face it, kids, men suffer from penis envy on quite another level than women do, a crucial matter if yours is black and mine is white: furthermore, no matter what Saint Paul may thunder, love is where you find it. A man can fall in love with a man: incarceration, torture, fire, and death, and, still more, the threat of these, have not been able to prevent it, and never will. It became a grave, a tragic matter, on the North American continent, where white power became indistinguishable from the question of sexual dominance. But the question of sexual dominance can exist only in the nightmare of that soul which has armed itself, totally, against the possibility of the changing motion of conquest and surrender, which is love.

The immense quantity of polish expended on *Guess Who's Coming to Dinner* is meant to blind one to its essential inertia and despair. A black person can make nothing of this film—except, perhaps, *Superfly*—and, when one tries to guess what white people make of it, a certain chill goes down the spine. A thirty-seven-year-old black doctor, for whom the word "prodigy" is simply ridiculously inadequate, has met a white girl somewhere in his travels, and they have come, together, to the home of the girl's parents, in San Francisco, to announce their intention to marry each other. Since the girl does not doubt, and has no reason to doubt, her parents' approval, this trip would not seem to be necessary. However, she may wish, merely, to exhibit her remarkable catch to San Francisco: or, to put it in less speculative terms, we are, again, at the mercy of a plot. The wonder doctor is Sidney Poitier, and the girl's parents are Spencer Tracy and Katharine Hepburn: which means that the question of parental blessing is immediately robbed of the remotest suspense: these winning, intelligent, and forward-looking people can certainly not object. The girl's mother, after an initial shock, is won over, almost at once. The father is dubious, cranky, and crotchety, but we know that his heart is in the right place—otherwise, Spencer Tracy would never have been cast in the part. The wonder doctor's parents (significantly) do not really pose a problem, and they enter the picture late—we will speak of them later.

The suspense, then, concerning this interracial marriage, can be created only by the black doctor. We gather that he has been married before, to a black woman, who died. This informs us that, in spite of his brilliance, he is not presumptuous, and he is not an upstart, unstable adventurer: nothing less than real love would have driven him so far beyond the boundaries of caste. This love is, also, quite remarkably self-effacing. He informs the girl's parents that, even though their daughter may be prepared to marry *him* without their consent, *he* will not marry *her* without it. The girl loves her parents too much, he explains, to be able to endure such a rupture; nor can he himself, for reasons of his own, bear to be the author of such pain.

Since history affords so few examples of this species of restraint on the part of the prospective bridegroom, perhaps we should take a closer look at him: and try to find out what he is actually saying. I scarcely have the heart to indicate the echoes to be found, here, of *In Abraham's Bosom* (yes: the supplicant of Paul Green's *In Abraham's Bosom*) nor do more than indicate the existence of Eugene O'Neill's *All God's Chillun Got Wings*, or the terror underlying *The Hairy Ape*: not now can I tell you: the road was rocky. The setting of *Guess Who's Coming to Dinner* is the key. We are on the heights of San Francisco—at a time not too far removed from the moment when the city of San Francisco reclaimed the land at Hunter's Point and urban-renewalized the niggers out of it. The difficult and terrified city, where the niggers are, lives far beneath these heights. The father is in a perfectly respectable, perhaps even admirable profession, and the mother runs an art gallery. The setting is a brilliant re-creation of a certain—and far from unattractive—level of American life. And the black doctor is saying, among other things, that his presence in this landscape (this hard-won Eden) will do nothing to threaten, or defile it—indeed, since in the event that he marries the girl, they are immediately going to the Far East, or some such place, he will not even be present. One can scarcely imagine striking a bargain more painless; and without even losing a daughter, who will, merely, in effect, be traveling, and broadening her education; keeping in touch via trans-Pacific telephone, and coming home to San Francisco from time to time, with her yet more various, toddling, and exotic acquisitions.

This moment in the film is handled with such skill that one would certainly prefer to believe it, if one could. Only the fact that one does not believe it prevents one from resenting it. No man in love is so easily prepared to surrender his beloved, or travel so many thousands of miles to do so: no one expects such behavior from Steve McQueen. Without belaboring this sufficiently glaring point, the basis for such suspense as the film may hope to claim having now been established, we are confronted with a series of classical tableaux:

We have already met the white, backward, uneducated taxi driver, mightily displeased by the glimpse he catches, in his rear-view mirror, of our lovers, kissing. He conveys his displeasure, failing to shake the doctor's cool: indeed, the doctor tips him.

We have already met the mother's assistant at the art gallery, a white woman, along with a particularly gruesome (and very cunningly used) example of modern art. The doctor toys with this dreadful object, as he toys with the woman's avid curiosity, and our lovers leave.

We meet the mother and the father, distressed domestic tête-à-tête, etc.—at which point we are informed of the doctor's staggering achievements—and now we meet the loyal nigger maid.

It so happened that I saw *The Birth of a Nation* and *Guess Who's Coming to Dinner* on the same day—the first in the morning, the second in the afternoon. It happened, also, that I saw both films in the company of a young African girl, a Cameroons journalist. This girl has never seen America, and, understandably, took my testimony concerning my country with enormous grains of salt.

Yet, it was not my testimony which presented us, on the same day, in two films divided from each other by something like half a century, with the same loyal nigger maid, playing the same role, and speaking the same lines. In *The Birth of a Nation*, the loyal nigger maid informs the nigger congressman that she don't like niggers who set themselves up above their station. When our black wonder doctor hits San Francisco, some fifty-odd years later, he encounters exactly the same maid, who tells him exactly the same thing, for the same reason, and in the same words, adding, merely, as a concession, no doubt, to modern times—she has come across our black hero, having entered his room without knocking, holding only a towel between his nakedness and her indignation—"and furthermore to that, you ain't even that handsome!" For she is a part of the family: she would appear to have no family of her own: and is clearly prepared to protect her golden-haired mistress from the clutches of this black ape by any means necessary.

The inclusion of this figure is absolutely obligatory—compulsive—no matter what the film imagines itself to be saying by means of this inclusion. How many times have we seen her! She is Dilsey, she is Mammy, in *Gone with the Wind*, and in *Imitation of Life*, and *The Member of the Wedding*—mother of sorrows, whore and saint, reaching a kind of apotheosis in *Requiem for a Nun*. (And yet, black men have mothers and sisters and daughters who are not like that at all!) In *Guess Who*, her presence is meant to be taken as comic, and the film seems to be using her to suggest that backward people can be found on both sides of the racial fence—a point which can scarcely be made so long as one is sitting on it. In any case, in life, she has a family, she may even have a doctor for a son, and she assuredly does not love the white family so deeply as they are compelled to suppose: she cannot, since she knows how bitterly her black family is endangered by her white one.

Then, there is the scene with the mother and the lady assistant at the art gallery, a scene which Miss Hepburn obviously relishes, and which she plays with a marvelously vindictive skill. The lady assistant is horrified at the news of this impending disastrous marriage, and is full of sympathy for the mother: who reacts with a cold, proud, and even rather terrified contempt. (This is probably the best scene in the film, and it juts out from it because of Hepburn's genuine indignation.) She walks the lady to her car, makes her get into the car, instructs her to pay herself her wages, and a bonus, to start her car motor, to get rid of the artistic monstrosity with which we have seen the doctor amusing himself earlier, and get permanently lost. One down, then, but several more to go, for, now, here come the doctor's father and mother.

The film's high polish does not entirely succeed in blinding us to a kind of incipient reality suggested by these two.

Though they come, principally, out of a Hollywood script-writer's imagination, they unexpectedly resist being manipulated into total irrelevance—or, in other words, it proved somewhat difficult to find a place for them in this so briefly troubled Eden.

The black mother and the white mother become allies at once, firmly opting for the happiness of their children. The black father and the white father, without becoming allies, nevertheless agree that their children should not marry. I forgot to mention the priest, who is, perhaps, the master stroke of the film. Though, as the film carefully informs us, the Tracy-Hepburn couple are not Catholic, this priest is their best friend, and he is, unequivocally, on the side of the young couple. The two crass, practical fathers find, therefore, that they have taken on those two formidable adversaries, the Church, and mother love—the last being also related to women's intuition. The Church, here, is truculent (rather than militant) and mocks the fears of the white father: and mother love, as projected by Bea Richards in her brief scene with Spencer Tracy, moderately poignant and perceptive. The outcome cannot really very much longer be left in doubt (the film has got to end) but before we can arrive at the film's resolution, there is another matter to be dealt with, and that involves the relationship of the black father to the black son.

It is here that the film's polish cracks—becomes, as it were, unglued. There is no way, simply, for so light and self-serving a fable to deal with a matter so weighty—and so painful. It is not enough for the father to feel that his son has gone mad, and is throwing away his life, or his future, because of a doomed infatuation. The crucial element in such a confrontation is the question—vivid, though nearly unspoken—between the father and the son: what did the father raise the son to respect? For the son can make his lonely decision now only by confronting the nature and the value of that gift. A black man who has raised a son who has achieved his own life, and a son who has also achieved worldly eminence, has great respect for that son. He will offer his judgment, but he will not attempt to impose his will. As for being frightened for that son, the father has been frightened so long that this fear has become no more remarkable to him than the fact that he has to shave; moreover, hiding his fear from his son has been one of the principal conditions of his life, as a father, and a man. And rarely does the father complain about the sacrifices he has made: the subject arrives during adolescence, when the father is attempting to prepare the son for the price *he* will have to pay for his life. All this takes place, anyway, in a kind of short-hand virtually impossible to translate for the bulk of white Americans. But, leaving all that aside, the father has absolutely no motive for this scene. The son is a world-famous doctor, thirty-seven years old, who has already been married, and who has lived all over the world; and who, if he marries the girl, is immediately taking her away with him, out of the United States. The father knows perfectly well that America is not the world: indeed, it would have to be a part of his pride that his effort has helped to release his son from the obscenely crippling pressures of his homeland. It can make absolutely no difference to him who his son marries: if the son is free and happy, the father is, too. And it is worth noting, perhaps, that the film appears completely to forget the wonder doctor's eminence, and the effect that this would have on his parents. As the parents of a world-famous man, they, indisputably, outrank their hosts, and might very well feel that the far from galvanizing fiancée is not worthy of their son: it is not the black parents who would be ill at ease.

But the American self-evasion, which is all that this country has as history, has created the myth on which this film is based, and this myth cannot endure so treacherous a perception; treacherous to the American self-image, and to what passes, in America, for self-esteem. Only yesterday, if, indeed, it was yesterday, the hotly contested white fiancée cried *death before dishonor!* (or *you yellow dogs!*) and ran out of this life, into the arms of Jesus, in order not to be defiled by the nigger's touch. Today—if it *is* today—she tells her mother, in a scene manipulated with such cool efficiency that it almost seems to be true, that, although she certainly wanted to sleep with her black fiancé, *he* was too honorable to touch *her*: in this day of so many liberations, make of this collision of inadmissible fantasies whatever you will. In any case, it is out of all this that the black son must say, finally, to his black father, and ignobly enough, "You're a colored man. I just want to be a man." Which means that a man exists only in the brutally limited lexicon of those who think of themselves as white, and imagine, therefore, that they control reality and rule the world. And the black son says this to his black father in spite of the fact that he, the wonder doctor, has had to become a living freak, a walking encyclopedia of rare medical knowledge, in order to have the question of his marriage to a white girl *discussed*. The assumptions of *The Last of the Mohicans* and *The Birth of a Nation* are very present here, and, if even the wonder doctor must undergo such trials in order to be able to touch his lady love, heaven help the high-school dropouts: so many of whom found themselves in Attica, for example, not impossibly for trying to be men. Heaven did not help those among the blacks who failed to master their pre-med courses on the day that the Republic, responsive to the will of heaven, decided to uphold what Rockefeller, in one of his nobler statements, described as "the impartial application of the law": he, too, clearly, is a movie fan.

The film does make one despairing attempt to suggest, after Galileo, that the earth may be turning: in that lamentable scene in the city when Tracy tastes a new flavor of ice cream and discovers that he likes it. This scene occurs in a drive-in, and is punctuated by Tracy's backing his car into the car of a young black boy. The black boy's resulting tantrum is impressive—and also entirely false, due to no fault of the actor (D'Urville Martin). The moral of the scene is *They're here now, and we have to deal with them*: or, *The natives are restless. What shall we do?*

Ah. What indeed—short, that is, of bombing them back into the stone age. As concerns *Guess Who's Coming to Dinner*, we can conclude that people have the right to marry whom they choose, especially if we know that they are leaving town as soon as dinner is over.

In Sol Stein's *The Childkeeper*, a short and remarkable novel, a forty-eight-year-old bank vice-president, and his wife, and three of their four children, spend a long weekend together in their country house. The children, who are adolescents, invite some of their adolescent friends, and, among these, is a black boy of nineteen, named Greco. The father finds himself paralyzed by his liberal, or, more accurately, humanitarian presumptions (presumptions by which he does not live) and by his apprehension that he really knows nothing about his children, nor (he both hopes and fears) they about him. The presence of the black boy, an exceedingly rude and dangerous visitor, drags to the surface the buried terrors of his life, and, helplessly, he kills the boy. He does not mean to kill him, but Eden has a price: and the death of the black boy brings about his own.

The question of identity is a question involving the most profound panic—a terror as primary as the nightmare of the mortal fall. This question can scarcely be said to exist among the wretched, who know, merely, that they are wretched and who bear it day by day—it is a mistake to suppose that the wretched do not know that they are wretched; nor does this question exist among the splendid, who know, merely, that they are splendid, and who flaunt it, day by day: it is a mistake to suppose that the splendid have any intention of surrendering their splendor. An identity is questioned only when it is menaced, as when the mighty begin to fall, or when the wretched begin to rise, or when the stranger enters the gates, never, thereafter, to be a stranger: the stranger's presence making *you* the stranger, less to the stranger than to yourself. Identity would seem to be the garment with which one covers the nakedness of the self: in which case, it is best that the garment be loose, a little like the robes of the desert, through which robes one's nakedness can always be felt, and, sometimes, discerned. This trust in one's nakedness is all that gives one the power to change one's robes.

Lawrence of Arabia, stemming, both dimly and helplessly, from T. E. Lawrence's *Seven Pillars of Wisdom*, is a kind of muted and updated, excruciatingly astute version of Rudyard Kipling's *Gunga Din*. The word "muted" does not refer to the musical score, which must be the loudest in the history of the cinema, and which is absolutely indispensable to the intention of the film.

The song says *There is trouble all over this world*: and our

ancestors, the English, made careful note of this, and pro-
ceeded to base their imperial policy on this relentless and utilitarian truth. Living on an island, they built boats, and where
trouble was, they sailed them; sometimes, they very carefully
brought the needed trouble with them, and very often, simply,
their presence was trouble enough. The English learned how
to use, and foment, trouble to their purposes, and this policy
was known as Divide and Rule. Alongside this, and justifying
it, was the concept and necessity of Civilization. I point this
out, calmly enough, because nothing in *Lawrence of Arabia*
really conveys the fact that the British were deliberately using,
and backing, an Arab rebellion in order to complete the dis-
memberment of the Ottoman Empire. This they managed to
do, without keeping any of their promises to the Arabs, to
the great sorrow and bewilderment of young Lawrence, who
does not understand, until Damascus, to what pragmatic ends
his idealism has been put. (The Sykes-Picot Treaty contained
a secret clause which divided the conquered territory between
England, France, and Russia. Lawrence, in his book, is aware
of this. But, "In revenge I vowed to make the Arab revolt the
engine of its own success, as well as hand-maid to our Egyptian campaign: and vowed to lead it so madly in the final
victory that expediency should counsel to the Powers a fair
settlement of the Arabs' moral claims.")

The film begins with a long, overhead shot of a motorcycle
in a sunlit square. A khaki-clad man appears and begins fooling around with the motorcycle: walks off, comes back. A
closer shot reveals that he is trying to get the motorcycle
started. He starts it, gets on it, and we ride with him through
the English countryside, on a sunny day. For those who know
that Lawrence died in a motorcycle accident, the film is beginning at the end of Lawrence's life: later on, we may ask
ourselves why.

The motorcycle goes off the road, crashes. We are then
present at Lawrence's funeral, a very impressive one, treated
to vehemently conflicting views of him—emanating from the
military—and the film begins.

Since the Empire must be kept in the background—and yet,
always be present, hence the overwhelming music—the great
burden of this film is on the shoulders of Lawrence, played

by Peter O'Toole. But the star of the film is the desert: the vast, technicolored backdrop of the desert meant to invest with splendor a stammering tale.

For, this overwhelming desert, though it exists geographically, and was actually filmed by an actual camera crew, sent there for that purpose, is put to a use which is as far from reality as are most of the people we encounter in it. The least real of these people is Lawrence himself. This is not O'Toole's fault: but so grave an adventure can scarcely be ascribed to the vagaries and idealism of a single man. Lawrence's courage and steadfastness are given as admirable, because hard-won— here, the film, unconsciously, rather patronizes Lawrence; his complexities are barely—or, rather, perhaps, endlessly—hinted at, that is to say never illuminated. His rapport with the Arabs is of great use to the British, whose attitude toward him, otherwise, is, at best, ambivalent. The film takes the view that he was a valiant, maverick, naïve and headstrong, brutally broken in battle, and betrayed, less by his country than by his inability to confront—as do his superiors—the hard facts of life: the hard facts of life, in this case, referring, principally, to the limits and exigencies of power. And it would appear to be true that Lawrence's concept of power existed almost entirely on a messianic level—indeed, on a level far more complex and painful than that—but it is almost impossible to pursue this speculation within the confines described by the film.

The film presents us with an inadvertent martyr to the cause of spreading civilization: the speeding of the light to those in darkness. One of the hazards of this endeavor is that of finding oneself in the hands of the infidels. This is what happens to Lawrence in the film (and in a far more fascinating and terrible way in his book). In the film, he is captured by the Turks, refuses the lustful attentions of a Turkish Bey, and is raped by the soldiers. This precipitates his subsequent slaughter of the fleeing Turkish Army. This slaughter destroys his soul, and, though the desert has now claimed him forever, he no longer has any role in the desert, and so must go home to England, dead, to die.

The film begins with the death of Lawrence in order to avoid, whether consciously or not, the deepest and most dangerous implications of this story. We are confronted with a fallen hero, and we trace the steps which lead him to his end. But the zeal which drove Lawrence into the desert does not begin at the point at which we meet him in the film, but farther back than that, in that complex of stratifications called England. Of this, Lawrence himself was most tormentedly aware.

The English can be said to exemplify the power of nostalgia to an uncanny degree. Nothing the world holds, from Australia to Africa, to America, India, to China, to Egypt, appears to have made the faintest imprint on the English soul: wherever the English are *is*—or will resist, out of perversity, or at its peril, becoming—England. (Not, on the other hand, of course, that it can ever truly *be* England: but it can try.) This is a powerful presumption, but why, then, the ruder recipient cannot but demand, do not the English stay in England? It would appear that this island people need endless corroboration of their worth: and the tragedy of their history has been their compulsion to make the world their mirror, and this to a degree not to be equalled in the history of any other people—and with a success, if that is the word, not to be equalled in the history of any other people. *I liked the things beneath me*—Lawrence, from *Seven Pillars of Wisdom*, is speaking—*and took my pleasures and adventures downward. There seemed a certainty in degradation, a final safety. Man could rise to any height, but there was an animal level beneath which he could not fall. It was a satisfaction on which to rest.*

The necessity, then, of those "lesser breeds without the law"—those wogs, barbarians, niggers—is this: one must not become more free, nor become more base than they: must not be used as they are used, nor yet use them as their abandonment allows one to use them: therefore, they must be civilized. But, when they *are* civilized, they may simply "spuriously imitate [the civilizer] back again," leaving the civilizer with "no satisfaction on which to rest."

Thus, it may be said that the weary melancholy underlying *Lawrence of Arabia* stems from the stupefying apprehension that, whereas England may have been doomed to civilize the world, no power under heaven can civilize England. I am using England, at the moment, arbitrarily, simply because England is responsible for Lawrence: but the principle illustrates the dilemma of all the civilizing, or colonizing powers, particularly now, as their power begins to be, at once, more tenuous and more brutal, and their vaunted identities revealed as being dubious indeed. The greater the public power, the greater the private, inadmissible despair; the greater this despair, the greater the danger to all human life. The camera remains on Lawrence's face a long time before he finally cries, *No prisoners!* and leads his men to massacre the Turks. This pause is meant to recall to us the intolerable mortification he has endured, and to make comprehensible the savagery of this English schoolboy.

But the mortification of an English schoolboy, in the desert, at the hands of infidels who refuse to be civilized, cannot be used to justify the bloody course of Empire, or the ruthless stratagems of power: this schoolboy is armed with the weight of a nation, and his mortification is, or should be, nothing to the point. If we grant that the Turks are, also, notoriously bloodthirsty, then we must equally grant that rape is not unknown in English public schools: there *is* no "animal level" beneath which "we" cannot fall. The truth is that Lawrence was deliberately formed and deliberately used, and, at that moment, superbly executed the real intentions of the state which had formed him. So, after all, do most of us, without even knowing it: sometimes, the unexpected results—given the short-sightedness of states, and statesmen—are immediate, immense, and retaliatory. For example, there may, one day, be a film, called *Chamberlain, at Munich,* in which we will learn, for the first time, of the mortifications Chamberlain endured and which compelled him, as Prime Minister of England, to sell, as it turned out, all of Europe to the then German Chancellor, in order to protect his island. Looking for all the world like the schoolboy he never ceased to be, he proclaimed to cheering crowds, upon his return from Munich, *"If at first you don't succeed, try, try again!"*

The crowds were cheering their own impending ordeal: one wonders how many of them survived the rage which their loyal schoolboy, superb epitome of themselves, had just unleashed against them.

*

In 1952, I was in America, just in time for the McCarthy era. I had never seen anything like it.

If I had ever really been able to hate white people, the era of that dimwitted, good-natured, flamboyant representative of the American people would have been pure heaven: for, not even the most vindictive hatred could have imagined the slimy depths to which the bulk of white Americans allowed themselves to sink: noisily, gracelessly, flatulent and foul with patriotism. Though cowardice was certainly the most vividly recognizable color in the tapestry, it was not mere cowardice one was watching, but something much worse, an absolute panic, absolutely infantile. Truman, the honest haberdasher and machine-made politician, in whose wisdom we had dropped the atomic bomb on Japan, had been elected President the year (1948) that I left America. Subsequently, my countrymen (who were still arguing among themselves as to this relationship—their relationship, that is, to blacks) decided to entrust their lives, their fortunes, and their sacred honor, not once, but twice, to Daddy Warbucks Eisenhower, who had nothing against McCarthy, and who was Papa to Richard Nixon. I began to feel a terrified pity for the white children of these white people: who had been sent, by their parents, to Korea, though their parents did not know why. Neither did their parents know why these miserable, incontestably inferior, rice-eating gooks refused to come to heel, and would not be saved. But *I* knew why. I came from a long line of miserable, incontestably inferior, rice-eating, chicken-stealing, hog-swilling niggers—who had acquired these skills in their flight from bondage—who still refused to come to heel, and who would not be saved. If two and two make four, then it is a very simple matter to recognize that people unable to be responsible for their own children, and who care so little about each other, are unlikely instruments for the salvation of the people whom they permit themselves the luxury of despising as inferior to themselves. Even in the case of Korea, we, the blacks at least, knew why our children were there: they had been sent there to be used, in exactly the same way, and for the same reasons, as the blacks had been so widely dispersed out of Africa—an incalculable investment of raw material in what was not yet known as the common market.

Each time the black discontent erupts within the continental limits of the United States—erupts, that is, to the extent of demanding a "police action"—the Republic claims "outside" interference. It is simply not conceivable that American blacks can be so unhappy (or so bright, or so brave) as seriously to menace the only social order that they know; a social order, moreover, in which they have achieved, or have been given—let's hear both points of view, please!—the highest standard of living of any black people in the world. Apart from pointing out that the black suicide rate began to rise impressively about a quarter of a century ago, we will not otherwise challenge this moving article of faith. Unluckily, Americans remain at the mercy of this misapprehension when attempting to deal with the world. They do not know how their slaves endured, nor how they endure, nor do they know what their slaves know about them—they do not dare to know it: and what they dare not know about Little Black Sambo is precisely what they do not dare to know about the world by which they are surrounded. Thus, the disaster in Korea had to be explained away. American error being unthinkable, and American might not to be questioned, the disaster could be explained away only by a species of *inside* interference: America was not being defeated, it was being betrayed, by disloyal Americans.

A disloyal American was any American who disapproved of the course his government was taking: though it is very important to stress that Charles Lindbergh, for example, who disapproved of the course his government was taking, and who addressed an America First Committee Rally in Madison Square Garden to prove it, was never considered anything less than a superb and loyal patriot: as is, today, Governor George Wallace, of Alabama, who would have agreed with Colonel Lindbergh that we were fighting on the wrong side. (Lindbergh's wife, the poetess, Anne Morrow Lindbergh, assured us that the inconveniences of the Third Reich—the foul-smelling camps, the ovens, the gas chambers, the slaughter of, among other human beings, the Jews—were "not in themselves the future," merely "scum on the wave of the future.") The American marked as disloyal was always someone whose disagreement with his government might have begun with his apprehension of the role of Franco's Spain, and Mussolini's Italy, and the Italian adventure in Ethiopia: someone who could see what these piratical rehearsals, carried out with the consent, and the power, of the Western world, meant for the future of the world. It was also someone who could see that it had not been Roosevelt, but a global war, necessitating a war economy, which ended the American, and, subsequently, the Western Depression. A disloyal American was anyone who really believed in equal justice under the law, and his testimony may have begun with the Scottsboro Case, or with the Peekskill riot. A disloyal American was anyone who believed it his right, and his duty, to attempt to feed the hungry, and clothe the naked, and visit those in prison, and he may have been fingered, so to speak, by any Southern senator: he was certainly being scrutinized by the late, and much lamented, J. Edgar Hoover, history's most highly paid (and most utterly useless) *voyeur*.

Americans, then, in order to prove their devotion to American ideals, began informing on each other. I had been living in Europe for nearly four years, and knew refugees from precisely this species of moral and actual nightmare, from Germany, Italy, Spain, and Russia, and Ethiopia: *Give us your poor!* But this species of refugee was not what the hymn of the Statue of Liberty had in mind.

Lives, careers, and loves were smashed on the rock of this cowardice. I was much younger then: the best I can say is that I was appalled, but not—alas—surprised. Still, it was horrible to be confirmed: out of this obscenely fomented hysteria, we are confronted with the nonsense of the pumpkin papers, the self-important paranoia of Whittaker Chambers, such nightshade creatures as Harvey Matusow, Elizabeth Bentley, and Harry Gold, and the breathtaking careers of those remarkable spies, Julius and Ethel Rosenberg: who are about to lose their lives, just the same, in order to astonish, halt, and purify, an erring nation. Yes: and there were others. Some knew it, and some didn't.

I wandered, then, in my confusion and isolation—for almost all the friends I had had were in trouble, and, therefore, in one way or another, *incommunicado*—into a movie, called *My Son, John*. And I will never forget it.

This movie stars Miss Helen Hayes, the late Van Heflin, and the late Robert Walker. Dean Jagger plays the American Legion husband. (Years and years ago, Dean Jagger had appeared in John Wexley's play about the Scottsboro Case, *They Shall Not Die!*: he played the young reporter whose love forces one of the poor white girls to retract her testimony that the black boys had raped her.)

The family is the American family one has seen and seen and seen again on the American screen: the somewhat stolid, but, at bottom, strong, decent, and loving head of the family; the somewhat scatterbrained, but, at bottom, shrewd, loving, and tough wife and mother; and the children of this remarkably unremarkable couple. In *My Son, John*, there are two sons. One of them plays football, which is, literally, all that we ever learn about him. The other son, John, who does not, apparently, play football, has flown the family coop, and has a job in Washington, where he appears to be doing very well. But they don't see very much of him anymore, which causes the mother some distress: she misses her son, John, and this to a somewhat disquieting extent—the movie seems to feel, however, that this morbid worry about the life of her grown son is the normal reaction of any normal American mother.

The mother's distress is considerably augmented by the arrival of the FBI, in the personable person of Van Heflin, who arrives to ask the family discreet questions concerning their maverick relative. Though this FBI agent is the soul of tact and understanding, the mother eventually perceives the gravity of the situation, and agrees to attempt to save her son. The salvation of her son depends on confession, for he is, indeed, a Communist agent: for the sake of her son's salvation, she must, therefore, cooperate with the FBI. For, if her son does not confess, he is lost: he is anathema. The film concentrates on the struggle in the soul of the mother between mother love and her larger duty. At one point in the film, she cheers him on, exactly as though he were on the football field, urging him to make the touchdown and save the team.

Nothing can possibly redeem so grisly a species of sentimental dishonesty, but Robert Walker's gleefully vicious parody of the wayward American son does a great deal to demystify it. The moment he enters the family house, he makes the reasons for his leaving it very clear: his American Legion father, his adoring mother, his football-playing brother, bore him shitless, and he simply does not want to be like them. This is heresy, of course, and Walker plays it for all it is worth, absolutely heartless and hilarious, acting out all of his mother's terrors, including, and especially, the role of flaming faggot, which is his father's terror, too. It is astonishing that he was allowed to get away with so broad and hostile a put-down—one very nearly expects him to turn up, in black-face, singing "Mammy"—but, on the other hand, this is probably exactly the way the film sees wayward sons. Once they have renounced the American virtues, they are, because of this renunciation, practically Communists already and able to incarnate everything we fear.

Virtue triumphs, at last, of course, but not before the erring son has come to a bloody end. He has been sacrificed to life's larger aims, that is, to the American way of life. The mother says to the father, at the close of the film—the father having more swiftly perceived, and faced, his son's defection—*You were more right than any of us, dear, because you thought with your heart.* This meant, in the context of those years—the harvest of which we have not done reaping—that Elizabeth Bentley and Matusow and Greenglass were also thinking with their hearts, and so were the friendly witnesses before the House Un-American Activities Committee, who threw their friends to the wolves, and so was Eisenhower, when he refused to intervene in the Rosenberg case. No crime had been proven against Ethel Rosenberg: she was considered to have masterminded her husband's crimes, though, clearly, there could be no proof of this, either, nor can it be said that there exists any proof of her husband's crimes. Eisenhower, nevertheless, asserted that leniency toward Ethel Rosenberg would mean, simply, that, thereafter, the Russians would recruit their spies from among women. Music up, slow dissolve (exterior, day) to close-up of the Statue of Liberty, fade-out, the end.

My first encounter with the FBI took place in 1945, in

Woodstock, New York, where I was living in a cabin in the woods. Neither of the two men resembled Van Heflin in the least.

It was early in the morning, they walked me out of the diner, and stood me against a wall. My color had already made me conspicuous enough in that town—this is putting it mildly indeed—and, from a distance, the townspeople stared. I had the feeling that they were waiting to be selected as members of the firing squad.

I had not the remotest notion as to why they had come looking for me. I knew of nothing which I could possibly have done to have attracted their attention. Much later in my life, I knew very well what I had done to attract their attention, and intended, simply, to keep on keeping on. In any case, once you *have* come to the attention of the FBI, they keep a friendly file on you, and your family, and your friends.

But, on this morning, I was terribly frightened, and I was desperately trying to keep one jump ahead of them—to guess what it was before they revealed it. If I could guess what it was, then I might know how to answer and know what to do.

It developed that they were looking for a boy who had deserted from the Marines. I knew no one answering that description, and I said so. They conveyed, very vividly, what they would do to me if I did not tell them the truth—what they could do to smart niggers like me. (I was a smart nigger because I worked, part-time, as an artist's model, and lived in an artist's colony, and had a typewriter in my shack.) My ass would be in a sling—this was among the gentler warnings. They frightened me, and they humiliated me—it was like being spat on, or pissed on, or gang-raped—but they made me hate them, too, with a hatred like hot ice, and all I knew, simply, was that, if I could figure out what they wanted, nothing could induce me to give it to them.

They showed me a series of photographs. From their questions, I realized that they were talking about something that had taken place in the city, during my last visit there. I had spent a lot of time in the restaurant, where I was still occasional waiter. And I had been to a party, briefly, with some friends of mine. One photograph rang a distant bell in my memory: and they saw this. I had seen the face somewhere, but I could not remember where. And, now, my problem was to remember where I had seen the face, and then double lock the memory out of their reach.

And, eventually, I *did* remember. The boy's name was Teddy. I had met him at a party, with some friends of mine—who were, really, friends of his; had seen him, in fact, only once, and very briefly. If I could scarcely remember his name, he would certainly have the same difficulty with mine, and, if he was a fugitive from justice, he would scarcely take a chance on coming to hide in my cabin.

I knew the name now, and I was determined not to reveal it. It was no part of my duty to help them trap the cat, and, no doubt, he had his reasons for deserting the Marines. But the interrogation was rugged, ruthless, and prolonged, and, eventually, the name slipped out: "Well, there was Carmen, and me, and Joe, and Teddy—"

"Teddy? Is this Teddy?"

I cursed myself, for, of course, they had known the name all along. My utterance of the name had confirmed something, and I had been helpful to them, after all. This frightened me in a new way, in a way that I had never been frightened before. I could see, suddenly, that they could keep me against this wall, under this sun, for the foreseeable future, and, finally, whatever I knew would be dragged out of me. But, in fact, thank God, or somebody, all I knew about the boy was his name. I did not even know his last name. And the afternoon wore on, with threats and curses. They came to my cabin, and searched it—I felt that they had searched it before.

When the interrogation was finally over, one of them took out a nickel and dropped it into my palm. With this nickel, the moment I had any news of Teddy I was to call him. I'd be a mighty sorry nigger if I didn't. I took the nickel, and I assured him that I would certainly call him the moment I had any news of Teddy. I thought, You can bet your ass I'll call you. Don't piss, don't shit, don't fuck, until I call you: do nothing till you hear from me.

They left me, finally, haunted the cabin, and roamed the town for two days. Teddy never appeared. I never spent the nickel, I threw it away.

*

Teddy was turned in. This, I learned much later, in New York, during my visit in 1952. One of the friends at that long-gone party really knew Teddy, and the FBI had come to see him, too, and had also given him a nickel. I was having dinner with this friend one night, and he told me, in the casual course of conversation, that he believed that Teddy had stolen his typewriter, and this had made him so angry that he had gone downstairs, to the drugstore, and dropped the nickel in the slot, and turned the deserter in.

Well. Perhaps he would have turned him in, anyway—human beings, including you and me, are capable of anything, and I might have turned him in. Being human, I certainly have no guarantee that betrayal is not among my possibilities, and, indeed, betrayal takes so many forms that I know myself to have been guilty of betrayal more than once. But I do not think that my friend—with whom I never broke bread again—would have spoken of it so lightly had it not been for the moral climate of the time. The artifacts of the time had helped create this climate, and the artificers of the time had become accomplices to this unspeakable immorality. I was an artificer, too, facing, therefore, a heavy question. I loved my country, but I could not respect it, could not, upon my soul, be reconciled to my country as it was. And I loved my work, had great respect for the craft which I was compelled to study, and wanted it to have some human use. It was beginning to be clear to me that these two loves might, never, in my life, be reconciled: no man can serve two masters.

3

Where the Grapes
of Wrath Are Stored

*I found a leak in my building,
and:
my soul has got to move.
I say:
my soul has got to move,
my soul has got to move.*

Song

At the top of 1968, over the vehement protests of my family and my friends, I flew to Hollywood to write the screenplay for *The Autobiography of Malcolm X.* My family and my friends were entirely right, but I was not (since I survived it) entirely wrong. Still, I think that I would rather be horse-whipped, or incarcerated in the forthright bedlam of Bellevue, than repeat the adventure—not, luckily, that I will ever be allowed to repeat it: it is not an adventure which one permits a friend, or brother, to attempt to survive twice. It was a gamble which I knew I might lose, and which I lost—a very bad day at the races: but I learned something.

Fox was then resolving the Cuban-American tension by means of a movie called *Ché!*. This enterprise gave us Omar Sharif, as Ché Guevara, and Jack Palance, as Fidel Castro: the resulting vaudeville team is not required to sing, or dance, nor is it permitted, using the words very loosely, to act. The United Fruit Company is not mentioned. John Foster Dulles is not mentioned, either, though he was the lawyer for said company, nor is his brother, Allen, who was the head of the CIA. In the person of Ché, we are confronted with a doomed, romantic clown. His attempts to awaken the peasants merely disturb them, and their goats: this observation, which is inexorably and inevitably true on one level, is absolutely false on the level at which the film uses it. In the person of Castro, we are confronted with a cigar-smoking, brandy-drinking maniac: a "spic," as clearly unsuited for political responsibility as the nigger congressmen of *The Birth of a Nation.*

Since both the film for which I had been hired, and *Ché!*
were controversial, courageous, revolutionary films, being
packaged for the consumer society, it was hoped that our film
would beat *Ché!* to the box-office. This was not among my
concerns. I had a fairly accurate idea of what Hollywood was
about to do with *Ché!*. (This is not black, bitter paranoia, but
cold, professional observation: you can make a fairly accurate
guess as to the direction a film is likely to take by observing
who is cast in it, and who has been assigned to direct it.) The
intention of *Ché!* was to make both the man, and his Bolivian
adventure, irrelevant and ridiculous; and to do this, furthermore, with such a syrup of sympathy that any incipient Ché
would think twice before leaving Mama, and the ever-ready
friend at the bank. Ché, in the film, is a kind of Lawrence of
Arabia, trapped on the losing side, and unable, even, to understand the natives he has, mistakenly, braved the jungles to
arouse. I had no intention of so betraying Malcolm, or *his*
natives. Yet, my producer had been advised, in an inter-office
memo which I, quite unscrupulously, intercepted, that the
writer (me) should be advised that the tragedy of Malcolm's
life was that he had been mistreated, early, by some whites,
and betrayed (later) by *many* blacks: emphasis in the original.
The writer was also to avoid suggesting that Malcolm's trip
to Mecca could have had any political implications, or repercussions.

Well. I had never before seen this machinery at such close
quarters, and I confess that I was both fascinated and challenged. Near the end of my Hollywood sentence, the studio
assigned me a "technical" expert, who was, in fact, to act as
my collaborator. This fact was more or less disguised at first,
but I was aware of it, and far from enthusiastic; still, by the
time the studio and I had arrived at this impasse, there was
no ground on which I could "reasonably" refuse. I liked the
man well enough—I had no grounds, certainly, on which to
dislike him. I didn't contest his "track record" as a screenwriter, and I reassured myself that he might be helpful: he was
signed, anyway, and went to work.

Each week, I would deliver two or three scenes, which he
would take home, breaking them—translating them—into
cinematic language, shot by shot, camera angle by camera

angle. This seemed to me a somewhat strangling way to make a film. My sense of the matter was that the screenwriter delivered as clear a blueprint as possible, which then became the point of departure for all the other elements involved in the making of a film. For example, surely it was the director's province to decide where to place the camera; and he would be guided in his decision by the dynamic of the scene. However: as the weeks wore on, and my scenes were returned to me, "translated," it began to be despairingly clear (to me) that all meaning was being siphoned out of them. It is very hard to describe this, but it is important that I try.

For example: there is a very short scene in my screenplay in which the central character, a young boy from the country, walks into a very quiet, very special Harlem bar, in the late afternoon. The scene is important because the "country" boy is Malcolm X, the bar is Small's Paradise, and the purpose of the scene is to dramatize Malcolm's first meeting with West Indian Archie—the numbers man who introduced Malcolm to the rackets. The interior evidence of Malcolm's book very strongly suggests a kind of father-son relationship between Archie and Malcolm: my problem was how to suggest this as briefly and effectively as possible.

So, in my scene, as written, Malcolm walks into the bar, dressed in the zoot-suit of the times, and orders a drink. He does not know how outrageously young and vulnerable he looks. Archie is sitting at a table with his friends, and they watch Malcolm, making jokes about him between themselves. But their jokes contain an oblique confession: they see themselves in Malcolm. They have all *been* Malcolm once. He does not know what is about to happen to him, but they do, because it has already happened to them. They have been seeing it happen to others, and enduring what has happened to them, for nearly as long as Malcolm has been on earth. Archie, particularly, is struck by something he sees in the boy. So, when Malcolm, stumbling back from the jukebox, stumbles over Archie's shoes, Archie uses this as a pretext to invite the boy over to the table. And that is all there is to the scene.

My collaborator brought it back to me, translated. It was really the same scene, he explained, but he had added a little action—thus, when Malcolm stumbles over Archie's shoes,

Archie becomes furious. Malcolm, in turn, becomes furious, and the scene turns into a shoot-out from *High Noon*, with everybody in the bar taking bets as to who will draw first. In this way, said my collaborator (with which judgment the studio, of course, agreed) everyone in the audience could *see* what Archie saw in Malcolm: he admired the "country boy's" guts.

We are to believe, then, on the basis of the "translated" scene, that a group of seasoned hustlers, in a very hip Harlem bar, allow a child from the country whom nobody knows to precipitate a crisis which may bring the heat down on everybody, and in which the child, by no means incidentally, may lose his life—while they take bets. West Indian Archie is so angry that a child stepped on his shoes that he forgets he has all that numbers money on him, and all those people waiting to be paid—both above and below the line. And, furthermore, this was not at all what Archie saw in Malcolm, nor was it what I wanted the audience to see.

The rewritten scene was much longer than the original scene, and, though it occurs quite early in the script, derailed the script completely. With all of my scenes being "translated" in this way, the script would grow bulkier than *War and Peace*, and the script, therefore, would have to be cut. And I saw how that would work. Having fallen into the trap of accepting "technical" assistance, I would not, at the cutting point, be able to reject it; and the script would then be cut according to the "action" line, and in the interest of "entertainment" values. How I got myself out of this fix doesn't concern us here—I simply walked out, taking my original script with me—but the adventure remained very painfully in my mind, and, indeed, was to shed a certain light for me on the adventure occurring through the American looking-glass.

Lady Sings the Blues is related to the black American experience in about the same way, and to the same extent that Princess Grace Kelly is related to the Irish potato famine: by courtesy. The film pretends to be based on Billie Holiday's autobiography, and, indeed, Billie's book may make a very fine film one day: a day, however, which I no longer expect to live long enough to see. The film that *has* been made is impeccably put together, with an irreproachable professional polish, and has one or two nice moments. It has absolutely nothing to do with Billie, or with jazz, or any other kind of music, or the risks of an artist, or American life, or black life, or narcotics, or the narcotics laws, or clubs, or managers, or policemen, or despair, or love. The script is as empty as a banana peel, and as treacherous.

It is scarcely possible to think of a black American actor who has not been misused: not one has ever been seriously challenged to deliver the best that is in him. The most powerful examples of this cowardice and waste are the careers of Paul Robeson and Ethel Waters. If they had ever been allowed really to hit their stride, they might immeasurably have raised the level of cinema and theater in this country. Their effect would have been, at least, to challenge the stultifyingly predictable tics of such overrated figures as Miss Helen Hayes, for example, and life, as one performer can sometimes elicit it from another, might more frequently have illuminated our stage and screen. It is pointless, however, to pursue this, and personally painful: Mr. Robeson is declining, in obscurity, and Miss Waters is singing in Billy Graham's choir. They might have been treated with more respect by the country to which they gave so much. But, then, we had to send telegrams to the Mayor of New York City, asking him to call off the cops who surrounded Billie's bedside—looking for heroin in her ice cream—and let the Lady die in peace.

What the black actor has managed to give are moments—indelible moments, created, miraculously, beyond the confines of the script: hints of reality, smuggled like contraband into a maudlin tale, and with enough force, if unleashed, to shatter the tale to fragments. The face of Ginger Rogers, for example, in *Tales of Manhattan*, is something to be placed in a dish, and eaten with a spoon—possibly a long one. If the face of Ethel Waters were placed in the same frame, the face of Little Eva would simply melt: to prevent this, the black performer has been sealed off into a vacuum. Inevitably, therefore, and as a direct result, the white performer is also sealed off and can never deliver the best that is in him, either. His plight is less obvious, but the results can be even more devastating. The black performer knows, at least, what the odds are, and knows that he must endure—even though he has done nothing to deserve—his fate. So does the white performer know this, as concerns himself, *his* possibilities, *his* merit, *his* fate, and he knows this on a somewhat less accessible and more chaotic and intimidating level. James Edwards, dead at the age of fifty-three, in a casting office, was a beautiful actor, and knew, at least, that he was an actor. Veronica Lake was a star, riding very high for a while there: she also died in relative obscurity, but it is doubtful that she knew as much.

The moments given us by black performers exist so far beneath, or beyond, the American apprehensions that it is difficult to describe them. There is the close-up of Sidney Poitier's face, for example, in *The Defiant Ones*, describing how his wife, "she say, be nice. Be nice." Black spectators supply the sub-text—the unspoken—out of their own lives, and the pride and anguish in Sidney's face at that moment strike deep. I do not know what happens in the breasts of the multitudes who think of themselves as white: but, clearly, they hold this anguish far outside themselves. There is the truth to be found in Ethel Waters's face at the end of *Member of the Wedding*, the Juano Hernandez of *Young Man with a Horn* and *Intruder in the Dust*, Canada Lee, in *Body and Soul*, the Rochester of *The Green Pastures* and *Tales of Manhattan*, and Robeson in everything I saw him do. You will note that I am deliberately avoiding the recent spate of so-called black films. I have seen very few of them, and, anyway, it would be virtually impossible to discuss them as films. I suspect their intention to be lethal indeed, and to be the subject of quite another investigation. Their entire purpose (apart from making money; and this money is not for blacks; in spite of the fact that some of these films appear to have been, at least in part, financed by blacks) is to stifle forever any possibility of such moments—or, in other words, to make black experience irrelevant and obsolete. And I may point out that this vogue, had it been remotely serious, had a considerable body of work on which to draw—from *Up From Slavery* to *Let Me Live*, from *The Auto-Biography of an Ex-Colored Man*, and *Cane*, to *Black Boy* to *Invisible Man* to *Blues Child Baby* to *The Bluest Eye* to *Soledad Brother*. An incomplete list, and difficult: but the difficulty is not in the casting.

My buddy, Ava Gardner, once asked me if I thought she could play Billie Holiday. I had to tell her that, though she was certainly "down" enough for it—courageous and honest and beautiful enough for it—she would almost certainly not be allowed to get away with it, since Billie Holiday had been widely rumored to be black, and she, Ava Gardner, was widely rumored to be white. I was not really making a joke, or, if I was, the joke was bitter: for I certainly know some black girls who are much, much whiter than Ava. Nor do I blame the black girls for this, for this utterly inevitable species of schizophrenia is but one of the many manifestations of the spiritual and historical trap, called racial, in which all Americans find themselves and against which some of us, some of the time, manage to arrive at a viable and honorable identity. I was really thinking of black actors and actresses, who would have been much embittered if the role of Billie Holiday had been played by a white girl: but, then, I had occasion to think of them later, too, when the tidal wave of "black" films arrived, using such a staggering preponderance of football players and models.

I had never been a Diana Ross fan, and received the news that she was to play Billie with a weary shrug of the shoulders. I could not possibly have been more wrong, and I pray the lady to accept from me my humble apologies—for my swift, and, alas, understandably cynical reaction. For, indeed, the most exasperating aspect of *Lady Sings the Blues*, for me, is that the three principals—Miss Ross, Billy Dee Williams, and Richard Pryor—are, clearly, ready, willing, and able to stretch out and go a distance not permitted by the film. And, even within this straitjacket, they manage marvelous moments, and a truth which is not in the script is sometimes glimpsed through them. Diana Ross, clearly, respected Billie too much to try to imitate her. She picks up on Billie's beat, and, for the rest, uses herself, with a moving humility and candor, to create a portrait of a woman overwhelmed by the circumstances of her life. This is not exactly Billie Holiday, but it *is* the role as written, and she does much more with it than the script deserves. So does Billy Dee, in the absolutely impossible role of Louis McKay, and so does Richard Pryor, in a role which appears to have been dreamed up by a nostalgic, aging jazz *aficionado.*

The film begins at the end, more or less: titles over, we watch a series of sepia stills of Billie being fingerprinted, and thrown, alone, into a padded cell. We pick up, then, on a gawky colored girl, alone in the streets of Harlem. She has been sent by her mother to a rooming house, which turns out to be a whorehouse. She does not stay there long—packs her bags, and gets dressed, in fact, as a particularly horny and vocal client is getting undressed. She has seen Louis in this establishment, or elsewhere: in any case, she has seen him. She later meets him again, in a dive where she is one of the singers, and where the singer is expected to pick up money off the tables with her, ah, sexual equipment. Billie cannot do this, which has its effect on the two men in her life, Louis, and Piano Man (Richard Pryor). It is at this point that Piano Man dubs her "Lady," and it is at this point that she has her first date with Louis. A few frames later, she is the black singer with a white band, touring the South. (Billie went on the road with Artie Shaw, but the film version of this adventure is not in Billie's book.) On the road, she encounters the Ku Klux Klan, and sees a lynching. One of the members of the band has been offering her drugs, but she has always refused. After the lynching—an image, and a moment, to which we shall return—she succumbs to the friendly pusher, and returns to New York, hooked. Louis tries to get her off drugs, but does not succeed. Desperate for a fix, she pulls a razor on him, to force him to give her her works; after which he asks her to leave his house. Her mother dies, she gets busted—I think, in that order—Louis returns, and helps bring her back to the living. He also realizes that she needs her career, and helps her to begin again. Since she cannot work in New York, they end up on the Coast, with Piano Man. Eventually, Louis has to leave, on business, and to arrange her date in Carnegie Hall. Left alone with Piano Man, she decides that she wants to "cop," and sends him out to buy the junk. They are broke, and so she gives him a ring, which he is to pawn, to pay for it. Piano Man cops, all right, but doesn't pawn the ring, and doesn't pay for the stuff, and is, therefore, beaten to death before her eyes. The patient and loving Louis comes to the Coast, and brings her back to New York, where she scores a triumph on the Carnegie Hall stage. As Billie is singing, *God Bless the Child*, and as thousands cheer, we learn, from blow-ups of newspaper items behind her, of her subsequent mis-adventures, and her death at the age of forty-four. And the film fades out, with a triumphant Billie, who is, already, how-ever, unluckily, dead, singing on-stage before a delirious au-dience—or, rather, two: one in the cinema Carnegie Hall, and one in the cinema where we are seated.

It is not every day that a film crams so much cake down one's throat, and yet leaves one with so much more to swallow.

Now, it is not enough to say that the film really has nothing to do with Billie Holiday, since the film's authority—and, therefore, its presumed authenticity—derives from the use of her name. It is not enough to say that the film does not re-create her journey: the question is why the film presents itself as her journey. Most of the people who knew, or saw, or heard Billie Holiday will be dying shortly before, or shortly after, this century dies. (Billie would now be sixty years old.) This film cannot be all that is left of her torment and courage and beauty and grace. And the moments of truth smuggled into the film by the actors form a kind of Rosetta stone which the future will not be able to read, as, indeed, the present cannot.

In the film, we meet Billie on the streets of New York. But we do not know that she was raped at ten, sentenced, as a result, to a "Catholic institution" where she beat her hands to "a bloody damn pulp" when she was locked in with the body of a dead girl. We do not know that she was virtually raped at twelve, and that, at thirteen, she was a "hip kitty." We do not know, from the film, that when she refuses to sleep with the horny and vocal Big Blue, he has her thrown in jail: we know nothing, in fact, of the kind of terror with which this girl lived almost from the time that she was born. The incident with Big Blue is reduced to low comedy, much as is the scene with Billie's mother when she tries on the extrava-gant hat. Billie's testimony concerning the meaning of this hat is not in the film: "all the big-time whores wore big red velvet hats then—she looked so pretty in it"—nor is the fact that it is the mother who has bought the hat, because "we were going to live like ladies." In the film, Billie auditions as a dancer, and is terrible, and she says so in the book. It is also during this audition that the piano player saves her by snarling, "Girl, can you sing?" and so she sings for the first time in public, and this turns out to be the beginning of her career.

But the scene, as recounted by Billie, and the scene as translated in the film have nothing whatever in common. In the film, for no immediately discernible reason, except, perhaps, ambition, Billie drops into a nearby club, and asks for an audition. She is dressed as Hollywood—though it should certainly know better by now, God knows—persistently imagines cheap whores to dress. She joins the chorus line, disastrously, ending with her black bottom stuck out—after which, etc., she sings, etc.

Billie's testimony is that she and her mother were about to be evicted in the morning and that it was as "cold as all hell that night, and I walked out without any kind of coat." She hits a joint, she is indeed allowed to dance, but solo, "and it was pitiful." Before they throw her out, the piano player does indeed say, " 'Girl, can you sing?'—So I asked him to play 'Trav'lin' All Alone'. That came closer than anything to the way I felt." And: "when I left the joint that night, I split with the piano player and still took home fifty-seven dollars—I went out and bought a whole chicken and some baked beans."

The scene, in the film, is far from being an improvement on Billie's testimony, and it has two curious results, neither of which are vouched for anywhere in Billie's book. One is the invention of Piano Man, who, according to the film, remains with Billie until his death. According to the book, she scarcely ever sees him again, nor, according to Billie's evidence, does he ever become one of her intimates. It is conceivable, of course, however preposterous, that this figure is meant to suggest a kind of distillation of Lester Young: but I do not have the heart to pursue that line of country. The other result is that the club-owner, a white man, becomes one of Billie's staunchest supporters, and closest friends. The book offers no corroborating evidence of this, either, though Billie speaks with great affection of such people as Tony Pastor and

Artie Shaw. But absolutely none of these people are even suggested in the film—these people who were so important to
her, along with Pigmeat Markham, and "Pops" Armstrong,
and Charlie Barnet—or the jazz atmosphere of that period of
Billie's life, and our lives. The film suggests nothing of the
terrifying economics of a singer's life, and you will not learn,
from the film, that Billie received no royalties for the records
she was making then: you will not learn that the music industry is one of the areas of the national life in which the
blacks have been most persistently, successfully, and brutally
ripped off. If you have never heard of the Apollo Theatre, you
will learn nothing of it from this film, nor what Billie's appearances there meant to her, or what a black audience means
to a black performer.

Now, obviously, the only way to translate the written word
to the cinema involves doing considerable violence to the
written word, to the extent, indeed, of forgetting the written
word. A film is meant to be seen, and, ideally, the less a film
talks, the better. The cinematic translation, nevertheless, however great and necessary the violence it is compelled to use on
the original form, is obliged to remain faithful to the intention, and the vision, of the original form. The necessary violence of the translation involves making very subtle and
difficult choices. The root motive of the choices made can be
gauged by the effect of these choices: and the effect of these
deliberate choices, deliberately made, must be considered as
resulting in a willed and deliberate act—that is, the film which
we are seeing is the film we are intended to see.

Why? What do the filmmakers wish us to learn?

Billie is very honest in her book, she hides nothing. We
know the effect of her father's death on her, for example, and
how her father died, and how, ultimately, this connected with
her singing of "Strange Fruit." We see her relationship with
her mother: "I didn't want to hurt her, and I didn't—until
three years before she died, when I went on junk." We know,
from her testimony, that she was in love with the husband
who turned her into a junkie, and we certainly know, from
her testimony, that she loved the Louis who did his best to
save her. I repeat: her testimony, for that is what we are compelled to deal with, and respect, and whatever others may

imagine themselves to know of these matters cannot compare with the testimony of the person who was there.

She testifies, too: "I had the white gowns, and the white shoes. And every night they'd bring me the white gardenias and the white junk. When I was on, I was on and nobody gave me any trouble. No cops, no treasury agents, nobody."

"I got into trouble," says Billie, "when I tried to get off."

Let us see what the film makes of all this: what we are meant to learn.

Billie's father is not in the film, and is mentioned, I think, only once: near the end of the film, when she and Piano Man are high—just before Piano Man is murdered—and they both crack up when Billie says that her father never beat her because he was never home.

In the book, her father is a jazz musician, mainly on the road, who, eventually, leaves home, divorces, and re-marries. But, when he was in town, Billie was able to blackmail him into giving her the rent money for her mother and herself. And she cared about him: "it wasn't the pneumonia that killed him, it was Dallas, Texas. That's where he was, and where he walked around, going from hospital to hospital, trying to get help. But none of them would even so much as take his temperature, or let him in [but] because he had been in the Army, had ruined his lungs and had records to prove it, they finally let him in the Jim Crow ward. By that time, it was too late." And, later: "a song was born which became my personal protest—'Strange Fruit'—when [Lewis Allen] showed me that poem, I dug it right off. It seemed to spell out all the things that had killed Pop."

This is quite forthright, and even contains, if one dares say so, a certain dramatic force. In the film, on the southern road, Billie leaves the bus to go relieve herself in the bushes. Wandering along the countryside, Billie suddenly sees, on the road just before her, grieving black people, and a black body hanging from a tree. The best that one can say for this moment is that it is mistaken, and the worst that it is callously false and self-serving—which may be a rude way of saying the same thing: luckily, it is brief. The scene operates to resolve, at one stroke, several problems, and without in the least involving or intimidating the spectator. The lynch scene is as remote as an

Indian massacre, occurring in the same landscape, and eliciting the same response: a mixture of pious horror, and gratified reassurance. The ubiquitous Ku Klux Klan appears, marching beside the bus in which the band is riding. The band is white, and they attempt to hide Billie, making, meanwhile, friendly gestures to their marching countrymen. But Billie, because of the strange fruit she has just seen hanging, is now beside herself, and deliberately makes herself visible, cursing and weeping against the Klan: she, and the musicians, make a sufficiently narrow, entirely cinematic escape. This scene is pure bullshit Hollywood-American fable, with the bad guys robed and the good guys casual: as a result, anyway, of all this unhealthy excitement, this understandable (and oddly reassuring) bitterness, Billie finally takes her first fix, and is immediately hooked.

This incident is not in the book: for the very good reason, certainly, that black people in this country are schooled in adversity long before white people are. Blacks perceive danger far more swiftly, and, however odd this may sound, then attempt to protect their white comrade from his white brothers: they know their white comrade's brothers far better than the comrade does. One of the necessities of being black, and knowing it, is to accept the hard discipline of learning to avoid useless anger, and needless loss of life: every mother and his mother's mother's mother's brother is needed.

The off-screen Billie faced down white sheriffs, and laughed at them, to their faces, and faced down white managers, cops, and bartenders. She was much stronger than this film can have any interest in indicating, and, as a victim, infinitely more complex.

Otherwise, she would never have been able to tell us, so simply, that she sang "Strange Fruit" for her father, and got hooked because she fell in love.

The film cannot accept—because it cannot use—this simplicity. That victim who is able to articulate the situation of the victim has ceased to be a victim: he, or she, has become a threat.

The victim's testimony must, therefore, be altered. But, since no one outside the victim's situation dares imagine the victim's situation, this testimony can be altered only after it has been delivered; and after it has become the object of some study. The purpose of this scrutiny is to emphasize certain striking details which can then be used to quite another purpose than the victim had in mind. Given the complexity of the human being, and the complexities of society, this is not difficult. (Or, it does not appear to be difficult: the endless revisions made in the victim's testimony suggest that the endeavor may be impossible. Wounded Knee comes to mind, along with "Swing Low, Sweet Chariot," and we have yet to hear from My Lai.) Thus, for example, ghetto citizens have been heard to complain, very loudly, of the damage done to their homes during any ghetto uprising, and a grateful Republic fastens on this as a benevolent way of discouraging future uprisings. But the truth is, and every ghetto citizen knows this, that no one trapped in the ghetto owns anything, since they certainly do not own the land. Anyone who doubts this has only to spend tomorrow walking through the ghetto nearest to his.

Once the victim's testimony is delivered, however, there is, thereafter, forever, a witness somewhere: which is an irreducible inconvenience for the makers and shakers and accomplices of this world. These run together, in packs, and corroborate each other. They cannot bear the judgment in the eyes of the people whom they intend to hold in bondage forever, and who know more about them than their lovers. This remote, public, and, as it were, principled, bondage is the indispensable justification of their own: when the prisoner is free, the jailer faces the void of himself.

If *Lady Sings the Blues* pretended to be concerned with the trials of a white girl, and starred, say, the late Susan Hayward (*I'll Cry Tomorrow*) or Bette Davis (*A Stolen Life*) or Olivia de Havilland (*To Each His Own*) or the late Judy Garland (*A Star Is Born*) or any of the current chicks, Billie's love for her father and for the husband who so fatally turned her on would be the film's entire motivation: *the guy that won you/has run off and undone you/that great beginning/has seen its final inning/*: as desperately falsified, but in quite another way. The situations of Lana Turner (in *The Postman Always Rings Twice*) or Barbara Stanwyck (in *Double Indemnity*) or Joan Crawford (in almost anything, but, especially, *Mildred Pierce*) are dictated, at bottom, by the brutally crass and commercial terms on which the heroine is to survive—are dictated, that is, by society. But, at the same time, the white chick is always, somehow, saved or strengthened or destroyed by love—society is out of it, beneath her: it matters not at all that the man she marries, or deserts, or murders, happens to own Rhodesia, or that *she* does: love is all.

But the private life of a black woman, to say nothing of the private life of a black man, cannot really be considered at all. To consider this forbidden privacy is to violate white privacy—by destroying the white dream of the blacks; to make black privacy a black and private matter makes white privacy real, for the first time: which is, indeed, and with a vengeance, to endanger the stewardship of Rhodesia. The situation of the white heroine must never violate the white self-image. Her situation must always transcend the inexorability of the social setting, so that her innocence may be preserved: Grace Kelly, when she shoots to kill, at the end of *High Noon*, for example, does not become a murderess. But the situation of the black heroine, to say nothing of that of the black hero, must always be left at society's mercy: in order to justify white history and in order to indicate the essential validity of the black condition.

Billie's account of her meeting with Louis McKay is very simple, even childlike, and very moving. Louis is asleep on a bench, a whore is lifting his wallet, and Billie prevents this, pretending that Louis, whom she has never seen in her life before, is her old man. And she gives Louis his wallet. Anyone surviving these mean streets knows something about that moment. It is not a moment which the film can afford, for it conveys, too vividly, how that victim, the black, yet refuses to be a victim, has another source of sustenance: Billie's morality, at that moment, indeed, threatens the very foundations of the Stock Exchange.

The film does not suggest that the obsolete and vindictive narcotics laws had anything to do with her fate: does not pick up the challenge implicit in her statement: *When I was on, I was on, and nobody bothered me. . . . I got into trouble when I tried to get off.* Neither does it suggest that the distinction between Big Business and Organized Crime is like the old ad, which asks, *Which twin has the Toni?* The film leaves us with the impression, and this is a matter of choices coldly and deliberately made, that a gifted, but weak and self-indulgent woman, brought about the murder of her devoted Piano Man because she was not equal, either to her gifts, or to the society which had made her a star, and, as the closing sequence proves, adored her.

There was a rite in our church, called *pleading the blood.*

When the sinner fell on his face before the altar, the soul of the sinner then found itself locked in battle with Satan: or, in the place of Jacob, wrestling with the angel. All of the forces of Hell rushed to claim the soul which had just been astonished by the light of the love of God. The soul in torment turned this way and that, yearning, equally, for the light and for the darkness: yearning, out of agony, for reconciliation— and for rest: for this agony is compounded by an unimaginable, unprecedented, unspeakable fatigue. Only the saints who had passed through this fire—the incredible horror of the fainting of the spirit—had the power to intercede, to "plead the blood," to bring the embattled and mortally endangered soul "through." The pleading of the blood was a plea to whosoever had loved us enough to spill his blood for us, that he might sprinkle the soul with his love once more, to give us power over Satan, and the love and courage to live out our days.

One of the songs we sang comes out of the last of the Egyptian plagues, the death of the firstborn: *when I see the blood, I will pass over you.* (There is a reason that blacks call each other "bloods.") Another of the songs is, at once, more remote, and yet more present: *somebody needs you, Lord, come by here!*

I had been prayed through, and I, then, prayed others through: had testified to having been born again, and, then, helped others to be born again.

The word "belief" has nearly no meaning anymore, in the recognized languages, and ineptly approaches the reality to which I am referring: for there can be no doubt that it is a reality. The blacks had first been claimed by the Christian church, and then excluded from the company of white Christians—from the fellowship of Christians: which taught us all that we needed to know about white Christians. The blacks did not so much use Christian symbols as recognize them— recognize them for what they were before the Christians came along—and, thus, reinvested these symbols with their original energy. The proof of this, simply, is the continued existence and authority of the blacks: it is through the creation of the black church that an unwritten, dispersed, and violated inheritance has been handed down. The word "revelation" has very little meaning in the recognized languages: yet, it is the only word for the moment I am attempting to approach. This moment changes one forever. One is confronted with the agony and the nakedness and the beauty of a power which has no beginning and no end, which contains you, and which you contain, and which will be using you when your bones are dust. One thus confronts a self both limited and boundless, born to die and born to live. The creature is, also, the creation, and responsible, endlessly, for that perpetual act of creation which is both the self and more than the self. One is set free, then, to live among one's terrors, hour by hour and day by day, alone, and yet never alone. *My soul is a witness!*—so one's ancestors proclaim, and in the deadliest of the midnight hours.

To live in connection with a life beyond this life means, in effect—in truth—that, frightened as one may be, and no matter how limited, or how lonely, and no matter how the deal, at last, goes down, no man can ever frighten you. This is why blacks can be heard to say, *I ain't got to do nothing but stay black, and die!*: which is, after all, a far more affirmative apprehension than *I'm free, white, and twenty-one.* The first proposition is changeless, whereas the second is at the mercy of time, weather, the dictionary, geography, and fashion. The custodian of an inheritance, which is what blacks have had to be, in Western culture, must hand the inheritance down the line. So, you, the custodian, recognize, finally, that your life does not belong to you: nothing belongs to you. This will not sound like freedom to Western ears, since the Western world pivots on the infantile, and, in action, criminal delusions of possession, and of property. But, just as *love is the only money*, as the song puts it, so this mighty responsibility is the only freedom. Your child does not belong to you, and you must prepare your child to pick up the burden of his life long before the moment when you must lay your burden down.

But the people of the West will not understand this until everything which they now think they have has been taken away from them. In passing, one may observe how remarkable it is that a people so quick and so proud to boast of what they have taken from others are unable to imagine that what they have taken from others can also be taken from them.

In our church, the Devil had many faces, all of them one's own. He was not always evil, rarely was he frightening—he was, more often, subtle, charming, cunning, and warm. So, one learned, for example, never to take the easy way out: whatever looked easy was almost certainly a trap. In short, the Devil was that mirror which could never be smashed. One had to look into the mirror every day—*good morning, blues/Blues, how do you do?/Well, I'm doing all right/Good morning/How are you?*—check it all out, and take it all in, and travel. The pleading of the blood was not, for us, a way of exorcising a Satan whom we knew could never sleep: it was to engage Satan in a battle which we knew could never end.

I first saw *The Exorcist*, in Hollywood, with a black friend of mine, who had his own, somewhat complex reasons for insisting that I see it: just so, one of my brothers had one day walked me into the film, *The Devils*, which he had already seen, saying, cheerfully, as we walked out, *Ain't that some shit? I just wanted you to see how sick these people are!* Both my friend and my brother had a point. I had already read *The Devils*; now, I forced myself to read *The Exorcist*—a difficult matter, since it is not written; then, I saw the film again, alone. I tried to be absolutely open to it, suspending judgment as totally as I could. For, after all, if I had once claimed to be "filled" with the Holy Ghost, and had once really believed, after all, that the Holy Ghost spoke through me, I could not, out of hand, arbitrarily sneer at the notion of demonic possession. The fact that I had been an adolescent boy when I believed all this did not really get me off the hook: I can produce no documents proving that I am not what I was.

My friend and I had a drink together, after we had seen the

film, and we discussed it at some length. He was most struck by the figure of the young priest: he found the key to this personage in a rather strange place, and his observation haunted me for weeks. Father Karras confesses, at one point, that he has lost his faith. "So, we must be careful," David said to me, "lest we lose our faith—and become possessed." He was no longer speaking of the film, nor was he speaking of the church.

I carried this somewhat chilling admonition away with me. When I saw the film again, I was most concerned with the audience. I wondered what they were seeing, and what it meant to them.

The film, or its ambience, reminded me of *The Godfather*, both being afflicted with the same pious ambiguity. Ambiguity is not quite the word, for the film's intention is not at all ambiguous; yet, hypocrisy is not quite the word, either, since it suggests a more deliberate and sophisticated level of cunning. *The Exorcist* is desperately compulsive, and compulsive, precisely, in the terror of its unbelief. The vast quantities of tomato paste expended in *The Godfather* are meant to suggest vast reservoirs of courage, devotion, and nobility, qualities with which the film is not in the least concerned—and which, apart from Brando's performance, are never present in it. (And, at that, it is probably more accurate to speak of Brando's *presence*, a pride, an agony, an irreducible dignity.) *The Exorcist* has absolutely nothing going for it, except Satan, who is certainly the star: I can say only that Satan was never like that when he crossed *my* path (for one thing, the evil one never so rudely underestimated me). His concerns were more various, and his methods more subtle. *The Exorcist* is not in the least concerned with damnation, an abysm far beyond the confines of its imagination, but with property, with safety, tax shelters, stocks and bonds, rising and falling markets, the continued invulnerability of a certain class of people, and the continued sanctification of a certain history. If *The Exorcist* itself believed this history, it could scarcely be reduced to so abject a dependence on special effects.

In Georgetown, in Washington, D.C., a young movie actress is shooting a film. She is forthright, and liberated, as can be gathered from her liberated language. The film she is making is involved with a student uprising—in the book, she describes it as *"dumb!"*: in the film, one of her lines suggests that the students work within the system. This line, however, is neatly balanced by another, which suggests that the political perceptions of this film-within-a-film may owe a great deal to Walt Disney.

Before this, we have encountered the aged priest, who will become the exorcist, digging in the ruins of northern Iraq. This opening sequence is probably the film's most effective, ruthlessly exploiting the uneasiness one cannot but feel when touched by the energy of distant gods, unknown. It sets up, with some precision, the spirit of the terror which informs the Christian-pagan argument: it may be something of a pity that Ingmar Bergman could not have guided the film from there. However, Max von Sydow, the exorcist—rather like Marlon Brando, in *The Godfather*—having been exhibited, is now put on ice, and, if we wish to await his return, we have no choice but to see the end of the movie.

The horror of the demonic possession begins with what sound, to the heroine, like rats in the attic. Her daughter's dresses are misplaced. Room temperatures change, alarmingly and inexplicably. Furniture is mysteriously moved about. Her daughter's personality changes, and obscenities she has never used before become a part of her speech. (Though she overhears the mother using some of them: over the trans-Atlantic telephone, to her father, who is estranged from her mother.) The daughter also plays around with a ouija board, and has made a friend in the spirit world, called Captain Howdy. The mother worries over all these manifestations, both worldly and other-worldly, of the mysteries now being confronted by her growing daughter with all of the really dreadful apathy of the American middle class, reassuring herself that nothing she has done, or left undone, has irreparably damaged her child; who will certainly grow up, therefore, to be as healthy as her mother and to make as much money. But, eventually, at a very posh Georgetown party, of which her mother is the hostess, this daughter comes downstairs in her nightgown, and, while urinating on the floor, tells a member of the party that he is going to die. After this, her affliction, or possession, develops apace.

The plot now compels us to consider a Jesuit priest, young, healthy, athletic, intelligent, presumably celibate, with a dying mother, and in trouble with his faith. His mother dies, alone, in a dingy flat in New York, where he has been compelled to leave her, and he is unable to forgive himself for this. There is the film director, a drunken, cursing agnostic, other priests, psychiatrists, doctors, a detective—well: all people we have met before, and there is very little to be said about them. One of the psychiatrists is nearly castrated by Regan, the daughter, who has abnormal strength while in the grip of Satan. Along with the mumbo-jumbo of levitating beds and discontented furniture and Wuthering Heights tempests, there is the moment when the daughter is compelled by Satan to masturbate with a crucifix, after which she demands that her mother lick her, after which she throws her mother across the room, after which the mother screams, after which she faints. It develops that the film director, dead in a mysterious accident, has actually been pushed, by Regan, through her bedroom window, to his death: again, while in the grip of Satan. All else having failed, the aged priest is called from his retreat to perform the exorcism: the young priest is his assistant. The strain of exorcising Satan proves too much for the aged priest, who has a heart attack, and dies. The young priest, still mad with guilt concerning the death of his mother, taunts Satan, daring him to stop picking on helpless little girls, and enter *him*. Satan does this with an eagerness which suggests that he, too, is weary of little girls and hurls the priest through the bedroom window, to his death, and, also, presumably, to eternal damnation; as to this last point, however, I really cannot be clear.

The young priest is tormented by guilt, and especially in reference to his mother, throughout the film: and Satan ruthlessly plays on this, sometimes speaking (through Regan) in the mother's voice, and sometimes incarnating her. And Satan also plays on the guilt of Regan's mother—her guilt concerning her failed marriage, her star status, her ambition, her relation to her daughter, her essentially empty and hypocritical and totally unanchored life: in a word, her emancipation. This uneasy, and even terrified guilt is the subtext of *The Exorcist*, which cannot, however, exorcise it since it never confronts it.

But this confrontation would have been to confront the

devil. The film terrified me on two levels. The first, as I have tried to indicate, involved my deliberate attempt to leave myself open to it, and to the extent, indeed, of re-living my adolescent holy-roller terrors. It was very important for me not to pretend to have surmounted the pain and terror of that time of my life, very important not to pretend that it left no mark on me. It marked me forever. In some measure I encountered the abyss of my own soul, the labyrinth of my destiny: these could never be escaped, to challenge these imponderables being, precisely, the heavy, tattered glory of the gift of God.

To encounter oneself is to encounter the other: and this is love. If I know that my soul trembles, I know that yours does, too: and, if I can respect this, both of us can live. Neither of us, truly, can live without the other: a statement which would not sound so banal if one were not endlessly compelled to repeat it, and, further, believe it, and act on that belief. My friend was quite right when he said, *So, we must be careful—lest we lose our faith—and become possessed.*

For, I have seen the devil, by day and by night, and have seen him in you and in me: in the eyes of the cop and the sheriff and the deputy, the landlord, the housewife, the football player: in the eyes of some junkies, the eyes of some preachers, the eyes of some governors, presidents, wardens, in the eyes of some orphans, and in the eyes of my father, and in my mirror. It is that moment when no other human being is real for you, nor are you real for yourself. This devil has no need of any dogma—though he can use them all—nor does he need any historical justification, history being so largely his invention. He does not levitate beds, or fool around with little girls: *we* do.

The mindless and hysterical banality of the evil presented in *The Exorcist* is the most terrifying thing about the film. The Americans should certainly know more about evil than that; if they pretend otherwise, they are lying, and any black man, and not only blacks—many, many others, including white children—can call them on this lie; he who has been treated *as* the devil recognizes the devil when they meet. At the end of *The Exorcist*, the demon-racked little girl murderess kisses the Holy Father, and she remembers nothing: she is departing with her mother, who will, presumably, soon make another film. The grapes of wrath are stored in the cotton fields and migrant shacks and ghettoes of this nation, and in the schools and prisons, and in the eyes and hearts and perceptions of the wretched everywhere, and in the ruined earth of Vietnam, and in the orphans and the widows, and in the old men, seeing visions, and in the young men, dreaming dreams: these have already kissed the bloody cross and will not bow down before it again: and have forgotten nothing.

St. Paul de Vence
July 29, 1975

OTHER ESSAYS

Contents

Smaller Than Life (Review: *There Was Once a Slave: The Heroic Story of Frederick Douglass,* by Shirley Graham; July 19, 1947) 577

History as Nightmare (Review: *Lonely Crusade,* by Chester Himes; October 25, 1947) 579

The Image of the Negro (Review: *Albert Sears,* by Millen Brand; *Kingsblood Royal,* by Sinclair Lewis; *The Path of Thunder,* by Peter Abrahams; *God is for White Folks,* by Will Thomas; *Quality,* by Cid Ricketts Sumner; April 1948) 582

Lockridge: 'The American Myth' (Review: *Raintree County,* by Ross Lockridge, Jr.; April 10, 1948) 588

Preservation of Innocence (Summer 1949) 594

The Negro at Home and Abroad (Review: *No Green Pastures,* by Roi Ottley; November 27, 1951) 601

The Crusade of Indignation (Review: *Negroes on the March,* by Daniel Guerin; *Goodbye to Uncle Tom,* by J. C. Furnas; July 7, 1956). 606

Sermons and Blues (Review: *Selected Poems of Langston Hughes;* March 29, 1959). 614

On Catfish Row: *Porgy and Bess* in the Movies (September 1959) 616

They Can't Turn Back (August 1960) 622

The Dangerous Road Before Martin Luther King (February 1961) 638

The New Lost Generation (July 1961) 659

The Creative Process (1962) 669

Color (December 1962). 673

A Talk to Teachers (December 21, 1963) 678

"This Nettle, Danger . . ." (February 1964) 687

Nothing Personal (1964) 692

Words of a Native Son (December 1964) 707

The American Dream and the American Negro
    (March 7, 1965) 714
On the Painter Beauford Delaney (1965) 720
The White Man's Guilt (August 1965) 722
A Report from Occupied Territory (July 11, 1966) 728
Negroes Are Anti-Semitic Because They're Anti-White
    (April 9, 1967) 739
White Racism or World Community? (October 1968) . . . 749
Sweet Lorraine (November 1969) 757
How One Black Man Came To Be an American
    (Review: *Roots*, by Alex Haley; September 26, 1976) . . . 762
An Open Letter to Mr. Carter (January 23, 1977) 766
Last of the Great Masters (Review: *The World of Earl Hines*,
    by Stanley Dance; October 16, 1977) 770
Every Good-bye Ain't Gone (December 19, 1977) 773
If Black English Isn't a Language, Then Tell Me, What Is?
    (July 29, 1979) 780
Open Letter to the Born Again (September 29, 1979) . . . 784
Dark Days (October 1980) 788
Notes on the House of Bondage (November 1, 1980) . . . 799
Introduction to *Notes of a Native Son, 1984*
    (April 18, 1984) 808
Freaks and the American Ideal of Manhood
    (January 1985) 814
The Price of the Ticket (1985) 830

Smaller Than Life

There Was Once a Slave. *The Heroic Story of Frederick Douglass.* By Shirley Graham. Julian Messner. $3.

In her biography of Frederick Douglass, Shirley Graham has gathered together an absolutely staggering number of details and has approached her subject with an all but breathless reverence and a high purpose—that of revealing the extent of the heroism of this former slave and his significance during the most crucial part of our history. Since she has won the Julian Messner Award for having written the best book combating intolerance in America, the larger implications of her subject are inescapable—the position of the Negro in American society today. Yet I cannot see that Miss Graham has made any contribution to interracial understanding, for she is so obviously determined to Uplift the Race that she makes Douglass a quite unbelievable hero and has robbed him of dignity and humanity alike. As serious biography this performance is very nearly ludicrous; and in the battle against intolerance it seems to me that the book's effect will be negligible.

Part of the trouble lies in the serious limitations of fictionalized biography. At best it usually manages to be simply a readable account of a historical figure: most often the validity of the characterization suffers in the degree that it is fictional. It is just not possible for a contemporary biographer to know what So-and-So said to his wife at the breakfast table in 1866, or how he felt walking through the woods, or his physiological reactions to heartbreak. The attempt, presumably made in order to bring the reader closer to the subject, actually operates to alienate the reader and to inject an element of unreality. And the false intimacy vulgarizes the subject.

Miss Graham begins her story when Douglass is sixteen and, wild-eyed with adoration, follows him till he drops some three hundred pages later. From the first sentence to the last his eyes are on a star; the people Sharing his Vision are sometimes allowed to be confused or misguided but are intrinsically noble, and all, with the same monotonous flash of insight, are struck with awe when they see him. The people who are against him are all bilious or drunken or devilishly clever, and it is Miss Graham's peculiar ability to create the impression, no matter what the facts, that these people too tremble at the mere mention of the name of Frederick Douglass. Miss Graham drags in the Forces of History, as many as she can lay her hands on, and as often as the mood strikes her dumps them on the reader and dashes on to the next Douglass triumph. In her account even history bends before the force of this man.

In Miss Graham's history book voices "crack like whips," people fight "like tigers," are "struck all of a heap"; hero and saint alike "shake with rage" or bite "trembling lips," in spite of which time "deals kindly" with them; and every one of them, even Lincoln, realizes that *"few men are like this Douglass!"* (Italics Miss Graham's). Douglass comes to painful, spasmodic life only when she allows him to speak for himself—as she, mercifully, often does, but not often enough.

There is a tradition among emancipated whites and progressive Negroes to the effect that no unpleasant truth concerning Negroes is ever to be told, a tradition as crippling and insidious as that other tradition that Negroes are never to be characterized as anything more than amoral, laughing clowns. Frederick Douglass was first of all a man—honest within the limitations of his character and his time, quite frequently misguided, sometimes pompous, gifted but not always a hero, and no saint at all. Miss Graham, in her frenzied efforts to make him (a) a Symbol of Freedom, and (b) an example of What the Negro Race Can Produce, has reduced a significant, passionate human being to the obscene level of a Hollywood caricature. Relations between Negroes and whites, like any other province of human experience, demand honesty and insight; they must be based on the assumption that there is one race and that we are all part of it.

The Nation, July 19, 1947

History as Nightmare

LONELY CRUSADE. By Chester Himes. New York: Alfred A. Knopf. 398 pages. $3.

IN *If He Hollers Let Him Go*, published in 1945, Chester Himes studied, with rage and sometimes with disturbing perception, the struggle and defeat of one Negro war-worker on the West Coast, our native tensions intensified by war and the protagonist's relationships with his upper-class mulatto girl and the sexual tensions between himself and a female white war-worker. It was one of those books for which it is difficult to find any satisfactory classification: not a good novel but more than a tract, relentlessly honest, and carried by the fury and the pain of the man who wrote it. It seemed to me then one of the few books written by either whites or Negroes about Negroes which considered the enormous role which white guilt and tension play in what has been most accurately called the American dilemma.

Lonely Crusade can almost be considered an expansion of the earlier novel. Much of the rage is gone and with it the impact, and the book is written in what is probably the most uninteresting and awkward prose I have read in recent years. Yet the book is not entirely without an effect and is likely to have an importance out of all proportion to its intrinsic merit. For, just as the earlier book was carried by rage, this book is carried by what seems to be a desperate, implacable determination to find out the truth, please God, or die.

In less than four hundred pages Mr. Himes undertakes to consider the ever-present subjective and subconscious terror of a Negro, a dislocation which borders on paranoia; the political morality of American Communists; the psychology of union politics; Uncle Tomism; Jews and Negroes; the vast sexual implications of our racial heritage; the difficulty faced by any Negro in his relationships with both light people and dark; and the position of the American white female in the whole unlovely structure. This is a tall order and if we give Mr. Himes an A for ambition—and a rather awe-stricken gasp for effort—we are forced also to realize that the book's considerable burden never really gets shoulder high. It is written almost as though the author were determined within one book, regardless of style or ultimate effect, to say all of the things he wanted to say about the American republic and the position of the Negro in it. Part of the failure of the book certainly lies in this fact, that far too much is attempted; and the story never really gets under way because of a complete lack of integration. Any one of its elements, perceptively studied, would make an impressive novel; and, further, because of the crudity of the story structure, the climax—the murder of a bigoted white man by his Negro stooge, an incident valid in itself and with terrible implications—fails of its effect and seems almost an afterthought; and the resolution—the holding aloft of the union banner—leaves one with that same embarrassed rage produced by a reading of *Invictus*. The book, nevertheless, has flashes of power and insight—the handling of the white girl's relation to Lee, for example, and Lee's sexual relationship with his wife; and one of the subsidiary characters, the Uncle Tom named Luther, is handled and seen so accurately that no white man, ever again, should dare to turn his back on any Negro he feels that he has bought and conquered.

I have already indicated that Mr. Himes seems capable of some of the worst writing on this side of the Atlantic, but his integrity has actually the cumulative effect of making him seem far wiser and more skillful than he is. The value of his book lies in its earnest effort to understand the psychology of oppressed and oppressor and their relationship to each other. It fails to raise his book to the level of *A Passage To India* but it does lend it an historical importance, not unlike that accorded to *Uncle Tom's Cabin* or, more recently, to *Native Son*. For, of all the spate of recent novels concerning racial oppression not one has exhibited any genuine understanding of its historical genesis or contemporary necessity or its psychological toll. One might over-simplify our racial heritage sufficiently to observe, and not at all flippantly, that its essentials would seem to be contained in the tableau of a black and white man facing each other and that the root of our trouble is between their legs. More and more it is impossible to discuss the Negro in America without also discussing American customs, morals and fears. *Lonely Crusade* is an ugly story but the story of American Negroes and white America's relation to them is a far uglier story and with more sinister implications than have yet found their way into print. It is no longer just a Negro's story, we have no longer the convenient symbol of a minstrel man and his wild guitar, or the Negro rapist, or the brave, black college student battling upward against all odds. Time moves too fast, human beings are too complex, yesterday's benevolence is more dangerous than a time bomb now. On that low ground where Negroes live something is happening: something which can be measured in decades and generations and which may spell our doom as a republic and almost certainly implies a cataclysm. Unlike Bigger Thomas, gone to his death cell, inarticulate and destroyed by his need for identification and for revenge, and with only the faintest intimation in that twilight of what had destroyed him and of what his life might have been, Mr. Himes' protagonist, Lee Gordon, sees what has happened and what is happening and watches helplessly the progress of his own disease. *And there is no path out.* In a group so pressed down, terrified and at bay and carrying generations of constricted, subterranean hostility, no real group identification is possible. Nor is there a Negro tradition to cling to in the sense that Jews may be said to have a tradition; this was left in Africa long ago and no-one remembers it now. Lee Gordon is forced back on himself, not even bitterness can serve him as a weapon any more. The impact of rejection and continual indignity on his personality is a personal one and this impact, multiplied, can destroy, not only himself, but an entire nation.

The minstrel man is gone and Uncle Tom is no longer to be trusted. Even Bigger Thomas is becoming irrelevant; we are faced with a black man as many faceted as we ourselves are, as individual, with our ambivalences and insecurities and our struggles to be loved. He is now an American and we cannot change that; it is our attitudes which must change both towards ourselves and him. "History," says Joyce, "is a nightmare from which I am struggling to awaken." We have all heard what happened to those who slept too long.

The New Leader, October 25, 1947

The Image of the Negro

ALBERT SEARS. By Millen Brand. New York, Simon and Schuster, 1947. 273 pp. $2.75.

KINGSBLOOD ROYAL. By Sinclair Lewis. New York, Random House, 1947. 348 pp. $3.00.

THE PATH OF THUNDER. By Peter Abrahams. New York, Harper, 1948. 278 pp. $2.75.

GOD IS FOR WHITE FOLKS. By Will Thomas. New York, Creative Age, 1947. 305 pp. $3.00.

QUALITY. By Cid Ricketts Sumner. New York, Bobbs-Merrill, 1947. 278 pp. $2.75. (Bantam Reprint, 1947. $.25.)

P ERHAPS the measure of the really stupendous inadequacy of the five novels under consideration here is the fact that, of them all, the most impressive and the most valid is Millen Brand's quite unremarkable *Albert Sears*. Reading these novels I was struck by an almost paralyzing desperation: What could one possibly say about them? What, in these days, is a novel? If it is conceded that *Kingsblood Royal* is a new low, even for the American liberal middlebrow, what then is one to say about *Albert Sears*, a resolutely undistinguished novel which, by virtue of its present company, seems graceful and perceptive and quite thoroughly worthwhile? The line between what might be called the personal or creative intellectual and that vast culture of the masses with which we are, willy-nilly, involved, is a precarious one: on the one hand there is corruption and on the other a remote vista closely resembling No Man's Land.

Granting the initial debasement of literary standards, the arrival of the protest novel was inevitable. The question forever posed by the existence of the protest novel—a kind of writing becoming nearly as formalized as those delicate vignettes written for the women's magazines—is whether or not its power as a corrective social force is sufficient to override its deficiencies as literature. It is better, it is said, to have a *Kingsblood Royal* or a *Gentleman's Agreement*, shoddy as they are, than nothing at all; it is an improvement over the un-realistic, hush-hush attitude of preceding generations. At least, the existence of these novels keeps urgent social questions in the public mind; no one can hide from them.

But this attractive and optimistic analysis poses questions of its own: How closely do these novels reflect the social ques-tions which—since, admittedly, they are not, by and large, good novels—are their sole reason for being? With what reality are they concerned, how is it probed, how translated, exactly what message is being brought to this amorphous pub-lic mind? Finally: is the "great work" these novels are presum-ably doing in the world quite worth the torture they are to read?

Albert Sears comes under the heading of a protest novel somewhat arbitrarily. Much, but not all, of the story is con-cerned with the efforts of a Negro family to move into a white neighborhood. The book differs from its fellows in that, if the struggle is recounted without distinction or power, it is also relatively free of the condescension and the infantile bitterness which forms the pulpy core of the other novels here. Mr. Brand is not really at ease when writing about the national problem, but one almost admires his occasional honest stiff-ness when one considers what nightmares of tolerance he might have evoked instead. On the basis of the work being considered, he is the only man here entitled to be called a novelist at all; and this is not because his novel indicates any very impressive talent or because of any startling insights, but merely because there is at work in Mr. Brand a more sensitive intelligence and a modest honesty and the ability to write a sentence. His story, as a matter of fact, is concerned not so much with Negroes as with the relationship between an ille-gitimate adolescent and his strong-willed father; on this level it is more controlled but no more illuminating than most sim-ilar studies produced in our time; and on this level it is not worth much discussion. The incident of the Manhurst family, which adds a kind of violent strength, also tears what there is of the novel to pieces, since it never quite fits in and it diverts rather than broadens our sympathy. To be sure, this is not so much Mr. Brand's defection as it is the inherited response of

our generation, which is inclined to see in every Negro a furious call to arms.

Here, nevertheless, Mr. Brand's novel has a valuable element, one which might one day be explored with some profit:
his protagonist, the young Albert, battles on the side of the
Negroes with no very clear aim and only because he is guilt-
ridden and anchorless, rejected from that white society in
which he was born and with which he struggles to get into
step. But his acceptance of the Manhursts is a desperate, transient act; it is neither noble nor liberal, it is not "American."
His friendship with the Negro family may continue or it may
not; in any case, both the battle and the identification have
been personal. The Manhursts do not represent a problem to
him, their blackness or whiteness is not his concern. They are
human beings to whom he has responded, who have afforded
him a shelter for a time. (Throughout the book the Manhursts
never attain the status of a "problem"; they are a nui-
sance—niggers who are bringing property values down—and
they are opposed in the usual ugly, shocking ways. But at the
end of the book they are still there; their neighbors are no
better for the experience but, having tried and failed, they are
resigned and have ceased to hurl brickbats; instead they are
looking about for other places to live.)

With *Kingsblood Royal* we descend abruptly into a kind of
lugubrious, sentimental nightmare. This is an ill-tempered,
tasteless, condescending novel, which, despite the great fame
of its author, might be dismissed as utterly without significance if it were not for the fact that three other novels, written
by people closer to the scene—two Negroes and a Southern
white woman—differ from it only in that they are not quite
so bald. These novels—*The Path of Thunder, God Is For White
Folks,* and *Quality*—have a great deal in common. They are
not, in the first place, so much concerned with Negroes as
they are with sex between the races and the doomed offspring
thereof. (Negroes are, as a matter of fact, considered with a
somewhat uneasy and disapproving affection.) The protagonists are manifestly superior, and are monotonously hounded
because of their dark blood, which in these novels has much
the same relevance as some mysterious, rather nasty, and im-

placable disease. In all except one of these novels, the protagonists are as fair as daylight: Neil Kingsblood "discovers" that he has Negro blood and must learn to face it; in *Quality*, the heroine, who has been "passing" in the North, comes home to the South and her illiterate granny to live among and learn to love her people; in *The Path of Thunder*, the locale of which is South Africa, Lanny, the hero, is quite dark, but turns out, after all, to be the son of the town's ruling white man; and in *God Is For White Folks*, Beau, the illegitimate son of a Southern plantation owner, eventually comes home to his dying father's bosom, bringing a Negro bride as irreproachably fair as himself to reign in the ancestral halls.

This approaches pure fantasy, an element familiar in fiction but never allied formally with sociology. Here we can make two charitable assumptions: one, that, after all, these things *do* happen; two, that the tasteless prose and the antique plots will present no obstacles to the public mind and are, perhaps, the safest vehicles for a humane and honest rage. But, probing more deeply, one finds that these novels are not essentially any more "advanced" than *The Birth of a Nation*; even the humane rage comes closer to approximating a kind of uncontrollable hysteria. These novels utilize—compulsively—a rather shabby trick: Treat Negroes as human beings, the novelists cry; but this contains a clause: there *are* some Negroes you ought to admire; and finally: many of them, most of the best of them, are not much darker than you are. This might be forgivable, were there not at the same time an exploitation of the more familiar myth which these novels are loudly engaged in tearing down.

Thus, when the heroine of *Quality* goes home—to a landscape not notably different from that made familiar by Margaret Mitchell—her greatest humiliation comes when she is treated in exactly the same manner as a dark, gin-drinking, razor-toting hussy—concerning whom the author, through the heroine's eyes, comments: "In a way [her hysteria] compensated for her ignorance, her low standing in the social scale. Maybe the same thing was true of the great mass of the colored people, simple, ignorant, yet uninhibited in their emotional expression." It is the heroine, with her great admixture of white blood, who will lead her people from these low grounds. Similarly, when Neil Kingsblood discovers his ancestry, his wife waits apprehensively for the signs—expecting him to turn into a "shambling, foolish" darky. But this does not happen and she sticks to him; after all, he has not really changed; he is as white as ever; he has merely become a crusader for a downtrodden people.

The really remarkable plots, counter-plots, and sub-plots that make these novels as impossible to remember as they are difficult to read, again betray an essential desperation. The plots are all concerned with the sexual aggressions of whites against blacks; these constitute, before the books begin, the essential *a priori* dilemma; they operate to burden every encounter within the novel proper with a clandestine, historic significance; the atmosphere inside which these people move is made heavy with unfulfilled desire. The considerable problem this presents to the American psyche is partially solved by keeping the protagonists as light as possible or, at any rate, making it abundantly clear that the Negro under discussion is not subject to the same passions and cannot therefore be bound by the same laws as saddle other Negroes. These novels are, really, exceedingly timorous studies of transgression, and they all have two sets of transgressors: the ancestors, who are a Negro woman and a white man; and the protagonists, who, in all cases but one, are a Negro man and a white woman. The exception is *Quality*, whose heroine forsakes her white would-be lover and is last seen making plans for a Negro hospital with a quite satisfyingly dark young doctor. In *Kingsblood Royal* the sting of transgression is removed by the complete innocence of the transgressor and the impossibility of taking his one-thirty-second Negro-ness seriously. *God Is For White Folks* ends in quite an impressive display of abrupt insanity, murders, and sudden deaths in which all of the elderly transgressors are destroyed and the lover and his lass, produced, incontrovertibly, by sin, are redeemed through blood and allowed to enter the manse. In *The Path of Thunder*, Lanny, despite his father's blood, is dark, and Sarie is fair, and they are shot to death in an old cabin; it is Lanny's father, incidentally, who shoots them.

But the quarrel here is not with the violent incident; or the violent death; or the difficulty of union between black and white. The reports of violence may not come in the nature of a revelation, but it is a real and valid aspect of the lives that Negroes lead. One suspects, however, that the very frequency and sameness of the reports operate on the public mind as a bludgeon, numbing the hypothetical response; it may, indeed, be insisted that unless the report has the urgency of a revelation, the report is worthless.

Out of whatever motives, we have here, in effect, merely *the exploitation of an ugly reality*. Finally, we are shown nothing, we feel nothing, nothing is illuminated. The worthlessness of these novels consists precisely in that they supposedly expose a reality that in actuality they conspire to mask. For this is not the reality: the reality is more sinister, more treacherous, and more profound than this; and it is, above all, more personal. In none of the foregoing has it been my purpose to resurrect or exploit the ancient bogeyman of sex between the races, but only to inquire how and why in the first place it became a bogeyman at all, and why, if it has been exorcised, it exerts yet, as the sole breath of life in these ambitious novels, so ferocious and unmistakable a force. It is a question we are inclined to dismiss with jeers: that old stuff! But the question has not been answered and the failure is significant.

These novels have in common a subterranean assumption, unspoken by the emancipated, but living in our culture and apparently shared by the novelists themselves: the assumption that whiteness is a kind of salvation and that blackness is a kind of death. Beneath this assumption, like the dark, fantastic sub-plots on which these books rely, are the centuries of fear and desire and hatred and shame that are peculiarly the province of the Puritan Anglo-Saxon and which have made the oppression of black by white a more complicated reality than these novels indicate. The exploration of this reality may yet produce a very powerful literature; we are, in the meantime, confronted with a phenomenon not even remotely literary, which is only one more aspect of an enduring inability to face the truth.

Commentary, April 1948

Lockridge: 'The American Myth'

I. THE BOOK AS SYMPTOM

Iᴎ his lifetime Ross Lockridge, Jr., came across a great many words and in *Raintree County* he has set down every one of them. It follows from this that his reading was prodigious: apparently almost every volume of American history ever published and most of the best (and much of the mediocre) writing of past epochs and our own: Shakespeare, Donne, Wolfe, Whitman, Joyce, Dos Passos. He heard—and remembered—almost every folk song, ballad and doggerel verse which can be called American; he accepted, with a really remarkable zest, all of the best American sentiments and practically listed all of the old, familiar aims and concepts. His book is as American, as banal and brave and cheerful as *The Battle Hymn of the Republic*, which, in fact, it resembles to an appalling degree; and, since *Raintree County* is not nearly so concise it is a good deal more difficult to get through without gagging.

Mr. Lockridge, then, is concerned with America. The jacket states reverently that he has attempted no less than a complete embodiment of the American Myth: an heroic undertaking indeed! His people are as invincibly American as the Fourth of July and it takes them 1066 pages to celebrate; everything that happens to them takes place in a fragrant, booming benevolent confusion called the Republic. The Hero is John Wyckliff Shawnessy, who is something of a cross between Lincoln, Mickey Rooney, Van Johnson and Shakespeare, with much in his makeup of the *Shropshire Lad*; though he does not, of course, ever allow himself such suicidal excesses of gloom. He and the book have moments that are genuine enough; perhaps the book's best moments are those concerned with Johnny's childhood. In spite of the fact that Mr. Lockridge writes far too much, there are times when he does not write badly. (It cannot honestly be said that he ever writes well.) His ear for speech is accurate if it is not sensitive; his characterization is vivid—like Sinclair Lewis, or, more accu-

rately, like Dickens, he depends on a series of carefully exaggerated foibles—but it is never revelatory; his people are as
clear as the sunlight in which they always seem to be bathed
and, ultimately, as static and uninteresting.

Incorporating the nature of the American Myth between
the covers of any novel is admittedly a gigantic task; and it is
made almost impossible by the fact that so many versions of
the same myth are used for so many warring purposes. Which
America will you have? There is America for the Indians—
which Mr. Lockridge mentions hastily and drops. There is
America for the people who settled the country, concerning
whom Mr. Lockridge is vehemently lyrical but no more startling than a Thanksgiving hymn. There is America for the
laborer, for the financier, America of the north and south,
America for the hillbilly, the urbanite, the farmer. And there
is America for the Protestant, the Catholic, the Jew, the Mexican, the Oriental and that arid sector which we have reserved
for the Negro. These Americas diverge significantly and sometimes dangerously and they have much in common. All of
them bound doubtfully together create a picture and a climate
not indicated in *Raintree County*. Mr. Lockridge is not entirely unaware of these national contradictions; he simply does
not know what to make of them. ('The Union forever!' he
cries desperately. 'O, beautiful, unanalyzable concept!')

At each impasse similar rhetoric is trotted out. The book,
which had no core to begin with, becomes as amorphous as
cotton candy under the drumming flow of words. These
words are designed less to illuminate than they are to conceal;
or, more accurately, Mr. Lockridge uses them as a kind of
shimmering web, hiding everything with an insistent radiance
and proving that, after all, everything is, or is going to be, all
right. This dependence on the Word, especially as illustrated
by this novel, strikes me as something quite peculiarly American. (In the beginning—and the Word was God.) Here is
evinced a remarkable and touching regard for all things written and an almost slavish respect for anyone who writes. This
does not, as one might think, lead to taste or discrimination
or insight: the devotion is unqualified. Mr. Lockridge behaves
in the presence of the Word like a child let loose in a well-
stocked ice-cream parlor. This allows him to speak, in the

same affectionate, admiring tone, of Shakespeare and Shawnessy, both boy poets. In the beginning one accepts this as a
gentle kind of mockery, but, later on, when Mr. Lockridge
has become more explicit about his concept of writing and his
attitude towards Shakespeare—whose greatest play, by virtue
of a dialect we have no room for here, concerned the shooting
of Abraham Lincoln and was, unhappily, never written—and
has further allowed us to read some of the work produced by
his Hero, one concludes that Mr. Lockridge was in earnest all
the time. This terrible, blind, indiscriminate dependence on
all things literary, which operates to dignify any and all rhetoric and makes of Shakespeare merely a superior rhetorician,
is an integral part of this novel; perhaps, indeed, *Raintree
County* would be inconceivable without it. An enduring part
of our myth is the right of everyone to be heard, and this
theoretical right has somehow become sufficiently debased so
that the mere act of verbalization is endowed with a wholly
disproportionate grandeur. This is due, in part perhaps, to the
national uneasiness in the presence of a work of art and it is
part of our culture, our popular culture: *in America anyone
can do anything.* The writer has, of course, failed unless he is
able to reach a large audience; if he is not sufficiently 'close'
to the people, sufficiently 'American' he is regarded with suspicion and dislike. We have, in effect, defied the individual out
of existence. At the same time there is a lurking distrust and
dissatisfaction with the product of this psychology; we are, as
a nation, accused of being artistically shallow. Hence, 'greater'
and 'greater' novels, 'mightier' movies, more 'searching' plays.
(We have done dreadful things to the adjective, too.) Long
articles appear in wide-selling periodicals concerning our native talent: we have artists, too, not one whit inferior to those
of other times and places, and ours are better paid. The re-
sultant confused struggling is further confounded by the necessity to be ultimately affirmative. (Weekly, Mr. Adams in the
Times charts the wretched path trodden by those writers who
are not.) Gloom must have a comedy relief, the acid comment
must be followed by a cheer. In a word, since a work of art,
literary art specifically, is almost always dangerous, we are aiming at a product which will be indisputably Art, which will be
resoundingly popular—and financially successful—and, so far

from being disturbing, will gratify the national ego and cause no-one—except, perhaps, our enemies—any trouble at all.

This is not, of course, new; it is remarkable only because the complacent mechanisms of our culture have made this attitude so widespread. There is observable now, moreover, to an extent unprecedented hitherto, an anxiety on the part of Americans concerning themselves and their heritage. This anxiety cannot yet be called probing; Americans are not noted for introspection and rather disapprove of it. Rather, we are approaching a state of mind which closely resembles shock. In Mr. Lockridge's Republic, whatever goes wrong—and nothing, of course, is irrevocably wrong—there is room for everyone and certain things are sure; but this is not any longer true in fact. Time has challenged us, our dream; and we find now that no one is very clear or specific about the nature of the dream. There were always contradictions, but we assumed that they would be taken care of; and since never before have we been in quite so important a position in the world, the contradictions have never been quite so glaring before. Something has gone wrong, no one quite knows where; no one knows where we are going; we seem to be headed in several directions at once. The strain is made a good deal more unbearable by the fact that Americans passionately believe in their avowed ideals, amorphous as they are, and are terrified of waking from a radiant dream. *Raintree County* is a kind of ultimate defense of the dreaming and the dream. It seeks to explain us to ourselves in the light of the irrevocable past. But this can only be done if the past is truly examined. Mr. Lockridge has, instead, given us the usual, superficial sunlight. He has exploited nearly every possible device to explain away all contradictions. He holds back the darkness by a perpetual insistence that darkness is not possible; or, at any rate, not possible in America, 'the last best hope of earth.'

If it is, indeed, the last, best hope we had better find out more about it. And this will demand an understanding which can only be arrived at through a thorough self-appraisal. This might, at once, make us less complacent and more mature; we might discover that affirmation consists of more than a handful of cheerful slogans. *Raintree County*, according to its author, cannot be found on any map; and it is always summer there. He might also have added that no one lives there any-more.

2. POSTSCRIPT: THE MAN

The death of Ross Lockridge, Jr. of carbon monoxide poisoning on the night of Saturday, March 6, wrote the grisliest possible finale to his ambitious novel. The newspaper accounts reported his suicide as the result of overwork: he put his whole heart into the book, we are told, and suffered a complete breakdown. Overworked suicides are by no means rare in what is known as the literary world; the history of writing is crammed with vignettes of the lonely, starving artist rushing gratefully to death; but it is not the kind of thing one expects from a young, superbly successful American novelist, certainly not the kind of thing predicted for the author of the Great American Novel. It must have been a savage blow to Mr. Adams.

Raintree County is nothing if not affirmative. It elects to weld into an inviolable unity these sprawling United States. (One is tempted to remark here: but the unity has always been taken for granted. Why the need now to prove that the United States of America is actually that?) In encompassing this aim Mr. Lockridge makes it apparent that he loves his country; and it becomes apparent that he does not really understand it and that he is disturbed. The disturbance—manifested, for instance, by those long tortured philosophical discussions between the Hero and Professor Webster Stiles—is perhaps the healthiest aspect of *Raintree County*. Here the disturbance is anterior and hidden; the author stacks his cards as best he can against the cynical Professor. It is as though the Professor were there to espouse the darkness so that Mr. Shawnessy can argue for the light. It is always apparent that one is expected to like the Professor but never to agree with him; he has, after all, renounced those virtues and those aspirations which form the blood and skeleton of the good life.

And these virtues, aspirations? We have all grown up with them; we learned them in Sunday School and in Boy Scout meetings; they have formed the basis for countless valedictories. These precepts are designed for our instruction and protection; they are designed to prove that life in the Republic is always green and fertile, that our hopes and our strivings form the noblest dream of all. Why, then, are we so loath to come to terms with it?

The gulf between our dream and the realities that we live with is something that we do not understand and do not wish to admit. It is almost as though we were asking that others look at what we want and turn their eyes, as we do, away from what we are. I am not, as I hope is clear, speaking of civil liberties, social equality, etc., where, indeed, a strenuous battle is yet carried on; I am speaking, instead, of a particular shallowness of mind, an intellectual and spiritual laxness, a terror of individual responsibility and a corresponding terror of change. This rigid refusal to look at ourselves may well destroy us; particularly now, since if we cannot understand ourselves we will not be able to understand anything.

Mr. Lockridge's death is an inconceivable end for the hero of *Raintree County*. He, who lived his zestful life through, was not slated, in the Lockridge scheme, to meet death at his own hand. This is the ultimate negation, antithetical to everything John Wyckliff Shawnessy so thoroughly believed in, whose initials, at the book's end, are written in the air.

"What is America?" Mr. Shawnessy asks the question and except to call it a noble dream the question is not answered. Since the book at every point evades the riddle of the human being the question is never really asked. The death of the hero of *Raintree County* admits an uncertainty and desperation the entire county would conspire to deny. But if America is a dream it is also a reality; a small dream is not enough to live by. We are not unlike the audience which assembled to hear the only political speech made by Mr. Shawnessy when he was running for office: they liked him, they knew it was a good speech. But they could not remember nor repeat a single word of it.

The New Leader, April 10, 1948

Preservation of Innocence

THE PROBLEM of the homosexual, so vociferously involved with good and evil, the unnatural as opposed to the natural, has its roots in the nature of man and woman and their relationship to one another. While at one time we speak of nature and at another of the nature of man, we speak on both occasions of something of which we know very little and we make the tacit admission that they are not one and the same. Between nature and man there is a difference; there is, indeed, perpetual war. It develops when we think about it that not only is a natural state perversely indefinable outside of the womb or before the grave but that it is not on the whole a state which is altogether desirable. It is just as well that we cook our food and are not baffled by water-closets and do not copulate in the public thoroughfare. People who have not learned this are not admired as natural but are feared as primitive or incarcerated as insane. We spend vast amounts of our time and emotional energy in learning how not to be natural and in eluding the trap of our own nature and it therefore becomes very difficult to know exactly what is meant when we speak of the unnatural. It is not possible to have it both ways, to use nature at one time as the final arbiter of human conduct and at another to oppose her as angrily as we do. As we are being inaccurate, perhaps desperately defensive and making, inversely, a most damaging admission when we describe as inhuman some reprehensible act committed by a human being, so we become hopelessly involved in paradox when we describe as unnatural something which is found in nature. A cat torturing a mouse to death is not described as inhuman for we assume that it is being perfectly natural; nor is a table condemned as being unnatural for we know that it has nothing to do with nature. What we really seem to be saying when we speak of the inhuman is that we cannot bear to be confronted with that fathomless baseness shared by all humanity and when we speak of the unnatural that we cannot imagine what vexations nature will dream up next. We have, in short, whenever nature is invoked to support our human divisions, every right to be suspicious, nature having betrayed only the most perplexing and untrustworthy interest in man and none whatever in his institutions. We resent this indifference and we are frightened by it; we resist it; we ceaselessly assert the miracle of our existence against this implacable power. Yet we know nothing of birth or death except that we remain powerless when faced by either. Much as we resent or threaten or cajole nature she refuses absolutely to relent; she may at any moment throw down the trump card she never fails to have hidden and leave us bankrupt. In time, her ally and her rather too explicit witness, suns rise and set and the face of the earth changes; at length the limbs stiffen and the light goes out of the eyes.

> And nothing 'gainst time's scythe may make defense
> Save breed to brave him when he takes thee hence.

We arrive at the oldest, the most insistent and the most vehement charge faced by the homosexual: he is unnatural because he has turned from his life-giving function to a union which is sterile. This may, in itself, be considered a heavy, even an unforgivable crime, but since it is not so considered when involving other people, the unmarried or the poverty-stricken or the feeble, and since his existence did not always invoke that hysteria with which he now contends, we are safe in suggesting that his present untouchability owes its motive power to several other sources. Let me suggest that his present debasement and our obsession with him corresponds to the debasement of the relationship between the sexes; and that his ambiguous and terrible position in our society reflects the ambiguities and terrors which time has deposited on that relationship as the sea piles seaweed and wreckage along the shore.

For, after all, I take it that no one can be seriously disturbed about the birth-rate: when the race commits suicide it will not be in Sodom. Nor can we continue to shout unnatural whenever we are confronted by a phenomenon as old as mankind, a phenomenon, moreover, which nature has maliciously repeated in all of her domain. If we are going to be natural then this is part of nature; if we refuse to accept this, then we have rejected nature and must find another criterion.

Instantly the Deity springs to mind, in much the same

manner, I suspect, that he sprang into being on the cold, black day when we discovered that nature cared nothing for us. His advent, which alone had the power to save us from nature and ourselves, also created a self-awareness and, therefore, tensions and terrors and responsibilities with which we had not coped before. It marked the death of innocence; it set up the duality of good-and-evil; and now Sin and Redemption, those mighty bells, began that crying which will not cease until, by another act of creation, we transcend our old morality. Before we were banished from Eden and the curse was uttered, "I will put enmity between thee and the woman", the homosexual did not exist; nor, properly speaking, did the heterosexual. We were all in a state of nature.

We are forced to consider this tension between God and nature and are thus confronted with the nature of God because He is man's most intense creation and it is not in the sight of nature that the homosexual is condemned, but in the sight of God. This argues a profound and dangerous failure of concept, since an incalculable number of the world's humans are thereby condemned to something less than life; and we may not, of course, do this without limiting ourselves. Life, it is true, is a process of decisions and alternatives, the conscious awareness and acceptance of limitations. Experience, nevertheless, to say nothing of history, seems clearly to indicate that it is not possible to banish or to falsify any human need without ourselves undergoing falsification and loss. And what of murder? A human characteristic, surely. Must we embrace the murderer? But the question must be put another way: is it possible not to embrace him? For he is in us and of us. We may not be free until we understand him.

The nature of man and woman and their relationship to one another fills seas of conjecture and an immense proportion of the myth, legend and literature of the world is devoted to this subject. It has caused, we gather, on the evidence presented by any library, no little discomfort. It is observable that the more we imagine we have discovered the less we know and that, moreover, the necessity to discover and the effort and self-consciousness involved in this necessity makes this relationship more and more complex. Men and women seem to function as imperfect and sometimes unwilling mirrors for one another; a falsification or distortion of the nature of the one is immediately reflected in the nature of the other. A division between them can only betray a division within the soul of each. Matters are not helped if we thereupon decide that men must recapture their status as men and that women must embrace their function as women; not only does the resulting rigidity of attitude put to death any possible communion, but, having once listed the bald physical facts, no one is prepared to go further and decide, of our multiple human attributes, which are masculine and which are feminine. Directly we say that women have finer and more delicate sensibilities we are reminded that she is insistently, mythically and even historically, treacherous. If we are so rash as to say that men have greater endurance, we are reminded of the procession of men who have gone to their long home while women walked about the streets—mourning, we are told, but no doubt, gossiping and shopping at the same time. We can pick up no novel, no drama, no poem; we may examine no fable nor any myth without stumbling on this merciless paradox in the nature of the sexes. This is a paradox which experience alone is able to illuminate and this experience is not communicable in any language that we know. The recognition of this complexity is the signal of maturity; it marks the death of the child and the birth of the man.

II

One may say, with an exaggeration vastly more apparent than real, that it is one of the major American ambitions to shun this metamorphosis. In the truly awesome attempt of the American to at once preserve his innocence and arrive at a man's estate, that mindless monster, the tough guy, has been created and perfected; whose masculinity is found in the most infantile and elementary externals and whose attitude towards women is the wedding of the most abysmal romanticism and the most implacable distrust. It is impossible for a moment to believe that any Cain or Chandler hero loves his girl; we are given overwhelming evidence that he wants her, but that is not the same thing and, moreover, what he seems to want is revenge; what they bring to each other is not even passion or sexuality but an unbelievably barren and wrathful grinding. They are surrounded by blood and treachery; and their bitter coupling, which has the urgency and precision of machine-gun fire, is heralded and punctuated by the mysterious and astounded corpse. The woman, in these energetic works, is the unknown quantity, the incarnation of sexual evil, the smiler with the knife. It is the man, who, for all his tommy-guns and rhetoric, is the innocent, inexplicably, compulsively and perpetually betrayed. Men and women have all but dis-appeared from our popular culture, leaving only this disturb-ing series of effigies with a motive power which we are told is sex, but which is actually a dream-like longing, an unful-fillment more wistful than that of the Sleeping Beauty await-ing the life-giving touch of the fated Prince. For the American dream of love insists that the Boy get the Girl; the tough guy has a disconcerting tendency to lapse abruptly into baby-talk and go off with Her—having first ascertained that she is not blood-guilty; and we are always told that this is what he *really* wants, to stop all this chasing around and settle down, to have children and a full life with a woman who, unhappily even when she appears, fails to exist. The merciless ingenuity of Mr. James M. Cain hit upon an effective solution to this problem in a recent novel by having his protagonist fall in love with a twelve year old, a female against whom no crime could be charged, who was not yet guilty of the shedding of blood and who thereafter kept herself pure for the hero until he returned from his exhausting and improbable trials. This preposterous and tasteless notion did not seem, in Mr. Cain's world, to be preposterous or tasteless at all, but functioned, on the con-trary, as an eminently fortunate and farsighted inspiration.

Mr. Cain, indeed, has achieved an enormous public and, I should hope, a not inconsiderable fortune on the basis of his remarkable preoccupation with the virile male. One may sug-gest that it was the dynamism of his material which trapped him into introducing, briefly, and with the air of a man wear-ing antiseptic gloves, an unattractive invert in an early novel, *Serenade*, who was promptly stabbed to death by the hero's mistress, a lusty and unlikely senorita. This novel contains a curious admission on the part of the hero to the effect that there is always somewhere a homosexual who can wear down the resistance of the normal man by knowing which buttons to press. This is presented as a serious and melancholy warning and it is when the invert of *Serenade* begins pressing too many buttons at once that he arrives at his sordid and bloody end. Thus is that immaculate manliness within us protected; thus summarily do we deal with any obstacle to the union of the Boy and the Girl. Can we doubt the wisdom of drawing the curtains when they finally come together? For the instant that the Boy and Girl become the Bride and Groom we are forced to leave them; not really supposing that the drama is over or that we have witnessed the fulfillment of two human beings, though we would like to believe this, but constrained by the knowledge that it is not for our eyes to witness the pain and the tempest that will follow. (For we *know* what follows; we know that life is not really like this at all.) What are we to say, who have already been betrayed, when this boy, this girl, discovers that the knife which preserved them for each other has unfitted them for experience? For the boy cannot know a woman since he has never become a man.

Hence, violence: that brutality which rages unchecked in our literature is part of the harvest of this unfulfillment, strident and dreadful testimony to our renowned and cherished innocence. Consider, in those extravagant denouncements which characterize those novels—to be more and more remarked on the bookshelves—which are concerned with homosexuality, how high a value we place on this dangerous attribute. In *The City and the Pillar* the avowed homosexual who is the protagonist murders his first and only perfect love when at length they meet again for he cannot bear to kill instead that desolate and impossible dream of love which he has carried in his heart so long. In *The Folded Leaf* the frail, introverted Lymie attempts suicide in an effort to escape the danger implicit in his love for Spud; a bloody act which, we are told, has purchased his maturity. In *The Fall of Valor* the god-like Marine defends his masculinity with a poker, leaving for dead the frightened professor who wanted him. These violent resolutions, all of them unlikely in the extreme, are compelled by a panic which is close to madness. These novels are not concerned with homosexuality but with the ever-present danger of sexual activity between men.

It is this unadmitted tension, longing and terror and wrath which creates their curiously mindless and pallid, yet smouldering atmosphere. It is a mistake, I think, that this subject matter sets them apart in any fruitful or significant way from anything written by James M. Cain or Laura Z. Hobson or Mary Jane Ward. They are alike in that they are wholly unable to recreate or interpret any of the reality or complexity of human experience; and that area which it is their self-avowed purpose to illuminate is precisely the area on which is thrown the most distorting light. As one may close *Gentleman's Agreement*, which is about Gentiles and Jews, having gained no insight into the mind of either; as *The Snake Pit* reveals nothing of madness and James M. Cain tells us nothing of men and women, so one may read any current novel concerned with homosexual love and encounter merely a procession of platitudes the ancestry of which again may be traced to The Rover Boys and their golden ideal of chastity. It is quite impossible to write a worthwhile novel about a Jew or a Gentile or a Homosexual, for people refuse, unhappily, to function in so neat and one-dimensional a fashion. If the novelist considers that they are no more complex than their labels he must, of necessity, produce a catalogue, in which we will find, neatly listed, all those attributes with which the label is associated; and this can only operate to reinforce the brutal and dangerous anonymity of our culture.

A novel insistently demands the presence and passion of human beings, who cannot ever be labeled. Once the novelist has created a human being he has shattered the label and, in transcending the subject matter, is able, for the first time, to tell us something about it and to reveal how profoundly all things involving human beings interlock. Without this passion we may all smother to death, locked in those airless, labeled cells, which isolate us from each other and separate us from ourselves; and without this passion when we have discovered the connection between that Boy-Scout who smiles from the subway poster and that underworld to be found all over America, vengeful time will be upon us.

Zero, Summer 1949

The Negro at Home and Abroad

NO GREEN PASTURES, by Roi Ottley. Scribner's. 234 pp. $3.00.

M R. OTTLEY takes us through England, France, Italy, Germany, through the Russian-dominated Balkan states, to Greece, Egypt, and Israel, triumphantly uncovering the black skeleton in the Old World's closet. One can scarcely imagine that this will greatly impress the Europeans, who have lived for generations on a continent absolutely phosphorescent with dry bones; but Mr. Ottley, twentieth-century American ("Negro though I am"), does not approve of skeletons, and he makes this disapproval manifest whenever they are found.

Unhappily, all skeletons have their histories, in the face of which nothing is more irrelevant than disapproval—to suggest the first limitation of Mr. Ottley's book. Secondly, he cannot make us believe that any American Negro is any longer allowed the luxury of looking at the world as though it were a simple matter of black against white. Only the backward peoples, i.e., natives under colonial domination, are able to do that. Finally, the journalistic method is not really so flexible as we suppose; it is capable of description but rarely of penetration. Because one feels that Roi Ottley is more intent upon proving his thesis—the existence of racial prejudice in Europe—than he is upon illuminating the root, manner, and reason for this prejudice, the point of *No Green Pastures* is lost: that American Negroes are better off than Negroes anywhere else in the world, and that Europe ought to clean house before trumpeting about our lynchings.

In the first place, racial prejudice in Europe is not news. Such an idea can only spring from an arbitrary juxtaposition of the situations of the Negro in Europe and the Negro in America—or, rather, out of an attempt to consider these two very different situations as though their history and motivations were the same. The racial lexicon of Europe is not that of America, and the significance of the Negro in the European imagination has very little to do with the displacement the Negro causes in the American mind.

According to Mr. Ottley, some Negro soldiers stationed in the Netherlands during the Second World War found, to their "shock" and "humiliation," at a Dutch celebration of Christmas, that a Dutchwoman had blackened her face with cork, impersonating "offensively" the black servant of *Sinterklaas*. But what else is a Dutchwoman likely to know about Negroes except that they are black, and—so far as she is concerned— have always been servants? One can scarcely say that she is actuated by malice against Negroes: She is not even thinking of Negroes; she is celebrating a traditional holiday in traditional fashion. No one, I suppose, will seriously suggest that because we in America no longer blacken our faces with burnt cork—to impersonate, say, Sambo—we are freer from racial prejudice than Europeans. On the contrary: The interracial manners and mores of America are infinitely more complex and cautious and vastly more sophisticated than those of Europe, and this is because America has been forced to contend with a peculiar and centuries-old racial tension which is no part of Europe's history.

For it is not, I trust, impolitic to point out that Negroes are not white but black. And further: According to the criteria of our civilization, and in their own eyes and in the memory of all men living, black men constitute a have-not nation. This is history, a nightmare from which one cannot hope to escape until one has apprehended its inexorable nature. Folklore and custom are the means used by the populace to perpetuate and even to revere their history, to which they owe their identity; and it is therefore fruitless to quarrel with white men because in ritual, myth, and fancy they allocate to black men the role which they have played and still play. This, as I take it, is one of the things that Mr. Ottley is talking about when he speaks of prejudice on the continent and in England. He means that white men harbor, in relation to black men, a certain unconscious assumption of superiority and that they look upon black men as travelers from another world.

This is, indeed, one of the causes of the bottomless anger of black men: that they have been forced to learn far more about whites than whites have ever found it necessary to learn about them. White men are allowed the luxury of never think-ing about blacks at all, until they happen to encounter one, whereas few black men anywhere live for very long without encountering, as an impossible obstacle forever, the idea, the presence, and the power of whites. In the mind of the black man the humanity of the white is never for an instant in ques-tion—it is to this blind humanity, precisely, that all his plight bears witness. The questions that the Negro lives with are how not to hate the white man, or, otherwise, how to hate him most effectively; how to fool him, cheat him, use him; how, in short, failing the possibility of a general overturn, to wrest for himself in the white man's world an honored place, or at any rate a bearable *Lebensraum*.

For this reason the white man, in his interracial encounters, cannot fail to cause in the breast of the black a certain fury, however deeply this fury may be hidden—when, out of an innocence which can scarcely at first be believed, the white man wishes to discover the spirit, aspirations, and personal history of the black stranger before him. The black, in the face of this innocence, and observing the extent of the white man's apprehensions, cannot but feel a certain bitter superiority of his own, and a certain contempt. And he cannot but find it very nearly unforgivable that, in the mind of the white man, who has cost him so much, his own humanity should occupy so little place or such a humiliating one. This is an aspect of the interracial reality which nearly everyone in Europe has been able to ignore and which we in America, with dubious success, are perpetually wishing out of existence.

But the great difference between the manifestations of race prejudice in America is involved with the power of the human personality—in this context the black personality, a phenom-enon with which Europe has never had to cope. The black man in Europe does not, in the first place, live there, and, economic and military necessities aside, he is not really con-sidered a European citizen. He lives in the colonies, which, whatever their importance to the economic well-being and however they may be administered, remain a matter of total indifference to the European man in the street; and he pursues in these colonies a way of life which is an utter and barbaric mystery. The Dutch Zwarte Piet is a far more genuinely mythological figure than the American Sambo—for Black Peter has never threatened the Dutch spiritual or social well-being. He does not live in Dutch houses, or go to Dutch schools, or walk Dutch streets. Few Dutchmen, I should hazard, have ever been forced to find an answer to the exasperating question as to whether or not they would let their sisters marry him. The black man exists for Europe almost entirely in the mind, in which cage he is, not surprisingly, a kind of archetypal Noble Savage, exotic, childlike, backward. Almost never has he leaped out of the image and into life, as so spectacularly happened in America—a country, it is sometimes useful to remember, which was settled by Europeans.

The European image of the black man rests finally, one must say, on ignorance, and, however expedient this ignorance may be, it is sustained by the objective conditions; whereas the American image of the Negro has been created out of our terrible experience, and is sustained by an anguished inability to come to terms with that experience, or to conquer the guilty fear and shame which have been its quite inevitable and self-perpetuating legacy. This heritage deprives us entirely of the kind of racial innocence which one finds in Europe. Europeans can blacken their faces with cork because the black man as a human being has no reality in their lives. He is not one of them. But he is *one of us*—and from this reality there is no escape.

Disastrously enough, this escape seems sometimes to be our most passionate wish. Mr. Ottley, who insists that our heritage is great, yet essays to place himself and us at a vast remove from all its more troubling aspects; which is to say that he does not wish to deal with it in all its implications, and so achieves that flatness of tone which is popularly taken as evidence of an unbiased mind. It is not, for example, enough to suggest that because "the bulk of blacks in Europe is abysmally poor," American Negroes are better off because some are able to drive a Cadillac. The history of the Negro in America is a heavier weight than this celebrated vehicle is able to carry. Both white and black in America, the one to evade his guilt and weight of responsibility, and the other to deny past humiliation and present trouble, make the same great error:

the reduction of black-white history in America to a kind of tableau of material progress.

This is a mere fragment of the truth, moreover a fragment which, when isolated from its complex of causes (and effects), becomes nothing less than a distortion. Neither the bitterness of our battles nor the reality of our victories can be conveyed in such a formulation, nor can we hope in so inadequate a language to clarify for Europe any of the complexities of American life. "What America has learned about race relations is of vital importance to a multicolored world," runs Mr. Ottley's concluding sentence. This is perfectly true, and yet the reader feels, by the time he has reached it, that all Mr. Ottley means to say is that America has learned that, given education (and the possibility of Cadillacs), American whites and Negroes can be polite to one another. Surely, out of the fantastic racial history acted out on our continent we must make something more meaningful than this. What we can make of our unique experience depends on our willingness to accept the bitterness in which this experience was gained—the price we paid, both black and white, and the effect it has had on us. We look upon this experience with shame, but it is out of what has been our greatest shame that we may be able to create one day our greatest opportunity.

Reporter, November 27, 1951

The Crusade of Indignation

NEGROES ON THE MARCH. A Frenchman's Report on the American Negro Struggle. By Daniel Guerin. George L. Weismann. $1.50.

GOODBYE TO UNCLE TOM. By J. C. Furnas. William Sloane Associates. $6.

T HE LOVE of money," St. Paul once wrote, with a fairly typical lack of precision, "is the root of all evil." This formulation seems to leave a great many evils out of account, and it does not even raise the question of just why the human heart, in which this love of money lives, should be so base. Nor does it raise the question of what money is, what is its power, what it means to people or states. With so many knotty questions thus neatly disposed of, people who share Paul's attitude about money can also believe—as he, being bigoted in quite another direction, did not—that people will be made better as their economic state improves. It is an extremely attractive theory, and most of us have at one time or another espoused it.

Only—in order to bring about this economic utopia, one needs a band of people who do not care about money—or power?—who will carry out the necessary operation of taking the money from those who now have an abundance of it and distributing it among those who have too little.

In this operation—the love of money persisting so tenaciously—blood is likely to be shed. And the shedding of blood will probably prove to be the operation's most real achievement. When things go back to what may be called normal, it will be seen that the people who were to be made better still persist in loving money and in trying—no matter what it may do to themselves, their neighbors, or their children—to make it.

People who approach the Negro problem from this doctrinaire point of view are always embarrassed by at least two facts. One is that Negroes love money quite as much as whites do, and rather more than they love one another. The other is that the people in America least attracted to the idea of a worker's state are the workers. They are not interested in themselves as workers—except in their clashes with management, in which they are represented by those other managers, the union leaders. They are interested in achieving what, in fact, can still be achieved at this period in American life: a measure of economic peace. Unless forced by outside pressure, they are not terribly concerned with what may be happening next door—among Negroes, for example.

In the Negro world, as in the white world, Negroes who have money band together and try to ignore the existence of their unluckier brothers. That is the way the love of money works. But neither money, nor the love of it, is the root of all evil. The importance of money is simply that power in the world does not exist without it and power in the world is what almost everyone would like to have.

The love of money thesis is the thesis of Daniel Guerin's *Negroes on The March*, and, since I find it impossible to take the thesis seriously, I find it rather difficult to discuss the book—which is, anyway, less a discussion of the American Negro's situation than a rather shrill diatribe against the capitalist system. No one with any pretension to intellectual honesty claims that the capitalist system is perfect, or is likely to be made so. It may indeed be doomed, and we may all be the slothful and pussy-footing creatures Mr. Guerin says we are. But his own tone is so extremely ungenerous that I cannot avoid a certain chill when I think of the probable fate of dissenters in his vari-colored brave new world. Here he is on Gunnar Myrdal, the Swedish social scientist whose *An American Dilemma* Mr. Guerin finds "feeble in *interpretation*". (All italics are Mr. Guerin's.) ". . . it does not explain *how, by whom, and why race prejudice was brought into being*." (It certainly does not; I, too, should like to read the book which does.) But Mydral's feebleness, it turns out, is blacker than mere incompetence: "Without calling into question Myrdal's good faith, we must nevertheless make the observation that his method is quite in harmony with the concerns of those who subsidized his work and serves their interests quite well. For what did the trustees of the Carnegie Foundation actually want?" What they didn't want was a "cause-and-effect relationship. . . . established between capitalist oppression and race prejudice." Bright students, or people who have heard this song before will already have guessed the reason, as follows: ". . . victims of race prejudice would be likely to draw conclusions dangerous to the established order." Nor would the awakened white workers have taken long to realize that their best interests lay in black-white solidarity. Myrdal's real task, according to Mr. Guerin, was to avoid saying anything which, by leading to such a holocaust, would displease and possibly destroy the Carnegie Foundation.

A man whose vision of the world remains as elementary as Mr. Guerin's can scarcely be trusted to help us understand it. It is true enough, for example, as far as it goes, that slavery was established and then abolished for economic reasons; but slavery did not come into the world along with capitalism any more than race prejudice did; and it need scarcely be said, at this late date, that where capitalism has been abolished slavery and race prejudice yet remain. It is also true—again, as far as it goes—that, as Mary McLeod Bethune said, "The voice of organized labor has become one of the most powerful in the land and unless we have a part in that voice our people will not be heard." But "our people" are then speaking as a part of organized labor. Labor's interests may often be identical with the Negro's interests; but Mr. Guerin fails to understand that, in the light of the white worker's desire to achieve greater status, his aims and those of the Negro often clash quite bitterly.

All this is changing, to be sure, but so very, very slowly, and in such unexpected ways that only a madman would dare to predict the final issue—if one can speak, in human affairs, of a final issue. The world in which people find themselves is not simply a vindictive plot imposed on them from above; it is also the world they have helped to make. They have helped to make, and help to sustain it by sharing the assumptions which hold their world together. Mr. Guerin's book, so far from having broken with any of the assumptions which have helped to cause such agony in the world—so far from being revolutionary or even "modern"—is a desperate cliche, is painfully, stiflingly old-fashioned. It is certainly not revolutionary today to suggest, that, whereas it was wrong for capitalists to murder workers, it is right for workers to murder capitalists; whereas it is wrong for whites to murder Negroes, Negroes may be pardoned for murdering whites. Mr. Guerin is unable to recognize a sadly persistent fact: the concepts contained in words like "freedom," "justice," "democracy" are not common concepts; on the contrary, they are rare. People are not born knowing what these are. It takes enormous and, above all, individual effort to arrive at the respect for other people that these words imply. Since Mr. Guerin lacks any sense of history, except as something to be manipulated, and has really no respect whatever for the human personality, he is unable to give us any sense of the perpetual interaction of these forces on one another. Without this sense all states become abstractions, and lawless ones at that.

Mr. Guerin wants us all to go out right away and begin preparing for the equitable new state which will succeed to the present inequitable one; and should the present state seem reluctant to wither away, he has no objection to setting it to the torch. One of his heroes, John Brown, is one of the minor villains in J. C. Furnas' admirable *Goodbye To Uncle Tom*. Mr. Furnas' attitude can be gathered from his comment that "What Mrs. Stowe and John Brown did was not to create the forces that would free the slave but to make sure that North and South went into their crisis in the least promising state of mind." In view of the enormous bitterness the Civil War has left us, this statement seems disquietingly close to the truth. It suggests that indignation and goodwill are not enough to make the world better. Clarity is needed, as well as charity, however difficult this may be to imagine, much less sustain, toward the other side. Perhaps the worst thing that can be said about social indignation is that it so frequently leads to the death of personal humility. Once that has happened, one has ceased to live in that world of men which one is striving so mightily to make over. One has entered into a dialogue with that terrifying deity, sometimes called History, previously, and perhaps again, to be referred to as God, to which no sacrifice in human suffering is too great.

Mr. Furnas maintains that, despite the world-renowned indignation of its author, *Uncle Tom's Cabin* is a shoddy and almost totally undocumented piece of fiction, which it is; and, further, that it is this book which has set the tone for the attitude of American whites toward Negroes for the last one hundred years. This may seem, at first, rather too heavy a weight to place on a single book. Yet when one considers this novel's enormous prestige and popularity, remembers that it was read for generations as though it were another Bible, that it is involved with the deepest, most lasting bitterness and the bloodiest conflict this nation has ever known; when one reflects, above all, how it flatters the popular mind, positively discouraging that mind from any tendency to think the matter through for itself—and this to such an extent that both pro and anti-Negro sentiment have read this book as scripture—one is forced to the conclusion that Mr. Furnas is almost certainly more nearly right than wrong. Add to this the impact of the "Tom" shows, which persisted, according to Mr. Furnas, until 1933, the last one being heard of in 1950, which definitively jettisoned whatever validity Mrs. Stowe's work might have had, and which introduced—with Topsy—that blackfaced comic-character who is the despair of Negro actors even today—well, at least it can be said that few indeed are the novels which can boast of such a long, varied and influential life, few the novels which the objective conditions conspired to keep in fashion for so long. Even today, Mr. Furnas places the annual sale of this novel at about 8,000 copies.

And, indeed, if anyone seriously doubts that the attitudes to be found in *Uncle Tom's Cabin* are still prevalent among us, he has only to wade or sit through that other publishing landmark and mammoth movie, *Gone With The Wind*, or see almost any other movie dealing with Negro life, or read almost any other novel on the same subject published in this country since 1852. Or simply: ask himself what he really knows about the American Negro, what he really feels about him. It is a question, after all, whether what we will here call the ordinary American of good will knows anything more about Negro life than what has filtered through to him via memories of an exemplary Negro maid, or the experience—for which he is almost certainly not prepared—of, say, some Billie Holiday records, perhaps a trip or two through Harlem, perhaps one or two Negro colleagues, or a Negro college friend. And what he *feels* concerning all this is a mystery, probably even to himself. The sad truth is that he has probably taken refuge from this exceedingly disturbing question in the arbitrary decision that Negroes are just like everybody else. But, obviously, and especially in this context, this is no truer than the sporadically old-fashioned notion that Negroes are inferior to everybody else: sporadically, because fashions in thought—in the breast and in the world—are subject to bewildering and shameful cycles. We have all had the experience of finding that our reactions and perhaps even our deeds have denied beliefs we thought were ours. And this is the danger of arriving at arbitrary decisions in order to avoid the risks of thought, of striking arbitrary attitudes. If the attitude is a cover, what it is covering will inevitably be revealed.

And exactly this, in fact, has happened so often that there is another, and very crucial difficulty encountered in interracial communication, in attempting to discover not *what*, but *who* the Negro is. In the first place, popular belief to the contrary, it is not enough to have been born a Negro to understand the history of Negroes in America. And, whereas whites have a complicated social machinery and a natural—and cultivated—mental and spiritual laziness operating to keep far from them any sense of how Negroes live; Negroes, beginning with the natural desire to escape the humiliations, the downright persecutions, which Negroes endure, end, often enough, by despising all the *other* Negroes who have brought them to this condition—a condition which they spend incalculable amounts of energy blotting out of their conscious minds. But they, naturally enough, therefore, also hate all whites, who make the world as bleak for them as does a cloud before the sun. This universal hatred, turning inward and feeding on itself, is not the least ghastly aspect of the heritage of the American Negro, for all that it remains, by its nature, so hidden. It is, for one thing, the absolute death of the communication which might help to liberate both Negroes and whites.

And all this, according to Mr. Furnas (and in the words of Abraham Lincoln) because of the "little woman who made this big war." Well, of course, not quite. Mr. Furnas, who clearly cannot stand the "little woman," makes the point that she was able to have such a tremendous effect because she was a mildly gifted woman who mirrored the assumptions of her time—and place—so perfectly. She helped to inspire and keep aflame the zeal in the general Northern breast to liberate those slaves, of whom they knew only that the souls belonged to God. Of the motives beneath the zeal she helped inspire, Mrs. Stowe knew nothing; it was not real to her that the war which was finally being fought was not being fought to free the slave, that it was a hand to hand contest between the North and the South for dominance. And when the slave was finally freed, it developed that his soul did indeed belong to God and that God could take it, for all the nation seemed to care.

For it is easy to proclaim all souls equal in the sight of God: it is hard to make men equal on earth, in the sight of men. This problem had never entered Mrs. Stowe's mind, for the reason that it had never entered her mind that the Negro could conceivably *be* an equal. She knew nothing about the Africa, to which projects were made to send him, as, when writing *Uncle Tom's Cabin*, she had known nothing of slavery beyond what she had gathered by reading and one or two short trips to Kentucky. Perhaps if she had known more about the slave's condition, and what this condition does to a people, she (and the nation) would have had a more realistic, more responsible view of what would probably happen when thousands of unlettered, abruptly homeless, totally vulnerable and unprepared people were turned loose upon the body politic. Mr. Furnas is not being unjust when he observes that the righteous zeal of Mrs. Stowe, like that of most of the Abolitionists, resembled that of an anti-vivisectionist committee. It had not entered their heads that they were fighting for the rights of men like themselves. They were fighting for the right of the "sons of Ethiopia, whatever . . . their natural stupidity . . . to stretch forth their hands to God." Of the right of the "sons of Ethiopia" to conquer that unquestioned "natural stupidity," of their right to work, live, vote, marry, and even to become unbelievers, they had never thought. We are until today struggling with many of the results of this righteous zeal in action.

One of the results is the continuing bitterness felt by the descendants of those "sons of Ethiopia," whom we have never yet, wholly, managed to regard as men. Perhaps nothing in

Goodbye To Uncle Tom more justifies the title than Mr. Furnas' unsentimental insistence that this must be done, and now, for no other reason than our common humanity, and that the way to begin is by taking a hard look at oneself.

The Nation, July 7, 1956

Sermons and Blues

SELECTED POEMS OF LANGSTON HUGHES. Drawings by E. McKnight Kauffer. 297 pp. New York: Alfred A. Knopf. $5.

EVERY TIME I read Langston Hughes I am amazed all over again by his genuine gifts—and depressed that he has done so little with them. A real discussion of his work demands more space than I have here, but this book contains a great deal which a more disciplined poet would have thrown into the waste-basket (almost all of the last section, for example).

There are the poems which almost succeed but which do not succeed, poems which take refuge, finally, in a fake simplicity in order to avoid the very difficult simplicity of the experience! And one sometimes has the impression, as in a poem like "Third Degree"—which is about the beating up of a Negro boy in a police station—that Hughes has had to hold the experience outside him in order to be able to write at all. And certainly this is understandable. Nevertheless, the poetic trick, so to speak, is to be within the experience and outside it at the same time—and the poem fails.

Mr. Hughes is at his best in brief, sardonic asides, or in lyrics like "Mother to Son," and "The Negro Speaks of Rivers." Or "Dream Variations":

> To fling my arms wide
> In some place of the sun,
> To whirl and to dance
> Till the white day is done.
> Then rest at cool evening
> Beneath a tall tree
> While night comes on gently,
>   Dark like me—
> That is my dream!
>
> To fling my arms wide
> In the face of the sun.
> Dance! Whirl! Whirl!

Till the quick day is done.
Rest at pale evening . . .
A tall, slim tree . . .
Night coming tenderly
Black like me.

I do not like all of "The Weary Blues," which copies, rather than exploits, the cadence of the blues, but it comes to a remarkable end. And I am also very fond of "Island," which begins "Wave of sorrow/Do not drown me now."

Hughes, in his sermons, blues and prayers, has working for him the power and the beat of Negro speech and Negro music. Negro speech is vivid largely because it is private. It is a kind of emotional shorthand—or sleight-of-hand—by means of which Negroes express, not only their relationship to each other, but their judgment of the white world. And, as the white world takes over this vocabulary—without the faintest notion of what it really means—the vocabulary is forced to change. The same thing is true of Negro music, which has had to become more and more complex in order to continue to express any of the private or collective experience.

Hughes knows the bitter truth behind these hieroglyphics: what they are designed to protect, what they are designed to convey. But he has not forced them into the realm of art where their meaning would become clear and overwhelming. "Hey, pop!/Re-bop!/Mop!" conveys much more on Lenox Avenue than it does in this book, which is not the way it ought to be.

Hughes is an American Negro poet and has no choice but to be acutely aware of it. He is not the first American Negro to find the war between his social and artistic responsibilities all but irreconcilable.

The New York Times Book Review,
March 29, 1959

On Catfish Row
"Porgy and Bess" in the Movies

GRANDIOSE, foolish, and heavy with the stale perfume of self-congratulation, the Hollywood-Goldwyn-Preminger production of *Porgy and Bess* lumbered into the Warner theater shortly before the death of Billie Holiday. These two facts are not, of course, related in any concrete or visible way. Yet, at the time I was watching Bess refuse Sporting Life's offer of "happy dust," Billie was in the hospital. A day or so later, I learned that she was under arrest for possession of heroin and that the police were at her bedside. A number of people, some of whom I knew, were trying to have the dying woman accorded more humane treatment. "She's sitting up today," said one of the last people to see her alive, "and if they don't bug her to death, she'll never die." Well, she *is* dead and I tend to concur with the woman who suggests that she was "bugged" to death. We are altogether too quick to disclaim responsibility for the fate which overtakes—so of-ten—so many gifted, driven, and erratic artists. Nobody pushed them to their deaths, we like to say. They jumped. Of course there is always some truth to this, but the pressures of the brutally indifferent world cannot be dismissed so speedily. Moreover, though we disclaim all responsibility for the failure of an artist, we are happy to take his success or survival as a flattering comment on ourselves. In fact, Billie was produced and destroyed by the same society. It had not the faintest intention of producing her and it did not intend to destroy her; but it has managed to do both with the same bland lack of concern.

But I do not intend to talk about Billie Holiday, who has gained her immortality dearly and who is in no need of any remarks of mine. She would have made a splendid, if some-what overwhelming Bess and, indeed, I should imagine that she was much closer to the original, whoever she was, of this portrait than anyone who has ever played or sung it. She was certainly much closer to it than Dorothy Dandridge, who plays the role, loosely speaking, in the present production. I am told that Miss Dandridge is a singer, though she seems never to have sung in the movies, but she is not an actress. Other people in *Porgy and Bess* are very gifted players indeed and under less depressing conditions have done admirable work; and there are others who give every indication of being able to act—if they could only find a director. In short, the saddest and most infuriating thing about the Hollywood production of *Porgy and Bess* is that Mr. Otto Preminger has a great many gifted people in front of his camera and not the remotest notion of what to do with any of them. The film cost upwards of six, or sixty, millions, or billions, of dollars but all that was needed for the present result was a little cardboard and a little condescension. As for the cardboard, consider the set, surely the most characterless in this opera's entire history; and as for condescension, consider the costumes, most of which seem to have been left over from one of those traveling "Tom" shows. All of this, needless to say, in color, on a screen a block wide, and in stereophonic sound—which last means that one is not allowed to listen to the music but is beaten over the head with it. The camera takes an interest in the proceedings which can best be described as discreet: trundling lamely behind Diahann Carroll, for example, while she mauls someone's heroically patient infant and waits for her man to be lost at sea. This event, like everything else in the movie, is so tastelessly overdone, so heavily telegraphed—rolling chords, dark sky, wind, ominous talk about hurricane bells, etc.—that there is really nothing left for the actors to do.

It is always necessary to suppose that the director knows more than his actors, knows, that is, how to get the best out of them, as individual performers and as an ensemble. This is a supposition which the facts do not always support. In the case of a white director called upon to direct a Negro cast, the supposition ceases—with very rare exceptions—to have any validity at all. The director *cannot* know anything about his company if he knows nothing about the life that produced them. We still live, alas, in a society mainly divided into black and white. Black people still do not, by and large, tell white people the truth and white people still do not want to hear it. By the time the cameras start rolling or rehearsals begin, the director is entirely at the mercy of his ignorance and of whatever system of theories or evasions he has evolved to cover his ignorance.

So is his company, which knows very well that, as he has no way of understanding the range of the Negro personality, he cannot possibly assess any given performer's potential. They know, in short, that in this limited sense, as in so many others, they are going to be ill-used and they resign themselves to it with as much sardonic good nature as they can muster. They are working, at least, and they will be seen; this part may lead to a better part or even better parts for others. So the disaster proceeds and the miracle is that even in so thoroughgoing a disaster as *Porgy and Bess* a couple of very effective moments are achieved. This is partly by virtue of the material. For we have not even mentioned the probable quality of the script on which the Negro performer will be working or the reasons that this script finds itself in production.

I like *Porgy and Bess* but I do not think it is a great American opera. We do not have one yet. It is—or it was, until Mr. Preminger got his hands on it—an extraordinarily vivid, good-natured, and sometimes moving show. It is the story of a Negro beggar-cripple and his prostitute-addict sweetheart and it takes place in a Charleston ghetto; and it owes its vitality to the fact that DuBose Heyward loved the people he was writing about. (By which I do not mean to imply that he loved all Negroes; he was a far better man than that.)

Just the same, it is a white man's vision of Negro life. This means that when it should be most concrete and searching it veers off into the melodramatic and the exotic. It seems to me that the author knew more about Bess than he understood and more about Porgy than he could face—than any of us, so far, can face. The idea of a Negro beggar-cripple who yet has enough force in his hands to kill a man and enough force in his body—to say nothing of his spirit—to possess a woman is surely an arresting one; as is the notion that this woman is, herself, because of her own uncontrollable drives, at the mercy of two whore masters, one of whom is a murderer and both of whom are dope addicts. And Heyward was not inventing all this but describing things that he had seen.

What has always been missing from George Gershwin's

opera is what the situation of Porgy and Bess says about the white world. It is because of this omission that Americans are so proud of the opera. It assuages their guilt about Negroes and it attacks none of their fantasies. Since Catfish Row is clearly such a charming place to live, there is no need for them to trouble their consciences about the fact that the people who live there are still not allowed to move anywhere else. Neither need they probe within their own lives to discover what the Negroes of Catfish Row really mean to them. But I am certainly not the first person to suggest that these Negroes seem to speak to them of a better life—better in the sense of being more honest, more open, and more free: in a word, more sexual. This is the cruelest fantasy of all, hard to forgive. It means that Negroes are penalized, and hideously, for what the general guilty imagination makes of them. This fantasy is at the bottom of almost all violence against Negroes; it is the reason they are not to be mixed in buses, houses, schools, jobs; they are to remain instead in Catfish Row, to have fish fries and make love. It is a fantasy which is tearing the nation to pieces and it is surely time we snapped out of it. For nobody in Catfish Row is having fish fries these days, and love is as rare and as difficult there as it has always been everywhere else. They struggle to pay the rent, the life insurance, the note due on the bedroom suite, the TV set, the refrigerator, the car. They worry about their children. They begin to hate each other, they turn to mysticism or to dope, they die there.

Obviously, neither Samuel Goldwyn nor Otto Preminger nor most of the audience for *Porgy and Bess* knows this, or wants to know it; and they would defend their production, I suppose, in the words of Mr. Preminger, as taking place in "a world which does not really exist." This is an entirely illegitimate defense, and, in any case, the people in front of the camera keep reminding one, most forcefully, of a *real* Catfish Row, real agony, real despair, and real love. Many of them have been there, after all, and they know. Out of one Catfish Row or another came the murdered Bessie Smith and the dead Billie Holiday and virtually every Negro performer this country has produced. Until today, no one wants to hear the story, and the Negro performer is still in battle with the white man's image of the Negro—which the white man clings to in order not to be forced to revise his image of himself. But in the Catfish Row where I was born, the truth, they said, will out. And certainly something comes "out" in Ruth Attaway's miming of "My Man's Gone Now," some genuine depth is touched which has nothing to do with the vulgar production in which she is, for the rest of the time, quite thanklessly trapped.

No one can admire Sidney Poitier more than I do, but he is entirely wrong for the role of Porgy. He does not succeed in making me believe that he is afraid of Crown, Crown's wounds, or the police, or buzzards—or, indeed, of anything else; nor do I believe for a moment that he is unable to get up off that cart and walk. The very qualities which lend him his distinction—his intelligence, virility, and grace—operate against him here. Yet he does do something else which is utterly remarkable, especially against the eery sexual chill emanating from Miss Dandridge: he makes me believe that he loves Bess. Poitier is, in fact, one of the very few actors on the American screen who is not compelled to spend most of his cinema time proving that he is not afraid of women. One is not compelled to watch him flexing his muscles and screwing up his courage in order to approach his mortal enemy and accomplish the unspeakable.

There is a great and instructive irony in this. That image one is compelled to hold of another person—in order, as I have said, to retain one's image of oneself—may become that person's trial, his cross, his death. It may or may not become his prison; but it inevitably becomes one's own. People who thought of Bessie Smith as a coarse black woman, and who let her die, were far less free than Bessie, who had escaped all their definitions by becoming herself. This is still the only way to become a man or a woman—or an artist. Now Billie Holiday has escaped forever from managers, landlords, locked hotels, fear, poverty, illness, and the watchdogs of morality and the law. "I had a long, long way to go," she used to sing. Well, she made it, all the way from Catfish Row, and no one has managed to define her yet. For the Negro is not a statistic or a problem or a fantasy: he is a person and it is simply not possible for one person to define another. Those who try soon find themselves trapped in their own definitions.

Whoever has found himself in a real Catfish Row knew that he had two choices, to live or to die, and some lived. If the day ever comes when the survivors of the place can be fooled into believing that the Hollywood cardboard even faintly resembles, or is intended to resemble, what it was like to be there, all our terrible and beautiful history will have gone for nothing and we will all be doomed to an unimaginable irreality. I prefer to believe that the day is coming when we will tell the truth about it—and ourselves. On that day, and not before that day, we can call ourselves free men.

Commentary, September 1959

They Can't Turn Back

I AM the only Negro passenger at Tallahassee's shambles of an airport. It is an oppressively sunny day. A black chauffeur, leading a small dog on a leash, is meeting his white employer. He is attentive to the dog, covertly very aware of me and respectful of her in a curiously watchful, waiting way. She is middle-aged, beaming and powdery-faced, delighted to see both the beings who make her life agreeable. I am sure that it has never occurred to her that either of them has the ability to judge her or would judge her harshly. She might almost, as she goes toward her chauffeur, be greeting a friend. No friend could make her face brighter. If she were smiling at me that way I would expect to shake her hand. But if I should put out my hand, panic, bafflement, and horror would then overtake that face, the atmosphere would darken, and danger, even the threat of death, would immediately fill the air.

On such small signs and symbols does the Southern cabala depend, and that is why I find the South so eerie and exhausting. This system of signs and nuances covers the mined terrain of the unspoken—the forever unspeakable—and everyone in the region knows his way across this field. This knowledge that a gesture can blow up a town is what the South refers to when it speaks of its "folkways." The fact that the gesture is not made is what the South calls "excellent race relations." It is impossible for any Northern Negro to become an adept of this mystery, not because the South's racial attitudes are not found in the North but because it has never been the North's necessity to construct an entire way of life on the legend of the Negro's inferiority. That is why the battle of Negro students for freedom here is really an attempt to free the entire region from the irrational terror that has ruled it for so long.

Of course, there are two points of view about the position of the Negro in the South and in this country, and what we have mainly heard for all these years has been the viewpoint of the white majority. The great significance of the present student generation is that it is through them that the point of view of the subjugated is finally and inexorably being expressed. What students are demanding is nothing less than a total revision of the ways in which Americans see the Negro, and this can only mean a total revision of the ways in which Americans see themselves.

The only other black man at the airport is one of the shapeless, shambling ones who seem always to be at Southern airports for the express purpose of making sure that I get my bags into the right taxicab—the right cab being the one that will take me. And he performs this function in the usual, headdown way. There is an alcove here with "Colored Waiting Room" printed above it. This makes me realize that a study of Federal directives regarding interstate travel would have been helpful only if I had come South to be a test case—that is, if I had come to *be* a story as opposed merely to writing one. As an interstate passenger, both I and the airport would be breaking the Federal law if I were to go into a colored waiting room.

I tell my taxi driver that I am going to the university. There is no need to specify which of the city's two universities I mean, and he tells me that there are people going out there all the time. *Oh, you people have caused a lot of talk*, he seems to be saying. He is a pallid, reddish type, around forty. I suppose, quite good-natured and utterly passive. There seems to be no point in asking what he thinks of the situation here. Even to mention it is to mark oneself as a troublemaker, which my typewriter, accent, and presence have already sufficiently done. Yet I have the feeling that he would love to say something about it—but perhaps if he did he would also be marked as a troublemaker. I volunteer a few comments about the landscape, in the faint hope of opening him up. The South *is* very beautiful but its beauty makes one sad because the lives that people live, and have lived here, are so ugly that now they cannot even speak to one another. It does not demand much reflection to be appalled at the inevitable state of mind achieved by people who dare not speak freely about those things which most disturb them.

The cab driver answers me pleasantly enough, taking his tone and also, alas, the limits of the conversation from me. We reach the campus of the Florida Agricultural and Me-

chanical University. It is a land-grant college. When it was
founded, in 1887, "by constitutional provision and legislative
enactment," it was the State Normal College for Colored.
Later on it became the Florida A. & M. College for Negroes.
After the Second World War—possibly, by this time, it had
become redundant—the "for Negroes" was dropped.

It is a very attractive campus, about a mile outside of town,
on the highest of Tallahassee's seven hills. My driver seems
very proud of the State of Florida for having brought it into
being. It is clear that he intends to disarm any criticism I may
have by his boasts about the dairy farm, the football field, the
guesthouse, the science buildings, the dormitories. He is particularly vocal about the football team, which seems to be,
here as on less beleaguered campuses, the most universally
respected of the university's achievements. F.A.M.U. turns
out, in fact, to be just as poor a center of learning as almost
any other university in this country. It is very nearly impossible, after all, to become an educated person in a country so
distrustful of the independent mind. The fact that F.A.M.U.
is a Negro university merely serves to demonstrate this American principle more clearly; and the pressure now being placed
on the Negro administration and faculty by the white Florida
State Board of Control further hampers the university's effectiveness as a training ground for future citizens. In fact, if
the Florida State Board of Control has its way, Florida will no
longer produce citizens, only black and white sheep. I do not
think or, more accurately, I refuse to think that it *will* have
its way but, at the moment, all that prevents this are the sorely
menaced students and a handful of even more sorely menaced
teachers and preachers.

My driver impresses upon me the newness of most of the
campus buildings. Later on I found out that these buildings
date from 1956, just two years after the Supreme Court declared the separate-but-equal statute to be invalid. The old
buildings, however, are dreadfully old and some of the faculty
live in barracks abandoned by the Air Force after the Second
World War. These too were "renovated" after the separate-
but-equal statute had been outlawed. During the time that
"separate-but-equal" was legal it did not matter how unequal
facilities for Negroes were. But now that the decree is illegal

the South is trying to make Negro facilities equal in order to keep them separate. From this it may not be unfair to conclude that a building, a campus or a system is considered renovated when it has merely been disguised. But I do not say any of this to my driver.

The university guesthouse is not expecting me; this frightens and angers me, and we drive to a motel outside of town. The driver and the Negro woman who runs the motel know each other in a casual, friendly way. I have only large bills and the driver has no change; but the woman tells him she will take the money I owe him out of my room rent and pay him when he comes again. They speak together exactly as though they were old friends, yet with this eerie distance between them. It is impossible to guess what they really think of each other.

Some students I met in New York had told me about Richard Haley. I had written him and he now arrives and places himself, shortly, as my ally and my guide. He and another member of F.A.M.U.'s staff had come to the airport earlier to meet me but had arrived too late. I tell him that I had concluded, from the fact that I was not met, that the F.A.M.U. people had not wanted me to come and had taken this way to let me know. Haley is a tall man in his early forties, who, shortly after I left Tallahassee, was dismissed from his position in the Music Department because he backed the student protest movement. He looked grave as I spoke, said he appreciated my bluntness and agreed that I might find hostility on the part of many of the people I was likely to meet. The events of the last few months had created great divisions in the Negro world. The F.A.M.U. president, for example, would not be glad to see me, for he and his supporters were hoping that the entire problem would somehow go away. These men are in an impossible position because their entire usefulness to the State of Florida depends on their ability to influence and control their students. But the students do not trust them, and this means the death of their influence and their usefulness alike. These men are as unable as is the State of Florida to find anything that will divert the students from their present course.

Until now the Negro college president's usefulness to the students, to the Negro community and to the state was determined by the number of alternatives to equality that he could produce out of the Southern hat. The docility of the students was the tacit price agreed upon for more funds, new buildings, more land. And these were tangible alternatives, for these things were hideously needed. As for curricular expansion, it usually came about in order to contain the discontent of Negro students. For example, at one time the state made no provision for the study of law at its Negro university. Students then applied, with every intention of testing the legality of the state's position, for instruction in white colleges. To prevent such testing, law was added to the Negro university curriculum. And what has happened is that precisely those dormitories, chemistry labs, and classrooms for which Negro presidents formerly bargained are now being built by the South in a doomed attempt to blunt the force of the Supreme Court decision against segregation. Therefore, the Negro college president has literally nothing more whatever to offer his students—except his support; if he gives this, of course, he promptly ceases to be a Negro college president. This is the death rattle of the Negro school system in the South. It is easy to judge those Negroes who, in order to keep their jobs, are willing to do everything in their power to subvert the student movement. But it is more interesting to consider what the present crisis reveals about the system under which they have worked so long.

For the segregated school system in the South has always been used by the Southern states as a means of controlling Negroes. When one considers the lengths to which the South has gone to prevent the Negro from ever becoming, or even feeling like, an equal, it is clear that the Southern states could not have used schools in any other way. This is one of the reasons, deliberate or not, that facilities were never equal. The demoralizing Southern school system also says a great deal about the indifference and irresponsibility of the North. The Negro presidents, principals and teachers would not be nearly so frightened of losing their jobs if the possibility of working in Northern schools were not almost totally closed to them.

Richard Haley found a room for me in town and introduced

me to the Tallahassee Inter-Civic Council, an organization
that makes no secret of its intention to remain in business
exactly as long as segregation does. It was called into existence
by a bus boycott in 1956. The Tallahassee boycott began five
months after the boycott in Montgomery, and in a similar
way, with the arrest of two Negro coeds who refused in a
crowded bus to surrender their seats to whites on the motor-
man's order. The boycott ran the same course, from cross-
burning, fury and intransigence on the part of the city and
bus officials, along with almost total and unexpected unanimity among the Negroes, to reprisal, intimidation and near-
bankruptcy of the bus company, which took its buses off the
streets for a month.

The Reverend C. K. Steele, president of the ICC, remembers that "those were rough days. Every time I drove my car
into the garage, I expected a bullet to come whizzing by my
head." He was not being fanciful: there are still bullet holes
in his living room window. The Reverend Daniel Speed, a
heavy, rough-looking man who might be completely terrifying
if he did not love to laugh and who owns a grocery store in
Tallahassee, organized the boycott motor pool, with the result
that all the windows were blown out of his store. The Speed
and Steele children are among the state's troublesome students. And Speed and Steele, along with Haley, are the people
whom the students most trust. Speed's support of the students
is particularly surprising in view of his extreme vulnerability as
a Negro businessman. "There has been," he told me, "much
reprisal," but he preferred that I remain silent about the
details.

Haley drove me to the hotel that he had found for me in
one of the two Negro sections of Tallahassee. This section
seems to be the more disreputable of the two, judging at least
from its long, unpaved streets, the gangs of loud, shabby men
and women, boys and girls, in front of the barbershops, the
poolroom, the Coffee House, the El Dorado Café and the
Chicken Shack. It is to this part of town that the F.A.M.U.
students come to find whisky—this is a dry county, which
means that whisky is plentiful and drunkards numerous—and
women who may or may not be wild but who are indisputably

available. My hotel is that hotel found in all small Southern towns—all small Southern towns, in any case, in which a hotel for Negroes exists. It is really only a rather large frame house, run by a widow who also teaches school in Quincy, a town not far away. It is doomed, of course, to be a very curious place, since everyone from N.A.A.C.P. lawyers, visiting church women and unfrocked preachers to traveling pimps and the simply, aimlessly, transiently amorous cannot possibly stay anywhere else. The widow knows this, which makes it impossible for her—since she is good-natured and also needs the money—to turn anyone away. My room is designed for sleeping—possibly—but not for work.

I type with my door open, because of the heat, and presently someone knocks, asking to borrow a pencil. But he does not really want a pencil, he is merely curious about who would be sitting at a typewriter so late at night—especially in this hotel. So I meet J., an F.A.M.U. student who is visiting a friend and also, somewhat improbably, studying for an exam. He is nineteen, very tall and slender, very dark, with extraordinarily intelligent and vivid brown eyes. It is, no doubt, only his youth and the curious combination of expectancy and vulnerability, which are among the attributes of youth, that cause me to think at once of my younger brothers when they were about his age.

He borrows the pencil and stands in the door a moment, being much more direct and curious about me than I am able to be about him. Nevertheless I learn that he is from a Florida town not very far away, has a sister but is the only son of very modestly situated people, is studying here on a scholarship and intends to become a bacteriologist. There is also about him something extremely difficult to describe because, while all of us have been there, no one wishes to remember it: the really agonizing privacy of the very young. They are only beginning to realize that the world is difficult and dangerous, that they are, themselves, tormentingly complex and that the years that stretch before them promise to be more dangerous than the years that are behind. And they always seem to be wrestling, in a private chamber to which no grownup has access, with monumental decisions.

Everyone laughs at himself once he has come through this

storm, but it is borne in on me, suddenly, that it *is* a storm, a storm, moreover, that not everyone survives and through which no one comes unscathed. Decisions made at this time always seem and, in fact, nearly always turn out to be decisions that determine the course and quality of a life. I wonder for the first time what it can be like to be making, in the adolescent dark, such decisions as this generation of students has made. They are in battle with more things than can be named. Not only must they summon up the force to face the law and the lawless—who are not, right now in Tallahassee, easily distinguishable—or the prospect of jail or the possibility of being maimed or killed; they are also dealing with problems yet more real, more dangerous and more personal than these: who they are, what they want, how they are to achieve what they want and how they are to reconcile their responsibilities to their parents with their responsibilities to themselves. Add to this exams; the peculiar difficulty of studying at all in so electric a situation; the curious demoralization that can occur in a youngster who is unable to respect his college president; and the enormous questions that, however dealt with or suppressed, must live in the mind of a student who is already, legally, a convict and is on a year's probation. These are all very serious matters, made the more serious by the fact that the students have so few models to emulate. The young grow up by watching and imitating their elders—it is their universal need to be able to revere them; but I submit that in this country today it is quite impossible for a young person to be speeded toward his maturity in this way. (This impossibility contains the key to what has been called "the beat generation.") What the elders have that they can offer the young is evidence, in their own flesh, of defeats endured, disasters passed and triumphs won. This is their moral authority, which, however mystical it may sound, is the only authority that endures; and it is through dealing with this authority that the young catch their first glimpse of what has been called the historical perspective. But this does not, and cannot exist, either privately or publicly, in a country that has told itself so many lies about its history, that, in sober fact, has yet to excavate its history from the rubble of romance. Nowhere is this clearer than in the South today, for if the tissue of myths that has for so long been propagated as Southern history had any actual validity, the white people of the South would be far less tormented people and the present generation of Negro students could never have been produced. And this is certainly one of the reasons that the example of Martin Luther King, Jr., means so much to these young people, even to those who know nothing about Gandhi and are not religious and ask hard questions about nonviolence. King is a serious man because the doctrine that he preaches is reflected in the life he leads. It is this acid test to which the young unfailingly put the old, this test, indeed, to which it is presently putting the country.

I suggest to J. that perhaps he and his friend would like a drink and we carry my half-bottle of bourbon down the hall. His friend turns out to be really his distant cousin and a gospel singer, and I begin to realize that J. himself is very religious in much the same way I remember myself as being. But once I myself had left the church I suppose I thought all young people had, forever. We talk, I somewhat lamely, about the religious standards J.'s family expects him to maintain. I can see, though I do not know if he can—yet—that he talks about these standards because he is beginning to wonder about his lifelong ability to live up to them. And this leads us, slowly, as the bourbon diminishes and the exam begins to be forgotten, to the incipient war between himself and his family and to his strange position on the F.A.M.U. campus. J. is one of those youngsters whose reality one tends to forget, who really believe in the Ten Commandments, for whom such words as "honor" and "truth" conjure up realities more real than the daily bread. From him I get my first picture of the campus, a picture that turns out to be quite accurate. The actively dissident students are a minority, though they have the tacit, potentially active support of the entire student body. J. is not one of the active students because he is going to school on a scholarship and is afraid of hurting his family by being thrown out of school. He himself confesses that the fact that he can be deterred by such a consideration means that he is "not ready for action yet." But it is very clear that this unreadiness troubles him greatly. "I don't know," he keeps saying, "I don't know what's the right thing to do." But he is also extremely unhappy on the campus because he is part of that minority of students who actually study. "You know," he says, with that rather bewildering abruptness of a youngster who has decided to talk, "the dean called me in one day and asked me why I didn't have any friends. He said: 'I notice you don't go out much for athletics.' I told him I didn't come to college to be an athlete, and anyway I walk all the time and I've got all the friends I need, everybody respects me and they leave me alone. I don't want to hang out with those kids. They come over here"—the section of town in which we were sitting—"every night. Well, I wasn't raised that way." And he looks defiant; he also looks bewildered. "I got the impression that he would like me better if I was more like all the other kids." And now he looks indignant. "Can you imagine that?"

I do not tell him how easily I can imagine that, and he gets around to saying that he would rather be in some other college—"farther north, in a bigger town. I don't like Tallahassee." But his parents want him to remain nearby. "But they're worried about my being here now, too, on account of the student sit-ins, so maybe—" He frowns. I get a glimpse of his parents, reading the newspapers, listening to the radio, burning up the long-distance wires each time Tallahassee is in the news. He tells me about the twelfth of March, 1960, when a thousand marching students were dispersed by tear gas bombs and thirty-five of them were arrested. "I was on the campus—of course I knew about it, the march, I mean. A girl came running back to campus, she was crying. It seemed the longest time before I could make any sense out of what she was saying and, Lord, I thought there was murder in that town." But he is most impressed by this fact: "I came over here that night and maybe you don't know it, but this part of town is always wide open but that night—" he gestures—"boy, nobody was in the streets. It was quiet. It was dark. It was like everybody'd died. I couldn't believe it—*nothing!*" He is silent. "I guess they were afraid." Then he looks at me quickly. "I don't blame them." I think that he means that he has no right to blame them. "I've got to make some kind of decision soon," he says.

I tell him that I am coming to the campus the next day,

and this elicits from him the names of students he wants me to meet, and also the names of Reverend Steele, Reverend Speed and Mr. Haley. I think it is safe to say that these three, along with one other person whom I cannot, for the person's sake, name—and it strikes me as horrendous that such a consideration should be necessary in this country—were the four Negro adults most respected by the students. This fact alone, since they are four utterly dedicated and intransigent people, ought to cause the municipality to reflect.

The next day I meet and briefly talk to A., lean, light-colored, taciturn, nineteen, from Ohio, a sociology major, who has been arrested for his part in the sit-ins and is on a year's probation. He is very matter-of-fact and quiet, very pleasant and respectful, and absolutely tense with the effort this costs him. Or perhaps I exaggerate, but I am always terribly struck by the abnormal self-containment of such young people. A. speaks about the possibility of transferring to another college. Somehow I do not get the impression that this possibility is very real to him, and then I realize that part of his tension is due to worry about his exams.

I also talk to V., eighteen, from Georgia, the skinniest child I have ever seen, who is also on a year's probation. He is rather bitter about the failure of the Negro community to respond as he had expected it to. "*I* haven't got to live with it," he tells me—somewhat unrealistically since, as it later turns out, his relatives are determined to keep him in Tallahassee and he will certainly be living with the problem for the next couple of years. "I did it for them. Looks like they don't appreciate it." He was appalled that the Negroes of Frenchtown—the section of town in which I am staying—should have vanished on the evening of March 12. I got the impression that he had rather expected them to meet the students in the street with trumpets drums and banners.

During the sit-ins of February the students had attempted, without success, to see the mayor and had spoken, without results, to the managers of the local Woolworth and McCrory dime stores. (As of this writing, the mayor of Tallahassee, who, I was told, uses the word "nigger" freely, has seen the students of his city only at lunch counters and in court.) It was to break the official and managerial silence that the sit-in of March 12 was organized. It was on this occasion that members of the White Citizens' Council, along with friends, sympathizers and people who "just happened to be in from the country for the day," met the students with baseball bats and knives. The good people of Tallahassee were not in the streets that day, of course; there were only the students, the police and the mob; and from this, which has now become a pattern in the South, I think it is safe to suggest that the convictions of the good people have less reality than the venom and panic of the worst. The police did not arrest any members of the mob but dispersed the students with tear gas and arrested, in all, thirty-five of them, twenty-nine Negroes and six whites.

Tallahassee has been quiet since March 12. The students felt that this time they themselves had been too quiet. Students from Tallahassee's two universities—Florida State, set up for whites, and Florida A. & M. for Negroes—are not allowed to visit each other's campuses. And so, on a Monday night during my May visit, they met in a church to make plans for a prayer meeting on the steps of the Capitol to remind the town that the students had no intention of giving up their struggle. There were about twenty students, in a ratio of about two Negroes to one white. It was a CORE meeting (the Congress of Racial Equality is an organization dedicated to bringing about change by passive resistance to social injustice), and Haley, Steele and the warrior to whom I can give no name were present as the Adult Leadership.

The prayer meeting had originally been the brain storm of R., a white student, foreign-born, very measured in speech, very direct in manner. There was first some uncertainty as to whether the prayer meeting should be held at all because of the pressure of exams and the homegoing plans of students, many of whom would have departed by Thursday.

There had also been the hope originally, since CORE is by now a dirty word in Tallahassee, of getting broader community support by asking the ministers of all faiths to give the news to their congregations and urge them to join the students. It was possible to gauge the depth of official hostility and community apathy by the discussion this suggestion precipitated.

One of the Negro students suggested that not all the ministers were to be trusted; one of them would surely feel it his duty to warn the police. A white coed student protested this vehemently, it being her view that there was no possible harm in an open prayer meeting—"It's just a y'all-come *prayer* meeting!"—and refused to believe that the police would not protect such spectacular piety. And this brought up the whole question of strategy: If the police were not warned, then the prayer meeting would have to be described as spontaneous. "But you can't," said a Negro coed, "*decide* to have a *spontaneous* prayer meeting. Especially not on the steps of the Capitol on Thursday at one o'clock." "Oh, it'll be spontaneous enough," said another student—my notes do not indicate his color—"by the time we start praying." D., a white coed, was against informing the police: "We love them dearly," she said with rather heavy sarcasm, "but I don't want them to get the impression that I'm asking their permission to do *anything*." "We're not asking their permission," said another white student. "We have every right to have prayer meeting and we're just informing them of it." "There's no reason," said the girl who felt that the police would not possibly do anything to peacefully praying people, "for them not to treat us just like they'd treat any other group of citizens."

This led to rather cynical laughter and someone, looking around the room, offered to name "oh, about twenty-five multicolored reasons." In all this there was no question of fear of the police; there was simply no belief whatever that they would act impartially or "that they might turn out," as Reverend Steele unconvincingly suggested, "to protect us." It is significant, I think, that none of the students, except for one lone girl—who turned out to be the daughter of a segregationist and who was therefore in a way defending her father against the imputation of villainy—believed that they could call on the police for protection. It was for this reason that it was decided not to ask the city's ministers to invite their congregations. "If too many people know, they'll just have time to call in all those people from the country and State troopers, and it'll be a mess," someone said. And this left open the great question of how, precisely, to handle the police. Was it, strategically speaking, better to inform them or better to give them no warning. "If you tell the police," said one Negro student, "it's just as good as telling the White Citizens' Council." Again it is significant that no one, white or black, contested this statement. It was finally decided not to inform the police and to arrive at the steps of the Capitol singly or in pairs. "That way they won't have time to get their boys together."

Now the prayer meeting, in fact, did not take place. Phones began ringing early in the morning of the scheduled day, warning that news of the plans had somehow leaked out and the students could expect great trouble if they tried to get to the Capitol.

A day later I talk with Haley and ask him what, in his judgment, is the attitude of most white people in the South. I confess myself baffled. Haley doesn't answer my question directly.

"What we're trying to do," he tells me, "is to sting their consciences a little. They don't want to think about it. Well, we must make them think about it.

"When they come home from work," Haley continues, "and turn on the TV sets and there *you* are—" he means *you the Negro*—"on your way to jail again, and they know, at the bottom of their hearts, that it's not because you've done anything wrong—something happens in them, something's got to happen in them. They're human beings, too, you know," and he smiles. We are standing in the hall of the university's music building.

It is near the end of the day and he is about to go and give an exam. I have heard him say what he has just told me more than once to some embittered and caustic student, trying with all his might to inculcate in the student that charity without which—and how this country proves it!—social change is meaningless. Haley always speaks very quietly. "We have to wake up all those people in the middle," he says. "Most white people in the South don't especially like the idea of integration, but they'll go along with it. By and by they'll get used to it."

And all this, I think to myself, will only be a page in history. I cannot help wondering what kind of page it will be, whether we are hourly, in this country now, recording our salvation or our doom.

I can tell from the way Haley looks at me that he knows that *I* am feeling rather caustic and embittered today. I wonder how *he* feels. I know that he is afraid of losing his job. I admire him much more than I can say for playing so quietly a chips-down game.

Haley goes off to give his exam and I walk outside, waiting for my taxi and watching the students. Only a decade and a half divide us, but what changes have occurred in those fifteen years! The world into which I was born must seem as remote to them as the flood. I watch them. Their walk, talk, laughter are as familiar to me as my skin, and yet there is something new about them. They remind me of all the Negro boys and girls I have ever known and they remind me of myself; but, really, I was never like these students. It took many years of vomiting up all the filth I'd been taught about myself, and half-believed, before I was able to walk on the earth as though I had a right to be here.

Well, they didn't have to come the way I came. This is what I've heard Negro parents say, with a kind of indescribable pride and relief, when one of their children graduated or won an award or sailed for Europe: began, in short, to move into the world as a free person. The society into which American Negro children are born has always presented a particular challenge to Negro parents. This society makes it necessary that they establish in the child a force that will cause him to *know* that the world's definition of his place and the means used by the world to make this definition binding are not for a moment to be respected. This means that the parent must prove daily, in his own person, how little the force of the world avails against the force of a person who is determined to be free. Now, this is a cruel challenge, for the force of the world is immense. That is why the vow *My children won't come like I came* is nothing less than a declaration of war, a declaration that has led to innumerable casualties. Generations of Negro children have said, as all the students here have said: "My Daddy taught me never to bow my head to nobody." But sometimes Daddy's head was bowed: frequently Daddy was destroyed.

These students were born at the very moment at which Europe's domination of Africa was ending. I remember, for example, the invasion of Ethiopia and Haile Selassie's vain appeal to the League of Nations, but they remember the Bandung Conference and the establishment of the Republic of Ghana.

Americans keep wondering what has "got into" the students. What has "got into" them is their history in this country. They are not the first Negroes to face mobs: they are merely the first Negroes to frighten the mob more than the mob frightens them. Many Americans may have forgotten, for example, the reign of terror in the 1920's that drove Negroes out of the South. Five hundred thousand moved North in one year. Some of the people who got to the North barely in time to be born are the parents of the students now going to school. This was forty years ago, and not enough has happened—not enough freedom has happened. But these young people are determined to make it happen and make it happen now. They cannot be diverted. It seems to me that they are the only people in this country now who really believe in freedom. Insofar as they can make it real for themselves, they will make it real for all of us. The question with which they present the nation is whether or not we really want to be free. It is because these students remain so closely related to their past that they are able to face with such authority a population ignorant of its history and enslaved by a myth. And by this population I do not mean merely the unhappy people who make up the Southern mobs. I have in mind nearly all Americans.

These students prove unmistakably what most people in this country have yet to discover: that time is real.

Mademoiselle, August 1960

The Dangerous Road Before
Martin Luther King

I FIRST met Martin Luther King, Jr. nearly three years ago now, in Atlanta, Georgia. He was there on a visit from his home in Montgomery. He was "holed up," he was seeing no one, he was busy writing a book—so I was informed by the friend who, mercilessly, at my urgent request, was taking me to King's hotel. I felt terribly guilty about interrupting him but not guilty enough to let the opportunity pass. Still, having been raised among preachers, I would not have been surprised if King had cursed out the friend, refused to speak to me, and slammed the door in our faces. Nor would I have blamed him if he had, since I knew that by this time he must have been forced to suffer many an admiring fool.

But the Reverend King is not like any preacher I have ever met before. For one thing, to state it baldly, I liked him. It is rare that one *likes* a world-famous man—by the time they become world-famous they rarely like themselves, which may account for this antipathy. Yet King is immediately and tremendously winning, there is really no other word for it; and there he stood, with an inquiring and genuine smile on his face, in the open door of his hotel room. Behind him, on a desk, was a wilderness of paper. He looked at his friend, he looked at me, I was introduced; he smiled and shook my hand and we entered the room.

I do not remember much about that first meeting because I was too overwhelmed by the fact that I was meeting him at all. There were millions of questions that I wanted to ask him, but I feared to begin. Besides, his friend had warned me not to "bug" him, I was not there in a professional capacity, and the questions I wanted to ask him had less to do with his public role than with his private life. When I say "private life" I am not referring to those maliciously juicy tidbits, those meaningless details, which clutter up the gossip columns and muddy everybody's mind and obliterate the humanity of the subject as well as that of the reader. I wanted to ask him how it felt to be standing where he stood, how he bore it, what complex of miracles had prepared him for it. But such questions can scarcely be asked, they can scarcely be answered.

And King does not like to talk about himself. I have described him as winning, but he does not give the impression of being particularly outgoing or warm. His restraint is not, on the other hand, of that icily uneasy, nerve-racking kind to be encountered in so many famous Negroes who have allowed their aspirations and notoriety to destroy their identities and who always seem to be giving an uncertain imitation of some extremely improbable white man. No, King impressed me then and he impresses me now as a man solidly anchored in those spiritual realities concerning which he can be so eloquent. This divests him of the hideous piety which is so prevalent in his profession, and it also saves him from the ghastly self-importance which until recently, was all that allowed one to be certain one was addressing a Negro leader. King cannot be considered a chauvinist at all, not even incidentally, or part of the time, or under stress, or subconsciously. What he says to Negroes he will say to whites; and what he says to whites he will say to Negroes. He is the first Negro leader in my experience, or the first in many generations, of whom this can be said; most of his predecessors were in the extraordinary position of saying to white men, *Hurry*, while saying to black men, *Wait*. This fact is of the utmost importance. It says a great deal about the situation which produced King and in which he operates; and, of course, it tells us a great deal about the man.

"He came through it all," said a friend of his to me, with wonder and not a little envy, "really unscarred. He never went around fighting with himself, like we all did." The "we" to whom this friend refers are all considerably older than King, which may have something to do with this lightly sketched species of schizophrenia; in any case, the fact that King really loves the people he represents and has—*therefore*—no hidden, interior need to hate the white people who oppose him has had and will, I think, continue to have the most far-reaching and unpredictable repercussions on our racial situation. It need scarcely be said that our racial situation is far more complex and dangerous than we are prepared to think of it as being—since our major desire is not to think of it at all—and King's role in it is of an unprecedented difficulty.

He is not, for example, to be confused with Booker T. Washington, whom we gratefully allowed to solve the racial problem singlehandedly. It was Washington who assured us, in 1895, one year before it became the law of the land, that the education of Negroes would not give them any desire to become equals; they would be content to remain—or, rather, after living for generations in the greatest intimacy with whites, to become—separate. It is a measure of the irreality to which the presence of the Negro had already reduced the nation that this utterly fantastic idea, which thoroughly controverts the purpose of education, which has no historical or psychological validity, and which denies all the principles on which the country imagines itself to have been founded, was not only accepted with cheers but became the cornerstone of an entire way of life. And this did not come about, by the way, merely because of the venom or villainy of the South. It could never have come about at all without the tacit consent of the North; and this consent robs the North, historically and actually, of any claim to moral superiority. The failure of the government to make any realistic provision for the education of tens of thousands of illiterate former slaves had the effect of dumping this problem squarely into the lap of one man—who knew, whatever else he may not have known, that the education of Negroes had somehow to be accomplished. Whether or not Washington believed what he said is certainly an interesting question. But he *did* know that he could accomplish his objective by telling white men what they wanted to hear. And it has never been very difficult for a Negro in this country to figure out what white men want to hear: he takes his condition as an echo of their desires.

There will be no more Booker T. Washingtons. And whether we like it or not, and no matter how hard or how long we oppose it, there will be no more segregated schools, there will be no more segregated anything. King is entirely right when he says that segregation is dead. The real question which faces the Republic is just how long, how violent, and how expensive the funeral is going to be; and this question it is up to the Republic to resolve, it is not really in King's hands. The sooner the corpse is buried, the sooner we can get around to the far more taxing and rewarding problems of integration, or what King calls community, and what I think of as the achievement of nationhood, or, more simply and cruelly, the growing up of this dangerously adolescent country.

I saw King again, later that same evening, at a party given by this same friend. He came late, did not stay long. I remember him standing in the shadows of the room, near a bookcase, drinking something nonalcoholic, and being patient with the interlocutor who had trapped him in this spot. He obviously wanted to get away and go to bed. King is somewhat below what is called average height, he is sturdily built, but is not quite as heavy or as stocky as he had seemed to me at first. I remember feeling, rather as though he were a younger, much-loved, and menaced brother, that he seemed very slight and vulnerable to be taking on such tremendous odds.

I was leaving for Montgomery the next day, and I called on King in the morning to ask him to have someone from the Montgomery Improvement Association meet me at the airport. It was he who had volunteered to do this for me, since he knew that I knew no one there, and he also probably realized that I was frightened. He was coming to Montgomery on Sunday to preach in his own church.

Montgomery is the cradle of the Confederacy, an unlucky distinction which no one in Montgomery is allowed to forget. The White House which symbolized and housed that short-lived government is still standing, and "people," one of the Montgomery ministers told me, "walk around in those halls and cry." I do not doubt it, the people of Montgomery having inherited nothing less than an ocean of spilt milk. The boycott had been over for a year by the time I got there, and had been ended by a federal decree outlawing segregation in the busses. Therefore, the atmosphere in Montgomery was extraordinary. I think that I have never been in a town so aimlessly hostile, so baffled and demoralized. Whoever has a stone to fling, and flings it, is then left without any weapons; and this was (and remains) the situation of the white people in Montgomery.

I took a bus ride, for example, solely in order to observe the situation on the busses. As I stepped into the bus, I suddenly remembered that I had neglected to ask anyone the price of a bus ride in Montgomery, and so I asked the driver. He gave me the strangest, most hostile of looks, and turned his face away. I dropped fifteen cents into the box and sat down, placing myself, delicately, just a little forward of the center of the bus. The driver had seemed to feel that my question was but another Negro trick, that I had something up my sleeve, and that to answer my question in any way would be to expose himself to disaster. He could not guess what I was thinking, and he was not going to risk further personal demoralization by trying to. And this spirit was the spirit of the town. The bus pursued its course, picking up white and Negro passengers. Negroes sat where they pleased, none very far back; one large woman, carrying packages, seated herself directly behind the driver. And the whites sat there, ignoring them, in a huffy, offended silence.

This silence made me think of nothing so much as the silence which follows a really serious lovers' quarrel: the whites, beneath their cold hostility, were mystified and deeply hurt. They had been betrayed by the Negroes, not merely because the Negroes had declined to remain in their "place," but because the Negroes had refused to be controlled by the town's image of them. And, without this image, it seemed to me, the whites were abruptly and totally lost. The very foundations of their private and public worlds were being destroyed.

I had never heard King preach, and I went on Sunday to hear him at his church. This church is a red brick structure, with a steeple, and it directly faces, on the other side of the street, a white, domed building. My notes fail to indicate whether this is the actual capitol of the state or merely a courthouse; but the conjunction of the two buildings, the steepled one low and dark and tense, the domed one higher and dead white and forbidding, sums up, with an explicitness a set designer might hesitate to copy, the struggle now going on in Montgomery.

At that time in Montgomery, King was almost surely the most beloved man there. I do not think that one could have entered any of the packed churches at that time, if King was present, and not have felt this. Of course, I think that King would be loved by his congregations in any case, and there is always a large percentage of church women who adore the young male pastor, and not always, or not necessarily, out of those grim, psychic motives concerning which everyone today is so knowledgeable. No, there was a feeling in this church which quite transcended anything I have ever felt in a church before. Here it was, totally familiar and yet completely new, the packed church, glorious with the Sunday finery of the women, solemn with the touching, gleaming sobriety of the men, beautiful with children. Here were the ushers, standing in the aisles in white dresses or in dark suits, with arm bands on. People were standing along each wall, beside the windows, and standing in the back. King and his lieutenants were in the pulpit, young Martin—as I was beginning to think of him—in the center chair.

When King rose to speak—to preach—I began to understand how the atmosphere of this church differed from that of all the other churches I have known. At first I thought that the great emotional power and authority of the Negro church was being put to a new use, but this is not exactly the case. The Negro church was playing the same role which it has always played in Negro life, but it had acquired a new power.

Until Montgomery, the Negro church, which has always been the place where protest and condemnation could be most vividly articulated, also operated as a kind of sanctuary. The minister who spoke could not hope to effect any objective change in the lives of his hearers, and the people did not expect him to. All they came to find, and all that he could give them, was the sustenance for another day's journey. Now, King could certainly give his congregation that, but he could also give them something more than that, and he had. It is true that it was *they* who had begun the struggle of which he was now the symbol and the leader; it is true that it had taken all of *their* insistence to overcome in him a grave reluctance to stand where he now stood. But it is also true, and it does not happen often, that once he had accepted the place they had prepared for him, their struggle became absolutely indistinguishable from his own, and took over and controlled his life. He suffered with them and, thus, he helped them to suffer. The joy which filled this church, therefore, was the joy achieved by people who have ceased to delude themselves about an intolerable situation, who have found their prayers for a leader miraculously answered, and who now know that they can change their situation, if they will.

And, surely, very few people had ever spoken to them as King spoke. King is a great speaker. The secret of his greatness does not lie in his voice or his presence or his manner, though it has something to do with all these; nor does it lie in his verbal range or felicity, which are not striking; nor does he have any capacity for those stunning, demagogic flights of the imagination which bring an audience cheering to its feet. The secret lies, I think, in his intimate knowledge of the people he is addressing, be they black or white, and in the forthrightness with which he speaks of those things which hurt and baffle them. He does not offer any easy comfort and this keeps his hearers absolutely tense. He allows them their self-respect—indeed, he insists on it.

"We know," he told them, "that there are many things wrong in the white world. But there are many things wrong in the black world, too. We can't keep on blaming the white man. There are many things we must do for ourselves."

He suggested what some of these were:

"I know none of you make enough money—but save some of it. And there are some things we've got to face. I know the situation is responsible for a lot of it, but do you know that Negroes are 10 per cent of the population of St. Louis and are responsible for 58 per cent of its crimes? We've got to face that. And we have to do something about our moral standards. And we've got to stop lying to the white man. Every time you let the white man think *you* think segregation is right, you are co-operating with him in doing *evil*.

"The next time," he said, "the white man asks you what you think of segregation, you tell him, Mr. Charlie, I think it's wrong and I wish you'd do something about it by nine o'clock tomorrow morning!"

This brought a wave of laughter and King smiled, too. But he had meant every word he said, and he expected his hearers to act on them. They also expected this of themselves, which is not the usual effect of a sermon; and that they are living up to their expectations no white man in Montgomery will deny.

There was a dinner in the church basement afterwards, where, for the first time, I met Mrs. King—light brown, delicate, really quite beautiful, with a wonderful laugh—and watched young Martin circulating among church members and visitors. I overheard him explaining to someone that bigotry was a disease and that the greatest victim of this disease was not the bigot's object, but the bigot himself. And these people could only be saved by love. In liberating oneself, one was also liberating them. I was shown, by someone else, the damage done to the church by bombs. King did not mention the bombing of his own home, and I did not bring it up. Late the next night, after a mass meeting in another church, I flew to Birmingham.

I did not see King again for nearly three years. I saw him in Atlanta, just after his acquittal by a Montgomery court of charges of perjury, tax evasion, and misuse of public funds. He had moved to Atlanta and was co-pastor, with his father, of his father's church. He had made this move, he told me, because the pressures on him took him away from Montgomery for such excessively long periods that he did not feel that he was properly fulfilling his ministerial duties there. An attempt had been made on his life—in the North, by a mysterious and deranged Negro woman; and he was about to receive, in the state of Georgia, for driving without a resident driver's license, a suspended twelve-month sentence.

And, since I had last seen him, the Negro student movement had begun and was irresistibly bringing about great shifts and divisions in the Negro world, and in the nation. In short, by the time we met again, he was more beleaguered than he had ever been before, and not only by his enemies in the white South. Three years earlier, I had not encountered very many people—I am speaking now of Negroes—who were really critical of him. But many more people seemed critical of him now, were bitter, disappointed, skeptical. None of this had anything to do—I want to make this absolutely clear—with his personal character or his integrity. It had to do with his effectiveness as a leader. King has had an extraordinary effect in the Negro world, and therefore in the nation, and is now in the center of an extremely complex cross fire.

He was born in Atlanta in 1929. He has Irish and Indian blood in his veins—Irish from his father's, Indian from his mother's side. His maternal grandfather built Ebenezer Baptist Church, which, as I have said, young Martin now co-pastors with his father. This grandfather seems to have been an extremely active and capable man, having been one of the NAACP leaders in Atlanta thirty or forty years ago, and having been instrumental in bringing about the construction of Atlanta's first Negro high school. The paternal grandfather is something else again, a poor, violent, and illiterate farmer who tried to find refuge from reality in drinking. He clearly had a great influence on the formation of the character of Martin, Sr., who determined, very early, to be as unlike his father as possible.

Martin, Sr. came to Atlanta in 1916, a raw, strapping country boy, determined, in the classic American tradition, to rise above his station. It could not have been easy for him in the Deep South of 1916, but he was, luckily, too young for the Army, and prices and wages rose during the war, and his improvident father had taught him the value of thrift. So he got his start. He studied in evening school, entered Atlanta's Morehouse College in 1925, and graduated in June of 1930, more than a year after Martin was born. (There are two other children, an older girl who now teaches at Spelman College, and a younger boy, pastor of a church in Noonan, Georgia.) By this time, Martin, Sr. had become a preacher, and was pastor of two small churches; and at about this time, his father-in-law asked him to become the assistant pastor of Ebenezer Baptist Church, which he did.

His children have never known poverty, and Martin, Sr. is understandably very proud of this. "My prayer," he told me, "was always: Lord, grant that my children will not have to come the way I did." They didn't, they haven't, the prayers certainly did no harm. But one cannot help feeling that a person as single-minded and determined as the elder Reverend King clearly is would have accomplished anything he set his hand to, anyway.

"I equipped myself to give them the comforts of life," he says. "Not to waste, not to keep up with the Joneses, but just to be comfortable. We've never lived in a rented house—and never ridden *too* long in a car on which payment was due."

He is naturally very proud of Martin, Jr. but he claims to be not at all surprised. "He sacrificed to make himself ready"—ready, that is, for a trial, or a series of trials, which might have been the undoing of a lesser man. Yet, though he is not surprised at the extraordinary nature of his son's eminence, he *was* surprised when, at college, Martin decided that he was called to preach. He had expected him to become a doctor or a lawyer because he always spoke of these professions as though he aspired to them.

As he had; and since, as I have said, King is far from garrulous on the subject of his interior life, it is somewhat difficult to know what led him to make this switch. He had already taken pre-medical and law courses. But he had been raised by a minister, an extremely strong-minded one at that, and in an extraordinarily peaceful and protected way. "Never," says his father, "has Martin known a fuss or a fight or a strike back in the home." On the other hand, there are some things from which no Negro can really be protected, for which he can only be prepared; and Martin, Sr. was more successful than most fathers in accomplishing this strenuous and delicate task. "I have never believed," he says, "that anybody was better than I." That this is true would seem to be proved by the career of his son, who *"never went around fighting with himself, like we all did."*

Here, speculation is really on very marshy ground, for the father must certainly have fought in himself some of the battles from which young Martin was protected. We have only to consider the era, especially in the South, to realize that this must be true. And it must have demanded great steadiness of mind, as well as great love, to hide so successfully from his children the evidence of these battles. And, since salvation, humanly speaking, is a two-way street, I suggest that, if the father saved the children, it was, almost equally, the children who saved him. It would seem that he was able, with rare success, to project onto his children, or at least onto one of them, a sense of life as he himself would have liked to live it, and somehow made real in their personalities principles on which he himself must often have found it extremely dangerous and difficult to act. Martin, Sr. is regarded with great ambivalence by both the admirers and detractors of his son, and I shall, alas, shortly have more to say concerning his generation; but I do not think that the enormous achievement sketched above can possibly be taken away from him.

Again, young Martin's decision to become a minister has everything to do with his temperament, for he seems always to have been characterized by his striking mixture of steadiness and peace. He apparently did the normal amount of crying in his childhood, for I am told that his grandmother "couldn't stand to see it." But he seems to have done very little complaining; when he was spanked, "he just stood there and took it"; he seems to have been incapable of carrying grudges; and when he was attacked, he did not strike back.

From King's own account, I can only guess that this decision was aided by the fact that, at Morehouse College, he was asked to lead the devotions. The relationship thus established between himself and his contemporaries, or between himself and himself, or between himself and God, seemed to work for him as no other had. Also, I think it is of the utmost importance to realize that King loves the South; many Negroes do. The ministry seems to afford him the best possible vehicle for the expression of that love. At that time in his life, he was discovering "the beauty of the South"; he sensed in the people "a new determination"; and he felt that there was a need for "a new, courageous witness."

But it could not have occurred to him, of course, that *he* would be, and in such an unprecedented fashion, that witness. When Coretta King—then Coretta Scott—met him in Boston, where he was attending Boston University and she was studying at the New England Conservatory of Music, she found him an earnest, somewhat too carefully dressed young man. He had gone from Morehouse to Crozer Theological Seminary in Pennsylvania; the latter institution was interracial, which may have had something to do with his self-consciousness. He was fighting at that time to free himself from all the stereotypes of the Negro, an endeavor which does not leave much room for spontaneity. Both he and Coretta were rather lonely in Boston, and for similar reasons. They were both very distinguished and promising young people, which means that they were also tense, self-conscious, and insecure. They were inevitably cut off from the bulk of the Negro community and their role among whites had to be somewhat ambiguous, for they were not being judged merely as themselves—or, anyway, they could scarcely afford to think so. They were responsible for the good name of all the Negro people.

Coretta had perhaps had more experience than Martin in this role. The more I spoke to her, the more I realized how her story illuminates that of her husband. She had come from Lincoln High in Marion, Alabama, to Antioch College in Ohio, part of one of the earliest groups of Negro students accepted there. She was thus, in effect, part of an experiment, and though she took it very well and can laugh about it now, she certainly must have had her share of exasperated and lonely moments. The social mobility of a Negro girl, especially in such a setting, is even more severely circumscribed than that of a Negro male, and any lapse or error on her part is far more dangerous. From Antioch, Coretta eventually came to Boston on a scholarship and by this time a certain hoydenish, tomboy quality in her had begun, apparently, to be confirmed. The atmosphere at Antioch had been entirely informal, which pleased Coretta; I gather that at this time in her life she was usually to be seen in sweaters, slacks, and scarves. It was a ferociously formal young man and a ferociously informal young girl who finally got together in Boston.

Martin immediately saw through Coretta's disguise, and informed her on their first or second meeting that she had all the qualities he wanted in a wife. Coretta's understandable tendency was to laugh at this; but this tendency was checked by the rather frightening suspicion that he meant it; if he had not meant it, he would not have said it. But a great deal had been invested in Coretta's career as a singer, and she did not feel that she had the right to fail all the people who had done so much to help her. "And I'd certainly never intended to marry a *minister*. It was true that he didn't seem like any of the ministers I'd met, but—still—I thought of how circumscribed my life might become." By circumscribed, she meant dull; she could not possibly have been more mistaken.

What had really happened, in Coretta's case, as in so many others, was that life had simply refused to recognize her private timetable. She had always intended to marry, but tidily, possibly meeting her husband at the end of a triumphant concert tour. However, here he was now, exasperatingly early, and she had to rearrange herself around this fact. She and Martin were married on June 18, 1953. By now, naturally, it is she whom Martin sometimes accuses of thinking too much about clothes. "People who are doing something don't have time to be worried about all that," he has informed her. Well, he certainly ought to know.

Coretta King told me that from the time she reached Boston and all during Martin's courtship, and her own indecision, she yet could not rid herself of a feeling that all that was happening had been, somehow, preordained. And one does get an impression, until this point in the King story at least, that inexorable forces which none of us really know anything about were shaping and preparing him for that fateful day in Montgomery. Everything that he will need has been delivered, so to speak, and is waiting to be used. Everything, including the principle of nonviolence. It was in 1950 that Dr. Mordecai W. Johnson of Howard University visited India. King heard one of the speeches Johnson made on his return, and it was from this moment that King became interested in Gandhi as a figure, and in nonviolence as a way of life. Later, in 1957, he would visit India himself.

But, so far, of course, we are speaking after the fact. Plans and patterns are always more easily discernible then. This is not so when we try to deal with the present, or attempt speculations about the future.

Immediately after the failure, last June, of Montgomery's case against him, King returned to Atlanta. I entered, late, on a Sunday morning, the packed Ebenezer Baptist Church, and King was already speaking.

He did not look any older, and yet there was a new note of anguish in his voice. He was speaking of his trial. He described the torment, the spiritual state of people who are committed to a wrong, knowing that it is wrong. He made the trials of these white people far more vivid than anything he himself might have endured. They were not ruled by hatred, but by terror; and, therefore, if community was ever to be achieved, these people, the potential destroyers of the person, must not be hated. It was a terrible plea—to the people; and it was a prayer. In *Varieties of Religious Experience*, William James speaks of vastation—of *being*, as opposed to merely regarding, the monstrous creature which came to him in a vision. It seemed to me, though indeed I may be wrong, that something like this had happened to young Martin Luther— that he had looked on evil a long, hard, lonely time. For evil is in the world: it may be in the world to stay. No creed and no dogma are proof against it, and indeed no person is; it is always the naked person, alone, who, over and over and over again, must wrest his salvation from these black jaws. Perhaps young Martin was finding a new and more somber meaning in the command: "Overcome evil with good." The command does not suggest that to overcome evil is to eradicate it.

King spoke more candidly than I had ever heard him speak before, of his bitterly assaulted pride, of his shame, when he found himself accused, before all the world, of having used and betrayed the people of Montgomery by stealing the money they had entrusted to him. "I knew it wasn't true— but who would believe me?"

He had canceled a speaking trip to Chicago, for he felt that he could not face anyone. And he prayed; he walked up and down in his study, alone. It was borne in on him, finally, that he had no right *not* to go, no right to hide. "I called the airport and made another reservation and went on to Chicago." He appeared there, then, as an accused man, and gave us no details of his visit, which did not, in any case, matter. For if he had not been able to face Chicago, if he had not won that battle with himself, he would have been defeated long before his entrance into that courtroom in Montgomery.

When I saw him the next day in his office, he was very different, kind and attentive, but far away. A meeting of the Southern Christian Leadership Conference was to begin that day, and I think his mind must have been on that. The beleaguered ministers of the Deep South were coming to Atlanta that day in order to discuss the specific situations which confronted them in their particular towns or cities, and King was their leader. All of them had come under immensely greater local pressure because of the student sit-in movement. Inevitably, they were held responsible for it, even though they might very well not have known until reading it in the papers that the students had carried out another demonstration. I do not mean to suggest that there is any question of their support of the students—they may or may not be responsible *for* them but they certainly consider themselves responsible *to* them. But all this, I think, weighed on King rather heavily.

He talked about his visit to India and its effect on him. He was hideously struck by the poverty, which he talked about in great detail. He was also much impressed by Nehru, who had, he said, extraordinary qualities of "perception and dedication and courage—far more than the average American politician." We talked about the South. "Perhaps 4 or 5 per cent of the people are to be found on either end of the racial scale"— either actively for or actively against desegregation; "the rest are passive adherents. The sin of the South is the sin of conformity." And he feels, as I do, that much of the responsibility for the situation in which we have found ourselves since 1954 is due to the failure of President Eisenhower to make any coherent, any guiding statement concerning the nation's greatest moral and social problem.

But we did not discuss the impending conference which, in any case, he could scarcely have discussed with me. And we did not discuss any of the problems which face him now and make his future so problematical. For he could not have discussed these with me, either.

That white men find King dangerous is well known. They can say so. But many Negroes also find King dangerous, but cannot say so, at least not publicly. The reason that the Negroes of whom I speak are trapped in such a stunning silence is that to say what they really feel would be to deny the entire public purpose of their lives.

Now, the problem of Negro leadership in this country has always been extremely delicate, dangerous, and complex. The term itself becomes remarkably difficult to define, the moment one realizes that the real role of the Negro leader, in the eyes of the American Republic, was not to make the Negro a first-class citizen but to keep him content as a second-class one. This sounds extremely harsh, but the record bears me out. And this problem, which it was the responsibility of the entire country to face, was dumped into the laps of a few men. Some of them were real leaders and some of them were false. Many of the greatest have scarcely ever been heard of.

The role of the genuine leadership, in its own eyes, was to destroy the barriers which prevented Negroes from fully participating in American life, to prepare Negroes for first-class citizenship, while at the same time bringing to bear on the Republic every conceivable pressure to make this status a reality. For this reason, the real leadership was to be found everywhere, in law courts, colleges, churches, hobo camps: on picket lines, freight trains, and chain gangs; and in jails. Not everyone who was publicized as a leader really was one. And many leaders who would never have dreamed of applying the term to themselves were considered by the Republic when it knew of their existence at all—to be criminals. This is, of course, but the old and universal story of poverty in battle with privilege, but we tend not to think of old and universal stories as occurring in our brand new and still relentlessly parochial land.

The real goal of the Negro leader was nothing less than the total integration of Negroes in all levels of the national life. But this could rarely be stated so baldly; it often could not be stated at all; in order to begin Negro education, for example, Booker Washington had found it necessary to state the exact opposite. The reason for this duplicity is that the goal contains the assumption that Negroes are to be treated, in all respects, exactly like all other citizens of the Republic. This is an idea which has always had extremely rough going in America. For one thing, it attacked, and attacks, a vast complex of special interests which would lose money and power if the situation of the Negro were to change. For another, the idea of freedom necessarily carries with it the idea of sexual freedom: the freedom to meet, sleep with, and marry whom one chooses. It would be fascinating, but I am afraid we must postpone it for the moment, to consider just why so many people appear to be convinced that Negroes would then immediately meet, sleep with, and marry white women; who, remarkably enough, are only protected from such undesirable alliances by the majesty and vigilance of the law.

The duplicity of the Negro leader was more than matched by the duplicity of the people with whom he had to deal. They, and most of the country, felt at the very bottom of their hearts that the Negro was inferior to them and, therefore, merited the treatment that he got. But it was not always politic to say this, either. It certainly could never be said over the bargaining table, where white and black men met.

The Negro leader was there to force from his adversary whatever he could get: new schools, new schoolrooms, new houses, new jobs. He was invested with very little power because the Negro vote had so very little power. (Other Negro leaders were trying to correct *that*.) It was not easy to wring concessions from the people at the bargaining table, who had, after all, no intention of giving their power away. People seldom do give their power away, forces beyond their control take their power from them; and I am afraid that much of the liberal cant about progress is but a sentimental reflection of this implacable fact. (Liberal cant about love and heroism also obscures, not to say blasphemes, the great love and heroism of many white people. Our racial story would be inconceivably more grim if these people, in the teeth of the most fantastic odds, did not continue to appear; but they were almost never, of course, to be found at the bargaining table.) Whatever concession the Negro leader carried away from the bargaining table was won with the tacit understanding that he, in return, would influence the people he represented in the direction that the people in power wished them to be influenced. Very often, in fact, he did not do this at all, but contrived to delude the white men (who are, in this realm, rather easily deluded) into believing that he had. But very often, too, he deluded himself into believing that the aims of white men in power and the desires of Negroes out of power were the same.

It was altogether inevitable, in short, that, by means of the extraordinary tableau I have tried to describe, a class of Negroes should have been created whose loyalty to their class was infinitely greater than their loyalty to the people from whom they had been so cunningly estranged. We must add, for I think it is important, that the Negro leader knew that he, too, was called "nigger" when his back was turned. The great mass of the black people around him were illiterate, demoralized, in want, and incorrigible. It is not hard to see that the Negro leader's personal and public frustrations would almost inevitably be turned against these people, for their misery, which formed the cornerstone of his peculiar power, was also responsible for his humiliation. And in Harlem, now, for example, many prominent Negroes ride to and from work through scenes of the greatest misery. They do not see this misery, though, because they do not want to see it. They defend themselves against an intolerable reality, which menaces them, by despising the people who are trapped in it.

The criticism, therefore, of the publicized Negro leadership—which is not, as I have tried to indicate, always the real leadership—is a criticism leveled, above all, against this class. They are, perhaps, the most unlucky bourgeoisie in the world's entire history, trapped, as they are, in a no man's land between black humiliation and white power. They cannot move backwards, and they cannot move forward, either.

One of the greatest vices of the white bourgeoisie on which they have modeled themselves is its reluctance to think, its distrust of the independent mind. Since the Negro bourgeoisie has so many things *not* to think about, it is positively afflicted with this vice. I should like at some other time to embark on a full-length discussion of the honorable and heroic role played by the NAACP in the national life, and point out to what extent its work has helped create the present ferment. But, for the moment, I shall have to confine my remarks to its organ, *The Crisis*, because I think it is incontestable that this magazine reveals the state of mind of the Negro bourgeoisie. *The Crisis* has the most exciting subject matter in the world at its fingertips, and yet manages to be one of the world's dullest magazines. When the Reverend James Lawson—who was expelled from Vanderbilt University for his sit-in activities—said this, or something like it, he caused a great storm of ill feeling. But he was quite right to feel as he does about *The Crisis*, and quite right to say so. And the charge is not answered by referring to the history of the NAACP.

Now, to charge *The Crisis* with dullness may seem to be a very trivial matter. It is not trivial, though, because this dullness is the result of its failure to examine what is really happening in the Negro world—its failure indeed, for that matter, to seize upon what is happening in the world at large. And I have singled it out because this inability is revelatory of the gap which now ominously widens between what we shall now have to call the official leadership and the young people who have begun what is nothing less than a moral revolution.

It is because of this gap that King finds himself in such a difficult position. The pressures on him are tremendous, and they come from above and below. He lost much moral credit, for example, especially in the eyes of the young, when he allowed Adam Clayton Powell to force the resignation of his (King's) extremely able organizer and lieutenant, Bayard Rustin. Rustin, also, has a long and honorable record as a fighter for Negro rights, and is one of the most penetrating and able men around. The techniques used by Powell—we will not speculate as to his motives—were far from sweet; but King was faced with the choice of defending his organizer, who was also his friend, or agreeing with Powell; and he chose the *latter* course. Nor do I know of anyone satisfied with the reasons given for the exclusion of James Lawson from the Southern Christian Leadership Conference. It would seem, certainly, that so able, outspoken, and energetic a man might prove of great value to this organization: why, then, is he not a part of it?

And there are many other questions, all of them ominous, and too many to go into here. But they all come, finally, it seems to me, to this tremendous reality: it is the sons and daughters of the beleaguered bourgeoisie—supported, in the most extraordinary fashion, by those old, work-worn men and women who were known, only yesterday, as "the country niggers"—who have begun a revolution in the consciousness of this country which will inexorably destroy nearly all that we now think of as concrete and indisputable. These young people have never believed in the American image of the Negro and have never bargained with the Republic, and now they never will. There is no longer any basis on which to bargain: for the myth of white supremacy is exploding all over the world, from the Congo to New Orleans. Those who have been watched and judged and described for so long are now watching and judging and describing for themselves. And one of the things that this means, to put it far too simply and bluntly, is that the white man on whom the American Negro has modeled himself for so long is vanishing. Because this white man was, himself, very largely a mythical creation: white men have never been, here, what they imagined themselves to be. The liberation of Americans from the racial anguish which has crippled us for so long can only mean, truly, the creation of a new people in this still-new world.

But the battle to achieve this has not ended, it has scarcely begun. Martin Luther King, Jr., by the power of his personality and the force of his beliefs, has injected a new dimension into our ferocious struggle. He has succeeded, in a way no Negro before him has managed to do, to carry the battle into the individual heart and make its resolution the province of the individual will. He has made it a matter, on both sides of the racial fence, of self-examination; and has incurred, therefore, the grave responsibility of continuing to lead in the path he has encouraged so many people to follow. How he will do this I do not know, but I do not see how he can possibly avoid a break, at last, with the habits and attitudes, stratagems and fears of the past.

No one can read the future, but we do know, as James has put it, that "all futures are rough." King's responsibility, and ours, is to that future which is already sending before it so many striking signs and portents. The possibility of liberation which is always real is also always painful, since it involves such an overhauling of all that gave us our identity. The Negro who will emerge out of this present struggle—whoever, indeed, this dark stranger may prove to be—will not be dependent, in any way at all, on any of the many props and crutches which help form our identity now. And neither will the white man. We will need every ounce of moral stamina we can find. For everything is changing, from our notion of politics to our notion of ourselves, and we are certain, as we begin history's strangest metamorphosis, to undergo the torment of being forced to surrender far more than we ever realized we had accepted.

Harper's, February 1961

The New Lost Generation

T HIS is an extremely difficult record to assess. Perhaps it begins for me in 1946, when my best friend took his life. He was an incandescent Negro boy of twenty-four, whose future, it had seemed to all of us, would unfailingly be glorious. He and I were Socialists, as were most of our friends, and we dreamed of this utopia, and worked toward it. We may have evinced more conviction than intelligence or skill, and more youthful arrogance than either, but we, nevertheless, had carried petitions about together, fought landlords together, worked as laborers together, been fired together, and starved together.

But for some time before his death, troubles graver than these had laid hold of my friend. Not only did the world stubbornly refuse his vision; it despised him for his vision, and scourged him for his color. Of course, it despised and scourged me, too, but I was different from my friend in that it took me nearly no time to despise the world right back and decide that I would accomplish, in time, with patience and cunning and by becoming indestructible, what I might not, in the moment, achieve by force or persuasion. My friend did not despise anyone. He really thought that people were good, and that one had only to point out to them the right path in order to have them, at once, come flocking to it in loudly rejoicing droves.

Before his death, we had quarreled very bitterly over this. I had lost my faith in politics, in right paths; if there *were* a right path, one might be sure (I informed him with great venom) that whoever was on it was simply asking to be stoned to death—by all the world's good people. I didn't give a damn, besides, *what* happened to the miserable, the unspeakably petty world. There was probably not a handful of decent people in it. My friend looked very saddened by these original reflections. He said that it seemed to him that I had taken the road which ended in fascism, tyranny, and blood.

So, I told him, have you. One fine day, you'll realize that people don't *want* to be better. So you'll have to make them better. And how do you think you'll go about it?

He said nothing to this. He was sitting opposite me, in a booth, in a Greenwich Village diner.

What about love? he asked me.

His question threw me off guard, and frightened me. With the indescribable authority of twenty-two, I snarled: Love! You'd better forget about that, my friend. That train has *gone*.

The moment I said this, I regretted it, for I remembered that he *was* in love: with a young white girl, also a Socialist, whose family was threatening to have him put in prison. And the week before, a handful of sailors had come across them in the subway and beaten him very badly.

He looked at me and I wanted to unsay what I had said, to say something else. But I could not think of anything which would not sound, simply, like unmanly consolation, which would not sound as though I were humoring him.

You're a poet, he said, and you don't believe in love.

And he put his head down on the table and began to cry.

We had come through some grueling things together, and I had never seen him cry. In fact, he went into and came out of battles laughing. We were in a hostile, public place. New York was fearfully hostile in those days, as it still is. He was my best friend, and for the first time in our lives I could do nothing for him; and it had been my ill-considered rage which had hurt him. I wanted to take it back, but I did not know how. I *would* have known how if I had been being insincere. But, though I know now that I was wrong, I did not know it then. I had meant what I had said, and my unexamined life would not allow me to speak otherwise. I really did not, then, as far as I knew, believe that love existed, except as useless pain; and the time was far from me when I would begin to see the contradiction implicit in the fact that I was bending all my forces, or imagined I was, to protect myself against it.

He wept; I sat there; no one, for a wonder, bothered us. By and by we paid, and walked out into the streets. This was the last time, but one, that I ever saw him; it was the very last time that we really spoke. A very short time after this, his body was found in the Hudson River. He had jumped from the George Washington Bridge.

Why do I begin my sketch of Americans abroad with this memory? I suppose that there must be many reasons. I certainly cannot hope to tell or, for that matter, to face them all. One reason, of course, is that I thought for a very long time that I had hastened him to his death. *You're a poet, and you don't believe in love.* But, leaving aside now this hideous and useless speculation, it is from the time of my friend's death that I resolved to leave America. There were two reasons for this. One was that I was absolutely certain, from the moment I learned of his death, that I, too, if I stayed here, would come to a similar end. I felt then, and, to tell the truth, I feel now, that he would not have died in such a way and certainly not so soon, if he had not been black. (Legally speaking. Physically, he was almost, but not quite, light enough to pass.) And this meant that he was the grimmest, until then, of a series of losses for which I most bitterly blamed the American republic. From the time of this death, I began to be afraid of enduring any more. I was afraid that hatred, and the desire for revenge would reach unmanageable proportions in me, and that my end, even if I should not physically die, would be infinitely more horrible than my friend's suicide.

He was not the only casualty of those days. There were others, white, friends of mine, who, at just about the time his indescribably colored body was recovered from the river, were returning from the world's most hideous war. Some were boys with whom I had been to high school. One boy, Jewish, sat with me all night in my apartment on Orchard Street, telling me about the camps he had seen in Germany and the Germans he had blasted off the face of the earth. I will never forget his face. I had once known it very well—shortly before, when we had been children. It was not a child's face now. He had *seen* what people would do to him—because he was a Jew; he knew what he had done to Germans; and not only could nothing be undone, it might very well be that this was all that the world could do or be, over and over again, forever. All political hopes and systems, then, seemed morally bankrupt: for, if Buchenwald was wrong, what, then, *really* made Hiroshima right? He shook his head, an old Jew already, an old man. If all visions of human nature are to be distrusted, and all hopes, what about love?

The people I knew found the most extraordinary ways of dealing with this question; but it was a real question. Girls who had been virgins when they married their husbands—and there were some, I knew them—sometimes had to have abortions before their husbands returned from overseas. The marriage almost never survived the returning pressures, and, very often, the mental equilibrium of the partners—or ex-partners—was lost, never to be regained. Men who had had homosexual adventures in CO camps, or in the service, could not accept what had happened to them, could not forget it, dared not discover if they desired to repeat it, and lapsed into a paralysis from which neither men nor women could rouse them. It was a time of the most terrifying personal anarchy. If one gave a party, it was virtually certain that someone, quite possibly oneself, would have a crying jag or have to be restrained from murder or suicide. It was a time of experimentation, with sex, with marijuana, and minor infringements of the law, such as "boosting" from the A&P and stealing electricity from Con Edison. I knew some people who had a stolen refrigerator for which they had no room and no use, and which they could not sell; it was finally shipped, I believe, of all places, to Cuba. But, finally, it seems to me that life was beginning to tell us who we were, and what life was—news no one has ever wanted to hear: and we fought back by clinging to our vision of ourselves as innocent, of love perhaps imperfect but reciprocal and enduring. And we did not know that the price of this was experience. We had been raised to believe in formulas.

In retrospect, the discovery of the orgasm—or, rather, of the orgone box—seems the least mad of the formulas that came to hand. It seemed to me—though I was, perhaps, already too bitterly innoculated against groups or panaceas—that people turned from the idea of the world being made better through politics to the idea of the world being made better through psychic and sexual health like sinners coming down the aisle at a revival meeting. And I doubted that their conversion was any more to be trusted than that. The converts, indeed, moved in a certain euphoric aura of well-being, which would not last. They had not become more generous, but less, not more open, but more closed. They ceased, totally, to listen and could only proselytize; nor did their private lives become discernibly less tangled. There are no formulas for the improvement of the private, or any other, life—certainly not the formula of more and better orgasms. (Who decides?) The people I had been raised among had orgasms all the time, and still chopped each other up with razors on Saturday nights.

By this wild process, then, of failure, elimination, and rejection, I, certainly, and most of the people whom I knew got to Europe, and, roughly speaking, "settled" there. Many of us have returned, but not all: it is important to remember that many expatriates vanish into the lives of their adopted country, to be flushed out only, and not always then, by grave international emergency. This applies especially, of course, to women, who, given the pressures of raising a family, rarely have time to be homesick, or guilty about "escaping" the problems of American life. Their first loyalties, thank heaven, are to the men they married and the children they must raise. But I know American couples, too, who have made their homes in Europe quite happily, and who have no intention of returning to this country. It is worth observing, too, that these people are nearly always marked by a lack of spite or uneasiness concerning this country which quite fails to characterize what I tend to think of as the "displaced" or "visible" expatriate. That is, remarkable as this may sound, it is not necessary to hate this country in order to have a good time somewhere else. In fact, the people who hate this country never manage, except physically, to leave it, and have a wretched life wherever they go.

And, of course, many of us have become, in effect, commuters; which is a less improbable state now than it was a decade ago. Many have neither returned nor stayed, but can be found in Village bars, talking about Europe, or in European bars, talking about America.

Apart from the G.I.'s who remained in Europe, thoughtfully using up all the cheap studios, and nearly all, as it turned out, of the available good will, we, who have been described (not very usefully) as the "new" expatriates, began arriving in Paris around '45, '46, '47, and '48. The character of the influx began to change very radically after that, if only because the newcomers had had the foresight to arm themselves with jobs:

American government jobs, which also meant that they had housing allowances and didn't care how much rent they paid. Neither, of course, did the French landlords, with the results that rents rose astronomically and we who had considered ourselves forever installed in the Latin Quarter found ourselves living all over Paris. But this, at least for some of us, turned out to be very healthy and valuable. We were in Paris, after all, because we had presumably put down all formulas and all safety in favor of the chilling unpredictability of experience.

Voyagers discover that the world can never be larger than the person that is in the world; but it is impossible to foresee this, it is impossible to be warned. It is only when time has begun spilling through his fingers like water or sand—carrying away with it, forever, dreams, possibilities, challenges, and hopes—that the young man realizes that he will not be young forever. If he wishes to paint a picture, raise a family, write a book, design a building, start a war—well, he does not have forever in which to do it. He has only a certain amount of time, and half of that time is probably gone already. As long as his aspirations are in the realm of the dream, he is safe; when he must bring them back into the world, he is in danger.

Precisely for this reason, Paris was a devastating shock. It was easily recognizable as Paris from across the ocean: that was what the letters on the map spelled out. This was not the same thing as finding oneself in a large, inconvenient, indifferent city. Paris, from across the ocean, looked like a refuge from the American madness; now it was a city four thousand miles from home. It contained—in those days—no doughnuts, no milk shakes, no Coca-Cola, no dry Martinis; nothing resembling, for people on our economic level, an American toilet; as for toilet paper, it was yesterday's newspaper. The concierge of the hotel did not appear to find your presence in France a reason for rejoicing; rather, she found your presence, and in particular your ability to pay the rent, a matter for the profoundest suspicion. The policemen, with their revolvers, clubs, and (as it turned out) weighted capes, appeared to be convinced of your legality only after the most vindictive scrutiny of your passport; and it became clear very soon that they were not kidding about the three-month period during which every foreigner had to buy a new visa or leave the country. Not a few astounded Americans, unable to call their embassy, spent the night in jail, and steady offenders were escorted to the border. After the first street riot, or its aftermath, one witnessed in Paris, one took a new attitude toward the Paris paving stones, and toward the café tables and chairs, and toward the Parisians, indeed, who showed no signs, at such moments, of being among the earth's most cerebral or civilized people. Paris hotels had never heard of central heating or hot baths or showers or clean towels and sheets or ham and eggs; their attitude toward electricity was demonic—once one had seen what they thought of as wiring one wondered why the city had not, long ago, vanished in flame; and it soon became clear that Paris hospitals had never heard of Pasteur. Once, in short, one found oneself divested of all the things that one had fled from, one wondered how people, meaning, above all, oneself, could possibly do without them.

And yet one did, of course, and in the beginning, and sporadically, thereafter, found these privations a subject for mirth. One soon ceased expecting to be warm in one's hotel room, and read and worked in the cafés. The French, at least insofar as student hotels are concerned, do not appear to understand the idea of a social visit. They expect one's callers to be vastly more intimate, if not utilitarian, than that, and much prefer that they register and spend the night. This aspect of Parisian life would seem vastly to simplify matters, but this, alas, is not the case. It merely makes it all but impossible to invite anyone to your hotel room. Americans do not cease to be Puritans when they have crossed the ocean; French girls, on the other hand, contrary to legend, tend, preponderantly, to be the marrying kind; thus, it was not long before we brave voyagers rather felt that we had been turned loose in a fair in which there was not a damn thing we could buy, and still less that we could sell.

And I think that when we began to be frightened in Paris, to feel baffled and betrayed, it was because we had failed, after all, somehow, and once again, to make the longed-for, magical human contact. It was on this connection with another human being that we had felt that our lives and our work depended. It had failed at home. We had thought we knew why. Everyone at home was too dry and too frightened, mercilessly pinned beneath the thumb of the Puritan God. Yet, here we were, surrounded by quite beautiful and sensual people, who did not, however, appear to find us beautiful or sensual. They said so. By the time we had been abroad two years, each of us, in one way or another, had received this message. It was one of the things that was meant when we were referred to as children. We had been perfectly willing to refer to all the other Americans as children—in the beginning; we had not known what it meant; we had not known that we were included.

By 1950 some of us had already left Paris for more promising ports of call, Tangiers for some, or Italy, or Spain; Sweden or Denmark or Germany for others. Some girls had got married and vanished; some had got married and vanished and reappeared—minus their husbands. Some people got jobs with the ECA and began a slow retreat back into the cocoon from which they had never quite succeeded in emerging. Some of us were going to pieces—spectacularly, as in my own case, quietly, in others. One boy, for example, had embarked on the career which I believe still engages him, that of laboriously writing extremely literary plays in English, translating them— laboriously—into French and Spanish, reading the trilingual results to a coterie of friends who were, even then, beginning to diminish, and then locking them in his trunk. Magazines were popping up like toadstools and vanishing like fog. Painters and poets of thin talent and no industry began to feel abused by the lack of attention their efforts elicited from the French, and made outrageously obvious—and successful— bids for the attention of visiting literary figures from the States, of whose industry, in any case, there could be no doubt. And a certain real malice now began to make itself felt in our attitudes toward the French, as well as a certain defensiveness concerning whatever it was we had come to Paris to do, and clearly were not doing. We were edgy with each other, too. Going, going, going, gone—were the days when we walked through Les Halles, singing, loving every inch of France, and loving each other; gone were the jam sessions in Pigalle, and our stories about the whores there; gone were the nights spent smoking hashish in Arab cafés; gone were the mornings which found us telling dirty stories, true stories, sad, and earnest stories, in grey, workingmen's cafés. It was all gone. We were secretive with each other. I no longer talked about my novel. We no longer talked about our love affairs, for either they had failed, were failing, or were serious. Above all, they were private—how can love be talked about? It is probably the most awful of all the revelations this little life affords. We no longer walked about, as a friend of mine once put it, in a not too dissimilar context, in "friendly groups of five thousand." We were splitting up, and each of us was going for himself. Or, if not precisely for himself, his own way: some of us took to the needle, some returned to the family business, some made loveless marriages, some ceased fleeing and turned to face the demons that had been on the trail so long. The luckiest among us were these last, for they managed to go to pieces and then put themselves back together with whatever was left. This may take away one's dreams, but it delivers one to oneself. Without this coming together, the longed-for love is never possible, for the confused personality can neither give nor take.

In my own case, I think my exile saved my life, for it inexorably confirmed something which Americans appear to have great difficulty accepting. Which is, simply, this: a man is not a man until he's able and willing to accept his own vision of the world, no matter how radically this vision departs from that of others. (When I say "vision," I do not mean "dream.") There are long moments when this country resembles nothing so much as the grimmest of popularity contests. The best thing that happened to the "new" expatriates was their liberation, finally, from any need to be smothered by what is really nothing more (though it may be something less) than mother love. It need scarcely, I hope, be said that I have no interest in hurling gratuitous insults at American mothers; they are certainly helpless, if not entirely blameless; and my point has nothing to do with them. My point is involved with the great emphasis placed on public approval here, and the resulting and quite insane system of penalties and rewards. It puts a premium on mediocrity and has all but slaughtered any concept of excellence. This corruption begins in the private life and unfailingly flowers in the public life. Europeans refer to Americans as children in the same way that American Negroes refer to them as children, and for the same reason: they mean that Americans have so little experience—experience referring not to *what* happens, but to *who*—that they have no key to the experience of others. Our current relations with the world forcibly suggest that there is more than a little truth to this. What Europe still gives an American—or gave us—is the sanction, if one can accept it, to become oneself. No artist can survive without this acceptance. But rare indeed is the American artist who achieved this without first becoming a wanderer, and then, upon his return to his own country, the loneliest and most blackly distrusted of men.

Esquire, July 1961

The Creative Process

PERHAPS the primary distinction of the artist is that he must actively cultivate that state which most men, necessarily, must avoid: the state of being alone. That all men *are*, when the chips are down, alone, is a banality—a banality because it is very frequently stated, but very rarely, on the evidence, believed. Most of us are not compelled to linger with the knowledge of our aloneness, for it is a knowledge which can paralyze all action in this world. There are, forever, swamps to be drained, cities to be created, mines to be exploited, children to be fed: and none of these things can be done alone. But the conquest of the physical world is not man's only duty. He is also enjoined to conquer the great wilderness of himself. The role of the artist, then, precisely, is to illuminate that darkness, blaze roads through that vast forest; so that we will not, in all our doing, lose sight of its purpose, which is, after all, to make the world a more human dwelling place.

The state of being alone is not meant to bring to mind merely a rustic musing beside some silver lake. The aloneness of which I speak is much more like the aloneness of birth or death. It is like the fearful aloneness which one sees in the eyes of someone who is suffering, whom we cannot help. Or it is like the aloneness of love, that force and mystery which so many have extolled and so many have cursed, but which no one has ever understood or ever really been able to control. I put the matter this way, not out of any desire to create pity for the artist—God forbid!—but to suggest how nearly, after all, is his state the state of everyone, and in an attempt to make vivid his endeavor. The states of birth, suffering, love, and death, are extreme states: extreme, universal, and inescapable. We all know this, but we would rather not know it. The artist is present to correct the delusions to which we fall prey in our attempts to avoid this knowledge.

It is for this reason that all societies have battled with that incorrigible disturber of the peace—the artist. I doubt that future societies will get on with him any better. The entire purpose of society is to create a bulwark against the inner and

the outer chaos, literally, in order to make life bearable and
to keep the human race alive. And it is absolutely inevitable
that when a tradition has been evolved, whatever the tradition
is, that the people, in general, will suppose it to have existed
from before the beginning of time and will be most unwilling
and indeed unable to conceive of any changes in it. They do
not know how they will live without those traditions which
have given them their identity. Their reaction, when it is suggested that they can or that they must, is panic. And we see
this panic, I think, everywhere in the world today, from the
streets of our own New Orleans to the grisly battleground of
Algeria. And a higher level of consciousness among the people
is the only hope we have, now or in the future, of minimizing
the human damage.

The artist is distinguished from all the other responsible
actors in society—the politicians, legislators, educators, scientists, et cetera—by the fact that he is his own test tube, his
own laboratory, working according to very rigorous rules,
however unstated these may be, and cannot allow any consideration to supersede his responsibility to reveal all that he can
possibly discover concerning the mystery of the human being.
Society must accept some things as real; but he must always
know that the visible reality hides a deeper one, and that all
our action and all our achievement rests on things unseen. A
society must assume that it is stable, but the artist must know,
and he must let us know, that there is nothing stable under
heaven. One cannot possibly build a school, teach a child, or
drive a car without taking some things for granted. The artist
cannot and must not take anything for granted, but must drive
to the heart of every answer and expose the question the answer hides.

I seem to be making extremely grandiloquent claims for a
breed of men and women historically despised while living and
acclaimed when safely dead. But, in a way, the belated honor
which all societies tender their artists proves the reality of the
point I am trying to make. I am really trying to make clear
the nature of the artist's responsibility to his society. The peculiar nature of this responsibility is that he must never cease
warring with it, for its sake and for his own. For the truth, in
spite of appearances and all our hopes, is that everything is

always changing and the measure of our maturity as nations and as men is how well prepared we are to meet these changes and, further, to use them for our health.

Now, anyone who has ever been compelled to think about it—anyone, for example, who has ever been in love—knows that the one face which one can never see is one's own face. One's lover—or one's brother, or one's enemy—sees the face you wear, and this face can elicit the most extraordinary reactions. We do the things we do, and feel what we feel, essentially because we must—we are responsible for our actions, but we rarely understand them. It goes without saying, I believe, that if we understood ourselves better, we would damage ourselves less. But the barrier between oneself and one's knowledge of oneself is high indeed. There are so many things one would rather not know! We become social creatures because we cannot live any other way. But in order to become social, there are a great many other things which we must not become, and we are frightened, all of us, of those forces within us which perpetually menace our precarious security. Yet, the forces are there, we cannot will them away. All we can do is learn to live with them. And we cannot learn this unless we are willing to tell the truth about ourselves, and the truth about us is always at variance with what we wish to be. The human effort is to bring these two realities into a relationship resembling reconciliation. The human beings whom we respect the most, after all—and sometimes fear the most—are those who are most deeply involved in this delicate and strenuous effort: for they have the unshakable authority which comes only from having looked on and endured and survived the worst. That nation is healthiest which has the least necessity to distrust or ostracize or victimize these people—whom, as I say, we honor, once they are gone, because, somewhere in our hearts, we know that we cannot live without them.

The dangers of being an American artist are not greater than those of being an artist anywhere else in the world, but they are very particular. These dangers are produced by our history. They rest on the fact that in order to conquer this continent, the particular aloneness of which I speak—the aloneness in which one discovers that life is tragic, and, *therefore*, unutterably beautiful—could not be permitted. And that this prohibition is typical of all emergent nations will be proven, I have no doubt, in many ways during the next fifty years. This continent now is conquered, but our habits and our fears remain. And, in the same way that to become a social human being one modifies and suppresses and, ultimately, without great courage, lies to oneself about all one's interior, uncharted chaos, so have we, as a nation, modified and suppressed and lied about all the darker forces in our history. We know, in the case of the person, that whoever cannot tell himself the truth about his past is trapped in it, is immobilized in the prison of his undiscovered self. This is also true of nations. We know how a person, in such a paralysis, is unable to assess either his weaknesses or his strengths, and how frequently indeed he mistakes the one for the other. And this, I think, we do. We are the strongest nation in the western world, but this is not for the reasons that we think. It is because we have an opportunity which no other nation has of moving beyond the Old World concepts of race and class and caste, and create, finally, what we must have had in mind when we first began speaking of the New World. But the price for this is a long look backward whence we came and an unflinching assessment of the record. For an artist, the record of that journey is most clearly revealed in the personalities of the people the journey produced. Societies never know it, but the war of an artist with his society is a lover's war, and he does, at his best, what lovers do, which is to reveal the beloved to himself, and with that revelation, make freedom real.

Creative America, 1962

Color

WHITE PEOPLE are not really white, but colored people can sometimes be extremely colored. In Negro speech, the word "colored" has very special reverberations. One may hear, in sorrow, "Man, that cat is just too colored." And this can mean, depending on the speaker, the situation, the subject, that the cat under discussion is coarse, overbearing, incompetent and so uncertain of his value that he is perpetually adopting the most outrageous and transparent affectations. This is one of the meanings of color in the psyche and the experience of the American Negro. But the same phrase can also be applied to someone who is direct, warm, unaffected and unconquerable—someone, who, like Duke Ellington, is able to move, without missing a beat or manifesting the slightest uneasiness, from Harlem corn bread to Buckingham Palace caviar and back again, *ad infinitum*. "The Duke knows who *is*, man": which reveals another aspect of the meaning of color among the people who constitute America's most tenacious and problematical minority.

At bottom, to be colored means that one has been caught in some utterly unbelievable cosmic joke, a joke so hideous and in such bad taste that it defeats all categories and definitions. One's only hope of supporting, to say nothing of surviving, this joke is to flaunt in the teeth of it one's own particular and invincible style. It is at this turning, this level, that the word color, ravaged by experience and heavy with the weight of peculiar spoils, returns to its first meaning, which is not *negro*, the Spanish word for black, but vivid, many-hued, e.g., the rainbow, and warm and quick and vital, e.g., life.

How hard it is though, to speak of Negro life in these terms, Negroes being so bitterly maligned and so brutally penalized for those very qualities of color which have helped them to endure. The Puritan dicta still inhabit and inhibit the American body and soul. Joy and sin have been synonyms here for so many generations that the former can now be defended only on therapeutic, i.e., pragmatic grounds, necessitating a similar metamorphosis for the latter. Now it is suggested that we Live—a little!—in order not to become too dangerously

Disturbed. (*Plus ça change*—) But no one has suggested—I would like to think that no one has dared—such a formula to Negroes, who do not yet dance or make love as a way of supporting Mental Health, and who are, indeed, in the main, thank heaven, incapable of making so deluded a connection. They have seen too many dancers, to say nothing of lovers, swept straight into the madhouse; dancing and love are meant to seem effortless, but are very difficult and dangerous activities.

To suggest that joy can be present, in any way, on any level, of Negro life offends, of course, immediately all of our social and sentimental assumptions. Joy is the fruit of Yankee thrift and virtue and makes its sweet appearance only after a lifetime of cruel self-denial and inveterate moneymaking. On the other hand, such a suggestion immediately justifies the immorality, the inequity of our social regulations: if the Negro is "happy" in his "place," as we still would be only too delighted to believe, then it becomes, in us, a virtue not only to keep him there but to frustrate, for the sake of his continued happiness and the protection of our property and our profits, any attempt of his to rise out of it.

Well, the Negro is *not* happy in his place, and white people aren't happy in their place, either—two very intimately related facts—but the unhappiness of white people seems never to rattle and resound more fiercely than in their pleasure mills. The world that mainly frequents white nightclubs seems afflicted with a strange uncertainty as to whether or not they are really having fun—they keep peeping at each other in order to find out. One's aware, in an eerie way, that there are barriers which must not be crossed, and that by these invisible barriers everyone is mesmerized. But it is quite impossible to discover where, in action, these barriers are to be found: nothing matches the abandon of those struggling to be free of invisible chains, who wish, at the same time, to remain socially safe. And nothing matches that joylessness, either.

In an uptown club, the invisible chains are mighty and the barriers are innumerable. But everyone in the club lives too intimately with impassable barriers of all kinds to need to watch them. They know exactly where the barriers are and they would like, simply, for a little while, to forget them. Again, they are threatened in so many ways that they cannot conceivably be threatened by anything that happens at the club. Violence is always a possibility, of course, but the point is that it is *always* a possibility, and one has had to learn to live with it. It is almost impossible to be threatened by social or sexual insult, the very style of Harlem Negroes being a kind of distillation and transcendence of all the insults they daily receive. And the necessity of a personal style, no matter how upsetting, is too well understood for anyone to be mocked for their clothes, or their manner—unless of course, either of these is considered too slavish an imitation of white people. Everything done by Negroes in this country is, in a way, done in imitation of white people, but everything depends on the manner and intention, and the degree of hardheadedness. A girl wearing a mink—or, more probably, a minkette—is admired for having achieved it in the first place. One assumes it could not have been easy. But she is pitied and despised if she supposes her minkette is her passport out of the black world. Girls who have ceased doing whatever it is that American Negro girls do to their hair and allowed it to resume its natural texture are very strongly admired in some circles, but looked on with some nervousness in most. Such a girl is no longer merely colored, but *somewhere else*, and she poses in her presence, by all that triumphantly kinky hair, the great problem of just *who* the American Negro is, and what his future is to be. Women are able, of course, to say, "Well, I like it on *her*. But I don't know if it would suit *me*." But Negro men are intimidated in another way altogether, having despised women with kinky hair for so long. And they are told, *You been so brainwashed by the white man, you even wanted your women to look white!* And this is not quite true, of course, so many of "our" women having been fairly white when they got here, but, on the other hand, it is true enough. And toward what standard of beauty ought black people now turn, especially as they exemplify, in themselves, so many different standards. The entire scene is rich and funny and sad, and both bound and free, like the heavy and resplendent matron wearing a complete Easter outfit, from head almost to toe, but with her shoes in her hand and her slippers on her feet. She had the shoes and she wanted everyone to know it; but her feet hurt. And she didn't care who knew *that*.

The atmosphere of a Harlem nightclub is curiously misleading because of the simplicity of the white world's assumptions. Color, for anyone who uses it, or is used by it, is a most complex, calculated and dangerous phenomenon. One will probably find more color in Smalls' Paradise, for example, even on an off night, than I, anyway, have usually managed to encounter in any nightclub downtown. It is not that the music is intrinsically so much better—always—but the people playing it and the people hearing it have more fun with it, and with each other. They know, on one level, everything concerning each other that there is to know: they are all black. And this produces an atmosphere of freedom which is exactly as real as the limits which have made it necessary. And what they don't know about each other, like who works where, or who sleeps with whom, doesn't matter. No one gives a damn, and this allows everyone to be himself—at the club. No one gives a damn because they know exactly how rough it is out there, when the club gates close. And while they are dancing and listening to the music and drinking and joking and laughing, with all their finery on, and looking so bold and free, they know who enters, who leaves, and on what errands: they are aware of the terrible and unreachable forces which yet rule their lives. In years past, and sometimes even now, musicians said for them what they themselves could not say, and helped them to endure the unendurable. But nothing is static. Now, unless Ray Charles or Nina Simone is down the street at the Apollo, one will have to go downtown to hear them. And not many of Harlem's Negroes go downtown for their entertainment because they do not feel welcome there.

The comparison between the relative spontaneity and freedom of whites and blacks is falsely stated. There are some relatively free and spontaneous white people, not very many; and some relatively free and spontaneous Negroes, not, in my experience, very many more. A person's freedom can only be judged in terms of his flexibility, his openness toward life; it is not his situation which makes him free, but himself. Some rare people become free through oppression; most do not.

Some people, at least equally rare, release themselves from the delusion that they were born free and go on to establish an approximation of that personal order which will allow them to become so. Most people are not able to look on each other as human beings, and, in spite of everything, to treat each other that way. Until this happens, freedom is only an empty word. In the meantime, what one's contrasting is a matter of style, i.e., ways of life, and contrasting these, moreover, in their most public manifestations. The atmosphere of a Harlem nightclub *must* be different from that of the Copacabana because of the way of life which has produced it, and the peculiar needs it serves. White nightclubs do not draw people from a community, but from all over this peculiar country. And white people are as isolated from each other in the nightclub as they are all over America, in their daily lives. A nightclub being no place to establish a human relationship, they walk out as untouched as they were when they walked in. It is this cumulative and grinding inability to reach out to others which makes nightclub life, downtown, so grim. But it is because the world looks on them with such guilt, that they seem freer in their pleasures than white people do. White Americans know very little about pleasure because they are so afraid of pain. But people dulled by pain can sing and dance till morning and find no pleasure in it.

Esquire, December 1962

A Talk to Teachers

L ET'S BEGIN by saying that we are living through a very dangerous time. Everyone in this room is in one way or another aware of that. We are in a revolutionary situation, no matter how unpopular that word has become in this country. The society in which we live is desperately menaced, not by Khrushchev, but from within. So any citizen of this country who figures himself as responsible—and particularly those of you who deal with the minds and hearts of young people— must be prepared to "go for broke." Or to put it another way, you must understand that in the attempt to correct so many generations of bad faith and cruelty, when it is operating not only in the classroom but in society, you will meet the most fantastic, the most brutal, and the most determined resistance. There is no point in pretending that this won't happen.

Now, since I am talking to schoolteachers and I am not a teacher myself, and in some ways am fairly easily intimidated, I beg you to let me leave that and go back to what I think to be the entire purpose of education in the first place. It would seem to me that when a child is born, if I'm the child's parent, it is my obligation and my high duty to civilize that child. Man is a social animal. He cannot exist without a society. A society, in turn, depends on certain things which everyone within that society takes for granted. Now, the crucial paradox which confronts us here is that the whole process of education occurs within a social framework and is designed to perpetuate the aims of society. Thus, for example, the boys and girls who were born during the era of the Third Reich, when educated to the purposes of the Third Reich, became barbarians. The paradox of education is precisely this—that as one begins to become conscious one begins to examine the society in which he is being educated. The purpose of education, finally, is to create in a person the ability to look at the world for himself, to make his own decisions, to say to himself this is black or this is white, to decide for himself whether there is a God in heaven or not. To ask questions of the universe, and then learn to live with those questions, is the way he achieves his own identity. But no society is really anxious to have that kind of person around. What societies really, ideally, want is a citizenry which will simply obey the rules of society. If a society succeeds in this, that society is about to perish. The obligation of anyone who thinks of himself as responsible is to examine society and try to change it and to fight it—at no matter what risk. This is the only hope society has. This is the only way societies change.

Now, if what I have tried to sketch has any validity, it becomes thoroughly clear, at least to me, that any Negro who is born in this country and undergoes the American educational system runs the risk of becoming schizophrenic. On the one hand he is born in the shadow of the stars and stripes and he is assured it represents a nation which has never lost a war. He pledges allegiance to that flag which guarantees "liberty and justice for all." He is part of a country in which anyone can become President, and so forth. But on the other hand he is also assured by his country and his countrymen that he has never contributed anything to civilization—that his past is nothing more than a record of humiliations gladly endured. He is assured by the republic that he, his father, his mother, and his ancestors were happy, shiftless, watermelon-eating darkies who loved Mr. Charlie and Miss Ann, that the value he has as a black man is proven by one thing only—his devotion to white people. If you think I am exaggerating, examine the myths which proliferate in this country about Negroes.

Now all this enters the child's consciousness much sooner than we as adults would like to think it does. As adults, we are easily fooled because we are so anxious to be fooled. But children are very different. Children, not yet aware that it is dangerous to look too deeply at anything, look at everything, look at each other, and draw their own conclusions. They don't have the vocabulary to express what they see, and we, their elders, know how to intimidate them very easily and very soon. But a black child, looking at the world around him, though he cannot know quite what to make of it, is aware that there is a reason why his mother works so hard, why his father is always on edge. He is aware that there is some reason why, if he sits down in the front of the bus, his father or

mother slaps him and drags him to the back of the bus. He
is aware that there is some terrible weight on his parents'
shoulders which menaces him. And it isn't long—in fact it
begins when he is in school—before he discovers the shape of
his oppression.

Let us say that the child is seven years old and I am his
father, and I decide to take him to the zoo, or to Madison
Square Garden, or to the U.N. Building, or to any of the
tremendous monuments we find all over New York. We get
into a bus and we go from where I live on 131st Street and
Seventh Avenue downtown through the park and we get into
New York City, which is not Harlem. Now, where the boy
lives—even if it is a housing project—is in an undesirable
neighborhood. If he lives in one of those housing projects of
which everyone in New York is so proud, he has at the front
door, if not closer, the pimps, the whores, the junkies—in a
word, the danger of life in the ghetto. And the child knows
this, though he doesn't know why.

I still remember my first sight of New York. It was really
another city when I was born—where I was born. We looked
down over the Park Avenue streetcar tracks. It was Park Avenue, but I didn't know what Park Avenue meant *downtown*.
The Park Avenue I grew up on, which is still standing, is dark
and dirty. No one would dream of opening a Tiffany's on that
Park Avenue, and when you go downtown you discover that
you are literally in the white world. It is rich—or at least it
looks rich. It is clean—because they collect garbage downtown. There are doormen. People walk about as though they
owned where they were—and indeed they do. And it's a great
shock. It's very hard to relate yourself to this. You don't know
what it means. You know—you know instinctively—that none
of this is for you. You know this before you are told. And
who is it for and who is paying for it? And why isn't it for
you?

Later on when you become a grocery boy or messenger and
you try to enter one of those buildings a man says, "Go to
the back door." Still later, if you happen by some odd chance
to have a friend in one of those buildings, the man says,
"Where's your package?" Now this by no means is the core
of the matter. What I'm trying to get at is that by this time

the Negro child has had, effectively, almost all the doors of opportunity slammed in his face, and there are very few things he can do about it. He can more or less accept it with an absolutely inarticulate and dangerous rage inside—all the more dangerous because it is never expressed. It is precisely those silent people whom white people see every day of their lives—I mean your porter and your maid, who never say anything more than "Yes Sir" and "No Ma'am." They will tell you it's raining if that is what you want to hear, and they will tell you the sun is shining if *that* is what you want to hear. They really hate you—really hate you because in their eyes (and they're right) you stand between them and life. I want to come back to that in a moment. It is the most sinister of the facts, I think, which we now face.

There is something else the Negro child can do, too. Every street boy—and I was a street boy, so I know—looking at the society which has produced him, looking at the standards of that society which are not honored by anybody, looking at your churches and the government and the politicians, understands that this structure is operated for someone else's benefit—not for his. And there's no room in it for him. If he is really cunning, really ruthless, really strong—and many of us are—he becomes a kind of criminal. He becomes a kind of criminal because that's the only way he can live. Harlem and every ghetto in this city—every ghetto in this country—is full of people who live outside the law. They wouldn't dream of calling a policeman. They wouldn't, for a moment, listen to any of those professions of which we are so proud on the Fourth of July. They have turned away from this country forever and totally. They live by their wits and really long to see the day when the entire structure comes down.

The point of all this is that black men were brought here as a source of cheap labor. They were indispensable to the economy. In order to justify the fact that men were treated as though they were animals, the white republic had to brainwash itself into believing that they were, indeed, animals and *deserved* to be treated like animals. Therefore it is almost impossible for any Negro child to discover anything about his actual history. The reason is that this "animal," once he suspects his own worth, once he starts believing that he is a man, has begun to attack the entire power structure. This is why America has spent such a long time keeping the Negro in his place. What I am trying to suggest to you is that it was not an accident, it was not an act of God, it was not done by well-meaning people muddling into something which they didn't understand. It was a deliberate policy hammered into place in order to make money from black flesh. And now, in 1963, because we have never faced this fact, we are in intolerable trouble.

The Reconstruction, as I read the evidence, was a bargain between the North and South to this effect: "We've liberated them from the land—and delivered them to the bosses." When we left Mississippi to come North we did not come to freedom. We came to the bottom of the labor market, and we are still there. Even the Depression of the 1930s failed to make a dent in Negroes' relationship to white workers in the labor unions. Even today, so brainwashed is this republic that people seriously ask in what they suppose to be good faith, "What does the Negro want?" I've heard a great many asinine questions in my life, but that is perhaps the most asinine and perhaps the most insulting. But the point here is that people who ask that question, thinking that they ask it in good faith, are really the victims of this conspiracy to make Negroes believe they are less than human.

In order for me to live, I decided very early that some mistake had been made somewhere. I was not a "nigger" even though you called me one. But if I was a "nigger" in your eyes, there was something about *you*—there was something *you* needed. I had to realize when I was very young that I was none of those things I was told I was. I was not, for example, happy. I never touched a watermelon for all kinds of reasons. I had been invented by white people, and I knew enough about life by this time to understand that whatever you invent, whatever you project, is you! So where we are now is that a whole country of people believe I'm a "nigger," and I *don't*, and the battle's on! Because if I am not what I've been told I am, then it means that *you're* not what you thought *you* were *either*! And that is the crisis.

It is not really a "Negro revolution" that is upsetting this country. What is upsetting the country is a sense of its own identity. If, for example, one managed to change the curriculum in all the schools so that Negroes learned more about themselves and their real contributions to this culture, you would be liberating not only Negroes, you'd be liberating white people who know nothing about their own history. And the reason is that if you are compelled to lie about one aspect of anybody's history, you must lie about it all. If you have to lie about my real role here, if you have to pretend that I hoed all that cotton just because I loved you, then you have done something to yourself. You are mad.

Now let's go back a minute. I talked earlier about those silent people—the porter and the maid—who, as I said, don't look up at the sky if you ask them if it is raining, but look into your face. My ancestors and I were very well trained. We understood very early that this was not a Christian nation. It didn't matter what you said or how often you went to church. My father and my mother and my grandfather and my grandmother knew that Christians didn't act this way. It was as simple as that. And if that was so there was no point in dealing with white people in terms of their own moral professions, for they were not going to honor them. What one did was to turn away, smiling all the time, and tell white people what they wanted to hear. But people always accuse you of reckless talk when you say this.

All this means that there are in this country tremendous reservoirs of bitterness which have never been able to find an outlet, but may find an outlet soon. It means that well-meaning white liberals place themselves in great danger when they try to deal with Negroes as though they were missionaries. It means, in brief, that a great price is demanded to liberate all those silent people so that they can breathe for the first time and *tell* you what they think of you. And a price is demanded to liberate all those white children—some of them near forty—who have never grown up, and who never will grow up, because they have no sense of their identity.

What passes for identity in America is a series of myths about one's heroic ancestors. It's astounding to me, for example, that so many people really appear to believe that the country was founded by a band of heroes who wanted to be free. That happens not to be true. What happened was that some people left Europe because they couldn't stay there any longer and had to go someplace else to make it. That's all. They were hungry, they were poor, they were convicts. Those who were making it in England, for example, did not get on the *Mayflower*. That's how the country was settled. Not by Gary Cooper. Yet we have a whole race of people, a whole republic, who believe the myths to the point where even today they select political representatives, as far as I can tell, by how closely they resemble Gary Cooper. Now this is dangerously infantile, and it shows in every level of national life. When I was living in Europe, for example, one of the worst revelations to me was the way Americans walked around Europe buying this and buying that and insulting everybody—not even out of malice, just because they didn't know any better. Well, that is the way they have always treated me. They weren't cruel, they just didn't know you were alive. They didn't know you had any feelings.

What I am trying to suggest here is that in the doing of all this for 100 years or more, it is the American white man who has long since lost his grip on reality. In some peculiar way, having created this myth about Negroes, and the myth about his own history, he created myths about the world so that, for example, he was astounded that some people could prefer Castro, astounded that there are people in the world who don't go into hiding when they hear the word "Communism," astounded that Communism is one of the realities of the twentieth century which we will not overcome by pretending that it does not exist. The political level in this country now, on the part of people who should know better, is abysmal.

The Bible says somewhere that where there is no vision the people perish. I don't think anyone can doubt that in this country today we are menaced—intolerably menaced—by a lack of vision.

It is inconceivable that a sovereign people should continue, as we do so abjectly, to say, "I can't do anything about it. It's the government." The government is the creation of the people. It is responsible to the people. And the people are responsible for it. No American has the right to allow the present government to say, when Negro children are being bombed and hosed and shot and beaten all over the deep South, that there is nothing we can do about it. There must have been a day in this country's life when the bombing of four children in Sunday School would have created a public uproar and endangered the life of a Governor Wallace. It happened here and there was no public uproar.

I began by saying that one of the paradoxes of education was that precisely at the point when you begin to develop a conscience, you must find yourself at war with your society. It is your responsibility to change society if you think of yourself as an educated person. And on the basis of the evidence—the moral and political evidence—one is compelled to say that this is a backward society. Now if I were a teacher in this school, or any Negro school, and I was dealing with Negro children, who were in my care only a few hours of every day and would then return to their homes and to the streets, children who have an apprehension of their future which with every hour grows grimmer and darker, I would try to teach them—I would try to make them know—that those streets, those houses, those dangers, those agonies by which they are surrounded, are criminal. I would try to make each child know that these things are the results of a criminal conspiracy to destroy him. I would teach him that if he intends to get to be a man, he must at once decide that he is stronger than this conspiracy and that he must never make his peace with it. And that one of his weapons for refusing to make his peace with it and for destroying it depends on what he decides he is worth. I would teach him that there are currently very few standards in this country which are worth a man's respect. That it is up to him to begin to change these standards for the sake of the life and the health of the country. I would suggest to him that the popular culture—as represented, for example, on television and in comic books and in movies—is based on fantasies created by very ill people, and he must be aware that these are fantasies that have nothing to do with reality. I would teach him that the press he reads is not as free as it says it is—and that he can do something about that, too. I would try to make him know that just as American history is longer, larger, more various, more beautiful, and more terrible than anything anyone has ever said about it, so is the world larger, more daring, more beautiful and more terrible, but principally larger—and that it belongs to him. I would teach him that he doesn't have to be bound by the expediencies of any given Administration, any given policy, any given time—that he has the right and the necessity to examine everything. I would try to show him that one has not learned anything about Castro when one says, "He is a Communist." This is a way of *not* learning something about Castro, something about Cuba, something, in fact, about the world. I would suggest to him that he is living, at the moment, in an enormous province. America is not the world and if America is going to become a nation, she must find a way—and this child must help her to find a way—to use the tremendous potential and tremendous energy which this child represents. If this country does not find a way to use that energy, it will be destroyed by that energy.

The Saturday Review, December 21, 1963

"This Nettle, Danger . . ."

A GREAT WRITER operates as an unimpeachable witness to one's own experience; and one of the reasons that great writers are so rare (and their careers, in the main, so stormy) is that almost no one wishes to have his experience corroborated. I suppose that one of the reasons for this is that one's actual experience cannot but assault one's self-image, one's aspirations and one's safety. We all attempt to live on the surface, where we assume we will be less lonely, whereas experience is of the depths and is dictated by what we really fear and hate and love as distinguished from what we think we *ought* to fear and hate and love. One can imagine, for example, that a Shakespeare, writing of the recent bloody events in Texas, would give us a very different version of those events from that which we are presently evolving; by which I do not mean to say that Shakespeare's version would be literally the true one—the literal truth, anyway, is almost always astoundingly misleading. But Shakespeare's version would differ from ours in one important and disturbing way. We would rather believe that evil comes into the world by means of a single man, can be laid at the door of Another; but Shakespeare knew, and all artists know, that evil comes into the world by means of some vast, inexplicable and probably ineradicable human fault. That is to say: the evil is, in some sense, ours, and we help to feed it by failing so often in our private lives to deal with our private truth—our own experience.

In any case, it is the writer's necessity to deal as truthfully as possible with his own experience, and it is his hope to enlarge this experience to contain the experience of others, of millions. Shakespeare did not write an autobiographical first novel, and he does not seem to have felt any necessity to publish abroad the more arresting details of his private life, with the result that we now say, somewhat plaintively, that we know very little about Shakespeare. I think we know as much as we need to know, and far more than we now know concerning our annotated, documented and gossip column'd contemporaries. In the case of these latter, we know, or think we know, where they hang out, what they think, whom they sleep with and whether or not they got along with their parents. These are profoundly irrelevant details, since we don't know what the person—or, perhaps in this context, one should rather say the subject—makes of them, what he sees in them, what he takes from them. Without knowing this, we know nothing, experience being less a matter of *what* happens than to *whom*: experience is created out of the effort to create oneself. Every man writes about his own Shakespeare—and his Shakespeare changes as he himself changes, grows as he grows—and the Shakespeare that I am reading at this stage of my life testifies, for me, to this effort and proves to me also that the sustenance for this effort can only be love.

Every writer in the English language, I should imagine, has at some point hated Shakespeare, has turned away from that monstrous achievement with a kind of sick envy. In my most anti-English days I condemned him as a chauvinist ("this England," indeed!) and because I felt it so bitterly anomalous that a black man should be forced to deal with the English language at all—should be forced to assault the English language in order to be able to speak—I condemned him as one of the authors and architects of my oppression. Again, in the way that some Jews bitterly and mistakenly resent Shylock, I was dubious about Othello (what did he see in Desdemona?) and bitter about Caliban. His great vast gallery of people, whose reality was as contradictory as it was unanswerable, unspeakably oppressed me. I was resenting, of course, the assault on my simplicity; and, in another way, I was a victim of that loveless education which causes so many schoolboys to detest Shakespeare. But I feared him, too, feared him because, in his hands, the English language became the mightiest of instruments. No one would ever write that way again. No one would ever be able to match, much less surpass, him.

Well, I was young and missed the point entirely, was unable to go behind the words and, as it were, the diction, to what the poet was saying. I still remember my shock when I finally *heard* these lines from the murder scene in "Julius Caesar." The assassins are washing their hands in Caesar's blood. Cassius says:

Stoop then, and wash.—How many ages hence
Shall this our lofty scene be acted over,
In states unborn and accents yet unknown!

What I suddenly heard, for the first time, was manifold. It was the voice of lonely, dedicated, deluded Cassius, whose life had never been real for me before—I suddenly seemed to know what this moment meant to him. But beneath and beyond that voice I also heard a note yet more rigorous and impersonal—and contemporary: that "lofty scene," in all its blood and necessary folly, its blind and necessary pain, was thrown into a perspective which has never left my mind. Just so, indeed, is the heedless state overthrown by men, who, in order to overthrow it, have had to achieve a desperate single-mindedness. And this single-mindedness, which we think of (why?) as ennobling, also operates, and much more surely, to distort and diminish a man—to distort and diminish us all even, or perhaps especially, those whose needs and whose energy made the overthrow of the state inevitable, necessary and just. And the terrible thing about this play, for me—it is not necessarily my favorite play, whatever that means, but it *is* the play which I first, so to speak, discovered—is the tension it relentlessly sustains between individual ambition, self-conscious, deluded, idealistic or corrupt, and the blind, mindless passion which drives the individual no less than it drives the mob. "I am Cinna the poet, I am Cinna the poet . . . I am not Cinna the conspirator"—that cry rings in my ears. And the mob's response: "Tear him for his bad verses!" And yet—though one howled with Cinna and felt his terrible rise, at the hands of his countrymen, to death, it was impossible to hate the mob. Or, worse than impossible, useless; for here we were, at once howling and being torn to pieces, the only receptacles of evil and the only receptacles of nobility to be found in all the universe. But the play does not even suggest that we have the perception to know evil from good or that such a distinction can ever be clear: "The evil that men do lives after them; The good is oft interred with their bones. . . ."

Once one has begun to suspect this much about the world—once one has begun to suspect, that is, that one is not, and never will be, innocent, for the reason that no one is—some of the self-protective veils between oneself and reality begin to fall away. It is probably of some significance, though we cannot pursue it here, that my first real apprehension of Shakespeare came when I was living in France, and thinking and speaking in French. The necessity of mastering a foreign language forced me into a new relationship to my own. (It was also in France, therefore, that I began to read the Bible again.) My quarrel with the English language had been that the language reflected none of my experience. But now I began to see the matter in quite another way. If the language was not my own, it might be the fault of the language; but it might also be my fault. Perhaps the language was not my own because I had never attempted to use it, had only learned to imitate it. If this were so, then it might be made to bear the burden of my experience if I could find the stamina to challenge it, and me, to such a test.

In support of this possibility, I had two mighty witnesses: my black ancestors, who evolved the sorrow songs, the blues and jazz, and created an entirely new idiom in an overwhelmingly hostile place; and Shakespeare, who was the last bawdy writer in the English language. What I began to see—especially since, as I say, I was living and speaking in French—is that it is experience which shapes a language; and it is language which controls an experience. The structure of the French language told me something of the French experience, and also something of the French expectations—which were certainly not the American expectations, since the French daily and hourly said things which the Americans could not say at all. (Not even in French.) Similarly, the language with which I had grown up had certainly not been the King's English. An immense experience had forged this language, it had been (and remains) one of the tools of a people's survival, and it revealed expectations which no white American could easily entertain. The authority of this language was in its candor, its irony, its density and its beat: this was the authority of the language which produced me, and it was also the authority of Shakespeare. Again, I was listening very hard to jazz and hoping, one day, to translate it into language, and Shakespeare's bawdiness became very important to me since bawdiness was one of the elements of jazz and revealed a tremendous, loving and realistic respect for the body, and that ineffable force which the body contains, which Americans have mostly lost, which I had experienced only among Negroes, and of which I had then been taught to be ashamed.

My relationship, then, to the language of Shakespeare revealed itself as nothing less than my relationship to myself and my past. Under this light, this revelation, both myself and my past began slowly to open, perhaps the way a flower opens at morning, but, more probably, the way an atrophied muscle begins to function, or frozen fingers to thaw. The greatest poet in the English language found his poetry where poetry is found: in the lives of the people. He could have done this only through love—by knowing, which is not the same thing as understanding, that whatever was happening to anyone was happening to him. It is said that his time was easier than ours, but I doubt it—no time can be easy if one is living through it. I think it is simply that he walked his streets and saw them, and tried not to lie about what he saw; his public streets and his private streets, which are always so mysteriously and inexorably connected; but he trusted that connection. And, though I, and many of us, have bitterly bewailed (and will again) the lot of an American writer—to be part of a people who have ears to hear and hear not, who have eyes to see and see not! I am sure that Shakespeare did the same. Only, he saw, as I think we must, that the people who produce the poet are not responsible to him: he is responsible to them. That is why he is called a poet. And his responsibility, which is also his joy and his strength and his life, is to defeat all labels and complicate all battles by insisting on the human riddle, to bear witness, as long as breath is in him, to that mighty, unnameable, transfiguring force which lives in the soul of man, and to aspire to do his work so well that when the breath has left him, the people—*all people!*—who search in the rubble for a sign or a witness will be able to find him there.

Show, February 1964

Nothing Personal

I USED to distract myself, some mornings before I got out of bed, by pressing the television remote control gadget from one channel to another. This may be the only way to watch TV: I certainly saw some remarkable sights. Blondes and brunettes and, possibly, redheads—my screen was colorless—washing their hair, relentlessly smiling, teeth gleaming like the grillwork of automobiles, breasts firmly, chillingly encased—packaged, as it were—and brilliantly uplifted, forever, all sagging corrected, forever, all middle age bulge—*middle age bulge!*—defeated, eyes as sensuous and mysterious as jelly beans, lips covered with cellophane, hair sprayed to the consistency of aluminum, girdles forbidden to slide up, stockings defeated in their subversive tendencies to slide down, to turn crooked, to snag, to run, to tear, hands prevented from aging by incredibly soft detergents, fingernails forbidden to break by superbly smooth enamels, teeth forbidden to decay by mysterious chemical formulas, all conceivable body odor, under no matter what contingency, prevented for twenty-four hours of every day, forever and forever and forever, children's bones knit strong by the foresight of vast bakeries, tobacco robbed of any harmful effects by the addition of mint, the removal of nicotine, the presence of filters and the length of the cigarette, tires which cannot betray you, automobiles which will make you feel proud, doors which cannot slam on those precious fingers or fingernails, diagrams illustrating—proving—how swiftly impertinent pain can be driven away, square-jawed youngsters dancing, other square-jawed youngsters, armed with guitars, or backed by bands, howling; all of this—and so much more!—punctuated by the roar of great automobiles, overtaking gangsters, the spatter of tommy-guns mowing them down, the rise of the organ as the Heroine braces herself to Tell All, the moving smile of the housewife who has just won a fortune in metal and crockery; news—news? from where?—dropping into this sea with the alertness and irrelevancy of pebbles, sex wearing an aspect so implacably dispiriting that even masturbation (by no means mutual) seems one of the possibilities that vanished in Eden, and murder one's last, best hope—sex of an appalling coyness, often in the form of a prophylactic cigarette being extended by the virile male toward the aluminum and cellophane girl. They happily blow smoke into each other's face, jelly beans, brilliant with desire, grillwork gleaming; perhaps—poor, betrayed exiles—they are trying to discover if, behind all that grillwork, all those barriers, either of them has a tongue.

Subsequently, in the longer and less explicit commercials in which these images are encased, the male certainly doesn't seem to have a tongue—perhaps one may say that the cat's got it; father knows best, these days, only in politics, which is the only place we ever find him, and where he proves to be—alas!—absolutely indistinguishable from the American boy. He doesn't even seem much closer to the grave—which fact, in the case of most of our most influential politicians, fills a great many people, all over the world, with despair.

And so it should. We have all heard the bit about what a pity it was that Plymouth Rock didn't land on the Pilgrims instead of the other way around. I have never found this remark very funny. It seems wistful and vindictive to me, containing, furthermore, a very bitter truth. The inertness of that rock meant death for the Indians, enslavement for the blacks, and spiritual disaster for those homeless Europeans who now call themselves Americans and who have never been able to resolve their relationship either to the continent they fled or to the continent they conquered. Leaving aside—as we, mostly, imagine ourselves to be able to do—those people to whom we quaintly refer as minorities, who, without the most tremendous coercion, coercion indistinguishable from despair, would ever have crossed the frightening ocean to come to this desolate place? I know the myth tells us that heroes came, looking for freedom; just as the myth tells us that America is full of smiling people. Well, heroes are always, by definition, looking for freedom, and no doubt a few heroes got here, too—one wonders how they fared; and though I rarely see anyone smiling here, I am prepared to believe that many people are, though God knows what it is they're smiling about; but the relevant truth is that the country was settled by a desperate, divided, and rapacious horde of people who were determined to forget their pasts and determined to make money. We certainly have not changed in this respect and this is proved by our faces, by our children, by our absolutely unspeakable loneliness, and the spectacular ugliness and hostility of our cities. Our cities are terribly unloved—by the people who live in them, I mean. No one seems to feel that the city belongs to him.

Despair: perhaps it is this despair which we should attempt to examine if we hope to bring water to this desert.

It is, of course, in the very nature of a myth that those who are its victims and, at the same time, its perpetrators, should, by virtue of these two facts, be rendered unable to examine the myth, or even to suspect, much less recognize, that it is a myth which controls and blasts their lives. One sees this, it seems to me, in great and grim relief, in the situation of the poor white in the Deep South. The poor white was enslaved almost from the instant he arrived on these shores, and he is still enslaved by a brutal and cynical oligarchy. The utility of the poor white was to make slavery both profitable and safe and, therefore, the germ of white supremacy which he brought with him from Europe was made hideously to flourish in the American air. Two world wars and a world-wide depression have failed to reveal to this poor man that he has far more in common with the ex-slaves whom he fears than he has with the masters who oppress them both for profit. It is no accident that ancient Scottish ballads and Elizabethan chants are still heard in those dark hills—talk about a people being locked in the past! To be locked in the past means, in effect, that one has no past, since one can never assess it, or use it: and if one cannot use the past, one cannot function in the present, and so one can never be free. I take this to be, as I say, the American situation in relief, the root of our unadmitted sorrow, and the very key to our crisis.

It has always been much easier (because it has always seemed much safer) to give a name to the evil without than to locate the terror within. And yet, the terror within is far truer and far more powerful than any of our labels: the labels change, the terror is constant. And this terror has something to do with that irreducible gap between the self one invents—the self one takes oneself as being, which is, however, and by definition, a provisional self—and the undiscoverable self

which always has the power to blow the provisional self to
bits. It is perfectly possible—indeed, it is far from uncommon—to go to bed one night, or wake up one morning, or
simply walk through a door one has known all one's life, and
discover, between inhaling and exhaling, that the self one has
sewn together with such effort is all dirty rags, is unusable, is
gone: and out of what raw material will one build a self again?
The lives of men—and, therefore, of nations—to an extent
literally unimaginable, depend on how vividly this question
lives in the mind. It is a question which can paralyze the mind,
of course; but if the question does *not* live in the mind, then
one is simply condemned to eternal youth, which is a synonym
for corruption.

Some rare days, often in the winter, when New York is
cheerfully immobilized by snow—cheerfully, because the
snow gives people an excuse to talk to each other, and they
need, God help us, an excuse—or sometimes when the frozen
New York spring is approaching, I walk out of my house toward no particular destination, and watch the faces that pass
me. Where do they come from? how did they become—these
faces—so cruel and so sterile? they are related to whom? they
are related to what? They do not relate to the buildings, certainly—no human being could; I suspect, in fact, that many
of us live with the carefully suppressed terror that these buildings are about to crash down on us; the nature of the movement of the people in the streets is certainly very close to
panic. You will search in vain for lovers. I have not heard
anyone singing in the streets of New York for more than
twenty years. By singing, I mean singing for joy, for the hell
of it. I don't mean the drunken, lonely, 4-AM keening which
is simply the sound of some poor soul trying to vomit up his
anguish and gagging on it. Where the people can sing, the
poet can live—and it is worth saying it the other way around,
too: where the poet can sing, the people can live. When a
civilization treats its poets with the disdain with which we treat
ours, it cannot be far from disaster; it cannot be far from the
slaughter of the innocents. Everyone is rushing, God knows
where, and everyone is looking for God knows what—but it
is clear that no one is happy here, and that something has
been lost. Only, sometimes, uptown, along the river, perhaps,

I've sometimes watched strangers here, here for a day or a week or a month, or newly transplanted, watched a boy and a girl, or a boy and a boy, or a man and a woman, or a man and a child, or a woman and a child; yes, *there* was something recognizable, something to which the soul responded, something to make one smile, even to make one weep with exultation. They were yet distinguishable from the concrete and the steel. One felt that one might approach them without freezing to death.

2

A European friend of mine and myself were arrested on Broadway, in broad daylight, while looking for a taxi. He had been here three days, had not yet mastered English, and I was showing him the wonders of the city of New York. He was impressed and bewildered, though he also seemed rather to wonder what purpose it served—when, suddenly, down from heaven, or up through the sidewalk, two plain-clothes men appeared, separated us, scarcely a word was spoken. I watched my friend, carried by the scruff of the neck, vanish into the crowd. Not a soul seemed to notice; apparently it happened every day. I was pushed into the doorway of a drugstore, and frisked, made to empty my pockets, made to roll up my sleeves, asked what I was doing around here—"around here" being the city in which I was born.

I am an old hand at this—policemen have always loved to pick me up and, sometimes, to beat me up—so I said nothing during this entire operation. I was worried about my friend, who might fail to understand the warmth of his reception in the land of the free; worried about his command of English, especially when confronted by the somewhat special brand used by the police. Neither of us carried knives or guns, neither of us used dope: so much for the criminal aspect. Furthermore, my friend was a married man, with two children, here on a perfectly respectable visit, and he had not even come from some dirty and disreputable place, like Greece, but from geometric and solvent Switzerland: so much for morals. I was not exactly a bum, either, so I wondered what the cop would say.

He seemed extremely disappointed that I carried no weapons, that my veins were not punctured—disappointed, and, therefore, more truculent than ever. I conveyed to him with some force that I was not precisely helpless and that I was perfectly able, and more than willing, to cause him a great deal of trouble. Why, exactly, had he picked us up?

He was now confused, afraid, and apologetic, which caused me to despise him from the bottom of my heart. He said— how many times have I heard it!—that there had been a call out to pick up two guys who looked just like us.

White and black, you mean?

Apart from my friends, I think I can name on the fingers of one hand all the Americans I have ever met who were able to answer a direct question, a real question: well, not exactly. Hell, no. He hadn't even known that the other guy was white. (He thought that he was Puerto Rican, which says something very interesting, I think, about the eye of the beholder—like, as it were, to like.)

Nevertheless, he was in a box—it was not going to be a simple matter of apologizing and letting me go. Unless he was able to find his friend and *my* friend, I was going to force him to arrest me and then bring charges for false arrest. So, not without difficulty, we found my friend, who had been released and was waiting in the bar around the corner from our house. He, also, had baffled his interlocutor; had baffled him by turning out to be exactly what he had said he was, which contains its own comment, I think, concerning the attitudes Americans have toward each other. He had given my friend a helpful tip: if he wanted to make it in America, it would be better for him not to be seen with niggers. My friend thanked him warmly, which brought a glow, I should imagine, to his simple heart—how we adore simplicity!— and has since made something of a point of avoiding white Americans.

I certainly can't blame him. For one thing, talking to Americans is usually extremely uphill work. We are afraid to reveal ourselves because we trust ourselves so little. American attitudes are appalling, but so are the attitudes of most of the people in the world. What is stultifying here is that the attitude is presented as the person; one is expected to justify the attitude in order to reassure the person—whom, alas, one has yet to meet, who is light-years away, in some dreadful, private labyrinth. And in this labyrinth the person is desperately trying *not* to find out what he *really* feels. Therefore, the truth cannot be told, even about one's attitudes: we live by lies. And not only, for example, about race—whatever, by this time, in this country, or, indeed, in the world, this word may mean—but about our very natures. The lie has penetrated to our most private moments, and the most secret chambers of our hearts.

Nothing more sinister can happen, in any society, to any people. And when it happens, it means that the people are caught in a kind of vacuum between their present and their past—the romanticized, that is, the maligned past, and the denied and dishonored present. It is a crisis of identity. And in such a crisis, at such a pressure, it becomes absolutely indispensable to discover, or invent—the two words, here, are synonyms—the stranger, the barbarian, who is responsible for our confusion and our pain. Once he is driven out—destroyed—then we can be at peace: those questions will be gone. Of course, those questions never go, but it has always seemed much easier to murder than to change. And this is really the choice with which we are confronted now.

I know that these are strong words for a sunlit, optimistic land, lulled for so long, and into such an euphoria, by prosperity (based on the threat of war) and by such magazines as *Reader's Digest*, and stirring political slogans, and Hollywood and television. (Communications whose role is not to communicate, but simply to reassure.) Nevertheless, I am appalled—for example—by the limpness with which the entire nation appears to have accepted the proposition that, in the city of Dallas, Texas, in which handbills were being issued accusing the late President Kennedy of treason, one would *need* a leftist lunatic with a gun to blow off the President's head. Leftists have a hard time in the south; there cannot be very many there; I, certainly, was never followed around southern streets by leftist lunatics, but state troopers. Similarly, there are a great many people in Texas, or, for that matter, in America, with far stronger reasons for wishing the President dead than any demented Castroite could have had. Quite apart, now, from what time will reveal the truth of this case to have been, it is reassuring to feel that the evil came from without and is in no way connected with the moral climate of America; reassuring to feel that the enemy sent the assassin from far away, and that we, ourselves, could never have nourished so monstrous a personality or be in any way whatever responsible for such a cowardly and bloody act. Well. The America of my experience has worshipped and nourished violence for as long as I have been on earth. The violence was being perpetrated mainly against black men, though—the strangers; and so it didn't count. But, if a society permits one portion of its citizenry to be menaced or destroyed, then, very soon, no one in that society is safe. The forces thus released in the people can never be held in check, but run their devouring course, destroying the very foundations which it was imagined they would save.

But we are unbelievably ignorant concerning what goes on in our country—to say nothing of what goes on in the rest of the world—and appear to have become too timid to question what we are told. Our failure to trust one another deeply enough to be able to talk to one another has become so great that people with these questions in their hearts do not speak them: our opulence is so pervasive that people who are afraid to lose whatever they think they have persuade themselves of the truth of a lie, and help disseminate it; and God help the innocent here, that man or woman who simply wants to love, and be loved. Unless this would-be lover is able to replace his or her backbone with a steel rod, he or she is doomed. This is no place for love. I know that I am now expected to make a bow in the direction of those millions of unremarked, happy marriages all over America, but I am unable honestly to do so because I find nothing whatever in our moral and social climate—and I am now thinking particularly of the state of our children—to bear witness to their existence. I suspect that when we refer to these happy and so marvelously invisible people, we are simply being nostalgic concerning the happy, simple, God-fearing life which we imagine ourselves once to have lived. In any case, wherever love is found, it unfailingly makes itself felt in the individual, the personal authority of the individual. Judged by this standard, we are a loveless nation. The best that can be said is that some of us are struggling.

And what we are struggling against is that death in the heart which leads not only to the shedding of blood, but which reduces human beings to corpses while they live.

3

Four AM can be a devastating hour. The day, no matter what kind of day it was, is indisputably over; almost instantaneously, a new day begins: and how will one bear it? Probably no better than one bore the day that is ending, possibly not as well. Moreover, a day is coming which one will not recall, the last day of one's life, and on that day one will *oneself* become as irrecoverable as all the days that have passed.

It is a fearful speculation—or, rather, a fearful knowledge—that, one day one's eyes will no longer look out on the world. One will no longer be present at the universal morning roll call. The light will rise for others, but not for you. Sometimes, at four AM, this knowledge is almost enough to force a reconciliation between oneself and all one's pain and error. Since, anyway, it will end one day, why not try it—life—one more time? *It's a long old road,* as Bessie Smith puts it, *but it's got to find an end.* And so, she wearily, doggedly, informs us, *I picked up my bag, baby, and I tried it again.* Her song ends on a very bitter and revealing note: *You can't trust nobody, you might as well be alone/Found my long-lost friend, and I might as well stayed at home!*

Still, she was driven to find that long-lost friend, to grasp again, with fearful hope, the unwilling, unloving, human hand. I think all of our voyages drive us there; for I have always felt that a human being could only be saved by another human being. I am aware that we do not save each other very often. But I am also aware that we save each other some of the time. And all that God can do, and all that I expect Him to do, is lend one the courage to continue one's journey and face one's end, when it comes, like a man.

For, perhaps—perhaps—between now and that last day, something wonderful will happen, a miracle, a miracle of coherence and release. And the miracle on which one's unsteady attention is focussed is always the same, however it may be stated, or however it may remain unstated. It is the miracle of love, love strong enough to guide or drive one into the great estate of maturity, or, to put it another way, into the apprehension and acceptance of one's own identity. For some deep and ineradicable instinct—I believe—causes us to know that it is only this passionate achievement which can outlast death, which can cause life to spring from death.

Nevertheless, sometimes, at four AM, when one feels that one has probably become simply incapable of supporting this miracle, with all one's wounds awake and throbbing, and all one's ghastly inadequacy staring and shouting from the walls and the floor—the entire universe having shrunk to the prison of the self—death glows like the only light on a high, dark, mountain road, where one has, forever and forever! lost one's way.—And many of us perish then.

But if one can reach back, reach down—into oneself, into one's life—and find there some witness, however unexpected or ambivalent, to one's reality, one will be enabled, though perhaps not very spiritedly, to face another day. (We used to sing in the church, *It's another day's journey, and I'm so glad, the world can't do me no harm!*) What one must be enabled to recognize, at four o'clock in the morning, is that one has no right, at least not for reasons of private anguish, to take one's life. All lives are connected to other lives and when one man goes, much more than the man goes with him. One has to look on oneself as the custodian of a quantity and a quality—oneself—which is absolutely unique in the world because it has never been here before and will never be here again. But it is extremely difficult, in this place and time, to look on oneself in this way. Where all human connections are distrusted, the human being is very quickly lost.

Four AM passes, the dangerous turning maneuvered once more; and here comes the sun or the rain and the hard, metallic, unrevealing light and sounds of life outside and movement in the streets. Cautiously, one peeks through the blinds, guessing at the weather. And, presently, out of the limbo of the bathroom steam and fog, one's face comes floating up again, from unimaginable depths. Here it comes, unreadable as ever, the patient bones steady beneath the skin, eyes veiling the mind's bewilderment and the heart's loss, only the lips cryptically suggesting that all is not well with the spirit which lives within this clay. Then one selects the uniform which one will wear. This uniform is designed to telegraph to others what to see so that they will not be made uncomfortable and probably hostile by being forced to look on another human being. The uniform must suggest a certain setting and it must dictate a certain air and it must also convey, however subtly, a dormant aggressiveness, like the power of a sleeping lion. It is necessary to make anyone on the streets think twice before attempting to vent his despair on you. So armed, one reaches the unloved streets.

The unloved streets. I have very often walked through the streets of New York fancying myself a kind of unprecedented explorer, trapped among savages, searching for hidden treasure; the trick being to discover the treasure before the savages discovered me; hence, my misleading uniform. After all, I have lived in cities in which stone urns on park parapets were not unthinkable, cities in which it was perfectly possible, and not a matter of taking one's life in one's hands, to walk through the park. How long would a stone urn last in Central Park? And look at the New York buildings, rising up like tyrannical eagles, glass and steel and aluminum smiting the air, jerry-built, inept, contemptuous; who can function in these buildings and for whose profit were they built? Unloved indeed: look at our children. They roam the streets, as arrogant and irreverent as business-men and as dangerous as those gangs of children who roamed the streets of bombed European cities after the last World War. Only, these children have no strange and grinning soldiers to give them chocolate candy or chewing gum, and no one will give them a home. No one has one to give, the very word no longer conveying any meaning, and, anyway, nothing is more vivid in American life than the fact that we have no respect for our children, nor have our children any respect for us. By being what we have become, by placing things above people, we broke their hearts early, and drove them away.

We have, as it seems to me, a very curious sense of reality—or, rather, perhaps, I should say, a striking addiction to irreality. How is it possible, one cannot but ask, to raise a child without loving the child? How is it possible to love the child if one does not know who one is? How is it possible for the child to grow up if the child is not loved? Children can survive without money or security or safety or things: but they are lost if they cannot find a loving example, for only this example can give them a touchstone for their lives. *Thus far and no further:* this is what the father must say to the child. If the child is not told where the limits are, he will spend the rest of his life trying to discover them. For the child who is not told where the limits are knows, though he may not know he knows it, that no one cares enough about him to prepare him for his journey.

This, I think, has something to do with the phenomenon, unprecedented in the world, of the ageless American boy; it has something to do with our desperate adulation of simplicity and youth—how bitterly betrayed one must have been in one's youth to suppose that it is a virtue to remain simple or to remain young!—and it also helps to explicate, to my mind at least, some of the stunning purposes to which Americans have put the imprecise science of psychiatry. I have known people in genuine trouble, who somehow managed to live with their trouble; and I cannot but compare these people— ex-junkies and jail-birds, sons of German Nazis, sons of Spanish generals, sons of Southern racists, blues singers and black matrons—with that fluid horde, in my professional and quasi-professional contacts, whose only real trouble is inertia, who work at the most disgraceful jobs in order to pay, for the luxury of someone else's attention, twenty-five dollars an hour. To my black and toughened, Puritan conscience, it seems an absolute scandal; and, again, this peculiar self-indulgence certainly has a dreadful effect on their children, whom they are quite unable to raise. And they cannot raise them because they have opted for the one commodity which is absolutely beyond human reach: safety. This is one of the reasons, as it seems to me, that we are so badly educated, for to become educated (as all tyrants have always known) is to become inaccessibly independent, it is to acquire a dangerous way of assessing danger, and it is to hold in one's hands a means of changing reality. This is not at all the same thing as "adjusting" to reality: the effort of "adjusting" to reality simply has the paradoxical effect of destroying reality, since it substitutes for one's own speech and one's own voice an

interiorized public cacophony of quotations. People are defeated or go mad or die in many, many ways, some in the
silence of that valley, *where I couldn't hear nobody pray*, and
many in the public, sounding horror where no cry or lament
or song or hope can disentangle itself from the roar. And so
we go under, victims of that universal cruelty which lives in
the heart and in the world, victims of the universal indifference to the fate of another, victims of the universal fear of
love, proof of the absolute impossibility of achieving a life
without love. One day, perhaps, unimaginable generations
hence, we will evolve into the knowledge that human beings
are more important than real estate and will permit this
knowledge to become the ruling principle of our lives. For I
do not for an instant doubt, and I will go to my grave believing, that we can build Jerusalem, if we will.

4

*The light that's in your eyes/Reminds me of the skies/That
shine above us every day*—so wrote a contemporary lover, out
of God knows what agony, what hope, and what despair. But
he saw the light in the eyes, which is the only light there is
in the world, and honored it and trusted it; and will always
be able to find it; since it is always there, waiting to be found.
One discovers the light in darkness, that is what darkness is
for; but everything in our lives depends on how we bear the
light. It is necessary, while in darkness, to know that there is
a light somewhere, to know that in oneself, waiting to be
found, there is a light. What the light reveals is danger, and
what it demands is faith. Pretend, for example, that you were
born in Chicago and have never had the remotest desire to
visit Hong Kong, which is only a name on a map for you;
pretend that some convulsion, sometimes called accident,
throws you into connection with a man or a woman who lives
in Hong Kong; and that you fall in love. Hong Kong will
immediately cease to be a name and become the center of
your life. And you may never know how many people live in
Hong Kong. But you will know that one man or one woman
lives there without whom you cannot live. And this is how
our lives are changed, and this is how we are redeemed.

What a journey this life is! dependent, entirely, on things unseen. If your lover lives in Hong Kong and cannot get to Chicago, it will be necessary for you to go to Hong Kong. Perhaps you will spend your life there, and never see Chicago again. And you will, I assure you, as long as space and time divide you from anyone you love, discover a great deal about shipping routes, air lanes, earthquake, famine, disease, and war. And you will always know what time it is in Hong Kong, for you love someone who lives there. And love will simply have no choice but to go into battle with space and time and, furthermore, to win.

I know we often lose, and that the death or destruction of another is infinitely more real and unbearable than one's own. I think I know how many times one has to start again, and how often one feels that one cannot start again. And yet, on pain of death, one can never remain where one is. The light. The light. One will perish without the light.

I have slept on rooftops and in basements and subways, have been cold and hungry all my life; have felt that no fire would ever warm me, and no arms would ever hold me. I have been, as the song says, *'buked and scorned* and I know that I always will be. But, my God, in that darkness, which was the lot of my ancestors and my own state, what a mighty fire burned! In that darkness of rape and degradation, that fine, flying froth and mist of blood, through all that terror and in all that helplessness, a living soul moved and refused to die. We really emptied oceans with a home-made spoon and tore down mountains with our hands. And if love was in Hong Kong, we learned how to swim.

It is a mighty heritage, it is the human heritage, and it is all there is to trust. And I learned this through descending, as it were, into the eyes of my father and my mother. I wondered, when I was little, how they bore it—for I knew that they had much to bear. It had not yet occurred to me that I also would have much to bear; but they knew it, and the unimaginable rigors of their journey helped them to prepare me for mine. This is why one must say Yes to life and embrace it wherever it is found—and it is found in terrible places; nevertheless, there it is: and if the father can say, *Yes, Lord*, the child can learn that most difficult of words, *Amen*.

For nothing is fixed, forever and forever and forever, it is not fixed; the earth is always shifting, the light is always changing, the sea does not cease to grind down rock. Generations do not cease to be born, and we are responsible to them because we are the only witnesses they have.

The sea rises, the light fails, lovers cling to each other, and children cling to us. The moment we cease to hold each other, the moment we break faith with one another, the sea engulfs us and the light goes out.

1964

Words of a Native Son

I'M involved in something rather dangerous: I think it's always dangerous for a writer to talk about his work. I don't mean to be coy or modest; I simply mean that there is so much about his work that he doesn't really understand and can't understand—because it comes out of certain depths concerning which, no matter what we think we know these days, we know very, very little. It comes out of the same depths that love comes or murder or disaster. It comes out of things which are almost impossible to articulate. That's the writer's effort. Every writer knows that he may work 24 hours a day, and for several years; without that he wouldn't be a writer; but without something that happens out of that effort, some freedom which arrives from way down in the depths, something which touches the page and brings the scene alive, he wouldn't be a writer.

It's dangerous in another way to talk about my work, because I'm a novelist and as I'm writing this I'm publicly involved in a Broadway play, and the record of novelists who have managed to write plays is so extremely discouraging that I won't even go into it. But for some reason I know I had to do the play. I have written one play before. I have had to re-examine that experience lately because it turned out to be important in a way that I didn't realize at the time. I wrote the play after I finished my first novel, when I knew I had to write something, but I knew I couldn't write another novel right away. I thought I would try a play. It took about three years to do and we produced it at Howard University. I was very casual about it. I went down to Howard about a week before we were supposed to open, saw the play, and almost died. It was the first time I realized that speeches don't necessarily work in the theater. I was suddenly bombarded with my own literature, an unbearable experience. I had to begin cutting because I realized that the actors could do many things in silence or could make one word, one gesture, count more than two or three pages of talk. I began to suspect, and this is what I'm struggling with now, that the two disciplines—the discipline of writing a novel and the discipline of writing a play—are so extremely different that it would have been luckier for me, in terms of the play, if I had been a violinist or a guitar player or a rock-'n'-roll singer or a plumber. My chances of writing a play would have been better if I had been in any of those professions.

Here's what I'm trying to get at when I refer to the two disciplines. Every artist is involved with one single effort, really, which is somehow to dig down to where reality is. We live, especially in this age and in this country and at this time, in a civilization which supposes that reality is something you can touch, that reality is tangible. The aspirations of the American people, as far as one can read the current evidence, depend very heavily on this concrete, tangible, pragmatic point of view. But every artist and, in fact, every person knows, deeper than conscious knowledge or speech can go, that beyond every reality there is another one which controls it. Behind my writing table, which is a tangible thing, there is a passion which created the table. Behind the electric light you might be reading by now, there was the passion of a man who once stole the fire in order to bring us this light. The things that people really do and really mean and really feel are almost impossible for them to describe, but these are the very things which are most important about them: These things control them and that is where reality is. What one tries to do in a novel is to show this reality.

Such effort would not be important if life were not important. But life *is* important, vastly more so than art; but without the passion of art, that portion of life we call civilization is in great danger when it begins, as we have, to neglect or to despise its artists. Artists are the only people in a society who can tell that society the truth about itself. When I was working on *Another Country*, which was the hardest thing I had done until that time, I had several problems in trying to get across, in trying to convey, what I felt was happening to us in this country. Not that this is unusual: In a sense, every work of art, if I may use that phrase, is a kind of metaphor for what the artist takes to be our condition. My principal problem, at least by hindsight, was how to handle my heroine, Ida, who in effect dictated a great deal of the book to me. And the first thing that I had to realize was that she, operating in New

York as she did, as Negro girls do, was an object of wonder and even some despair—and some distrust—to all the people around her, including people who were very fond of her—Vivaldo, her lover, and their friends. I had somehow to make the reader see what was happening to this girl. I knew that a girl like Ida would not be able to say it for herself, but I also knew that no reader will believe you if you simply tell him what you want him to know. You must make him see it for himself. He must somehow be trapped into the reality you want him to submit to and you must achieve a kind of rigorous discipline in order to walk the reader to the guillotine without his knowing it.

Now, in order to get what I wanted I had to invent Rufus, Ida's brother, who had not been present at the original conception. Rufus was the only way that I could make the reader see what had happened to Ida and what was controlling her in all her relationships, why she was so difficult, why she was so uncertain, why she suffered so; and of course the reason she was suffering was because of what had happened to her brother, because her brother was dead. She was not about to forgive anybody for it. And this rage was about to destroy her. In order to get this across, I had to put great lights around Ida and keep the reader at a certain distance from her. I had to let him see what Vivaldo thought, what Cass thought, what Eric thought, but what Ida thought had to remain for all of them the mystery which it is in life, and had to be, therefore, a kind of mystery for the reader, too, who had to be fascinated by her and wonder about her and care about her and try to figure out what was driving her to where she was so clearly going. And I think that in some ways, Ida, finally, when she does talk to her lover, says things which she would not have been able to say in any other way or under any other pressure, and I had somehow to get her to that pressure. In a novel you can suggest a great deal. You *must* suggest a great deal. There is something in a novel which we'll have to refer to here as the setting. The setting is the climate. For example, it is unimportant in a novel to describe the room. It is unimportant in a novel to describe the characters. It doesn't really matter whether they have blue eyes or brown hair or whatever. You have to make the reader see them with just enough detail

not to blot the picture out. Try to sketch the character in, let
the reader do the rest. That's not as lazy or irresponsible as it
may sound. I mean that the character's reality has to come
from something deeper than his physical attributes and therefore the setting in which he operates has to come from something deeper than that, too. The New York of *Another
Country* never really existed except in *Another Country*. The
bar in which Cass and Vivaldo have their crucial scene when
Cass tells him about her husband is one of a million cocktail
bars; all that is described in that scene, I think, is some peanuts
on the table. And you can do that in a novel because the
reader has been in a bar like that and the reader has been in
New York streets: there are some nerves you must press which
will operate to make him see what you want him to see, and
this, in a way, is the setting.

But you cannot do that in a play. Everything in a play has
to be terribly concrete, terribly visible. The church in which I
was born operates in one way in *Go Tell It on the Mountain*,
mainly as a presence, I think, as a weight, as a kind of affliction
for all those people who are in it, who are in fact trapped in
it and don't know how to get out. But in my play there is
another church. And I suddenly saw it. I don't know if I can
make this clear to you. On a back road in Mississippi or Louisiana or some place in the deep South, we were wandering
around talking to various people, and there was a small church
sitting by itself. I was very oppressed that day by things we'd
seen and I was very aware that I was in the deep South and
had been very close to my father's birthplace. It suddenly
struck me that this church must have been very much like the
church in which my father preached before he came North. I
looked into the window and suddenly saw my set. It was a
country church. I saw that if I could select the details which
would be most meaningful for what I was trying to do, then
in a sense, that part of my problem was solved. And I saw
something else. I always have some idea of where I want to
go. I even sometimes have my last chapter or my last line, a
kind of very rough and untrustworthy map. But I don't know
quite how I'm going to get there. In the working out of
a novel, you work it out in terms of dialog and conflicts,
and again, this is power of suggestion, this is hitting on the

readers' nerves—nerves which we all have in common. In a play, you're doing the same thing. But you're doing it in such a different way that, for example, a white woman in my play, who is a somewhat older woman, married to a murderer, which is part of what the play is about, has to be revealed in very different ways. And I began to see her by watching certain people, by watching for her, watching for my character, which is what you start doing, really, once this character has captured your attention. You look at everybody around you in another way. You suddenly are looking for some revelatory and liberating detail. And if you're working on a play—I don't know if I'm making this clear—you suddenly watch people in a very physical way. You watch the way they light their cigarettes, you watch the way they cross a room, you observe, for the first time, whether or not this person is bowlegged and you begin to think that you can tell by the way a person combs his or her hair, by the beat of a pause, by the things they do or do not say, what is going on inside them. You're watching for the ways in which people reveal themselves in their day-to-day life. What Freud called—I think I'm right about this—the psychopathology of everyday life. So that as I began watching for my woman in the South, I began to see her, too. I have a very good actress friend. I began to watch her, as if she were going to play the part. How would she walk into the door with groceries, and how would she look at their child: how would she look at her husband whom she loves, whom she understands, whom she knows to be a murderer? How would she do it? And I began to see that there would be very small things she would do and very peculiar things that she would say to reveal her torment. I began to see that this is what we all do, all of the time, all of us, including you and me. That whatever is really driving us is what can never, never, never be hidden and is there to see if one wants to see it. The trouble is, of course, that most of us are afraid of that level of reality. It seems to threaten us, because we think we can be safe. And this brings me to something much deeper; for when you've gotten this far, you see something which every writer is really seeing over and over and over again, at pressures of varying intensity. And he is *really* telling the same story over and over and over again, trying different ways to tell it and trying to get more and more and more of it out. As I write this, I am trying to tell it in a play set in the deep South.

But one afternoon in Harlem I understood something more about my story and about myself. My brother and some other people and my nephew were on the block where I grew up. It hasn't changed much in these last 38 years of progress. And we also visited a funeral parlor nearby. A boy had died, a boy of 27 who had been on the needle and who was a friend of my nephew's. I don't know why this struck me so much today, but it did. Perhaps because my nephew was there— I don't know. We walked to the block where we grew up. There's a railing on that block, an iron railing with spikes. It's green now, but when I was a child, it was black. And at one point in my childhood—I must have been very, very young—I watched a drunken man falling down, being teased by children, falling next to that railing. I remember the way his blood looked against the black, and for some reason I've never forgotten that man. Today I began to see why. There's a dead boy in my play, it really pivots on a dead boy. The whole action of the play is involved with an effort to discover how this death came about and who really, apart from the man who physically did the deed, was responsible for it. The action of the play involves the terrible discovery that no one was innocent of it, neither black nor white. All had a hand in it, as we all do. But this boy is all the ruined children that I have watched all my life being destroyed on streets up and down this nation, being destroyed as we sit here, and being destroyed in silence. This boy is, somehow, my subject, my torment, too. And I think he must also be yours. I've begun to be obsessed more and more by a line that comes from William Blake. It says, "A dog starved at his master's gate/Predicts the ruin of the State."

The story that I hope to live long enough to tell, to get it out somehow whole and entire, has to do with the terrible, terrible damage we are doing to all our children. Because what is happening on the streets of Harlem to black boys and girls is also happening on all American streets to everybody. It's a terrible delusion to think that any part of this republic can be safe as long as 20,000,000 members of it are as menaced as they are. The reality I am trying to get at is that the humanity

of this submerged population is equal to the humanity of anyone else, equal to yours, equal to that of your child. I know
when I walk into a Harlem funeral parlor and see a dead boy
lying there. *I know*, no matter what the social scientists say,
or the liberals say, that it is extremely unlikely that he would
be in his grave so soon if he were not black. That is a terrible
thing to have to say. But, if it is so, then the people who are
responsible for this are in a terrible condition. Please take
note. I'm not interested in anybody's guilt. Guilt is a luxury
that we can no longer afford. I know you didn't do it, and I
didn't do it either, but I am responsible for it because I am a
man and a citizen of this country and you are responsible for
it, too, for the very same reason: As long as my children face
the future that they face, and come to the ruin that they come
to, your children are very greatly in danger, too. They are
endangered above all by the moral apathy which pretends it
isn't happening. This does something terrible to us. Anyone
who is trying to be conscious must begin to be conscious of
that apathy and must begin to dismiss the vocabulary which
we've used so long to cover it up, to lie about the way things
are. We must make the great effort to realize that there is no
such thing as a Negro problem—but simply a menaced boy.
If we could do this, we could save this country, we could save
the world. Anyway, that dead boy is my subject and my responsibility. And yours.

Playboy, December 1964

The American Dream and the American Negro

I FIND MYSELF, not for the first time, in the position of a kind of Jeremiah. It would seem to me that the question before the house is a proposition horribly loaded, that one's response to that question depends on where you find yourself in the world, what your sense of reality is. That is, it depends on assumptions we hold so deeply as to be scarcely aware of them.

The white South African or Mississippi sharecropper or Alabama sheriff has at bottom a system of reality which compels them really to believe when they face the Negro that this woman, this man, this child must be insane to attack the system to which he owes his entire identity. For such a person, the proposition which we are trying to discuss here does not exist.

On the other hand, I have to speak as one of the people who have been most attacked by the Western system of reality. It comes from Europe. That is how it got to America. It raises the question of whether or not civilizations can be considered equal, or whether one civilization has a right to subjugate— in fact, to destroy—another.

Now, leaving aside all the physical factors one can quote— leaving aside the rape or murder, leaving aside the bloody catalogue of oppression which we are too familiar with anyway—what the system does to the subjugated is to destroy his sense of reality. It destroys his father's authority over him. His father can no longer tell him anything because his past has disappeared.

In the case of the American Negro, from the moment you are born every stick and stone, every face, is white. Since you have not yet seen a mirror, you suppose you are, too. It comes as a great shock around the age of 5, 6 or 7 to discover that the flag to which you have pledged allegiance, along with everybody else, has not pledged allegiance to you. It comes as a great shock to see Gary Cooper killing off the Indians and, although you are rooting for Gary Cooper, that the Indians are you.

It comes as a great shock to discover that the country which is your birthplace and to which you owe your life and identity has not, in its whole system of reality, evolved any place for you. The disaffection and the gap between people, only on the basis of their skins, begins there and accelerates throughout your whole lifetime. You realize that you are 30 and you are having a terrible time. You have been through a certain kind of mill and the most serious effect is again not the catalogue of disaster—the policeman, the taxi driver, the waiters, the landlady, the banks, the insurance companies, the millions of details 24 hours of every day which spell out to you that you are a worthless human being. It is not that. By that time you have begun to see it happening in your daughter, your son or your niece or your nephew. You are 30 by now and nothing you have done has helped you escape the trap. But what is worse is that nothing you have done, and as far as you can tell nothing you *can* do, will save your son or your daughter from having the same disaster and from coming to the same end.

We speak about expense. There are several ways of addressing oneself to some attempt to find out what that word means here. From a very literal point of view, the harbors and the ports and the railroads of the country—the economy, especially in the South—could not conceivably be what they are if it had not been (and this is still so) for cheap labor. I am speaking very seriously, and this is not an overstatement: I picked cotton, I carried it to the market, I built the railroads under someone else's whip for nothing. For nothing.

The Southern oligarchy which has still today so very much power in Washington, and therefore some power in the world, was created by my labor and my sweat and the violation of my women and the murder of my children. This in the land of the free, the home of the brave. None can challenge that statement. It is a matter of historical record.

In the Deep South you are dealing with a sheriff or a landlord or a landlady or the girl at the Western Union desk. She doesn't know quite whom she is dealing with—by which I mean, if you are not part of a town and if you are a Northern nigger, it shows in millions of ways. She simply knows that it is an unknown quantity and she wants to have nothing to do with it. You have to wait a while to get your telegram. We have all been through it. By the time you get to be a man it is fairly easy to deal with.

But what happens to the poor white man's, the poor white woman's, mind? It is this: they have been raised to believe, and by now they helplessly believe, that no matter how terrible some of their lives may be and no matter what disaster overtakes them, there is one consolation like a heavenly revelation—at least they are not black. I suggest that of all the terrible things that could happen to a human being that is one of the worst. I suggest that what has happened to the white Southerner is in some ways much worse than what has happened to the Negroes there.

Sheriff Clark in Selma, Ala., cannot be dismissed as a total monster; I am sure he loves his wife and children and likes to get drunk. One has to assume that he is a man like me. But he does not know what drives him to use the club, to menace with the gun and to use the cattle prod. Something awful must have happened to a human being to be able to put a cattle prod against a woman's breasts. What happens to the woman is ghastly. What happens to the man who does it is in some ways much, much worse. Their moral lives have been destroyed by the plague called color.

This is not being done 100 years ago, but in 1965 and in a country which is pleased with what we call prosperity, with a certain amount of social coherence, which calls itself a civilized nation and which espouses the notion of freedom in the world. If it were white people being murdered, the Government would find some way of doing something about it. We have a civil rights bill now. We had the 15th Amendment nearly 100 years ago. If it was not honored then, I have no reason to believe that the civil rights bill will be honored now.

The American soil is full of the corpses of my ancestors, through 400 years and at least three wars. Why is my freedom, my citizenship, in question now? What one begs the American people to do, for all our sakes, is simply to accept our history.

It seems to me when I watch Americans in Europe that what they don't know about Europeans is what they don't know about me. They were not trying to be nasty to the French girl, rude to the French waiter. They did not know that they hurt their feelings: they didn't have any sense that this particular man and woman were human beings. They walked over them with the same sort of bland ignorance and condescension, the charm and cheerfulness, with which they had patted me on the head and which made them upset when I was upset.

When I was brought up I was taught in American history books that Africa had no history and that neither had I. I was a savage about whom the least said the better, who had been saved by Europe and who had been brought to America. Of course, I believed it. I didn't have much choice. These were the only books there were. Everyone else seemed to agree. If you went out of Harlem the whole world agreed. What you saw was much bigger, whiter, cleaner, safer. The garbage was collected, the children were happy. You would go back home and it would seem, of course, that this was an act of God. You belonged where white people put you.

It is only since World War II that there has been a counter-image in the world. That image has not come about because of any legislation by any American Government, but because Africa was suddenly on the stage of the world and Africans had to be dealt with in a way they had never been dealt with before. This gave the American Negro, for the first time, a sense of himself not as a savage. It has created and will create a great many conundrums.

One of the things the white world does not know, but I think I know, is that black people are just like everybody else. We are also mercenaries, dictators, murderers, liars. We are human, too. Unless we can establish some kind of dialogue between those people who enjoy the American dream and those people who have not achieved it, we will be in terrible trouble. This is what concerns me most. We are sitting in this room and we are all civilized; we can talk to each other, at least on certain levels, so that we can walk out of here assuming that the measure of our politeness has some effect on the world.

I remember when the ex-Attorney General, Mr. Robert Kennedy, said it was conceivable that in 40 years in America we might have a Negro President. That sounded like a very emancipated statement to white people. They were not in Harlem when this statement was first heard. They did not hear the laughter and bitterness and scorn with which this statement was greeted. From the point of view of the man in the Harlem barber shop, Bobby Kennedy only got here yesterday and now he is already on his way to the Presidency. We were here for 400 years and now he tells us that maybe in 40 years, if you are good, we may let you become President.

Perhaps I can be reasoned with, but I don't know—neither does Martin Luther King—none of us knows how to deal with people whom the white world has so long ignored, who don't believe anything the white world says and don't entirely believe anything I or Martin say. You can't blame them.

It seems to me that the City of New York has had, for example, Negroes in it for a very long time. The City of New York was able in the last 15 years to reconstruct itself, to tear down buildings and raise great new ones, and has done nothing whatever except build housing projects, mainly in the ghettoes, for the Negroes. And of course the Negroes hate it. The children can't bear it. They want to move out of the ghettoes. If American pretensions were based on more honest assessments of life, it would not mean for Negroes that when someone says "urban renewal" some Negroes are going to be thrown out into the streets, which is what it means now.

It is a terrible thing for an entire people to surrender to the notion that one-ninth of its population is beneath them. Until the moment comes when we, the Americans, are able to accept the fact that my ancestors are both black and white, that on that continent we are trying to forge a new identity, that we need each other, that I am not a ward of America, I am not an object of missionary charity, I am one of the people who built the country—until this moment comes there is scarcely any hope for the American dream. If the people are denied participation in it, by their very presence they will wreck it. And if that happens it is a very grave moment for the West.

The New York Times Magazine,
March 7, 1965

On the Painter Beauford Delaney

I LEARNED about light from Beauford Delaney, the light contained in every thing, in every surface, in every face. Many years ago, in poverty and uncertainty, Beauford and I would walk together through the streets of New York City. He was then, and is now, working all the time, or perhaps it would be more accurate to say that he is *seeing* all the time; and the reality of his seeing caused me to begin to see. Now, what I began to see was not, at that time, to tell the truth, his painting; that came later; what I saw, first of all, was a brown leaf on black asphalt, oil moving like mercury in the black water of the gutter, grass pushing itself up through a crevice in the sidewalk. And because I was seeing it with Beauford, because Beauford caused me to see it, the very colours underwent a most disturbing and salutary change. The brown leaf on the black asphalt, for example—what colours were these, really? To stare at the leaf long enough, to try to apprehend the leaf, was to discover many colours in it; and though black had been described to me as the absence of light, it became very clear to me that if this were true, we would never have been able to see the colour; black: the light is trapped in it and struggles upward, rather like that grass pushing upward through the cement. It was humbling to be forced to realise that the light fell down from heaven, on everything, on everybody, and that the light was always changing. Paradoxically, this meant for me that memory is a traitor and that life does not contain the past tense: the sunset one saw yesterday, the leaf that burned, or the rain that fell, have not really been seen unless one is prepared to see them every day. As Beauford is, to his eternal credit, and for our health and hope.

Perhaps I am so struck by the light in Beauford's paintings because he comes from darkness—as I do, as, in fact, we all do. But the darkness of Beauford's beginnings, in Tennessee, many years ago, was a black-blue midnight indeed, opaque, and full of sorrow. And I do not know, nor will any of us ever really know, what kind of strength it was that enabled him to make so dogged and splendid a journey. In any case, from

Tennessee, he eventually came to Paris (I have the impression that he walked and swam) and for a while lived in a suburb of Paris, Clamart. It was at this time that I began to see Beauford's painting in a new way, and it was also at this time that Beauford's paintings underwent a most striking metamorphosis into freedom. I know this sounds extremely subjective; but let it stand; it is not really as subjective as it sounds. There was a window in Beauford's house in Clamart before which we often sat—late at night, early in the morning, at noon. This window looked out on a garden; or, rather, it would have looked out on a garden if it had not been for the leaves and branches of a large tree which pressed directly against the window. Everything one saw from this window, then, was filtered through these leaves. And this window was a kind of universe, moaning and wailing when it rained, light of the morning, and as blue as the blues when the last light of the sun departed.

Well, that life, that light, that miracle, are what I began to see in Beauford's paintings, and this light began to stretch back for me over all the time we had known each other, and over much more time than that, and this light held the power to illuminate, even to redeem and reconcile and heal. For Beauford's work leads the inner and the outer eye, directly and inexorably, to a new confrontation with reality. At this moment one begins to apprehend the nature of his triumph. And the beauty of his triumph, and the proof that it is a real one, is that he makes it ours. Perhaps I should not say, flatly, what I believe—that he is a great painter, among the very greatest; but I do know that great art can only be created out of love, and that no greater lover has ever held a brush.

Transition, 1965

The White Man's Guilt

I HAVE often wondered, and it is not a pleasant wonder, just what white Americans talk about with one another.

I wonder this because they do not, after all, seem to find very much to say to *me*, and I concluded long ago that they found the color of my skin inhibitory. This color seems to operate as a most disagreeable mirror, and a great deal of one's energy is expended in reassuring white Americans that they do not see what they see.

This is utterly futile, of course, since they *do* see what they see. And what they see is an appallingly oppressive and bloody history, known all over the world. What they see is a disastrous, continuing, present, condition which menaces them, and for which they bear an inescapable responsibility. But since, in the main, they seem to lack the energy to change this condition, they would rather not be reminded of it. Does this mean that, in their conversations with one another, they merely make reassuring sounds? It scarcely seems possible, and yet, on the other hand, it seems all too likely. In any case, whatever they bring to one another, it is certainly not freedom from guilt. The guilt remains, more deeply rooted, more securely lodged, than the oldest of old trees.

And to have to deal with such people can be unutterably exhausting, for they, with a really dazzling ingenuity, a tireless agility, are perpetually defending themselves against charges which one, disagreeable mirror though one may be, has not, really, for the moment, made. One does not *have* to make them. The record is there for all to read. It resounds all over the world. It might as well be written in the sky. One wishes that Americans, white Americans, would read, for their own sakes, this record, and stop defending themselves against it. Only then will they be enabled to change their lives.

The fact that they have not yet been able to do this—to face their history, to change their lives—hideously menaces this country. Indeed, it menaces the entire world.

White man, hear me! History, as nearly no one seems to know, is not merely something to be read. And it does not refer merely, or even principally, to the past. On the contrary, the great force of history comes from the fact that we carry it within us, are unconsciously controlled by it in many ways, and history is literally *present* in all that we do. It could scarcely be otherwise, since it is to history that we owe our frames of reference, our identities, and our aspirations. And it is with great pain and terror that one begins to realize this. In great pain and terror one begins to assess the history which has placed one where one is, and formed one's point of view. In great pain and terror because, thereafter, one enters into battle with that historical creation, Oneself, and attempts to re-create oneself according to a principle more humane and more liberating: one begins the attempt to achieve a level of personal maturity and freedom which robs history of its tyrannical power, and also changes history.

But, obviously, I am speaking as an historical creation which has had bitterly to contest its history, to wrestle with it, and finally accept it, in order to bring myself out of it. My point of view certainly is formed by my history, and it is probable that only a creature despised by history finds history a questionable matter. On the other hand, people who imagine that history flatters them (as it does, indeed, since they wrote it) are impaled on their history like a butterfly on a pin and become incapable of seeing or changing themselves, or the world.

This is the place in which it seems to me, most white Americans find themselves. Impaled. They are dimly, or vividly, aware that the history they have fed themselves is mainly a lie, but they do not know how to release themselves from it, and they suffer enormously from the resulting personal incoherence. This incoherence is heard nowhere more plainly than in those stammering, terrified dialogues which white Americans sometime entertain with that black conscience, the black man in America. The nature of this stammering can be reduced to a plea: Do not blame *me*, I was not there. I did not do it. My history has nothing to do with Europe or the slave trade. Anyway, it was *your* chiefs who sold *you* to *me*. I was not present on the middle passage, I am not responsible for the textile mills of Manchester, or the cotton fields of Mississippi. Besides, consider how the English, too, suffered in those mills and in those awful cities! I *also* despise the governors of southern states and the sheriffs of southern counties, and I *also* want your child to have a decent education and rise as high as his capabilities will permit. I have nothing against you, nothing! What have *you* got against *me*? *What do you want?* But, on the same day, in another gathering, and in the most private chamber of his heart, always, the white American remains proud of that history for which he does not wish to pay, and from which, materially, he has profited so much.

On that same day, in another gathering, and in the most private chamber of his heart always, the black American finds *himself* facing the terrible roster of his lost: The dead, black junkie; the defeated, black father; the unutterably weary, black mother; the unutterably ruined, black girl. And one begins to suspect an awful thing: that people believe that they *deserve* their history, and that when they operate on this belief, they perish. But one knows that they can scarcely avoid believing that they deserve it: one's short time on this earth is very mysterious and very dark and very hard. I have known many black men and women and black boys and girls who really believed that it was better to be white than black, whose lives were ruined or ended by this belief; and I, myself, carried the seeds of this destruction within me for a long time.

Now if I, as a black man, profoundly believe that I deserve my history and deserve to be treated as I am, then I must also, fatally, believe that white people deserve their history and de-serve the power and the glory which their testimony and the evidence of my own senses assure me that they have. And if black people fall into this trap, the trap of believing that they deserve their fate, white people fall into the yet more stunning and intricate trap of believing that they deserve *their* fate, and their comparative safety and that black people, therefore, need only do as white people have done to rise to where white people now are. But this simply cannot be said, not only for reasons of politeness or charity, but also because white people carry in them a carefully muffled fear that black people long to do to others what has been done to them. Moreover, the history of white people has led them to a fearful, baffling place where they have begun to lose touch with reality—to lose touch, that is, with themselves—and where they certainly are not truly happy, for they know they are not truly safe. They do not know how this came about; they do not dare examine how this came about. On the one hand, they can scarcely dare to open a dialogue which must, if it is honest, become a personal confession—a cry for help and healing, which is, really, I think, the basis of all dialogues—and, on the other hand, the black man can scarcely dare to open a dialogue which must, if it is honest, become a personal confession which, fatally, contains an accusation. And yet, if neither of us cannot do this, each of us will perish in those traps in which we have been struggling for so long.

The American situation is very peculiar, and it may be without precedent in the world. No curtain under heaven is heavier than that curtain of guilt and lies behind which white Americans hide. That curtain may prove to be yet more deadly to the lives of human beings than that Iron Curtain of which we speak so much, and know so little. The American curtain is color. Color. White men have used this word, this concept, to justify unspeakable crimes, not only in the past, but in the present. One can measure very neatly the white American's distance from his conscience—from himself—by observing the distance between White America and Black America. One has only to ask oneself who established this distance, who is this distance designed to protect, and from what is this distance designed to offer protection?

I have seen all this very vividly, for example, in the eyes of southern law enforcement officers barring, let us say, the door to a courthouse. There they stood, comrades all, invested with the authority of the community, with helmets, with sticks, with guns, with cattle prods. Facing them were unarmed black people—or, more precisely, they were faced by a group of unarmed people arbitrarily called black, whose color really ranged from the Russian steppes to the Golden Horn to Zanzibar. In a moment, because he could resolve the situation in no other way, this sheriff, this deputy, this honored American citizen, began to club these people down. Some of these people might have been related to him by blood. They are assuredly related to the black mammy of his memory and the black playmates of his childhood. And for a moment, therefore, he seemed nearly to be pleading with the people facing him not to force him to commit yet another crime and not to make yet deeper that ocean of blood in which his conscience was drenched, in which his manhood was perishing. The people did not go away, of course; once a people arise, they never go away (a fact which should be included in the Marine handbook). So the club rose, the blood came down, and his bitterness and his anguish and his guilt were compounded.

And I have seen it in the eyes of rookie cops in Harlem— rookie cops who were really the most terrified people in the world, and who had to pretend to themselves that the black junkie, the black mother, the black father, the black child were of different human species than themselves. The southern sheriff, the rookie cop, could, and I suspect still can only deal with their lives and their duties by hiding behind the color curtain—a curtain which, indeed, eventually becomes their principal justification for the lives they lead.

They thus will barricade themselves behind this curtain and continue in their crime, in the great unadmitted crime of what they have done to themselves.

White man, hear me! A man is a man, a woman is a woman, a child is a child. To deny these facts is to open the doors on a chaos deeper and deadlier, and, within the space of a man's lifetime, more timeless, more eternal, than the medieval vision of Hell. White man, you have already arrived at this unspeakable blasphemy in order to make money. You cannot endure the things you acquire—the only reason you continually acquire them, like junkies on hundred dollar a day habits—and your money exists mainly on paper. God help you on that day when the population demands to know what is behind that paper. But, even beyond this, it is terrifying to consider the precise nature of the things you have bought with the flesh you have sold—of what you continue to buy with the flesh you continue to sell. To what, precisely, are you headed? To what human product, precisely, are you devoting so much ingenuity, so much energy?

In Henry James' novel, *The Ambassadors*, published not long before James' death, the author recounts the story of a middle-aged New Englander, assigned by his middle-aged bride-to-be, a widow, the task of rescuing from the flesh-pots of Paris her only son. She wants him to come home to take over the direction of the family factory. In the event, it is the

middle-aged New Englander, The Ambassador, who is seduced, not so much by Paris as by a new and less utilitarian
view of life. He counsels the young man to "live, live all you
can; it is a mistake not to." Which I translate as meaning
"trust life, and it will teach you, in joy and sorrow, all you
need to know." Jazz musicians know this. The old men and
women of Montgomery—those who waved and sang and
wept and could not join the marching, but had brought so
many of us to the place where we could march—know this.
But white Americans do not know this. Barricaded inside their
history, they remain trapped in that factory to which, in Henry
James' novel, the son returns. We never know what this factory produces, for James never tells us. He only conveys to us
that the factory, at an unbelievable human expense, produces
unnameable objects.

Ebony, August 1965

A Report from Occupied Territory

O N APRIL 17, 1964, in Harlem, New York City, a young salesman, father of two, left a customer's apartment and went into the streets. There was a great commotion in the streets, which, especially since it was a spring day, involved many people, including running, frightened, little boys. They were running from the police. Other people, in windows, left their windows, in terror of the police because the police had their guns out, and were aiming the guns at the roofs. Then the salesman noticed that two of the policemen were beating up a kid: "So I spoke up and asked them, 'why are you beating him like that?' Police jump up and start swinging on me. He put the gun on me and said, 'get over there.' I said, 'what for?'"

An unwise question. Three of the policemen beat up the salesman in the streets. Then they took the young salesman, whose hands had been handcuffed behind his back, along with four others, much younger than the salesman, who were handcuffed in the same way, to the police station. There: "About thirty-five I'd say came into the room, and started beating, punching us in the jaw, in the stomach, in the chest, beating us with a padded club—spit on us, call us niggers, dogs, animals—they call us dogs and animals when I don't see why we are the dogs and animals the way they are beating us. Like they beat me they beat the other kids and the elderly fellow. They throw him almost through one of the radiators. I thought he was dead over there."

"The elderly fellow" was Fecundo Acion, a 47-year-old Puerto Rican seaman, who had also made the mistake of wanting to know why the police were beating up children. An adult eyewitness reports, "Now here come an old man walking out a stoop and asked one cop, 'say, listen, sir, what's going on out here?' The cop turn around and smash him a couple of times in the head." And one of the youngsters said, "He get that just for a question. No reason at all, just for a question."

No one had, as yet, been charged with any crime. But the nightmare had not yet really begun. The salesman had been so badly beaten around one eye that it was found necessary to hospitalize him. Perhaps some sense of what it means to live in occupied territory can be suggested by the fact that the police took him to Harlem Hospital themselves—nearly nineteen hours after the beating. For fourteen days, the doctors at Harlem Hospital told him that they could do nothing for his eye, and he was removed to Bellevue Hospital, where for fourteen days, the doctors tried to save the eye. At the end of fourteen days it was clear that the bad eye could not be saved and was endangering the good eye. All that could be done, then, was to take the bad eye out.

As of my last information, the salesman is on the streets again, with his attaché case, trying to feed his family. He is more visible now because he wears an eye patch; and because he questioned the right of two policemen to beat up one child, he is known as a "cop hater." Therefore, "I have quite a few police look at me now pretty hard. My lawyer he axe (asked) me to keep somebody with me at all times 'cause the police may try to mess with me again."

You will note that there is not a suggestion of any kind of appeal to justice, and no suggestion of any recompense for the grave and gratuitous damage which this man has endured. His tone is simply the tone of one who has miraculously survived—he might have died; as it is, he is merely half blind. You will also note that the patch over his eye has had the effect of making him, more than ever, the target of the police. It is a dishonorable wound, not earned in a foreign jungle but in the domestic one—not that this would make any difference at all to the nevertheless insuperably patriotic policeman—and it proves that he is a "bad nigger." ("Bad niggers," in America, as elsewhere, have always been watched and have usually been killed.) The police, who have certainly done their best to kill him, have also provided themselves with a pretext *derisoire* by filing three criminal charges against him. He is charged with beating up a schoolteacher, upsetting a fruit stand, and assaulting the (armed) police. Furthermore, he did all of these things in the space of a single city block, and simultaneously.

The salesman's name is Frank Stafford. At the time all this happened, he was 31 years old. And all of this happened, all

of this and a great deal more, just before the "long, hot summer" of 1964 which, to the astonishment of nearly all New
Yorkers and nearly all Americans, to the extremely verbal anguish of *The New York Times*, and to the bewilderment of the
rest of the world, eventually erupted into a race riot. It was
the killing of a 15-year-old Negro boy by a white policeman
which overflowed the unimaginably bitter cup.

As a result of the events of April 17, and of the police performance that day, and because Harlem is policed like occupied territory, six young Negro men, the oldest of whom is
20, are now in prison, facing life sentences for murder. Their
names are Wallace Baker, Daniel Hamm, Walter Thomas,
Willie Craig, Ronald Felder and Robert Rice. Perhaps their
names don't matter. They might be my brothers: they might
also be yours. My report is based, in part, on Truman Nelson's
The Torture of Mothers (The Garrison Press, 15 Olive Street,
Newburyport, Mass., with an introduction by Maxwell
Geismar). *The Torture of Mothers* is a detailed account of the
case which is now known as the case of The Harlem Six. Mr.
Nelson is *not*, as I have earlier misled certain people into believing, a white Southern novelist, but a white Northern one.
It is a rather melancholy comment, I think, on the Northern
intellectual community, and it reveals, rather to my despair,
how little I have come to expect of it that I should have been
led so irresistibly into this error. In a way, though, I certainly
have no wish to blame Mr. Nelson for *my* errors; he is, nevertheless, somewhat himself to blame. His tone makes it clear
that he means what he says and he knows what he means. The
tone is rare. I have come to expect it only of Southerners—
or mainly from Southerners—since Southerners must pay so
high a price for their private and their public liberation. But
Mr. Nelson actually comes from New England, and is what
another age would have called an abolitionist. No Northern
liberal would have been capable of it because the Northern
liberal considers himself as already saved, whereas the white
Southerner has to pay the price for his soul's salvation out of
his own anguish and in his own flesh and in the only time he
has. Mr. Nelson wrote the book in an attempt to create publicity and public indignation; whatever money the book makes
goes into the effort to free The Harlem Six. I think the book

is an extraordinary moral achievement, in the great American tradition of Tom Paine and Frederick Douglass, but I will not be so dishonest as to pretend that I am writing a book review. No, I am writing a report, which is also a plea for the recognition of our common humanity. Without this recognition, our common humanity will be proved in unutterable ways. My report is also based on what I myself know, for I was born in Harlem and raised there. Neither I, nor my family, can be said ever really to have left; we are—*perhaps*—no longer as totally at the mercy of the cops and the landlords as once we were: in any case, our roots, our friends, our deepest associations are there, and "there" is only about fifteen blocks away.

This means that I also know, in my own flesh, and know, which is worse, in the scars borne by many of those dearest to me, the thunder and fire of the billy club, the paralyzing shock of spittle in the face; and I know what it is to find oneself blinded, on one's hands and knees, at the bottom of the flight of steps down which one has just been hurled. I know something else: these young men have been in jail for two years now. Even if the attempts being put forth to free them should succeed, what has happened to them in these two years? People are destroyed very easily. Where is the civilization and where, indeed, is the morality which can afford to destroy so many?

There was a game played for some time between certain highly placed people in Washington and myself before the administration changed and the Great Society reached the planning stage. The game went something like this: around April or May, that is as the weather began to be warmer, my phone would ring. I would pick it up and find that Washington was on the line.

Washington: What are you doing for lunch—oh, say, tomorrow, Jim?

Jim: Oh—why—I guess I'm free.

Washington: Why don't you take the shuttle down? We'll send a car to the airport. One o'clock all right?

Jim: Sure. I'll be there.

Washington: Good. Be glad to see you.

So there I would be the next day, like a good little soldier, seated (along with other good little soldiers) around a luncheon table in Washington. The first move was not mine to make, but I knew very well why I had been asked to be there.

Finally, someone would say—we would probably have arrived at the salad—"say, Jim. What's going to happen this summer?"

This question, translated, meant: Do you think that any of those unemployed, unemployable Negroes who are going to be on the streets all summer will cause us any trouble? What do you think we should do about it? But, later on, I concluded that I had got the second part of the question wrong; they really meant, what was *I* going to do about it?

Then I would find myself trying patiently to explain that the Negro in America can scarcely yet be considered—for example—as a part of the labor unions—and he is certainly not so considered by the majority of these unions—and that, therefore, he lacks that protection and that incentive. The jobs that Negroes have always held, the lowest jobs, the most menial jobs, are now being destroyed by automation. No remote provision has yet been made to absorb this labor surplus. Furthermore, the Negro's education, North and South, remains, almost totally, a segregated education, which is but another way of saying that he is taught the habits of inferiority every hour of every day that he lives. He will find it very difficult to overcome these habits. Furthermore, every attempt he makes to overcome them will be painfully complicated by the fact that the ways of being, the ways of life of the despised and rejected, nevertheless contain an incontestable vitality and authority. This is far more than can be said of the middle class which, in any case, and whether it be black or white, does not dare to cease despising him. He may prefer to remain where he is, given such unattractive choices, which means that he either remains in limbo, or finds a way to use the system in order to beat the system. Thus, even when opportunities—my use of this word is here limited to the industrialized, competitive, contemporary North American sense—hitherto closed to Negroes begin, very grudgingly, to open up, few can be found to qualify for them for the reasons sketched above, and also because it demands a very rare person, of any color, to risk madness and heartbreak in an attempt to achieve the impossible. (I know Negroes who have gone literally mad because they wished to become commercial air-line pilots.) Nor is this the worst.

The children, having seen the spectacular defeat of their fathers—having seen what happens to any bad nigger and, still more, what happens to the good ones—cannot listen to their fathers and certainly will not listen to the society which is responsible for their orphaned condition. What to do in the face of this deep and dangerous estrangement? It seemed to me—I would say, sipping coffee and trying to be calm—that the principle of what had to be done was extremely simple; but before anything could be done, the principle had to be grasped. The principle on which one had to operate was that the government which can force me to pay my taxes and force me to fight in its defense anywhere in the world *does not have the authority* to say that it cannot protect my right to vote or my right to earn a living or my right to live anywhere I choose. Furthermore, no nation, wishing to call itself free, can possibly survive so massive a defection. What to do? Well, there is a real estate lobby in Albany, for example, and this lobby, which was able to rebuild all of New York, downtown, and for money, in less than twenty years, is also responsible for Harlem and the condition of the people there, and the condition of the schools there, and the future of the children there. What to do? Why is it not possible to attack the power of this lobby? Are their profits more important than the health of our children? What to do? Are textbooks printed in order to teach children, or are the contents of these textbooks to be controlled by the Southern oligarchy and the commercial health of publishing houses? What to do? Why are Negroes and Puerto Ricans virtually the only people pushing trucks in the garment center, and what union has the right to trap and victimize Negroes and Puerto Ricans in this way? None of these things (I would say) could possibly be done without the consent, in fact, of the government, and we in Harlem know this even if some of you profess not to know how such a hideous state of affairs came about. If some of these things are not begun—I would say—then, of course, we will be sitting on a powder keg all summer. Of course, the powder keg may blow up; it will be a miracle if it doesn't.

They thanked me. They didn't believe me, as I conclude, since nothing was ever done. The summer was always violent. And in the spring, the phone began to ring again.

Now, what I have said about Harlem is true of Chicago, Detroit, Washington, Boston, Philadelphia, Los Angeles and San Francisco—is true of every Northern city with a large Negro population. And the police are simply the hired enemies of this population. They are present to keep the Negro in his place and to protect white business interests, and they have no other function. They are, moreover—even in a country which makes the very grave error of equating ignorance with simplicity—quite stunningly ignorant; and, since they know that they are hated, they are always afraid. One cannot possibly arrive at a more sure-fire formula for cruelty.

This is why those pious calls to "respect the law," always to be heard from prominent citizens each time the ghetto explodes, are so obscene. The law is meant to be my servant and not my master, still less my torturer and my murderer. To respect the law, in the context in which the American Negro finds himself, is simply to surrender his self-respect.

On April 17, some school children overturned a fruit stand in Harlem. This would have been a mere childish prank if the children had been white—had been, that is, the children of that portion of the citizenry for whom the police work and who have the power to control the police. But these children were black, and the police chased them and beat them and took out their guns; and Frank Stafford lost his eye in exactly the same way The Harlem Six lost their liberty—by trying to protect the younger children. Daniel Hamm, for example, tells us that ". . . we heard children scream. We turned around and walked back to see what happened. I saw this policeman with his gun out and with his billy in his hand. I like put myself in the way to keep him from shooting the kids. Because first of all he was shaking like a leaf and jumping all over the place. And I thought he might shoot one of them."

He was arrested, along with Wallace Baker, carried to the police station, beaten—"six and twelve at a time would beat us. They got so tired beating us they just came in and started spitting on us—they even bring phlegm up and spit on me."

This went on all day. In the evening, Wallace Baker and Daniel Hamm were taken to Harlem Hospital for X rays and then carried back to the police station, where the beating continued all night. They were eventually released, with the fruit-stand charges pending, in spite of the testimony of the fruit-stand owner. This fruit-stand owner had already told the police that neither Wallace Baker nor Daniel Hamm had ever been at his store and that they certainly had had nothing to do with the fruit-stand incident. But this had no effect on the conduct of the police. The boys had already attracted the attention of the police, long before the fruit-stand riot, and in a perfectly innocent way. They are pigeon fanciers and they keep—kept—pigeons on the roof. But the police are afraid of everything in Harlem and they are especially afraid of the roofs, which they consider to be guerrilla outposts. This means that the citizens of Harlem who, as we have seen, can come to grief at any hour in the streets, and who are not safe at their windows, are forbidden the very air. They are safe only in their houses—or were, until the city passed the No Knock, Stop and Frisk laws, which permit a policeman to enter one's home without knocking and to stop anyone on the streets, at will, at any hour, and search him. Harlem believes, and I certainly agree, that these laws are directed against Negroes. They are certainly not directed against anybody else. One day, "two carloads of detectives came and went up on the roof. They pulled their guns on the kids and searched them and made them all come down and they were going to take them down to the precinct." But the boys put up a verbal fight and refused to go and attracted quite a crowd. "To get these boys to the precinct we would have to shoot them," a policeman said, and "the police seemed like they was embarrassed. Because I don't think they expected the kids to have as much sense as they had in speaking up for themselves." They refused to go to the precinct, "and they didn't," and their exhibition of the spirit of '76 marked them as dangerous. Occupied territory is occupied territory, even though it be found in that New World which the Europeans conquered; and it is axiomatic, in occupied territory, that any act of resistance, even though it be executed by a child, be answered at once, and with the full weight of the occupying forces. Furthermore, since the police, not at all surprisingly, are abysmally incompetent—for neither, in fact, do they have any respect for the law, which is not surprising, either—Harlem and all of New York City is full of unsolved crimes. A crime, as we know, is solved when someone is arrested and convicted. It is not indispensable, but it is useful, to have a confession. If one is carried back and forth from the precinct to the hospital long enough, one is likely to confess to anything.

Therefore, ten days later, following the slaying of Mrs. Margit Sugar in Mr. and Mrs. Sugar's used-clothing store in Harlem, the police returned and took Daniel Hamm away again. This is how his mother tells it: "I think it was three (detectives) come up and they asked are you Danny Hamm? And he says yes and right away—gun right to the head and slapping him up, one gun here and one here—just all the way down the hall—beating him and knocking him around with the gun to his head." The other boys were arrested in the same way, and, again of course, they were beaten; but this arrest was a far greater torture than the first one had been because some of the mothers did not know where the boys were, and the police, who were holding them, refused for many hours to say that they were holding them. The mothers did not know of what it was their children were accused until they learned, via television, that the charge was murder. At that time in the state of New York, this charge meant death in the electric chair.

Let us assume that all six boys are guilty as (eventually) charged. Can anyone pretend that the manner of their arrest, or their treatment, bears any resemblance to equal justice under the law? The Police Department has loftily refused to "dignify the charges." But can anyone pretend that they would dare to take this tone if the case involved, say, the sons of Wall Street brokers? I have witnessed and endured the brutality of the police many more times than once—but, of course, I cannot prove it. I cannot prove it because the Police Department investigates itself, quite as though it were answerable only to itself. But it cannot be allowed to be answerable only to itself; it must be made to answer to the community which pays it, and which it is legally sworn to protect; and if American Negroes are not a part of the American community, then all of the American professions are a fraud.

This arrogant autonomy, which is guaranteed the police, not only in New York, *by the most powerful forces in American life*—otherwise, they would not dare to claim it, would, indeed, be unable to claim it—creates a situation which is as close to anarchy as it already, visibly, is close to martial law.

Here is Wallace Baker's mother speaking, describing the night that a police officer came to her house to collect the evidence which he hoped would prove that her son was guilty of murder. The late Mrs. Sugar had run a used-clothing store and the policeman was looking for old coats. "Nasty as he was that night in my house. He didn't ring the bell. So I said, have you got a search warrant? He say, no, I don't have no search warrant and I'm going to search anyway. Well, he did. So I said, will you please step out of this room till I get dressed? He wouldn't leave." This collector of evidence against the boys was later arrested on charges of possessing and passing counterfeit money (he pleaded guilty to a misdemeanor, "conspiring" to pass counterfeit money). The officer's home in Hartsdale, N. Y., is valued at $35,000, he owns two cars, one a Cadillac, and when he was arrested, had $1,300 in his pockets. But the families of The Harlem Six do not have enough money for counsel. The court appointed counsel, and refused to allow the boys counsel of their own choice, even though the boys made it clear that they had no confidence in their court-appointed counsel, and even though four leading civil rights lawyers had asked to be allowed to handle the case. The boys were convicted of first-degree murder, and are now ending their childhood and may end their lives in jail.

These things happen, in all our Harlems, every single day. If we ignore this fact, and our common responsibility to change this fact, we are sealing our doom. Here is the boy, Daniel Hamm, speaking—speaking of his country, which has sworn to bring peace and freedom to so many millions: "They don't want us here. They don't want us—period! All they want us to do is work on these penny-ante jobs for them—and that's *it*. And beat our heads in whenever they feel like it. They don't want us on the street 'cause the World's Fair is coming. And they figure that all black people are hoodlums anyway, or bums, with no character of our own. So they put us off the streets, so their friends from Europe, Paris or Vietnam—wherever they come from—can come and see this supposed-to-be great city."

There is a very bitter prescience in what this boy—this "bad nigger"—is saying, and he was not born knowing it. We taught it to him in seventeen years. He is draft age now, and if he were not in jail, would very probably be on his way to Southeast Asia. Many of his contemporaries are there, and the American Government and the American press are extremely proud of them. They are dying there like flies; they are dying in the streets of all our Harlems far more hideously than flies. A member of my family said to me when we learned of the bombing of the four little girls in the Birmingham Sunday school, "Well, they don't need us for work no more. Where are they building the gas ovens?" Many Negroes feel this; there is no way not to feel it. Alas, we know our countrymen, municipalities, judges, politicians, policemen and draft boards very well. There is more than one way to skin a cat, and more than one way to get bad niggers off the streets. No one in Harlem will ever believe that The Harlem Six are guilty—God knows their guilt has certainly not been proved. Harlem knows, though, that they have been abused and possibly destroyed, and Harlem knows why—we have lived with it since our eyes opened on the world. One is in the impossible position of being unable to believe a word one's countrymen say. "I can't believe what you say," the song goes, "because I see what you do"—and one is also under the necessity of escaping the jungle of one's situation into any other jungle whatever. It is the bitterest possible comment on our situation now that the suspicion is alive in so many breasts that America has at last found a way of dealing with the Negro problem. *"They don't want us—period!"* The meek shall inherit the earth, it is said. This presents a very bleak image to those who live in occupied territory. The meek Southeast Asians, those who remain, shall have their free elections, and the meek American Negroes—those who survive—shall enter the Great Society.

The Nation, July 11, 1966

Negroes Are Anti-Semitic Because They're Anti-White

WHEN we were growing up in Harlem our demoralizing series of landlords were Jewish, and we hated them. We hated them because they were terrible landlords, and did not take care of the building. A coat of paint, a broken window, a stopped sink, a stopped toilet, a sagging floor, a broken ceiling, a dangerous stairwell, the question of garbage disposal, the question of heat and cold, of roaches and rats—all questions of life and death for the poor, and especially for those with children—we had to cope with all of these as best we could. Our parents were lashed down to futureless jobs, in order to pay the outrageous rent. We knew that the landlord treated us this way only because we were colored, and he knew that we could not move out.

The grocer was a Jew, and being in debt to him was very much like being in debt to the company store. The butcher was a Jew and, yes, we certainly paid more for bad cuts of meat than other New York citizens, and we very often carried insults home, along with the meat. We bought our clothes from a Jew and, sometimes, our secondhand shoes, and the pawnbroker was a Jew—perhaps we hated him most of all. The merchants along 125th Street were Jewish—at least many of them were; I don't know if Grant's or Woolworth's are Jewish names—and I well remember that it was only after the Harlem riot of 1935 that Negroes were allowed to earn a little money in some of the stores where they spent so much.

Not all of these white people were cruel—on the contrary, I remember some who were certainly as thoughtful as the bleak circumstances allowed—but all of them were exploiting us, and that was why we hated them.

But we also hated the welfare workers, of whom some were white, some colored, some Jewish, and some not. We hated the policemen, not all of whom were Jewish, and some of whom were black. The poor, of whatever color, do not trust the law and certainly have no reason to, and God knows we didn't. "If you *must* call a cop," we said in those days, "for

God's sake, make sure it's a white one." We did not feel that the cops were protecting us, for we knew too much about the reasons for the kinds of crimes committed in the ghetto; but we feared black cops even more than white cops, because the black cop had to work so much harder—on *your* head—to prove to himself and his colleagues that he was not like all the other niggers.

We hated many of our teachers at school because they so clearly despised us and treated us like dirty, ignorant savages. Not all of these teachers were Jewish. Some of them, alas, were black. I used to carry my father's union dues downtown for him sometimes. I hated everyone in that den of thieves, especially the man who took the envelope from me, the envelope which contained my father's hard-earned money, that envelope which contained bread for his children. "Thieves," I thought, "every one of you!" And I know I was right about that, and I have not changed my mind. But whether or not all these people were Jewish, I really do not know.

The Army may or may not be controlled by Jews; I don't know and I don't care. I know that when I worked for the Army I hated all my bosses because of the way they treated me. I don't know if the post office is Jewish but I would certainly dread working for it again. I don't know if Wanamaker's was Jewish, but I didn't like running their elevator, and I didn't like any of their customers. I don't know if Nabisco is Jewish, but I didn't like cleaning their basement. I don't know if Riker's is Jewish, but I didn't like scrubbing their floors. I don't know if the big, white bruiser who thought it was fun to call me "Shine" was Jewish, but I know I tried to kill him—and he stopped calling me "Shine." I don't know if the last taxi driver who refused to stop for me was Jewish, but I know I hoped he'd break his neck before he got home. And I don't think that General Electric or General Motors or R.C.A. or Con Edison or Mobiloil or Coca-Cola or Pepsi-Cola or Firestone or the Board of Education or the textbook industry or Hollywood or Broadway or television—or Wall Street, Sacramento, Dallas, Atlanta, Albany, or Washington—are controlled by Jews. I think they are controlled by Americans, and the American Negro situation is a direct result of this control. And anti-Semitism among Negroes, inevitable as it may be, and understandable, alas, as it is, does not operate to menace this control, but only to confirm it. It is not the Jew who controls the American drama. It is the Christian.

The root of anti-Semitism among Negroes is, ironically, the relationship of colored peoples—all over the globe—to the Christian world. This is a fact which may be difficult to grasp, not only for the ghetto's most blasted and embittered inhabitants, but also for many Jews, to say nothing of many Christians. But it is a fact, and it will not be ameliorated—in fact, it can only be aggravated—by the adoption, on the part of colored people now, of the most devastating of the Christian vices.

Of course, it is true, and I am not so naive as not to know it, that many Jews despise Negroes, even as their Aryan brothers do. (There are also Jews who despise Jews, even as their Aryan brothers do.) It is true that many Jews use, shamelessly, the slaughter of the 6,000,000 by the Third Reich as proof that they cannot be bigots—or in the hope of not being held responsible for their bigotry. It is galling to be told by a Jew whom you know to be exploiting you that he cannot possibly be doing what you know he is doing because he is a Jew. It is bitter to watch the Jewish storekeeper locking up his store for the night, and going home. Going, with *your* money in his pocket, to a clean neighborhood, miles from you, which you will not be allowed to enter. Nor can it help the relationship between most Negroes and most Jews when part of this money is donated to civil rights. In the light of what is now known as the white backlash, this money can be looked on as conscience money merely, as money given to keep the Negro happy in his place, and out of white neighborhoods.

One does not wish, in short, to be told by an American Jew that his suffering is as great as the American Negro's suffering. It isn't, and one knows that it isn't from the very tone in which he assures you that it is.

For one thing, the American Jew's endeavor, whatever it is, has managed to purchase a relative safety for his children, and a relative future for them. This is more than your father's endeavor was able to do for you, and more than your endeavor has been able to do for your children. There are days when it can be exceedingly trying to deal with certain white musical or theatrical celebrities who may or may not be Jewish—what, in show business, is a name?—but whose preposterous incomes cause one to think bitterly of the fates of such people as Bessie Smith or King Oliver or Ethel Waters. Furthermore, the Jew can be proud of his suffering, or at least not ashamed of it. His history and his suffering do not begin in America, where black men have been taught to be ashamed of everything, especially their suffering.

The Jew's suffering is recognized as part of the moral history of the world and the Jew is recognized as a contributor to the world's history: this is not true for the blacks. Jewish history, whether or not one can say it is honored, is certainly known: the black history has been blasted, maligned, and despised. The Jew is a white man, and when white men rise up against oppression, they are heroes: when black men rise, they have reverted to their native savagery. The uprising in the Warsaw ghetto was not described as a riot, nor were the participants maligned as hoodlums: the boys and girls in Watts and Harlem are thoroughly aware of this, and it certainly contributes to their attitude toward the Jews.

But, of course, my comparison of Watts and Harlem with the Warsaw ghetto will be immediately dismissed as outrageous. There are many reasons for this, and one of them is that while America loves white heroes, armed to the teeth, it cannot abide bad niggers. But the bottom reason is that it contradicts the American dream to suggest that any gratuitous, unregenerate horror can happen here. We make our mistakes, we like to think, but we are getting better all the time.

Well, to state it mildly, this is a point of view which any sane or honest Negro will have some difficulty holding. Very few Americans, and this includes very few Jews, wish to believe that the American Negro situation is as desperate and dangerous as it is. Very few Americans, and very few Jews, have the courage to recognize that the America of which they dream and boast is not the America in which the Negro lives. It is a country which the Negro has never seen. And this is not merely a matter of bad faith on the part of Americans.

Bad faith, God knows, abounds, but there is something in the American dream sadder and more wistful than that.

No one, I suppose, would dream of accusing the late Moss Hart of bad faith. Near the end of his autobiography, "Act One," just after he has become a successful playwright, and is riding home to Brooklyn for the first time in a cab, he reflects:

"I stared through the taxi window at a pinch-faced 10-year-old hurrying down the steps on some morning errand before school, and I thought of myself hurrying down the streets on so many gray mornings out of a doorway and a house much the same as this one. My mind jumped backward in time and then whirled forward, like a many-faceted prism—flashing our old neighborhood in front of me, the house, the steps, the candy store—and then shifted to the skyline I had just passed by, the opening last night, and the notices I still hugged tightly under my arm. It was possible in this wonderful city for that nameless little boy—for any of its millions—to have a decent chance to scale the walls and achieve what they wished. Wealth, rank, or an imposing name counted for nothing. The only credential the city asked was the boldness to dream."

But this is not true for the Negro, and not even the most successful or fatuous Negro can really feel this way. His journey will have cost him too much, and the price will be revealed in his estrangement—unless he is very rare and lucky—from other colored people, and in his continuing isolation from whites. Furthermore, for every Negro boy who achieves such a taxi ride, hundreds, at least, will have perished around him, and not because they lacked the boldness to dream, but because the Republic despises their dreams.

Perhaps one must be in such a situation in order really to understand what it is. But if one is a Negro in Watts or Harlem, and knows why one is there, and knows that one has been sentenced to remain there for life, one can't but look on the American state and the American people as one's oppressors. For that, after all, is exactly what they are. They have corralled you where you are for their ease and their profit, and are doing all in their power to prevent you from finding out enough about yourself to be able to rejoice in the only life you have.

*

One does not wish to believe that the American Negro can feel this way, but that is because the Christian world has been misled by its own rhetoric and narcoticized by its own power.

For many generations the natives of the Belgian Congo, for example, endured the most unspeakable atrocities at the hands of the Belgians, at the hands of Europe. Their suffering occurred in silence. This suffering was not indignantly reported in the Western press, as the suffering of white men would have been. The suffering of this native was considered necessary, alas, for European, Christian dominance. And, since the world at large knew virtually nothing concerning the suffering of this native, when he rose he was not hailed as a hero fighting for his land, but condemned as a savage, hungry for white flesh. The Christian world considered Belgium to be a civilized country; but there was not only no reason for the Congolese to feel that way about Belgium; there was no possibility that they could.

What will the Christian world, which is so uneasily silent now, say on that day which is coming when the black native of South Africa begins to massacre the masters who have massacred him so long? It is true that two wrongs don't make a right, as we love to point out to the people we have wronged. But *one* wrong doesn't make a right, either. People who have been wronged will attempt to right the wrong; they would not be people if they didn't. They can rarely afford to be scrupulous about the means they will use. They will use such means as come to hand. Neither, in the main, will they distinguish one oppressor from another, nor see through to the root principle of their oppression.

In the American context, the most ironical thing about Negro anti-Semitism is that the Negro is really condemning the Jew for having become an American white man—for having become, in effect, a Christian. The Jew profits from his status in America, and he must expect Negroes to distrust him for it. The Jew does not realize that the credential he offers, the fact that he has been despised and slaughtered, does not increase the Negro's understanding. It increases the Negro's rage.

For it is not here, and not now, that the Jew is being slaughtered, and he is never despised, here, as the Negro is, *because* he is an American. The Jewish travail occurred across the sea and America rescued him from the house of bondage. But America *is* the house of bondage for the Negro, and no country can rescue him. What happens to the Negro here happens to him *because* he is an American.

When an African is mistreated here, for example, he has recourse to his embassy. The American Negro who is, let us say, falsely arrested, will find it nearly impossible to bring his case to court. And this means that *because* he is a native of this country—"one of our niggers"—he has, effectively, no recourse and no place to go, either within the country or without. He is a pariah in his own country and a stranger in the world. This is what it means to have one's history and one's ties to one's ancestral homeland totally destroyed.

This is not what happened to the Jew and, therefore, he has allies in the world. That is one of the reasons no one has ever seriously suggested that the Jew be nonviolent. There was no need for him to be nonviolent. On the contrary, the Jewish battle for Israel was saluted as the most tremendous heroism. How can the Negro fail to suspect that the Jew is really saying that the Negro deserves his situation because he has not been heroic enough? It is doubtful that the Jews could have won their battle had the Western powers been opposed to them. But such allies as the Negro may have are themselves struggling for their freedom against tenacious and tremendous Western opposition.

This leaves the American Negro, who technically represents the Western nations, in a cruelly ambiguous position. In this situation, it is not the American Jew who can either instruct him or console him. On the contrary, the American Jew knows just enough about this situation to be unwilling to imagine it again.

Finally, what the American Negro interprets the Jew as saying is that one must take the historical, the impersonal point of view concerning one's life and concerning the lives of one's kinsmen and children. "We suffered, too," one is told, "but we came through, and so will you. In time."

In whose time? One has only one life. One may become reconciled to the ruin of one's own life, but to become reconciled to the ruin of one's children's lives is not reconciliation. It is the sickness unto death. And one knows that such counselors are not present on these shores by following this advice. They arrived here out of the same effort the American Negro is making: they wanted to live, and not tomorrow, but today. Now, since the Jew is living here, like all the other white men living here, he wants the Negro to wait. And the Jew sometimes—often—does this in the name of his Jewishness, which is a terrible mistake. He has absolutely no relevance in this context as a Jew. His only relevance is that he is white and values his color and uses it.

He is singled out by Negroes not because he acts differently from other white men, but because he doesn't. His major distinction is given him by that history of Christendom, which has so successfully victimized both Negroes and Jews. And he is playing in Harlem the role assigned him by Christians long ago: he is doing their dirty work.

No more than the good white people of the South, who are really responsible for the bombings and lynchings, are ever present at these events, do the people who really own Harlem ever appear at the door to collect the rent. One risks libel by trying to spell this out too precisely, but Harlem is really owned by a curious coalition which includes some churches, some universities, some Christians, some Jews, and some Negroes. The capital of New York is Albany, which is not a Jewish state, and the Moses they sent us, whatever his ancestry, certainly failed to get the captive children free.

A genuinely candid confrontation between American Negroes and American Jews would certainly prove of inestimable value. But the aspirations of the country are wretchedly middle-class and the middle class can never afford candor.

What is really at question is the American way of life. What is really at question is whether Americans already have an identity or are still sufficiently flexible to achieve one. This is a painfully complicated question, for what now appears to be the American identity is really a bewildering and sometimes demoralizing blend of nostalgia and opportunism. For example, the Irish who march on St. Patrick's Day, do not, after all, have any desire to go back to Ireland. They do not intend to go back to live there, though they may dream of going back there to die. Their lives, in the meanwhile, are here, but they cling, at the same time, to those credentials forged in the Old World, credentials which cannot be duplicated here, credentials which the American Negro does not have. These credentials are the abandoned history of Europe—the abandoned and romanticized history of Europe. The Russian Jews here have no desire to return to Russia either, and they have not departed in great clouds for Israel. But they have the authority of knowing it is there. The Americans are no longer Europeans, but they are still living, at least as they imagine, on that capital.

That capital also belongs, however, to the slaves who created it for Europe and who created it here; and in that sense, the Jew must see that he is part of the history of Europe, and will always be so considered by the descendant of the slave. Always, that is, unless he himself is willing to prove that this judgment is inadequate and unjust. This is precisely what is demanded of all the other white men in this country, and the Jew will not find it easier than anybody else.

The ultimate hope for a genuine black-white dialogue in this country lies in the recognition that the driven European serf merely created another serf here, and created him on the basis of color. No one can deny that the Jew was a party to this, but it is senseless to assert that this was because of his Jewishness. One can be disappointed in the Jew if one is romantic enough—for not having learned from his history; but if people did learn from history, history would be very different.

All racist positions baffle and appall me. None of us are that different from one another, neither that much better nor that much worse. Furthermore, when one takes a position one must attempt to see where that position inexorably leads. One must ask oneself, if one decides that black or white or Jewish people are, by definition, to be despised, is one willing to murder a black or white or Jewish baby: for *that* is where the position leads. And if one blames the Jew for having become a white American, one may perfectly well, if one is black, be speaking out of nothing more than envy.

If one blames the Jew for not having been ennobled by

oppression, one is not indicting the single figure of the Jew but the entire human race, and one is also making a quite breathtaking claim for oneself. I know that my own oppression did not ennoble me, not even when I thought of myself as a practicing Christian. I also know that if today I refuse to hate Jews, or anybody else, it is because I know how it feels to be hated. I learned this from Christians, and I ceased to practice what the Christians practiced.

The crisis taking place in the world, and in the minds and hearts of black men everywhere, is not produced by the star of David, but by the old, rugged Roman cross on which Christendom's most celebrated Jew was murdered. And not by Jews.

The New York Times Magazine, April 9, 1967

White Racism or World Community?

SINCE I am not a theologian in any way whatever, I probably ought to tell you what my credentials are. I never expected to be standing in such a place, because I left the pulpit twenty-seven years ago. That says a good deal, I suppose, about my relationship to the Christian Church. And in a curious way that is part of my credentials. I also address you in the name of my father, who was a Baptist minister, who gave his life to the Christian faith, with some very curious and stunning and painful results. I address you as one of those people who have always been outside it, even though one tried to work in it. I address you as one of the creatures, one of God's creatures, whom the Christian Church has most betrayed. And I want to make it clear to you that though I may have to say some rather difficult things here this afternoon, I want to make it understood that in the heart of the absolutely necessary accusation there is contained a plea. The plea was articulated by Jesus Christ himself, who said, "Insofar as you have done it unto the least of these, you have done it unto me."

Now it would seem to me that the nature of the confrontation, the actual historical confrontation between the non-white peoples of the world and the white peoples of the world, between the Christian Church and those people outside the Christian Church who are unable to conceive themselves as being equally the sons of God, the nature of that confrontation is involved with the nature of the experience which a black person represents vis-à-vis the Cross of Christ, and vis-à-vis that enormous structure which is called the Church. Because I was born in a Christian culture, I never considered myself to be totally a free human being. In my own mind, and in fact, I was told by Christians what I could do and what I could become and what my life was worth. Now, this means that one's concept of human freedom is in a sense frozen or strangled at the root. This has to do, of course, with the fact that though he was born in Nazareth under a very hot sun, and though we know that he spent his life beneath that sun, the Christ I was presented with was presented to me with blue eyes and blond hair, and all the virtues to which I, as a black man, was expected to aspire had, by definition, to be white. This may seem a very simple thing and from some points of view it might even seem to be a desirable thing. But in fact what it did was make me very early, make us, the blacks, very early distrust our own experience and refuse, in effect, to articulate that experience to the Christians who were our oppressors. That was a great loss for me, as a black man. I want to suggest that it was also a great loss for you, as white people. For example, in the church I grew up in, we sang a song that that man who was hung on a Roman cross between two thieves would have understood better than most church prelates. We sang—and we knew what we meant when we sang it—"I've been rebuked and I've been scolded." We won our Christianity, our faith, at the point of a gun, not because of the example afforded by white Christians, but in spite of it. It was very difficult to become a Christian if you were a black man on a slave ship, and the slave ship was called 'The Good Ship Jesus.' These crimes, for one must call them crimes, against the human being have brought the church and the entire Western world to the dangerous place we find ourselves in today. Because if it is true that your testimony as Christians has proven invalid; if it is true that my importance in the Christian world was not as a living soul, dear to the sight of God, but as a means of making money, and representatively more sinister than that too representing some terrifying divorce between the flesh and the spirit; if that is true (and it would be very difficult to deny the truth of this) then at this moment in the world's history it becomes necessary for me, for my own survival, not to listen to what you say but to watch very carefully what you do, not to read your pronouncements but to go back to the source and to check it for myself. And if that is so, then it may very well mean that the revolution which was begun two thousand years ago by a disreputable Hebrew criminal may now have to be begun again by people equally disreputable and equally improbable. It's got to be admitted that if you are born under the circumstances in which most black people in the West are born, that means really black people over the entire world, when you look around you, having attained something resembling adulthood, it is perfectly true that you can see that the destruction of the Christian Church as it is presently constituted may not only be desirable but necessary.

If you have grown to be, let us say, thirty years old in a Christian nation and you understand what has happened to you and your brothers, your mother, your father, your sisters and the ways in which you are menaced, not precisely by the wickedness of Christians, but by the wickedness of white people; most people are not wicked, most people are terribly lazy, most people are terribly afraid of acting on what they know. I think everyone knows that no child is a criminal, I think everyone knows that all children are sacred, and yet the Christian world, until today, victimises all black children and destroys them because they are not white. This is done in many ways. One of the most important ways in which it is done is the way in which the history of black people, which means then the history of the Christian world, is taught Christians, in order to justify the means by which they rose to power, have had to convince themselves, and have had to try to convince me, that when Africa was "discovered," as Christians so quaintly put it, and when I was discovered and brought away to be used like an animal, we have had to agree, the Christian Church had to conspire with itself to say that I preferred slavery to my own condition and that I really liked the role I played in Western culture. Until at last the Christian Church has got to pretend that black South African miners are pleased to go into the mines and bring out the diamonds and the wealth, all the wealth which belongs to Africa, to dig it up for nothing and give it to Europe. We all know, no matter what we say, no matter how we may justify it or hide from this fact, every human being knows, something in him knows, and this is what Christ was talking about; no one wants to be a slave. Black people have had to adjust to incredible vicissitudes and involve in fantastic identity against incredible odds. But those songs we sang, and sing, and our dances and the way we talk to each other, betray a terrifying pain, a pain so great that most Western people, most white Westerners, are simply baffled by it and paralysed by it, because they do not dare imagine what it would be like to be a black father, and what a black father would have to tell a black son in order for the black son to live at all.

Now, this is not called morality, this is not called faith, this has nothing to do with Christ. It has to do with power, and part of the dilemma of the Christian Church is the fact that it opted, in fact, for power and betrayed its own first principles which were a responsibility to every living soul, the assumption of which the Christian Church's basis, as I understand it, is that *all* men are the sons of God and that *all* men are free in the eyes of God and are victims of the commandment given to the Christian Church, "Love one another as I have loved you." And if that is so, the Church is in great danger not merely because the black people say it is but because people are always in great danger when they know what they should do, and refuse to act on that knowledge. To try to make it as clear as I can; we hear a great deal these days of a young black man called Stokely Carmichael, we gather from the public press that Stokely's a very dangerous, radical, black fanatic racist. Not long ago we heard much the same thing about the late Malcolm X, and neither was the late Martin Luther King the most popular man in his country.

But everyone overlooks the fact that Stokely Carmichael began his life as a Christian and for many, many years, unnoticed by the world's press, was marching up and down highways in my country, in the deep south, spent many many years being beaten over the head and thrown in jail, singing "We shall overcome," and meaning it and believing it, doing day by day and hour by hour precisely what the Christian Church is supposed to do, to walk from door to door, to feed the hungry, to speak to those who are oppressed, to try to open the gates of prisons for all those who are imprisoned. And a day came, inevitably, when this young man grew weary of petitioning a heedless population and said in effect, what all revolutionaries have always said, I petitioned you and petitioned you, and you can petition for a long, long time, but the moment comes when the petitioner is no longer a petitioner but has become a beggar. And at that moment one concludes, you will not do it, you cannot do it, it is not in you to do it, and therefore I must do it. When Stokely talks about black power, he is simply translating into the black idiom what the English said hundreds of years ago and have always proclaimed as their guiding principle, black power translated means the self-determination of people. It means that, nothing more and nothing less. But it is astounding, and it says a great deal about Christendom, that whereas black power, the conjunction of the word 'black' with the word 'power', frightens everybody, no one in Christendom appears seriously to be frightened by the operation and the nature of white power. Stokely may make terrifying speeches (though they are not terrifying to me, I must say) and Stokely may be, though I don't believe it, a racist in reverse, but in fact he's not nearly as dangerous as the people who now rule South Africa, he's not nearly as dangerous as many of the people who govern my own poor country. He's only insisting that he is present only once on this earth as a man, not as a creation of the Christian conscience, not as a fantasy in the Christian mind, not as an object of missionary charity, not as something to be manipulated or defined by others, but as a man himself, on this earth, under the sky, on the same lonely journey we all must make, alone. He (I am using him as an example) by insisting on the sacredness of his soul, by demanding his soul's salvation, is closer to the Hebrew prophet than, let us say arbitrarily, another eminent Christian, the Governor of Alabama. And in the same way it is perfectly possible twenty years from now that the Christian Church, if indeed it lasts that long, will be appalled by some of the things some of the sons of the late Martin Luther King may have to say. After all, speaking now again as a creation of the Christian Church, as a black creation of the Christian Church, I watched what the Christian Church did to my father, who was in the pulpit all the years of his life, I watched the kind of poverty, the kind of hopeless poverty, which was not an act of God, but an act of the State, against which he and his children struggled, I watched above all, and this is what is crucial, the ways in which white power can destroy black minds, and what black people are now fighting against, precisely that. We watched too many of us being destroyed for too long and destroyed where it really matters, not only in chain gangs, and in prisons and on needles, not only do I know, and every black person knows, hundreds of people, thousands of people, perishing in the streets of my nation as we stand here, perishing, for whom there is no hope, perishing in the jails of my country, and not only my country. For one reason, and one reason only, because they are black and because the structure into which they were born, the Christian structure, had determined and fore-ordained that destruction, to maintain its power. Now, of course, this, from the point of view of anyone who takes the preaching of the man from Galilee seriously, is very close to being the sin against the Holy Ghost, for which you will remember there is no forgiveness.

It seems to me, then, that the most serious thing that has happened in the world today and in the Christian conscience is that Christians, having rationalized their crimes for so long, though they live with them every day and see the evidence of them every day, they put themselves out of touch with themselves. There is a sense in which it can be said that my black flesh is the flesh that St. Paul wanted to have mortified. There is a sense in which it can be said that very long ago, for a complex of reasons, but among them power, the Christian personality split itself in two, split itself into dark and light, in fact, and it is now bewildered, at war with itself, is literally unable to comprehend the force of such a woman as Mahalia Jackson, who does not sound like anyone in Canterbury Cathedral, unable to accept the depth of sorrow, out of which a Ray Charles comes, unable to get itself in touch with itself, with its selfless totality. From my point of view, it seems to me that the flesh and the spirit are one; it seems to me that when you mortify the one, you have mortified the other. It would seem to me that the morality by which the Christian Church claims to live, I mean the public morality, that morality governing our sexual relations and the structure of the family, is terribly inadequate for what the world, and people in the world, must deal with now.

One of the things that happened, it seems to me, with the rise of the Christian Church, was precisely the denial of a certain kind of spontaneity, a certain kind of joy, a certain kind of freedom, which a man can only have when he is in touch with himself, his surroundings, his women and his children. It seems to me that this shows very crucially in the nature, the structure of our politics and in the personalities of our children, who would like to learn, if I may put it this way, how to sing the blues, because the blues are not a racial creation, the blues are an historical creation produced by the confrontation precisely between the pagan, the black pagan from Africa, and the alabaster cross. I am suggesting that the nature of the lies the Christian Church has always helplessly told about me are only a reflection of the lies the Christian Church has always helplessly told itself, to itself, about itself.

I am saying that when a person, when a people, are able to persuade themselves that another group or breed of men are less than men, they themselves become less than men and have made it almost impossible for themselves to confront reality and to change it. If I deny what I know to be true, if I deny that that white child next to me is simply another child, and if I pretend that that child, because its colour is white, deserves destruction, I have begun the destruction of my own personality and I am beginning the destruction of my own children. I think that if we have a future, we must now begin to tremble for some of the children of some of our contemporaries. I tremble frankly for the children of all white South Africans, who will not deserve their fate. I tremble for that day that is coming when some non-white nations, for example Vietnam, are able to pay the West back—they have a long and bloody bill to pay. I tremble when I wonder if there is left in the Christian civilizations (and only these civilizations can answer this question—I cannot) the moral energy, the spiritual daring, to atone, to repent, to be born again; if it is possible, if there is enough leaven in the loaf, to cause us to discard our actual and historical habits, to cause us to take our places with that criminal Jew, for He was a criminal, who was put to death by Rome between two thieves, because He claimed to be the Son of God. That claim was a revelation and a revolution because it means that we are all the sons of God. That is a challenge, that's the hope. It is only by attempting to face that challenge that one can begin to expand and transform God's nature which has to be forever an act of creation on the part of every human being. It is important to bear in mind that we are responsible for our soul's salvation, not the Bishop, not the priest, not my mother, ultimately it is each man's responsibility alone in his own chamber before his own gods to deal with his health and his sickness, to deal with his life and his death. When people cannot do this with themselves, they very quickly cannot do it with others. When one begins to live by habit and by quotation, one has begun to stop living.

Finally, the mandate of this body is not merely goodwill, not merely paper resolutions. If one believes in the Prince of Peace one must stop committing crimes in the name of the Prince of Peace. The Christian Church still rules this world, it still has the power, to change the structure of South Africa. It has the power, if it will, to prevent the death of another Martin Luther King junior. It has the power, if it will, to force my Government to cease dropping bombs in South-East Asia. These are crimes committed in the name of the Christian Church, and no more than we have absolved the Germans for saying "I didn't know it," "I didn't know what it was about," "I knew of people having been taken away in the night, but it has nothing to do with me." We were very hard on the Germans about that. But Germany is also a Christian nation, and what the Germans did in the Second World War, since they are human and we are human too, there is no guarantee that we are not doing that, right now. When a structure, a State or a Church or a country, becomes too expensive for the world to afford, when it is no longer responsive to the needs of the world, that structure is doomed. If the Christian faith does not recover its Lord and Saviour Jesus Christ, we shall discover the meaning of what he meant when he said, "Insofar as have done it unto the least of these, you have done it unto me."

Address to the World Council of Churches,
July 7, 1968

Sweet Lorraine

HAT's the way I always felt about her, and so I won't apologize for calling her that now. *She* understood it: in that far too brief a time when we walked and talked and laughed and drank together, sometimes in the streets and bars and restaurants of the Village, sometimes at her house, sometimes at my house, sometimes gracelessly fleeing the houses of others; and sometimes seeming, for anyone who didn't know us, to be having a knock-down, drag-out battle. We spent a lot of time arguing about history and tremendously related subjects in her Bleecker Street and, later, Waverly Place flats. And often, just when I was certain that she was about to throw me out, as being altogether too rowdy a type, she would stand up, her hands on her hips (for these down-home sessions she always wore slacks), and pick up my empty glass as though she intended to throw it at me. Then she would walk into the kitchen, saying, with a haughty toss of her head, "Really, Jimmy. You ain't *right*, child!" With which stern put-down, she would hand me another drink and launch into a brilliant analysis of just why I wasn't "right." I would often stagger down her stairs as the sun came up, usually in the middle of a paragraph and always in the middle of a laugh. That marvelous laugh. That marvelous face. I loved her, she was my sister and my comrade. Her going did not so much make me lonely as make me realize how lonely we were. We had that respect for each other which perhaps is only felt by people on the same side of the barricades, listening to the accumulating thunder of the hooves of horses and the treads of tanks.

The first time I ever saw Lorraine was at the Actors' Studio, in the Winter of '58–'59. She was there as an observer of the Workshop Production of *Giovanni's Room*. She sat way up in the bleachers, taking on some of the biggest names in the American theatre because she had liked the play and they, in the main, hadn't. I was enormously grateful to her, she seemed to speak for me; and afterward she talked to me with a gentleness and generosity never to be forgotten. A small, shy, determined person, with that strength dictated by abso-

lutely impersonal ambition: she was not trying to "make it"—
she was trying to keep the faith.

We really met, however, in Philadelphia, in 1959, when *A
Raisin In The Sun* was at the beginning of its amazing career.
Much has been written about this play; I personally feel that
it will demand a far less guilty and constricted people than the
present-day Americans to be able to assess it at all; as an historical achievement, anyway, no one can gainsay its importance. What is relevant here is that I had never in my life seen
so many black people in the theatre. And the reason was that
never in the history of the American theatre had so much of
the truth of black people's lives been seen on the stage. Black
people ignored the theatre because the theatre had always ignored them.

But, in *Raisin*, black people recognized that house and all
the people in it—the mother, the son, the daughter and the
daughter-in-law—and supplied the play with an interpretative
element which could not be present in the minds of white
people: a kind of claustrophobic terror, created not only by
their knowledge of the house but by their knowledge of the
streets. And when the curtain came down, Lorraine and I
found ourselves in the backstage alley, where she was immediately mobbed. I produced a pen and Lorraine handed me
her handbag and began signing autographs. "It only happens
once," she said. I stood there and watched. I watched the
people, who loved Lorraine for what she had brought to
them; and watched Lorraine, who loved the people for what
they brought to *her*. It was not, for her, a matter of being
admired. She was being corroborated and confirmed. She was
wise enough and honest enough to recognize that black
American artists are in a very special case. One is not merely
an artist and one is not judged merely as an artist: the black
people crowding around Lorraine, whether or not they considered her an artist, assuredly considered her a witness. This
country's concept of art and artists has the effect, scarcely
worth mentioning by now, of isolating the artist from the
people. One can see the effect of this in the irrelevance of so
much of the work produced by celebrated white artists; but
the effect of this isolation on a black artist is absolutely fatal.
He *is*, already, as a black American citizen, isolated from most

of his white countrymen. At the crucial hour, he can hardly look to his artistic peers for help, for they do not know enough about him to be able to correct him. To continue to grow, to remain in touch with himself, he needs the support of that community from which, however, all of the pressures of American life incessantly conspire to remove him. And when he is effectively removed, he falls silent—and the people have lost another hope.

Much of the strain under which Lorraine worked was produced by her knowledge of this reality, and her determined refusal to be destroyed by it. She was a very young woman, with an overpowering vision, and fame had come to her early—she must certainly have wished, often enough, that fame had seen fit to drag its feet a little. For fame and recognition are not synonyms, especially not here, and her fame was to cause her to be criticized very harshly, very loudly, and very often by both black and white people who were unable to believe, apparently, that a really serious intention could be contained in so glamorous a frame. She took it all with a kind of astringent good humor, refusing, for example, even to consider defending herself when she was being accused of being a "slum lord" because of her family's real-estate holdings in Chicago. I called her during that time, and all she said—with a wry laugh—was, "My God, Jimmy, do you realize you're only the second person who's called me today? And you know how my phone kept ringing *before*!" She was not surprised. She was devoted to the human race, but she was not romantic about it.

When so bright a light goes out so early, when so gifted an artist goes so soon, we are left with a sorrow and wonder which speculation cannot assuage. One's filled for a long time with a sense of injustice as futile as it is powerful. And the vanished person fills the mind, in this or that attitude, doing this or that. Sometimes, very briefly, one hears the exact inflection of the voice, the exact timbre of the laugh—as I have, when watching the dramatic presentation, *To Be Young, Gifted and Black*, and in reading through these pages. But I do not have the heart to presume to assess her work, for all of it, for me, was suffused with the light which was Lorraine. It is possible, for example, that *The Sign In Sidney Brustein's*

Window attempts to say too much; but it is also exceedingly probable that it makes so loud and uncomfortable a sound because of the surrounding silence; not many plays, presently, risk being accused of attempting to say too much! Again, *Brustein* is certainly a very *willed* play, unabashedly didactic: but it cannot, finally, be dismissed or categorized in this way because of the astonishing life of its people. It positively courts being dismissed as old-fashioned and banal and yet has the unmistakable power of turning the viewer's judgment in on himself. *Is all this true or not true?* the play rudely demands; and, unforgivably, leaves us squirming before this question. One cannot quite answer the question negatively, one risks being caught in a lie. But an affirmative answer imposes a new level of responsibility, both for one's conduct and for the fortunes of the American state, and one risks, therefore, the disagreeable necessity of becoming "an insurgent again." For Lorraine made no bones about asserting that art has a purpose, and that its purpose was action: that it contained the "energy which could change things."

It would be good, selfishly, to have her around now, that small, dark girl, with her wit, her wonder, and her eloquent compassion. I've only met one person Lorraine couldn't get through to, and that was the late Bobby Kennedy. And, as the years have passed since that stormy meeting—Lorraine talks about it in these pages, so I won't go into it here—I've very often pondered what she then tried to convey—that a holocaust is no respecter of persons; that what, today, seems merely humiliation and injustice for a few, can, unchecked, become Terror for the many, snuffing out white lives just as though they were black lives; that if the American state could not protect the lives of black citizens, then, presently, the entire State would find itself engulfed. And the horses and tanks are indeed upon us, and the end is not in sight. Perhaps it is just as well, after all, that she did not live to see with the outward eye what she saw so clearly with the inward one. And it is not at all farfetched to suspect that what she saw contributed to the strain which killed her, for the effort to which Lorraine was dedicated is more than enough to kill a man.

I saw Lorraine in her hospital bed, as she was dying. She tried to speak, she couldn't. She did not seem frightened or sad, only exasperated that her body no longer obeyed her; she smiled and waved. But I prefer to remember her as she was the last time I saw her on her feet. We were at, of all places, the PEN Club, she was seated, talking, dressed all in black, wearing a very handsome wide, black hat, thin, and radiant. I knew she had been ill, but I didn't know, then, how seriously. I said, "Lorraine, baby, you look beautiful, how in the world do you do it?" She was leaving, I have the impression she was on a staircase, and she turned and smiled that smile and said, "It helps to develop a serious illness, Jimmy!" and waved and disappeared.

How One Black Man Came To Be an American

A REVIEW OF "ROOTS"

I CANNOT guess what Alex Haley's countrymen will make of his birthday present to us during this election and Bicentennial year. One is tempted to say that it could scarcely have come at a more awkward time—what with the conventions, the exhibition of candidates, the dubious state of this particular and perhaps increasingly dubious union, and the American attempt, hopelessly and predictably schizophrenic, of preventing total disaster, for white people and for the West, in South Africa. There is a carefully muffled pain and panic in the nation, which neither candidate, neither party, can coherently address, being, themselves, but vivid symptoms of it.

What most significantly fills this void, or threatens to, is the presence, in America, of the world's first genuine black Westerner. Created here in pain and darkness, remnant of slaughter, his hour may, at last, and in mysterious, unprecedented ways, have begun to strike. Certainly a bell is tolling now for all that the Western peoples imagined would last forever. This electoral contest, taking place in an arena which is, presently, at the very center of the troubled world, seems to have invested the black vote with a power, and exhibits toward it a respect, which the black vote has never, in the memory of the living, had before. This has not happened before now for the very simple reason that, until now, Americans were able to prevent it from happening. They cannot prevent it now simply because—they cannot; it is not because the Americans have seen a great light. They need the moral authority of their former slaves, who are the only people in the world who know anything about them and who may be, indeed, the only people in the world who really care anything about them.

In any event, and no matter how diversely, and with what contradictions, the black vote is cast in the 24 years left of this century's life, the impact of the visible, overt, black presence on the political machinery of this country alters, forever, the weight and the meaning of the black presence in the world.

This means that the black people of this country bear a mighty responsibility—which, odd as it may sound, is nothing new— and face an immediate future as devastating, though in a different way, as the past which has led us here: I am speaking of the beginning of the end of the black diaspora, which means that I am speaking of the beginning of the end of the world as we have suffered it until now.

The world of Alex Haley's book begins in Gambia West Africa in 1750 with the birth of one of his ancestors, Kunta Kinte, born of Omoro and Binta Kinte, of the Mandinka tribe, and of the Muslim faith. In the re-creation of this time and place, Haley succeeds beautifully where many have failed. He must have studied and sweated hard to achieve such ease and grace, for he would appear to have been born in his ancestral village and to be personally acquainted with everybody there. The public ceremonies of this people are revealed as a precise and coherent mirror of their private and yet connected imaginations. And these ceremonies, imaginations, however removed in time, are yet, for a black man anyway, naggingly familiar and present. I say, for a black man, but these ceremonies, these imaginations are really universal, finally inescapably as old and deep as the human race. The tragedy of the people doomed to think of themselves as white lies in their denial of these origins: they become incoherent because they can never stammer from whence they came.

There exists, in West African life, what I have heard described as the "eight day" ceremony. This ceremony takes place eight days after the birth of the child, during which time the father—alone—has to give his child a name. This name is both a gift and a challenge, for it is hoped that the child will make his own some of the positive qualities that the name implies (very like, if you will, and yet entirely unlike people naming their children after movie stars). On the eighth day, in the presence of the village, the child is named: "[Omoro] lifted up the infant and as all watched, whispered three times into his son's ear the name he had chosen for him. It was the first time the name had ever been spoken as this child's name, for Omoro's people felt that each human being should be the first to know who he was."

Now, nothing like this has ever happened to me, or to any

American black I know, and, yet, something like this surely happened somehow, somewhere, for the tenacity with which a black man, or woman, can insist on not being called "out of their name" has something of this tone. And even way up here in the 20th century, Muhammad Ali will not be the only one to respond to the moment that the father lifted his baby up with his face to the heavens, and said softly, "Behold—the only thing greater than yourself."

We know that Kunta will be kidnapped, and brought to America, and yet, we have become so engrossed in his life in the village, and so fond of him, that the moment comes as a terrible shock. We, too, would like to kill his abductors. We are in his skin, and in his darkness, and, presently, we are shackled with him, in his terror, rage, and pain, his stink, and the stink of others, on the ship which brings him here. It can be said that we know the rest of the story—how it turned out, so to speak, but frankly, I don't think that we do know the rest of the story. It *hasn't* turned out yet, which is the rage and pain and danger of this country. Alex Haley's taking us back through time to the village of his ancestors is an act of faith and courage, but this book is also an act of love, and it is this which makes it haunting.

The density of the African social setting eventually gives way to the shrill incoherence of the American one. Haley makes no comment on this contrast, there being indeed none to make, apart from that made by the remarkable people we meet on these shores, who, born here, are yet striving, as the song puts it, "to make it my home."

The American setting is as familiar as the back of one's hand. Yet, as Haley's story unfolds, the landscape begins to be terrifying, unutterably strange and bleak, a cloud hanging over it day and night. Without ever seeming to, and with a compassion as haunting as the sorrow songs which helped produce him, Haley makes us aware of the disaster overtaking not the black nation, but the white one. One will not, for example, soon forget the fiddler, who had been told by his master—who was considered to be a "good" master—that he could buy his freedom, and how he worked for 30 years to buy it. But when he brought the money to his master, his master regretfully informed him that he could take the money only as a down payment on the fiddler's freedom because the price of slaves had risen so high that he would be cheating himself if he allowed his slave to buy his freedom for so little. This is the same master who later sells Kunta's daughter as punishment for her having aided a runaway slave, and who, as Kunta is beaten nearly unconscious, as the girl's mother lies prostrate, and as the sheriff drags the girl away, walks, head downward, into his house. What, one can't but wonder, can be waiting for him in that house. Perhaps, all hard things considered, it was wealthier in the slaves' cabins. We had to face whatever was in there, and, while we might call each other nigger, we knew that a man was not a thing.

"Roots" is a study of continuities, of consequences, of how a people perpetuate themselves, how each generation helps to doom, or helps to liberate, the coming one—the action of love, or the effect of the absence of love, in time. It suggests, with great power, how each of us, however unconsciously, can't but be the vehicle of the history which has produced us. Well, we can perish in this vehicle, children, or we can move on up the road.

The New York Times Book Review,
September 26, 1976

An Open Letter to Mr. Carter

I HAVE a thing to tell you, but with a heavy heart, for it is not a new thing.

In North Carolina, as I write, nine black men and one white woman are under sentences of a total of 282 years in various prisons on various charges, including arson. The Rev. Ben Chavis, who was 29 years old yesterday, is the best known of the Wilmington 10.

In Charlotte, three black men are on bail and facing sentences, equally savage, on charges equally preposterous.

I will not insult your intelligence by discussing the details of the cases.

It must be relatively rare to find ten people (who have never before committed any offense) who merit 282 years in prison. As for Ben Chavis, the courts have totally failed to indicate what he has done to merit 34.

James Earl Grant was arrested in the more liberal city of Charlotte, accused with two others of burning down the Lazy B riding stables in which fifteen horses died. He merited a mere 25. The other two men got a total of 30 years in the 1972 trial—the fire was in 1968.

In any event, some of the most pertinent details of the cases are to be found in major newspapers and in the Congressional Record: Messrs. John Conyers Jr., Ronald V. Dellums and Charles B. Rangel speaking.

And the mother of Ben Chavis, speaking from a church in Raleigh, N.C., has the most pertinent question, especially in light of the fact that her son is a Christian minister: "You in the Christian church, will you be diligent in keeping them from getting my son?"

And the entire horror evolved from the manner in which a Wilmington judge decided to desegregate a Wilmington high school, and the fact that the black students wished to declare the birthday of the late Dr. Martin Luther King Jr. a day of mourning.

I have said that it is not a new thing I have to tell you, and, indeed, most of it is not new for me. I might in my own mind, as I write, be speaking of the Scottsboro Boys: where I came in, so to speak.

If I know, you must certainly know of the silent pact made between the North and the South, after Reconstruction, the purpose of which was—and is—to keep the nigger in his place.

If I know, then you must certainly know, that keeping the nigger in his place was the most extraordinarily effective way of keeping the poor white in his place, and also, of keeping him poor:

The situation of the Wilmington 10 and of the Charlotte 3 is a matter of Federal collusion, and would not be possible without that collusion.

When those black children and white children and black men and white men and black women and white women were marching, behind Martin, up and down those dusty roads, trespassing, trespassing wherever they were, in the wrong waiting room, at the wrong coffee counter, in the wrong department store, in the wrong toilet, and were carried off to jail, they found themselves before *federally* appointed judges, who gave them the maximum sentence.

Some people died beneath that sentence, some went mad, some girls will never become pregnant again. Some of us, following Martin, and, however we may sometimes have disagreed with him, feeling his love, and believing *I have a dream!* could sometimes raise in an evening $30,000 or $40,000 or $50,000—yes: which was gone in bail-bond money in the morning. And, yes, my friend, that is called collusion. The kids would die in the chain gang, and we would drop dead on the road. Or, as my friend the actress Miss Ruby Dee once put it to me, after four girls were killed in the 1963 bombing of the Birmingham Sunday School, and as we were trying to organize a protest rally—to demand, in fact—that the American people, in the light of so dreadful an event, declare Christmas a day of mourning, of atonement: *"Soon, there won't be enough black people to go around."*

I was present at the culmination of the voter-registration drive in Selma, Alabama, not so very long ago. My friend James Forman had been organizing for six months, or thereabouts; it is not easy, in such a town, where virtually every white man considers that he owns every black man. (I am speaking with the utmost restraint and will not attempt to describe the events of that day.) Nevertheless, hundreds of people came out early in the morning and lined up in front of the courthouse.

In Selma, there are two courthouses, the state courthouse and a Federal courthouse, and they face each other across a narrow street—catty-corner to these two buildings is a recruiting station (*Uncle Sam wants you!*).

The sheriff, armed, forced us to move from one side of the street to the other—that is, to the steps of the Federal courthouse. "We" are now, among others, Representative John Conyers, my brother David, and myself. Representatives of the Justice Department and the Federal Bureau of Investigation are standing on the steps with us, under the American flag. (We have already seen the sheriff and his deputies beat up two black boys and hurl them into a truck—but they were on the wrong side of the street.)

The sheriff crosses the street and demands that we leave the steps of the Federal courthouse. I ask the Justice Department, or the F.B.I., if he has any right to throw us off *Federal* property. *No*, is the answer, *but we can't do anything about it.*

I am watching the recruiting station. We'll move inside because the alternative is slaughter. It is 4:30 and the whistle blows; it means the courthouse is closed. The people who have been standing there all day long, only 12 of whom have been allowed to enter the courthouse, and none of whom have been registered, turn and walk away.

The F.B.I. wishes to know if any one of us would like to sign an affidavit. *I signed my affidavit in Korea* says my brother, and turns away to watch the departing people.

When we marched on Montgomery, the Confederate flag was flying from the dome of the Capitol: this gesture can be interpreted as *insurrection*. But when Muhammad Ali decided to be *true to his faith* and refused to join the Army, the wrath of an entire Republic was visited on his head, he was stripped of his title, and was not allowed to work. In short, his countrymen decided to break him, and it is not their virtue that they failed. It is *his* virtue.

I am not so much trying to bring to your mind the suffering

of a despised people—a very comforting notion, after all, for most Americans—as the state and the fate of a nation of which you are the elected leader. The situations of the Wilmington 10, and the Charlotte 3, are very small symptoms of the monstrous and continuing wrong for which you, as the elected leader, are now responsible.

Too many of us are in jail, my friend; too many of us are starving, too many of us can find no door open. And I was in Charlotte, 20 years ago, three years after the Supreme Court made segregation in education illegal, when it was decided that *separate* could not, by definition, be *equal*. Charlotte then begged for time, and time, indeed, has passed. I was in Boston a few months ago and Boston, now, is begging for time. Across the entire question of the education of our children—*all* our children—is dragged the entirely false issue of busing. A child's future does not change because he is bused into another neighborhood.

Well, I dared to write you this letter out of the concrete necessity of bringing to your attention the situations of the Wilmington 10 and the Charlotte 3. I repeat, their situation is but a very small indication of the wretched in this country: the nonwhite, the Indian, the Puerto Rican, the Mexican, the Oriental. Consider that we may all have learned, by now, all that we can learn from you and may not want to become like you. At this hour of the world's history it may be that you, now, have something to learn from us.

I must add, in honor, that I write to you because I love our country: And you, in my lifetime, are the only president to whom I would have written.

The New York Times, January 23, 1977

Last of the Great Masters

THE WORLD OF EARL HINES
By Stanley Dance.
Illustrated. 324 pp. New York:
Charles Scribner's Sons. Cloth, $15.95. Paper, $7.95.

TONI MORRISON, that handsome and perceptive lady, once remarked that, in spite of all the other elements which more immediately meet the eye, she was struck by the quantity of "sheer intelligence" which went into the forging of black life in America—without which "intelligence," simply, none of us would have survived. Similarly, while reading Earl "Fatha" Hines's vast and beautiful document, I am struck by the *sheer* generosity of the man, and the people he lived with, whom he shares with us. Hines is describing hard trials, good times, bad times, narrow escapes—but the book is never petty or mean and never bitter. Such generosity may also be a function of the intelligence; it gives life, certainly, heals, and saves.

In "The World of Earl Hines," Stanley Dance, the British jazz critic and author of "The World of Duke Ellington" and "The World of Swing," has compiled Earl Hines's taped record of his life and music. It is an oral history—spanning 72 years, from Hines's birth in Duquesne, Pa., through his rise to prominence as a pianist, singer and bandleader in the 1920's, his "rediscovery" in the late 50's, and on to his present acclaim as "the last of the great masters." Complementing Hines's own words are Dance's interviews with other jazz greats who knew and played with Hines; Dizzy Gillespie, Teddy Wilson, Budd Johnson and Billy Eckstine are among those who give their impressions of "Fatha."

But it is difficult to assess or discuss so loaded and tremendous a record. It is impossible to do justice to a book in which one meets King Oliver, Louis Armstrong, Valaida Snow, Duke Ellington, Count Basie, Benny Goodman, Dizzy Gillespie, Nat Cole, Sarah Vaughan, Ethel Waters ("she used some language I won't use here") Ella Fitzgerald (on opening nights, "a nervous wreck"), Charlie Parker ("It was too bad he got mixed up with the wrong crowd. He was a fine boy and there was nothing wrong with him at all when it came to his character. All the harm he did he did to himself.") And Jack Teagarden and Johnny Hodges, and Joe Louis, and the dapper Billy Eckstine taking very literally a Southern cafe owner's warning: "You can't drink it in here." "I'm not going to drink it in here," Mr. E. replied, and threw the coffee all over the man.

For there is the reality of life on the American road, for Earl Hines and all his swinging, singing boys and girls. ("When we traveled by train through the South, they would send a porter back to our car to let us know when the dining room was cleared, and then we would all go in together. We couldn't eat when we wanted to. We had to eat when they were ready for us.") It certainly demands something extraordinary in the way of generosity to describe the endless humiliation and the omnipresent danger as vividly as Hines does, and yet so laconically and so without bitterness. The men and women in this book were creating the only musical vocabulary this country has. They were creating American *classical* music. There isn't any other, and the American attempts to deny this have led, among other disasters, to the melancholy rise and fall of the late Elvis Presley, who was so highly paid for having a black sound in a white body. Utter madness, of course, but it does a lot to illuminate the economic situation of black musicians, who have, alas, black sounds in black bodies.

And, it seems to me, it is because these men were doing something, and knew what they were doing, that they could call upon such vast reserves of generosity, be so free of bitterness and evince so little need to prove their manhood. It would not appear that they were tormented by the question of their manhood. They would appear to have known that they were men, to have been raised to know it and to have rejoiced in their identity. In any case—another of the melancholy facts the Republic overlooks—a man's identity can never be threatened by a child, and all racists are children. A man's life can be threatened and taken: But part of the price of being a man is knowing that.

These black and—in spite of the fame of some—so largely unknown bards of yesterday and today ("this marvel of social organization," as Ralph Ellison puts it) have given more to the world than anyone can say; are responsible, literally, for generations. They gave our sorrow and danger back to us, transformed, and they helped us to embrace and triumph over it. They gave us back our joy, and we could give it to our children. Out of the depths of the midnight hour, we could laugh. *"One never knows,"* says the bemused Fats Waller, *"do one?"*

Yes. I, too, have said that I would exchange all the blues to save one starving child. I was wrong, not only because the exchange is not in my power, but because this singing of the Lord's song in so strange a land has saved more children than anyone will ever know, and the beginning is not yet in sight.

The New York Times Book Review,
October 16, 1977

Every Good-bye Ain't Gone

I AM writing this note just 29 years after my first departure from America. It was raining—naturally. My mother had come downstairs, and stood silently, arms folded, on the stoop. My baby sister was upstairs, weeping. I got into the cab, waved, and drove away.

It may be impossible for anyone to tell the truth about his past. You drag your past with you everywhere, or it drags you. Therefore, the simplest thing for me to say concerning that first departure from America is that I had no choice. It was not the heroic departure of a prodigy. Time was to prove (and how!) that I was a prodigal son indeed, but, by the time the fatted calf came my way, intimacy with too many dubious hamburgers had caused me to lose my appetite. I *did* want the people I loved to know how much I loved them, especially that little girl weeping on the top floor of that tenement: I will say that. And my departure, which, especially in my own eyes, stank of betrayal, was my only means of proving, or redeeming, that love, my only hope. Or, in other words, I knew then that I was a writer, but did not know if I could last long enough to prove it. And, if I loved the people I loved, I also knew that they loved me, did not deserve and could scarcely afford the spectacle of the firstborn as a disaster. That seems a grandiose way of putting it, yet it is the only honest way for *me* to put it; and it is not really grandiose at all—it comes out of the life I saw all around me. The song says, *motherless children have a hard time!* And so do the fatherless, and the brotherless. The firstborn knows this first, and, therefore, the accident of being the firstborn is also a reality, and I took it very seriously.

For, in the years that I—we—were growing up in Harlem, Harlem was still, essentially, a southern community, but lately, and violently, driven north. The people had dragged the South with them, *in* them, to the northern ghetto, and one of the results of this was that all of the children belonged to all of the elders. If, for example, a grown-up, even a very young grown-up, caught me doing something I should not have been doing, blocks from my house, he, or she, would

773

whip my behind and carry me, howling, to my house, to tell my mother or father why I had been whipped. Mama or Daddy would thank the person, and then whip my behind again. It is a hard way to learn, perhaps, but there are no easy ways, and so I learned that I was supposed to be an "example." That didn't make sense to me in the beginning—I hated what seemed to me to be an injustice—but it made sense to me later. We were *all* expected to be examples to each other. The eldest was expected to do his best to protect those behind him from being destroyed by the bloody discoveries the eldest had already made. The price for this was astronomical: that the eldest did not allow *himself* to be destroyed.

This was quite an assignment for a black, defenseless-looking high school graduate who—to remain within the confines of the mentionable—had had feet, fists, tables, clubs, and chairs bounced off his only head, and who, by the time of November, 1948, trusted no one, and knew that he trusted no one, knew that this distrust was suicidal, and also knew that there was no question any longer of his *life* in America: his violent destruction could be taken as given; it was a matter of time. By the time I was 22, I was a survivor—a survivor, furthermore, with murder in his heart.

A man with murder in his heart will murder, or be murdered—it comes to the same thing—and so I knew I had to leave. Somewhere else, anywhere else, the question of my life might still be open, but in my own country that question was closed.

Well, I was lucky—the black people I grew up with would say I was blessed. Some things had happened to me because I was black, and some things had happened to me because I was *me*, and I had to discover the demarcation line, if there was one. It seemed to me that such a demarcation line must certainly exist, but it was also beginning to be borne in on me that it was certainly not easy to find: and perhaps, indeed, when found, not to be trusted. How to perceive, define, a line nearly too thin for the naked eye, so mercurial, and so mighty. Only a really shattered, scotch- or martini-guzzling, upward-mobility-struck house nigger could possibly deny the relentless tension of the black condition. Being black affected one's life span, insurance rates, blood pressure, lovers, children, every dangerous hour of every dangerous day. There was absolutely no way *not* to be black without ceasing to exist. But it frequently seemed that there was no way to *be* black, either, without ceasing to exist.

For one of the ways of being black is to accept what the world tells you about your mother and your father, your brother and your sister; and what that world tells you—in many ways, from the language of the lawgiver to the language of the liberal—is that "your" people deserve, in effect, their fate. Your fate—"your" people's fate—involves being, forever, a little lower than these particular angels, angels who, nevertheless, are always ready to give you a helping hand.

Well, this is, after all, but another way of observing that it is exceedingly difficult for most of us to discard the assumptions of the society in which we were born, in which we live, to which we owe our identities; very difficult to defeat the trap of circumstance, which is, also, the web of safety; virtually impossible, if not completely impossible, to envision the future, except in those terms which we think we already know. Most of us are about as eager to be changed as we were to be born, and go through our changes in a similar state of shock.

Including this writer, of course, who was far, however, years ago, from being able to forgive himself for being so irretrievably human. The power of the social definition is that it becomes, fatally, one's own—but it took time, and much deep water, to make me see this. Rage and misery can be a source of comfort, simply because one has lived with rage and misery for so long.

But to accept this rage and misery as a source of comfort is to enter one of the vicious circles of hell. One does not, after all, forgive the world for this horror, nor can one forgive oneself. Because one cannot forgive oneself, one cannot forgive others, or, even, really, *see* others—one is always striking out at the wrong person, for only some other, poor, doomed innocent, obviously, is likely to be in striking range. One's self-esteem begins to shrivel, one's hope for the future begins to crack. In reacting against what the world calls you, you endlessly validate its judgment.

I had not conceived, then, that I had only to study the

hieroglyphic of my circumstances if I wished to decipher my inheritance. *Circumstances:* a rather heavy word, when you consider it, connecting, for me, by means of Ezekiel's *wheel in the middle of a wheel*, with the iron, inescapable truth of revolutions—we black folk say, what goes around, comes around. Circumstances, furthermore, are complicated, simplified, and, ultimately, defined by the person's reaction to these circumstances—for no one, no matter how it may seem, simply *endures* his circumstances. If we are what our circumstances make us, we are, also, what we make of our circumstances. This is, perhaps, the key to history, since *we* are history, and since the tension of which I am speaking is so silent and so private, with effects so unforeseeable, and so public.

In any case, the Americans' ladder is not Jacob's ladder, their pillow is not Jacob's pillow. Armed with this legacy, this testament, and this envelope which I had not yet opened, I went to France.

November 11, 1948: rain, fatigue, panic, the absolute certainty of being dashed to death on the vindictive tooth of the Eiffel Tower, which we circled, it seemed to me, for hours. I do not remember feeling the remotest exhilaration. I had a few "friends" in Paris, and $40 in my pocket, and expected a little less from my friends than I did from the $40. I was wrong, I must tell you at once, as to my friends, who were far more present than I would have dared allow myself to hope—my first lesson, perhaps, in humility; perhaps the first opening of a certain door. For the people who were nice to me were very nice to me without, if you see what I mean, being *nice:* They forced me to recognize that they cared about me. This was a bewildering, a paralyzing, revelation, and I know that I was not very graceful. The Bronx, Brooklyn, Texas, Princeton, and Alabama accents stammered out a need and anguish like my own: If I were ever to grow up, ever, then I had to hear my accent in the accent of others, and to recognize that anguish was not a province which I had discovered only yesterday, alone. On the other hand, I was right about the $40, which melted in a day, and there I was, in Paris, on my ass.

My ass, mister, *mine:* and I was glad. In spite of everything—the cops, the concierges, the hotels, the alleys, the joints, eventually the hospital, finally the jail—I was glad. If the demarcation line existed, then I had to be somewhat close to it, for I refused to believe that I could be so abject as to blame my trials, those crises which I myself perpetually precipitated, on my color. Furthermore, I could not dare to see that the question of the demarcation line was a false question and that I could hide behind it, paralyzed, vindictive, and guilty, for the rest of my life.

It was not for this, however, that I had left a small girl crying on the top floor of a Harlem tenement.

There *was* a demarcation line, to be walked every hour of every day. The demarcation line was my apprehension of, and, therefore, my responsibility for, my own experience: the chilling vice versa of what I had made of my experience and what that experience had made of me. I will owe the French a debt forever, for example, if only because, during one of my passionately insane barroom brawls, I suddenly realized that the Frenchman I was facing had not the remotest notion—and could not possibly have had the remotest notion—of the tension in my mind between *Orléans*, a French city, and *New Orleans*, where my father had been born, between *louis*, the coin, and *Louis*, the French king, for whom was named the state of Louisiana, the result of which celebrated purchase had been the death of so many black people. Neither did any African, as far as I could tell, at that moment of my own time and space, have any notion of this tension and torment. But what I began to see was that, if they had no notion of *my* torment, I certainly had no notion of theirs, and that I was treating people exactly as I had been treated at home.

In order to keep the faith—climbing Jacob's ladder—I came home, to go to Little Rock and Charlotte, and so forth and so on, in 1957, and was based in America from 1957 to 1970.

I have been in and out of my country, in and out of various cauldrons, for a very long time, long enough to see the doctrine of white supremacy return, like a plague, to the continent which spawned it. This is not a bitter statement. It comes, to tell the truth, out of love, for I am thinking of the children. I watch—here, for example—French and Algerian children trying to become friends with each other, reacting to, but not yet understanding, the terrors of their parents, and very far indeed from having any notion of the terrors of the state. They have no way of knowing that the state is menaced and shaken to the degree, precisely, that they, themselves, the presumed victims, or at least, the wards of the state, make manifest their identity—which is not what it might be, either for better or for worse, if they were still in Algeria. They cannot possibly know that they, ex-slave and ex-master, cannot be used as their fathers were used—that all identities, in short, are in question, are about to be made new.

Every good-bye ain't gone: human history reverberates with violent upheaval, uprooting, arrival and departure, hello and good-bye. Yet, I am not certain that anyone ever leaves home. When "home" drops below the horizon, it rises in one's breast and acquires the overwhelming power of menaced love.

In my early years in Paris, I met and became friends with an elderly man who had left Germany in something like 1933 to become a hunted refugee because he had refused, in any way whatever, to be a part of the criminal Nazi state. I admired this man very much, and his pain was very vivid to me. God knows one couldn't quarrel with his reasons for leaving Germany, and yet his repudiated homeland was present in everything he said and did. The French landscape, which he loved as I did, could console, could even nearly reconcile: but it could not replace the landscape he carried in his heart. In the early fifties his mother was dying and wanted to see her son one last time, and I took my friend to the railroad station. I never, never forgot that moment. I wondered if that was going to happen to me. I wanted to go home, I wanted to see *my* mother and my brothers and my sisters and my friends—but the novel wasn't finished (it seemed, indeed, that it would *never* be finished), and that was the only trophy I could carry home. All my love was in it, and the reason for my journey.

I suspect, though I certainly cannot prove it, that every life moves full circle—toward revelation: You begin to see, and even rejoice to see, what you always saw. You can even tell anguish to sit down, and shut up, you're busy right now— and anguish, as you should certainly know by now, ain't to go nowhere. It might go around the corner, on a particularly bright day, and there *are* those days: but anguish has your number, knows, to paraphrase the song, where you live. It's a difficult relationship, but mysteriously indispensable. It teaches you.

So. I *could* talk about the European panic, which takes so monotonous a form: but what is happening in Europe, now, to blacks, and to other, unprecedented niggers, has been happening for a very long time. Once I began to recover from my delirium, it was the first thing in Europe that I clearly saw: so it would be dishonest to pretend that this crisis, a global crisis, has anything to do with my motives or my movement now. I will say that my baby sister is a grown, married woman now, with an exceedingly swift and cunning son who has not the faintest intention of allowing me to forget that I'm his uncle: so, for me, for all of us, I believe, that dreadful day in November of '48 is redeemed.

Neither do I want anyone to suppose that I think that the gem of the ocean has kept any of its promises, but my ancestors counseled me to *keep the faith*: and I promised, I vowed, that I would. If I am a part of the American house, and I am, it is because my ancestors paid—*striving to make it my home*— so unimaginable a price: and I have seen some of the effects of that passion everywhere I have been, all over this world. That music is everywhere, resounds, resounds: and tells me that now is the moment, for me, to return to the eye of the hurricane.

New York, December 19, 1977

If Black English Isn't a Language,
Then Tell Me, What Is?

S T. PAUL DE VENCE, France—The argument concerning
the use, or the status, or the reality, of black English is
rooted in American history and has absolutely nothing to do
with the question the argument supposes itself to be posing.
The argument has nothing to do with language itself but with
the *role* of language. Language, incontestably, reveals the
speaker. Language, also, far more dubiously, is meant to define
the other—and, in this case, the other is refusing to be defined
by a language that has never been able to recognize him.

People evolve a language in order to describe and thus control their circumstances, or in order not to be submerged by
a reality that they cannot articulate. (And, if they cannot articulate it, they *are* submerged.) A Frenchman living in Paris
speaks a subtly and crucially different language from that of
the man living in Marseilles; neither sounds very much like a
man living in Quebec; and they would all have great difficulty
in apprehending what the man from Guadeloupe, or Martinique, is saying, to say nothing of the man from Senegal—
although the "common" language of all these areas is French.
But each has paid, and is paying, a different price for this
"common" language, in which, as it turns out, they are not
saying, and cannot be saying, the same things: They each have
very different realities to articulate, or control.

What joins all languages, and all men, is the necessity to
confront life, in order, not inconceivably, to outwit death: The
price for this is the acceptance, and achievement, of one's temporal identity. So that, for example, though it is not taught
in the schools (and this has the potential of becoming a political issue) the south of France still clings to its ancient and
musical Provençal, which resists being described as a "dialect." And much of the tension in the Basque countries, and
in Wales, is due to the Basque and Welsh determination not
to allow their languages to be destroyed. This determination
also feeds the flames in Ireland for among the many indignities

the Irish have been forced to undergo at English hands is the English contempt for their language.

It goes without saying, then, that language is also a political instrument, means, and proof of power. It is the most vivid and crucial key to identity: It reveals the private identity, and connects one with, or divorces one from, the larger, public, or communal identity. There have been, and are, times, and places, when to speak a certain language could be dangerous, even fatal. Or, one may speak the same language, but in such a way that one's antecedents are revealed, or (one hopes) hidden. This is true in France, and is absolutely true in England: The range (and reign) of accents on that damp little island make England coherent for the English and totally incomprehensible for everyone else. To open your mouth in England is (if I may use black English) to "put your business in the street": You have confessed your parents, your youth, your school, your salary, your self-esteem, and, alas, your future.

Now, I do not know what white Americans would sound like if there had never been any black people in the United States, but they would not sound the way they sound. *Jazz*, for example, is a very specific sexual term, as in *jazz me, baby*, but white people purified it into the Jazz Age. *Sock it to me*, which means, roughly, the same thing, has been adopted by Nathaniel Hawthorne's descendants with no qualms or hesitations at all, along with *let it all hang out* and *right on! Beat to his socks*, which was once the black's most total and despairing image of poverty, was transformed into a thing called the Beat Generation, which phenomenon was, largely, composed of *uptight*, middle-class white people, imitating poverty, trying to *get down*, to get *with it*, doing their *thing*, doing their despairing best to be *funky*, which we, the blacks, never dreamed of doing—we *were* funky, baby, like *funk* was going out of style.

Now, no one can eat his cake, and have it, too, and it is late in the day to attempt to penalize black people for having created a language that permits the nation its only glimpse of reality, a language without which the nation would be even more *whipped* than it is.

I say that the present skirmish is rooted in American history, and it is. Black English is the creation of the black diaspora. Blacks came to the United States chained to each other, but from different tribes: Neither could speak the other's language. If two black people, at that bitter hour of the world's history, had been able to speak to each other, the institution of chattel slavery could never have lasted as long as it did. Subsequently, the slave was given, under the eye, and the gun, of his master, Congo Square, and the Bible—or, in other words, and under these conditions, the slave began the formation of the black church, and it is within this unprecedented tabernacle that black English began to be formed. This was not, merely, as in the European example, the adoption of a foreign tongue, but an alchemy that transformed ancient elements into a new language: *A language comes into existence by means of brutal necessity, and the rules of the language are dictated by what the language must convey.*

There was a moment, in time, and in this place, when my brother, or my mother, or my father, or my sister, had to convey to me, for example, the danger in which I was standing from the white man standing just behind me, and to convey this with a speed, and in a language, that the white man could not possibly understand, and that, indeed, he cannot understand, until today. He cannot afford to understand it. This understanding would reveal to him too much about himself, and smash that mirror before which he has been frozen for so long.

Now, if this passion, this skill, this (to quote Toni Morrison) "sheer intelligence," this incredible music, the mighty achievement of having brought a people utterly unknown to, or despised by "history"—to have brought this people to their present, troubled, troubling, and unassailable and unanswerable place—if this absolutely unprecedented journey does not indicate that black English is a language, I am curious to know what definition of language is to be trusted.

A people at the center of the Western world, and in the midst of so hostile a population, has not endured and transcended by means of what is patronizingly called a "dialect." We, the blacks, are in trouble, certainly, but we are not doomed, and we are not inarticulate because we are not compelled to defend a morality that we know to be a lie.

The brutal truth is that the bulk of the white people in America never had any interest in educating black people, except as this could serve white purposes. It is not the black child's language that is in question, it is not his language that is despised: It is his experience. A child cannot be taught by anyone who despises him, and a child cannot afford to be fooled. A child cannot be taught by anyone whose demand, essentially, is that the child repudiate his experience, and all that gives him sustenance, and enter a limbo in which he will no longer be black, and in which he knows that he can never become white. Black people have lost too many black children that way.

And, after all, finally, in a country with standards so untrustworthy, a country that makes heroes of so many criminal mediocrities, a country unable to face why so many of the nonwhite are in prison, or on the needle, or standing, futureless, in the streets—it may very well be that both the child, and his elder, have concluded that they have nothing whatever to learn from the people of a country that has managed to learn so little.

The New York Times, July 29, 1979

Open Letter to the Born Again

I MET Martin Luther King Jr. before I met Andrew Young. I know that Andy and I met only because of Martin. Andy was, in my mind, and not because he ever so described himself, Martin's "right-hand man." He was present—absolutely present. He saw what was happening. He took upon himself his responsibility for knowing what he knew, and for seeing what he saw. I have heard Andy attempt to describe himself only once: when he was trying to clarify something about me, to someone else. So, I learned, one particular evening, what his Christian ministry meant to him. Let me spell that out a little.

The text comes from the New Testament, Matthew 25:40: *Inasmuch as ye have done it unto one of the least of these my brethren, ye have done it unto me.*

I am in the strenuous and far from dull position of having news to deliver to the Western world—for example: *black* is not a synonym for *slave*. Do not, I counsel you, attempt to defend yourselves against this stunning, unwieldy and undesired message. You will hear it again: indeed, this is the only message the Western world is likely to be hearing from here on out.

I put it in this somewhat astringent fashion because it is necessary, and because I speak, now, as the grandson of a slave, a direct descendant of a born-again Christian. *My conversion*, as Countee Cullen puts it, *came high-priced/I belong to Jesus Christ*. I am also speaking as an ex-minister of the Gospel, and, therefore, as one of the born again. I was instructed to feed the hungry, clothe the naked and visit those in prison. I am far indeed from my youth, and from my father's house, but I have not forgotten these instructions, and I pray upon my soul that I never will. The people who call themselves "born again" today have simply become members of the richest, most exclusive private club in the world, a club that the man from Galilee could not possibly hope—or wish—to enter.

Inasmuch as ye have done it unto the least of these my brethren, ye have done it unto me. That is a hard saying. It is hard

to live with that. It is a merciless description of our responsibility for one another. It is that hard light under which one
makes the moral choice. That the Western world has forgotten
that such a thing as the moral choice exists, my history, my
flesh, and my soul bear witness. So, if I may say so, does the
predicament into which the world's most celebrated born-
again Christian has managed to hurl Mr. Andrew Young.

Let us not belabor the obvious truth that what the Western
world calls an "energy" crisis ineptly disguises what happens
when you can no longer control markets, are chained to your
colonies (instead of vice versa), are running out of slaves (and
can't trust those you think you still have), can't, upon rigorously sober reflection, really send the Marines, or the Royal
Navy, anywhere, or risk a global war, have no allies—only
business partners, or "satellites"—and have broken every
promise you ever made, anywhere, to anyone. I know what I
am talking about: my grandfather never got the promised
"forty acres, and a mule," the Indians who survived *that* holocaust are either on reservations or dying in the streets, and
not a single treaty between the United States and the Indian
was ever honored. That is quite a record.

Jews and Palestinians know of broken promises. From the
time of the Balfour Declaration (during World War I) Palestine was under five British mandates, and England promised
the land back and forth to the Arabs or the Jews, depending
on which horse seemed to be in the lead. The Zionists—as
distinguished from the people known as Jews—using, as
someone put it, the "available political machinery," i.e., colonialism, e.g., the British Empire—promised the British that,
if the territory were given to them, the British Empire would
be safe forever.

But absolutely no one cared about the Jews, and it is worth
observing that non-Jewish Zionists are very frequently anti-
Semitic. The white Americans responsible for sending black
slaves to Liberia (where they are still slaving for the Firestone
Rubber Plantation) did not do this to set them free. They
despised them, and they wanted to get rid of them. Lincoln's
intention was not to "free" the slaves but to "destabilize" the
Confederate Government by giving their slaves reason to "de-
fect." The Emancipation Proclamation freed, precisely, those

slaves who were not under the authority of the President of what could not yet be insured as a Union.

It has always astounded me that no one appears to be able to make the connection between Franco's Spain, for example, and the Spanish Inquisition; the role of the Christian church or—to be brutally precise, the Catholic Church—in the history of Europe, and the fate of the Jews; and the role of the Jews in Christendom and the discovery of America. For the discovery of America coincided with the Inquisition, and the expulsion of the Jews from Spain. Does no one see the connection between *The Merchant of Venice* and *The Pawnbroker*? In both of these works, as though no time had passed, the Jew is portrayed as doing the Christian's usurious dirty work. The first white man I ever saw was the Jewish manager who arrived to collect the rent, and he collected the rent because he did not own the building. I never, in fact, saw any of the people who owned any of the buildings in which we scrubbed and suffered for so long, until I was a grown man and famous. None of them were Jews.

And I was not stupid: the grocer and the druggist were Jews, for example, and they were very very nice to me, and to us. They were never really white, for me. The cops were white. The city was white. The threat was white, and God was white. Not for even a single split second in my life did the despicable, utterly cowardly accusation that "the Jews killed Christ" reverberate. I knew a murderer when I saw one, and the people who were trying to kill me were not Jews.

But the state of Israel was not created for the salvation of the Jews; it was created for the salvation of the Western interests. This is what is becoming clear (I must say that it was always clear to me). The Palestinians have been paying for the British colonial policy of "divide and rule" and for Europe's guilty Christian conscience for more than thirty years.

Finally: there is absolutely—repeat: *absolutely*—no hope of establishing peace in what Europe so arrogantly calls the Middle East (how in the world would Europe know? having so dismally failed to find a passage to India) without dealing with the Palestinians. The collapse of the Shah of Iran not only revealed the depth of the pious Carter's concern for "human rights," it also revealed who supplied oil to Israel, and to whom Israel supplied arms. It happened to be, to spell it out, white South Africa.

Well. The Jew, in America, is a white man. He has to be, since I am a black man, and, as he supposes, his only protection against the fate which drove him to America. But he is still doing the Christian's dirty work, and black men know it.

My friend, Mr. Andrew Young, out of tremendous love and courage, and with a silent, irreproachable, indescribable nobility, has attempted to ward off a holocaust, and I proclaim him a hero, betrayed by cowards.

The Nation, September 29, 1979

Dark Days

I HIT the streets when I was seven. It was the middle of the Depression and I learned how to sing out of hard experience. To be black was to confront, and to be forced to alter, a condition forged in history. To be white was to be forced to digest a delusion called white supremacy. Indeed, without confronting the history that has either given white people an identity or divested them of it, it is hardly possible for anyone who thinks of himself as white to know what a black person is talking about at all. Or to know what education is.

Not one of us—black or white—knows how to walk when we get here. Not one of us knows how to open a window, unlock a door. Not one of us can master a staircase. We are absolutely ignorant of the almost certain results of falling out of a five-story window. None of us comes here knowing enough not to play with fire. Nor can one of us drive a tank, fly a jet, hurl a bomb, or plant a tree.

We must be taught all that. We have to learn all that. The irreducible price of learning is realizing that you do not know. One may go further and point out—as any scientist, or artist, will tell you—that the more you learn, the less you know; but that means that you have begun to accept, and are even able to rejoice in, the relentless conundrum of your life.

What happens, black poet Langston Hughes asks, *to a dream deferred?* What happens, one may now ask, when a reality finds itself on a collision course with a fantasy? For the white people of this country have become, for the most part, sleepwalkers, and their somnambulation is reflected in the caliber of U.S. politics and politicians. And it helps explain why the blacks, who walked all those dusty miles and endured all that slaughter to get the vote, are now not voting.

Education occurs in a context and has a very definite purpose. The context is mainly unspoken, and the purpose very often unspeakable. But education can never be aimless, and it cannot occur in a vacuum.

I went to school in Harlem, quite a long time ago, during

a time of great public and private strain and misery. Yet I was somewhat luckier than the Harlem children are today. I was going to school in the Thirties, after the stock market crash. My family lived on Park Avenue, just above the uptown railroad tracks. The poverty of my childhood differed from poverty today in that the TV set was not sitting in front of our faces, forcing us to make unbearable comparisons between the room we were sitting in and the rooms we were watching; neither were we endlessly being told what to wear and drink and buy. We knew that we were poor, but then, everybody around us was poor.

The stock market crash had very little impact on our house. We had made no investments, and we wouldn't have known a stockbroker if one had patted us on the head. The market was part of the folly that always seemed to be overtaking white people, and it was always leading them to the same end. They wept briny tears, they put pistols to their heads or jumped out of windows. *That's just like white folks,* was my father's contemptuous judgment, and we took our cue from him and felt no pity whatever. *You reap what you sow,* Daddy said, grimly, carrying himself and his lunch box off to the factory, while we carried *our* lunch boxes off to school and, soon, into the streets, where my brother and I shined shoes and sold shopping bags. Mama went downtown or to the Bronx to clean white ladies' apartments.

Yet there *is* a moment from that time that I remember today and will probably always remember—a photograph from the center section of the *Daily News*. We were starving, people all over the country were starving. Yet here were several photographs of farmers, somewhere in America, slaughtering hogs and pouring milk onto the ground in order to force prices up (or keep them up), in order to protect their profits. I was much too young to know what to make of this beyond the obvious. People were being forced to starve, and being driven to death, for the sake of money.

One might say that my recollection of this photograph marks a crucial moment in my education; but one must also say that my education must have begun long before that moment, and dictated my reaction to the photograph. My education began, as does everyone's, with the people who towered over me, who were responsible for me, who were forming me. They were the people who loved me, in their fashion—whom I loved, in mine. These were people whom I had no choice but to imitate and, in time, to outwit. One realizes later that there is no one to outwit but oneself.

When I say that I was luckier than the children are today, I am deliberately making a very dangerous statement, a statement that I am willing, even anxious, to be called on. A black boy born in New York's Harlem in 1924 was born of southerners who had but lately been driven from the land, and therefore was born into a southern community. And this was incontestably a community in which every parent was responsible for every child. Any grown-up, seeing me doing something he thought was wrong, could (and did) beat my behind and then carry me home to my Mama and Daddy and tell them why he beat my behind. Mama and Daddy would thank him and then beat my behind again.

I learned respect for my elders. And I mean respect. I do not mean fear. In spite of his howling, a child can tell when the hand that strikes him means to help him or to harm him. A child can tell when he is loved. One sees this sense of confidence emerge, slowly, in the conduct of the child—the first fruits of his education.

Every human being born begins to be *civilized* the moment he or she is born. Since we all arrive here absolutely helpless, with no way of getting a decent meal or of moving from one place to another without human help (and human help exacts a human price), there is no way around that. But this is civilization with a small *c*. Civilization with a large *C* is something else again. So is education with a small *e* different from Education with a large *E*. In the lowercase, education refers to the relations that actually obtain among human beings. In the uppercase, it refers to power. Or, to put it another way, my father, mother, brothers, sisters, lovers, friends, sons, daughters civilize me in quite another way than the state intends. And the education I can receive from an afternoon with Picasso, or from taking one of my nieces or nephews to the movies, is not at all what the state has in mind when it speaks of Education.

For I still remember, lucky though I was, that reality altered when I started school. My mother asked me about one of my teachers: was she white or colored? My answer, which was based entirely on a child's observation, was that my teacher was "a little bit colored and a little bit white." My mother laughed. So did the teacher. I have no idea how she might react today. In fact, my answer had been far more brutally accurate than I could have had any way of knowing. But I wasn't penalized or humiliated for my unwitting apprehension of the Faulknerian torment.

Harlem was not an all-black community during the time I was growing up. It was only during the Second World War that Harlem began to become entirely black. This transformation had something to do, in part, with the relations between black and white soldiers called together under one banner. These relations were so strained and volatile that, however equal the soldiers might be deemed, it was thought best to keep them separate when off the base. And Harlem, officially or not, was effectively off limits for white soldiers.

Harlem's transformation relates to the military in another way. The Second World War ended the Depression by throwing America into a war economy. We are in a war economy still, and we are only slightly embarrassed by the difficulty of officially declaring a Third World War. But where there's a will, I hate to suggest, there's often a way.

When I was growing up there were Finns, Jews, Poles, West Indians, and various other exotics scattered all over Harlem. We could all be found eating as much as we could hold in Father Divine's restaurants for fifteen cents. I fought every campaign of the Italian-Ethiopian War with the oldest son of the Italian fruit and vegetable vendor who lived next door to us. I lost. Inevitably. He knew who had the tanks.

The new prosperity caused many people to pack their bags and go. Some blacks got as far as Queens, Jamaica, or the Bronx. One might say that a certain rupture began during this time. We began to lose each other. The whites who left moved directly into the American mainstream, as we like to say, without the complexity of the smallest regret and without a backward look. The blacks moved into limbo. The doors opened

for white people and (especially) for their children. The
schools, the unions, industry, and the arts were not opened
for blacks. Not then, and not now.

This meant—means—that the black family had moved onto
yet another sector of a vast and endless battlefield. The people
I am speaking of came mainly from the South. They had been
driven north by the sheer impossibility of remaining in the
South. They came with nothing. And the good Lord knows
it was a hard journey. Their children had never seen the South;
their challenges came from the hard pavements of a hostile
city, and their parents had no arms with which to protect them
from its devastation.

When I went to work as a civilian for the Army in 1942, I
earned about three times as much in a week as my father ever
had. This was not without its effect on my father. His authority was being eroded, he was being cheated of the reality
of his role. And I, of course, had absolutely no way of understanding the ferocious complexity of his reaction. I did not
understand the depth and power and reality of his pain.

The blacks who moved out of Harlem were not received
with open arms by their countrymen. They were mocked and
despised, and their children were in greater danger than ever.
No friendly neighbor was likely to correct the child. The child
would either rise up into a seeming responsibility and respect-
ability, one step ahead of paranoia, or drop down to the needle and the prison. And since there is not a single institution
in this country that is not a racist institution—beginning with
the churches, and by no means ignoring the unions—blacks
were unable to seize the tools with which they could forge a
genuine autonomy.

The new prosperity also brought in the blight of housing
projects to keep the nigger in his place. Whites, thinking "If
you can't beat them, stone them," dumped drugs into the
ghetto, and what had once been a community began to fragment. The space between people grew wider. The question of
identity became a paralyzing one. Being "accepted" could
cause even greater anguish, and was a more deadly danger,
than being spat on as a nigger.

I was luckier in school than the children are today. My situation, however grim, was relatively coherent. I was not yet lost. Though most of my teachers were white, many were black. And some of the white teachers were very definitely on the Left. They opposed Franco's Spain, and Mussolini's Italy, and Hitler's Third Reich. For these extreme opinions, several were placed on blacklists and drummed out of the academic community—to the everlasting shame of that community.

The black teachers, paradoxically, were another matter. They were laconic about politics but single-minded about the future of black students. Many of them were survivors of the Harlem Renaissance and wanted us black students to know that we could do, become, anything. We were not, in any way whatever, to be limited by the Republic's estimation of black people. *They* had refused to be defined that way, and they had, after all, paid some dues.

I did not, then, obviously, really know who some of these people were. Gertrude E. Ayers, for example, my principal at P.S. 24, was the first black principal in the history of New York City schools. I did not know, then, what this meant. Dr. Kenneth Clark informed me in the early Sixties that Ayers was the only one until 1963. And there was the never-to-be-forgotten Mr. Porter, my black math teacher, who soon gave up any attempt to teach me math. I had been born, apparently, with some kind of deformity that resulted in a total inability to count. From arithmetic to geometry, I never passed a single test. Porter took his failure very well and compensated for it by helping me run the school magazine. He assigned me a story about Harlem for this magazine, a story that he insisted demanded serious research. Porter took me downtown to the main branch of the public library at Forty-second Street and waited for me while I began my research. He was very proud of the story I eventually turned in. But I was so terrified that afternoon that I vomited all over his shoes in the subway.

The teachers I am talking about accepted my limits. I could begin to accept them without shame. I could trust them when they suggested the possibilities open to me. I understood why they changed the list of colleges they had hoped to send me to, since I was clearly never going to become either an athlete or a businessman.

I was an exceedingly shy, withdrawn, and uneasy student.

Yet my teachers somehow made me believe that I could learn. And when I could scarcely see for myself any future at all, my teachers told me that the future was mine. The question of color was but another detail, somewhere between being six feet tall and being six feet under. In the long meantime, everything was up to me.

Every child's sense of himself is terrifyingly fragile. He is really at the mercy of his elders, and when he finds himself totally at the mercy of his peers, who know as little about themselves as he, it is because his peers' elders have abandoned them. I am talking, then, about morale, that sense of self *with which the child must be invested*. No child can do it alone.

But children, I submit, cannot be fooled. They can only be betrayed by adults, not fooled—for adults, unlike children, are fooled very easily, and only because they wish to be. Children—innocence being both real and monstrous—intimidate, harass, blackmail, terrify, and sometimes even kill one another. But no child can fool another child the way one adult can fool another. It would be impossible, for example, for children to bring off the spectacle—the scandal—of the Republican or Democratic conventions. They do not have enough to hide—or, if you like, to flaunt.

I remember being totally unable to recite the Pledge of Allegiance until I was seven years old. Why? At seven years old I was certainly not a card-carrying Communist, and no one had told me not to recite "with liberty and justice for all." In fact, my father thought that I should recite it for safety's sake. But I knew that he believed it no more than I, and that *his* recital of the pledge had done nothing to contribute to his safety, to say nothing of the tormented safety of his children.

How did I know that? How does any child know that? I knew it from watching my father's face, my father's hours, days, and nights. I knew it from scrubbing the floors of the tenements in which we lived, knew it from the eviction notices, knew it from the bitter winters when the landlords gave us no heat, knew it from my mother's face when a new child was born, knew it by contrasting the kitchens in which my mother was employed with *our* kitchen, knew it from the kind of desperate miasma in which you grow up learning that you have been born to be despised. Forever.

It remains impossible to describe the Byzantine labyrinth black people find themselves in when they attempt to save their children. A high school diploma, which had almost no meaning in my day, nevertheless suggested that you had been to school. But today it operates merely as a credential for jobs—for the most part nonexistent—that demand virtually nothing in the way of education. And the attendance certificate merely states that you have been through school without having managed to learn anything.

The educational system of this country is, in short, designed to destroy the black child. It does not matter whether it destroys him by stoning him in the ghetto or by driving him mad in the isolation of Harvard. And whoever has survived this crucible is a witness to the power of the Republic's educational system.

It is an absolute wonder and an overwhelming witness to the power of the human spirit that any black person in this country has managed to become, in any way whatever, educated. The miracle is that some have stepped out of the rags of the Republic's definitions to assume the great burden and glory of their humanity and of their responsibility for one another.

It is an extraordinary achievement to be trapped in the dungeon of color and to dare to shake down its walls and to step out of it, leaving the jailhouse keeper in the rubble.

But for the black man with the attaché case, or for the black boy on the needle, it has always been the intention of the Republic to promulgate and guarantee his dependence on this Republic. For although one cannot really be educated to believe a lie, one can be forced to surrender to it.

And there is, after all, no reason *not* to be dependent on one's country or, at least, to maintain a viable and fruitful relationship with it. But this is not possible if you see your country and your country does not see you. It is not possible if the entire effort of your countrymen is an attempt to destroy your sense of reality.

*

This is an election year, I am standing in the streets of Harlem, Newark, or Watts, and I have been asked a question.

Now, what am I to say concerning the presidential candidates, season after ignoble season? Carter has learned to sing *Let my people go*, speaking of the hostages in Iran, while taking no responsibility at all for the political prisoners all over his home state of Georgia. He is prepared for massive retaliation against the Ayatollah Khomeini but, after Miami, can only assure the city's blacks that violence is not the answer. This despite the fact that in the event of "massive retaliation," blacks will assuredly be sent to fight in Iran—and for what? Despite the news of the acquittal of the four Miami policemen who beat the black man McDuffie to death. That news made page 24 of *The New York Times*. The uprising resulting from the acquittal made page one.

The ghetto man, woman, or child who may already wonder why curbing inflation means starving him out of existence (or into the Army) may also wonder why violence is right for Carter, or for any other white man, but wrong for the black man. The ghetto people I am talking to, or about, are not at all stupid, and if I lie to them, how can I teach them?

Dark days. Recently I was back in the South, more than a quarter of a century after the Supreme Court decision that outlawed segregation in the Republic's schools, a decision to be implemented with "all deliberate speed." My friends with whom I had worked and walked in those dark days are no longer in their teens, or even their thirties. Their children are now as old as their parents were then, and, obviously, some of my comrades are now roughly as old as I, and I am facing sixty. Dark days, for we know how much there is to be done and how unlikely it is that we will live another sixty years. We know, for that matter, how utterly improbable it is—indeed, miraculous—that we can still have a drink, or a pork chop, or a laugh together.

I walked into an Alabama courtroom, in Birmingham, where my old friend the Reverend Fred Shuttlesworth was sitting. I had not seen him in more than twenty years; his church was bombed shortly after I last saw him. Now, something like twenty-two years later, the man accused of bombing the church was on trial. The Reverend Shuttlesworth was very cool, much cooler than I, given that the trial had been delayed twenty-two years. How slowly the mills of justice grind if one is black. What in the world can possibly happen in the mind and heart of a black student, observing, who must stumble out of this courtroom and back to Yale?

It was a desegregated(!) courtroom, and it was certainly a mock trial. The only reason the defendant, J. B. Stoner, was not legally, openly acquitted was that the jury—mostly women, and one exceedingly visible black man dressed in a canary-colored suit (I had the feeling that no one ever addressed a word to him)—could not quite endorse Stoner's conviction (among his many others about blacks) that being born a Jew should be made a crime "punishable by death—legally." (He hastened to add, "I'm against illegal violence.") Forced to admit—by the reading of newspaper quotes—that he had crowed, upon hearing of the assassination of Martin Luther King Jr., "Well, he's a good nigger *now*," Stoner said, "Hell, that ain't got nothing to do with violence. The man was already dead."

He was not acquitted, but he received the minimum sentence—ten years—and is free on bail.

If I put this travesty back to back with the case of—for example—the Wilmington Ten, I will begin to suggest to my students the meaning of *education*.

On the first day of class last winter at Bowling Green State University, where I was a visiting writer-in-residence, one of my white students, in a racially mixed class, asked me, "Why does the white hate the nigger?"

I was caught off guard. I simply had not had the courage to open the subject right away. I underestimated the children, and I am afraid that most of the middle-aged do. The subject, I confess, frightened me, and it would never have occurred to me to throw it at them so nakedly. No doubt, since I am not totally abject, I would have found a way to discuss what we refer to as interracial tension. What my students made me realize (and I consider myself eternally in their debt) was that the notion of interracial tension hides a multitude of delusions and is, in sum, a cowardly academic formulation. In the ensuing discussion the children, very soon, did not need me at all, except as a vaguely benign adult presence. They began talking to one another, and they were not talking about race. They were talking of their desire to know one another, their need to know one another; each was trying to enter into the experience of the other. The exchanges were sharp and remarkably candid, but never fogged by an unadmitted fear or hostility. They were trying to become whole. They were trying to put themselves and their country together. They would be facing hard choices when they left this academy. And why was it a condition of American life that they would then be forced to be strangers?

The reality, the depth, and the persistence of the delusion of white supremacy in this country causes any real concept of education to be as remote, and as much to be feared, as change or freedom itself. What black men here have always known is now beginning to be clear all over the world. Whatever it is that white Americans want, it is not freedom—neither for themselves nor for others.

It's you who'll have the blues, Langston Hughes said, *not me. Just wait and see.*

Esquire, October 1980

Notes on the House of Bondage

GABRIEL'S TRUMPET is a complex metaphor. Poor Gabriel is not only responsible for *when we dead awaken*—heavy enough—but he must also blow that trumpet *to wake the children sleeping*.

The children are always ours, every single one of them, all over the globe; and I am beginning to suspect that whoever is incapable of recognizing this may be incapable of morality. Or, I am saying, in other words, that we, the elders, are the only models children have. What we see in the children is what they have seen in us—or, more accurately perhaps, what they *see* in us.

I, too, find that a rather chilling formulation, but I can find no way around it. How am I, for example, to explain to any of my tribe of nieces and nephews and great-nieces and great-nephews how it happens that in a nation so boastfully autonomous as the United States we are reduced to the present Presidential candidates? I certainly do not want them to believe that Carter or Reagan—*or* Anderson—are the best people this country can produce. That despair would force me onto the road taken by the late, Guyana-based Jim Jones. But there they are, the pea-nut farmer and the third-rate, failed, ex-Warner Brothers contract player, both as sturdy and winning as Wheaties, and as well equipped to run the world as I am to run a post office.

There they are. And there is, also, the question, *Who you going to vote for, Uncle Jimmy?*

It can be said, of course—and let me say it before you do—that I am speaking as a black American. My testimony can, therefore, be dismissed out of hand by reason of my understandable (thank you) but quite unreasonable bitterness.

Well, I have had my bitter moments, certainly, days and ways, but I do not think that I can usefully be described as a bitter man. I would not be trying to write this if I were, for the bitter do not, mainly, speak: they, suddenly and quite unpredictably, act. The bitter can be masters, too, at telling you what you want to hear because they *know* what you want to hear. And how do they know that?

Well, some of them know it because they must raise their children and bring them to a place, somehow, where the American guile and cowardice cannot destroy them. No black citizen (!) of what is left of Harlem supposes that either Carter, or Reagan, or Anderson has any concern for them at all, except as voters—that is, to put it brutally, except as instruments, or dupes—and, while one hates to say that the black citizens are right, one certainly cannot say that they are wrong.

One has merely to look up and down the streets of Harlem; walk through the streets and into what is left of the houses; consider the meaning of this willed, inhuman and criminal devastation, and look into the faces of the children. *Who you going to vote for, Uncle Jimmy?*

John Brown, I have sometimes been known to say, but that flippant rage is, of course, no answer.

But, if we're to change our children's lives and help them to liberate themselves from the jails and hovels—the mortal danger—in which our countrymen have placed us, the vote does not appear to be the answer, either. It has certainly not been the answer until now.

Here one finds oneself on treacherous ground indeed. I am, legally anyway, an adult, a somewhat battered survivor of this hard place, and have never expected my power to vote to have any effect whatever on my life, and it hasn't. On the other hand, I have been active in voter registration drives in the South because the acquisition of the vote, there and then, and even if only for local aims, was too crucial and profound a necessity even to be argued. Nor can it be denied that the sheer tenacity of the black people in the South, their grace under pressure (to put it far too mildly) and the simple fact of their presence in the voting booth profoundly challenged, if it did not expose, the obscene Southern mythology.

Thus, though there is certainly no New South yet, the old one has no future, and neither does the "old" North. The situation of the black American is a direct (and deliberate) result of the collusion between the North and South and the Federal Government. A black man in this country does not live under a two-party system but a four-party system. There is the Republican Party in the South, and there is the Republican Party in the North; there is the Democratic Party in the

North and the Democratic Party in the South. These entities are Tweedledum and Tweedledee as concerns the ways they have been able, historically, to manipulate the black presence, the black need. At the same time, both parties were (are) protected from the deepest urgencies of black need by the stance of the Federal Government, which could (can) always justify both parties, and itself, by use of the doctrine of "States' rights."

In the South, then, the Republican Party was the *nigra's* friend, and, in the North, it was the Democrats who lovingly dried our tears. But, however liberal Northern Democrats might seem to be, nothing was allowed to menace the party unity—certainly not niggers—with the result that the presumed or potential power of the black vote in the North was canceled out by the smirk on the faces of the candidates in the South. The party had won—was in—and we were out. What it came to was that, as long as blacks in the South could not vote, blacks in the North could have nothing to vote for. A very clever trap, which only now, and largely because of the black vote in the South, may be beginning to be sprung.

The American institutions are all bankrupt in that they are unable to deal with the present—resembling nothing so much as Lot's wife. When Americans look out on the world, they see nothing but dark and menacing strangers who appear to have no sense of rhythm at all, nor any respect or affection for white people; and white Americans really do not know what to make of all this, except to increase the defense budget.

This panic-stricken saber rattling is also for the benefit of the domestic darker brother. The real impulse of the bulk of the American people toward their former slave is lethal: if he cannot be used, he should be made to disappear. When the American people, Nixon's no-longer-silent majority, revile the Haitian, Cuban, Turk, Palestinian, Iranian, they are really cursing the nigger, and the nigger had better know it.

The vote does not work for a black American the way it works for a white one, for the despairingly obvious reason that whites, in general, are welcomed to America, and blacks, in general, are not. Yet, risking a seeming contradiction, one may go further and point out that America's egalitarian image is very important to American self-esteem. Therefore, blacks from the West Indies, say, or Africa, who arrive with no social or political quarrels with the United States, who have already been formed by the island, or village community, and who bring their mercantile skills with them, are likely to fare much better here than Sambo does—for a brief and melancholy season. Since the entire country is bizarre beyond belief, the black immigrant does not quarrel with its customs, considering that these customs have nothing to do with him. He sticks to his kith and kin, and saves his pennies, and is the apple of the white American eye, for he proves that the Yankee-Puritan virtues are all that one needs to prosper in this brave new world.

This euphoria lasts, at most, a generation. In my youth, the West Indians, who assured American blacks that *they*, the West Indians, had never been slaves, ran their stores, saved their pennies, went bankrupt and, as a community, disappeared— or, rather, became a part of the larger black community. Later on, the Puerto Ricans were hurled into this fire and, after the brief, melancholy and somewhat violent season, we began to compare notes, and share languages, and now here come, among others, the Haitians, and the beginning of the end of the doctrine of divide-and-rule, at least as concerns the dark people of the West.

The white person of the West is quite another matter. His presence in America, in spite of vile attacks on "the foreign-born," poses no real problem. Within a generation, at most two, he is at home in his new country and climbing that ladder. If there is trouble in the Irish, Italian or Polish ward, say, the trouble can be contained and eliminated because the demands of these white people do not threaten the fabric of American society. This proved to be true during even the bloodiest of the worker-industrial clashes: white workers opted for being white first and workers second—and, in the land of the free and the home of the brave, who said that they had to remain workers? It was easy enough to turn the white worker against the black worker by threatening to put the black man in the white man's job, at a lower salary. Once the white worker had fallen into this trap, the rest was child's play: the black was locked out of the unions, the unions and big business got in bed together and, whenever there was trouble in the ghetto, white America, as one man, cried, *What does the Negro want?* Billy clubs, tear gas, guns and cold-blooded murder imposed a sullen order, and a grateful Republic went back to sleep.

This has been the American pattern for all of the years that I have been on earth, and, of course, for generations before that, and I have absolutely no reason to believe that this leopard has changed his spots. Nixon was elected, after all, received his "mandate," by means of the Omnibus Crime Bill and the "Safe Streets Act" ("safe streets" meaning *keep the nigger in his place*) and his crony, the late and much lamented Gov. Nelson Rockefeller, who was responsible for the Attica slaughter, passed the Hitlerian "No-Knock Stop and Frisk Law," which brought every black person in New York a little closer to the madhouse and the grave. The Nixon career was stopped by Watergate, God be praised, and by the intervention of a black man, thank our ancestors; but Attorney General John Mitchell had already corralled several thousands of us, black and white, in a ballpark.

The United States is full of ballparks. My black vote, which has not yet purchased my autonomy, may yet, if I choose to use it, keep me out of the ballpark long enough to figure out some other move. Or for the children to make a move. Or for aid to come from somewhere. My vote will probably not get me a job or a home or help me through school or prevent another Vietnam or a third World War, but it may keep me here long enough for me to see, and use, the turning of the tide—for the tide has got to turn. And, since I am not the only black man to think this way, if Carter is re-elected, it will be by means of the black vote, and it will not be a vote for Carter. It will be a coldly calculated risk, a means of buying time. Perhaps only black people realize this, but we are dying, here, out of all proportion to our numbers, and with no respect to age, dying in the streets, in the madhouse, in the tenement, on the roof, in jail and in the Army. This is not by chance, and it is not an act of God. It is a result of the action of the American institutions, all of which are racist: it is revelatory of the real and helpless impulse of most white Americans toward black people.

Therefore, in a couple of days, blacks may be using the vote to outwit the Final Solution. Yes. The Final Solution. No black person can afford to forget that the history of this country is genocidal, from where the buffalo once roamed to where our ancestors were slaughtered (from New Orleans to New York, from Birmingham to Boston) and to the Caribbean to Hiroshima and Nagasaki to Saigon. Oh, yes, let freedom ring.

Why are you voting for Carter, Uncle Jimmy? Well, don't, first of all, take this as an endorsement. It's meant to be a hard look at the options, which, however, may no longer exist by the time you read this, may no longer exist as I write.

I lived in California when Ronald Reagan was Governor, and that was a very ugly time—the time of the Black Panther harassment, the beginning (and the end) of the Soledad Brothers, the persecution, and trial, of Angela Davis. That, all that, and much more, but what I really found unspeakable about the man was his contempt, his brutal contempt, for the poor.

Perhaps because he is a Southerner, there lives in Carter still—I think—an ability to be tormented. This does not necessarily mean much, so many people preferring torment to action, or responsibility, and it is, furthermore, a very real question (for some; some would say that it's not a question at all) as to how much of Carter belongs to Carter. But if he can still be tormented, he can be made to pause—the machinery can be made to pause—and we will have to find a way to use that pause.

It is terror that informs the American political and social scene—the terror of leaving the house of bondage. It isn't a terror of seeing *black* people leave the house of bondage, for white people think that they *know* that this cannot *really* happen, not even to Leontyne Price, or Mohammad Ali, who are, after all, "exceptions," with white blood, and mortal. No, white people had a much better time in the house of bondage than we did, and God bless their souls, they're going to miss it—all that adulation, adoration, ease, with nothing to do but fornicate, kill Indians, breed slaves and make money. Oh, there were rough times, too, as *Shane*, *True Grit* and *Rocky* inform us, but the rules of the game were clear, and the rewards demanded nothing more complex than stamina. God was a businessman, like all "real" Americans, and understood that "business was business." The American innocence was unassailable, fixed forever, for it was not a crime to kill a black or a red or a yellow man. On the contrary, it might be, and was most often so considered, a duty. It was not a crime to rape a black or red or yellow woman—it was sport; besides, *niggers ought to be glad we pump some white blood into their kids every once in a while.* The lowest white man was more exalted than the most articulate or eminent black: an exceedingly useful article of faith both for the owners of the Southern fields and the bosses in the Northern sweatshops, who worked this exalted creature past senility to death.

Thus, what the house of bondage accomplished for what we will call the classic white American was the destruction of his moral sense, except in relation to whites. But it also destroyed his sense of reality and, therefore, his sense of white people had to be as compulsively one-dimensional as his vision of blacks. The result is that white Americans have been one another's jailers for generations, and the attempt at individual maturity is the loneliest and rarest of the American endeavors. (This may also be why a "boyish" look is a very decided advantage in the American political and social arena.)

Well, the planet is destroying the American fantasies; which does not give the Americans the right to destroy the planet. I don't know if it is possible to speak coherently concerning what my disturbed countrymen want, but I hazard that, although the Americans are certainly capable of precipitating Armageddon, their most desperate desire is to make time stand still. If time stands still, it can neither judge nor accuse nor exact payment; and, indeed, this is precisely the bargain the black presence was expected to strike in the white Republic. It is why the black face had always to be a happy face.

Recently, the only two black shows on Broadway were minstrel shows. There was a marvelous current between the blacks on the stage and the blacks in the audience. Both knew why the white audience was there, and to watch white audiences being reassured by a minstrel show can be grotesque and sorrowful beyond belief. But the minstrel show is really no different from the TV screen which celebrates, night after night and year after year and decade after decade, the slaughter of the Native American and pretends (in spite of *Roots,* which demands a separate assessment) that the black enslavement never occurred.

Well. It did occur, and *is* occurring all up and down America, as I write, and is crossing borders and being exported to various "underdeveloped" portions of the globe. But this endeavor cannot succeed, with force or without it, because the center of the earth has shifted. The British Prime Minister, for example, is a grotesque anachronism, and the world is not holding its breath waiting to see what will happen in England; England's future will be determined by what is happening in the world.

I am speaking of the breakup—the end—of the so-overextended Western empire. I am thinking of the black and nonwhite peoples who are shattering, redefining and re-creating history—making all things new—simply by declaring their presence, by delivering their testimony. The empire never intended that this testimony should be heard, but, *if I hold my peace, the very stones will cry out.*

One can speak, then, of the fall of an empire at that moment when, though all of the paraphernalia of power remain intact and visible and seem to function, neither the citizen-subject within the gates nor the indescribable hordes outside it believe in the morality or the reality of the kingdom anymore—when no one, any longer, anywhere, aspires to the empire's standards.

This is the charged, the dangerous, moment, when everything must be re-examined, must be made new; when nothing at all can be taken for granted. One looks again at the word "famine." At this hour of the world's history, famine must be considered a man-made phenomenon and one looks at who is starving. There is nothing even faintly ridiculous, or unfair, in these apprehensions, which are produced by nothing less than Western history. Our former guides and masters are among the most ruthless creatures in mankind's history, slaughtering and starving one another to death long before they discovered the blacks. If the British were willing to starve Ireland to death—which they did, in order to protect the profits of British merchants—why would the West be reluctant to starve Africa out of existence? Especially since the generation facing famine now is precisely that generation that will begin the real and final liberation of Africa from Europe. It is, in any case, perfectly clear that the earth's populations can be fed if—or, rather, when—we alter our priorities. We can irrigate deserts and feed the entire earth for the price we are paying to build bombs that we will be able to use, in any event, only once; after which whoever is left will have to begin doing what I am suggesting now. It would be nice if we could, for once, make it easy on ourselves.

The elders, especially at this moment of our black-white history, are indispensable to the young, and vice versa. It is of the utmost importance, for example, that I, the elder, do not allow myself to be put on the defensive. The young, no matter how loud they get, have no real desire to humiliate their elders and, if and when they succeed in doing so, are lonely, crushed and miserable, as only the young can be.

Someone my age, for example, may be pleased and proud that Carter has blacks in his Cabinet. A younger person may wonder just what their function is in such a Cabinet. They will be keenly aware, too, that blacks called upon to represent the Republic are, very often, thereby prohibited from representing blacks. A man my age, schooled in adversity and skilled in compromise, may choose not to force the issue of defense spending versus the bleak and criminal misery of the black *and* white populations here, but a younger man may say, out loud, that he will not fight for a country that has *never* fought for him and, further, that the myth and menace of global war are nothing more and nothing less than a coward's means of distracting attention from the real crimes and concerns of this Republic. And I may have to visit him in prison, or suffer with him there—no matter. The irreducible miracle is that we have sustained each other a very long time, and come a long, long way together. We have come to the end of a language and are now about the business of forging a new one. For we have survived, children, the very last white country the world will ever see.

The Nation, November 1, 1980

Introduction to
Notes of a Native Son, 1984

IT WAS Sol Stein, high school buddy, editor, novelist, playwright, who first suggested this book. My reaction was not enthusiastic: as I remember, I told him that I was too young to publish my memoirs.

I had never thought of these essays as a possible book. Once they were behind me, I don't, in fact, think that I thought of them at all. Sol's suggestion had the startling and unkind effect of causing me to realize that time had passed. It was as though he had dashed cold water in my face.

Sol persisted, however, and so did the dangers and rigors of my situation. I had returned from Paris, in 1954, out of motives not at all clear to me. I had promised a Swiss friend a visit to the land of my birth, but that, I think, has to be recognized as a pretext: it fails to have the weight of a motive. I find no objective reason for my return to America at that time—I am not sure that I can find the subjective one, either.

Yet, here I was, at the top of 1954, several months shy of thirty, scared to death, but happy to be with my family and my friends. It was my second return since my departure, in 1948.

I had returned in 1952, with my first novel, stayed long enough to show it to my family, and to sell it, and, then, I hauled on out of here. In 1954, I came back with *The Amen Corner*, and I was working on *Giovanni's Room*—which had broken off from what was to become *Another Country*.

Actually, '54–'55, in spite of frightening moments, and not only in retrospect, was a great year. I had, after all, survived something—the proof was that I was working. I was at the Writer's Colony, Yaddo, in Saratoga Springs, when my buddy, Marlon Brando, won the Oscar, and I watched Bette Davis present it to him, and kiss him, on TV. The late Owen Dodson called me there, from Washington, D.C., to say that he was directing, at Howard University, a student production of my play. I went to Washington, where I met the late, great E. Franklin Frazier and the great Sterling Brown. Howard was the first college campus I had ever seen, and, without these men, I do not know what would have become of my morale. The play, thank God, was a tremendous seven- or ten-day wonder, playing to standing room only on the last night, in spite of a reluctant, not yet Black faculty ("This play will set back the Speech Department by thirty years!"), a bewildered *Variety* ("What do you think Negroes in the North will think of this play?"), and the fact that it was not to be seen again for nearly ten years. And I had fallen in love. I was happy— the world had never before been so beautiful a place.

There was only one small hitch. I—we—didn't have a dime, no pot, nor no window.

Sol Stein returned to the attack. We had agreed on nine essays, he wanted a tenth, and I wrote the title essay between Owen's house and the Dunbar Hotel. Returned to New York, where I finished *Giovanni's Room*. Publisher's Row, that hot-bed of perception, looked on the book with horror and loath-ing, refused to touch it, saying that I was a young *Negro* writer, who, if he published this book, would alienate his au-dience and ruin his career. They would not, in short, publish it, as a favor to me. I conveyed my gratitude, perhaps a shade too sharply, borrowed money from a friend, and myself and my lover took the boat to France.

I had never thought of myself as an essayist: the idea had never entered my mind. Even—or, perhaps, especially now— I find it hard to re-create the journey.

It has something to do, certainly, with what I was trying to discover and, also, trying to avoid. If I was trying to discover myself—on the whole, when examined, a somewhat dubious notion, since I was also trying to avoid myself—there was, certainly, between that self and me, the accumulated rock of ages. This rock scarred the hand, and all tools broke against it. Yet, there was a *me*, somewhere: I could feel it, stirring within and against captivity. The hope of salvation—identity— depended on whether or not one would be able to decipher and describe the rock.

One song cries, *"lead me to the rock that is higher than I,"* and another cries, *"hide me in the rock!"* and yet another pro-claims, *"I got a home in that rock."* Or, *"I ran to the rock to hide my face: the rock cried out, no hiding place!"*

The accumulated rock of ages deciphered itself as a part of my inheritance—a part, mind you, not the totality—but, in order to claim my birthright, of which my inheritance was but a shadow, it was necessary to challenge and claim the rock. Otherwise, the rock claimed me.

Or, to put it another way, my inheritance was particular, specifically limited and limiting: my birthright was vast, connecting me to all that lives, and to everyone, forever. But one cannot claim the birthright without accepting the inheritance.

Therefore, when I began, seriously, to write—when I knew I was committed, that this would be my life—I had to try to describe that particular condition which was—is—the living proof of my inheritance. And, at the same time, with that very same description, I had to claim my birthright. I am what time, circumstance, history, have made of me, certainly, but I am, also, much more than that. So are we all.

The conundrum of color is the inheritance of every American, be he/she legally or actually Black or White. It is a fearful inheritance, for which untold multitudes, long ago, sold their birthright. Multitudes are doing so, until today. This horror has so welded past and present that it is virtually impossible and certainly meaningless to speak of it as occurring, as it were, in time. It can be, and it has been, suicidal to attempt to speak of this to a multitude, which, assuming it knows that time exists, believes that time can be outwitted.

Something like this, anyway, has something to do with my beginnings. I was trying to locate myself within a specific inheritance and to use that inheritance, precisely, to claim the birthright from which that inheritance had so brutally and specifically excluded me.

It is not pleasant to be forced to recognize, more than thirty years later, that neither this dynamic nor this necessity have changed. There have been superficial changes, with results at best ambiguous and, at worst, disastrous. Morally, there has been no change at all and a moral change is the only real one. *"Plus ça change,"* groan the exasperated French (who should certainly know), *"plus c'est le même chose."* (The more it changes, the more it remains the same.) At least they have the style to be truthful about it.

The only real change vividly discernible in this present, unspeakably dangerous chaos is a panic-stricken apprehension on the part of those who have maligned and subjugated others for so long that the tables have been turned. Not once have the Civilized been able to honor, recognize, or describe the Savage. He is, practically speaking, the source of their wealth, his continued subjugation the key to their power and glory. This is absolutely and unanswerably true in South Africa—to name but one section of Africa—and, as to how things fare for Black men and women; here, the Black has become, economically, all but expendable and is, therefore, encouraged to join the Army, or, a notion espoused, I believe, by Daniel Moynihan and Nathan Glazer, to become a postman—to make himself useful, for Christ's sake, while White men take on the heavy burden of ruling the world.

Well. *Plus ça change.* To say nothing, speaking as a Black citizen, regarding his countrymen, of *friends like these.*

There is an unadmitted icy panic coiled beneath the scaffolding of these present days, hopes, endeavors. I have said that the Civilized have never been able to honor, recognize, or describe the Savage. Once they had decided that he was savage, there was nothing to honor, recognize or describe. But the savages describe the Europeans, who were not yet, when they landed in the New(!) World, White, as *the people from heaven.* Neither did the savages in Africa have any way of foreseeing the anguished diaspora to which they were about to be condemned. Even the chiefs who sold Africans into slavery could not have had any idea that this slavery was meant to endure forever, or for at least *a thousand years.* Nothing in the savage experience could have prepared them for such an idea, any more than they could conceive of the land as something to be bought and sold. (As I cannot believe that people are actually buying and selling air space above the towers of Manhattan.)

Nevertheless, all of this happened, and is happening. Out of this incredible brutality, we get the myth of the happy darky and *Gone With the Wind.* And the North Americans appear to believe these legends, which they have created and which absolutely nothing in reality corroborates, until today. And when these legends are attacked, as is happening now—all over a globe which has never been and never will be White—

my countrymen become childishly vindictive and unutterably dangerous.

The unadmitted panic of which I spoke above is created by the terror that the Savage can, now, describe the Civilized: the only way to prevent this is to obliterate humanity. This panic proves that neither a person nor a people can do anything without knowing what they are doing. Neither can anyone avoid paying for the choices he or she has made. It is savagely, if one may say so, ironical that the only proof the world—mankind—has ever had of White supremacy is in the Black face and voice: that face never scrutinized, that voice never heard. The eyes in that face prove the unforgivable and unimaginable horror of being a captive in the promised land, but also prove that *trouble don't last always*: and the voice, once filled with a rage and pain that corroborated the reality of the jailer, is addressing another reality, in other tongues. The people who think of themselves as White have the choice of becoming human or irrelevant.

Or—as they are, indeed, already, in all but actual fact: obsolete. For, if trouble don't last always, as the Preacher tells us, neither does Power, and it is on the fact or the hope or the myth of Power that that identity which calls itself White has always seemed to depend.

I had just turned thirty-one when this book was first published, and, by the time you read this, I will be sixty. I think that quite remarkable, but I do not mention it, now, as an occasion for celebrations or lamentations. I don't feel that I have any reason to complain: emphatically, the contrary, to leave it at that, and no matter what tomorrow brings. Yet, I have reason to reflect—one always does, when forced to take a long look back. I remember many people who helped me in indescribable ways, all those years ago, when I was the pop-eyed, tongue-tied kid, in my memory sitting in a corner, on the floor. I was having a rough time in the Village, where the bulk of the populace, egged on by the cops, thought it was great fun to bounce tables and chairs off my head, and I soon stopped talking about my "constitutional" rights. I am, I suppose, a survivor.

A survivor of what? In those years, I was told, when I became terrified, vehement, or lachrymose: *It takes time, Jimmy.*

It takes time. I agree: I still agree: though it certainly didn't take much time for some of the people I knew then—in the Fifties—to turn tail, to decide to make it, and drape themselves in the American flag. A wretched and despicable band of cowards, whom I once trusted with my life—*friends like these!*

But we will discuss all that another day. When I was told, it takes time, when I was young, I was being told it will take time before a Black person can be treated as a human being here, but it will happen. We will help to make it happen. We promise you.

Sixty years of one man's life is a long time to deliver on a promise, especially considering all the lives preceding and surrounding my own.

What has happened, in the time of my time, is the record of my ancestors. No promise was kept with them, no promise was kept with me, nor can I counsel those coming after me, nor my global kinsmen, to believe a word uttered by my morally bankrupt and desperately dishonest countrymen.

"And," says Doris Lessing, in her preface to *African Stories,* *"while the cruelties of the white man toward the black man are among the heaviest counts in the indictment against humanity, colour prejudice is not our original fault, but only one aspect of the atrophy of the imagination that prevents us from seeing ourselves in every creature that breathes under the sun."*

Amen. *En avant.*

18 April 1984
Amherst, Massachusetts

Freaks and the American
Ideal of Manhood

To BE ANDROGYNOUS, *Webster's* informs us, is to have both male and female characteristics. This means that there is a man in every woman and a woman in every man. Sometimes this is recognized only when the chips are, brutally, down—when there is no longer any way to avoid this recognition. But love between a man and a woman, or love between any two human beings, would not be possible did we not have available to us the spiritual resources of both sexes.

To be androgynous does not imply both male and female sexual equipment, which is the state, uncommon, of the hermaphrodite. However, the existence of the hermaphrodite reveals, in intimidating exaggeration, the truth concerning every human being—which is why the hermaphrodite is called a freak. The human being does not, in general, enjoy being intimidated by what he/she finds in the mirror.

The hermaphrodite, therefore, may make his/her living in side shows or brothels, whereas the merely androgynous are running banks or filling stations or maternity wards, churches, armies or countries.

The last time you had a drink, whether you were alone or with another, you were having a drink with an androgynous human being; and this is true for the last time you broke bread or, as I have tried to suggest, the last time you made love.

There seems to be a vast amount of confusion in the Western world concerning these matters, but love and sexual activity are not synonymous: Only by becoming inhuman can the human being pretend that they are. The mare is not obliged to love the stallion, nor is the bull required to love the cow. They are doing what comes naturally.

But this by no means sums up the state or the possibilities of the human being in whom the awakening of desire fuels imagination and in whom imagination fuels desire. In other words, it is not possible for the human being to be as simple as a stallion or a mare, because the human imagination is perpetually required to examine, control and redefine reality, of which we must assume ourselves to be the center and the key. Nature and revelation are perpetually challenging each other; this relentless tension is one of the keys to human history and to what is known as the human condition.

Now, I can speak only of the Western world and must rely on my own experience, but the simple truth of this universal duality, this perpetual possibility of communion and completion, seems so alarming that I have watched it lead to addiction, despair, death and madness. Nowhere have I seen this panic more vividly than in my country and in my generation.

The American idea of sexuality appears to be rooted in the American idea of masculinity. Idea may not be the precise word, for the idea of one's sexuality can only with great violence be divorced or distanced from the idea of the self. Yet something resembling this rupture has certainly occurred (and is occurring) in American life, and violence has been the American daily bread since we have heard of America. This violence, furthermore, is not merely literal and actual but appears to be admired and lusted after, and the key to the American imagination.

All countries or groups make of their trials a legend or, as in the case of Europe, a dubious romance called "history." But no other country has ever made so successful and glamorous a romance out of genocide and slavery; therefore, perhaps the word I am searching for is not idea but ideal.

The American *ideal*, then, of sexuality appears to be rooted in the American ideal of masculinity. This ideal has created cowboys and Indians, good guys and bad guys, punks and studs, tough guys and softies, butch and faggot, black and white. It is an ideal so paralytically infantile that it is virtually forbidden—as an unpatriotic act—that the American boy evolve into the complexity of manhood.

The exigencies created by the triumph of the Industrial Revolution—or, in other terms, the rise of Europe to global dominance—had, among many mighty effects, that of commercializing the roles of men and women. Men became the propagators, or perpetrators, of property, and women became the means by which that property was protected and handed down. One may say that this was nothing more than the ancient and universal division of labor—women nurtured the tribe, men battled for it—but the concept of property had undergone a change. This change was vast and deep and sinister.

For the first time in human history, a man was reduced not merely to a thing but to a thing the value of which was determined, absolutely, by that thing's commercial value. That this pragmatic principle dictated the slaughter of the native American, the enslavement of the black and the monumental rape of Africa—to say nothing of creating the wealth of the Western world—no one, I suppose, will now attempt to deny.

But this principle also raped and starved Ireland, for example, as well as Latin America, and it controlled the pens of the men who signed the Declaration of Independence—a document more clearly commercial than moral. This is how, and why, the American Constitution was able to define the slave as three-fifths of a man, from which legal and commercial definition it legally followed that a black man "had no rights a white man was bound to respect."

Ancient maps of the world—when the world was flat—inform us, concerning that void where America was waiting to be discovered, HERE BE DRAGONS. Dragons may not have been here then, but they are certainly here now, breathing fire, belching smoke; or, to be less literary and Biblical about it, attempting to intimidate the mores, morals and morality of this particular and peculiar time and place. Nor, since this country is the issue of the entire globe and is also the most powerful nation currently to be found on it, are we speaking only of this time and place. And it can be said that the monumental struggles being waged in our time and not only in this place resemble, in awesome ways, the ancient struggle between those who insisted that the world was flat and those who apprehended that it was round.

Of course, I cannot possibly imagine what it can be like to have both male and female sexual equipment. That's a load of family jewels to be hauling about, and it seems to me that it must make choice incessant or impossible—or, in terms unavailable to me, unnecessary. Yet, not to be frivolous concerning what I know I cannot—or, more probably, dare not—imagine, I hazard that the physically androgynous state must create an all-but-intolerable loneliness, since we all exist, after all, and crucially, in the eye of the beholder. We all react to and, to whatever extent, become what that eye sees. This judgment begins in the eyes of one's parents (the crucial, the definitive, the all-but-everlasting judgment), and so we move, in the vast and claustrophobic gallery of Others, on up or down the line, to the eye of one's enemy or one's friend or one's lover.

It is virtually impossible to trust one's human value without the collaboration or corroboration of that eye—which is to say that no one can live without it. One can, of course, instruct that eye as to what to see, but this effort, which is nothing less than ruthless intimidation, is wounding and exhausting: While it can keep humiliation at bay, it confirms the fact that humiliation is the central danger of one's life. And since one cannot risk love without risking humiliation, love becomes impossible.

I hit the streets when I was about six or seven, like most black kids of my generation, running errands, doing odd jobs. This was in the black world—my turf—which means that I felt protected. I think that I really was, though poverty is poverty and we were, if I may say so, among the truly needy, in spite of the tins of corned beef we got from home relief every week, along with prunes. (Catsup had not yet become a vegetable; indeed, I don't think we had ever heard of it.) My mother fried corned beef, she boiled it, she baked it, she put potatoes in it, she put rice in it, she disguised it in corn bread, she boiled it in soup(!), she wrapped it in cloth, she beat it with a hammer, she banged it against the wall, she threw it onto the ceiling. Finally, she gave up, for nothing could make us eat it anymore, and the tins reproachfully piled up on the shelf above the bathtub—along with the prunes, which we also couldn't eat anymore. While I won't speak for my brothers and sisters, I can't bear corned-beef hash or prunes even today.

Poverty. I remember one afternoon when someone dropped a dime in front of the subway station at 125th Street and Lenox Avenue and I and a man of about 40 both scrambled for it. The man won, giving me a cheerful goodbye as he sauntered down the subway steps. I was bitterly disappointed, a dime being a dime, but I laughed, too.

The truly needy. Once, my father gave me a dime—the last dime in the house, though I didn't know that—to go to the store for kerosene for the stove, and I fell on the icy streets and dropped the dime and lost it. My father beat me with an iron cord from the kitchen to the back room and back again, until I lay, half-conscious, on my belly on the floor.

Yet—strange though it is to realize this, looking back—I never felt threatened in those years, when I was growing up in Harlem, my home town. I think this may be because it was familiar; the white people who lived there then were as poor as we, and there was no TV setting our teeth on edge with exhortations to buy what we could never hope to afford.

On the other hand, I was certainly unbelievably unhappy and pathologically shy, but that, I felt, was nobody's fault but mine. My father kept me in short pants longer than he should have, and I had been told, and I believed, that I was ugly. This meant that the idea of myself as a sexual possibility, or target, as a creature capable of inciting desire or capable of desire, had never entered my mind. And it entered my mind, finally, by means of the rent made in my short boy-scout pants by a man who had lured me into a hallway, saying that he wanted to send me to the store. That was the very last time I agreed to run an errand for any stranger.

Yet I was, in peculiar truth, a very lucky boy. Shortly after I turned 16, a Harlem racketeer, a man of about 38, fell in love with me, and I will be grateful to that man until the day I die. I showed him all my poetry, because I had no one else in Harlem to show it to, and even now, I sometimes wonder what on earth his friends could have been thinking, confronted with stingy-brimmed, mustachioed, razor-toting Poppa and skinny, popeyed Me when he walked me (rarely) into various shady joints, I drinking ginger ale, he drinking brandy. I think I was supposed to be his nephew, some nonsense like that, though he was Spanish and Irish, with curly black hair. But I knew that he was showing me off and wanted his friends to be happy for him—which, indeed, if the way they treated me can be taken as a barometer, they were. They seemed to feel that this was his business—that he would be in trouble if it became *their* business.

And though I loved him, too—in my way, a boy's way—I was mightily tormented, for I was still a child evangelist, which everybody knew, Lord. My soul looks back and wonders.

For what this really means is that all of the American categories of male and female, straight or not, black or white, were shattered, thank heaven, very early in my life. Not without anguish, certainly; but once you have discerned the meaning of a label, it may seem to define you for others, but it does not have the power to define you to yourself.

This prepared me for my life downtown, where I quickly discovered that my existence was the punch line of a dirty joke.

The condition that is now called gay was then called queer. The operative word was *faggot* and, later, pussy, but those epithets really had nothing to do with the question of sexual preference: You were being told simply that you had no balls.

I certainly had no desire to harm anyone, nor did I understand how anyone could look at me and suppose me physically capable of *causing* any harm. But boys and men chased me, saying I was a danger to their sisters. I was thrown out of cafeterias and rooming houses because I was "bad" for the neighborhood.

The cops watched all this with a smile, never making the faintest motion to protect me or to disperse my attackers; in fact, I was even more afraid of the cops than I was of the populace.

By the time I was 19, I was working in the Garment Center. I was getting on very badly at home and delayed going home after work as long as possible. At the end of the workday, I would wander east, to the 42nd Street Library. Sometimes, I would sit in Bryant Park—but I discovered that I could not sit there long. I fled, to the movies, and so discovered 42nd Street. Today that street is exactly what it was when I was an adolescent: It has simply become more blatant.

There were no X-rated movies then, but there were, so to speak, X-rated audiences. For example, I went in complete innocence to the Apollo, on 42nd Street, because foreign films were shown there—*The Lower Depths, Childhood of Maxim*

Gorky, La Bête Humaine—and I walked out as untouched (by human hands) as I had been when I walked in. There were the stores, mainly on Sixth Avenue, that sold "girlie" magazines. These magazines were usually to be found at the back of the store, and I don't so much remember them as I remember the silent men who stood there. They stood, it seemed, for hours, with the magazines in their hands and a kind of miasma in their eyes. There were all kinds of men, mostly young and, in those days, almost exclusively white. Also, for what it's worth, they were heterosexual, since the images they studied, at crotch level, were those of women.

Actually, I guess I hit 42nd Street twice and have very nearly blotted the first time out. I was not at the mercy of the street the first time, for, though I may have dreaded *going* home, I hadn't *left* home yet. Then, I spent a lot of time in the library, and I stole odds and ends out of Woolworth's—with no compunction at all, due to the way they treated us in Harlem. When I went to the movies, I imagine that a combination of innocence and terror prevented me from too clearly apprehending the action taking place in the darkness of the Apollo—though I understood it well enough to remain standing a great deal of the time. This cunning stratagem failed when, one afternoon, the young boy I was standing behind put his hand behind him and grabbed my cock at the very same moment that a young boy came up behind me and put his cock against my hand: Ignobly enough, I fled, though I doubt that I was missed. The men in the men's room frightened me, so I moved in and out as quickly as possible, and I also dimly felt, I remember, that I didn't want to "fool around" and so risk hurting the feelings of my uptown friend.

But if I was paralyzed by guilt and terror, I cannot be judged or judge myself too harshly, for I remember the faces of the men. These men, so far from being or resembling faggots, looked and sounded like the vigilantes who banded together on weekends to beat faggots up. (And I was around long enough, suffered enough, and learned enough to be forced to realize that this was very often true. I might not have learned this if I had been a white boy; but sometimes a white man will tell a black boy anything, everything, weeping briny tears. He knows that the black boy can never betray him, for no one will believe his testimony.)

These men looked like cops, football players, soldiers, sailors, Marines or bank presidents, admen, boxers, construction workers; they had wives, mistresses and children. I sometimes saw them in other settings—in, as it were, the daytime. Sometimes they spoke to me, sometimes not, for anguish has many days and styles. But I had first seen them in the men's room, sometimes on their knees, peering up into the stalls, or standing at the urinal stroking themselves, staring at another man, stroking, and with this miasma in their eyes. Sometimes, eventually, inevitably, I would find myself in bed with one of these men, a despairing and dreadful conjunction, since their need was as relentless as quicksand and as impersonal, and sexual rumor concerning blacks had preceded me. As for sexual roles, these were created by the imagination and limited only by one's stamina.

At bottom, what I had learned was that the male desire for a male roams everywhere, avid, desperate, unimaginably lonely, culminating often in drugs, piety, madness or death. It was also dreadfully like watching myself at the end of a long, slow-moving line: Soon I would be next. All of this was very frightening. It was lonely and impersonal and demeaning. I could not believe—after all, I was only 19—that I could have been driven to the lonesome place where these men and I met each other so soon, to stay.

The American idea of masculinity: There are few things under heaven more difficult to understand or, when I was younger, to forgive.

During the Second World War (the first one having failed to make the world safe for democracy) and some time after the Civil War (which had failed, unaccountably, to liberate the slave), life for niggers was fairly rough in Greenwich Village. There were only about three of us, if I remember correctly, when I first hit those streets, and I was the youngest, the most visible, and the most vulnerable.

On every street corner, I was called a faggot. This meant that I was despised, and, however horrible this is, it is clear.

What was *not* clear at that time of my life was what motivated the men and boys who mocked and chased me; for, if they found me when they were alone, they spoke to me very differently—frightening me, I must say, into a stunned and speechless paralysis. For when they were alone, they spoke very gently and wanted me to take them home and make love. (They could not take *me* home; they lived with their families.) The bafflement and the pain this caused in me remain beyond description. I was far too terrified to be able to accept their propositions, which could only result, it seemed to me, in making myself a candidate for gang rape. At the same time, I was moved by their loneliness, their halting, nearly speechless need. But I did not understand it.

One evening, for example, I was standing at the bottom of the steps to the Waverly Place subway station, saying goodbye to some friends who were about to take the subway. A gang of boys stood at the top of the steps and cried, in high, feminine voices, "Is this where the fags meet?"

Well. This meant that I certainly could not go back upstairs but would have to take the subway with my friends and get off at another station and maneuver my way home. But one of the gang saw me and, without missing a beat or saying a word to his friends, called my name and came down the steps, throwing one arm around me and asking where I'd been. He had let me know, some time before, that he wanted me to take him home—but I was surprised that he could be so open before his friends, who for their part seemed to find nothing astonishing in this encounter and disappeared, probably in search of other faggots.

The boys who are left of that time and place are all my age or older. But many of them are dead, and I remember how some of them died—some in the streets, some in the Army, some on the needle, some in jail. Many years later, we managed, without ever becoming friends—it was too late for that—to be friendly with one another. One of these men and I had a very brief, intense affair shortly before he died. He was on drugs and knew that he could not live long. "What a waste," he said, and he was right.

One of them said, "My God, Jimmy, you were moving so fast in those years, you never stopped to talk to me."

I said, "That's right, baby; I didn't stop because I didn't want you to think that I was trying to seduce you."

"Man," he said, indescribably, "why didn't you?"

But the queer—not yet gay—world was an even more intimidating area of this hall of mirrors. I knew that I was in the hall and present at this company—but the mirrors threw back only brief and distorted fragments of myself.

In the first place, as I have said, there were very few black people in the Village in those years, and of that handful, I was decidedly the most improbable. Perhaps, as they say in the theater, I was a hard type to cast; yet I was eager, vulnerable, and lonely. I was terribly shy, but boys *are* shy. I am saying that I don't think I felt absolutely, irredeemably grotesque—nothing that a friendly wave of the wand couldn't alter—but I was miserable. I moved through that world very quickly; I have described it as "my season in hell," for I was never able to make my peace with it.

It wasn't only that I didn't wish to seem or sound like a woman, for it was this detail that most harshly first struck my eye and ear. I am sure that I was afraid that I already seemed and sounded too much like a woman. In my childhood, at least until my adolescence, my playmates had called me a sissy. It seemed to me that many of the people I met were making fun of women, and I didn't see why. *I* certainly needed all the friends I could get, male *or* female, and women had nothing to do with whatever my trouble might prove to be.

At the same time, I had already been sexually involved with a couple of white women in the Village. There were virtually no black women there when I hit those streets, and none who needed or could have afforded to risk herself with an odd, raggedy-assed black boy who clearly had no future. (The first black girl I met who dug me I fell in love with, lived with and almost married. But I met her, though I was only 22, many light-years too late.)

The white girls I had known or been involved with—different categories—had paralyzed me, because I simply did not know what, apart from my sex, they wanted. Sometimes it was great, sometimes it was just moaning and groaning; but, ultimately, I found myself at the mercy of a double fear. The fear of the world was bearable until it entered the bedroom.

But it sometimes entered the bedroom by means of the motives of the girl, who intended to civilize you into becoming an appendage or who had found a black boy to sleep with because she wanted to humiliate her parents. Not an easy scene to play, in any case, since it can bring out the worst in both parties, and more than one white girl had already made me know that her color was more powerful than my dick.

Which had nothing to do with how I found myself in the gay world. I would have found myself there anyway, but perhaps the very last thing this black boy needed were clouds of imitation white women and speculations concerning the size of his organ: speculations sometimes accompanied by an attempt at the laying on of hands. "*Ooo!* Look at him! He's cute—he doesn't like you to touch him there!"

In short, I was black in that world, and I was used that way, and by people who truly meant me no harm.

And they could *not* have meant me any harm, because they did not see me. There were exceptions, of course, for I also met some beautiful people. Yet even today, it seems to me (possibly because I am black) very dangerous to model one's opposition to the arbitrary definition, the imposed ordeal, merely on the example supplied by one's oppressor.

The object of one's hatred is never, alas, conveniently outside but is seated in one's lap, stirring in one's bowels and dictating the beat of one's heart. And if one does not know this, one risks becoming an imitation—and, therefore, a continuation—of principles one imagines oneself to despise.

I, in any case, had endured far too much debasement willingly to debase myself. I had absolutely no fantasies about making love to the last cop or hoodlum who had beaten the shit out of me. I did not find it amusing, in any way whatever, to act out the role of the darky.

So I moved on out of there.

In fact, I found a friend—more accurately, a friend found *me*—an Italian, about five years older than I, who helped my morale greatly in those years. I was told that he had threatened to kill anyone who touched me. I don't know about that, but people stopped beating me up. Our relationship never seemed to worry him or his friends or his women.

My situation in the Village stabilized itself to the extent that

I began working as a waiter in a black West Indian restaurant, The Calypso, on MacDougal Street. This led, by no means incidentally, to the desegregation of the San Remo, an Italian bar and restaurant on the corner of MacDougal and Bleecker. Every time I entered the San Remo, they threw me out. I had to pass it all the time on my way to and from work, which is, no doubt, why the insult rankled.

I had won the Saxton Fellowship, which was administered by Harper & Brothers, and I knew Frank S. MacGregor, the president of Harper's. One night, when he asked me where we should have dinner, I suggested, spontaneously, the San Remo.

We entered, and they seated us and we were served. I went back to MacGregor's house for a drink and then went straight back to the San Remo, sitting on a bar stool in the window. The San Remo thus began to attract a varied clientele, indeed—so much so that Allen Ginsberg and company arrived there the year I left New York for Paris.

As for the people who ran and worked at the San Remo, they never bothered me again. Indeed, the Italian community never bothered me again—or rarely and, as it were, by accident. But the Village was full of white tourists, and one night, when a mob gathered before the San Remo, demanding that I come out, the owners closed the joint and turned the lights out and we sat in the back room, in the dark, for a couple of hours, until they judged it safe to drive me home.

This was a strange, great and bewildering time in my life. Once I was in the San Remo, for example, I was *in*, and anybody who messed with me was *out*—that was all there was to it, and it happened more than once. And no one seemed to remember a time when I had not been there.

I could not quite get it together, but it seemed to me that I was no longer black for them and they had ceased to be white for me, for they sometimes introduced me to their families with every appearance of affection and pride and exhibited not the remotest interest in whatever my sexual proclivities chanced to be.

They had fought me very hard to prevent this moment, but perhaps we were all much relieved to have got beyond the obscenity of color.

Matters were equally bewildering, though in a different way, at The Calypso. All kinds of people came into our joint —I am now referring to white people—and one of their most vivid aspects, for me, was the cruelty of their alienation. They appeared to have no antecedents nor any real connections.

"Do you really *like* your mother?" someone asked me, seeming to be astounded, totally disbelieving the possibility.

I was astounded by the question. Certainly, my mother and I did not agree about everything, and I knew that she was very worried about the dangers of the life I lived, but that was normal, since I was a boy and she was a woman. Of course she was worried about me: She was my *mother*. But she knew I wasn't crazy and that I would certainly never do anything, deliberately, to hurt her. Or my tribe, my brothers and sisters, who were probably worried about me, too.

My family was a part of my life. I could not imagine life without them, might never have been able to reconcile myself to life without them. And certainly one of the reasons I was breaking my ass in the Village had to do with my need to try to move us out of our dangerous situation. I was perfectly aware of the odds—my father had made that very clear—but he had also given me my assignment. "Do you really *like* your mother?" did not cause me to wonder about my mother or myself but about the person asking the question.

And perhaps because of such questions, I was not even remotely tempted by the possibilities of psychiatry or psychoanalysis. For one thing, there were too many schools—Freud, Horney, Jung, Reich (to suggest merely the tip of that iceberg)—and, for another, it seemed to me that anyone who thought seriously that I had any desire to be "adjusted" to this society had to be ill; too ill, certainly, as time was to prove, to be trusted.

I sensed, then—without being able to articulate it—that this dependence on a formula for safety, for that is what it was, signaled a desperate moral abdication. People went to the shrink in order to find justification for the empty lives they led and the meaningless work they did. Many turned, helplessly, hopefully, to Wilhelm Reich and perished in orgone boxes.

*

I seem to have strayed a long way from our subject, but our subject is social and historical—and continuous. The people who leaped into orgone boxes in search of the perfect orgasm were later to turn to acid. The people so dependent on psychiatric formulas were unable to give their children any sense of right or wrong—indeed, this sense was in themselves so fragile that during the McCarthy era, more than one shrink made a lot of money by convincing his patients, or clients, that their psychic health demanded that they inform on their friends. (Some of these people, after their surrender, attempted to absolve themselves in the civil rights movement.)

What happened to the children, therefore, is not even remotely astonishing. The flower children—who became the Weather Underground, the Symbionese Liberation Army, the Manson Family—are creatures from this howling inner space.

I am not certain, therefore, that the present sexual revolution is either sexual or a revolution. It strikes me as a reaction to the spiritual famine of American life. The present androgynous "craze"—to underestimate it—strikes me as an attempt to be honest concerning one's nature, and it is instructive, I think, to note that there is virtually no emphasis on overt sexual activity. There is nothing more boring, anyway, than sexual activity as an end in itself, and a great many people who came out of the closet should reconsider.

Such figures as Boy George do not disturb me nearly so much as do those relentlessly hetero (sexual?) keepers of the keys and seals, those who know what the world needs in the way of order and who are ready and willing to supply that order.

This rage for order can result in chaos, and in this country, chaos connects with color. During the height of my involvement in the civil rights movement, for example, I was subjected to hate mail of a terrifying precision. Volumes concerning what my sisters, to say nothing of my mother, were capable of doing; to say nothing of my brothers; to say nothing of the monumental size of *my* organ and what I did with it. Someone described, in utterly riveting detail, a scene he swore he had witnessed (I *think* it was a *he*—such mail is rarely signed) on the steps of houses in Baltimore of niggers fucking their dogs.

At the same time, I was also on the mailing list of one of the more elegant of the K.K.K. societies, and I still have some of that mail in my files. Someone, of course, eventually realized that the organization should not be sending that mail to this particular citizen, and it stopped coming—but not before I had had time to be struck by the similarity of tone between the hate mail and the mail of the society, and not before the society had informed me, by means of a parody of an Audubon Society postcard, what it felt and expected me to feel concerning a certain "Red-breasted" Martin Luther King, Jr.

The Michael Jackson cacophony is fascinating in that it is not about Jackson at all. I hope he has the good sense to know it and the good fortune to snatch his life out of the jaws of a carnivorous success. He will not swiftly be forgiven for having turned so many tables, for he damn sure grabbed the brass ring, and the man who broke the bank at Monte Carlo has nothing on Michael. All that noise is about America, as the dishonest custodian of black life and wealth; and blacks, especially males, in America; and the burning, buried American guilt; and sex and sexual roles and sexual panic; money, success and despair—to all of which may now be added the bitter need to find a head on which to place the crown of Miss America.

Freaks are called freaks and are treated as they are treated—in the main, abominably—because they are human beings who cause to echo, deep within us, our most profound terrors and desires.

Most of us, however, do not appear to be freaks—though we are rarely what we appear to be. We are, for the most part, visibly male or female, our social roles defined by our sexual equipment.

But we are all androgynous, not only because we are all born of a woman impregnated by the seed of a man but because each of us, helplessly and forever, contains the other— male in female, female in male, white in black and black in white. We are a part of each other. Many of my countrymen appear to find this fact exceedingly inconvenient and even unfair, and so, very often, do I. But none of us can do anything about it.

Playboy, January 1985

The Price of the Ticket

M Y SOUL looks back and wonders how I got over—indeed: but I find it unexpectedly difficult to remember, in detail, how I got started. I will never, for example, forget Saul Levitas, the editor of *The New Leader*, who gave me my first book review assignment sometime in 1946, nor Mary Greene, a wonderful woman, who was his man Friday: but I do not remember exactly how I met them.

I *do* remember how my life in Greenwich Village began—which is, essentially, how my career began—for it began when I was fifteen.

One day, a DeWitt Clinton H.S. running buddy, Emile Capouya, played hookey without me and went down to Greenwich Village and made the acquaintance of Beauford Delaney. The next day, he told me about this wonderful man he had met, a black—then, Negro, or Colored—painter and said that I must meet him: and he gave me Beauford Delaney's address.

I had a Dickensian job, after school, in a sweat shop on Canal Street, and was getting on so badly at home that I dreaded going home: and, so, sometime later, I went to 181 Greene Street, where Beauford lived then, and introduced myself.

I was terrified, once I had climbed those stairs and knocked on that door. A short, round brown man came to the door and looked at me. He had the most extraordinary eyes I'd ever seen. When he had completed his instant X-ray of my brain, lungs, liver, heart, bowels, and spinal column (while I had said, usefully, "Emile sent me") he smiled and said, "Come in," and opened the door.

He opened the door all right.

Lord, I was to hear Beauford sing, later, and for many years, *open the unusual door*. My running buddy had sent me to the right one, and not a moment too soon.

I walked through that door into Beauford's colors—on the easel, on the palette, against the wall—sometimes turned to the wall—and sometimes (in limbo?) covered by white sheets. It was a small studio (but it didn't seem small) with a black pot-bellied stove somewhere near the two windows. *I* remember two windows, there may have been only one: there *was* a fire escape which Beauford, simply by his presence, had transformed, transmuted into the most exclusive terrace in Manhattan or Bombay.

I walked into music. I had grown up with music, but, now, on Beauford's small black record player, I began to hear what I had never dared or been able to hear. Beauford never gave me any lectures. But, in his studio and because of his presence, I really began to *hear* Ella Fitzgerald, Ma Rainey, Louis Armstrong, Bessie Smith, Ethel Waters, Paul Robeson, Lena Horne, Fats Waller. He could inform me about Duke Ellington and W. C. Handy, and Josh White, introduce me to Frankie Newton and tell tall tales about Ethel Waters. And these people were not meant to be looked on by me as celebrities, but as a part of Beauford's life and as part of my inheritance.

I may have been with Beauford, for example, the first time I saw Paul Robeson, in concert, and in *Othello*: but I know that he bought tickets for us—really, for me—to see and hear Miss Marian Anderson, at Carnegie Hall.

Because of her color, Miss Anderson was not allowed to sing at The Met, nor, as far as The Daughters of The American Revolution were concerned, anywhere in Washington where white people might risk hearing her. Eleanor Roosevelt was appalled by this species of patriotism and arranged for Marian Anderson to sing on the steps of the Lincoln Memorial. This was a quite marvellous and passionate event in those years, triggered by the indignation of one woman who had, clearly, it seemed to me, married beneath her.

By this time, I was working for the Army—or the Yankee dollar!—in New Jersey. I hitchhiked, in sub-zero weather, out of what I will always remember as one of the lowest and most obscene circles of Hell, into Manhattan: where both Beauford and Miss Anderson were on hand to inform me that I had no right to permit myself to be defined by so pitiful a people. Not only was I not born to be a slave: I was not born to hope to become the equal of the slave-master. They had, the masters, incontestably, the rope—in time, with enough, they would hang themselves with it. They were not to hang *me*: *I* was to see to that. If Beauford and Miss Anderson were a part of my inheritance, I was a part of their hope.

I still remember Miss Anderson, at the end of that concert, in a kind of smoky yellow gown, her skin copper and tan, roses in the air about her, roses at her feet. Beauford painted it, an enormous painting, he fixed it in time, for me, forever, and he painted it, he said, for me.

Beauford was the first walking, living proof, for me, that a black man could be an artist. In a warmer time, a less blasphemous place, he would have been recognized as my Master and I as his Pupil. He became, for me, an example of courage and integrity, humility and passion. An absolute integrity: I saw him shaken many times and I lived to see him broken but I never saw him bow.

His example operated as an enormous protection: for the Village, then, and not only for a boy like me, was an alabaster maze perched above a boiling sea. To lose oneself in the maze was to fall into the sea. One saw it around one all the time: a famous poet of the twenties and thirties grotesquely, shamelessly, cadging drinks, another relic living in isolation on opium and champagne, someone your own age suddenly strung out or going under a subway train, people you ate with and drank with suddenly going home and blowing their brains out or turning on the gas or leaping out of the window. And, racially, the Village was vicious, partly because of the natives, largely because of the tourists, and absolutely because of the cops.

Very largely, then, because of Beauford and Connie Williams, a beautiful black lady from Trinidad who ran the restaurant in which I was a waiter, and the jazz musicians I loved and who referred to me, with a kind of exasperated affection, as "the kid," I was never entirely at the mercy of an environment at once hostile and seductive. They knew about dope, for example—I didn't: but the pusher and his product were kept far away from me. I needed love so badly that I could as easily have been hit with a needle as persuaded to share a joint of marijuana. And, in fact, Beauford and the others let me smoke with them from time to time. (But there were people they warned me *not* to smoke with.)

The only real danger with marijuana is that it can lead to rougher stuff, but this has to do with the person, not the weed. In my own case, it could hardly have become a problem, since I simply could not write if I were "high." Or, rather, I could, sometimes all night long, the greatest pages the world had ever seen, pages I tore up the moment I was able to read them.

Yet, I learned something about myself from these irredeemable horrors: something which I might not have learned had I not been forced to know that I was valued. I repeat that Beauford never gave me any lectures, but he didn't have to—he expected me to accept and respect the value placed upon me. Without this, I might very easily have become the junky which so many among those I knew were becoming then, or the Bellevue or Tombs inmate (instead of the visitor) or the Hudson River corpse which a black man I loved with all my heart was shortly to become.

Shortly: I was to meet Eugene sometime between 1943 and 1944 and "run" or "hang" with him until he hurled himself off the George Washington Bridge, in the winter of 1946. We were never lovers: for what it's worth, I think I wish we had been.

When he was dead, I remembered that he had, once, obliquely, suggested this possibility. He had run down a list of his girl friends: those he liked, those he *really* liked, one or two with whom he might really be in love, and, then, he said, "I wondered if I might be in love with you."

I wish I had heard him more clearly: an oblique confession is always a plea. But I was to hurt a great many people by being unable to imagine that anyone could possibly be in love with an ugly boy like me. To be valued is one thing, the recognition of this assessment demanding, essentially, an act of the will. But love is another matter: it is scarcely worth observing what a mockery love makes of the will. Leaving all that alone, however: when he was dead, I realized that I would have done anything whatever to have been able to hold him in this world.

Through him, anyway, my political life, insofar as I can claim, formally, to have had one, began. He was a Socialist—a member of the Young People's Socialist League (YPSL) and urged me to join, and I did. I, then, outdistanced him by becoming a Trotskyite—so that I was in the interesting position (at the age of nineteen) of being an anti-Stalinist when America and Russia were allies.

My life on the Left is of absolutely no interest. It did not last long. It was useful in that I learned that it may be impossible to indoctrinate me; also, revolutionaries tend to be sentimental and I hope that I am not. This was to lead to very serious differences between myself and Eugene, and others: but it was during this period that I met the people who were to take me to Saul Levitas, of *The New Leader*, Randall Jarrell, of *The Nation*, Elliott Cohen and Robert Warshow, of *Commentary*, and Philip Rahv, of *Partisan Review*.

These men are all dead, now, and they were all very important to my life. It is not too much to say that they helped to save my life. (As Bill Cole, at Knopf, was later to do when the editor assigned *Go Tell It On The Mountain* had me on the ropes.) And their role in my life says something arresting concerning the American dilemma, or, more precisely, perhaps, the American torment.

I had been to two black newspapers before I met these people and had simply been laughed out of the office: I was a shoeshine boy who had never been to college. I don't blame these people, God knows that I was an unlikely cub reporter: yet, I still remember how deeply I was hurt.

On the other hand, around this time, or a little later, I landed a job as messenger for New York's liberal newspaper, *PM*. It is perhaps worth pointing out that *PM* had a man of about my complexion (dark) in the tower, under whom I worked, a coal black Negro in the cellar, whom nobody ever saw, and a very fair Negro on the city desk, in the window. My career at *PM* was very nearly as devastating as my career as a civilian employee of the US Army, except that *PM* never (as far as I know) placed me on a blacklist. If the black newspapers had considered me absolutely beyond redemption, *PM* was determined to save me: I cannot tell which attitude caused me the more bitter anguish.

Therefore, though it may have cost Saul Levitas nothing to hurl a book at a black boy to see if he could read it and be articulate concerning what he had read, I took it as a vote of confidence and swore that I would give him my very best shot. And I loved him—the old man, as I sometimes called him (to his face) and I think—I know—that he was proud of me, and that he loved me, too.

It was a very great apprenticeship. Saul required a book review a week, which meant that I had to read and write all the time. He paid me ten or twenty dollars a shot: Mary Greene would sometimes coerce him into giving me a bonus. Then he would stare at her, as though he could not believe that she, his helper, could be capable of such base treachery and look at me more tragically than Julius Caesar looked at Brutus and sigh—and give me another five or ten dollars.

As for the books I reviewed—well, no one, I suppose, will ever read them again. It was after the war, and the Americans were on one of their monotonous conscience "trips": be kind to niggers, for Christ's sake, be kind to Jews! A high, or turning point of some kind was reached when I reviewed Ross Lockridge's sunlit and fabulously successful *Raintree County*. The review was turned in and the author committed suicide before the review was printed. I was very disagreeably shaken by this, and Saul asked me to write a postscript—which I did. That same week I met the late Dwight MacDonald, whom I admired very much because of his magazine, *Politics*, who looked at me with wonder and said that I was "very smart." This pleased me, certainly, but it frightened me more.

But no black editor could or would have been able to give me my head, as Saul did then: partly because he would not have had the power, partly because he could not have afforded—or needed—Saul's politics, and partly because part of the price of the black ticket is involved—fatally—with the dream of becoming white.

This is not possible, partly because white people are not white: part of the price of the white ticket is to delude themselves into believing that they are. The political position of *my old man*, for example, whether or not he knew it, was dictated by his (in his case) very honorable necessity not to break faith with the Old World. One may add, in passing, that the Old World, or Europe, has become nothing less than an American superstition, which accounts, if anything can, for an American vision of Russia so Talmudic and self-serving that it has absolutely nothing to do with any reality occurring under the sun.

But the black American must find a way to keep faith with, and to excavate, a reality much older than Europe. Europe has never been, and cannot be, a useful or valid touchstone for the American experience because America is not, and never can be, white.

My father died before Eugene died. When my father died, Beauford helped me to bury him and I then moved from Harlem to the Village.

This was in 1943. We were fighting the Second World War. *We:* who was this *we?*

For this war was being fought, as far as I could tell, to bring freedom to everyone with the exception of Hagar's children and the "yellow-bellied Japs."

This was not a matter, merely, of my postadolescent discernment. It had been made absolutely clear to me by the eighteen months or so that I had been working for the Army, in New Jersey, by the anti-Japanese posters to be found, then, all over New York, and by the internment of the Japanese.

At the same time, one was expected to be "patriotic" and pledge allegiance to a flag which had pledged no allegiance to you: it risked becoming your shroud if you didn't know how to keep your distance and stay in your "place."

And all of this was to come back to me much later, when Cassius Clay, a.k.a. Muhammad Ali, refused to serve in Vietnam because he was a Muslim—in other words, for religious reasons—and was stripped of his title, while placards all over New York trumpeted, *Be true to your faith!*

I have never been able to convey the confusion and horror and heartbreak and contempt which every black person I then knew felt. Oh, we dissembled and smiled as we groaned and cursed and did our duty. (And we *did* our duty.) The romance of treason never occurred to us for the brutally simple reason that you can't betray a country you don't have. (Think about it.) Treason draws its energy from the conscious, deliberate betrayal of a trust—as we were not trusted, we could not betray. And we did not wish to be traitors. We wished to be citizens.

We: the black people of this country, then, with particular emphasis on those serving in the Armed Forces. The way blacks were treated in, and by, an American Army spreading freedom around the globe was the reason for the heartbreak and contempt. Daddy's youngest son, by his first marriage, came home, on furlough, to help with the funeral. When these young men came home, in uniform, they started talking: and one sometimes trembled, for their sanity and for one's own. One trembled, too, at another depth, another incoherence, when one wondered—as one could not fail to wonder—what *nation* they represented. My brother, describing his life in uniform, did not seem to be representing the America his uniform was meant to represent—: he had never seen the America his uniform was meant to represent. Had anyone? did he know, had he met, anyone who had? Did anyone *live* there? judging from the great gulf fixed between their conduct and their principles, it seemed unlikely.

Was it worth his life?

For he, certainly, on the other hand, represented something much larger than himself and something in him knew it: otherwise, he would have been broken like a match-stick and lost or have surrendered the power of speech. *A nation within a nation:* this thought wavered in my mind, I think, all those years ago, but I did not know what to make of it, it frightened me.

We: my family, the living and the dead, and the children coming along behind us. This was a complex matter, for I was not living with my family in Harlem, after all, but "downtown," in the "white world," in alien and mainly hostile territory. On the other hand, for me, then, Harlem was almost as alien and in a yet more intimidating way and risked being equally hostile, although for very different reasons. This truth cost me something in guilt and confusion, but it was the truth. It had something to do with my being the son of an evangelist and having been a child evangelist, but this is not all there was to it—that is, guilt is not all there was to it.

The fact that this particular child had been born when and where he was born had dictated certain expectations. The child does not really know what these expectations are—does not know how real they are—until he begins to fail, challenge, or defeat them. When it was clear, for example, that the pulpit, where I had made so promising a beginning, would not be my career, it was hoped that I would go on to college. This was never a very realistic hope and—perhaps because I knew this—I don't seem to have felt very strongly about it. In any case, this hope was dashed by the death of my father.

Once I had left the pulpit, I had abandoned or betrayed my role in the community—indeed, my departure from the pulpit and my leaving home were almost simultaneous. (I had abandoned the ministry in order not to betray myself by betraying the ministry.)

Once it became clear that I was not going to go to college, I became a kind of two-headed monstrosity of a problem. Without a college education, I could, clearly, never hope to become a writer: would never acquire the skills which would enable me to conquer what was thought of as an all-white world. This meant that I would become a half-educated handyman, a vociferous, bitter ruin, spouting Shakespeare in the bars on Saturday night and sleeping it off on Sunday.

I could see this, too. I saw it all around me. There are few things more dreadful than dealing with a man who knows that he is going under, in his own eyes, and in the eyes of others. Nothing can help that man. What is left of that man flees from what is left of human attention.

I fled. I didn't want my Mama, or the kids, to see me like that.

And if all this seems, now, ridiculous and theatrical apprehension on the part of a nineteen-year-old boy, I can say only that it didn't seem remotely ridiculous then. A black person in this democracy is certain to endure the unspeakable and the unimaginable in nineteen years. It is far from an exaggeration to state that many, and by the deliberate will and action of the Republic, are ruined by that time.

White Americans cannot, in the generality, hear this, any more than their European ancestors, and contemporaries, could, or can. If I say that my best friend, black, Eugene, who took his life at the age of twenty-four, had been, until that moment, a survivor, I will be told that he had "personal" problems. Indeed he did, and one of them was trying to find a job, or a place to live, in New York. If I point out that there is certainly a connection between his death (when I was twenty-two) and my departure for Paris (when *I* was twenty-four) I will be condemned as theatrical.

But I am really saying something very simple. The will of the people, or the State, is revealed by the State's institutions. There was not, then, nor is there, now, a single American institution which is not a racist institution. And racist institutions—the unions, for one example, the Church, for another, and the Army—or the military—for yet another, are meant to keep the nigger in his place. Yes: we have lived through avalanches of tokens and concessions but white power remains white. And what it appears to surrender with one hand it obsessively clutches in the other.

I know that this is considered to be heresy. Spare me, for Christ's *and* His Father's sake, any further examples of American white progress. When one examines the use of this word in this most particular context, it translates as meaning that those people who have opted for being white congratulate themselves on their generous ability to return to the slave that freedom which they never had any right to endanger, much less take away. For this dubious effort, and still more dubious achievement, they congratulate themselves and expect to be congratulated—: in the coin, furthermore, of black gratitude, gratitude not only that my burden is—(slowly, but it takes time) being made lighter but my joy that white people are improving.

My black burden has not, however, been made lighter in the sixty years since my birth or the nearly forty years since the first essay in this collection was published and my joy, therefore, as concerns the immense strides made by white people is, to say the least, restrained.

Leaving aside my friends, the people I love, who cannot, usefully, be described as either black or white, they are, like life itself, thank God, many many colors, I do not feel, alas, that my country has any reason for self-congratulation.

If I were still in the pulpit which some people (and they may be right) claim I never left, I would counsel my countrymen to the self-confrontation of prayer, the cleansing breaking of the heart which precedes atonement. This is, of course, impossible. Multitudes are capable of many things, but atonement is not one of them.

A multitude is, I suppose, by definition, an anonymous group of people bound or driven together by fears (I wrote "tears") and hopes and needs which no individual member could face or articulate alone.

On the one hand, for example, mass conversions are notoriously transitory: within days, the reformed—"saved"—whore, whoremonger, thief, drunkard, have ventilated their fears and dried their tears and returned to their former ways. Nor do the quite spectacularly repentant "born again" of the present hour give up this world to follow Jesus. No, they take Jesus with them into the marketplace where He is used as proof of their acumen and as their Real Estate Broker, now, and, as it were, forever.

But it does not demand a mass conversion to persuade a mob to lynch a nigger or stone a Jew or mutilate a sexual heretic. It demands no conversion at all: in the very same way that the act demands no courage at all. That not one member of the mob could or would accomplish the deed alone is not merely, I think, due to physical cowardice but to cowardice of another order. To destroy a nigger, a kike, a dyke, or a faggot, by one's own act alone is to have committed a communion and, above all, to have made a public confession more personal, more total, and more devastating than any act of love: whereas the orgasm of the mob is drenched in the blood of the lamb.

A mob is not autonomous: it executes the real will of the people who rule the State. The slaughter in Birmingham, Alabama, for example, was not, merely, the action of a mob. That blood is on the hands of the state of Alabama: which sent those mobs into the streets to execute the will of the State. And, though I know that it has now become inconvenient and impolite to speak of the American Jew in the same breath with which one speaks of the American black (*I hate to say I told you so,* sings the right righteous Reverend Ray Charles, *but: I told you so*), I yet contend that the mobs in the streets of Hitler's Germany were in those streets not only by the will of the German State, but by the will of the western world, including those architects of human freedom, the British, and the presumed guardian of Christian and human morality, the Pope. The American Jew, if I may say so—and I say so with love, whether or not you believe me—makes the error of believing that his Holocaust ends in the New World, where mine begins. My diaspora continues, the end is not in sight, and I certainly cannot depend on the morality of this panic-stricken consumer society to bring me out of—: Egypt.

A mob cannot afford to doubt: that the Jews killed Christ or that niggers want to rape their sisters or that anyone who fails to make it in the land of the free and the home of the brave deserves to be wretched. But these ideas do not come from the mob. They come from the state, which creates and manipulates the mob. The idea of black persons as property, for example, does not come from the mob. It is not a spontaneous idea. It does not come from the people, who knew better, who thought nothing of intermarriage until they were penalized for it: this idea comes from the architects of the American State. These architects decided that the concept of Property was more important—more real—than the possibilities of the human being.

In the church I come from—which is not at all the same church to which white Americans belong—we were counselled, from time to time, to do our first works over. Though the church I come from and the church to which most white Americans belong are both Christian churches, their relationship—due to those pragmatic decisions concerning Property made by a Christian State sometime ago—cannot be said to involve, or suggest, the fellowship of Christians. We do not, therefore, share the same hope or speak the same language.

To do your first works over means to reexamine everything. Go back to where you started, or as far back as you can, examine all of it, travel your road again and tell the truth about it. Sing or shout or testify or keep it to yourself: but *know whence you came.*

This is precisely what the generality of white Americans cannot afford to do. They do not know how to do it—: as I must suppose. They come through Ellis Island, where *Giorgio* becomes *Joe, Pappavasiliu* becomes *Palmer, Evangelos* becomes *Evans, Goldsmith* becomes *Smith* or *Gold,* and *Avakian* becomes *King.* So, with a painless change of name, and in the twinkling of an eye, one becomes a white American.

Later, in the midnight hour, the missing identity aches. One can neither assess nor overcome the storm of the middle passage. One is mysteriously shipwrecked forever, in the Great New World.

The slave is in another condition, as are his heirs: *I told Jesus it would be all right/If He changed my name.*

If *He* changed my name.

The Irish middle passage, for but one example, was as foul as my own, and as dishonorable on the part of those responsible for it. But the Irish became white when they got here and began rising in the world, whereas I became black and began sinking. The Irish, therefore and thereafter—again, for but one example—had absolutely no choice but to make certain that I could not menace their safety or status or identity: and, if I came too close, they could, with the consent of the governed, kill me. Which means that we can be friendly with each other anywhere in the world, except Boston.

What a monumental achievement on the part of those heroes who conquered the North American wilderness!

The price the white American paid for his ticket was to become white—: and, in the main, nothing more than that, or, as he was to insist, nothing less. This incredibly limited not to say dimwitted ambition has choked many a human being to death here: and this, I contend, is because the white American has never accepted the real reasons for his journey. I know very well that my ancestors had no desire to come to this place: but neither did the ancestors of the people who became white and who require of my captivity a song. They require of me a song less to celebrate my captivity than to justify their own.

1985

CHRONOLOGY

NOTE ON THE TEXTS

NOTES

Chronology

1924   Born James Arthur Jones on August 2 in Harlem Hospital, New York City, the son of Emma Berdis Jones and a father he will never know. (Mother moved from Deal Island, Maryland, around the turn of the century and lived briefly in Philadelphia before moving to New York City.)

1925–28   Receives name James Arthur Baldwin after mother marries David Baldwin in 1927. (Stepfather, a Baptist preacher in Harlem who also works at a bottling factory, moved from New Orleans to New York City in the early 1920s with his mother, Barbara Ann Baldwin, a former slave, and son Samuel Baldwin, who is about 12 years old.) Family lives in Harlem apartment. Brother George born.

1929–34   Sister Barbara born. Baldwin begins attending Public School 24 in 1929, where he is encouraged in his studies by school principal, Gertrude E. Ayer. Brother Wilmer is born in 1930, brother David in 1931, and sister Gloria in 1933; during this time step-grandmother dies and Samuel, after a dispute with his father, leaves home for good. Baldwin helps mother care for growing family. Family is forced by lack of money to move several times, always within Harlem, and occasionally to accept relief. Orilla Miller, a WPA Theater Project worker in the public schools, encourages Baldwin in his reading and takes him to movies, museums, and plays.

1935–38   Sister Ruth born in 1935. Baldwin enters Frederick Douglass Junior High School (P.S. 139) in September 1935, where he is influenced by teacher and literary club adviser Countee Cullen, a leading poet of the Harlem Renaissance. Contributes essays, sketches, poems, and stories to school magazine *The Douglass Pilot* and becomes one of its editors. Visits midtown library often and reads voraciously; his favorite novels are Stowe's *Uncle Tom's Cabin* and Dickens' *A Tale of Two Cities*. Sister Elizabeth born in 1937. Researches history of Harlem for essay "Harlem—Then and Now." Attends Pentecostalist churches with family of school friend Arthur Moore; undergoes a conversion experience, becomes a young minister at Fireside Pentecostal Assembly, and for next three years preaches there regularly. Enters De Witt Clinton High School, a prestigious public school in the Bronx, in September 1938.

1939–41 Works on school journal *The Magpie* along with friends Emile Capouya, Sol Stein, and Richard Avedon; Baldwin's contributions include stories "Woman at the Well," "Mississippi Legend," "Incident in London," and an interview with Countee Cullen, "Rendezvous with Life." Grows troubled at not knowing his real father. Finds it hard to concentrate on schoolwork and fails some courses but does well in English and history. Through Capouya meets Beauford Delaney, an artist living in Greenwich Village; he introduces Baldwin to the art world there, teaches him about music—including blues and jazz, which are forbidden by stepfather at home—and becomes a lifelong friend. Stepfather's health begins to fail. With Capouya's support, Baldwin leaves the church, preaching his last sermon at the end of senior year.

1942–44 Awarded high school diploma in January 1942. Takes laboring job at army depot under construction in Belle Mead, near Princeton, New Jersey, where Capouya is also employed. Rooms with local family but visits New York on weekends and regularly sends money to family. Fired from Belle Mead job; returns home and finds work at a meatpacking plant. Stepfather dies on July 29, 1943, the same day that sister Paula is born. Baldwin loses the meatpacking job. Moves to Greenwich Village to concentrate on writing, staying at first with Delaney and other friends. Works as waiter at Calypso restaurant and enjoys the company of artists and writers who gather there. Has liaisons with both men and women. Around this time tells Capouya that he thinks of himself as homosexual. Becomes good friend of Eugene Worth and meets young actor Marlon Brando while taking a theater class. Begins a novel that he calls "Crying Holy" and "In My Father's House" (later *Go Tell It on the Mountain*). Meets Richard Wright in late 1944; he reads Baldwin's manuscript and recommends it to an editor at Harper and Brothers.

1945–48   Receives $500 grant from Harper's Eugene F. Saxton Memorial Trust in November 1945. Works on novel; a draft is rejected by both Harper and Doubleday. Eugene Worth commits suicide by jumping from George Washington Bridge in the winter of 1946; Baldwin is deeply upset and later uses the incident in *Another Country*. Baldwin begins regularly writing reviews for *The Nation* and *The New Leader*, and in 1948 *Commentary* publishes his essay "The Harlem Ghetto" and story "Previous Condition." Drafts novel "Ignorant Armies," which he abandons. Reads widely in French, Russian, and American literature including Balzac, Flaubert, Dostoevsky, Henry Miller, Walt Whitman, and Henry James. Wins Rosenwald fellowship to do book on Harlem in collaboration with photographer Theodore Pelatowski, whom he met through Avedon (it is never completed). Moves to Paris in November 1948. Sees Richard Wright, who moved to France in 1947, and meets Themistocles Hoetis and Asa Beneviste, friends of Wright who are planning to publish a little magazine called *Zero*, and journalist Otto Friedrich. Stays first at Hôtel de Rome then finds less expensive room at Hôtel de Verneuil, where he makes a number of friends including English socialist Mary Keen and Norwegian journalist Gidske Anderson. Meets Truman Capote, Saul Bellow, and Herbert Gold around this time. Explores the works of Henry James.

1949–50   "Everybody's Protest Novel" (*Zero*, Spring 1949, and *Partisan Review*, June 1949), attacking Stowe's *Uncle Tom's Cabin* and including criticism of Wright's *Native Son*, strains his relationship with Wright. Finds job in summer as clerk for an American lawyer. Works sporadically on his novel (later called *Go Tell It on the Mountain*), then starts another, "So Long at the Fair," about Greenwich Village, which he abandons. Continues writing essays. When clerking job ends in late September, accepts a loan from American acquaintance Frank Price as advance against the publication of his novel. Takes trip with Hoetis and Anderson in fall but becomes ill in the south of France and is hospitalized twice for treatment of inflamed gland. Reads Shakespeare and the Bible during recuperation. Back in Paris is jailed for eight days in December in connection with a friend's theft of a bedsheet; charges are dismissed (later writes of the incident in "Equal in Paris").

Falls in love with Lucien Happersberger, a young Swiss living in Paris.

1951–52   Meets Mary Painter, an economist at the American embassy, with whom he forms an enduring friendship. Low on funds, continues writing for journals but makes little progress on novel. "Many Thousands Gone" (*Partisan Review*, Nov.–Dec. 1951), an explicit attack on Wright, leads to painful break between the writers. Spends three months in winter of 1951–52 with Happersberger at his family's cottage in Loèche-les-Bains in the Bernese Alps, where he completes *Go Tell It on the Mountain*. When Knopf expresses interest in the novel, borrows money from Marlon Brando and sails to New York in June. Receives $250 advance from Knopf and another $750 when revised novel is accepted in July. Meets Ralph Ellison. Spends time with family and friends and begins a play, *The Amen Corner*. Back in France, becomes godfather to Luc James Happersberger, son of Lucien and Suzy Happersberger, who were married earlier in the year. Writes essay "Stranger in the Village," based on stay in Loèche-les-Bains (*Harper's Magazine*, Oct. 1953).

1953   Completes draft of *The Amen Corner*. *Go Tell It on the Mountain* is published by Knopf in May; receives congratulatory letter from Langston Hughes, with laudatory reviews enclosed. Knopf declines to publish play but requests another novel. Spends time with entertainers including Gordon Heath, Bernard Hassell, Bobby Short, Inez Cavanaugh, and meets Maya Angelou around this time. Sees writers including Chester Himes, Gardner Smith, and Frank Yerby. Beauford Delaney moves to France in late summer and settles in Clamart, outside of Paris, where Baldwin sees him often. Goes to Les Quatre-Chemins, near Grasse, for Christmas and remains until March 1954; works on new novel that becomes *Giovanni's Room*.

1954–55   Wins Guggenheim fellowship and returns to New York in June 1954. Agrees to prepare a collection of his essays and reviews at the request of Sol Stein, now an editor at Beacon Press. Works on play, novel, and essays at MacDowell Colony in Peterboro, New Hampshire, and in 1955 at Yaddo in Saratoga Springs, New York. Lucien Happersberger arrives for a visit. Further revises *The Amen Corner* during rehearsals at Howard University, where it is staged by Owen Dodson's Howard Players in May 1955. Meets E. Franklin Frazier and Sterling Brown. Returns to Europe in summer. *Giovanni's Room*, which was rejected by Knopf and several other publishers earlier in 1955, is accepted by Dial Press in New York and Michael Joseph in London. *Notes of a Native Son* (11 essays) published by Beacon in late 1955.

1956   Accepts National Institute of Arts and Letters Award and *Partisan Review* fellowship. At request of editor Philip Rahv of *Partisan Review*, writes "Faulkner and Desegregation." Meets and begins friendship with Norman and Adele Mailer. Covers First Conference of Negro-African Writers and Artists; held at the Sorbonne in September, it is sponsored by *Présence Africaine*, a journal of the Négritude movement, and attended by delegates from Africa, the United States, and the Caribbean. Travels to Corsica where he writes article on the conference ("Princes and Powers," *Encounter*, Jan. 1957) and works on new novel, *Another Country*. *Giovanni's Room*, published by Dial in fall, goes into second printing in six weeks.

1957–58   "Sonny's Blues" appears in *Partisan Review*, summer 1957. Sails to New York in July and in September makes first trip to the Deep South on assignment for *Partisan Review* and *Harper's Magazine*. Interviews children who are integrating public schools in Charlotte, North Carolina, and sees Martin Luther King Jr. in Atlanta, Georgia. Travels through Alabama visiting Birmingham (where he meets the Rev. Fred Shuttlesworth), Little Rock, Tuskeegee, and Montgomery (meets Coretta Scott King), and Nashville, Tennessee. Back in New York for casting of Lee Strasberg's Actors Studio workshop production of *Giovanni's Room*, meets Lorraine Hansberry, Rip Torn, and Engin Cezzar, a young Turkish actor cast as Giovanni. At MacDowell Colony, writes essay on southern trip and works on adaptation of novel (staged in May 1958). Through old friend Sam Floyd, leases New York apartment at 81 Horatio Street. Accepts Elia Kazan's invitation to learn more about theater by apprenticing on his productions of Archibald MacLeish's *JB* and Tennessee Williams' *Sweet Bird of Youth*. Returns to Paris for summer of 1958.

1959   Awarded two-year Ford Foundation grant to complete
            Another Country. Hires William "Tony" Maynard as a pri-
            vate secretary. Travels to Sweden to interview film director
            Ingmar Bergman in October. Back in Paris, meets Jean
            Genet and is impressed by his play *Les Nègres* (*The Blacks*).
            "A Letter from the South: Nobody Knows My Name"
            published in *Partisan Review.*

1960   Travels in May to Tallahassee, Florida, to cover sit-in
            movement; meets members of the Congress of Racial
            Equality (CORE), and interviews students at Florida Ag-
            ricultural and Mechanical University, a historically black
            school ("They Can't Turn Back," *Mademoiselle*, Aug.
            1960). In Paris for summer, works on *Another Country*
            and second essay collection, *Nobody Knows My Name.*
            Spends time with William and Rose Styron and moves in
            late fall into studio at their home in Connecticut (uses it
            as his base through summer of 1961). Also sees James and
            Gloria Jones. Speaks at *Esquire Magazine* symposium on
            the writer in America held in San Francisco in October;
            spends time with John Cheever and Philip Roth. After
            sudden death of Richard Wright on November 28, returns
            to France to do research for essays on him (collected in
            Nobody Knows My Name as "Alas, Poor Richard").

1961   Second essay collection, *Nobody Knows My Name: More
            Notes of a Native Son*, published by Dial in summer to
            excellent reviews. Gives speeches, including address to
            CORE rally in Washington, D.C., in June, and makes ra-
            dio and television appearances. Meets Black Muslim lead-
            ers Malcolm X and Elijah Muhammad. Visits Israel and
            Istanbul, Turkey, where he sees family of Engin Cezzar
            and meets David Leeming (will stay in Istanbul often in
            following years). Completes *Another Country* in Decem-
            ber. Spends Christmas in Paris with Mary Painter, then
            goes to Loèche-les-Bains for filming of "Stranger in the
            Village" by Swiss television.

1962   Attends White House dinner honoring American Nobel
            laureates in April. Begins friendship with Katherine Anne
            Porter. *Another Country*, published by Dial in June to
            mixed reviews, becomes a national bestseller. Travels to
            Africa in July with sister Gloria, who works as his assistant.

Visits Dakar, Senegal; Conakry, Guinea; and Freetown, Sierra Leone. "Letter from a Region in My Mind," published in *The New Yorker* November 17, receives wide attention (essay is printed as "Down at the Cross" in *The Fire Next Time*).

1963   Undertakes lecture tour for CORE. In Jackson, Mississippi, meets James Meredith, the first African American student at the University of Mississippi, and Medgar Evers, state field secretary for the National Association for the Advancement of Colored People (NAACP); accompanies Evers on investigation of a reported lynching. Travels through the South giving talks, often held in churches. *The Fire Next Time*, collecting two essays, published by Dial in January to wide acclaim. Makes television and radio appearances, gives numerous interviews. Wins George Polk Memorial Award for outstanding magazine journalism in April and is subject of *Time* cover story on May 17. Continues lecture tour in New York and California, where he sees half-brother Samuel Baldwin for first time in 30 years. Photo-story on CORE tour appears in *Life* on May 24. Wires Attorney General Robert F. Kennedy on May 12 to protest police assaults on peaceful civil rights demonstrators in Birmingham, Alabama, and blames the violence in part on inaction by President John F. Kennedy. Meets with Robert Kennedy at his home in McLean, Virginia, on May 23. Brings a group of civil rights leaders and entertainers, including freedom rider Jerome Smith, Dr. Kenneth Clark, attorney Clarence B. Jones, Edwin C. Berry of the Chicago Urban League, Lorraine Hansberry, Harry Belafonte, Lena Horne, Rip Torn, and Henry Morgenthau, to meeting with Robert Kennedy and Burke Marshall, head of the Justice Department's Civil Rights Division, held at Kennedy's New York City apartment on May 24. Works on new play, *Blues for Mr. Charlie*, dedicating it to Medgar Evers, who was assassinated in Jackson on June 12, and plans a collaborative book project with Richard Avedon. Participates in March on Washington, a major demonstration for civil rights, in August. Along with brother David assists James Forman and Student Non-Violent Coordinating Committee (SNCC) in drive to register black voters in Selma, Alabama, in October. As part of a group that also includes Thurgood Marshall,

Harry Belafonte, and Sidney Poitier, goes to Nairobi in December for celebration of Kenya's independence.

1964–65   Elected to National Institute of Arts and Letters in February 1964. *Blues for Mr. Charlie*, directed by Burgess Meredith and starring Pat Hingle, Al Freeman Jr., Diana Sands, and Rip Torn, runs at ANTA Theater in New York City from April 23 to August 29, 1964. The play is published by Dial and *Nothing Personal*, with photographs by Richard Avedon, by Atheneum in 1964. In Cambridge Union Society debate at Cambridge University on February 18, 1965, successfully supports motion that "the American dream is at the expense of the American Negro"; opposition is led by William F. Buckley Jr. Malcolm X is assassinated February 21, 1965, in New York City. Participates in civil rights march from Selma to Montgomery, Alabama, led by Martin Luther King Jr. in late March. Speaking engagements include the New School for Social Research and Harvard University. Prepares story collection *Going To Meet the Man* (published by Dial in December). *The Amen Corner* opens April 16 at the Barrymore Theater in New York (runs for 48 performances) and another production of it tours in Europe and Israel. Spends holiday season in Istanbul with friends.

1966–67   Writes essays "Negroes Are Anti-Semitic Because They're Anti-White" and "Anti-Semitism and Black Power." Meets Eldridge Cleaver and Huey Newton. Agrees to write scenario for screen adaptation of *The Autobiography of Malcolm X* for producer Marvin Worth at Columbia Pictures.

1968–69   Visits Tony Maynard in Hamburg, Germany, where he is awaiting extradition to the United States on charges of murder (works on his behalf over several years; charges against Maynard are dismissed in 1974). Becomes a target of criticism by radical activists and is attacked by Eldridge Cleaver in *Soul on Ice*. Appears before congressional subcommittee with Betty Shabazz to propose establishment of a national commission on black history and culture. Works on *Malcolm X* script in Hollywood. Sees Martin Luther King Jr. and Andrew Young in Los Angeles in March during their fundraising drive for Poor People's

Campaign. Play *The Amen Corner* and novel *Tell Me How Long the Train's Been Gone* published by Dial. Martin Luther King Jr. is assassinated on April 4, 1968, in Memphis; Baldwin attends funeral April 9 in Atlanta. Has disputes with Columbia executives over *Malcolm X* script, and they assign screenwriter Arnold Perl to work with him. Addresses assembly of the World Council of Churches in Uppsala, Sweden, on "White Racism or World Community" in July. Writes article "The Price May Be Too High" (*The New York Times Magazine*, Feb. 2, 1969) on the problems of a black writer in a world controlled by whites. Quits the Columbia project in spring; continues working on his own script. In Istanbul directs Turkish stage production of John Herbert's *Fortune and Men's Eyes*.

1970–71   Ill with hepatitis for several weeks. Sedat Pakay makes short documentary film, *James Baldwin from Another Place*, in Istanbul in May 1970. Visits New York to record a conversation with Margaret Mead in August (transcription is published by Lippincott in 1971 as *A Rap on Race*). Becomes ill again and is hospitalized in Paris in October 1970; on advice of Mary Painter, goes to St. Paul-de-Vence, near Nice, to recuperate. Writes "An Open Letter to My Sister, Miss Angela Davis" (*New York Review of Books*, Jan. 7, 1971) after Davis is indicted for kidnapping and murder in connection with the August 1970 shootings at the San Rafael, California, courthouse (she is acquitted in 1972). Buys a large house on 10 acres of land in St. Paul-de-Vence. Hires Bernard Hassell to oversee the estate. Often sees actors Yves Montand and Simone Signoret and has numerous guests. Appears with poet Nikki Giovanni on Ellis Haizlipp's television program *Soul* (transcription is published by Lippincott as *A Dialogue* in 1973).

1972–74   *No Name in the Street* and *One Day When I Was Lost: A Scenario Based on "The Autobiography of Malcolm X"* published by Dial in 1972. Writes screenplay "The Inheritance" (never produced). Helps care for Beauford Delaney, whose mental faculties are failing; writes catalog tribute for major retrospective exhibition of his work in Paris. Becomes close to artist Yoran Cazac. Interviewed in August 1973, along with Josephine Baker, by Henry Louis Gates Jr., at this time a correspondent for *Time* magazine (editor declines to print Gates' story, calls Baldwin "passé"). Novel *If Beale Street Could Talk*, inspired by life of Tony Maynard, published by Dial in 1974. Awarded centennial medal for the "artist as prophet" from Cathedral of St. John the Divine in New York City in March 1974. Celebrates 50th birthday with family and friends in St. Paul-de-Vence.

1975–77 Works on long essay on movies, *The Devil Finds Work*, and children's book, *Little Man, Little Man: A Story of Childhood*, with illustrations by Yoran Cazac; both are published by Dial in 1976. Contributes to American bicentennial symposium *The Nature of a Humane Society* in October 1976; other participants include Toni Morrison, Archibald Cox, Arthur Schlesinger, and Coretta Scott King. Continues publishing in periodicals and gives many interviews.

1978 Teaches spring course in contemporary literature at Bowling Green College in Ohio, first long stay in the United States since 1969 (will return to teach at the college for fall semesters of 1979 and 1981). Awarded Martin Luther King Memorial Medal for "lifelong dedication to humanitarian ideals" at City College of New York. Vacations on Cape Cod before returning to France.

1979–80 Completes novel *Just Above My Head* (published in fall 1979 by Dial). Goes into seclusion after learning of Beauford Delaney's death in Paris on March 26, 1979. Teaches class at University of California, Berkeley, in spring, and speaks at Los Angeles, Santa Barbara, and San Diego campuses; meets Thomas A. Dorsey and sees Angela Davis. Begins writing and lecturing on "Black English." In France in summer writes "Open Letter to the Born Again" (*The Nation*, Sept. 29, 1979) after Andrew Young resigns as U.S. ambassador to the United Nations following disclosure of his unauthorized meetings with representatives of the Palestine Liberation Organization. Gives talks at Youngstown and Wayne state universities in February 1980. Travels to the University of Florida in Gainesville for meeting of African Literature Association, where he participates in conversation on the "African Aesthetic" with Nigerian writer Chinua Achebe. Travels through South accompanied by Dick Fontaine and Pat Hartley, who make a television documentary of his trip (*I Heard It Through the Grapevine*, released in 1982).

1981–82   Spends several weeks in Atlanta researching series of murders of black children for essay "The Evidence of Things Not Seen" (*Playboy*, Dec. 1981).

1983–84   *Jimmy's Blues: Selected Poems* published by Michael Joseph in 1983 (also published in New York by St. Martin's Press in 1985). Begins teaching in the Afro-American studies department at University of Massachusetts, Amherst, in fall 1983 (later teaches alternate semesters to make time for writing and speaking engagements). Hospitalized in Boston for exhaustion in late summer of 1984. Works on play "The Welcome Table." Writes "Freaks and the American Ideal of Manhood" (*Playboy*, Jan. 1985).

1985–86   *Go Tell It on the Mountain* dramatized on public television's *American Playhouse* in January 1985. *The Evidence of Things Not Seen* (expanded version of his 1981 essay) published by Holt, Rinehart and Winston and *The Price of the Ticket: Collected Non-Fiction, 1948–1985* by St. Martin's Press in 1985. Completes last year of teaching in June 1986. Travels to France where he is made an officer of the Legion of Honor in ceremony presided over by President François Mitterand on June 19. Travels with brother David in October to the Soviet Union for international conference. Suffers from weakness and persistent sore throat. Goes to London for production of *The Amen Corner* (it runs for seven months).

1987   Returns to St. Paul-de-Vence and undergoes tests that reveal cancer of the esophagus. Treatments including surgery on April 25 make it possible to eat. Feels well until middle of summer and works on "The Welcome Table" and other projects. As condition worsens, is cared for by brother David, aided by visiting relatives and friends. Enjoys seeing guests and speaks regularly by phone with mother. Interviewed by Quincy Troupe in November and later that month insists on hosting a Thanksgiving dinner party, although he is too weak to walk to table. Dies at home on December 1 with David, Happersberger, and Hassell at bedside. After viewings in St. Paul-de-Vence and Harlem and funeral service at Episcopal Cathedral of St. John the Divine, with eulogists including Toni Morrison, Maya Angelou, and Amiri Baraka, buried December 8 in Ferncliff Cemetery, Hartsdale, New York.

Note on the Texts

This volume of essays by James Baldwin presents the texts of *Notes of a Native Son* (1955), *Nobody Knows My Name: More Notes of a Native Son* (1961), *The Fire Next Time* (1963), *No Name in the Street* (1972), and *The Devil Finds Work* (1976), followed by a selection of 36 essays published between 1948 and 1985.

Most of Baldwin's earliest published writings were reviews and essays that appeared in publications such as *Commentary*, *The Nation*, *The New Leader*, and the Paris-based journal *Zero*. In 1954, Sol Stein, an editor at Beacon Press, proposed that Baldwin collect these reviews and articles in book form. In preparing the collection Baldwin revised and retitled some of the essays, and arranged the contents along thematic lines. He also chose to use "Autobiographical Notes," written in late 1952, as a preface. The essays in *Notes of a Native Son* originally appeared as follows: "Everybody's Protest Novel," *Zero*, Spring 1949; "Many Thousands Gone," *Partisan Review*, November–December 1951; "Carmen Jones: The Dark Is Light Enough," *Commentary*, January 1955, with the title "Life Straight in De Eye"; "The Harlem Ghetto," *Commentary*, February 1948; "Journey to Atlanta," *The New Leader*, October 9, 1948; "Notes of a Native Son," *Harper's*, November 1955, with the title "Me and My House"; "Encounter on the Seine: Black Meets Brown," *The Reporter*, June 6, 1950, with the title "The Negro in Paris"; "A Question of Identity," *Partisan Review*, July–August 1954; "Equal in Paris," *Commentary*, March 1955; "Stranger in the Village," *Harper's*, October 1953. The book was published by Beacon Press in late 1955. The present volume prints the text of the first 1955 Beacon printing.

Nobody Knows My Name, Baldwin's second collection of essays, was published by Dial Press in July 1961. Like *Notes of a Native Son*, it includes revised versions of several of the previously published essays. "The Discovery of What It Means to Be an American" originally appeared in *The New York Times Book Review*, January 25, 1959; "Princes and Powers" in *Encounter*, January 1957; "Fifth Avenue, Uptown: A Letter from Harlem" in *Esquire*, July 1960; "East River, Downtown: Postscript to a Letter from Harlem" in *The New York Times Magazine*, March 12, 1961, with the title "A Negro Assays the Negro Mood"; "A Fly in Buttermilk" in *Harper's*, October 1958, with the title "The Hard Kind of Courage"; "Nobody Knows My Name: A Letter from the South" in *Partisan Review*, Winter 1959; "Faulkner and Desegregation" in *Partisan Review*, Fall 1956. "In

Search of a Majority" was adapted from an address delivered at Kal-amazoo College, February 1960, and first appeared in print in *Nobody Knows My Name*. "The Male Prison" originally appeared in *The New Leader*, December 13, 1954, with the title "Gide as Husband and Homosexual." "Notes for a Hypothetical Novel" was adapted from an address delivered at an *Esquire* magazine symposium on "Writing in America Today" held at San Francisco State College, October 22–24, 1960, and appeared in print for the first time in *Nobody Knows My Name*. "The Northern Protestant" was originally published in *Esquire*, April 1960, with the title "The Precarious Vogue of Ingmar Bergman." Two of the three sections of "Alas, Poor Richard" originally appeared in periodical form: "Eight Men" in *Reporter*, March 16, 1961, with the title "The Survival of Richard Wright," and "The Exile" in *Encounter*, April 1961, with the title "Richard Wright" (a French translation of "Richard Wright" appeared in *Preuves*, Feb-ruary 1961, entitled "Richard Wright, tel que je l'ai connu"). The concluding section, "Alas, Poor Richard," was published for the first time in *Nobody Knows My Name*. "The Black Boy Looks at the White Boy" originally appeared in *Esquire*, May 1961. The present volume prints the text of the first 1961 printing of *Nobody Knows My Name*.

The Fire Next Time collected two previously published essays: "Down at the Cross," which appeared in *The New Yorker*, November 17, 1962, under the title "Letter from a Region in My Mind," and attracted wide attention, and "A Letter to My Nephew," which ap-peared in *The Progressive*, December 1962. *The Fire Next Time* was published by Dial Press in early 1963. This volume prints the text of the first 1963 printing.

No Name in the Street was written between 1969 and 1972, when Baldwin was living in Istanbul and St. Paul-de-Vence, France, and was published by Dial Press in May 1972. The text printed here is that of the first 1972 printing. *The Devil Finds Work* was written in 1974 and 1975, while Baldwin was living in France. He finished the manuscript on July 29, 1975, and the book was published early in 1976 by Dial Press. The text printed here is that of the first 1976 printing.

The present volume offers a selection of 36 essays in a section titled "Other Essays." The texts printed here are taken from their original publication in periodicals or books. (Twenty-five of these essays, in-dicated by * below, were collected in *The Price of the Ticket*, published in 1985, and one was published for the first time as the introduction to that volume.) The following list gives the source of each text.

"Smaller Than Life." *The Nation*, July 19, 1947.

"History as Nightmare." *The New Leader*, October 25, 1947.

"The Image of the Negro." *Commentary*, April 1948.

*"Lockridge: 'The American Myth.' " *The New Leader*, April 10, 1948.
"Preservation of Innocence." *Zero*, Summer 1949.
"The Negro at Home and Abroad." *Reporter*, November 27, 1951.
*"The Crusade of Indignation." *The Nation*, July 7, 1956.
"Sermons and Blues," *The New York Times Book Review*, March 29, 1959.
*"On Catfish Row: *Porgy and Bess* in the Movies." *Commentary*, September 1959.
*"They Can't Turn Back." *Mademoiselle*, August 1960.
*"The Dangerous Road Before Martin Luther King." *Harper's*, February 1961.
*"The New Lost Generation." *Esquire*, July 1961.
*"The Creative Process." From The National Culture Center, *Creative America* (New York: Ridge Press, 1962).
*"Color." *Esquire*, December 1962.
*"A Talk to Teachers." *Saturday Review*, December 21, 1963. Originally an address delivered on October 16, 1963, in New York City.
" 'This Nettle, Danger . . .'." *Show*, February 1964.
*Text of *Nothing Personal*. New York: Atheneum, 1964.
*"Words of a Native Son." *Playboy*, December 1964.
*"The American Dream and the American Negro." *The New York Times Magazine*, March 7, 1965. Based on remarks by Baldwin in a debate held at Cambridge University, February 18, 1965.
"On the Painter Beauford Delaney." *Transition* 4:18 (1965).
*"The White Man's Guilt." *Ebony*, August 1965.
*"A Report from Occupied Territory." *The Nation*, July 11, 1966.
*"Negroes Are Anti-Semitic Because They're Anti-White." *The New York Times Magazine*, April 9, 1967.
*"White Racism or World Community?" Transcript of an address delivered to the fourth international assembly of the World Council of Churches, Uppsala, Sweden, July 7, 1968, that appeared in *Ecumenical Review*, October 1968.
*"Sweet Lorraine." *Esquire*, November 1969.
*"How One Black Man Came To Be an American: A Review of Roots." *The New York Times Book Review*, September 26, 1976.
*"An Open Letter to Mr. Carter." *The New York Times*, January 23, 1977.
"Last of the Great Masters," *The New York Times Book Review*, October 16, 1977.
*"Every Good-bye Ain't Gone." *New York*, December 19, 1977.
*"If Black English Isn't a Language, Then Tell Me, What Is?" *The New York Times*, July 29, 1979.
*"Open Letter to the Born Again." *The Nation*, September 29, 1979.
*"Dark Days." *Esquire*, October 1980.
*"Notes on the House of Bondage." *The Nation*, November 1, 1980.
"Introduction to *Notes of a Native Son*." Boston: Beacon Press, 1984.
*"Freaks and the American Ideal of Manhood." *Playboy*, January 1985. (Titled "Here Be Dragons" in *The Price of the Ticket*.)

*"The Price of the Ticket." Introduction to *The Price of the Ticket: Collected Nonfiction 1948–1985* (New York: St. Martin's, 1985).

This volume presents the texts of the original printings chosen for inclusion here, but it does not attempt to reproduce features of their typographic design, such as display capitalization of chapter openings. The texts are printed without change, except for the correction of typographical errors. Spelling, punctuation, and capitalization are often expressive features, and they are not altered, even when inconsistent or irregular. Except for clearly typographical errors, the spelling and usage of foreign words and phrases are left as they appear in the original texts. The following is a list of typographical errors corrected, cited by page and line number: 5.31, Saxon; 148.17, strucure; 158.17, to with; 173.10, Jr.; 205.7, takes; 206.8, Citizen's; 210.37, Citizen's; 233.10, through out; 243.1, affection; 251.17, Hime's; 255.40, magazine,; 265.6–7, anemicly; 270.8, things; 281.6–7, condescenion; 294.38, *though*; 303.10, them; 309.16, favor,; 320.36, sit-in-movement; 324.23, said.; 329.9, realiz; 330.20. soicety; 345.24, war); 371.38, indeed:; 373.17–18, eveything; 377.36, through; 393.13, reverbating; 410.1, those which; 421.32, motion; 429.11, fortune,; 435.21, wordly; 464.24, take is; 472.37, undefineable; 479.6, though; 508.29, mysogynistic; 548.14, interrrogation; 551.14, *Ché!*; 551.14–15, *Lawrence of Arabia*; 553.27, according the; 556.5, Billy; 579.8, protagonists'; 580.17, girls'; 580.28, opressed; 580.36–37, observe, sentials...in and; 580.36–37, is its; 589.27, flows; 590.8, has,; 590.38, dangerous; 592.21, acutally; 592.32, him; has; 597.13, It; 598.16, tendancy; 598.27, exhausting [##] improbable; 599.3, many,; 599.7, Gan; 599.15, all).; 599.22, reknowned; 599.23, denoucements; 599.25, bookselves; 607.29, *interpretation*; 607.30, Guerin's).; 607.33, does).; 692.11, sensous; 720.29–30, everyday; 740.16, everyone; 752.34, headless; 780.17, lving; 831.33, where; 838.33–34, anymore.

Notes

In the notes below, the reference numbers denote page and line of this volume (the line count includes headings). No note is made for material included in standard desk-reference books such as Webster's *Collegiate*, *Biographical*, and *Geographical* dictionaries. Biblical references are keyed to the King James Version. Quotations from Shakespeare are keyed to *The Riverside Shakespeare*, ed. G. Blakemore Evans (Boston: Houghton Mifflin, 1974). Footnotes in the text were in the originals. For further background and references to other studies, see *Conversations with James Baldwin* (Jackson: University Press of Mississippi, 1989), ed. Fred L. Stanley and Louis H. Pratt; Fern Marja Eckmann, *The Furious Passage of James Baldwin* (New York: M. Evans & Co., Inc., 1966); David Leeming, *James Baldwin* (New York: Alfred A. Knopf, 1994); Fred L. Stanley and Nancy V. Stanley, *James Baldwin: A Reference Guide* (Boston: G. K. Hall & Co., 1980); W. J. Weatherby, *James Baldwin: Artist on Fire* (New York: Donald I. Fine, Inc., 1989).

NOTES OF A NATIVE SON

7.13–15   ("You . . . curse.")]   Shakespeare, *The Tempest*, I.ii.263–64.

16.10–11   *The Best . . . Lives*]   William Wyler's 1946 adaptation of Mac-Kinley Kantor's *Glory for Me*, about veterans resuming civilian life.

19.1   *Many . . . Gone*]   Title of an emancipation song that begins: "No more auction block for me, / No more, no more, / No more auction block for me: / Many thousands gone."

23.34–36   *Kingsblood . . . Go*]   For Baldwin's discussions of *Kingsblood Royal* and *If He Hollers Let Him Go*, see pages 582 and 579, respectively, in this volume.

25.6   WPA]   The Works Progress Administration, a federal agency created under the Emergency Relief Appropriation Act of 1935 to provide public jobs for the unemployed; it was severely cut back in 1937 and 1939 and dissolved in 1943.

33.35–36   Lucifer . . . heaven.]   Cf. Milton, *Paradise Lost* (1667), I.269.

37.1–2   *Stormy . . . Sky*]   *Stormy Weather* (1943), based on the career of dancer Bill "Bojangles" Robinson, with stars including Robinson, Lena Horne, Fats Waller, Ada Brown, Cab Calloway, and *Cabin in the Sky* (1943) about a gambler reformed by a dream in which God and Satan battle over his soul, with stars including Eddie "Rochester" Anderson, Ethel Waters, Lena Horne, and Louis Armstrong.

44.36   *PM*]   New York City illustrated tabloid newspaper (1940–48) that carried no advertising and was formatted as a news magazine.

45.24   *Watch . . . Rhine*]   Lillian Hellman's play about German refugees hounded in the U.S. by Nazis; it was filmed in 1943.

45.32–39   George S. Schuyler . . . daughter]   African American journalist, author, and editor (1895–1977), and his daughter, concert pianist and composer Philippa Duke Schuyler (1932–69).

57.17–18   Sister Rosetta Tharpe]   Tharpe sang with Lucky Millinder's big band in the 1940s.

97.11   Arletty]   Stage name of Arlette-Léonie Bathia, famous for her roles in Cocteau's adaptation of *A Streetcar Named Desire* (1949) and in films of Marcel Carné.

101.23–24   *tricoteuse . . . ax*]   *Tricoteuse*: knitter (cf. Madame Defarge knitting a stitch for every head that falls at the guillotine in Dickens' *A Tale of Two Cities*).

104.29   *les étudiants*]   Students.

108.7   *Plus tard.*]   Later.

108.21   *receleur*]   Receiver of stolen goods.

111.1   *l'affaire . . . lit*]   The affair of the bed sheet.

111.6   *monoprix*]   Name of a chain of discount stores.

112.30–31   *"Vous . . . extrait"*]   "Get ready. You are coming out." *Extrait* is literally translated "extracted."

117.31   *épicerie*]   Grocery.

119.36–38   Joyce . . . awaken.]   In James Joyce's *Ulysses* (1922): "History, Stephen said, is a nightmare from which I am trying to awake."

123.33   *le sale nègre*]   French: the dirty nigger.

NOBODY KNOWS MY NAME

137.5–6   It is . . . James observed]   From an 1872 letter quoted in a biographical note in Percy Lubbock's *Letters of Henry James* (Vol. 1, 1920).

141.11   Little Rock]   In defiance of a federal court desegregation order, Governor Orval Faubus in September 1957 called out the state national guard to prevent nine black students from beginning classes at the previously all-white Central High School in Little Rock, Arkansas. The students were allowed to enter the school on October 2, 1957, after President Dwight D. Eisenhower dispatched U.S. paratroopers to the city and federalized the Arkansas national guard.

143.33–34   Leopold Senghor] Senghor was a leader of the *Nègritude* movement with Aimé Césaire and Guinean poet Léon Dumas and a founder of the magazine *Présence Africaine* along with Césaire and Alioune Diop; Richard Wright assisted in these undertakings. Senghor was later president of Senegal, 1960–80.

144.5   Bandung] In Indonesia, site in April 1955 of the first conference of nonaligned nations.

144.39–40   *accablé des complexes*] Ridden with complexes.

147.6   John Davis] John A. Davis was director of the American Information Committee on Race and Caste.

147.17–18   Cook . . . Ivy] Cook taught at Howard University and Fontaine at the University of Pennsylvania, Bond was president of Lincoln University, and Ivy was the editor of *The Crisis*, the journal of the National Association for the Advancement of Colored People.

157.14   *et dépassement*] And surpassing.

160.19   George Lamming] Barbadian novelist and poet who had immigrated to England, Lamming was known especially for autobiographical works, including *In the Castle of My Skin* (1953).

161.14–15   Amos Tutuola] Nigerian author of prose epics and fantastic stories including *The Palm-Wine Drinkard and His Dead Palm-Wine Tapster in the Dead's Town* (1952).

162.7   Cheik Anta Diop] Senegalese historian; among his books are *Black Africa* (1960) and *The African Origin of Civilization* (1967).

167.20–21   *au lieu . . . autres.*] Instead of always being defined by others.

180.7–8   death . . . Lumumba] The Kasavubu government of the Republic of the Congo announced on February 13, 1961, that former prime minister Patrice Lumumba had been killed while attempting to flee from Katanga, where he had been held since January 1961. A United Nations investigation later concluded that Lumumba had been murdered by his Congolese opponents.

187.30–31   day-to-day . . . Scottsboro case] On March 25, 1931, nine black youths, aged 13 to 20, were accused of having raped two young white women on a freight train in northern Alabama. They were tried in Scottsboro, Alabama, beginning on April 6, 1931, and on April 9 eight of the defendants were sentenced to death (the case of the 13-year-old resulted in a mistrial when a jury deadlocked over whether to impose the death penalty). The Communist party of the United States immediately denounced the outcome as a legal lynching and made the case the focus of a nationwide propaganda campaign, while engaging in a fierce and eventually successful struggle with the NAACP over which organization would represent the defendants on appeal. In 1932 the U.S. Supreme Court overturned the verdicts on the grounds that the inadequate counsel provided to the accused at their trial violated their right to due process under the Fourteenth Amendment. Two defendants were re-tried and again sentenced to death in 1933, despite the recantation by one of the alleged victims of her previous testimony (the trials of the remaining de-fendants were postponed pending the appeal of the new conviction). The U.S. Supreme Court overturned one of the new convictions in 1935, ruling that the systematic exclusion of blacks from grand and trial jury duty violated the right to equal protection of the law under the Fourteenth Amendment. All of the defendants were then reindicted by Alabama authorities. Four of the defen-dants were retried and convicted between January 1936 and July 1937; one was sentenced to death (commuted in 1938 to life imprisonment), one to 99 years in prison, and two to 75-year terms. A fifth defendant received 20 years for assaulting a deputy while in custody, and charges against the remaining four were dropped in July 1937. Four of the imprisoned men were paroled between 1943 and 1950; a fifth escaped in 1948 to Michigan, where the governor refused to have him extradited to Alabama.

198.32   Angelo Herndon]   A labor organizer affiliated with the Commu-nist party who led a march in Georgia to protest racial discrimination, Hern-don was convicted in 1933 of inciting insurrection and sentenced to 20 years in prison under an antebellum law. The U.S. Supreme Court reversed his conviction in 1937.

198.37   Willie McGhee, Emmett Till]   Willie McGee was convicted in 1949 of raping Willamette Hawkins, a white woman, and sentenced to death. The U.S. Supreme Court refused to review McGee's case and despite international protests he was electrocuted in Laurel, Mississippi, on May 8, 1951. Emmett Till, a 14-year-old from Chicago, in August 1955 was taken at gunpoint from the home of relatives near Money, Mississippi, and later shot to death. J. W. Milam and Roy Bryant, the husband of a woman whom Till allegedly insulted, were acquitted of the crime by an all-white jury. Two months later they ex-plained their motives for committing the murder to Alabama journalist William Huie, who paid them $4,000 for the story (*Look*, Jan. 24, 1956).

202.34   Black Monday]   In *Brown* v. *Board of Education* (of Topeka, Kan-sas), decided on Monday, May 17, 1954, the Supreme Court unanimously ruled that segregation in public schools violated the equal protection clause of the Fourteenth Amendment and that the doctrine of "separate but equal" set forth in the *Plessy* v. *Ferguson* railway segregation case (1896) had "no place" in pubic education.

204.30   "the oldest have borne most."]   *King Lear*, V.iii.326.

209.1   *Faulkner and Desegregation*]   Written in response to remarks at-tributed to Faulkner in an interview with Russell Howe published in *The Re-porter*, March 22, 1956, and two pieces written by Faulkner that urged voluntary integration in the South to prevent northern intervention ("Letter to the Editor," *Life*, March 26, 1956, and "On Fear: The South in Labor," *Harper's*, June 1956).

211.31–32   interview . . . *Reporter*]   Alarmed by rising tensions over court-ordered integration at the University of Alabama, Faulkner drank heavily during the interview. He later repudiated the published piece, which he said included "statements which no sober man would make, nor it seems to me, any sane man believe."

225.7–9   Two Italians . . . Scottsboro case]   Nicola Sacco and Bartolomeo Vanzetti, anarchist Italian immigrants convicted of murder and armed robbery in 1920 and executed in 1927 despite international protests that their guilt had not been proven. For the Scottsboro case, see note 187.30–31.

240.24   *The Face*]   *Ansiktet* (*The Face*; 1958) was released in the United States as *The Magician* (see page 240.2).

263.17   the ECA]   The Economic Cooperation Administration, established by President Harry Truman in April 1948 to administer the European Recovery Program (the Marshall Plan). One of its objectives was to contain the spread of communism.

277.15   Suzuki rhythm]   Cf. Suzuki Daisetsu (1870–1966), a major interpreter of Zen Buddhism in the West.

278.21–31   At lilac . . . chairs.]   *On the Road* (1957), Pt. 3, Chap. 1.

279.1–4   Backwater . . . mo.']   "Backwater Blues," recorded 1927 by Bessie Smith (1895–1937).

282.36–37   piece . . . in *Esquire*]   "Superman Comes to the Supermart" (Nov. 1960).

THE FIRE NEXT TIME

287.2–3   *"God . . . time!"*]   From the spiritual "Got a Home in That Rock."

294.37–39   *The very . . . off.*]   In the spiritual that begins "You got a right, / I got a right, / We all got a right / To the tree of life."

296.3–10   Take up . . . you.]   In *The White Man's Burden* (1899).

308.37   "Elmer Gantry"]   Sinclair Lewis' novel (1927) about religious hypocrisy.

333.35   Birchites]   Members of the ultra-right-wing John Birch Society, founded 1958 by candy manufacturer Robert Welch and his business associates.

345.29–31   "The problem . . . line."]   *The Souls of Black Folk* (1903), "The Forethought."

NO NAME IN THE STREET

358.39   Leonard Lyons]   Author of the syndicated Broadway column "The Lyons Den," 1934–74.

368.4   *coûte que coûte*]   Come what may; cost what it will.

370.29   *Mission To Moscow*]   Pro-Soviet film (1943) based on the book (1941) by Joseph Davies.

373.37   *The Wages of Fear*]   *Le Salaire de la Peur* (1953), Henri-Georges Clouzot's film of Georges Arnaud's novel, starring Yves Montand, about drivers paid by a Central American oilfield manager to transport nitroglycerin over dangerous terrain.

380.31   Faulkner's declared intention]   See note 211.31–32.

383.7   covering, for *Encounter*]   "Princes and Powers" (pp. 143–69 in this volume).

387.17–18   Mr. and Mrs. Bates]   L. C. Bates, editor of the *Arkansas State Press*, a black newspaper, and Daisy Bates, president of the Arkansas chapter of the NAACP.

389.13–14   Dante's . . . *many*.]   *Inferno*, III.55–57.

393.32   Reverend Shuttlesworth]   Baptist minister and civil rights activist Fred L. Shuttlesworth, first president of the Alabama Christian Movement for Human Rights and a founder with Martin Luther King Jr. of the Montgomery Improvement Association (MIA) for the organization of a boycott against segregated buses in Montgomery, Alabama. The MIA was succeeded in 1957 by the Southern Christian Leadership Conference.

408.14–15   Robert Williams . . . East.]   A black militant, Williams fled to Cuba, and later lived in China and Africa, after being indicted in connection with the alleged kidnapping of a white couple during an outbreak of racial violence in North Carolina in 1961.

412.35   *black like me*]   In Langston Hughes' "Dream Variations" (1926; see page 615.5 in this volume).

414.21   bombing . . . school]   On September 15, 1963, a bomb exploded during Sunday school hour at the Sixteenth Street Baptist Church in Birmingham, Alabama; four girls were killed and 14 other persons wounded by the blast. The church had been a gathering place for schoolchildren participating in nonviolent civil rights demonstrations that spring.

433.19   a Stennis, a Maddox, a Wallace]   Pro-segregationsts Senator John Stennis of Mississippi, Georgia governor Lester Maddox, and Alabama governor George Wallace.

434.18   April 6]   In 1968.

436.7–8   *à la lanterne!*]   "To the lamppost!" (lynching cry during the French Revolution).

438.34   archbishop]   Patrick A. O'Boyle, archbishop of Washington, D.C., refused to give the opening invocation at the March on Washington until Student Nonviolent Coordinating Committee chairman John Lewis was persuaded to tone down what was described as the "scorched earth" language of his prepared speech.

457.16–17   Fred Hampton and Mark Clark]   Illinois Black Panther Party chairman Fred Hampton and Peoria leader Mark Clark were shot to death in a late-night police raid on Hampton's Chicago apartment December 4, 1969. Hampton was shot in the head while lying in bed.

475.13   fate . . . Maynard]   Maynard's case was reopened in March 1973 after an informant admitted that he had been coached by the New York district attorney's office to testify falsely that Maynard had confessed in prison to the murder. When Maynard's lawyers sought a fourth trial in January 1974, it was revealed that the prosecution had suppressed information about its chief witness's history of mental illness. Maynard was released on April 4, 1974, after his conviction for manslaughter was set aside due to the suppression of evidence in the previous three trials; the case was dismissed on August 23, 1974.

475.14–18   Attica . . . that.]   A five-day riot by 1,200 inmates at Attica State Correctional Institution in Attica, New York, ended on September 13, 1971, when the prison was retaken on the order of Governor Nelson Rockefeller after negotiations with the prisoners broke down. Thirty-three inmates and 10 of their hostages were killed in the action and another 80 persons wounded.

THE DEVIL FINDS WORK

491.35   Scottsboro boys]   See note 187.30–31.

492.2   Angelo Herndon's]   See note 198.32.

500.20   Bogart, *as Sam Spade*]   In John Huston's 1941 film of Dashiell Hammett's *The Maltese Falcon.*

500.30   *Ghosts*]   Henrik Ibsen's play (1881).

505.2–3   *Who . . . Fly*]   From the nursery rhyme "Who Killed Cock Robin?"

505.9   *I Shall . . . Graves*]   *J'irai cracher sur vos tombes* (1959) released in the U.S. as *I Spit on Your Graves.* The novel (1946) by French author, dramatist, songwriter, and jazz musician Boris Vian (1920–59) had been banned in France 1949.

522.23   Attica uprising]   See note 475.14–18.

524.3–4   T. S. Eliot . . . reality.] In *Murder in the Cathedral* (1935), part II, and *Four Quartets: Burnt Norton*, part I.

524.10   *Raisin in the Sun*] Lorraine Hansberry's play (1959) was directed by Lloyd Richards and the movie (Columbia Pictures, 1961) by Daniel Petrie.

533.12   Dilsey] Maid in William Faulkner's *The Sound and the Fury* (1929).

544.29   pumpkin papers] State department documents that Whittaker Chambers testified had been given to him by Alger Hiss while Chambers was a Soviet espionage agent, so-called because microfilm copies of the papers were hidden by Chambers in a hollowed-out pumpkin.

554.34–35   Little Eva] Daughter of a slaveholder in Harriet Beecher Stowe's *Uncle Tom's Cabin* (1852).

OTHER ESSAYS

581.36–37   "History . . . awaken."] See note 119.36–38.

582.36   *Gentleman's Agreement*] Laura Hobson's novel (1941) about anti-Semitism.

588.28   *Shropshire Lad*] A. E. Housman's poems (1896) addressed to or spoken by a soldier or farm boy, and mostly set in Shropshire, a "land of lost content."

590.34   Mr. Adams] J. Donald Adams, editor of *The New York Times Book Review*.

595.13–14   *And nothing . . . hence.*] Closing of Shakespeare's Sonnet 12.

598.22–23   Cain . . . recent novel] *The Butterfly* (1947).

600.6   Ward] Author of *The Snake Pit* (1946).

602.7   *Sinterklaas*] Saint Nicholas.

611.37–38   Lincoln . . . war."] On Stowe's visit to the White House in 1862, according to the recollections of her son.

637.4–5   Bandung Conference] See note 144.5.

640.7   became the law] In the Supreme Court decision in the case of *Plessy* v. *Ferguson* (see note 202.34).

641.21   Montgomery Improvement Association] See note 393.32.

666.17   ECA] See note 263.17.

684.33   Bible says somewhere] In Proverbs 29:18.

687.1   *"This Nettle, Danger . . . "*] Cf. Shakespeare, *I Henry IV*, II.iii.9–10: "out of this nettle, danger, we pluck this flower, safety."

688.17–18   "this England,"]   Shakespeare, *Richard II*, II.i.50.

692.1   *Nothing Personal*]   The book includes photographs by Richard Avedon.

711.21   the psychopathology . . . life.]   English title of Freud's *Zur Psychopathologie des Alltagslebens* (1904).

712.31–32   "A dog . . . State."]   "Auguries of Innocence," lines 8–9.

714.1–2   *The American . . . Negro*]   A slightly condensed transcript of Baldwin's argument in support of the motion "The American dream is at the expense of the American Negro" before the Cambridge Union Society of Cambridge University, February 18, 1965; William F. Buckley Jr. opposed the proposition.

720.1   *Beauford Delaney*]   Delaney, whose paintings focus on African American scenes, attended art schools in Boston and studied with Thomas Hart Benton, John Sloan, and Don Freeman. His work was exhibited at galleries, museums, and expositions in New York City, Chicago, Newark, and Paris, and collections of it are now held by major institutions including New York's Whitney Museum, the Newark Museum, and Morgan State College in Baltimore.

729.33   *derisoire*]   Derisive, mocking.

738.15   bombing of 4 little girls]   See note 414.21.

739.26   Harlem riot of 1935]   The violence of March 20–21, 1935, sparked by a rumor that a white shopkeeper had killed a black teenager, was largely directed at local stores; more than 200 were damaged.

750.14   scolded]   Perhaps a transcription error for "scorned"; cf. page 705.21 in this volume.

752.40   Stokely . . . black power]   Carmichael, while a leader of the Student Nonviolent Coordinating Committee (SNCC), publicly enunciated the concept of "black power" at a major Mississippi civil rights march organized by James Meredith in June 1966.

754.9–11   sin . . . forgiveness.]   Cf., e.g., Matthew 12:31–32, Mark 3:29–30; the "sin" against the Holy Ghost has been interpreted as the willful denunciation as evil of that which is manifestly good, thus exhibiting a spirit that is beyond repentance.

759.36–37   *To Be . . . Black*]   Subtitled *An Informal Autobiography of Lorraine Hansberry* (1969); the work was compiled and edited from writings of Hansberry (1930–65) by her ex-husband Robert Nemiroff.

766.8   the Wilmington 10.]   An editorial note keyed here in *The New York Times* reads: "The Wilmington 10 were convicted in 1972 of firebombing a grocery store during 1971 racial disturbances. The jury consisted of 10 whites and two blacks; the judge would not agree that Ku Klux Klan membership was cause for rejecting prospective jurors, and the principal prosecution witness was a young black who had been held in a state mental hospital before he agreed to testify. The United Church of Christ, of which Mr. Chavis had been an employee, said in October that the principal witness had recanted his testimony. The Federal District Court for the eastern district of North Carolina is considering the Church's request for bail and a new trial for the 10." The convictions were overturned by a Federal Court of Appeals on December 4, 1980, after the 10 had served prison terms.

766.21   in 1968.]   An editorial note keyed here in *The New York Times* reads: "In the case of the Charlotte 3, a trial judge refused to order a new trial after it was learned that the Federal Government had secretly paid $4,000 to each of the prosecution's two main witnesses and given them immunity from prosecution on other charges. The judge said the payments and immunity were in return for testimony in another trial (in which James Earl Grant was also convicted) and thus did not affect the fairness of the Lazy B trial."

784.25–27   *My conversion . . . Jesus Christ.*]   "Heritage" (1925), lines 89–90.

786.11   *The Pawnbroker*]   Novel (1961) by Edward Lewis Wallant; Sidney Lumet's film version appeared in 1965.

788.25–26   *What . . . deferred?*]   In the poem "Harlem" in *Montage of a Dream Deferred* (1951).

814.1–2   *Freaks . . . Manhood*]   Titled "Here Be Dragons" in *The Price of the Ticket.*

816.17–18   no rights . . . respect]   Cf. Chief Justice Roger B. Taney, in his opinion in *Dred Scott* v. *Sandford* (1857).

Library of Congress Cataloging-in-Publication Data

James, Baldwin, 1924–1987.
  [Essays. Selections]
  Collected essays / James Baldwin.
      p.   cm. — (The Library of America ; 98)
  Partial Contents: Notes of a native son — Nobody knows my name —
The fire next time — No name in the street — The devil finds work.
  ISBN 1–883011–52–3 (alk. paper)
  I. Title. II. Title: Notes of a native son. III. Title: Nobody
knows my name. IV. Title: Fire next time. V. Title: No name in the
street. VI. Title: Devil finds work. VII. Series
  PS3552.A45A16   1998   97–23496
  813′.54—dc21   CIP

THE LIBRARY OF AMERICA SERIES

Library of America fosters appreciation of America's literary heritage by publishing, and keeping permanently in print, authoritative editions of America's best and most significant writing. An independent nonprofit organization, it was founded in 1979 with seed funding from the National Endowment for the Humanities and the Ford Foundation.

1. Herman Melville: Typee, Omoo, Mardi
2. Nathaniel Hawthorne: Tales & Sketches
3. Walt Whitman: Poetry & Prose
4. Harriet Beecher Stowe: Three Novels
5. Mark Twain: Mississippi Writings
6. Jack London: Novels & Stories
7. Jack London: Novels & Social Writings
8. William Dean Howells: Novels 1875–1886
9. Herman Melville: Redburn, White-Jacket, Moby-Dick
10. Nathaniel Hawthorne: Collected Novels
11 & 12. Francis Parkman: France and England in North America
13. Henry James: Novels 1871–1880
14. Henry Adams: Novels, Mont Saint Michel, The Education
15. Ralph Waldo Emerson: Essays & Lectures
16. Washington Irving: History, Tales & Sketches
17. Thomas Jefferson: Writings
18. Stephen Crane: Prose & Poetry
19. Edgar Allan Poe: Poetry & Tales
20. Edgar Allan Poe: Essays & Reviews
21. Mark Twain: The Innocents Abroad, Roughing It
22 & 23. Henry James: Literary Criticism
24. Herman Melville: Pierre, Israel Potter, The Confidence-Man, Tales & Billy Budd
25. William Faulkner: Novels 1930–1935
26 & 27. James Fenimore Cooper: The Leatherstocking Tales
28. Henry David Thoreau: A Week, Walden, The Maine Woods, Cape Cod
29. Henry James: Novels 1881–1886
30. Edith Wharton: Novels
31 & 32. Henry Adams: History of the U.S. during the Administrations of Jefferson & Madison
33. Frank Norris: Novels & Essays
34. W.E.B. Du Bois: Writings
35. Willa Cather: Early Novels & Stories
36. Theodore Dreiser: Sister Carrie, Jennie Gerhardt, Twelve Men

37. Benjamin Franklin: Writings (2 vols.)
38. William James: Writings 1902–1910
39. Flannery O'Connor: Collected Works
40, 41, & 42. Eugene O'Neill: Complete Plays
43. Henry James: Novels 1886–1890
44. William Dean Howells: Novels 1886–1888
45 & 46. Abraham Lincoln: Speeches & Writings
47. Edith Wharton: Novellas & Other Writings
48. William Faulkner: Novels 1936–1940
49. Willa Cather: Later Novels
50. Ulysses S. Grant: Memoirs & Selected Letters
51. William Tecumseh Sherman: Memoirs
52. Washington Irving: Bracebridge Hall, Tales of a Traveller, The Alhambra
53. Francis Parkman: The Oregon Trail, The Conspiracy of Pontiac
54. James Fenimore Cooper: Sea Tales
55 & 56. Richard Wright: Works
57. Willa Cather: Stories, Poems, & Other Writings
58. William James: Writings 1878–1899
59. Sinclair Lewis: Main Street & Babbitt
60 & 61. Mark Twain: Collected Tales, Sketches, Speeches, & Essays
62 & 63. The Debate on the Constitution
64 & 65. Henry James: Collected Travel Writings
66 & 67. American Poetry: The Nineteenth Century
68. Frederick Douglass: Autobiographies
69. Sarah Orne Jewett: Novels & Stories
70. Ralph Waldo Emerson: Collected Poems & Translations
71. Mark Twain: Historical Romances
72. John Steinbeck: Novels & Stories 1932–1937
73. William Faulkner: Novels 1942–1954
74 & 75. Zora Neale Hurston: Novels, Stories, & Other Writings
76. Thomas Paine: Collected Writings
77 & 78. Reporting World War II: American Journalism
79 & 80. Raymond Chandler: Novels, Stories, & Other Writings

81. Robert Frost: Collected Poems, Prose, & Plays

82 & 83. Henry James: Complete Stories 1892–1910

84. William Bartram: Travels & Other Writings

85. John Dos Passos: U.S.A.

86. John Steinbeck: The Grapes of Wrath & Other Writings 1936–1941

87, 88, & 89. Vladimir Nabokov: Novels & Other Writings

90. James Thurber: Writings & Drawings

91. George Washington: Writings

92. John Muir: Nature Writings

93. Nathanael West: Novels & Other Writings

94 & 95. Crime Novels: American Noir of the 1930s, 40s, & 50s

96. Wallace Stevens: Collected Poetry & Prose

97. James Baldwin: Early Novels & Stories

98. James Baldwin: Collected Essays

99 & 100. Gertrude Stein: Writings

101 & 102. Eudora Welty: Novels, Stories, & Other Writings

103. Charles Brockden Brown: Three Gothic Novels

104 & 105. Reporting Vietnam: American Journalism

106 & 107. Henry James: Complete Stories 1874–1891

108. American Sermons

109. James Madison: Writings

110. Dashiell Hammett: Complete Novels

111. Henry James: Complete Stories 1864–1874

112. William Faulkner: Novels 1957–1962

113. John James Audubon: Writings & Drawings

114. Slave Narratives

115 & 116. American Poetry: The Twentieth Century

117. F. Scott Fitzgerald: Novels & Stories 1920–1922

118. Henry Wadsworth Longfellow: Poems & Other Writings

119 & 120. Tennessee Williams: Collected Plays

121 & 122. Edith Wharton: Collected Stories

123. The American Revolution: Writings from the War of Independence

124. Henry David Thoreau: Collected Essays & Poems

125. Dashiell Hammett: Crime Stories & Other Writings

126 & 127. Dawn Powell: Novels

128. Carson McCullers: Complete Novels

129. Alexander Hamilton: Writings

130. Mark Twain: The Gilded Age & Later Novels

131. Charles W. Chesnutt: Stories, Novels, & Essays

132. John Steinbeck: Novels 1942–1952

133. Sinclair Lewis: Arrowsmith, Elmer Gantry, Dodsworth

134 & 135. Paul Bowles: Novels, Stories, & Other Writings

136. Kate Chopin: Complete Novels & Stories

137 & 138. Reporting Civil Rights: American Journalism

139. Henry James: Novels 1896–1899

140. Theodore Dreiser: An American Tragedy

141. Saul Bellow: Novels 1944–1953

142. John Dos Passos: Novels 1920–1925

143. John Dos Passos: Travel Books & Other Writings

144. Ezra Pound: Poems & Translations

145. James Weldon Johnson: Writings

146. Washington Irving: Three Western Narratives

147. Alexis de Tocqueville: Democracy in America

148. James T. Farrell: Studs Lonigan Trilogy

149, 150, & 151. Isaac Bashevis Singer: Collected Stories

152. Kaufman & Co.: Broadway Comedies

153. Theodore Roosevelt: Rough Riders, An Autobiography

154. Theodore Roosevelt: Letters & Speeches

155. H. P. Lovecraft: Tales

156. Louisa May Alcott: Little Women, Little Men, Jo's Boys

157. Philip Roth: Novels & Stories 1959–1962

158. Philip Roth: Novels 1967–1972

159. James Agee: Let Us Now Praise Famous Men, A Death in the Family, Shorter Fiction

160. James Agee: Film Writing & Selected Journalism

161. Richard Henry Dana Jr.: Two Years Before the Mast & Other Voyages

162. Henry James: Novels 1901–1902

163. Arthur Miller: Plays 1944–1961

164. William Faulkner: Novels 1926–1929

165. Philip Roth: Novels 1973–1977

166 & 167. American Speeches: Political Oratory

168. Hart Crane: Complete Poems & Selected Letters

169. Saul Bellow: Novels 1956–1964
170. John Steinbeck: Travels with Charley & Later Novels
171. Capt. John Smith: Writings with Other Narratives
172. Thornton Wilder: Collected Plays & Writings on Theater
173. Philip K. Dick: Four Novels of the 1960s
174. Jack Kerouac: Road Novels 1957–1960
175. Philip Roth: Zuckerman Bound
176 & 177. Edmund Wilson: Literary Essays & Reviews
178. American Poetry: The 17th & 18th Centuries
179. William Maxwell: Early Novels & Stories
180. Elizabeth Bishop: Poems, Prose, & Letters
181. A. J. Liebling: World War II Writings
182. American Earth: Environmental Writing Since Thoreau
183. Philip K. Dick: Five Novels of the 1960s & 70s
184. William Maxwell: Later Novels & Stories
185. Philip Roth: Novels & Other Narratives 1986–1991
186. Katherine Anne Porter: Collected Stories & Other Writings
187. John Ashbery: Collected Poems 1956–1987
188 & 189. John Cheever: Complete Novels & Collected Stories
190. Lafcadio Hearn: American Writings
191. A. J. Liebling: The Sweet Science & Other Writings
192. The Lincoln Anthology
193. Philip K. Dick: VALIS & Later Novels
194. Thornton Wilder: The Bridge of San Luis Rey & Other Novels 1926–1948
195. Raymond Carver: Collected Stories
196 & 197. American Fantastic Tales
198. John Marshall: Writings
199. The Mark Twain Anthology
200. Mark Twain: A Tramp Abroad, Following the Equator, Other Travels
201 & 202. Ralph Waldo Emerson: Selected Journals
203. The American Stage: Writing on Theater
204. Shirley Jackson: Novels & Stories
205. Philip Roth: Novels 1993–1995
206 & 207. H. L. Mencken: Prejudices
208. John Kenneth Galbraith: The Affluent Society & Other Writings 1952–1967
209. Saul Bellow: Novels 1970–1982
210 & 211. Lynd Ward: Six Novels in Woodcuts
212. The Civil War: The First Year
213 & 214. John Adams: Revolutionary Writings
215. Henry James: Novels 1903–1911
216. Kurt Vonnegut: Novels & Stories 1963–1973
217 & 218. Harlem Renaissance Novels
219. Ambrose Bierce: The Devil's Dictionary, Tales, & Memoirs
220. Philip Roth: The American Trilogy 1997–2000
221. The Civil War: The Second Year
222. Barbara W. Tuchman: The Guns of August, The Proud Tower
223. Arthur Miller: Plays 1964–1982
224. Thornton Wilder: The Eighth Day, Theophilus North, Autobiographical Writings
225. David Goodis: Five Noir Novels of the 1940s & 50s
226. Kurt Vonnegut: Novels & Stories 1950–1962
227 & 228. American Science Fiction: Nine Novels of the 1950s
229 & 230. Laura Ingalls Wilder: The Little House Books
231. Jack Kerouac: Collected Poems
232. The War of 1812
233. American Antislavery Writings
234. The Civil War: The Third Year
235. Sherwood Anderson: Collected Stories
236. Philip Roth: Novels 2001–2007
237. Philip Roth: Nemeses
238. Aldo Leopold: A Sand County Almanac & Other Writings
239. May Swenson: Collected Poems
240 & 241. W. S. Merwin: Collected Poems
242 & 243. John Updike: Collected Stories
244. Ring Lardner: Stories & Other Writings
245. Jonathan Edwards: Writings from the Great Awakening
246. Susan Sontag: Essays of the 1960s & 70s
247. William Wells Brown: Clotel & Other Writings
248 & 249. Bernard Malamud: Novels & Stories of the 1940s, 50s, & 60s
250. The Civil War: The Final Year
251. Shakespeare in America

252. Kurt Vonnegut: Novels 1976–1985
253 & 254. American Musicals 1927–1969
255. Elmore Leonard: Four Novels of the 1970s
256. Louisa May Alcott: Work, Eight Cousins, Rose in Bloom, Stories & Other Writings
257. H. L. Mencken: The Days Trilogy
258. Virgil Thomson: Music Chronicles 1940–1954
259. Art in America 1945–1970
260. Saul Bellow: Novels 1984–2000
261. Arthur Miller: Plays 1987–2004
262. Jack Kerouac: Visions of Cody, Visions of Gerard, Big Sur
263. Reinhold Niebuhr: Major Works on Religion & Politics
264. Ross Macdonald: Four Novels of the 1950s
265 & 266. The American Revolution: Writings from the Pamphlet Debate
267. Elmore Leonard: Four Novels of the 1980s
268 & 269. Women Crime Writers: Suspense Novels of the 1940s & 50s
270. Frederick Law Olmsted: Writings on Landscape, Culture, & Society
271. Edith Wharton: Four Novels of the 1920s
272. James Baldwin: Later Novels
273. Kurt Vonnegut: Novels 1987–1997
274. Henry James: Autobiographies
275. Abigail Adams: Letters
276. John Adams: Writings from the New Nation 1784–1826
277. Virgil Thomson: The State of Music & Other Writings
278. War No More: American Antiwar & Peace Writing
279. Ross Macdonald: Three Novels of the Early 1960s
280. Elmore Leonard: Four Later Novels
281. Ursula K. Le Guin: The Complete Orsinia
282. John O'Hara: Stories
283. The Unknown Kerouac: Rare, Unpublished & Newly Translated Writings
284. Albert Murray: Collected Essays & Memoirs
285 & 286. Loren Eiseley: Collected Essays on Evolution, Nature, & the Cosmos
287. Carson McCullers: Stories, Plays & Other Writings
288. Jane Bowles: Collected Writings
289. World War I and America: Told by the Americans Who Lived It
290 & 291. Mary McCarthy: The Complete Fiction
292. Susan Sontag: Later Essays
293 & 294. John Quincy Adams: Diaries
295. Ross Macdonald: Four Later Novels
296 & 297. Ursula K. Le Guin: The Hainish Novels & Stories
298 & 299. Peter Taylor: The Complete Stories
300. Philip Roth: Why Write? Collected Nonfiction 1960–2014
301. John Ashbery: Collected Poems 1991–2000
302. Wendell Berry: Port William Novels & Stories: The Civil War to World War II
303. Reconstruction: Voices from America's First Great Struggle for Racial Equality
304. Albert Murray: Collected Novels & Poems
305 & 306. Norman Mailer: The Sixties
307. Rachel Carson: Silent Spring & Other Writings on the Environment
308. Elmore Leonard: Westerns
309 & 310. Madeleine L'Engle: The Kairos Novels
311. John Updike: Novels 1959–1965
312. James Fenimore Cooper: Two Novels of the American Revolution
313. John O'Hara: Four Novels of the 1930s
314. Ann Petry: The Street, The Narrows
315. Ursula K. Le Guin: Always Coming Home
316 & 317. Wendell Berry: Collected Essays
318. Cornelius Ryan: The Longest Day, A Bridge Too Far
319. Booth Tarkington: Novels & Stories
320. Herman Melville: Complete Poems
321 & 322. American Science Fiction: Eight Classic Novels of the 1960s
323. Frances Hodgson Burnett: The Secret Garden, A Little Princess, Little Lord Fauntleroy
324. Jean Stafford: Complete Novels
325. Joan Didion: The 1960s & 70s
326. John Updike: Novels 1968–1975
327. Constance Fenimore Woolson: Collected Stories
328. Robert Stone: Dog Soldiers, Flag for Sunrise, Outerbridge Reach
329. Jonathan Schell: The Fate of the Earth, The Abolition, The Unconquerable World
330. Richard Hofstadter: Anti-Intellectualism in American Life, The Paranoid Style in American Politics, Uncollected Essays 1956–1965

This book is set in 10 point Linotron Galliard,
a face designed for photocomposition by Matthew Carter
and based on the sixteenth-century face Granjon. The paper is acid-free
lightweight opaque that will not turn yellow or brittle with age.
The binding is sewn, which allows the book to open easily and lie flat.
The binding board is covered in Brillianta, a woven rayon cloth
made by Van Heek–Scholco Textielfabrieken, Holland.
Composition by The Clarinda Company.
Printing by Sheridan Grand Rapids, Grand Rapids, MI.
Binding by Dekker Bookbinding, Wyoming, MI.
Designed by Bruce Campbell.

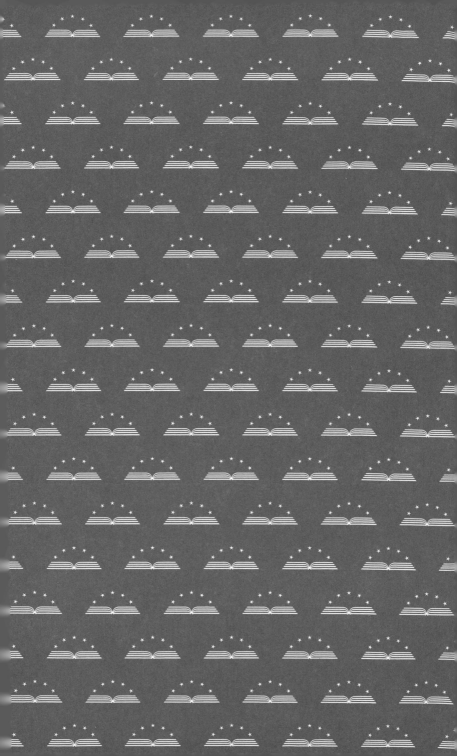